aboard	탑승하여, 배 위로	abroad	해외에(서)
access	접근[접속]하다, 접근	assess	평가하다, 재다
adapt	적응시키다, 적응하다	adopt	채택하다, 입양하다
addiction	중독	addition	추가, 덧셈
aesthetic	미학의, 미(美)의	authentic	진짜의, 진정한
affect	영향을 미치다, 감정	effect	가져오다, 결과, 영향, 효과
alley	골목	ally	동맹국, 협력자, 지지하다
annual	매년의, 연간의	annul	취소하다
appeal	매력, 간청	appear	나타나다, ~인 것 같다
arise	생기다, 발생하다	arouse	불러일으키다
artificial	인공의, 인위적인	artistic	예술적인
assault	폭행, 공격, 괴롭히다	assort	분류하다, 구분하다
bald	대머리인	bold	대담한, 용감한
barrel	통, 배럴	barren	척박한, 황량한
beat	이기다, 때리다	bit	조금, 약간
beside	~의 옆에	besides	게다가, ~이외에도
borrow	빌리다, 차용하다	burrow	굴을 파다
breadth	폭, 넓이	breath	숨, 호흡
bribe	뇌물, 뇌물을 주다	bride	신부
cancel	취소하다, 무효화하다	cancer	암
cite	인용하다, 예로 들다	site	장소, (인터넷) 사이트
cloth	옷감, 직물, 천	clothes	옷, 의복
clown	광대	crown	왕관, 왕위에 앉히다
coast	해안, 해변, 연안	cost	값, (값·비용이) ~이다
collect	모으다, 수집하다	correct	맞는, 옳은, 바로잡다
command	명령, 명령하다	commend	칭찬하다, 추천하다
competent	유능한, 적격인	competitive	경쟁의
complement	보충하다, 보충	compliment	칭찬하다, 칭찬
confident	자신 있는	confidential	비밀의, 기밀의
confirm	확인하다, 승인하다	conform	따르다, 순응하다

conscience	양심	conscious	의식하는
considerable	상당한, 중요한	considerate	사려 깊은
council	의회, 협의회	counsel	조언, 상담을 하다
curb	억제하다, 억제	curve	곡선, 곡선을 이루다
daily	매일 일어나는, 일일	dairy	낙농업, 유제품의
dedicate	바치다, 헌신하다	delicate	연약한, 섬세한
deep	깊은, 깊이	dip	살짝 담그다, 내려가다
deprive	빼앗다	derive	끌어내다, 얻다, 유래하다
desert	사막, 버리다	dessert	디저트, 후식
devote	바치다, 헌신하다	devout	독실한
die	죽다, 사망하다	dye	염색하다
discreet	신중한, 분별 있는	discrete	분리된, 별개의
distinct	별개의, 뚜렷한	instinct	본능, 직감
emigrate	이주하다, 이민	immigrate	이민 오다, 와서 살다
emphasize	강조하다, 역설하다	empathize	공감하다, 감정 이입하다
ethical	윤리[도덕]의	ethnic(al)	민족의
expand	확장하다, 확대되다	expend	(돈·시간을) 쏟다
extend	확장하다, 연장하다	extent	정도, 크기
fail	실패하다, ~하지 못하다	fair	타당한, 공정하게, 박람회
fertile	비옥한, 다산의	futile	헛된, 쓸데없는
find	찾다, 발견하다	found	설립하다, 기초를 쌓다
firm	회사, 딱딱한	form	종류, 유형, 형성되다
flesh	살, 과육	fresh	신선한, 생생한
fury	분노, 격분	furry	털로 덮인, 털 같은
garage	차고, 주차장	garbage	쓰레기(장)
greed	탐욕, 식탐	grid	격자무늬, 격자판
imaginable	상상할 수 있는	imaginary	가상적인
immense	엄청난, 어마어마한	immerse	담그다, ~에 몰두하다
imply	암시하다, 내포하다	infer	추론하다, 유추하다
industrial	산업의, 공업의	industrious	근면한, 부지런한

ingenious	독창적인, 정교한	ingenuous	솔직한, 숨김없는	personal	개인의, 개인적인	personnel	직원의, 직원
inhabit	살다, 거주하다	inhibit	억제하다, ~하지 못하게 하다	phase	단계, 시기	phrase	구, 구절
instigate	선동하다, 부추기다	investigate	조사하다, 수사하다	poem	시	poet	시인
intend	의도하다, 의미하다	intent	몰두하는, 의도	pole	막대기, 극	pore	구멍
invaluable	매우 귀중한	valueless	하찮은, 가치 없는	politic	현명한, 신중한	political	정치적인, 정당의
invent	발명하다	invert	뒤집다, 도치시키다	pray	기도하다	prey	먹이, 사냥감
irrigate	물을 대다, 관개하다	irritate	짜증나게 하다, 자극하다	principal	주요한, (단체의) 장	principle	원리, 원칙
label	표, 라벨을 붙이다	labo(u)r	노동, 노동의	probe	조사하다, 조사	prove	입증하다, 증명하다
lay	놓다, (알을) 낳다	lie	눕다, 거짓말하다, 거짓말	propel	나아가게 하다	proper	적절한, 정당한
lead	이끌다, 납	lid	뚜껑	qualify	자격을 얻다, 자격을 주다	quantify	양을 나타내다, 수량화하다
lessen	줄이다, 줄다	lesson	수업, 교훈	quota	한도, 몫	quote	인용하다
level	정도, 수준, 평평한	lever	지레, 지렛대로 움직이다	raise	올리다, 일으키다	rise	오르다, 증가
literal	문자 그대로의	literate	글을 읽고 쓸 줄 아는	real	진짜의, 현실적인	rear	뒤쪽, 뒤쪽의
literary	문학의, 문학적인	literacy	글을 읽고 쓸 줄 아는 능력	reality	현실, 실재	realty	부동산, 물적 재산
loose	느슨한, 헐렁한	lose	잃다, 지다	require	필요하다, 요구하다	inquire	묻다, 조사하다
mass	덩어리, 대규모의	mess	엉망진창인 상태	respectable	존경할 만한, 훌륭한	respective	각자의, 각각의
mean	뜻하다, 비열한	means	수단, 방법	responsible	책임이 있는	responsive	즉각 반응하는
mediation	조정, 중재	meditation	명상, 심사숙고	role	역할	roll	통, 구르다
meld	섞이다, 섞다	melt	녹다, 녹이다	rot	썩다, 썩히다	rote	암기
miner	광부	minor	적은, 미성년자, 부전공	royal	왕실의, 왕의	loyal	충성스러운
momentary	순간적인, 잠깐의	momentous	중대한	sail	항해하다, 돛	sale	판매, 매출, 영업
moss	이끼	moth	나방	sand	모래, 모래사장	send	보내다, 발송하다
mound	언덕, 무더기	mount	오르다, 증가하다	saw	톱, 톱질하다	sew	바느질하다, (바느질로) 만들다
neural	신경(계통)의	neutral	중립의	scrap	조각, 폐기하다	scrape	긁다, 긁기
noble	고결한, 귀족	novel	소설, 새로운	sensible	분별 있는, 합리적인	sensitive	민감한, 예민한
numeral	숫자, 수사	numerous	많은	sole	유일한, 단 하나의	sore	아픈, 상처
objective	목적, 객관적인	objection	이의, 반대	soul	영혼, 정신, 마음	sour	신, 상하다
odd	이상한, 홀수의	odds	가능성, 역경	successful	성공한, 성공적인	successive	연속하는
own	소유하다, 자신의	owe	빚지고 있다	sympathy	동정, 연민, 공감	empathy	감정 이입, 공감
pare	벗기다, 깎다	pear	배	vague	모호한, 애매한	vogue	유행
peak	절정, 정점, 봉우리	peek	훔쳐 보다	vain	헛된, 하찮은	vein	정맥, 혈관
peel	벗기다, 껍질	pill	알약	virtual	사실상의, 가상의	virtue	미덕, 덕
persevere	버티다, 이겨내다	preserve	보존하다	wonder	궁금해하다, 놀라움	wander	돌아다니다

정답표

01회
2018년 11월 학력평가 　　문제편 p.2 해설편 p.1

01 ②	02 ④	03 ②	04 ③	05 ①
06 ③	07 ②	08 ③	09 ④	10 ④
11 ④	12 ②	13 ③	14 ②	15 ⑤
16 ①	17 ⑤			

02회
2019년 3월 학력평가 　　문제편 p.5 해설편 p.6

01 ②	02 ③	03 ①	04 ③	05 ②
06 ④	07 ①	08 ③	09 ⑤	10 ④
11 ③	12 ⑤	13 ②	14 ①	15 ②
16 ①	17 ④			

03회
2019년 6월 학력평가 　　문제편 p.8 해설편 p.10

01 ②	02 ②	03 ①	04 ④	05 ①
06 ④	07 ⑤	08 ④	09 ⑤	10 ②
11 ③	12 ⑤	13 ②	14 ④	15 ③
16 ⑤	17 ④			

04회
2019년 9월 학력평가 　　문제편 p.11 해설편 p.15

01 ③	02 ⑤	03 ②	04 ③	05 ②
06 ③	07 ①	08 ④	09 ④	10 ④
11 ③	12 ④	13 ⑤	14 ①	15 ②
16 ②	17 ④			

05회
2019년 11월 학력평가 　　문제편 p.14 해설편 p.20

01 ③	02 ②	03 ⑤	04 ④	05 ⑤
06 ②	07 ④	08 ⑤	09 ⑤	10 ③
11 ①	12 ②	13 ①	14 ③	15 ⑤
16 ②	17 ⑤			

06회
2020년 3월 학력평가 　　문제편 p.17 해설편 p.26

01 ⑤	02 ④	03 ⑤	04 ④	05 ②
06 ③	07 ①	08 ④	09 ④	10 ③
11 ②	12 ③	13 ①	14 ②	15 ⑤
16 ⑤	17 ③			

07회
2020년 6월 학력평가 　　문제편 p.20 해설편 p.31

01 ①	02 ②	03 ④	04 ④	05 ①
06 ②	07 ③	08 ④	09 ⑤	10 ④
11 ②	12 ①	13 ⑤	14 ②	15 ④
16 ④	17 ③			

08회
2020년 9월 학력평가 　　문제편 p.23 해설편 p.36

01 ⑤	02 ②	03 ④	04 ⑤	05 ①
06 ④	07 ⑤	08 ③	09 ④	10 ④
11 ④	12 ②	13 ④	14 ②	15 ④
16 ④	17 ④			

09회
2020년 11월 학력평가 　　문제편 p.26 해설편 p.41

01 ④	02 ②	03 ①	04 ⑤	05 ④
06 ③	07 ⑤	08 ④	09 ⑤	10 ⑤
11 ①	12 ①	13 ②	14 ④	15 ③
16 ②	17 ④			

10회
2021년 3월 학력평가 　　문제편 p.29 해설편 p.46

01 ⑤	02 ②	03 ②	04 ④	05 ⑤
06 ②	07 ⑤	08 ②	09 ③	10 ③
11 ②	12 ①	13 ④	14 ④	15 ②
16 ④	17 ④			

11회
2021년 6월 학력평가 　　문제편 p.32 해설편 p.51

01 ③	02 ③	03 ②	04 ④	05 ①
06 ②	07 ③	08 ④	09 ④	10 ⑤
11 ④	12 ②	13 ①	14 ⑤	15 ④
16 ①	17 ③			

12회
2021년 9월 학력평가 　　문제편 p.35 해설편 p.55

01 ③	02 ③	03 ④	04 ⑤	05 ②
06 ③	07 ⑤	08 ③	09 ⑤	10 ②
11 ③	12 ②	13 ②	14 ④	15 ①
16 ①	17 ④			

13회
2021년 11월 학력평가 　　문제편 p.38 해설편 p.61

01 ③	02 ②	03 ④	04 ④	05 ⑤
06 ②	07 ②	08 ⑤	09 ④	10 ④
11 ②	12 ②	13 ①	14 ⑤	15 ①
16 ③	17 ⑤			

14회
2022년 3월 학력평가 　　문제편 p.41 해설편 p.66

01 ①	02 ①	03 ④	04 ⑤	05 ④
06 ③	07 ①	08 ②	09 ④	10 ②
11 ④	12 ①	13 ②	14 ①	15 ②
16 ①	17 ④			

15회
2022년 6월 학력평가 　　문제편 p.44 해설편 p.70

01 ⑤	02 ②	03 ④	04 ④	05 ⑤
06 ④	07 ①	08 ⑤	09 ④	10 ④
11 ②	12 ②	13 ④	14 ①	15 ⑤
16 ②	17 ③			

16회
2022년 9월 학력평가 　　문제편 p.47 해설편 p.75

01 ①	02 ①	03 ④	04 ⑤	05 ⑤
06 ⑤	07 ④	08 ⑤	09 ③	10 ③
11 ⑤	12 ②	13 ②	14 ①	15 ③
16 ⑤	17 ③			

17회
2022년 11월 학력평가 　　문제편 p.50 해설편 p.80

01 ④	02 ③	03 ⑤	04 ④	05 ⑤
06 ④	07 ⑤	08 ⑤	09 ④	10 ⑤
11 ②	12 ④	13 ④	14 ③	15 ④
16 ④	17 ④			

18회
2023년 3월 학력평가 　　문제편 p.53 해설편 p.85

01 ④	02 ①	03 ④	04 ③	05 ①
06 ④	07 ②	08 ③	09 ④	10 ②
11 ①	12 ②	13 ②	14 ④	15 ③
16 ③	17 ④			

19회
2023년 6월 학력평가 　　문제편 p.56 해설편 p.90

01 ②	02 ⑤	03 ①	04 ③	05 ④
06 ②	07 ①	08 ③	09 ③	10 ④
11 ②	12 ③	13 ①	14 ④	15 ③
16 ⑤	17 ②			

20회
2023년 9월 학력평가 　　문제편 p.59 해설편 p.95

01 ⑤	02 ③	03 ②	04 ④	05 ①
06 ①	07 ⑤	08 ④	09 ④	10 ②
11 ②	12 ①	13 ②	14 ④	15 ⑤
16 ②	17 ④			

21회
2023년 11월 학력평가 　　문제편 p.62 해설편 p.100

01 ②	02 ②	03 ④	04 ⑤	05 ⑤
06 ③	07 ⑤	08 ④	09 ④	10 ②
11 ②	12 ④	13 ①	14 ④	15 ②
16 ④	17 ④			

22회
2024년 3월 학력평가 　　문제편 p.65 해설편 p.105

01 ②	02 ④	03 ①	04 ④	05 ⑤
06 ③	07 ②	08 ④	09 ⑤	10 ①
11 ④	12 ④	13 ④	14 ④	15 ②
16 ⑤	17 ③			

23회
2024년 6월 학력평가 　　문제편 p.68 해설편 p.110

01 ④	02 ②	03 ④	04 ⑤	05 ④
06 ①	07 ③	08 ⑤	09 ⑤	10 ①
11 ④	12 ⑤	13 ②	14 ①	15 ⑤
16 ②	17 ④			

24회
2024년 9월 학력평가 　　문제편 p.71 해설편 p.115

01 ⑤	02 ③	03 ②	04 ⑤	05 ⑤
06 ②	07 ⑤	08 ④	09 ⑤	10 ③
11 ②	12 ①	13 ②	14 ④	15 ①
16 ②	17 ④			

MOTHERTONGUE
마더텅출판사
since1999.4.1.

 **정답표** ━━━━━━━━━━━━━━━━━━━━━━━━━━━━━

01회
2018년 11월 학력평가 · 문제편 p.2 해설편 p.1

01 ②	02 ④	03 ②	04 ③	05 ①
06 ③	07 ②	08 ③	09 ④	10 ④
11 ④	12 ④	13 ④	14 ②	15 ⑤
16 ①	17 ⑤			

02회
2019년 3월 학력평가 · 문제편 p.5 해설편 p.6

01 ②	02 ④	03 ①	04 ④	05 ②
06 ④	07 ④	08 ③	09 ⑤	10 ④
11 ③	12 ④	13 ②	14 ①	15 ②
16 ①	17 ④			

03회
2019년 6월 학력평가 · 문제편 p.8 해설편 p.10

01 ②	02 ②	03 ④	04 ④	05 ①
06 ④	07 ⑤	08 ④	09 ④	10 ②
11 ③	12 ④	13 ④	14 ④	15 ③
16 ⑤	17 ④			

04회
2019년 9월 학력평가 · 문제편 p.11 해설편 p.15

01 ③	02 ⑤	03 ②	04 ③	05 ②
06 ③	07 ③	08 ④	09 ④	10 ④
11 ⑤	12 ②	13 ⑤	14 ①	15 ②
16 ②	17 ④			

05회
2019년 11월 학력평가 · 문제편 p.14 해설편 p.20

01 ③	02 ②	03 ④	04 ④	05 ⑤
06 ②	07 ④	08 ④	09 ⑤	10 ④
11 ①	12 ④	13 ②	14 ③	15 ①
16 ②	17 ⑤			

06회
2020년 3월 학력평가 · 문제편 p.17 해설편 p.26

01 ⑤	02 ④	03 ⑤	04 ④	05 ②
06 ③	07 ④	08 ④	09 ④	10 ③
11 ①	12 ③	13 ④	14 ②	15 ⑤
16 ⑤	17 ③			

07회
2020년 6월 학력평가 · 문제편 p.20 해설편 p.31

01 ①	02 ②	03 ④	04 ④	05 ①
06 ②	07 ②	08 ④	09 ④	10 ④
11 ②	12 ①	13 ④	14 ②	15 ③
16 ④	17 ③			

08회
2020년 9월 학력평가 · 문제편 p.23 해설편 p.36

01 ⑤	02 ②	03 ④	04 ⑤	05 ①
06 ④	07 ⑤	08 ⑤	09 ④	10 ④
11 ④	12 ②	13 ①	14 ④	15 ①
16 ④	17 ④			

09회
2020년 11월 학력평가 · 문제편 p.26 해설편 p.41

01 ④	02 ②	03 ④	04 ④	05 ④
06 ③	07 ⑤	08 ④	09 ⑤	10 ③
11 ①	12 ①	13 ④	14 ④	15 ③
16 ②	17 ④			

10회
2021년 3월 학력평가 · 문제편 p.29 해설편 p.46

01 ⑤	02 ④	03 ②	04 ④	05 ⑤
06 ④	07 ⑤	08 ②	09 ③	10 ⑤
11 ③	12 ①	13 ④	14 ④	15 ②
16 ④	17 ④			

11회
2021년 6월 학력평가 · 문제편 p.32 해설편 p.51

01 ②	02 ②	03 ②	04 ④	05 ①
06 ②	07 ⑤	08 ④	09 ④	10 ④
11 ④	12 ⑤	13 ①	14 ④	15 ④
16 ④	17 ③			

12회
2021년 9월 학력평가 · 문제편 p.35 해설편 p.55

01 ③	02 ④	03 ②	04 ⑤	05 ②
06 ④	07 ⑤	08 ④	09 ⑤	10 ③
11 ④	12 ①	13 ②	14 ④	15 ①
16 ④	17 ④			

13회
2021년 11월 학력평가 · 문제편 p.38 해설편 p.61

01 ③	02 ②	03 ②	04 ④	05 ⑤
06 ②	07 ②	08 ⑤	09 ④	10 ①
11 ②	12 ②	13 ①	14 ⑤	15 ①
16 ②	17 ⑤			

14회
2022년 3월 학력평가 · 문제편 p.41 해설편 p.66

01 ①	02 ①	03 ②	04 ⑤	05 ③
06 ③	07 ④	08 ②	09 ④	10 ③
11 ④	12 ①	13 ②	14 ①	15 ②
16 ①	17 ④			

15회
2022년 6월 학력평가 · 문제편 p.44 해설편 p.70

01 ⑤	02 ②	03 ②	04 ④	05 ⑤
06 ④	07 ①	08 ⑤	09 ④	10 ④
11 ②	12 ②	13 ②	14 ①	15 ③
16 ②	17 ③			

16회
2022년 9월 학력평가 · 문제편 p.47 해설편 p.75

01 ①	02 ②	03 ④	04 ⑤	05 ④
06 ⑤	07 ④	08 ⑤	09 ③	10 ③
11 ③	12 ⑤	13 ②	14 ①	15 ④
16 ⑤	17 ③			

17회
2022년 11월 학력평가 · 문제편 p.50 해설편 p.80

01 ④	02 ⑤	03 ⑤	04 ④	05 ⑤
06 ③	07 ⑤	08 ⑤	09 ④	10 ②
11 ②	12 ①	13 ⑤	14 ③	15 ③
16 ④	17 ④			

18회
2023년 3월 학력평가 · 문제편 p.53 해설편 p.85

01 ②	02 ②	03 ④	04 ③	05 ①
06 ②	07 ④	08 ⑤	09 ④	10 ④
11 ①	12 ②	13 ②	14 ①	15 ①
16 ③	17 ④			

19회
2023년 6월 학력평가 · 문제편 p.56 해설편 p.90

01 ①	02 ⑤	03 ①	04 ⑤	05 ⑤
06 ②	07 ⑤	08 ④	09 ⑤	10 ②
11 ②	12 ③	13 ①	14 ①	15 ②
16 ⑤	17 ②			

20회
2023년 9월 학력평가 · 문제편 p.59 해설편 p.95

01 ⑤	02 ③	03 ②	04 ④	05 ①
06 ①	07 ⑤	08 ④	09 ③	10 ②
11 ④	12 ①	13 ⑤	14 ②	15 ⑤
16 ②	17 ④			

21회
2023년 11월 학력평가 · 문제편 p.62 해설편 p.100

01 ②	02 ③	03 ⑤	04 ⑤	05 ⑤
06 ③	07 ⑤	08 ⑤	09 ②	10 ②
11 ②	12 ②	13 ①	14 ③	15 ②
16 ④	17 ④			

22회
2024년 3월 학력평가 · 문제편 p.65 해설편 p.105

01 ③	02 ②	03 ①	04 ④	05 ⑤
06 ②	07 ②	08 ⑤	09 ⑤	10 ①
11 ④	12 ①	13 ②	14 ②	15 ②
16 ⑤	17 ③			

23회
2024년 6월 학력평가 · 문제편 p.68 해설편 p.110

01 ②	02 ①	03 ①	04 ④	05 ④
06 ①	07 ③	08 ③	09 ⑤	10 ①
11 ④	12 ⑤	13 ④	14 ④	15 ⑤
16 ②	17 ③			

24회
2024년 9월 학력평가 · 문제편 p.71 해설편 p.115

01 ⑤	02 ③	03 ③	04 ④	05 ④
06 ②	07 ⑤	08 ④	09 ⑤	10 ③
11 ④	12 ①	13 ②	14 ④	15 ①
16 ②	17 ④			

목차 ————————————————

모바일로 교재 MP3 이용하기

마더텅의 교재 MP3는 모바일
스트리밍/다운로드를 지원합니다.

이용방법 1
스마트폰으로 QR 코드 스캔!

이용방법 2
① 주소창에 **www.toptutor.co.kr**
   또는 포털에서 [마더텅] 검색
② 상단 메뉴 학습자료실 →
   [무료동영상강의] 클릭
③ 무료 동영상 강의에서
   [학년], [시리즈], [과목], [교재]
   선택 후 원하는 동영상 강의 수강

특별 제공
① 다양한 빠르기의 MP3 파일 지원!
난이도를 조절하여 듣기 실력을 향상시켜 보세요!
[MP3] ① 원배속 ② 1.1배속 ③ 1.25배속 ④ 1.5배속

② 문항별 분할 MP3 파일 지원!
효율적인 학습을 위해 모든 회차의 각 문항별
MP3 파일 다운로드를 지원합니다.

영어 듣기 MP3 파일 다운로드 안내

한국교육과정평가원 홈페이지
www.suneung.re.kr

자료마당 〉 기출문제 〉 해당 모의평가 및
수능 MP3 파일 다운로드

서울특별시교육청 홈페이지
www.sen.go.kr

교육정보 〉 학력평가 자료 〉 해당
학력평가 MP3 파일 다운로드

* 또는 마더텅 홈페이지(www.toptutor.co.kr)
  '고등—교재자료실'에서 해당 교재 게시글의
  링크 확인 후 클릭하시면 다운로드 페이지로
  연결됩니다.
* 다운로드 과정에서 어려움을 겪으신 분들은,
  마더텅 고객센터(1661-1064)로 연락 바랍니다.

01 2018년 11월 학력평가

MP3
25BL2_A01

동영상 강의
25BL2_L01

1번부터 17번까지는 듣고 답하는 문제입니다. 1번부터 15번까지는 한 번만 들려주고, 16번부터 17번까지는 두 번 들려줍니다. 방송을 잘 듣고 답을 하시기 바랍니다.

01
고2 2018년 11월 3번

다음을 듣고, 남자가 하는 말의 목적으로 가장 적절한 것을 고르시오.

① 동물 공연 일정을 안내하려고
② 동물원 관람 규칙을 설명하려고
③ 동물원에 새로 온 동물들을 소개하려고
④ 변경된 동물원 운영 시간을 공지하려고
⑤ 멸종 위기 동물 보호의 중요성을 강조하려고

02
고2 2018년 11월 4번

대화를 듣고, 여자의 의견으로 가장 적절한 것을 고르시오.

① 성인이 되면 경제적으로 독립해야 한다.
② 청소년 시기에 가족 간의 대화가 중요하다.
③ 신문 기사를 통해 경제관념을 기를 수 있다.
④ 부모가 바람직한 소비 습관을 가르쳐야 한다.
⑤ 구매 목록 작성으로 충동구매를 막을 수 있다.

03
고2 2018년 11월 5번

대화를 듣고, 두 사람의 관계를 가장 잘 나타낸 것을 고르시오.

① 환자 - 간호사
② 학생 기자 - 의사
③ 사진작가 - 모델
④ 봉사 단체 직원 - 자원봉사자
⑤ 중학생 - 보건 교사

04
고2 2018년 11월 6번

대화를 듣고, 그림에서 대화의 내용과 일치하지 않는 것을 고르시오.

05
고2 2018년 11월 7번

대화를 듣고, 여자가 남자에게 부탁한 일로 가장 적절한 것을 고르시오.

① 탁구채 빌려주기
② 이삿짐 옮겨 주기
③ 이웃 소개해 주기
④ 저녁 식사 초대하기
⑤ 집 청소 도와주기

06
고2 2018년 11월 9번

대화를 듣고, 여자가 지불할 금액을 고르시오. [3점]

① $63
② $70
③ $72
④ $80
⑤ $88

07

고2 2018년 11월 8번

대화를 듣고, 남자가 아이스 스케이트를 타러 갈 수 <u>없는</u> 이유를 고르시오.

① 쇼핑몰에 가기로 해서
② 여행 가방을 싸야 해서
③ 발표 준비를 해야 해서
④ 아르바이트를 해야 해서
⑤ 친구를 마중 나가야 해서

08

고2 2018년 11월 10번

대화를 듣고, Global Student Card에 관해 언급되지 <u>않은</u> 것을 고르시오.

① 발급 가능 연령　　② 유효 기간　　③ 발급 비용
④ 발급 필요 서류　　⑤ 발급 소요 기간

09

고2 2018년 11월 11번

Clearwater University 5km Run에 관한 다음 내용을 듣고, 일치하지 <u>않는</u> 것을 고르시오.

① 모든 학생과 교직원이 참가할 수 있다.
② 학생의 경우 참가비는 5달러이다.
③ 물과 간식이 제공될 것이다.
④ 점심 식사 전에 음악회가 있을 것이다.
⑤ 학교 웹 사이트나 도서관에서 신청 가능하다.

10

고2 2018년 11월 12번

다음 표를 보면서 대화를 듣고, 두 사람이 관람할 영화를 고르시오.

Limestone Movie Theater

	Title	Genre	Special Feature	Starting Time
①	*Love Really*	Drama	None	10 a.m.
②	*Funny Guys*	Comedy	None	1 p.m.
③	*Behind You*	Horror	3D	3 p.m.
④	*Space Wars*	Action	4D	6 p.m.
⑤	*Dinosaurs*	Animation	4D	8 p.m.

11

고2 2018년 11월 1번

대화를 듣고, 남자의 마지막 말에 대한 여자의 응답으로 가장 적절한 것을 고르시오.

① No, I don't know how to speak French.
② Well, we need to cross the street.
③ Good. I love to cook for myself.
④ Yeah, the food was really great.
⑤ Sorry. I already ate lunch.

12

고2 2018년 11월 2번

대화를 듣고, 여자의 마지막 말에 대한 남자의 응답으로 가장 적절한 것을 고르시오.

① Sure. I'd love to go there with you.
② Well, I wonder if we can get tickets.
③ Yeah, I've already finished my painting.
④ No, you won't be late for the exhibition.
⑤ Cheer up. You can go there another time.

13

대화를 듣고, 남자의 마지막 말에 대한 여자의 응답으로 가장 적절한 것을 고르시오. 3점

Woman: _____

① Okay. I like to read books about parenting.

② I don't agree. We're not prepared to raise dogs.

③ All right. I'll tell Amy that we'll take one of her puppies.

④ Never mind. You'll have another chance to have a puppy.

⑤ Sure. Pet owners should protect their pets from diseases.

14

대화를 듣고, 여자의 마지막 말에 대한 남자의 응답으로 가장 적절한 것을 고르시오. 3점

Man: _____

① Yeah. Let me know if you cannot find your way to the library.

② I agree. I'll update all the information as soon as possible.

③ Too bad. The renovation is taking longer than I expected.

④ Sorry. You cannot borrow more than five books at once.

⑤ Right. You can use all the library facilities for free.

15

다음 상황 설명을 듣고, Peter가 Stella에게 할 말로 가장 적절한 것을 고르시오.

Peter: _____

① You'd better take some cough medicine.

② What do you think about the new office?

③ We should cooperate to get the best result.

④ We need to purchase another copy machine.

⑤ Why don't we get some plants for fresh air?

[16~17] 다음을 듣고, 물음에 답하시오.

16

여자가 하는 말의 주제로 가장 적절한 것은?

① foods to reduce depression in the winter

② necessity of exercising during cold winters

③ healthy recipes for various enjoyable foods

④ ways to select foods with adequate nutrition

⑤ important functions of protein in the human body

17

언급된 식품이 아닌 것은?

① 연어   ② 계란   ③ 바나나

④ 요거트   ⑤ 호두

02 2019년 3월 학력평가

MP3   동영상 강의

2SBL2_A02   2SBL2_L02

😊 1번부터 17번까지는 듣고 답하는 문제입니다. 1번부터 15번까지는 한 번만 들려주고, 16번부터 17번까지는 두 번 들려줍니다. 방송을 잘 듣고 답을 하시기 바랍니다.

01
고2 2019년 3월 3번

다음을 듣고, 남자가 하는 말의 목적으로 가장 적절한 것을 고르시오.

① 올바른 안경 착용 및 관리 방법에 대해 알려 주려고
② 전자기기를 활용한 효과적인 학습법을 안내하려고
③ 어린이의 시력을 보호하는 방법을 소개하려고
④ 어린이의 야외 활동 시 보호자의 동반을 권유하려고
⑤ 성장기에 균형 있는 영양 섭취가 중요함을 강조하려고

02
고2 2019년 3월 4번

대화를 듣고, 여자의 의견으로 가장 적절한 것을 고르시오.

① 가격과 품질이 반드시 비례하는 것은 아니다.
② 의류는 매장에서 직접 입어 보고 사는 것이 좋다.
③ 정해진 예산 내에서 소비하는 습관을 가져야 한다.
④ 인터넷에 있는 상품 평가를 그대로 믿어서는 안 된다.
⑤ 인터넷을 통한 구매는 신뢰할 수 있는 곳에서 해야 한다.

03
고2 2019년 3월 5번

대화를 듣고, 두 사람의 관계를 가장 잘 나타낸 것을 고르시오.

① 광고 방송 담당자 — 의뢰인
② 광고 제작자 — 광고 모델
③ 식당 주인 — 주방장
④ 식당 종업원 — 손님
⑤ 방송 프로듀서 — 뉴스 진행자

04
고2 2019년 3월 6번

대화를 듣고, 그림에서 대화의 내용과 일치하지 않는 것을 고르시오.

05
고2 2019년 3월 7번

대화를 듣고, 남자가 할 일로 가장 적절한 것을 고르시오.

① 손님 명단 확인하기   ② 수건 교체하기
③ 오븐 속 음식 확인하기   ④ 냉장고에 케이크 넣기
⑤ 화장실에 화장지 갖다 놓기

06
고2 2019년 3월 9번

대화를 듣고, 여자가 지불할 금액을 고르시오.

① $30   ② $38   ③ $42
④ $48   ⑤ $50

정답과 해설 : 01~06 6~7

07

대화를 듣고, 남자가 여자와 함께 수리 센터에 갈 수 <u>없는</u> 이유를 고르시오.

① 교수님과 약속이 있어서
② 우편물을 수령해야 해서
③ 컴퓨터를 사러 가야 해서
④ 특별 강연을 들어야 해서
⑤ 테니스 강습을 받아야 해서

08

대화를 듣고, Romance City에 관해 언급되지 <u>않은</u> 것을 고르시오.

① 첫 방영 날짜   ② 주연 배우   ③ 줄거리
④ 감독   ⑤ 원작 소설

09

Redland Festival에 관한 다음 내용을 듣고, 일치하지 <u>않는</u> 것을 고르시오. 3점

① 건강을 증진하기 위한 과일 축제이다.
② Blue River Park에서 열리는 연례행사이다.
③ 과일 뷔페를 무제한 이용할 수 있다.
④ 입장료에 스포츠 활동 비용이 포함된다.
⑤ 사전 예약이 필요하다.

10

다음 표를 보면서 대화를 듣고, 여자가 주문할 헤어드라이어를 고르시오.

Best-Selling Hair Dryers

	Model	Power (wattage)	Material	Price	Cool Shot Setting
①	A	1,450	ceramic	$30	×
②	B	1,600	ceramic	$35	○
③	C	1,650	ionic	$40	×
④	D	1,700	ionic	$45	○
⑤	E	1,800	ionic	$53	○

11

대화를 듣고, 남자의 마지막 말에 대한 여자의 응답으로 가장 적절한 것을 고르시오.

① Right. He became a doctor to help people.
② No way. I don't think he sprained his ankle.
③ Yes. He just told me to relax for a few days.
④ Of course. You should have been more careful.
⑤ No. I didn't know that you were in the hospital.

12

대화를 듣고, 여자의 마지막 말에 대한 남자의 응답으로 가장 적절한 것을 고르시오.

① No problem. I made a reservation yesterday.
② Thanks. The food will be served in a minute.
③ I'm sorry. I won't be able to attend the party.
④ Okay. When are you going to throw the party?
⑤ Great. Can you tell me the name of the restaurant?

13

고2 2019년 3월 13번

대화를 듣고, 남자의 마지막 말에 대한 여자의 응답으로 가장 적절한 것을 고르시오. 3점

Woman: _____

① Not at all. We should empty the boxes first.
② Yes. We can keep clothes from getting dusty.
③ No way. We should keep pants and shirts separately.
④ Great. We can donate unnecessary clothes to charities.
⑤ No. We should never put our clothes in a box.

14

고2 2019년 3월 14번

대화를 듣고, 여자의 마지막 말에 대한 남자의 응답으로 가장 적절한 것을 고르시오. 3점

Man: _____

① That's awesome! It'll be very helpful.
② No, thanks. This app is not suitable for me.
③ Unbelievable! Your workout schedule is too tight.
④ Don't worry. You can use another fitness center.
⑤ I see. Maybe I can help you download the app.

15

고2 2019년 3월 15번

다음 상황 설명을 듣고, Willy가 수리 기사에게 할 말로 가장 적절한 것을 고르시오.

Willy: _____

① How much should I pay for the repair?
② You left one of your tools in my house.
③ I'm afraid the heater stopped working again.
④ Would you turn up the temperature for me?
⑤ Could you come and fix the heating system?

[16~17] 다음을 듣고, 물음에 답하시오.

16

고2 2019년 3월 16번

여자가 하는 말의 주제로 가장 적절한 것은?

① home appliances made smarter with technology
② ways of upgrading smart home appliances
③ how to buy smart home appliances online
④ benefits of energy-efficient home appliances
⑤ negative impacts of AI technologies on humans

17

고2 2019년 3월 17번

언급된 가전제품이 아닌 것은?

① washing machines   ② refrigerators
③ speakers   ④ air conditioners
⑤ vacuum cleaners

03 | 2019년 6월 학력평가

MP3 　동영상 강의
2SBL2_A03　2SBL2_L03

1번부터 17번까지는 듣고 답하는 문제입니다. 1번부터 15번까지는 한 번만 들려주고, 16번부터 17번까지는 두 번 들려줍니다. 방송을 잘 듣고 답을 하시기 바랍니다.

01 고2 2019년 6월 3번

다음을 듣고, 여자가 하는 말의 목적으로 가장 적절한 것을 고르시오.

① 새로운 수영 강사를 모집하려고
② 오후 수영 강좌 개설을 안내하려고
③ 강좌 등록 기간에 대해 공지하려고
④ 수영장 공사에 대한 양해를 구하려고
⑤ 수영 대회에 참가할 것을 권장하려고

02 고2 2019년 6월 4번

대화를 듣고, 남자의 의견으로 가장 적절한 것을 고르시오.

① 작문 실력은 상상력이 바탕이 되어야 한다.
② 글을 잘 쓰기 위해서는 독서를 많이 해야 한다.
③ 독해를 잘 하기 위해서는 속독법을 익혀야 한다.
④ 작가가 되기 위해서는 많은 자료 수집이 필요하다.
⑤ 풍부한 어휘 사용은 글의 내용을 다채롭게 해준다.

03 고2 2019년 6월 5번

대화를 듣고, 두 사람의 관계를 가장 잘 나타낸 것을 고르시오.

① 도서관 사서 - 학생　　② 작가 - 출판사 직원
③ 문학 평론가 - 기자　　④ 영화 감독 - 신인 배우
⑤ 문학 교사 - 학부모

04 고2 2019년 6월 6번

대화를 듣고, 그림에서 대화의 내용과 일치하지 않는 것을 고르시오.

05 고2 2019년 6월 7번

대화를 듣고, 여자가 할 일로 가장 적절한 것을 고르시오.

① 간식 구매하기　　② 여벌 옷 챙기기
③ 등산화 빌리기　　④ 여행 가방 챙기기
⑤ 친구 집 방문하기

06 고2 2019년 6월 9번

대화를 듣고, 여자가 지불할 금액을 고르시오. 3점

① $46　　② $54　　③ $60
④ $64　　⑤ $70

정답과 해설 : 01~06 10~12

07

대화를 듣고, 남자가 직장을 옮기려고 하는 이유를 고르시오.

① 다른 지방으로 이사를 가게 되어서
② 여가 시간을 더 많이 가지고 싶어서
③ 다른 회사에서 일할 것을 제안 받아서
④ 일에 대한 더 많은 보수를 받기 위해서
⑤ 새롭게 도전하여 능력을 개발하고 싶어서

10

다음 표를 보면서 대화를 듣고, 두 사람이 구입할 전기 주전자를 고르시오.

Electric Kettles

	Model	Capacity	Price	Color	Material
①	A	1 liter	$20	Pink	Plastic
②	B	1.5 liters	$25	White	Glass
③	C	1.5 liters	$27	Blue	Plastic
④	D	2 liters	$29	Black	Glass
⑤	E	2 liters	$32	Brown	Glass

08

대화를 듣고, Cat Fair에 관해 언급되지 <u>않은</u> 것을 고르시오.

① 행사 장소
② 행사 날짜
③ 티켓 가격
④ 기념품 지급
⑤ 특별 이벤트

11

대화를 듣고, 여자의 마지막 말에 대한 남자의 응답으로 가장 적절한 것을 고르시오.

① The book is easy to read.
② It needs more parking spaces.
③ It has various sportswear brands.
④ I am touched by the story of the movie.
⑤ My friends love to go shopping together.

09

Great Light Festival에 관한 다음 내용을 듣고, 일치하지 <u>않는</u> 것을 고르시오.

① 유명한 조명 예술가들이 참여한다.
② 큰 크리스마스 트리 앞에서 사진을 찍을 수 있다.
③ 12월 1일부터 한 달 동안 열린다.
④ 티켓은 온라인으로만 구매할 수 있다.
⑤ 조명이 들어오는 시간은 오후 6시부터 오후 10시까지이다.

12

대화를 듣고, 남자의 마지막 말에 대한 여자의 응답으로 가장 적절한 것을 고르시오.

① Right, the whole room is too bright.
② Cleaning will be finished in a minute.
③ Okay, wash your hair in the bathroom.
④ The carpenter is expected to arrive here.
⑤ Then, I'll go and buy a new one right now.

13

대화를 듣고, 여자의 마지막 말에 대한 남자의 응답으로 가장 적절한 것을 고르시오. 3점

Man: _____

① Let's invite other members to our club.
② You can make election campaign posters for me.
③ Don't worry, I'll vote against her in this election.
④ Be sure to wash your drawing tools after the contest.
⑤ Please check if she runs for student council president.

14

대화를 듣고, 남자의 마지막 말에 대한 여자의 응답으로 가장 적절한 것을 고르시오. 3점

Woman: _____

① I'm learning Spanish by reading comic books.
② He said setting a big goal should be done first.
③ Yeah, little things are sometimes hard to achieve.
④ Exactly. Small steps eventually lead to big ones.
⑤ I know. Using many examples is efficient for studying.

15

다음 상황 설명을 듣고, Sarah가 Peter에게 할 말로 가장 적절한 것을 고르시오.

Sarah: _____

① Let's practice on stage when nobody is there.
② How about going to watch a play with your friends?
③ Why don't you practice acting in front of your family?
④ You'd better talk with the teacher and change your role.
⑤ Spending a lot of time memorizing the script is important.

[16~17] 다음을 듣고, 물음에 답하시오.

16

남자가 하는 말의 주제로 가장 적절한 것은?

① importance of movies in human life
② animals that are friendly to humans
③ process of creating movie characters
④ reasons animations are getting popular
⑤ movies where animals are the main focus

17

언급된 동물이 아닌 것은?

① dog   ② lion   ③ dinosaur
④ rabbit   ⑤ pig

※ 최신 영어 영역 시험의 듣기 문항 순서 변경에 따라 회차 내 문항 순서를 재배치하였습니다.

04 2019년 9월 학력평가

MP3
2SBL2_A04

동영상 강의
2SBL2_L04

1번부터 17번까지는 듣고 답하는 문제입니다. 1번부터 15번까지는 한 번만 들려주고, 16번부터 17번까지는 두 번 들려줍니다. 방송을 잘 듣고 답을 하시기 바랍니다.

01
고2 2019년 9월 3번

다음을 듣고, 남자가 하는 말의 목적으로 가장 적절한 것을 고르시오.

① 사이버폭력 예방 교육일정을 공지하려고
② 학생들에게 학교 홈페이지 가입을 독려하려고
③ 학교 공식 소셜 미디어 페이지 개설을 알리려고
④ 학교 홈페이지 디자인 개선에 대한 의견을 공모하려고
⑤ 소셜 미디어 사용 시 개인 정보 보호 방법을 안내하려고

02
고2 2019년 9월 4번

대화를 듣고, 여자의 의견으로 가장 적절한 것을 고르시오.

① 청중의 특성에 맞는 연설 주제의 선택이 필요하다.
② 시각 자료의 활용은 청중의 집중을 유도할 수 있다.
③ 연설자의 목소리 톤은 연설의 내용에 따라 달라야 한다.
④ 대본을 보지 않고 연설하는 것은 설득력을 높일 수 있다.
⑤ 연설 연습 시 녹화를 활용하면 전달력 향상에 도움이 된다.

03
고2 2019년 9월 5번

대화를 듣고, 두 사람의 관계를 가장 잘 나타낸 것을 고르시오.

① 학생 - 사서교사
② 독자 - 소설가
③ 출판사 편집자 - 삽화가
④ 관객 - 무용가
⑤ 시나리오 작가 - 영화감독

04
고2 2019년 9월 6번

대화를 듣고, 그림에서 대화의 내용과 일치하지 않는 것을 고르시오.

05
고2 2019년 9월 7번

대화를 듣고, 남자가 여자에게 부탁한 일로 가장 적절한 것을 고르시오.

① 책 구입하기
② 번역본 검토하기
③ 책 포장하기
④ 이메일 보내기
⑤ 번역 앱 추천하기

06
고2 2019년 9월 9번

대화를 듣고, 남자가 지불할 금액을 고르시오. 3점

① $11
② $13
③ $15
④ $18
⑤ $21

07

고2 2019년 9월 8번

대화를 듣고, 여자가 개를 키울 수 없는 이유를 고르시오.

① 낮에 개를 돌볼 사람이 없어서
② 부모님이 허락하지 않아서
③ 개를 키울 마당이 없어서
④ 동생이 개를 무서워해서
⑤ 개 알레르기가 있어서

08

고2 2019년 9월 10번

대화를 듣고, World Food Festival에 관해 언급되지 않은 것을 고르시오.

① 개최 장소　　　　② 개최 일시
③ 프로그램 종류　　④ 반입 금지 물품
⑤ 주차 요금

09

고2 2019년 9월 11번

Arusha National Park Tour에 관한 다음 내용을 듣고, 일치하지 않는 것을 고르시오.

① 1일 투어 프로그램이다.
② 호수와 산의 풍경을 즐길 수 있다.
③ 다양한 야생 동물을 볼 수 있다.
④ 승차 장소와 하차 장소가 다르다.
⑤ 종료 시간은 날씨에 따라 달라질 수 있다.

10

고2 2019년 9월 12번

다음 표를 보면서 대화를 듣고, 두 사람이 구매할 Air Fryer를 고르시오.

Air Fryer

	Model	Price	Automatic Switch Off	Capacity (liters)	Warranty
①	A	$59	×	2	1 year
②	B	$68	○	2	1 year
③	C	$84	○	4	1 year
④	D	$95	○	4	2 years
⑤	E	$109	×	5	2 years

11

고2 2019년 9월 1번

대화를 듣고, 여자의 마지막 말에 대한 남자의 응답으로 가장 적절한 것을 고르시오.

① Sorry. I have plans tonight.
② I always buy tickets online.
③ You can do better next time.
④ You must have watched it a lot.
⑤ Actually, I wouldn't recommend it.

12

고2 2019년 9월 2번

대화를 듣고, 남자의 마지막 말에 대한 여자의 응답으로 가장 적절한 것을 고르시오.

① That's okay. You can deliver it tomorrow.
② Why don't you call the delivery person?
③ Don't worry. I'll return it for you.
④ Can you help me with packing?
⑤ Let's open the package now.

정답과 해설 : 07~12 17~19

13

대화를 듣고, 여자의 마지막 말에 대한 남자의 응답으로 가장
적절한 것을 고르시오.

Man: _____

① I hope you'll get better.

② I'm afraid I failed the exam.

③ Sometimes stress can be helpful.

④ Sure. I'll buy you some chocolate.

⑤ Okay. I'll exercise when I'm stressed.

14

대화를 듣고, 남자의 마지막 말에 대한 여자의 응답으로 가장
적절한 것을 고르시오. 3점

Woman: _____

① Don't worry. It'll only filter out the ads.

② Be careful. Don't trust online ads too much.

③ You're right. I'll consider using the program.

④ That can put your private information at risk.

⑤ Downloading the program will slow your
computer.

15

다음 상황 설명을 듣고, Eve가 Tom에게 할 말로 가장 적절한
것을 고르시오. 3점

Eve: _____

① You should find a job related to your field of
study.

② How about getting help from a career
counselor?

③ Do some research before choosing your major.

④ If I were you, I'd focus on studying history.

⑤ Why don't you apply for an internship?

[16~17] 다음을 듣고, 물음에 답하시오.

16

여자가 하는 말의 주제로 가장 적절한 것은?

① useful tips to finding parking spaces in cities
quickly

② efforts in Europe to handle air pollution from
traffic

③ impacts of greenhouse gases on the
environment

④ causes of traffic jams in European capital cities

⑤ various renewable energy sources in Europe

17

언급된 나라가 아닌 것은?

① Denmark ② France ③ Belgium
④ Switzerland ⑤ Germany

05 2019년 11월 학력평가

1번부터 17번까지는 듣고 답하는 문제입니다. 1번부터 15번까지는 한 번만 들려주고, 16번부터 17번까지는 두 번 들려줍니다. 방송을 잘 듣고 답을 하시기 바랍니다.

01 고2 2019년 11월 3번

다음을 듣고, 남자가 하는 말의 목적으로 가장 적절한 것을 고르시오.

① 행정실 운영 시간 변경을 안내하려고
② 불법 주차 집중 단속 기간을 공지하려고
③ 신설된 자전거 주차 시설에 대해 알려주려고
④ 도서관 설립을 위한 모금 행사를 홍보하려고
⑤ 자전거 통학 시 보호 장비 착용을 독려하려고

02 고2 2019년 11월 4번

대화를 듣고, 여자의 의견으로 가장 적절한 것을 고르시오.

① 외국 여행을 할 때 현지 문화를 존중해야 한다.
② 여행을 가기 전에 여행자 보험에 가입해야 한다.
③ 과소비를 줄이기 위해 지출 계획을 세워야 한다.
④ 관광객 유치를 위해 관광 상품을 다양화해야 한다.
⑤ 응급 처치 방법을 익혀 응급 상황에 대비해야 한다.

03 고2 2019년 11월 5번

대화를 듣고, 두 사람의 관계를 가장 잘 나타낸 것을 고르시오.

① 박물관 큐레이터 - 관람객 ② 사진작가 - 비평가
③ 메이크업 아티스트 - 고객 ④ 화가 - 기자
⑤ 미술 교사 - 학생

04 고2 2019년 11월 6번

대화를 듣고, 그림에서 대화의 내용과 일치하지 않는 것을 고르시오.

05 고2 2019년 11월 7번

대화를 듣고, 여자가 할 일로 가장 적절한 것을 고르시오.

① 현수막 걸기 ② 유인물 출력하기
③ 마이크 준비하기 ④ 프로젝터 점검하기
⑤ 간식 구입하기

06 고2 2019년 11월 9번

대화를 듣고, 남자가 지불할 금액을 고르시오.

① $80 ② $90 ③ $92
④ $98 ⑤ $100

07
고2 2019년 11월 8번

대화를 듣고, 여자가 커피 박람회에 갈 수 없는 이유를 고르시오.

① 홍보 동영상을 제작해야 해서
② 커피 원두를 사러 가야 해서
③ 제빵 수업을 지도해야 해서
④ 벼룩시장에 참여해야 해서
⑤ 병원 진료를 받아야 해서

08
고2 2019년 11월 10번

대화를 듣고, Forest Walk에 관해 언급되지 않은 것을 고르시오.

① 목적
② 시작 시간
③ 준비 물품
④ 신청 방법
⑤ 최대 참가 인원

09
고2 2019년 11월 11번

Langford Night Market에 관한 다음 내용을 듣고, 일치하지 않는 것을 고르시오.

① 9월 1일부터 시작한다.
② 올해 주제는 세계 음식 축제이다.
③ 라이브 음악 공연이 매일 밤 열린다.
④ 어린이를 위한 특별 공간이 있다.
⑤ 비가 와도 일정대로 진행된다.

10
고2 2019년 11월 12번

다음 표를 보면서 대화를 듣고, 여자가 주문할 컴퓨터 의자를 고르시오.

Computer Chairs

	Model	Price	Material	Height	Headrest
①	A	$110	Leather	Changeable	○
②	B	$95	Leather	Fixed	×
③	C	$80	Fabric	Changeable	○
④	D	$75	Fabric	Changeable	×
⑤	E	$70	Fabric	Fixed	×

11
고2 2019년 11월 1번

대화를 듣고, 남자의 마지막 말에 대한 여자의 응답으로 가장 적절한 것을 고르시오.

① Yes. I've already bought the train ticket.
② No. I can't go to the meeting tomorrow.
③ Cheer up. You can do better next time.
④ That's okay. You can stay in my home.
⑤ I see. I hope mom gets better soon.

12
고2 2019년 11월 2번

대화를 듣고, 여자의 마지막 말에 대한 남자의 응답으로 가장 적절한 것을 고르시오.

① You're right. I hope the weather is fine.
② Sure. You'll like my pictures of the festival.
③ Sorry. I was not allowed to take any pictures.
④ No more. You've already had enough apples.
⑤ Absolutely! I'd love to taste your pies.

13

대화를 듣고, 여자의 마지막 말에 대한 남자의 응답으로 가장 적절한 것을 고르시오. [3점]

Man: _____

① Alright. I'll get it and bring it to you right away.
② Exactly. I should have brought the documents.
③ I'm sorry. None of us are available that day.
④ Certainly. It'll take 30 minutes to finish my test.
⑤ Don't worry. He'll drop you there before the test.

14

대화를 듣고, 남자의 마지막 말에 대한 여자의 응답으로 가장 적절한 것을 고르시오. [3점]

Woman: _____

① Right. You can ignore his selfish and rude behavior.
② Okay. I'll try to get him more motivated in learning.
③ Yes. I should make time each day to spend with him.
④ Certainly. I'll ask him to share his toys with his brother.
⑤ I see. You need to encourage him to fall asleep on his own.

15

다음 상황 설명을 듣고, Mike가 Amy에게 할 말로 가장 적절한 것을 고르시오. [3점]

Mike: _____

① You need to develop your logical thinking for discussions.
② I'd like to recommend you for the leader of this book club.
③ Could you make more of an effort to find new club members?
④ Why don't you keep reading journals to improve your writing?
⑤ You should be responsible about reading books for club activities.

[16~17] 다음을 듣고, 물음에 답하시오.

16

여자가 하는 말의 주제로 가장 적절한 것은?

① roles of robots in rescuing animals
② robots inspired by real world animals
③ methods to ensure good animal welfare
④ robots competing for jobs in our society
⑤ animals helping improve medical science

17

언급된 동물이 <u>아닌</u> 것은?

① snake   ② bat   ③ ant
④ dog   ⑤ frog

06 | 2020년 3월 학력평가

1번부터 17번까지는 듣고 답하는 문제입니다. 1번부터 15번까지는 한 번만 들려주고, 16번부터 17번까지는 두 번 들려줍니다. 방송을 잘 듣고 답을 하시기 바랍니다.

01
고2 2020년 3월 3번

다음을 듣고, 남자가 하는 말의 목적으로 가장 적절한 것을 고르시오.

① 병실 사용 시 유의 사항을 설명하려고
② 병문안 시 면회 시간 준수를 당부하려고
③ 병원 내 새로운 편의 시설을 소개하려고
④ 병원 주변 도로 통제 구역을 공지하려고
⑤ 병원 일부 출입구의 사용 제한을 안내하려고

02
고2 2020년 3월 4번

대화를 듣고, 여자의 의견으로 가장 적절한 것을 고르시오.

① 꾸준한 봉사 활동은 자아 존중감을 높인다.
② 남을 가르칠 때 자신감을 갖는 것이 중요하다.
③ 학습량과 교과 성적이 정비례하는 것은 아니다.
④ 남을 가르치는 것은 자신의 학습에 도움이 된다.
⑤ 알고 있는 것과 가르치는 것은 별개의 문제이다.

03
고2 2020년 3월 5번

대화를 듣고, 두 사람의 관계를 가장 잘 나타낸 것을 고르시오.

① 뉴스 제보자 — 기자
② 해외 특파원 — 방송 제작자
③ 동아리 담당 교사 — 방송 작가
④ 방송 광고 의뢰인 — 촬영 감독
⑤ 방송국 견학 학생 — 뉴스 진행자

04
고2 2020년 3월 6번

대화를 듣고, 그림에서 대화의 내용과 일치하지 않는 것을 고르시오.

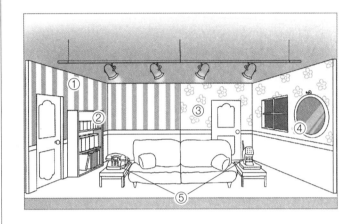

05
고2 2020년 3월 7번

대화를 듣고, 남자가 여자에게 부탁한 일로 가장 적절한 것을 고르시오.

① 퇴임식장 예약하기
② 사진 파일 보내주기
③ 점심 식사 주문하기
④ 행사 사진 촬영하기
⑤ 신문 기사 작성하기

06
고2 2020년 3월 9번

대화를 듣고, 여자가 지불할 금액을 고르시오. 3점

① $36   ② $45   ③ $54
④ $63   ⑤ $72

07

대화를 듣고, 남자가 배드민턴 레슨에 갈 수 없는 이유를 고르시오.

① 독감 예방 주사를 맞아서
② 발표 준비를 해야 해서
③ 수면 시간이 부족해서
④ 왼쪽 발목을 다쳐서
⑤ 진료 예약이 있어서

08

대화를 듣고, Dream Bio Research Project에 관해 언급되지 않은 것을 고르시오.

① 연구원 수　　② 예산 규모　　③ 연구 목적
④ 연구 장소　　⑤ 연구 기간

09

Marathon Reading Program에 관한 다음 내용을 듣고, 일치하지 않는 것을 고르시오.

① 학생, 교사, 학부모를 대상으로 한다.
② 오후 2시에 시작한다.
③ 학생들은 독서 감상문을 써야 한다.
④ 간식과 음료는 제공되지 않는다.
⑤ 이번 주 금요일까지 신청해야 한다.

10

다음 표를 보면서 대화를 듣고, 여자가 주문할 휴대용 스피커와 마이크 세트를 고르시오.

Portable Speaker & Microphone Sets

	Model	Price	Running Time	Color	Clip Microphone
①	A	$65	8 hours	White	×
②	B	$70	10 hours	Grey	○
③	C	$80	11 hours	White	○
④	D	$85	12 hours	Red	×
⑤	E	$110	15 hours	Grey	○

11

대화를 듣고, 여자의 마지막 말에 대한 남자의 응답으로 가장 적절한 것을 고르시오.

① Sorry, but our recipe is a secret.
② Sure. I'd like to buy this dressing.
③ No thanks. We don't need the recipe.
④ Yes, I can make you the vegetable soup.
⑤ Okay, I'll bring you the salad right away.

12

대화를 듣고, 남자의 마지막 말에 대한 여자의 응답으로 가장 적절한 것을 고르시오.

① I have no more clothes to donate.
② You can pick them up this afternoon.
③ Let me check if we can accept them.
④ I forgot to separate whites and colors.
⑤ Please bring the receipt to get a refund.

정답과 해설 : 07~12 27~29

13

고2 2020년 3월 13번

대화를 듣고, 여자의 마지막 말에 대한 남자의 응답으로 가장 적절한 것을 고르시오. 3점

Man: _____

① Okay. We'll let you have a one-month break.

② Please come for a medical checkup after a month.

③ Sorry. You'd better look for another sports center.

④ Sure. You can take the swimming lesson next week.

⑤ We offer a 20% discount for an annual membership.

14

고2 2020년 3월 14번

대화를 듣고, 남자의 마지막 말에 대한 여자의 응답으로 가장 적절한 것을 고르시오. 3점

Woman: _____

① We can throw a farewell party for him.

② I have another picture that I've almost finished.

③ I don't think I can exhibit my painting this time.

④ He already submitted his painting for the exhibition.

⑤ I believe all the families will come to the exhibition.

15

고2 2020년 3월 15번

다음 상황 설명을 듣고, Ryan이 Amy에게 할 말로 가장 적절한 것을 고르시오.

Ryan: _____

① I won't break my promises to the students.

② We should use the school facilities more often.

③ I'll do my best whether I win or lose the election.

④ You need to put all your belongings in the locker now.

⑤ We'd better find out if the school can replace the lockers.

[16~17] 다음을 듣고, 물음에 답하시오.

16

고2 2020년 3월 16번

여자가 하는 말의 주제로 가장 적절한 것은?

① the origin of the ancient Olympic Games

② the positive effects of the Olympic Games

③ the selection process for the Olympic athletes

④ reasons why some Olympic Games were cancelled

⑤ changes to the sports events in the Olympic Games

17

고2 2020년 3월 17번

언급된 스포츠 종목이 아닌 것은?

① soccer ② tennis ③ wrestling
④ handball ⑤ taekwondo

07 2020년 6월 학력평가

MP3
25BL2_A07

동영상 강의
25BL2_L07

😊 1번부터 17번까지는 듣고 답하는 문제입니다. 1번부터 15번까지는 한 번만 들려주고, 16번부터 17번까지는 두 번 들려줍니다. 방송을 잘 듣고 답을 하시기 바랍니다.

01
고2 2020년 6월 3번

다음을 듣고, 남자가 하는 말의 목적으로 가장 적절한 것을 고르시오.

① 오디션 개최를 공지하려고
② 뮤지컬 공연을 홍보하려고
③ 과제 제출 방법을 설명하려고
④ 재능 기부 방법을 안내하려고
⑤ 연극 수업 참여를 독려하려고

02
고2 2020년 6월 4번

대화를 듣고, 여자의 의견으로 가장 적절한 것을 고르시오.

① 기억력은 반복적인 학습을 통해 향상된다.
② 책을 읽을 때 음악을 듣는 것은 도움이 된다.
③ 꾸준한 독서 습관을 형성하는 것이 중요하다.
④ 음악 감상은 아동의 창의력 발달에 효과적이다.
⑤ 청력 보호를 위해 적절한 음량 조절이 필요하다.

03
고2 2020년 6월 5번

대화를 듣고, 두 사람의 관계를 가장 잘 나타낸 것을 고르시오.

① 배관공 - 집주인
② 식당 지배인 - 요리사
③ 관광 안내원 - 관광객
④ 부동산 중개인 - 고객
⑤ 인테리어 디자이너 - 의뢰인

04
고2 2020년 6월 6번

대화를 듣고, 그림에서 대화의 내용과 일치하지 않는 것을 고르시오.

05
고2 2020년 6월 7번

대화를 듣고, 여자가 할 일로 가장 적절한 것을 고르시오.

① 케이크 주문하기
② 감사 편지 쓰기
③ 영상 편집하기
④ 파티 공지하기
⑤ 교실 꾸미기

06
고2 2020년 6월 9번

대화를 듣고, 여자가 지불할 금액을 고르시오. 3점

① $30
② $36
③ $40
④ $45
⑤ $50

07
고2 2020년 6월 8번

대화를 듣고, 남자가 전시회에 갈 수 없는 이유를 고르시오.

① 봉사활동을 해야 해서
② 축구 경기를 해야 해서
③ 과학 과제를 해야 해서
④ 아르바이트를 해야 해서
⑤ 기말고사 준비를 해야 해서

08
고2 2020년 6월 10번

대화를 듣고, Flea Market에 관해 언급되지 않은 것을 고르시오.

① 개최 일시   ② 행사 장소   ③ 판매자 참가비
④ 신청 방법   ⑤ 판매 가능 물품

09
고2 2020년 6월 11번

Highland Movie Night에 관한 다음 내용을 듣고, 일치하지 않는 것을 고르시오.

① 매월 개최하는 행사이다.
② Highland 주민에게는 무료이다.
③ Lincoln 도서관에서 열린다.
④ 사전에 등록해야 한다.
⑤ 음식물 반입이 허용된다.

10
고2 2020년 6월 12번

다음 표를 보면서 대화를 듣고, 남자가 구매할 여행 가방을 고르시오.

Suitcases

	Model	Size(inch)	Price	Color	Free Gift
①	A	18	$80	white	travel pillow
②	B	24	$100	white	umbrella
③	C	26	$130	black	umbrella
④	D	28	$160	black	travel pillow
⑤	E	30	$210	white	umbrella

11
고2 2020년 6월 1번

대화를 듣고, 남자의 마지막 말에 대한 여자의 응답으로 가장 적절한 것을 고르시오.

① Yes. They look nice on you.
② Yeah. Let's go shop for them.
③ Right. Thanks for inviting me.
④ Sorry. I can't go to the party.
⑤ No. I didn't take the shoes yet.

12
고2 2020년 6월 2번

대화를 듣고, 여자의 마지막 말에 대한 남자의 응답으로 가장 적절한 것을 고르시오.

① All right! It's perfect for walking outside.
② Wonderful! The movie is a must-see.
③ Thanks. I'll park the car by myself.
④ Sorry. I didn't check the weather.
⑤ Whew! I can't walk any longer.

정답과 해설 : 07~12 32~34

13

대화를 듣고, 여자의 마지막 말에 대한 남자의 응답으로 가장 적절한 것을 고르시오. 3점

Man: _____

① That's true. I'll buy a new camera next week.
② Too bad. I will be disappointed if you can't come.
③ Really? You should tell your boss about the concert.
④ Never mind. The concert will be rescheduled anyway.
⑤ You're right. I'll just watch the video after the concert.

14

대화를 듣고, 남자의 마지막 말에 대한 여자의 응답으로 가장 적절한 것을 고르시오. 3점

Woman: _____

① Certainly! You are the best driver ever.
② Great. Let's check the bus schedule then.
③ No worries. It'll be the best season for us.
④ Of course. The bus fares are too expensive.
⑤ No problem. We'll be able to change the flight.

15

다음 상황 설명을 듣고, Katie가 Brian에게 할 말로 가장 적절한 것을 고르시오.

Katie: _____

① You'd better change your eating habits.
② We should choose the topic of the project.
③ Why don't we try an online survey instead?
④ Could you collect the copies for the survey?
⑤ I've already made the questions for the survey.

[16~17] 다음을 듣고, 물음에 답하시오.

16

여자가 하는 말의 주제로 가장 적절한 것은?

① lucky numbers in ancient times
② numbers that bring wealth to people
③ relationship between numbers and religion
④ symbolic meanings of numbers across cultures
⑤ danger of using favorite numbers in passwords

17

언급된 숫자가 아닌 것은?

① four   ② seven   ③ nine
④ ten   ⑤ thirteen

※ 최신 영어 영역 시험의 듣기 문항 순서 변경에 따라 회차 내 문항 순서를 재배치하였습니다.

08 2020년 9월 학력평가

MP3 2SBL2_A08   동영상 강의 2SBL2_L08

👂 1번부터 17번까지는 듣고 답하는 문제입니다. 1번부터 15번까지는 한 번만 들려주고, 16번부터 17번까지는 두 번 들려줍니다. 방송을 잘 듣고 답을 하시기 바랍니다.

01
고2 2020년 9월 3번

다음을 듣고, 남자가 하는 말의 목적으로 가장 적절한 것을 고르시오.

① 축제 장소 변경을 공지하려고
② 교내 동아리 부원을 모집하려고
③ 교내 축제 홍보문구를 공모하려고
④ 동아리 전시회 관람을 독려하려고
⑤ 축제 참가신청 방법을 안내하려고

02
고2 2020년 9월 4번

대화를 듣고, 여자의 의견으로 가장 적절한 것을 고르시오.

① 다양한 신체활동은 어린이의 창의력 신장에 필수적이다.
② 그림 그리기는 어린이의 집중력 향상에 도움이 된다.
③ 그림책을 읽어 주는 것은 자녀의 정서 안정에 좋다.
④ 부모와의 많은 대화는 자녀의 언어발달을 촉진한다.
⑤ 독서는 어린이의 상상력을 키우는 데 효과가 있다.

03
고2 2020년 9월 5번

대화를 듣고, 두 사람의 관계를 가장 잘 나타낸 것을 고르시오.

① 디자이너 - 패션모델
② 영화감독 - 영화배우
③ 출판사 직원 - 소설가
④ 잡지사 기자 - 웹툰 작가
⑤ 미술관 큐레이터 - 화가

04
고2 2020년 9월 6번

대화를 듣고, 그림에서 대화의 내용과 일치하지 <u>않는</u> 것을 고르시오.

05
고2 2020년 9월 7번

대화를 듣고, 남자가 여자에게 부탁한 일로 가장 적절한 것을 고르시오.

① 인터넷 연결 예약하기
② 컴퓨터 수리 맡기기
③ 영수증 재발급 받기
④ 가전제품 교환하기
⑤ 청소업체 연락하기

06
고2 2020년 9월 9번

대화를 듣고, 남자가 지불할 금액을 고르시오. [3점]

① $41   ② $46   ③ $51
④ $56   ⑤ $60

07

고2 2020년 9월 8번

대화를 듣고, 여자가 보드게임을 하러 갈 수 없는 이유를 고르시오.

① 병문안을 가야 해서
② 시험공부를 해야 해서
③ 방과 후 수업이 있어서
④ 생일 파티에 참석해야 해서
⑤ 스키용품을 사러 가야 해서

08

고2 2020년 9월 10번

대화를 듣고, Comedy Allstars에 관해 언급되지 않은 것을 고르시오.

① 공연 장소
② 공연 시작일
③ 관람료
④ 출연자
⑤ 티켓 예매 방법

09

고2 2020년 9월 11번

Organic Fair에 관한 다음 내용을 듣고, 일치하지 않는 것을 고르시오.

① 3일 동안 열린다.
② 다양한 유기농 제품이 전시된다.
③ 현장에서 제품 구매 시 할인을 받을 수 있다.
④ 유기농 비누 만들기 수업은 오후에 진행된다.
⑤ 온라인 사전 등록 시 무료로 입장할 수 있다.

10

고2 2020년 9월 12번

다음 표를 보면서 대화를 듣고, 여자가 구입할 무선 이어폰을 고르시오.

Wireless Earbuds

	Model	Price	Play Time (from a single charge)	Noise Canceling	Color
①	A	$135	5 hours	×	Silver
②	B	$145	8 hours	×	Silver
③	C	$160	8 hours	○	White
④	D	$180	10 hours	○	Black
⑤	E	$205	10 hours	○	Black

11

고2 2020년 9월 1번

대화를 듣고, 남자의 마지막 말에 대한 여자의 응답으로 가장 적절한 것을 고르시오.

① It was shipped to the wrong address.
② I'd like to pick up the book in person.
③ I couldn't find the book in that section.
④ It's damaged. Several pages are missing.
⑤ No problem. I'll pay with this credit card.

12

고2 2020년 9월 2번

대화를 듣고, 여자의 마지막 말에 대한 남자의 응답으로 가장 적절한 것을 고르시오.

① I don't think Italian food is healthy.
② I believe what looks good tastes good.
③ My aunt recently taught me the recipe.
④ Remember that too many cooks spoil the soup.
⑤ You should have followed the recipe I gave you.

13

대화를 듣고, 남자의 마지막 말에 대한 여자의 응답으로 가장 적절한 것을 고르시오. 3점

Woman:

① Bad posture can cause increased tension in your back.

② Be careful when you lift up something heavy.

③ Here are some tips for sleeping problems.

④ Too much exercise can lead to muscle ache.

⑤ Taking regular breaks while studying will help you focus.

14

대화를 듣고, 여자의 마지막 말에 대한 남자의 응답으로 가장 적절한 것을 고르시오. 3점

Man:

① Sure. I'll be careful not to forget the citations.

② Thank you. I'll start reading editorials on that site.

③ Summarizing articles isn't easy, but it works for me.

④ You're right. Nothing is better than writing by myself.

⑤ I agree. Not all information on the Web is trustworthy.

15

다음 상황 설명을 듣고, Brian이 Jennifer에게 할 말로 가장 적절한 것을 고르시오.

Brian:

① We should work out together more often.

② Don't waste money buying so many tumblers.

③ We'd better drink more water while we exercise.

④ When does the convenience store near the gym close?

⑤ Why don't you get a tumbler and bring it to the gym?

[16~17] 다음을 듣고, 물음에 답하시오.

16

남자가 하는 말의 주제로 가장 적절한 것은?

① superfoods for anti-aging

② key nutrients for kids' growth

③ effects of vitamins on the body

④ foods to protect kids' eye health

⑤ importance of eating a balanced diet

17

언급된 식품이 아닌 것은?

① carrots ② cheese ③ blueberries

④ almonds ⑤ salmon

09 2020년 11월 학력평가

1번부터 17번까지는 듣고 답하는 문제입니다. 1번부터 15번까지는 한 번만 들려주고, 16번부터 17번까지는 두 번 들려줍니다. 방송을 잘 듣고 답을 하시기 바랍니다.

01

다음을 듣고, 남자가 하는 말의 목적으로 가장 적절한 것을 고르시오.

① 기초 체력 향상을 위한 운동법을 설명하려고
② 체육 대회 참가 시 필요한 준비물을 공지하려고
③ 체육관 공사로 인한 수업 장소 변경을 알리려고
④ 체육 수업 시간에 준수해야 할 규칙을 안내하려고
⑤ 무리한 운동으로 인한 부상의 위험성을 경고하려고

02

대화를 듣고, 여자의 의견으로 가장 적절한 것을 고르시오.

① 족욕을 하는 것은 건강에 도움이 된다.
② 발 건강을 위해서 양말을 신어야 한다.
③ 운동 종목에 적합한 신발을 선택해야 한다.
④ 계절에 맞는 소재의 양말을 구입해야 한다.
⑤ 높은 굽의 신발은 척추에 무리를 줄 수 있다.

03

대화를 듣고, 두 사람의 관계를 가장 잘 나타낸 것을 고르시오.

① 가수 - 안무가
② 작곡가 - 작사가
③ 성우 - 녹음 기사
④ 방송 작가 - 프로듀서
⑤ 뮤지컬 배우 - 음향 감독

04

대화를 듣고, 그림에서 대화의 내용과 일치하지 않는 것을 고르시오.

05

대화를 듣고, 남자가 여자에게 부탁한 일로 가장 적절한 것을 고르시오.

① 집안 청소하기
② 저녁 식사 준비하기
③ 부모님 마중 나가기
④ 비행기 도착 시간 확인하기
⑤ 자동차에 주유하기

06

대화를 듣고, 여자가 지불할 금액을 고르시오. 3점

① $72
② $80
③ $90
④ $100
⑤ $108

07

대화를 듣고, 남자가 스터디 모임에 참여할 수 없는 이유를 고르시오.

① 영어 수업을 들어야 해서
② 학교 도서관에 가야 해서
③ 봉사 활동에 참여해야 해서
④ 다친 다리를 치료해야 해서
⑤ 건강 검진을 받아야 해서

08

대화를 듣고, Lakeville Campground에 관해 언급되지 않은 것을 고르시오.

① 주변 자연환경   ② 편의 시설   ③ 이용료
④ 이용 시간   ⑤ 예약 방법

09

Circus Experience Festival에 관한 다음 내용을 듣고, 일치하지 않는 것을 고르시오.

① 11월 20일에 시작해서 3일 동안 지속된다.
② 마술과 저글링을 포함한 다양한 체험 활동을 제공할 것이다.
③ 각 활동의 참가자 수를 10명으로 제한할 것이다.
④ 포토존에서 서커스 광대들과 함께 사진을 찍을 수 있다.
⑤ 기념품으로 무료 티셔츠를 증정할 것이다.

10

다음 표를 보면서 대화를 듣고, 여자가 구입할 무선 마이크 세트를 고르시오.

Wireless Microphone Sets

	Product	Receiving Distance	Headset	Color	Price
①	A	10m	not included	White	$50
②	B	20m	included	Silver	$65
③	C	30m	included	Red	$80
④	D	40m	included	Gold	$90
⑤	E	50m	not included	Black	$100

11

대화를 듣고, 남자의 마지막 말에 대한 여자의 응답으로 가장 적절한 것을 고르시오.

① No problem. Just let me know when you're ready.
② I'm afraid I can't. I lost my library card yesterday.
③ Sure. You can borrow my books anytime you want.
④ I'm sorry. The sunlight is too strong to go outside.
⑤ Of course. I'm going to walk to the library myself.

12

대화를 듣고, 여자의 마지막 말에 대한 남자의 응답으로 가장 적절한 것을 고르시오.

① I see. I'll take another road then.
② Really? Go to the hospital right now.
③ That's too bad. You should've left earlier.
④ Sorry. I got a speeding ticket on the highway.
⑤ Okay. I'll make a reservation for the restaurant.

13

대화를 듣고, 남자의 마지막 말에 대한 여자의 응답으로 가장 적절한 것을 고르시오.

Woman: _____

① Not really. I should change my major.

② I agree. I'd rather major in mathematics.

③ Oh, no. Let me call them and check again.

④ I got it. Popularity of the major is important.

⑤ Terrific! I can be a successful business person.

14

대화를 듣고, 여자의 마지막 말에 대한 남자의 응답으로 가장 적절한 것을 고르시오. 3점

Man: _____

① Don't worry. I know they'll definitely support your opinion.

② Of course not. We're not able to switch our club leaders now.

③ I understand. I'm going to look for another research topic then.

④ All right. That way we'll satisfy more members than last time.

⑤ Never mind. We can reschedule a time for our group discussion.

15

다음 상황 설명을 듣고, Melissa가 Bob에게 할 말로 가장 적절한 것을 고르시오. 3점

Melissa: _____

① Make sure to set the password for your credit card.

② You have to check if the Internet connection is stable.

③ Why don't you keep your security program up-to-date?

④ Don't illegally access other people's personal information.

⑤ How about adding the items to your online shopping cart?

[16~17] 다음을 듣고, 물음에 답하시오.

16

여자가 하는 말의 주제로 가장 적절한 것은?

① blooming seasons for flowers

② implied meanings of flowers

③ ways to make flower beds

④ origins of national flowers

⑤ steps for planting flowers

17

언급된 꽃이 <u>아닌</u> 것은?

① carnations　　② tulips　　③ irises

④ roses　　⑤ daisies

정답과 해설 : 13~17 44~46

※ 고2 2021년 3월 학력평가 시험지와 문항 순서가 동일합니다.

옆 QR 코드를 가리고 찍으세요.

10 2021년 3월 학력평가

MP3
동영상 강의

2SBL2_A10   2SBL2_L10

😊 1번부터 17번까지는 듣고 답하는 문제입니다. 1번부터 15번까지는 한 번만 들려주고, 16번부터 17번까지는 두 번 들려줍니다. 방송을 잘 듣고 답을 하시기 바랍니다.

01

다음을 듣고, 여자가 하는 말의 목적으로 가장 적절한 것을 고르시오.

① 학부모 간담회 일정 변경을 공지하려고
② 현장 학습에 동행해 줄 것을 부탁하려고
③ 학부모 동의서 온라인 제출 방법을 안내하려고
④ 현장 학습 장소에 관한 학부모의 의견을 구하려고
⑤ 현장 학습 학부모 동의서 확인 및 제출을 요청하려고

02

대화를 듣고, 남자의 의견으로 가장 적절한 것을 고르시오.

① 오디오 북은 다른 활동을 하면서 듣기에 편리하다.
② 오디오 북은 책의 내용을 깊이 이해하는 데 도움이 된다.
③ 운동을 할 때는 오디오 북보다 음악을 듣는 것이 더 낫다.
④ 도서관은 다양한 장르의 오디오 북을 구비해야 한다.
⑤ 오디오 북은 조용한 장소에서 들을 필요가 있다.

03

대화를 듣고, 두 사람의 관계를 가장 잘 나타낸 것을 고르시오.

① 수영 코치 — 선수
② 서핑 강사 — 강습생
③ 인명 구조 요원 — 관광객
④ 기상청 직원 — 기상 캐스터
⑤ 서핑용품점 주인 — 거래처 직원

04

대화를 듣고, 그림에서 대화의 내용과 일치하지 않는 것을 고르시오.

05

대화를 듣고, 여자가 남자에게 부탁한 일로 가장 적절한 것을 고르시오.

① 아기 모자 뜨기
② 유인물 가져오기
③ 동아리 모임 날짜 정하기
④ 비누 만들기 재료 구입하기
⑤ 과학 실험실 사용 허락받기

06

대화를 듣고, 남자가 지불할 금액을 고르시오. 3점

① $60
② $65
③ $70
④ $75
⑤ $80

07

대화를 듣고, 여자가 취업 면접 특강에 갈 수 없는 이유를 고르시오.

① 전공 강의를 들어야 해서
② 진로 센터를 방문해야 해서
③ 취업 면접을 보러 가야 해서
④ 도서관 아르바이트를 해야 해서
⑤ 컴퓨터 능력 시험에 응시해야 해서

08

대화를 듣고, West Lake Fun Run에 관해 언급되지 않은 것을 고르시오.

① 개최 날짜   ② 코스 길이   ③ 출발 시간
④ 참가비   ⑤ 모금액 용도

09

Sleep Under the Sea에 관한 다음 내용을 듣고, 일치하지 않는 것을 고르시오.

① 상어 터널 안에서 잘 기회가 있을 것이다.
② 직원 전용 구역 방문은 포함되지 않는다.
③ 돌고래에 관한 3D 영화를 볼 수 있을 것이다.
④ 15세 미만 어린이는 성인과 동반해야 한다.
⑤ 저녁 식사와 아침 식사가 제공될 것이다.

10

다음 표를 보면서 대화를 듣고, 두 사람이 주문할 자전거 헬멧을 고르시오.

Bike Helmets

	Model	Weight (grams)	Price	LED Lights	Color
①	A	620	$25	×	Blue
②	B	550	$30	×	Yellow
③	C	420	$45	○	Blue
④	D	310	$55	○	Yellow
⑤	E	240	$75	○	White

11

대화를 듣고, 남자의 마지막 말에 대한 여자의 응답으로 가장 적절한 것을 고르시오.

① It was a three-day camping trip.
② We were not able to camp at home.
③ My father put it up in the living room.
④ I bought it at a camping gear store nearby.
⑤ The weather was so nice for sleeping out in the tent.

12

대화를 듣고, 여자의 마지막 말에 대한 남자의 응답으로 가장 적절한 것을 고르시오.

① Yes. I'll give you a call when I'm available.
② Well, you're not doing any project at the moment.
③ All right. We can talk now since the visitor just left.
④ Why not? You can join the project anytime.
⑤ Sure. I have 30 minutes for you now.

13

대화를 듣고, 남자의 마지막 말에 대한 여자의 응답으로 가장 적절한 것을 고르시오.

Woman: _____

① You're right. He's been eating too much lately.

② That's not fair. I don't want to walk him all week.

③ Sorry. I don't have time to take him to the vet now.

④ Okay. I'll take him out for a walk on weekends then.

⑤ Not really. Too much exercise is not good for his health.

14

대화를 듣고, 여자의 마지막 말에 대한 남자의 응답으로 가장 적절한 것을 고르시오. [3점]

Man: _____

① I don't think so. The competition is only one week away.

② Of course. We'd better focus on preparing for the exam.

③ So I used it in the last online debate competition.

④ Then I should get used to using it for debating.

⑤ Don't worry. I had my laptop fixed already.

15

다음 상황 설명을 듣고, Lisa가 Kevin에게 할 말로 가장 적절한 것을 고르시오. [3점]

Lisa: _____

① Why don't we interview the new history teacher?

② Let's put your caricature of Mr. Jackson in the article.

③ We should write an article about the caricature contest.

④ I wonder if you can draw more caricatures of the students.

⑤ How about taking a photo of Mr. Jackson during the interview?

[16~17] 다음을 듣고, 물음에 답하시오.

16

남자가 하는 말의 주제로 가장 적절한 것은?

① unique local foods that are popular worldwide

② importance of family gatherings on New Year's Day

③ the most common New Year's resolutions across cultures

④ various ways of celebrating the New Year around the world

⑤ efforts to preserve traditional recipes in different countries

17

언급된 나라가 <u>아닌</u> 것은?

① Spain ② Denmark ③ Mexico
④ France ⑤ Greece

11 | 2021년 6월 학력평가

1번부터 17번까지는 듣고 답하는 문제입니다. 1번부터 15번까지는 한 번만 들려주고, 16번부터 17번까지는 두 번 들려줍니다. 방송을 잘 듣고 답을 하시기 바랍니다.

01

다음을 듣고, 여자가 하는 말의 목적으로 가장 적절한 것을 고르시오.

① 도서관의 새로운 행사를 홍보하려고
② 자판기 관리 도우미 학생을 모집하려고
③ 자판기 사용 시 규칙에 대해 안내하려고
④ 자판기 설치 일정이 연기된 것을 알리려고
⑤ 학교 식당을 깨끗이 사용할 것을 당부하려고

02

대화를 듣고, 남자의 의견으로 가장 적절한 것을 고르시오.

① 올바른 역사관을 가지는 것이 중요하다.
② 암기력은 학습 효과를 높이는 데 중요한 요인이다.
③ 역사 만화책을 읽는 것이 역사 공부에 도움이 된다.
④ 다양한 주제의 독서를 통해 창의력을 키울 수 있다.
⑤ 만화 그리기는 아이들의 상상력을 풍부하게 해 준다.

03

대화를 듣고, 두 사람의 관계를 가장 잘 나타낸 것을 고르시오.

① 신문 기자 - 화가
② 방송 진행자 - 요리사
③ 식료품점 직원 - 농부
④ 촬영 감독 - 배우
⑤ 식당 주인 - 손님

04

대화를 듣고, 그림에서 대화의 내용과 일치하지 <u>않는</u> 것을 고르시오.

05

대화를 듣고, 여자가 할 일로 가장 적절한 것을 고르시오.

① 머리띠 사기
② 깃발 주문하기
③ 응원가 고르기
④ 깃발에 팀 이름 쓰기
⑤ 남동생에게 도움 요청하기

06

대화를 듣고, 남자가 지불할 금액을 고르시오. [3점]

① $70
② $100
③ $140
④ $160
⑤ $180

07

대화를 듣고, 여자가 영화관에 갈 수 없는 이유를 고르시오.

① 시험이 끝나지 않아서
② 가족들과 캠핑을 가야 해서
③ 어머니 생일 파티가 있어서
④ 프레젠테이션을 준비해야 해서
⑤ 영화 티켓을 구할 수가 없어서

08

대화를 듣고, Friday Night Walk에 관해 언급되지 않은 것을 고르시오.

① 행사 목적   ② 코스 종류   ③ 참가비
④ 기념품   ⑤ 신청 방법

09

Advanced English Reading Camp에 관한 다음 내용을 듣고, 일치하지 않는 것을 고르시오.

① 8월 6일부터 8일까지 개최된다.
② 영어 원어민 교사 2명이 참석한다.
③ 온라인으로 사전 등록을 해야 한다.
④ 누구나 무료로 참가할 수 있다.
⑤ 참가 인원은 최대 20명으로 제한된다.

10

다음 표를 보면서 대화를 듣고, 두 사람이 구입할 책장을 고르시오.

<Bookcases>

	Model	Material	Number of Shelves	Color	Price
①	A	plastic	3	white	$40
②	B	metal	3	white	$50
③	C	metal	4	red	$60
④	D	wood	4	white	$80
⑤	E	wood	5	red	$100

11

대화를 듣고, 남자의 마지막 말에 대한 여자의 응답으로 가장 적절한 것을 고르시오.

① Of course. I promise to help her.
② No. I can't find a clothes shop nearby.
③ I'm sorry. I'm busy cooking dinner now.
④ No problem. Tell me when you're ready.
⑤ Okay. I'll buy what you asked for tomorrow.

12

대화를 듣고, 여자의 마지막 말에 대한 남자의 응답으로 가장 적절한 것을 고르시오.

① Wow! Welcome back from your honeymoon.
② Okay. My friends gave me this birthday card.
③ Sorry. I almost forgot that you got married last month.
④ That's too bad. I hope you'll get better from your cold.
⑤ Absolutely. I'm excited to see you in your wedding dress.

13

대화를 듣고, 남자의 마지막 말에 대한 여자의 응답으로 가장 적절한 것을 고르시오. [3점]

Woman: _____

① If you want, you can borrow mine.
② My microphone is different from yours.
③ Well, your package has already arrived.
④ Making a good first impression is important.
⑤ No way. This is the lowest price I can offer.

14

대화를 듣고, 여자의 마지막 말에 대한 남자의 응답으로 가장 적절한 것을 고르시오. [3점]

Man: _____

① You are late. You should take a taxi, instead.
② That's nice. Swimming will make you healthier.
③ You're right. Walking is better than riding a bike.
④ If so, you should go to the repair shop and fix it.
⑤ Don't worry. I can teach you how to ride a bicycle.

15

다음 상황 설명을 듣고, Lucy가 Mike에게 할 말로 가장 적절한 것을 고르시오.

Lucy: _____

① We can't afford to go on an overseas trip.
② Why don't we stay home for our vacation?
③ Don't forget to call me when you get there.
④ How about planning out our trip in advance?
⑤ You should finish your work before the deadline.

[16~17] 다음을 듣고, 물음에 답하시오.

16

남자가 하는 말의 주제로 가장 적절한 것은?

① teas that are good for health
② snacks that go well with teas
③ various ways to grow tea plants
④ different tea etiquettes around the world
⑤ list of countries that consume a lot of tea

17

언급된 차가 <u>아닌</u> 것은?

① green tea   ② lemon tea   ③ rose tea
④ mint tea   ⑤ black tea

정답과 해설 : 13~17 54~55

12 2021년 9월 학력평가

MP3 동영상 강의

2SBL2_A12   2SBL2_J12

 1번부터 17번까지는 듣고 답하는 문제입니다. 1번부터 15번까지는 한 번만 들려주고, 16번부터 17번까지는 두 번 들려줍니다. 방송을 잘 듣고 답을 하시기 바랍니다.

01

다음을 듣고, 남자가 하는 말의 목적으로 가장 적절한 것을 고르시오.

① 학교 급식 일정 변경을 알리려고
② 학교 식당 이용 시 주의 사항을 안내하려고
③ 학교 급식 설문 조사 기간 연장을 공지하려고
④ 설문 조사로 선정된 학교 급식 메뉴를 소개하려고
⑤ 학교 급식 개선을 위한 토론회 참석을 요청하려고

02

대화를 듣고, 여자의 의견으로 가장 적절한 것을 고르시오.

① 꾸준한 독서는 집중력 향상에 효과적이다.
② 학생의 연령에 맞는 도서 추천이 중요하다.
③ 소설을 읽는 것은 공감 능력 향상에 도움이 된다.
④ 학생의 흥미를 유발할 수 있는 독서 교육이 필요하다.
⑤ 창의적인 글쓰기를 위해 다양한 주제의 소설을 읽어야 한다.

03

대화를 듣고, 두 사람의 관계를 가장 잘 나타낸 것을 고르시오.

① 호텔 직원 - 투숙객
② 음반 제작자 - 밴드 연주자
③ 유치원 교사 - 학부모
④ 파티 플래너 - 의뢰인
⑤ 레크리에이션 강사 - 수강생

04

대화를 듣고, 그림에서 대화의 내용과 일치하지 <u>않는</u> 것을 고르시오.

05

대화를 듣고, 여자가 남자에게 부탁한 일로 가장 적절한 것을 고르시오.

① 에어컨 수리 요청하기
② 야구 경기 티켓 구매하기
③ 주문한 음식 찾아오기
④ 박물관 투어 취소하기
⑤ 식사 장소 예약하기

06

대화를 듣고, 여자가 지불할 금액을 고르시오.

① $36
② $40
③ $45
④ $50
⑤ $63

07

대화를 듣고, 남자가 도서관에 갈 수 없는 이유를 고르시오.

① 독서 토론을 위해 책을 읽어야 해서
② 학생회 회의에 참석해야 해서
③ 병원 진료를 받아야 해서
④ 동아리 면접을 준비해야 해서
⑤ 말하기 대회 대본을 작성해야 해서

08

대화를 듣고, Electronics Fair에 관해 언급되지 않은 것을 고르시오.

① 프로그램   ② 장소   ③ 종료일
④ 참가 업체   ⑤ 티켓 가격

09

Jump and Grow Together에 관한 다음 내용을 듣고, 일치하지 않는 것을 고르시오.

① 신입생 11명으로 팀을 구성해야 한다.
② 각 팀은 세 번의 점프 기회를 갖는다.
③ 10월 첫 번째 토요일에 열린다.
④ 학교 체육관에서 개최된다.
⑤ 행사 당일에 참가 신청이 가능하다.

10

다음 표를 보면서 대화를 듣고, 여자가 구입할 Monitor Stand를 고르시오.

Monitor Stand

	Model	Price	Material	Storage Drawer	USB Ports
①	A	$20	Plastic	○	2
②	B	$23	Metal	×	2
③	C	$25	Metal	×	3
④	D	$28	Metal	○	3
⑤	E	$35	Plastic	○	4

11

대화를 듣고, 남자의 마지막 말에 대한 여자의 응답으로 가장 적절한 것을 고르시오.

① Too bad. When did you break your watch?
② Sorry. I couldn't join the meeting yesterday.
③ Exactly. Should we go back to work right now?
④ Thanks. It was a good opportunity to learn more.
⑤ Sure. Why don't we go out to get some fresh air?

12

대화를 듣고, 여자의 마지막 말에 대한 남자의 응답으로 가장 적절한 것을 고르시오.

① We don't always need a car to travel.
② That's why I practiced a lot this time.
③ I'm glad you didn't get stuck in traffic.
④ Make sure to arrive on time for your test.
⑤ I forgot my identification card for the test.

정답과 해설 : 07~12 57~59

13

대화를 듣고, 남자의 마지막 말에 대한 여자의 응답으로 가장 적절한 것을 고르시오. 3점

Woman: _____

① No thanks. I can make my own infographics.

② Of course. I'll send it to you right away.

③ Sorry. I forgot to download it yesterday.

④ I see. You mean the shorter, the better.

⑤ Okay. I'll put the graph onto this page.

14

대화를 듣고, 여자의 마지막 말에 대한 남자의 응답으로 가장 적절한 것을 고르시오. 3점

Man: _____

① You should have taken more pictures at the top.

② I would have regretted it if I'd missed this view.

③ The trail is flat enough to hike without equipment.

④ The original plan is important, but safety comes first.

⑤ I've done this hike before, so I know it isn't dangerous.

15

다음 상황 설명을 듣고, Amanda가 Natalie에게 할 말로 가장 적절한 것을 고르시오. 3점

Amanda: _____

① It's dangerous to use headphones while riding a scooter.

② I think you should check your scooter regularly.

③ Walking to school is better for your health.

④ A license is required to ride an electric scooter.

⑤ Turning up music might distract you from studying.

[16~17] 다음을 듣고, 물음에 답하시오.

16

남자가 하는 말의 주제로 가장 적절한 것은?

① animals' abilities to count

② reasons for animals' migrating

③ hunting habits of wild animals

④ necessity of protecting animal rights

⑤ ways to conserve endangered animals

17

언급된 동물이 아닌 것은?

① wolves　　② frogs　　③ chickens

④ snakes　　⑤ desert ants

정답과 해설 : 13~17 59~60

※ 고2 2021년 11월 학력평가 시험지와 문항 순서가 동일합니다.

옆 QR 코드를 가리고 찍으세요.

13 2021년 11월
학력평가

MP3

25BL2_A13

동영상 강의

25BL2_L13

😊 1번부터 17번까지는 듣고 답하는 문제입니다. 1번부터 15번까지는 한 번만 들려주고, 16번부터 17번까지는 두 번 들려줍니다. 방송을 잘 듣고 답을 하시기 바랍니다.

01

다음을 듣고, 남자가 하는 말의 목적으로 가장 적절한 것을 고르시오.

① 도서관 홈페이지 개설을 홍보하려고
② 도서관 운영 시간 연장을 공지하려고
③ 도서관 재개관 날짜 연기를 안내하려고
④ 도서관 환경 조성 아이디어를 공모하려고
⑤ 도서관 벽 공사로 인한 소음에 대해 사과하려고

02

대화를 듣고, 여자의 의견으로 가장 적절한 것을 고르시오.

① 방학 계획표에는 매일 해야 할 일을 포함해야 한다.
② 방학 계획을 세울 때는 일의 중요도를 고려해야 한다.
③ 규칙적인 생활 습관이 시간 활용의 효율성을 높여준다.
④ 학생들의 시간 관리 방법에 대한 교육을 강화해야 한다.
⑤ 방학 중에는 다양한 체험 활동을 해보는 것이 필요하다.

03

대화를 듣고, 두 사람의 관계를 가장 잘 나타낸 것을 고르시오.

① 자동차 정비사 - 운전자
② 렌터카 회사 직원 - 고객
③ 운전면허 강사 - 수강생
④ 공항 주차 요원 - 여행객
⑤ 보험 설계사 - 보험 계약자

04

대화를 듣고, 그림에서 대화의 내용과 일치하지 <u>않는</u> 것을 고르시오.

05

대화를 듣고, 남자가 여자를 위해 할 일로 가장 적절한 것을 고르시오.

① 캠핑장 예약하기
② 일기 예보 확인하기
③ 모기 퇴치제 가져오기
④ 바비큐 물품 구매하기
⑤ 휴대용 스피커 빌려주기

06

대화를 듣고, 남자가 지불할 금액을 고르시오.

① $38
② $40
③ $42
④ $44
⑤ $50

07

대화를 듣고, 여자가 One-Day Baking Class에 참여할 수 없는 이유를 고르시오.

① 독후감을 작성해야 해서
② 사촌 집들이에 가야 해서
③ 영화 시사회에 초대받아서
④ 배우 사인회에 가기로 해서
⑤ 수영 수업을 수강해야 해서

08

대화를 듣고, Charity Carol Concert에 관해 언급되지 않은 것을 고르시오.

① 공연 장소   ② 공연 팀
③ 티켓 판매금 기부처   ④ 티켓 판매 시작일
⑤ 최대 관람 인원

09

Drone Photo Contest에 관한 다음 내용을 듣고, 일치하지 않는 것을 고르시오.

① 2017년에 처음 시작된 대회이다.
② 사진과 드론을 좋아하는 누구나 참가할 수 있다.
③ 3개의 사진 분야가 있을 것이다.
④ 우승자에게 최신형 컴퓨터를 줄 것이다.
⑤ 우승 사진은 웹 사이트에 게시될 것이다.

10

다음 표를 보면서 대화를 듣고, 여자가 주문할 향수를 고르시오.

Women's Perfume

	Product	Price	Scent	Size (ml)	Free Gift
①	A	$60	citrus	30	pouch
②	B	$70	woody	30	hand mirror
③	C	$80	earthy	50	pouch
④	D	$90	floral	50	pouch
⑤	E	$110	fruity	70	hand mirror

11

대화를 듣고, 여자의 마지막 말에 대한 남자의 응답으로 가장 적절한 것을 고르시오.

① I already bought two apple pies.
② I think five apples will be enough.
③ The recipe is too difficult to follow.
④ You can buy them at the supermarket.
⑤ It's safe to put them in the refrigerator.

12

대화를 듣고, 남자의 마지막 말에 대한 여자의 응답으로 가장 적절한 것을 고르시오.

① Sorry. I'm afraid I'm allergic to seafood.
② Really? We need to think of another place.
③ Never mind. The conference was canceled.
④ Why not? You'd better begin the remodeling.
⑤ Thanks. I really enjoyed the dinner you cooked.

13

대화를 듣고, 여자의 마지막 말에 대한 남자의 응답으로 가장 적절한 것을 고르시오. 3점

Man: _____

① Don't worry. I'll send you the locations of the stores I often use.
② Thanks. I liked the cups you bought at the zero-waste shop.
③ Definitely. We started reducing waste thanks to your effort.
④ That's okay. I'll show you how to recycle this packaging.
⑤ It's on me. Feel free to buy what you really want.

14

대화를 듣고, 남자의 마지막 말에 대한 여자의 응답으로 가장 적절한 것을 고르시오. 3점

Woman: _____

① Sorry. As for me, taking a subway is better than a bus.
② No worries. I'm sure you'll do a great job on the project.
③ Too bad. We should have canceled that walking program.
④ I agree. You can keep your life healthy by taking enough rest.
⑤ Great. That way, I can exercise even if I have a busy schedule.

15

다음 상황 설명을 듣고, Amy가 Mr. Green에게 할 말로 가장 적절한 것을 고르시오. 3점

Amy: _____

① Is it possible for me to visit you to see what you do at work?
② Would you help me prepare a presentation on an architect?
③ Could you allow me to take part in designing a building?
④ Are you trying to find a job in the field of architecture?
⑤ Why don't you give a lecture at school on Career Day?

[16~17] 다음을 듣고, 물음에 답하시오.

16

여자가 하는 말의 주제로 가장 적절한 것은?

① differences between stars and planets
② effective ways to observe planets at night
③ origins of planets' names from Roman gods
④ ancient people who first discovered planets
⑤ environmental and weather conditions of planets

17

언급된 행성이 아닌 것은?

① Mercury　　② Jupiter　　③ Mars
④ Neptune　　⑤ Saturn

정답과 해설 : 13~17 64~65

※ 고2 2022년 3월 학력평가 시험지와 문항 순서가 동일합니다.

14 2022년 3월 학력평가

😊 1번부터 17번까지는 듣고 답하는 문제입니다. 1번부터 15번까지는 한 번만 들려주고, 16번부터 17번까지는 두 번 들려줍니다. 방송을 잘 듣고 답을 하시기 바랍니다.

01

다음을 듣고, 남자가 하는 말의 목적으로 가장 적절한 것을 고르시오.

① 수도관 수리로 음수대를 이용할 수 없다는 것을 알리려고
② 수도관 수리 일정이 변경되는 것을 공지하려고
③ 음수대 이용 시 질서를 지킬 것을 당부하려고
④ 물을 자주 마시는 것의 중요성을 강조하려고
⑤ 음수대가 추가로 설치된 장소를 안내하려고

02

대화를 듣고, 여자의 의견으로 가장 적절한 것을 고르시오.

① 파스텔 색상의 옷을 입으면 더 친근해 보인다.
② 공식적인 자리에는 어두운 색상의 옷이 어울린다.
③ 밝은 표정으로 인사하면 친근한 인상을 줄 수 있다.
④ 다양한 디자인의 옷을 통해 개성을 표현할 수 있다.
⑤ 기분이 우울할 때는 파스텔 색상의 옷을 입는 것이 좋다.

03

대화를 듣고, 두 사람의 관계를 가장 잘 나타낸 것을 고르시오.

① 관광객 - 관광 안내원   ② 사진작가 - 미술관 큐레이터
③ 화가 - 화가 지망생   ④ 관람객 - 박물관 관장
⑤ 촬영 감독 - 배우

04

대화를 듣고, 그림에서 대화의 내용과 일치하지 않는 것을 고르시오.

05

대화를 듣고, 남자가 여자를 위해 할 일로 가장 적절한 것을 고르시오.

① 파일 수정하기   ② 파일 출력하기
③ 유인물 복사하기   ④ 유인물 검토하기
⑤ 발표 일정 확인하기

06

대화를 듣고, 여자가 지불할 금액을 고르시오. 3점

① $48   ② $55   ③ $78
④ $80   ⑤ $83

07

대화를 듣고, 남자가 이번 토요일에 쇼핑하러 갈 수 없는 이유를 고르시오.

① 학교 축제에 쓸 동영상 제작을 도와야 해서
② 도서관에 봉사 활동을 하러 가야 해서
③ 장기 자랑 대회 예행연습을 해야 해서
④ 장기 자랑 대회 사회를 맡아야 해서
⑤ 무대 의상을 제작해야 해서

08

대화를 듣고, Modern Architecture Expo에 관해 언급되지 않은 것을 고르시오.

① 개최 장소   ② 주최 기관   ③ 개최 기간
④ 입장료   ⑤ 강연자 수

09

2022 Opera in School에 관한 다음 내용을 듣고, 일치하지 않는 것을 고르시오.

① *Romeo and Juliet*을 공연할 것이다.
② 3월 25일 학교 강당에서 열릴 것이다.
③ 공연은 45분간 진행될 것이다.
④ 질의응답 시간 전에 가수들과 사진을 찍을 수 있다.
⑤ 참석하려면 사전에 등록해야 한다.

10

다음 표를 보면서 대화를 듣고, 두 사람이 구입할 미니 오븐을 고르시오.

Mini Ovens

	Model	Price	Capacity (liters)	Weight (kilograms)	Baking Pan
①	A	$92	9	6.0	×
②	B	$93	10	6.5	○
③	C	$95	12	5.5	×
④	D	$98	13	5.0	○
⑤	E	$110	13	4.5	○

11

대화를 듣고, 여자의 마지막 말에 대한 남자의 응답으로 가장 적절한 것을 고르시오.

① I can go to the gym and exercise with you.
② I lift weights at the gym three times a week.
③ Joining a team sport is a good way to stay active.
④ I do push-ups and squats for 30 minutes every day.
⑤ Diet is just as important as exercise to stay in shape.

12

대화를 듣고, 남자의 마지막 말에 대한 여자의 응답으로 가장 적절한 것을 고르시오.

① The person who gets the most votes will be the winner.
② I'm so happy to be chosen as the best dancer.
③ It's hard for me to make my dance video.
④ I can help you upload the video to the website.
⑤ I'm looking for a good dance competition to enter.

13

대화를 듣고, 여자의 마지막 말에 대한 남자의 응답으로 가장 적절한 것을 고르시오. 3점

Man: _____

① Okay, I'll visit the repair cafe you recommended before.
② Well, I saw a repair cafe next to the post office.
③ Sure, you can easily find a place to volunteer at.
④ Yes, the new bike shop offers good deals.
⑤ Sorry, but I'm too busy to fix your bike.

14

대화를 듣고, 남자의 마지막 말에 대한 여자의 응답으로 가장 적절한 것을 고르시오. 3점

Woman: _____

① My dad has the same problem. I'll tell him about the app.
② Don't eat too much fruit. It raises your blood sugar level.
③ That's true. Exercise helps lower your blood sugar level.
④ Why not? I've been using this app for months.
⑤ You're right. I should control my screen time.

15

다음 상황 설명을 듣고, Sandra가 Mr. Wilson에게 할 말로 가장 적절한 것을 고르시오.

Sandra: _____

① Will you tell me how to run the student council meetings?
② Can we hold a sports competition for student health?
③ Please provide new sports equipment to students.
④ Is it possible for you to join our regular meetings?
⑤ Let us enter the sports league on behalf of our school.

[16~17] 다음을 듣고, 물음에 답하시오.

16

여자가 하는 말의 주제로 가장 적절한 것은?

① animals that can survive without food for a long time
② ways animals manage to adapt to extreme weather
③ impacts of climate change on animals' habitats
④ techniques animals use to avoid predators
⑤ unique hunting skills of various animals

17

언급된 동물이 아닌 것은?

① crocodiles   ② spiders   ③ penguins
④ dolphins   ⑤ sharks

15

2022년 6월
학력평가

MP3
25BL2_A15

동영상 강의
25BL2_L15

1번부터 17번까지는 듣고 답하는 문제입니다. 1번부터 15번까지는 한 번만 들려주고, 16번부터 17번까지는 두 번 들려줍니다. 방송을 잘 듣고 답을 하시기 바랍니다.

01

다음을 듣고, 남자가 하는 말의 목적으로 가장 적절한 것을 고르시오.

① 교내 밴드 공연을 홍보하려고
② 교장 선생님의 퇴임을 축하하려고
③ 변경된 음악 수업 장소를 안내하려고
④ 지역 오케스트라의 단원을 모집하려고
⑤ 새로운 음악 선생님의 부임을 알리려고

02

대화를 듣고, 여자의 의견으로 가장 적절한 것을 고르시오.

① 반복적인 학습을 통해 시험에서의 실수를 줄일 수 있다.
② 적당량의 초콜릿 섭취는 불안감 완화에 도움이 된다.
③ 단 음식을 많이 먹으면 호르몬의 균형이 깨진다.
④ 초콜릿의 효능에 대한 과학적 연구가 필요하다.
⑤ 의약품 남용에 대한 규제를 강화해야 한다.

03

대화를 듣고, 두 사람의 관계를 가장 잘 나타낸 것을 고르시오.

① 여행사 직원 - 여행객
② 헤어 디자이너 - 고객
③ 가구 제작자 - 의뢰인
④ 화가 - 모델
⑤ 영화감독 - 배우

04

대화를 듣고, 그림에서 대화의 내용과 일치하지 <u>않는</u> 것을 고르시오.

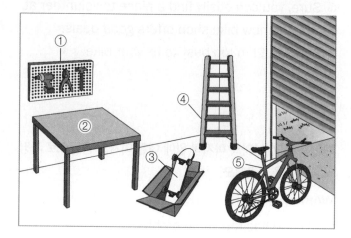

05

대화를 듣고, 남자가 할 일로 가장 적절한 것을 고르시오.

① 날씨 확인하기
② 렌트카 예약하기
③ 호텔 방 변경하기
④ 비행기표 예매하기
⑤ 할인 쿠폰 다운받기

06

대화를 듣고, 여자가 지불할 금액을 고르시오. 3점

① $30
② $35
③ $40
④ $45
⑤ $50

정답과 해설: 01~06 70~72

07

대화를 듣고, 여자가 벼룩시장에 갈 수 <u>없는</u> 이유를 고르시오.

① 결혼식에서 피아노를 연주해야 해서
② 빵집에서 아르바이트를 해야 해서
③ 티셔츠를 교환하러 가야 해서
④ 건강 검진을 받아야 해서
⑤ 과제를 제출해야 해서

08

대화를 듣고, Brantown Community Picnic에 관해 언급되지 <u>않은</u> 것을 고르시오.

① 일시　　　② 장소　　　③ 참가비
④ 증정품　　⑤ 신청 방법

09

Space Science Camp에 관한 다음 내용을 듣고, 일치하지 <u>않는</u> 것을 고르시오.

① 8월 21일부터 8월 23일까지 진행된다.
② 우주 여행에 관한 특별 강연이 있다.
③ 참가자에게는 별을 관측할 기회가 있다.
④ 예약 페이지는 캠프 3주 전에 열린다.
⑤ 참가비는 1인당 50달러이다.

10

다음 표를 보면서 대화를 듣고, 두 사람이 구매할 식기세척기를 고르시오.

Dishwashers

	Model	Price	Color	Type	Warranty Period
①	A	$650	black	portable	6 months
②	B	$680	black	built-in	6 months
③	C	$720	white	portable	1 year
④	D	$760	silver	built-in	1 year
⑤	E	$850	silver	built-in	2 years

11

대화를 듣고, 남자의 마지막 말에 대한 여자의 응답으로 가장 적절한 것을 고르시오.

① It's important to grow a lot of plants for the Earth.
② You need to water them once every three days.
③ Too much sunlight can be bad for the plants.
④ I'd better save water for the environment.
⑤ We should drink one liter of water a day.

12

대화를 듣고, 여자의 마지막 말에 대한 남자의 응답으로 가장 적절한 것을 고르시오.

① Sorry. I've already made a reservation at that restaurant.
② Oh, no. I must find another place as soon as possible.
③ Great. Let's have the phone fixed right now.
④ No way! It is too far away to go there.
⑤ Thanks. I'll definitely go to your party.

13

대화를 듣고, 남자의 마지막 말에 대한 여자의 응답으로 가장 적절한 것을 고르시오. [3점]

① Don't worry. I've already ordered it.
② You're right. I'll take care of it tomorrow.
③ My fault! I wrote the wrong address on it.
④ I'm sorry. I'll wake you up early next time.
⑤ Sure. You'd better return the borrowed item now.

14

대화를 듣고, 여자의 마지막 말에 대한 남자의 응답으로 가장 적절한 것을 고르시오. [3점]

① Okay. Then, I need to hurry up and register.
② Sorry. You can only register for it in person.
③ Thank you. I recommended them to my friend.
④ No worries. You can get over your fear of water.
⑤ Fantastic! The swimming instructor is professional.

15

다음 상황 설명을 듣고, Amy가 Jerry에게 할 말로 가장 적절한 것을 고르시오.

Amy: _____

① I think you can get them done by today.
② Do you know any way to get there in time?
③ Would you pick up my son from kindergarten for me?
④ I can't wait to see you at the kindergarten talent show.
⑤ You need not bring anything to the housewarming party.

[16~17] 다음을 듣고, 물음에 답하시오.

16

남자가 하는 말의 주제로 가장 적절한 것은?

① misunderstandings about recycled products
② processes and outputs of recycling
③ issues caused by waste pollution
④ the history of recycling systems
⑤ tips for reducing trash

17

언급된 소재가 아닌 것은?

① paper   ② metals   ③ fabrics
④ glass   ⑤ plastics

정답과 해설 : 13~17 74~75

※ 고2 2022년 9월 학력평가 시험지와 문항 순서가 동일합니다.

16 2022년 9월 학력평가

MP3
2SBL2_A16

동영상 강의
2SBL2_L16

1번부터 17번까지는 듣고 답하는 문제입니다. 1번부터 15번까지는 한 번만 들려주고, 16번부터 17번까지는 두 번 들려줍니다. 방송을 잘 듣고 답을 하시기 바랍니다.

01

다음을 듣고, 여자가 하는 말의 목적으로 가장 적절한 것을 고르시오.

① 설문조사 참여를 독려하려고
② 설문조사 결과를 공유하려고
③ 설문조사 기간 변경을 공지하려고
④ 학교 홈페이지 가입을 요청하려고
⑤ 학교 홈페이지 점검 시간을 안내하려고

02

대화를 듣고, 남자의 의견으로 가장 적절한 것을 고르시오.

① 논쟁은 더 나은 결정을 위한 기회가 된다.
② 의사 결정에 있어서 전원의 합의가 필수적이다.
③ 고민이 있을 때는 전문가에게 조언을 구해야 한다.
④ 리더로서 팀원들과 수평적 관계를 유지하는 것이 중요하다.
⑤ 팀 프로젝트의 성공을 위해서는 리더의 결단력이 필요하다.

03

대화를 듣고, 두 사람의 관계를 가장 잘 나타낸 것을 고르시오.

① 학생 - 문화 인류학 교수
② 미술관 관장 - 건축가
③ 여행 작가 - 삽화가
④ 신문 기자 - 전시 기획자
⑤ 구호 활동가 - 후원자

04

대화를 듣고, 그림에서 대화의 내용과 일치하지 <u>않는</u> 것을 고르시오.

05

대화를 듣고, 남자가 할 일로 가장 적절한 것을 고르시오.

① 포스터 인쇄하기
② MC 선발하기
③ 무대 설치하기
④ 졸업생에게 전화하기
⑤ 댄스팀 스케줄 정하기

06

대화를 듣고, 여자가 지불할 금액을 고르시오. 3점

① $13
② $14
③ $15
④ $16
⑤ $17

07

대화를 듣고, 남자가 락 페스티벌에 가지 <u>않는</u> 이유를 고르시오.

① 밴드 연습을 해야 해서
② 결혼식에 참석해야 해서
③ 할인 티켓이 매진되어서
④ 선물 살 돈을 모아야 해서
⑤ 라인업이 마음에 들지 않아서

08

대화를 듣고, Nova's Guide to the Stars에 관해 언급되지 <u>않은</u> 것을 고르시오.

① 장소   ② 참가 비용   ③ 활동 내용
④ 운영 기간   ⑤ 신청 방법

09

2022 London Public Library Event에 관한 다음 내용을 듣고, 일치하지 <u>않는</u> 것을 고르시오.

① 작가를 초청한다.
② 10월 27일에 열린다.
③ 현장 접수가 가능하다.
④ 참여 가능 인원은 최대 50명이다.
⑤ 질문을 이메일로 미리 보낼 수 있다.

10

다음 표를 보면서 대화를 듣고, 남자가 구입할 휴대용 접이식 의자를 고르시오.

Portable Folding Chair

	Model	Weight (kg)	Color	Number of Cup Holders	Carry Bag
①	A	3.2	white	1	○
②	B	2.3	white	2	○
③	C	2.1	gray	2	○
④	D	1.8	gray	2	×
⑤	E	1.6	black	1	×

11

대화를 듣고, 남자의 마지막 말에 대한 여자의 응답으로 가장 적절한 것을 고르시오.

① The person sitting behind me kept kicking my seat.
② You should have called the staff to help you.
③ I was so into it that it went by so fast.
④ I'm sorry you couldn't enjoy it.
⑤ I can't wait to see the movie.

12

대화를 듣고, 여자의 마지막 말에 대한 남자의 응답으로 가장 적절한 것을 고르시오.

① No way. We need the international program.
② Don't worry. I can exchange my book with yours.
③ Not bad. That's a good example of a topic sentence.
④ I understand. I was really nervous during the presentation.
⑤ Okay. Let's find one that is easy and interesting to talk about.

13

대화를 듣고, 여자의 마지막 말에 대한 남자의 응답으로 가장 적절한 것을 고르시오. 3점

Man: _____

① I'm sorry. I can give you a 10% discount, instead.
② Yes, please. I hope the new speaker works.
③ That's okay. But you'll need the receipt.
④ Never mind. I just got a full refund.
⑤ Thanks. But I fixed it already.

14

대화를 듣고, 남자의 마지막 말에 대한 여자의 응답으로 가장 적절한 것을 고르시오. 3점

Woman: _____

① It's nothing. I'm glad I could help.
② Excuse me. But I'm afraid I can't repair it.
③ I'm sorry. I missed an important phone call.
④ Sure. I can help you to make an appointment.
⑤ You're right. We should not waste our resources.

15

다음 상황 설명을 듣고, Amelia가 엄마에게 할 말로 가장 적절한 것을 고르시오.

Amelia: _____

① Do you have any good ideas regarding the presentation?
② Why don't you take Anna home before it gets too late?
③ I think we can finish the rest of the work tomorrow.
④ Could you please pick me up at Anna's house?
⑤ Tell me if you want to hang out with Anna.

[16~17] 다음을 듣고, 물음에 답하시오.

16

남자가 하는 말의 주제로 가장 적절한 것은?

① ways to encourage people to become vegetarians
② health risks associated with a poorly planned diet
③ the various reasons why people become vegetarians
④ the recommended daily amount of essential nutrients
⑤ food sources for vegetarians to prevent nutrient deficiency

17

언급된 영양소가 아닌 것은?

① protein　　② omega-3　　③ calcium
④ iron　　⑤ vitamin B12

17

2022년 11월
학력평가

1번부터 17번까지는 듣고 답하는 문제입니다. 1번부터 15번까지는 한 번만 들려주고, 16번부터 17번까지는 두 번 들려줍니다. 방송을 잘 듣고 답을 하시기 바랍니다.

01

다음을 듣고, 여자가 하는 말의 목적으로 가장 적절한 것을 고르시오.

① 자전거 전용 도로의 정비 일정을 공지하려고
② 자전거 안전 장비 착용의 중요성을 강조하려고
③ 공유 자전거 주차장의 설치 장소를 안내하려고
④ 공유 자전거를 지정된 장소에 주차할 것을 당부하려고
⑤ 친환경적인 교통수단을 이용해 등교할 것을 권장하려고

02

대화를 듣고, 남자의 의견으로 가장 적절한 것을 고르시오.

① 눈병 예방을 위해 정기적인 안과 검진을 받아야 한다.
② 적절한 휴식은 작업의 집중도를 높이는 데 도움이 된다.
③ 지나치게 밝은 컴퓨터 화면은 눈 건강에 해로울 수 있다.
④ 너무 작은 글씨를 읽는 것은 눈의 피로를 유발할 수 있다.
⑤ 시력 보호를 위해 화면과의 적당한 거리 유지가 필요하다.

03

대화를 듣고, 두 사람의 관계를 가장 잘 나타낸 것을 고르시오.

① 동화 작가 - 삽화가
② 악기 조율사 - 연주가
③ 학부모 - 유치원 교사
④ 피아노 강사 - 수강생
⑤ 중고 용품점 직원 - 손님

04

대화를 듣고, 그림에서 대화의 내용과 일치하지 <u>않는</u> 것을 고르시오.

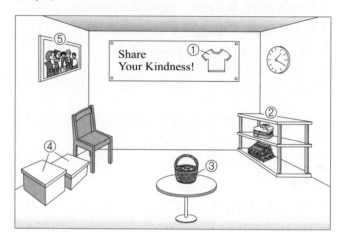

05

대화를 듣고, 남자가 할 일로 가장 적절한 것을 고르시오.

① 명단 출력하기
② 의자 가져오기
③ 동영상 내려받기
④ 구급상자 확인하기
⑤ 실험용 장갑 가져오기

06

대화를 듣고, 여자가 지불할 금액을 고르시오. [3점]

① $27
② $34
③ $36
④ $37
⑤ $40

정답과 해설 : 01~06 80~82

07

대화를 듣고, 남자가 레일 바이크를 타러 갈 수 <u>없는</u> 이유를 고르시오.

① 가족 모임에 가야 해서
② 축구 연습을 해야 해서
③ 아르바이트를 해야 해서
④ 연극 의상을 제작해야 해서
⑤ 뮤지컬 오디션이 예정되어 있어서

08

대화를 듣고, Winter Robot Camp에 관해 언급되지 <u>않은</u> 것을 고르시오.

① 기간   ② 장소   ③ 준비물
④ 운영 프로그램   ⑤ 등록 방법

09

Go Greener Festival에 관한 다음 내용을 듣고, 일치하지 <u>않는</u> 것을 고르시오.

① 11월 11일부터 13일까지 진행된다.
② 환경에 관한 노래가 연주된다.
③ 무대는 재활용된 재료로 제작된다.
④ 물병을 가져오면 음료를 무료로 받을 수 있다.
⑤ 주차장 이용이 불가능하다.

10

다음 표를 보면서 대화를 듣고, 두 사람이 주문할 직소 퍼즐 세트를 고르시오.

Jigsaw Puzzle Sets

	Set	Title of Painting	Number of Puzzle Pieces	Price	Frame
①	A	*Mona Lisa*	1,000	$44	wooden
②	B	*Starry Night*	800	$38	wooden
③	C	*Water Lilies*	700	$35	wooden
④	D	*Birth of Venus*	600	$33	metal
⑤	E	*Sunflowers*	400	$30	metal

11

대화를 듣고, 여자의 마지막 말에 대한 남자의 응답으로 가장 적절한 것을 고르시오.

① It was too late to learn something new.
② It was my aunt who taught me calligraphy.
③ I used to teach my little brother handwriting.
④ I didn't know you had the same hobby as me.
⑤ I bought a special brush for calligraphy online.

12

대화를 듣고, 남자의 마지막 말에 대한 여자의 응답으로 가장 적절한 것을 고르시오.

① I see. I'll register for the available course.
② No way. I'm not interested in water activities.
③ No problem. I'll let you choose the 7 p.m. class.
④ Wonderful. It's my pleasure to teach scuba diving.
⑤ Really? I've already signed up for the Friday course.

13

대화를 듣고, 여자의 마지막 말에 대한 남자의 응답으로 가장 적절한 것을 고르시오. 3점

Man: _____

① It'll be helpful to deliver DIY furniture.
② I'll fix your computer by using the manual.
③ I've already mastered how to put it together.
④ I'd like you to buy a brand new bookcase online.
⑤ I should find a video for assembling the bookcase.

14

대화를 듣고, 남자의 마지막 말에 대한 여자의 응답으로 가장 적절한 것을 고르시오.

Woman: _____

① Definitely. We should avoid eating only vegetables.
② Sorry. I prefer good-looking vegetables to ugly ones.
③ Good. Let's see if the vegetables we need are for sale.
④ Exactly. Ugly vegetables are not appropriate for eating.
⑤ Excellent. I like the ugly vegetables you bought for me.

15

다음 상황 설명을 듣고, Sofia가 Henry에게 할 말로 가장 적절한 것을 고르시오. 3점

Sofia: _____

① You need to look at reviews when choosing books.
② Why don't you show an example of a presentation?
③ How about giving students a choice in their books?
④ I recommend you assign a book report to students.
⑤ You should give students time to work with others.

[16~17] 다음을 듣고, 물음에 답하시오.

16

남자가 하는 말의 주제로 가장 적절한 것은?

① migration patterns of various birds
② bird diversity affected by city growth
③ everyday expressions related to birds
④ bird symbolism used in different cultures
⑤ impact of birds on agricultural development

17

언급된 새가 아닌 것은?

① eagle   ② crane   ③ owl
④ sparrow   ⑤ hummingbird

정답과 해설 : 13~17 84~85

※ 고2 2023년 3월 학력평가 시험지와 문항 순서가 동일합니다.

18 2023년 3월 학력평가

1번부터 17번까지는 듣고 답하는 문제입니다. 1번부터 15번까지는 한 번만 들려주고, 16번부터 17번까지는 두 번 들려줍니다. 방송을 잘 듣고 답을 하시기 바랍니다.

01

다음을 듣고, 여자가 하는 말의 목적으로 가장 적절한 것을 고르시오.

① 학교 실내 체육관의 임시 폐쇄를 안내하려고
② 학교 실내 체육관의 방과 후 이용을 권장하려고
③ 학교 실내 체육관 개관 10주년 기념식에 초대하려고
④ 학교 실내 체육관 시설 보수를 위한 의견을 모으려고
⑤ 학교 실내 체육관 이용 후 운동 기구 정리를 당부하려고

02

대화를 듣고, 남자의 의견으로 가장 적절한 것을 고르시오.

① 주위 환경과 대비되는 색의 등산복을 입는 것이 안전하다.
② 얇은 옷을 여러 겹 입으면 기온 변화에 대비할 수 있다.
③ 등산로를 벗어나 산행하면 자연을 훼손할 위험이 있다.
④ 등산복을 고를 때 방수 기능이 있는지 확인해야 한다.
⑤ 등산 전에 하는 준비 운동은 부상의 위험을 줄인다.

03

대화를 듣고, 두 사람의 관계를 가장 잘 나타낸 것을 고르시오.

① 사진작가 - 모델
② 휴대 전화 판매원 - 손님
③ 제품 디자이너 - 제조업자
④ 노트북 수리 기사 - 의뢰인
⑤ 택배 배달원 - 고객 센터 직원

04

대화를 듣고, 그림에서 대화의 내용과 일치하지 <u>않는</u> 것을 고르시오.

05

대화를 듣고, 남자가 여자를 위해 할 일로 가장 적절한 것을 고르시오.

① 도서관에 데려다주기
② 에세이 검토해 주기
③ 프린터 설치해 주기
④ 출력물 가져다주기
⑤ 수리 센터에 연락해 주기

06

대화를 듣고, 여자가 지불할 금액을 고르시오. 3점

① $36
② $39
③ $47
④ $52
⑤ $55

07

대화를 듣고, 남자가 내일 봉사 활동에 같이 갈 수 없는 이유를 고르시오.

① 봉사 활동 장소가 너무 멀어서
② 독감 예방 주사를 맞지 않아서
③ 가족과 저녁 식사를 해야 해서
④ 참여 가능한 나이가 되지 않아서
⑤ 스포츠 프로그램에 참여해야 해서

08

대화를 듣고, Nari Island 패키지 여행에 관해 언급되지 않은 것을 고르시오.

① 여행 기간　　② 방문 장소　　③ 최소 출발 인원
④ 이동 수단　　⑤ 가격

09

Afterschool Math Festival에 관한 다음 내용을 듣고, 일치하지 않는 것을 고르시오.

① 다음 주 월요일부터 3일간 진행된다.
② 9개의 활동 중 3개까지 참가할 수 있다.
③ 모든 활동의 예상 소요 시간은 같다.
④ 강연에 참석한 학생에게 강연자의 책이 무료로 제공된다.
⑤ 구내식당에서 특별한 간식과 음료가 제공된다.

10

다음 표를 보면서 대화를 듣고, 두 사람이 구매할 자외선 칫솔 소독기를 고르시오.

UV Toothbrush Sanitizers

	Model	Number of Slots	Built-in Battery	Drying Function	Price
①	A	3	×	×	$39
②	B	4	○	○	$48
③	C	4	×	×	$40
④	D	5	○	×	$50
⑤	E	6	○	○	$54

11

대화를 듣고, 여자의 마지막 말에 대한 남자의 응답으로 가장 적절한 것을 고르시오.

① Yes. You should stop watering it for a while.
② No, thanks. I can't keep a plant at home.
③ I agree. Those colorful leaves look nice.
④ Sure. I think gardening is a good hobby.
⑤ No. It's easy to grow plants indoors.

12

대화를 듣고, 남자의 마지막 말에 대한 여자의 응답으로 가장 적절한 것을 고르시오.

① I'm afraid I handed in my paper late.
② If so, applying hand cream might help.
③ Be careful when you use fabric scissors.
④ Well, the gloves are too big for my son.
⑤ Let's bring a paper grocery bag this time.

정답과 해설 : 07~12 87~89

13

대화를 듣고, 여자의 마지막 말에 대한 남자의 응답으로 가장 적절한 것을 고르시오. [3점]

Man: _____

① Okay. Let me go over to collect the boxes.

② Good idea. I hope they listen to our suggestion.

③ I see it differently. Those towels can be reused.

④ Never mind. I can go to the post office by myself.

⑤ Not really. Students must clean their own bedroom.

14

대화를 듣고, 남자의 마지막 말에 대한 여자의 응답으로 가장 적절한 것을 고르시오. [3점]

Woman: _____

① Don't worry. I can help you create a virtual lecture hall.

② Don't you remember? We've rented the same place.

③ Not yet. I need to sign up for a conference soon.

④ No way. Metaverse is not just for online games.

⑤ Why not? The audience loved your presentation.

15

다음 상황 설명을 듣고, Jane이 David에게 할 말로 가장 적절한 것을 고르시오.

Jane: _____

① I'm sure you can play the solo part beautifully.

② It's all my fault. I should have been more careful.

③ How about giving your solo part to someone else?

④ Too bad. We should postpone our concert for a week.

⑤ I will do my best to participate in the Spring Concert.

[16~17] 다음을 듣고, 물음에 답하시오.

16

남자가 하는 말의 주제로 가장 적절한 것은?

① reasons national flags have simple designs and colors

② geographical features affecting the national identity

③ common colors and their meanings in national flags

④ most frequently used symbols in national flags

⑤ differences in color preference across cultures

17

언급된 색이 아닌 것은?

① red   ② blue   ③ white
④ black   ⑤ green

정답과 해설 : 13~17 89~90

19 2023년 6월 학력평가

MP3
25BL2_A19

동영상 강의
25BL2_L19

1번부터 17번까지는 듣고 답하는 문제입니다. 1번부터 15번까지는 한 번만 들려주고, 16번부터 17번까지는 두 번 들려줍니다. 방송을 잘 듣고 답을 하시기 바랍니다.

01

다음을 듣고, 남자가 하는 말의 목적으로 가장 적절한 것을 고르시오.

① 보고서 작성 시 유의 사항을 안내하려고
② 화학 실험의 중요성을 강조하려고
③ 과제 제출 마감일을 공지하려고
④ 과학 보고서 주제를 소개하려고
⑤ 수강 신청 방법을 설명하려고

02

대화를 듣고, 여자의 의견으로 가장 적절한 것을 고르시오.

① 아이를 안아주는 것은 아이의 불안감을 덜어준다.
② 수면 시간에 아이에게 우유를 주는 것은 피해야 한다.
③ 아이에게 장난감을 주는 것은 인지 발달을 촉진한다.
④ 올바른 수면 습관 형성을 위해 부모와 아이는 함께 자야 한다.
⑤ 좋아하는 물건을 주는 것은 아이가 혼자 자는 데 도움이 된다.

03

대화를 듣고, 두 사람의 관계를 가장 잘 나타낸 것을 고르시오.

① 작곡가 - 가수
② 지휘자 - 피아니스트
③ 프로듀서 - 방송 작가
④ 광고 기획자 - 뮤지컬 배우
⑤ 영화 감독 - 음향 기사

04

대화를 듣고, 그림에서 대화의 내용과 일치하지 <u>않는</u> 것을 고르시오.

05

대화를 듣고, 여자가 할 일로 가장 적절한 것을 고르시오.

① 학생 사진 찍기
② 동아리 이름 바꾸기
③ 소개 글 작성하기
④ 마스코트 이미지 보내기
⑤ 동아리 활동집 인쇄하기

06

대화를 듣고, 남자가 지불할 금액을 고르시오. [3점]

① $80
② $90
③ $100
④ $108
⑤ $120

정답과 해설 : 01~06 90~92

07

대화를 듣고, 여자가 이사를 가려는 이유를 고르시오.

① 아픈 아버지를 돌보기 위해서
② 회사와 가까운 곳으로 가려고
③ 이웃과 사이가 좋지 않아서
④ 부모님으로부터 독립하려고
⑤ 집 계약 기간이 만료되어서

08

대화를 듣고, Blueway Spelling Bee Competition에 관해 언급되지 않은 것을 고르시오.

① 주최 기관　　② 참가 대상　　③ 참가 비용
④ 신청 방법　　⑤ 모집 인원

09

Ocean World에 관한 다음 내용을 듣고, 일치하지 않는 것을 고르시오.

① 주제는 심해 탐험이다.
② 오전 10시부터 오후 6시까지 운영된다.
③ 중앙 홀에서 영상을 시청할 수 있다.
④ 물고기 모양의 쿠키를 만들 수 있다.
⑤ 사전 예약제로 운영된다.

10

다음 표를 보면서 대화를 듣고, 두 사람이 구매할 보안 카메라를 고르시오.

Security Cameras

	Model	Price	Connectivity	Placement	Special Feature
①	A	$270	wired	indoor	motion detection
②	B	$300	wireless	indoor	sound detection
③	C	$400	wireless	indoor & outdoor	motion detection
④	D	$470	wireless	indoor & outdoor	sound detection
⑤	E	$520	wired	indoor & outdoor	motion detection

11

대화를 듣고, 남자의 마지막 말에 대한 여자의 응답으로 가장 적절한 것을 고르시오. 3점

① Never mind. I can't wait to see them speaking in the contest.
② Definitely! I'm sure your message will be clearly delivered.
③ Of course. I'm honored to make a speech as the captain.
④ Oh, no! I can't come to your graduation ceremony.
⑤ Sure. I'll add your brilliant idea to my script.

12

대화를 듣고, 여자의 마지막 말에 대한 남자의 응답으로 가장 적절한 것을 고르시오.

① Why not? I'll certainly go with you.
② I'm sorry. I can't find them anywhere.
③ Don't worry. You can use mine if you want.
④ Not really. I don't need to use them right now.
⑤ Forget about it. He'll use my earphones anyway.

13

대화를 듣고, 남자의 마지막 말에 대한 여자의 응답으로 가장 적절한 것을 고르시오.

Woman:

① How kind of her! I was worried that I wouldn't find it.
② Then, I'll tell her it was my fault, not yours.
③ Could you stop by again when it's raining?
④ Thanks for lending me your brand-new umbrella.
⑤ Why don't you ask her what she wants to do next time?

14

대화를 듣고, 여자의 마지막 말에 대한 남자의 응답으로 가장 적절한 것을 고르시오. 3점

Man:

① Thanks for letting me know. I should try using them.
② It tastes good. I'm curious about the recipe for this juice.
③ Don't worry. I don't care about the kinds of straws I use.
④ You're right. I'd better not use a silicone straw from now on.
⑤ I've tried all of them already, but I still prefer paper straws.

15

다음 상황 설명을 듣고, Nick이 Annie에게 할 말로 가장 적절한 것을 고르시오.

Nick:

① I'd like to replace my content with yours right away.
② We'd better ask our professor about which source to trust.
③ Your information is different from what's on the Internet.
④ You should have done more research for the presentation.
⑤ I believe that Van Gogh started painting in his early teens.

[16~17] 다음을 듣고, 물음에 답하시오.

16

여자가 하는 말의 주제로 가장 적절한 것은?

① resources used to design houses
② how to launch a design company
③ types and classifications of colors
④ artistic value of using various colors
⑤ effective use of colors for brand design

17

언급된 색깔이 아닌 것은?

① red　　　② yellow　　　③ orange
④ green　　　⑤ blue

※ 고2 2023년 9월 학력평가 시험지와 문항 순서가 동일합니다.

20

2023년 9월
학력평가

MP3
2SBL2_A20

동영상 강의
2SBL2_L20

😊 1번부터 17번까지는 듣고 답하는 문제입니다. 1번부터 15번까지는 한 번만 들려주고, 16번부터 17번까지는 두 번 들려줍니다. 방송을 잘 듣고 답을 하시기 바랍니다.

01

다음을 듣고, 남자가 하는 말의 목적으로 가장 적절한 것을 고르시오.

① 학생회 운영 방침을 설명하려고
② 학교 웹사이트 활용을 독려하려고
③ 진학 설명회 일정 변경을 공지하려고
④ 교내 봉사 활동 시 유의점을 안내하려고
⑤ 캠퍼스 투어 행사 자원봉사자를 모집하려고

02

대화를 듣고, 여자의 의견으로 가장 적절한 것을 고르시오.

① 휴대 전화는 정기적으로 소독해야 한다.
② 학생 대상 스마트 기기 활용 교육을 강화해야 한다.
③ 화면이 깨진 휴대 전화는 되도록 빨리 수리해야 한다.
④ 숙면을 위해 취침 전 전자 기기 사용을 자제해야 한다.
⑤ 휴대 전화 화면 밝기는 주변 밝기에 맞게 조절해야 한다.

03

대화를 듣고, 두 사람의 관계를 가장 잘 나타낸 것을 고르시오.

① 방송 연출가 - 배우
② 영화 각본가 - 과학자
③ 신문 기자 - 환경 운동가
④ 영화감독 - 영화 비평가
⑤ 잡지 구독자 - 잡지 편집장

04

대화를 듣고, 그림에서 대화의 내용과 일치하지 않는 것을 고르시오.

05

대화를 듣고, 남자가 할 일로 가장 적절한 것을 고르시오.

① 상자 가져오기
② 거실 청소하기
③ 전구 구입하기
④ 세탁물 맡기기
⑤ 바이올린 레슨 신청하기

06

대화를 듣고, 여자가 지불할 금액을 고르시오. [3점]

① $45
② $50
③ $55
④ $72
⑤ $80

정답과 해설 : 01~06 95~97

07

대화를 듣고, 남자가 식당에서 식사를 하지 **못한** 이유를 고르시오.

① 반려견을 데려가서
② 예약을 하지 않아서
③ 보수 공사 중이어서
④ 대기자가 너무 많아서
⑤ 음식 재료가 다 떨어져서

08

대화를 듣고, Home Organization Class에 관해 언급되지 **않은** 것을 고르시오.

① 장소　　　　② 일시　　　　③ 수강료
④ 수강 인원　　⑤ 준비물

09

2023 Board Game Design Contest에 관한 다음 내용을 듣고, 일치하지 **않는** 것을 고르시오.

① 참가 연령에 제한이 없다.
② 1라운드에서는 게임 소개 영상을 제출해야 한다.
③ 2라운드에서는 게임 디자이너의 도움을 받지 못한다.
④ 최종 우승자는 1,000달러를 받는다.
⑤ 9월 15일에 등록이 마감된다.

10

다음 표를 보면서 대화를 듣고, 두 사람이 주문할 제품을 고르시오.

Electric Mug Warmer Sets

	Set	Price	Mug Material	Mug Capacity	LED Display
①	A	$26	Glass	250ml	×
②	B	$32	Ceramic	350ml	○
③	C	$37	Ceramic	450ml	×
④	D	$42	Stainless Steel	550ml	○
⑤	E	$55	Stainless Steel	590ml	×

11

대화를 듣고, 남자의 마지막 말에 대한 여자의 응답으로 가장 적절한 것을 고르시오.

① Sorry. You can't put up the poster here.
② Sure. I'll create one and send it to you.
③ No. This QR code doesn't seem to work.
④ Right. Just scan the QR code and sign up.
⑤ Yes. You can participate in the auditions, too.

12

대화를 듣고, 여자의 마지막 말에 대한 남자의 응답으로 가장 적절한 것을 고르시오.

① Then, I'll apply for the poetry club.
② Yeah, I can recommend a good club for you.
③ No way. We can't accept any new members.
④ Great! I'll see you at the history club after school.
⑤ Really? Thank you for allowing me to join this club.

정답과 해설 : 07~12 97~99

13

대화를 듣고, 남자의 마지막 말에 대한 여자의 응답으로 가장 적절한 것을 고르시오. 3점

Woman: _____

① Okay. I'll go there to check if I can find more caps.
② Wait. I forgot to separate the caps from the bottles.
③ Good. We can use bottle caps for our artwork.
④ No worries. I've already taken out the trash.
⑤ No, thanks. We have enough toothbrushes.

14

대화를 듣고, 여자의 마지막 말에 대한 남자의 응답으로 가장 적절한 것을 고르시오. 3점

Man: _____

① Don't worry. I'll exchange those shoes for a smaller size.
② I got it. I'll buy a size seven for your hiking shoes.
③ I'm sorry. The shoe model you want is not on sale.
④ Absolutely. Check your shoes before you go hiking.
⑤ You're right. I'll wait for a sale to buy the shoes.

15

다음 상황 설명을 듣고, Kate가 Claire에게 할 말로 가장 적절한 것을 고르시오.

Kate: _____

① I think we should follow the dress code.
② Let's ask the clerk for a refund for the dress.
③ Why don't we buy tickets for the orchestra concert?
④ We'd better practice harder for the upcoming concert.
⑤ How about renting dresses instead of buying new ones?

[16~17] 다음을 듣고, 물음에 답하시오.

16

여자가 하는 말의 주제로 가장 적절한 것은?

① various ways to reduce wedding costs
② different wedding traditions across countries
③ cultural meaning of wedding reception food
④ changing marriage trends around the world
⑤ history of wedding dresses in different countries

17

언급된 나라가 아닌 것은?

① Germany   ② Cuba   ③ China
④ Nigeria   ⑤ Australia

21

2023년 11월
학력평가

MP3

동영상 강의

25BL2_A21

25BL2_L21

1번부터 17번까지는 듣고 답하는 문제입니다. 1번부터 15번까지는 한 번만 들려주고, 16번부터 17번까지는 두 번 들려줍니다. 방송을 잘 듣고 답을 하시기 바랍니다.

01

다음을 듣고, 남자가 하는 말의 목적으로 가장 적절한 것을 고르시오.

① 모터쇼 임시 주차장 운영을 안내하려고
② 방송국 방문 등록 방법을 설명하려고
③ 모터쇼 입장 시간 변경을 알려주려고
④ 공영 주차장 요금 인상을 공지하려고
⑤ 라디오 행사 지원 팀을 모집하려고

02

대화를 듣고, 여자의 의견으로 가장 적절한 것을 고르시오.

① 충분한 영양 섭취를 위해 다양한 과일을 먹어야 한다.
② 식사 전에 과일을 먹는 것이 건강에 도움이 된다.
③ 과일을 먹기 전에 껍질을 깨끗이 씻어야 한다.
④ 규칙적인 생활 습관이 체중 관리에 중요하다.
⑤ 늦은 밤중에 먹는 음식은 숙면을 방해한다.

03

다음을 듣고, 남자가 하는 말의 요지로 가장 적절한 것을 고르시오.

① 환경 교육 프로그램에 적극적으로 참여해야 한다.
② 쉽게 분해될 수 있는 플라스틱 제품 개발이 필요하다.
③ 플라스틱 쓰레기를 줄이기 위해 텀블러를 가지고 다녀야 한다.
④ 플라스틱병 재활용률을 높이려는 새로운 정책이 요구된다.
⑤ 텀블러 구매 시 유해 성분 포함 여부를 확인해야 한다.

04

대화를 듣고, 그림에서 대화의 내용과 일치하지 않는 것을 고르시오.

05

대화를 듣고, 여자가 할 일로 가장 적절한 것을 고르시오.

① 과학실 촬영하기
② 영상에 자막 넣기
③ 홍보 문구 만들기
④ 선생님 인터뷰하기
⑤ 배경 음악 선택하기

06

대화를 듣고, 남자가 지불할 금액을 고르시오. 3점

① $45   ② $60   ③ $65
④ $75   ⑤ $90

정답과 해설 : 01~06 100~102

07

대화를 듣고, 여자가 기타 동호회에 참석하지 **못한** 이유를 고르시오.

① 기타에 문제가 생겨서
② 늦게까지 일해야 해서
③ 손가락에 통증이 있어서
④ 프로젝트에 참여해야 해서
⑤ 새 연주법을 익히지 못해서

08

대화를 듣고, 2023 Laser Light Show에 관해 언급되지 **않은** 것을 고르시오.

① 주제   ② 기간   ③ 장소
④ 예매 방법   ⑤ 입장료

09

Highville Fashion Pop-up Stores에 관한 다음 내용을 듣고, 일치하지 **않는** 것을 고르시오.

① 12월 29일부터 3일 동안 진행될 것이다.
② 5층에서 열릴 것이다.
③ 장갑과 니트 모자를 포함한 패션 상품을 구매할 수 있다.
④ 전 상품에 대해 60퍼센트 할인을 제공할 것이다.
⑤ 모든 구매 고객에게 무료 커피 쿠폰을 줄 것이다.

10

다음 표를 보면서 대화를 듣고, 남자가 구매할 하이킹 스틱을 고르시오.

Hiking Sticks

	Model	Price	Material	Foldable	Color
①	A	$37	Bamboo	×	Brown
②	B	$39	Aluminum	○	Blue
③	C	$43	Carbon Fiber	×	Black
④	D	$47	Aluminum	○	Brown
⑤	E	$52	Carbon Fiber	○	Blue

11

대화를 듣고, 여자의 마지막 말에 대한 남자의 응답으로 가장 적절한 것을 고르시오.

① Don't worry. You can't miss the auditorium.
② Good idea. I'll go check if it's available.
③ Right. I want to sign up for your class.
④ No problem. I can change my recipe.
⑤ Yes. You'll win the contest next time.

12

대화를 듣고, 남자의 마지막 말에 대한 여자의 응답으로 가장 적절한 것을 고르시오.

① Not really. I'm still working on my report.
② Sorry. I can't issue you a library card now.
③ Great! I'm going to download and try it out.
④ Absolutely! I'll return your books tomorrow.
⑤ I agree. I should read different kinds of books.

13

대화를 듣고, 여자의 마지막 말에 대한 남자의 응답으로 가장 적절한 것을 고르시오. 3점

Man: _____

① Of course. I'll post them after you're done.

② Why not? I should search for online reviews.

③ Okay. I want to buy some pictures on auction.

④ I see. I can buy a bigger closet for your room.

⑤ No. I couldn't find anyone who wanted to buy them.

14

대화를 듣고, 남자의 마지막 말에 대한 여자의 응답으로 가장 적절한 것을 고르시오.

Woman: _____

① No wonder. She needs to practice more.

② Sorry to hear that. I hope she gets well soon.

③ It's no big deal. I'll give her advice on the facilities.

④ What a shame! I should've gone to the concert with you.

⑤ True. You'd better stay in the hospital a couple more days.

15

다음 상황 설명을 듣고, Ms. Parker가 Eric에게 할 말로 가장 적절한 것을 고르시오. 3점

Ms. Parker: _____

① You should check the nutrition facts label before consumption.

② You'd better drink more water to improve concentration.

③ You need to use meditation to ease students' worries.

④ How about separating water bottles for recycling?

⑤ Why don't you plan a schedule when you study?

[16~17] 다음을 듣고, 물음에 답하시오.

16

여자가 하는 말의 주제로 가장 적절한 것은?

① how to conveniently use airport facilities

② ways to get through airport security faster

③ futuristic airports designed by famous architects

④ airports named after well-known people in the world

⑤ guides for domestic-to-international airport transfer

17

언급된 도시가 아닌 것은?

① Chicago　　② Nairobi　　③ Paris

④ Jakarta　　⑤ Buenos Aires

※ 고2 2024년 3월 학력평가 시험지와 문항 순서가 동일합니다.

22 2024년 3월 학력평가

MP3   동영상 강의

25BL2_A22   25BL2_L22

😊 1번부터 17번까지는 듣고 답하는 문제입니다. 1번부터 15번까지는 한 번만 들려주고, 16번부터 17번까지는 두 번 들려줍니다. 방송을 잘 듣고 답을 하시기 바랍니다.

01

다음을 듣고, 남자가 하는 말의 목적으로 가장 적절한 것을 고르시오.

① 꽃 사진 촬영 동아리 회원을 모집하려고
② 꽃 사진 촬영 시 유의 사항을 당부하려고
③ 꽃 사진 촬영 행사가 취소됨을 공지하려고
④ 꽃 사진 촬영에 적합한 장비를 소개하려고
⑤ 꽃 사진을 촬영하기에 좋은 장소를 안내하려고

02

대화를 듣고, 여자의 의견으로 가장 적절한 것을 고르시오.

① 플래시 카드를 퀴즈에 활용하면 단어를 즐겁게 익힐 수 있다.
② 퀴즈를 내는 활동을 통해 학습자의 약점을 파악할 수 있다.
③ 단어 학습에 가장 효과적인 방법은 개인마다 차이가 있다.
④ 그림과 글이 함께 포함된 플래시 카드는 학습에 효과적이다.
⑤ 플래시 카드를 활용한 단어 학습 프로그램 개발이 필요하다.

03

다음을 듣고, 남자가 하는 말의 요지로 가장 적절한 것을 고르시오.

① 깔끔한 방을 유지하기 위해 필요 없는 물건을 없애야 한다.
② 쓰레기를 버릴 때는 환경에 미칠 악영향을 고려해야 한다.
③ 공간의 기능과 종류에 따라 효과적인 정리 방법이 다르다.
④ 사용하지 않는 물건은 보관하기보다 기부하는 것이 낫다.
⑤ 상자를 이용하면 물건을 효과적으로 보관할 수 있다.

04

대화를 듣고, 그림에서 대화의 내용과 일치하지 않는 것을 고르시오.

05

대화를 듣고, 여자가 남자에게 부탁한 일로 가장 적절한 것을 고르시오.

① 설문 결과 정리하기   ② 원인 조사하기
③ 그래프 제작하기   ④ 사진 고르기
⑤ 데이터 전송하기

06

대화를 듣고, 남자가 지불할 금액을 고르시오. 3점

① $25   ② $29   ③ $31
④ $34   ⑤ $36

정답과 해설 : 01~06 105~107

07

대화를 듣고, 여자가 공연 동영상 파일을 보내줄 수 <u>없는</u> 이유를 고르시오.

① 동영상을 촬영하지 않아서
② 부원들의 동의를 구해야 해서
③ 동영상 파일을 갖고 있지 않아서
④ 공연을 성공적으로 마치지 못해서
⑤ 학교 홍보 영상에 나오고 싶지 않아서

08

대화를 듣고, 학급 캠핑에 관해 언급되지 <u>않은</u> 것을 고르시오.

① 참여 학생 수 ② 날짜 ③ 대여 물품
④ 비용 ⑤ 도착 시간

09

2024 AI Expo에 관한 다음 내용을 듣고, 일치하지 <u>않는</u> 것을 고르시오.

① 5월 27일과 28일에 진행된다.
② 올해의 주제는 학교에서의 AI 활용이다.
③ 50개가 넘는 국가에서 채택된 AI 기술을 경험할 수 있다.
④ AI가 그려 주는 초상화를 받을 수 있다.
⑤ 웹사이트에서 20% 할인된 가격에 입장권을 구입할 수 있다.

10

다음 표를 보면서 대화를 듣고, 두 사람이 구매할 사진첩을 고르시오.

Photo Albums

	Model	Cover Material	Pages	Cover Color	Price
①	A	paper	20	white	$16
②	B	paper	30	blue	$19
③	C	fabric	30	white	$22
④	D	fabric	40	blue	$25
⑤	E	leather	40	brown	$30

11

대화를 듣고, 여자의 마지막 말에 대한 남자의 응답으로 가장 적절한 것을 고르시오.

① Fishing on the boat was the best for me.
② My grandparents visited us last weekend.
③ I am so glad that you had a great time.
④ It took too long to get to the island.
⑤ Some activities were canceled.

12

대화를 듣고, 남자의 마지막 말에 대한 여자의 응답으로 가장 적절한 것을 고르시오.

① Good idea. I'll go to the bookstore tomorrow.
② I'm sorry, but I haven't finished reading that book.
③ That's okay. I've already returned the book to the library.
④ Not at all. I would be able to go to her birthday party.
⑤ Thank you. I've always wanted to write a book myself.

정답과 해설 : 07~12 107~108

13

대화를 듣고, 여자의 마지막 말에 대한 남자의 응답으로 가장 적절한 것을 고르시오. [3점]

Man: _____

① Don't worry. You can pay with a credit card.

② I see. Then this one is a perfect choice for him.

③ It'll be fine. Your husband can drop by and pick it up.

④ Really? You'd better apply sunscreen before going out.

⑤ Exactly. A product with strong sun protection is better.

14

대화를 듣고, 남자의 마지막 말에 대한 여자의 응답으로 가장 적절한 것을 고르시오. [3점]

Woman: _____

① Right. It's better to hide weaknesses whenever possible.

② Good luck. Show them who you are, and you'll make it.

③ Of course. You can handle your homework effectively.

④ I agree. You can make your schedule using a planner.

⑤ Be careful! A weakness keeps you from growing up.

15

다음 상황 설명을 듣고, Lucy가 James에게 할 말로 가장 적절한 것을 고르시오.

Lucy: _____

① Why don't we start a campaign to ban the use of plastic?

② How about making posters with me about recycling?

③ Will you prepare for the student council meeting?

④ I want your opinion on the school art festival.

⑤ Let me tell you how to recycle properly.

[16~17] 다음을 듣고, 물음에 답하시오.

16

남자가 하는 말의 주제로 가장 적절한 것은?

① historical events that inspired inventions

② how inventions are unexpectedly created

③ hidden stories behind scientific inventions

④ unique inventions based on cultural identities

⑤ inventions that affected human life and history

17

언급된 발명품이 <u>아닌</u> 것은?

① wheel ② printing press ③ steam engine

④ light bulb ⑤ telephone

23 2024년 6월 학력평가

MP3
2SBL2_A23

동영상 강의
2SBL2_L23

1번부터 17번까지는 듣고 답하는 문제입니다. 1번부터 15번까지는 한 번만 들려주고, 16번부터 17번까지는 두 번 들려줍니다. 방송을 잘 듣고 답을 하시기 바랍니다.

01

다음을 듣고, 여자가 하는 말의 목적으로 가장 적절한 것을 고르시오.

① 휴식의 중요성을 강조하려고
② 직업 상담 전문가를 모집하려고
③ 스트레스 받는 이유를 설명하려고
④ 회사의 상담 프로그램을 홍보하려고
⑤ 상담 프로그램의 일정 변경을 공지하려고

02

대화를 듣고, 남자의 의견으로 가장 적절한 것을 고르시오.

① 운동을 마친 후 스트레칭을 하는 것이 필요하다.
② 천천히 걷는 것은 근육통 완화에 도움이 된다.
③ 과도한 스트레칭은 부상을 유발할 수 있다.
④ 자신의 몸에 맞는 식단을 구성하는 것이 중요하다.
⑤ 몸과 마음의 건강을 위해 규칙적인 운동을 해야 한다.

03

다음을 듣고, 여자가 하는 말의 요지로 가장 적절한 것을 고르시오.

① 감정 일기 쓰기는 자신의 감정을 이해하는 데 도움이 된다.
② 자신의 감정을 절제하며 의견을 전달하는 것이 필요하다.
③ 타인과의 유대감은 감정 일기의 공유를 통해 증진된다.
④ 일기 쓰기는 규칙적인 생활 습관 형성에 효과적이다.
⑤ 가족과의 대화로 부정적인 감정을 해소할 수 있다.

04

대화를 듣고, 그림에서 대화의 내용과 일치하지 <u>않는</u> 것을 고르시오.

05

대화를 듣고, 남자가 할 일로 가장 적절한 것을 고르시오.

① 저녁 식사 요리하기
② 여분 접시 확인하기
③ 와인 준비하기
④ 케이크 사러 가기
⑤ 공항에 마중 나가기

06

대화를 듣고, 여자가 지불할 금액을 고르시오. 3점

① $14
② $19
③ $24
④ $28
⑤ $33

07

대화를 듣고, 남자가 송별회에 참석할 수 <u>없는</u> 이유를 고르시오.

① 동생을 돌봐야 해서
② 클럽 활동에 가야 해서
③ 마라톤에 참가해야 해서
④ 병원 진료를 받아야 해서
⑤ 교수님과 면담을 해야 해서

08

대화를 듣고, Noodle Cooking Contest에 관해 언급되지 <u>않은</u> 것을 고르시오.

① 참가 대상
② 대회 날짜
③ 대회 장소
④ 우승 상금
⑤ 지원 방법

09

Library Plus에 관한 다음 내용을 듣고, 일치하지 <u>않는</u> 것을 고르시오.

① 도서관 자원봉사자들이 책을 집으로 배송한다.
② 도서관 회원은 무료로 이용할 수 있다.
③ 한 번에 최대 5권의 책을 빌릴 수 있다.
④ 전화로 대출 기간을 연장할 수 있다.
⑤ 직접 도서관에 방문하여 책을 반납해야 한다.

10

다음 표를 보면서 대화를 듣고, 두 사람이 구매할 반지를 고르시오.

Gold Rings

	Model	Price	Color	Stone	Gift-Wrapping Service
①	A	$300	White	Ruby	×
②	B	$330	Yellow	Ruby	×
③	C	$350	White	Emerald	○
④	D	$380	Rose	Ruby	○
⑤	E	$430	Rose	Emerald	×

11

대화를 듣고, 남자의 마지막 말에 대한 여자의 응답으로 가장 적절한 것을 고르시오. 3점

① Sorry. We can't finish our art class project today.
② Oh, it's such a shame that you missed the chance.
③ I don't think so. The tickets are not that expensive.
④ Yeah, just let me make sure it's okay with my mom first.
⑤ Why not? My mom and I don't have any plans on Sunday.

12

대화를 듣고, 여자의 마지막 말에 대한 남자의 응답으로 가장 적절한 것을 고르시오.

① Good idea. You can cook instead of me.
② My fault! I should have paid for the dinner.
③ Unfortunately, the restaurant is closed tonight.
④ Okay, then I guess we should cancel our plans.
⑤ Right. I'll check if there's any public parking nearby.

13

대화를 듣고, 남자의 마지막 말에 대한 여자의 응답으로 가장 적절한 것을 고르시오. [3점]

Woman: _____

① Right. Let's ask him if he can help us with the interview.
② I agree. That's why I want to go to the event to see him.
③ Wow, I can see that you've read so many of his books.
④ Yeah, I'm glad that your new book got published.
⑤ No. Negative reviews could help my career.

14

대화를 듣고, 여자의 마지막 말에 대한 남자의 응답으로 가장 적절한 것을 고르시오.

Man: _____

① Don't worry. He'll get his driver's license soon.
② Really? I didn't know you were interested in my car.
③ Oh, no. Then I should take my car to the repair shop.
④ No problem. We can schedule a time with my brother.
⑤ Never mind. I'm going to buy a different one tomorrow.

15

다음 상황 설명을 듣고, Bill이 Susan에게 할 말로 가장 적절한 것을 고르시오.

Bill: _____

① I think you need to find the right time to relax.
② Getting good grades is not the most important thing.
③ There must be many benefits to studying at the library.
④ Why don't you make a study plan to prepare for exams?
⑤ How about changing where you study to regain your focus?

[16~17] 다음을 듣고, 물음에 답하시오.

16

남자가 하는 말의 주제로 가장 적절한 것은?

① various drawing styles used by artists
② objects used as symbols in Western art
③ impact of religious objects on Western culture
④ changes in painting tools through history
⑤ how to paint objects in a realistic way

17

언급된 사물이 아닌 것은?

① mirrors   ② candles   ③ shells
④ books   ⑤ flowers

※ 고2 2024년 9월 학력평가 시험지와 문항 순서가 동일합니다.

24 | 2024년 9월 학력평가

MP3 　 동영상 강의

2SBL2_A24 　 2SBL2_L24

😊 1번부터 17번까지는 듣고 답하는 문제입니다. 1번부터 15번까지는 한 번만 들려주고, 16번부터 17번까지는 두 번 들려줍니다. 방송을 잘 듣고 답을 하시기 바랍니다.

01
다음을 듣고, 여자가 하는 말의 목적으로 가장 적절한 것을 고르시오.

① 미술 대회 작품을 공모하려고
② 직원 채용 일정을 안내하려고
③ 전시회 취소에 대해 항의하려고
④ 어린이 미술관 건립을 제안하려고
⑤ 미술관 무료 입장 행사를 홍보하려고

02
대화를 듣고, 남자의 의견으로 가장 적절한 것을 고르시오.

① 식물을 실내에 두면 호흡기 건강에 해로울 수 있다.
② 지나치게 높은 온도는 실내 식물에 악영향을 미친다.
③ 식물에게 말하는 것은 식물이 자라는 데 도움이 된다.
④ 상대방의 목소리를 통해 건강 상태를 파악할 수 있다.
⑤ 적절한 인사말은 대화를 자연스럽게 시작하는 데 필요하다.

03
다음을 듣고, 남자가 하는 말의 요지로 가장 적절한 것을 고르시오.

① 과일과 채소는 색깔에 따라 효능이 다르다.
② 규칙적인 식사는 혈당 수치 조절에 도움이 된다.
③ 식사 직후의 과일 섭취는 소화 문제를 유발할 수 있다.
④ 일상생활의 스트레스는 소화 불량을 악화시킬 수 있다.
⑤ 음식물 섭취만으로 하루 권장 비타민양을 채울 수 있다.

04
대화를 듣고, 그림에서 대화의 내용과 일치하지 <u>않는</u> 것을 고르시오.

05
대화를 듣고, 여자가 할 일로 가장 적절한 것을 고르시오.

① 운동 장비 대여하기　② 축구공 개수 확인하기
③ 스포츠 클럽 방문하기　④ 경기 규칙 유인물 만들기
⑤ 자원봉사자들에게 전화하기

06
대화를 듣고, 남자가 지불할 금액을 고르시오. 3점

① $24　② $28　③ $30
④ $38　⑤ $40

07

대화를 듣고, 여자가 대회에 출품할 사진을 촬영하지 <u>못한</u> 이유를 고르시오.

① 카메라가 고장나서
② 몸 상태가 좋지 않아서
③ 촬영하기에 날씨가 나빠서
④ 과학 캠프와 일정이 겹쳐서
⑤ 적합한 촬영 장소를 찾지 못해서

08

대화를 듣고, Poetry Magic에 관해 언급되지 <u>않은</u> 것을 고르시오.

① 출연자   ② 일시   ③ 장소
④ 기념품   ⑤ 등록 방법

09

Short-form Video Course에 관한 다음 내용을 듣고, 일치하지 <u>않는</u> 것을 고르시오.

① 무료 온라인 강좌이다.
② 세 단계로 이루어져 있다.
③ 웹사이트에서 등록할 수 있다.
④ 언제든지 반복해서 수강할 수 있다.
⑤ 모든 참가자의 작품에 대해 피드백을 제공한다.

10

다음 표를 보면서 대화를 듣고, 두 사람이 주문할 백색 소음 기계를 고르시오.

White Noise Machine

	Model	Price	Number of White Noise Tracks	Color	Alarm Function
①	A	$42	20	Silver	×
②	B	$38	18	White	×
③	C	$35	15	White	○
④	D	$30	12	Black	○
⑤	E	$25	8	Black	×

11

대화를 듣고, 여자의 마지막 말에 대한 남자의 응답으로 가장 적절한 것을 고르시오.

① Yeah. Our delivery has just arrived.
② Alright. Let's sign up for the membership.
③ Oh, no. I forgot to renew our membership.
④ Great. The shopping mall is close to our home.
⑤ Okay. I'll consider reducing my online shopping.

12

대화를 듣고, 남자의 마지막 말에 대한 여자의 응답으로 가장 적절한 것을 고르시오.

① Sure. I'll bring my tumbler next time.
② I'm afraid not. We're out of paper cups.
③ No worries. I already prepared the drinks.
④ Sorry. The cafe doesn't offer any discount.
⑤ Why not? Let's get a refund for the tumbler.

정답과 해설 : 07~12 116~118

13

대화를 듣고, 여자의 마지막 말에 대한 남자의 응답으로 가장 적절한 것을 고르시오.

Man: _____

① Good choice. This shirt looks great on you!
② Okay. We'd better go buy your shirt right away.
③ Really? I didn't know the rehearsal was canceled.
④ Well, why not wear a white shirt for the show?
⑤ Oh, I'm sorry that I missed your performance.

14

대화를 듣고, 남자의 마지막 말에 대한 여자의 응답으로 가장 적절한 것을 고르시오. 3점

Woman: _____

① I agree that we should walk our dogs often.
② I'm glad that my dog loved staying at the pet hotel.
③ I'd really appreciate it if you could take care of him.
④ It's better to pack only necessary things for traveling.
⑤ I recommend you bring your dog to the animal hospital.

15

다음 상황 설명을 듣고, David가 Emily에게 할 말로 가장 적절한 것을 고르시오. 3점

David: _____

① Can you look for different music for the last scene?
② I think we need to practice more for the musical.
③ Please check the schedule for the final stage.
④ Would you mind if I change some scenes?
⑤ I want you to play the main character.

[16~17] 다음을 듣고, 물음에 답하시오.

16

여자가 하는 말의 주제로 가장 적절한 것은?

① traditional ways to preserve foods
② possible origins of famous desserts
③ health concerns about ready-made foods
④ controversy over the cost of popular desserts
⑤ newly-invented desserts with special ingredients

17

언급된 나라가 아닌 것은?

① Scotland　　② Italy　　③ Egypt
④ France　　⑤ Sweden

01 2018년 11월 학력평가
딕테이션

녹음을 듣고, 빈칸에 알맞은 말을 쓰시기 바랍니다. 빈칸은 문제풀이에 핵심이 되는 키워드와 헷갈리기 쉬운 발음에 표시되어 있으니 이 점에 유의하여 듣기 바랍니다.

01
고2 2018년 11월 3번

M: Good morning. Welcome to Sunshine Zoo. I'm Mr. Johnson, the head of the zookeepers. We're working hard to _____ _____ _____ of tourists and animals. Before the tour, we kindly request that you keep _____ _____ _____ in mind. First, don't feed the animals or throw things at the cages as it can make them sick or _____ a lot of stress to them. Second, turn off the camera flash while taking pictures of the animals because it can _____ them. Lastly, don't leave young kids unattended. They might get lost and enter _____ areas. I hope you enjoy your tour.

02
고2 2018년 11월 4번

W: Honey, you're home early.

M: Hi, sweetie. Where is Cathy?

W: She went shopping with her friends.

M: Hmm.... She's been going shopping a lot lately. She must have spent all of her _____.

W: I think so. She asked me for more money yesterday. I'm worried that she doesn't think about how she spends her money.

M: I'm worried, too. She'll have to learn how to manage her money on her own.

W: Yeah. I think it's the _____ _____ _____ _____ to teach their child how to do that.

M: You're right. We should help Cathy to be _____ smart.

W: Of course. Home should be the place to gain _____ _____ _____.

M: I agree. Let's talk to her when she comes back home.

03
고2 2018년 11월 5번

W: Hello, sir. Thank you for sitting down with me today.

M: Hello, Erin. Thank you for coming here.

W: No problem. As I mentioned on the phone, I'm _____ _____ _____ about you for our school newspaper.

M: Yes, that's right.

W: So, I'd like to know what first attracted you to this job.

M: A documentary about _____ that I saw in a middle school science class inspired me.

W: I see. And I heard that you do medical volunteer work every summer.

M: I do. Some of the nurses at my hospital _____ _____ _____ _____ living in isolated areas.

W: That's so impressive. Finally, do you have any advice for students who want to be _____, like I do?

M: Well, always remember to put others' needs before your own.

W: That's an important point. Can I take pictures of you with the nurses for our article?

M: Sure. Please come this way.

04

M: Hi, Kelly. Have you finished preparing for the skit contest this Friday?

W: Yes, I almost have. Take a look. The banner with balloons at the _____ _____ _____ _____ looks good, doesn't it?

M: Yeah, it looks neat. What's the sofa on the stage for?

W: It's for the first skit.

M: Okay. The _____ trophy on the table looks cool. Is it for the winning class?

W: Exactly. The winning class will also get to perform at the school festival.

M: That's amazing. And what's the _____ for? I haven't seen it before.

W: It was set up for the contest yesterday. It'll be used between skits.

M: Wonderful! Who is the girl _____ glasses?

W: That's Judy. She's a staff member from another class.

M: I see. The contest will be really fun.

W: You should come and watch.

05

M: Hello, Alice. How are you?

W: Hi, Chris. I'm doing great. I'm _____ _____ _____ this new neighborhood.

M: Good. Have you met any of your other neighbors?

W: I met a few. I had dinner with my next door neighbors Tim and Julie last Saturday.

M: That's nice. I know the couple well. I _____ _____ with them at the community center.

W: Community center? Where is it?

M: It's next to the post office. I go there to play table tennis every weekend.

W: That sounds interesting. I like playing table tennis, too.

M: Then, why don't you _____ me this Saturday?

W: I'd like to, but I threw my racket away before moving here. _____ _____ _____ me one?

M: Sure. I have an extra.

W: Thank you.

06

M: Hello, how may I help you?

W: _____ _____ _____ _____ tickets for the next Greenville city bus tour, please.

M: There's one departing at 11 a.m. Is that time okay with you?

W: Sounds great. How much is the fare?

M: A ticket for an adult is $_____ per person.

W: Okay. How much is it for a child?

M: It's $20. How many tickets do you need?

W: _____ adults and one child. And I downloaded a coupon from your website. Can I use it?

M: Sure, with that you can save 10% _____ _____ _____ _____.

W: Sounds good. I'll use the coupon.

M: All right. How would you like to pay?

W: By credit card.

07

W: Jake, our presentation is finally over. I feel so relieved.

M: So do I. And what will you do now?

W: I'm _____ _____ going ice skating.

M: That sounds fun. Where can you do that?

W: There's an ice-rink at the _____ where I have my part-time job.

M: Really? How is it?

W: It's nice and big! There's also a discount for students. Why don't we go ice skating together today?

M: I _____ I could, but I can't go.

W: Why? Do you have something else to do?

M: Yes, I'm going _____ _____ _____ to Busan with my friends tomorrow. So I have to _____ my bag.

W: No problem. We can go ice skating next time. Have a nice trip!

M: Thanks. See you later.

08

W: Jim, take a look at this. I got a 'Global Student Card.'

M: Oh, let me see it. Can all students get one?

W: Only students from _____ _____ _____ years old can get one. It proves that we're students when travelling abroad.

M: It sounds useful. I might get one myself.

W: That's a good idea. Once you have it, it's

_____ _____ _____ three years.

M: I see. What do I need to do to get one issued?

W: You need to _____ a copy of your student ID card and an application form to the school office.

M: How long does it take to get it issued?

W: _____ _____ _____ about two weeks, and you'll receive it by mail.

M: Okay. Thank you for the information.

W: You're welcome. You can go right now before the office closes.

M: I _____ _____ _____ try. See you!

09

[Chime bell rings.]

W: Hello, everyone. This is Jane Parker from Clearwater University broadcasting center. The Clearwater University 5km Run will be held on _____ _____ to celebrate the school's 50th anniversary. All students and faculty members can participate in the run. It'll start at 10 a.m. and participants will run a course through the campus. The _____ _____ is $5 for students and $15 for faculty members. A bottle of water and a small snack will be provided. The run will be finished around noon, and _____ _____ there will be a music concert in the main hall at 2 p.m. If you're interested, you can sign up through the university website or in the school library _____ _____. Thank you.

10

고2 2018년 11월 12번

W: Brian, we're off work tomorrow. Do you have any plans?

M: I was thinking of going to see a movie at the Limestone Movie Theater. There're several _____ movies.

W: Really? Can I come with you?

M: Sure. Let me see. *[Pause]* We can see the timetable on the mobile app. These are the only tickets left.

W: Why don't we try 'Funny Guys'? I saw the _____. It looked interesting.

M: Oh, I've already seen it. How about a horror movie?

W: Hmm... I'm not really _____ _____ that kind of movie.

M: Okay. I've never seen a 3D or 4D movie before. Do you want to try out a movie with _____ _____?

W: I'd love to. Then I think that leaves us with two choices.

M: Okay. Hmm, this movie starts a little late for me. Let's see the one that starts _____.

W: It must be this one then. What do you think?

M: Great. I look forward to it.

11

고2 2018년 11월 1번

M: Tina, what _____ _____ _____ to have for lunch?

W: Well, how about the new French restaurant across the street?

M: Oh, I've heard about it. _____ _____ _____ to that place?

W: (Yeah, the food was really great.)

12

고2 2018년 11월 2번

W: Hey, Mike. I got _____ _____ for the art exhibition this Saturday.

M: Oh, you must be excited. You really like paintings.

W: Yeah. Let's _____ _____ and learn more about paintings.

M: (Sure. I'd love to go there with you.)

13

고2 2018년 11월 13번

M: Honey, what are you looking at?

W: Look at these puppies in this picture.

M: They're so cute. _____ puppies are they?

W: They're my cousin Amy's.

M: There're five of them! It must be difficult for her to raise all of them.

W: That's why she asked _____ _____ _____ to raise one. She knows I like dogs.

M: Really? That would be a good idea.

W: Yeah, but are you sure we can _____ _____ _____ _____ it?

M: Of course. I raised a dog when I was a kid.

W: Oh, I didn't know that you had a pet. I'll be able to take good care of it with your help.

M: Definitely. Our children will also be happy to know that _____ _____ a puppy.

W: (All right. I'll tell Amy that we'll take one of her puppies.)

14

[Phone rings.]

M: Hello? How can I help you?

W: Hello. I'd like to ask about the library _____.

M: You're talking to the right person. How may I help you?

W: I just checked the public library homepage, but I'm _____ _____ finding some information.

M: I apologize. What would you like to know?

W: It says the library is going to _____ after the renovation on the 15th of November. But what time does it open on that day?

M: It will open at 9 a.m. and close at 6 p.m.

W: Okay. I plan to borrow books on that day. Can I use the library card that I have now?

M: I'm afraid not. We _____ a new system.

W: Oh, how can I get a new card?

M: Come to the check-out desk and we'll give you one.

W: All right. I think _____ _____ _____ on the website would be helpful.

M: (I agree. I'll update all the information as soon as possible.)

15

M: Peter and Stella are working in the same office. Their office is _____ _____ computers, copy machines, and other office supplies, so there's always lots of dust in the office. They _____ _____ open the windows for some fresh air several times a day, but nowadays they can't because of severe and frequent fine dust. Because of this, Stella suffers from _____ _____, so Peter tries to think about how to improve air quality in the office. One day, Peter finds out that some plants help _____ the air. So, Peter wants to suggest to Stella that they _____ _____ _____ in their office. In this situation, what would Peter most likely say to Stella?

Peter: (Why don't we get some plants for fresh air?)

16~17

W: Hello, everyone. I'm Wilma Moore from Margaret Medical Center. As the days get shorter during winter, many people find themselves _____ _____. What can we do about it? I'd like to recommend some _____ _____ _____ that can help you deal with this problem. First, salmon, a popular cold-water _____, can help fight depression. Salmon is rich in omega-3 fatty acids that improve symptoms _____ _____ depression. Second, eating eggs daily can help fight many kinds of _____ _____. Eggs are one of the few foods that contain vitamin D, which can _____ depression. Third, if you eat a few bananas a day, it can keep you happy and _____ the symptoms of depression. Bananas are known to contain a type of protein that helps you relax, improving your mood. Lastly, yogurt also can be effective in beating the _____ _____. The protein and calcium in yogurt can ease anxiety. Try these foods and they'll lift you up when you're down. I hope you stay healthy during the cold winter.

02 2019년 3월 학력평가 딕테이션

녹음을 듣고, 빈칸에 알맞은 말을 쓰시기 바랍니다. 빈칸은 문제풀이에 핵심이 되는 키워드와 헷갈리기 쉬운 발음에 표시되어 있으니 이 점에 유의하여 듣기 바랍니다.

01

고2 2019년 3월 3번

M: Hello, everyone. These days, children tend to have _____ _____ because of too much time spent on digital devices, and many parents are worried about it. However, there are things you can _____ _____ _____ your child's eyes healthy. First of all, set screen time limits for your child. Second, provide your child with _____ foods, such as vegetables, fruits, nuts, and fish. They contain nutrients that are good for your child's eyes. Third, have your child wear _____ _____ when they play outside in the sun. Last but not least, have your child's eyes _____ regularly. Remember that prevention is better than cure. Thank you.

02

고2 2019년 3월 4번

W: Are you trying to buy something online, Neil?

M: Yes, Mom. I just found a nice _____ online.

W: What is it?

M: This black leather jacket. They sell it for only $60.

W: That's very cheap, but did you check if the shop is _____?

M: No, I didn't. Do I have to?

W: Well, you need to be cautious. There could be online sellers you _____.

M: You mean they could take my money without delivering my order?

W: Yeah. That's why you need to buy things _____ _____ _____ online shops.

M: Okay, Mom. I'll check that before I buy the jacket.

03

고2 2019년 3월 5번

[Cell phone rings.]

M: Hello, Ms. Johnson.

W: Hello, Mr. Baker. I'd like to talk to you about the _____ _____ _____ _____.

M: You mean the new menu commercial?

W: Yes. I think there's a problem with it.

M: Really? May I ask what that is?

W: Well, according to our contract, the commercial is supposed to be _____ before the evening news on your station.

M: Yes, I remember that.

W: But the commercial was not _____ yesterday.

M: Is that true?

W: Yes. I checked it myself.

M: Okay, Ms. Johnson. I'll talk with our staff about that and _____ the problem.

W: Thank you. I want you to do it as soon as possible.

04

M: Grace, come look at this showcase. These items were donated by sports stars who graduated from here.

W: Great! Who is the man in the _____ picture frame?

M: That's Larry Smith, the best player on the national baseball team.

W: There's a baseball bat _____ _____ the picture frame. Is it one of his?

M: Yes. He hit his 100th home run with that bat.

W: Oh, really? Whose glove is it in front of the _____?

M: It's Larry's, too. He used it when he was in high school.

W: I see. The basketball in the middle has a _____ K on it. What does it stand for?

M: You know the basketball player Kevin Jackson? K is his initial.

W: I didn't know he was a graduate of your school.

M: Look at his _____ _____ _____ _____. That's the very trophy he received as MVP.

W: Wow! You must be very proud of your graduates.

05

W: Honey, I'm so excited that we're finally having a _____ party.

M: Me, too.

W: The guests will arrive soon. Is everything ready?

M: Yes, almost. You've checked the _____, haven't you?

W: Yes, I have. The chicken is roasting nicely.

M: Good. The strawberry cake is in the _____. Hmm.... I think everything is all set. I'll take one last look at the bathroom.

W: Oh, I _____ _____ _____ the towels with fresh ones.

M: No problem. I'll take care of the towels. How about the _____ paper?

W: Don't worry. I've already replaced it with a new roll.

M: Good!

06

M: Emma, _____ _____ out of shampoo.

W: Really? Then I'll order some online now. [Pause]

M: What's the price of the shampoo we usually use?

W: It's $_____ a bottle at this online store. How many bottles do you want me to order?

M: How about _____ bottles?

W: Okay. Do we have anything else to buy?

M: Hmm, let me think. Oh, didn't you say you need to buy toothbrushes?

W: That's right. It's $10 _____ _____ _____ of four toothbrushes.

M: Then, let's order two packs.

W: Okay. I have a $2 _____ coupon, so I'll use it.

M: That's good. Is there a delivery charge?

W: No, there's no delivery charge for orders over $20. I'll place the order now.

07

W: Hi, Max. Where are you going?

M: I'm going to a print shop. My printer at home is

_____ _____ _____.

W: Oh, that must be annoying.

M: You're telling me. I have to fix it right away. Is

there any place nearby that can _____

_____?

W: There's one near the post office. I'm going there

today to have my laptop fixed.

M: Really? What time are you going? I'd like to go

with you _____ _____.

W: I'm going there at around 5 p.m. after Professor

Simon's special lecture.

M: 5 p.m.? I'm afraid I can't go with you then.

W: Oh, you have a tennis lesson today, don't you?

M: No, the lesson is tomorrow. Actually I have

_____ _____ _____

Professor Watson.

W: I see. Then, I'll text you the phone number of the

repair shop.

M: Thank you.

08

M: Maria, what are you watching?

W: I'm watching the preview of the new TV drama,

Romance City.

M: *Romance City*? When does it start?

W: The _____ _____ will be aired

on March 9th.

M: Oh, it's this Saturday!

W: Yes. My favorite actor, Liam Collins, is the

_____ _____.

M: Oh, he is? I like him, too.

W: The director is Sam Adams. He also

_____ *Dreamcatcher*.

M: Really? I loved that drama.

W: You know what? *Romance City* is _____

_____ the best-selling novel of the

same title.

M: Have you read the novel?

W: Of course. I enjoyed it very much.

09

W: Hello, listeners. Are you looking for something

to do this summer? Then, how about going

to the Redland Festival? It is a fruit festival to

_____ good health. This festival is an

annual event held in Blue River Park. This year, it

will _____ _____ on Saturday,

July 13th, from 10 a.m. to 8 p.m. During the

festival, an _____ fruit buffet will be

provided all day long. You can also participate in

sports activities such as soccer and badminton.

The $10 _____ fee includes sports

activities as well as the fruit buffet. Reservations

are _____ _____. Come enjoy

this fun festival. Thank you.

10

M: Claire, look at this. Five best-selling hair dryers are on sale at this online store.

W: Good. I was going to buy a new one.

M: Why don't you choose one with a _____ wattage? The higher the wattage, the faster you dry your hair.

W: You're right. I'll choose one with _____ watts or more.

M: Which material is better, ionic or ceramic?

W: The ionic model is _____ _____ my hair type. So, I'll get an ionic one.

M: I think the price is also important.

W: I agree. I'll buy a model _____ _____ $50.

M: Then, you have only two models to choose from.

W: I think it's better to choose one with a _____ _____ setting.

M: Yeah, with that function, you can dry your hair with cool air.

W: Okay, then, I'll order this one.

11

M: Esther, I heard from Jack that you _____ _____ _____.

W: Yeah, I fell down and twisted my ankle.

M: That sounds painful. Did you _____ _____ _____?

W: (Yes. He just told me to relax for a few days.)

12

W: What are you looking at on your smartphone, Jason?

M: Oh, I'm looking for a _____ to have my mother's birthday party.

W: Really? I know a nice Italian _____ _____.

M: (Great. Can you tell me the name of the restaurant?)

13

W: Daniel, what are you _____ _____ in the closet?

M: I'm looking for my spring pants and shirts. Where are they, Mom?

W: All your spring clothes are in the box here.

M: [Pause] Wow, you _____ all my spring clothes in this box!

W: Yeah. Look at what's written on the box.

M: Oh, it says "Daniel's spring clothes."

W: There are many good things about _____ off-season clothes in separate boxes.

M: I think we can easily find the clothes we need when the _____ change.

W: That's right. It also prevents the fading of colors.

M: I see. Is there _____ _____ _____?

W: (Yes. We can keep clothes from getting dusty.)

14

M: Honey, I'm home. What are you doing?

W: I'm doing yoga.

M: Aren't you going to the yoga center today?

W: No, I'm not going there any longer. It's _____ _____ from here.

M: But don't you think it's better to do yoga at the center?

W: Yes, but I don't want to _____ my time on the road.

M: If you exercise at home alone, you might lose interest.

W: Maybe, but I've found a nice fitness app and _____ _____ on my smartphone.

M: A fitness app? What does it do for you?

W: It helps _____ _____ _____ my workout schedule, provides personalized information, and so on.

M: (That's awesome! It'll be very helpful.)

15

M: Willy is a student who lives alone in a house near his university. Returning home after school, he finds that the _____ _____ of his house is very low. It feels quite chilly. He turns on the heating system, but it doesn't work. Willy _____ a repairman and asks him to come and fix it. The repairman comes and fixes the problem. Willy says thanks to him and _____ for the repair. After the repairman leaves, Willy finds that one of the repairman's _____ is on the floor. Willy calls the repairman again to let him _____ about this. In this situation, what would Willy most likely say to the repairman?

Willy: (You left one of your tools in my house.)

16~17

W: Hello, everyone. _____ _____ like Artificial Intelligence, it is possible to digitize homes. Today, I'd like to introduce to you household appliances _____ _____ with the help of technology. First are smart washing machines. Smart _____ with AI techniques can sense the different types of fabric so they regulate the washing _____ and detergent. They can even send an alert when detergent is out of stock. Next are smart _____. They allow the user to monitor food items inside. They can even show relevant recipes that can be made with those items. There are also smart speakers. Speakers controlled by _____ _____ can do various tasks such as creating a play list and searching the Internet. Lastly, robotic _____ _____ can automatically clean the tight and usually overlooked spaces that are hard to access in traditional ways. Now, let's watch a video about these smart home appliances.

03 2019년 6월 학력평가
딕테이션

MP3

2SBL2_A03

🙂 녹음을 듣고, 빈칸에 알맞은 말을 쓰시기 바랍니다. 빈칸은 문제풀이에 핵심이 되는 키워드와 헷갈리기 쉬운 발음에 표시되어 있으니 이 점에 유의하여 듣기 바랍니다.

01
고2 2019년 6월 3번

W: Hello, I'm Grace Cooper, the manager of the Dolphin Swimming Center. We always _____ your love and support for the center. I have a wonderful _____ for all our members. So far, swimming classes have been held only in the mornings and evenings. Since the number of members _____ _____, many people have asked for new afternoon classes. Finally, we decided to meet your needs. From next month, there will be two classes opening _____ _____ _____. The instructor will be Mr. Jones. I hope this is good news for our members. For more information about the new afternoon classes, check the center's website. Thank you for listening.

02
고2 2019년 6월 4번

M: Hi, Katie. What can I help you with?

W: Hello, Mr. Smith. I want to show you my _____ to get your advice.

M: Let me see. [Pause] You have creative ideas in your writing!

W: Thanks, but I think I need to _____ _____ _____ _____.

M: Hmm, that requires a lot of effort. Do you read a lot?

W: No, I don't have much time to read.

M: It's the _____ _____ you could do to improve your writing.

W: Why is that? How could reading help my writing?

M: Well, by reading books, you get a _____ of how stories flow.

W: Oh, I'd never thought of that.

M: More importantly, you can learn a lot of _____ to use for your writing!

W: If that's so, I'll make time to read more books.

03
고2 2019년 6월 5번

W: Hello, what can I do for you?

M: I went to the _____ _____, but I couldn't find *Romeo and Juliet* by Shakespeare.

W: Let me check.... [Typing sound] Oh, someone just borrowed it.

M: Oh, no. I really need it for my school _____. When can I borrow the book, then?

W: I'm not sure, but it is supposed to be _____ _____ _____ _____.

M: Then, are there any other books by Shakespeare? My teacher wants me to write a book _____ on a work by Shakespeare.

W: Okay. [Typing sound] We have several books by Shakespeare. How about *Hamlet*?

M: Oh, I've heard about that story. I'll read that book instead, then.

W: *Hamlet* is in literature section H. I can show you _____ _____ _____ if you want.

M: No, that's okay. I can go get it. Thank you so much.

W: You're welcome.

04

W: Andrew, have a look at this picture.

M: Wow, it is a really nice room. Whose is this?

W: Mine. My family moved into a new house last week, and I decorated the room by myself.

M: You did a great job! I especially like the curtains with the _____ _____ on the window.

W: Thank you. I thought these curtains would make my room stylish.

M: Good choice. The _____ _____ on the bed is so cute.

W: These days I fall asleep hugging her.

M: How sweet! What is this lamp for?

W: I put the lamp _____ the bed to read before going to sleep.

M: That's a good idea. It also gives the room a nice atmosphere.

W: The _____ _____ on the bookshelf looks beautiful, doesn't it?

M: It really does. And the _____ _____ on the wall goes well with the room.

W: I'm happy to hear that you like my room.

05

W: Tom, did you pack everything for tomorrow's _____ trip?

M: I'm almost done, Mom. I just need a few more things.

W: Good! Don't forget to pack some _____ _____!

M: Sure, I did. Just in case!

W: Well done! What about hiking boots? Didn't you say you were going to borrow Jake's?

M: Yes, he told me to pick them up in the afternoon.

W: That's so _____ of him. Anything else?

M: There is just one more important thing left. I have to go to the _____ store to buy some snacks!

W: Snacks are important. I'm going to the grocery store right now. I _____ _____ _____ for you if you want.

M: Could you? That would be great!

W: Sure, sweetie. No problem.

M: Then all I have to do is get the boots from Jake!

06

M: Hi, may I help you?

W: Hello. I'm looking for shampoo.

M: Do you have a _____ brand in mind?

W: No, I actually don't. Could you recommend me one?

M: Let's see. This brand _____ _____ _____ a new shampoo and it's on sale.

W: Great! So how much is it?

M: Originally, it was _____ dollars per bottle, but for this week only, if you buy three, you get 10% off the total price of the shampoo.

W: Awesome. I'll have _____ then.

M: Alright. Just to let you know, this brand also has another special promotion only for today!

W: Oh, really? What's the promotion about?

M: All customers who buy from this brand can get this body cleanser for _____ dollars.

W: That's great! Then I'll have three bottles of shampoo and one body cleanser. Here's my credit card.

07

W: Hey, Mark! You look _____. What's up?

M: I'm thinking of leaving my job.

W: Why? Did you get a job offer from another company?

M: Not yet, but I've _____ _____ to some other companies.

W: I thought you were satisfied with your work and salary.

M: Well, the pay is good and I'm comfortable with this job.

W: Then, why do you want to leave?

M: If I don't look for a new _____, I will get used to doing the same easy job and I won't develop.

W: You mean you want to _____ _____ _____ by challenging yourself with different work, don't you?

M: Exactly. I would be happier with a job that can help me improve my career.

W: I understand, but you'd better make the _____ after considering the matter carefully.

M: Thank you for your advice.

08

M: Rose, I've heard that you have a cat. Will you go to Cat Fair with me?

W: Cat Fair? Sounds interesting.

M: It'll be very useful. You can buy cat food and toys at cheap prices there.

W: Oh, I want to go. _____ _____ _____ be held?

M: It will be held in Coex Hall.

W: That's not far from here. When is it?

M: It's on the _____ of June. Are you available?

W: Luckily, I'm free that day. I wonder how much the tickets _____.

M: They are 10 dollars per person.

W: I see. Will there be any special events?

M: Yes! A famous cat _____ will be there to answer questions on cat health.

W: That sounds great. I look forward to going!

09

W: Hello, CBC radio listeners! I'm Grace Wilson, the manager of the Great Light Festival. I'm happy to let you know about this event. Famous light artists will join to show their work. The _____ of the event is 'Christmas.' There will be a big Christmas tree _____ with beautiful lights, and you can take nice pictures in front of it. The festival will be held _____ _____ _____ from December 1st at Skyline Park. Tickets for the festival are 20 dollars each and can only be _____ _____ _____ _____. The lighting hours will be from 6 p.m. to 10 p.m. I hope that many people come and enjoy the festival. Thank you.

10

고2 2019년 6월 12번

M: Amy, look at this flyer. _____
_____ are on sale!

W: Really? That's great! I think it is a good time to buy a new one.

M: Yeah, let's see. *[Pause]* This one looks cute but maybe it's too small for us.

W: You're right. We drink a lot of tea. It should be _____ _____ 1.5 liters.

M: Hmm, this one is too expensive. I don't want to spend more than $_____ on a kettle.

W: Me, either. Then we have three options. Which color do you like?

M: I don't think black _____ _____ in our kitchen.

W: I agree. It makes the kitchen too dark.

M: What about the material? There is a plastic one and a glass one.

W: We have used a plastic one before. It's better to try the other material _____ _____.

M: Good point. Then let's buy this one.

11

고2 2019년 6월 1번

W: Kevin, have you been to the _____ _____ _____ downtown?

M: Yes, I went there with my family last weekend. It was really nice.

W: Oh, really? What is _____ _____ it?

M: (It has various sportswear brands.)

12

고2 2019년 6월 2번

M: Oh, Susan! The _____ in the bathroom went out.

W: I know, but don't worry. We only have to replace the light bulb. I'll buy one tomorrow.

M: But, it's _____ _____ _____ the bathroom.

W: (Then, I'll go and buy a new one right now.)

13

고2 2019년 6월 13번

W: Willy, what are you doing?

M: Hi, Kelly! I'm making plans to _____ _____ _____ of student council.

W: Really? I'm guessing there will be strong competition among the _____.

M: What do you mean by that?

W: I heard Angela is also going to run for the position. She is popular among her classmates, you know.

M: I didn't know she was interested. I thought she was a _____ girl.

W: Her friends are rather enthusiastic about making her student council president.

M: Good for her! I hope my friends help me, too.

W: I want to _____ you in any way I can. Is there anything I can do?

M: You got first prize in the _____ contest, didn't you?

W: Yeah, but how can that help you?

M: (You can make election campaign posters for me.)

14

M: Katie, how was school today?

W: Great, Dad. We had a special lecture about a new study _____.

M: That must have been helpful for you! You have been worried about your grades these days.

W: Yeah, I have. Now I'm going to make a new study plan _____ _____ what I learned today.

M: What did you learn? Tell me about it.

W: The lecturer is the author of the book *Just Start Small*. He said we should start small if we want to get good grades.

M: Start small? That doesn't make sense to me.

W: Let me give you an example. _____ just one simple Spanish sentence after lunch is not difficult, is it?

M: Right, that doesn't seem like much _____.

W: But if I do it for a month steadily, I will be able to speak thirty Spanish sentences in total.

M: Then that's _____ _____ _____ _____.

W: (Exactly. Small steps eventually lead to big ones.)

15

W: Sarah and Peter are supposed to _____ in *Beauty and the Beast* on stage at the school festival. While practicing together, Peter looks really _____. His voice is too small and he even forgets what he should say from time to time. Sarah is worried about Peter, so she asks him to _____ his problem with her. Peter says that he is afraid of acting in front of many people. Then, Sarah remembers her _____ from last year. When she felt the same way, she used to practice while her

_____ _____ _____

_____, and she found it really helpful. Now, Sarah wants to suggest that he practice as she did. In this situation, what would Sarah most likely say to Peter?

Sarah: (Why don't you practice acting in front of your family?)

16~17

M: Hello, students. Yesterday we looked at movies where robots and _____ talk and act like human beings. Today we're going to talk about movies where animals _____

_____ _____ _____.

The 1961 film, *101 Dalmatians*, is a Walt Disney classic. A dog, Pongo, played a lovable role in this _____ _____. But animal movies aren't just about dogs. The movie, *Lion King*, tells the story of a young _____, Simba. He becomes the king after overcoming many difficulties. *Jurassic Park* is a 1993 American science _____ film directed by Steven Spielberg. You can feel big thrills while watching many _____ _____. In *Babe*, a cute little pig made a strong impression on lots of moviegoers. What's the best animal _____ movie? If you think your favorite animal film is missing, go ahead and share it with us!

04 2019년 9월 학력평가
딕테이션

🙂 녹음을 듣고, 빈칸에 알맞은 말을 쓰시기 바랍니다. 빈칸은 문제풀이에 핵심이 되는 키워드와 헷갈리기 쉬운 발음에 표시되어 있으니 이 점에 유의하여 듣기 바랍니다.

01

고2 2019년 9월 3번

M: Good morning, students! I'm Principal Brad Smith. We're pleased to announce the _____ of our school's official social media page on U-Channel! For better communication about school news, _____ _____, and upcoming events, we've started this social media page as our newest communication tool. We'll _____ to use our other notification tools, including the school website, letters home, and emails. The U-Channel page will be _____ _____ _____ allowing for quick and immediate updates accessible on your computer or mobile phone. As always, if you have any questions, please _____ _____ to ask. Thank you.

02

고2 2019년 9월 4번

W: Justin, how's your speech coming along?

M: I don't think it's going so well, Ms. Jones.

W: What's wrong? I know you've been working really hard.

M: I think the script and the _____ _____ are good, but something about my delivery is still awkward.

W: Have you _____ _____ a video of yourself practicing your speech?

M: No, I haven't. Why?

W: Seeing how you deliver your speech can help you correct your _____ points.

M: How can it help?

W: When you watch a video of yourself giving the speech, you can see what kinds of _____ you make and hear how you sound.

M: Oh, you mean that I can fix something strange in my delivery if I see myself do it on video?

W: Exactly! You can _____ your delivery through this method.

M: Thank you. I'll try that now.

03

고2 2019년 9월 5번

M: Excuse me, are you Anna Zimmerman? I can't believe I'm seeing you here!

W: Oh, hello. Have we met before?

M: No, but I'm a _____ _____ of yours.

W: Thank you. I love meeting my fans.

M: I just finished your _____ _____, *The Beautiful Days*. I read the whole thing in a day.

W: I'm flattered. What did you like most?

M: I really liked the part where Emma and Jason first dance.

W: That's my favorite moment, too. It took me more than two weeks to _____ _____ _____.

M: Wow! It was worth it. It was so beautifully described. I hope this book will be made into a movie.

W: I'm so glad you like it that much.

M: I think you're one of the best _____ in the world. Can I get your autograph, please?

W: Sure.

04

M: Hey, Vicky. Looks like your club's face painting booth is ready for the school festival.

W: I just finished it. Please have a look.

M: Okay. [Pause] You chose the roof with a _____ pattern. I love it.

W: Thanks. What do you think of the banner _____ _____ _____?

M: The one that says "face painting" on it? It looks really nice.

W: I wanted our booth's activity to be really clear. I designed it myself.

M: Really? You did a great job. Oh, there's _____ _____ _____ in the booth.

W: Right. That's where we'll do face painting. We also have _____ _____ next to the table. Do you think it's enough?

M: It looks like it'll be enough. That's a nice _____ _____ outside the booth.

W: Yes. I want visitors to take photos of themselves there.

M: Cool! It'll be a great place to record memories of the festival.

W: I think so, too. I hope many students visit my booth.

05

M: Good morning, Ms. Stevenson.

W: Hi, Minsu, how's your group project going? I heard that you're sending books to Nepal.

M: It's going well. We bought Korean folk tale books, and we're _____ them into English.

W: Are you going to remake the books in English?

M: No. We're planning to put the translations next to the _____ _____.

W: That sounds really difficult.

M: It is. But thanks to a translation app, we've been able to finish our _____ _____.

W: That's good! Does that mean you're almost ready to send the books?

M: Actually, that's why I came to see you. We're not sure if our English translation sounds natural. Would you _____ _____ the first draft of our translation?

W: No problem. I'm happy to help you. When do you need me to finish by?

M: Well, we'll package the books next month.

W: If you email me the translation this week, then I'll give you the _____ by the end of this month.

M: Thank you so much.

06

W: Hi. How can I help you?

M: I'm looking for vegetable seeds for my garden. Can you recommend some vegetables that are easy _____ _____?

W: Sure. How about lettuce or tomatoes?

M: How much are they?

W: Lettuce seeds are three dollars for one packet, and tomato seeds are _____ dollars for one packet.

M: Sounds good. I'll buy two packets of tomato seeds.

W: Okay. Do you need anything else?

M: I also need fertilizer.

W: I'd recommend this _____ fertilizer. It's one of our best sellers.

M: How much is it?

W: It was originally ten dollars a bottle, but we're offering a _____ percent discount on this fertilizer.

M: Great! I'll take one bottle. Here's my _____ card.

07

W: What a cute dog! Is it yours?

M: Yes. I _____ him from an animal rescue center.

W: I've always wanted a dog. But I can't have one.

M: Why? Are you allergic to animal hair?

W: I'm only allergic to cat hair. Dogs are _____ fine.

M: What's the problem, then? Your house has a big backyard, so I think it's a perfect place for dogs.

W: I think so, too. It's a really dog-friendly _____.

M: Do your parents not like dogs?

W: No, they love dogs. But I'm worried about a dog _____ _____ during the day.

M: Is there nobody who can look after a dog?

W: There is _____ _____ _____ _____ during the day. My parents work, and my brother and I go to school.

M: Oh, I see. That's why you can't get a dog.

08

M: Katie, what are you doing?

W: I'm looking at a _____ for the World Food Festival. Do you remember the event I talked about before?

M: Yeah. You said we can enjoy different types of foods from around the world. Where will it be?

W: It'll be _____ _____ the central park in Orange County.

M: That's not far from here. Is it on a weekend?

W: Yes. It's on Sunday, September 22nd and _____ at 10 a.m.

M: I've never been to a food festival before. What kind of programs does this one have?

W: There are _____ _____ for foods from all around the world and a variety of folk shows. Would you like to go with me?

M: I'd love to. [Pause] Hmm... we should probably drive there. Will there be _____ _____?

W: The brochure says there will be a parking lot. It'll cost five dollars to park there for the whole day.

M: Perfect! Let's take my car. I'll pick you up.

W: Okay. I'll see you then.

09

W: Hello, everyone. I'm Jessica Parker. Today, I'm here to tell you about the Arusha National Park Tour. It's a one-day tour program. This park is _____ between Kilimanjaro and Mount Meru. You can enjoy breathtaking views of lakes and mountains. Also, you can see _____ _____ such as monkeys, buffalos, and elephants. At 7 a.m., you will be picked up at the East entrance of the park to begin the tour. The _____ location will be the same as the pick-up location. The tour ends around 9 p.m., but that may change _____ _____ weather conditions. I hope you won't miss this tour.

10

M: Honey, what are you looking at?

W: A website that sells air fryers. I want one so we can cook more healthily.

M: Good idea. We can fry foods _____ _____ _____ if we buy one. How much do you think we should spend?

W: Well, I don't want to spend more than _____ dollars.

M: Okay. Then how about these models?

W: Hmm... it's safer to buy one that will turn off if it gets too hot.

M: You're right. Let's choose one with the _____ _____ _____ function.

W: What about capacity? My friend bought one that could only hold two liters. She regretted not buying a bigger one.

M: In that case, we should get one with a capacity of _____ _____ four liters. Now we have these two to choose from.

W: They both look good. But I think the one with the _____ _____ is better.

M: I agree. Let's order this one.

11

W: What did you do last weekend?

M: I _____ the movie *The Universe*.

W: Oh, really? I'm planning to watch that with my friend tonight. How _____ _____ _____ it?

M: (Actually, I wouldn't recommend it.)

12

M: Mom, I'm home. Did my package _____ this afternoon?

W: No. I've been home all day, but nothing came.

M: That's strange. I got a text message that says my package _____ _____.

W: (Why don't you call the delivery person?)

13

W: Hey, Brian, are you eating chocolate again? You've been eating a lot of chocolate these days.

M: Yeah, but I can't stop. I eat sweets _____ _____ _____.

W: What's going on?

M: I've been busy preparing for my final exams, and I have too many assignments.

W: I understand. But eating sweets doesn't really help _____ stress. It does more harm than good.

M: I know. Do you have any idea about what I can do instead?

W: Maybe you can try _____ _____ _____. Those have helped me a lot.

M: Really? That sounds like a better way to deal with my stress because it's healthier.

W: Definitely. _____ _____ will be much more helpful than eating chocolate.

M: (Okay. I'll exercise when I'm stressed.)

14

W: Jay, why do you look so _____?

M: I've been surfing the Internet, but there are so many ads.

W: What kinds of ads?

M: Pop-up advertisements. Whenever I open a new website, ads pop up. It takes a lot of time for me to close all of them.

W: That _____ _____ _____ to me, too. Maybe I can help you.

M: Is there a way to stop them?

W: I'm using a program that _____ pop-up advertisements.

M: Is it difficult to use?

W: It's very simple and easy. Just install a pop-up blocker on your computer, and it'll _____ ads from popping up.

M: That sounds good. But what if I can't see important pop-up messages _____ _____ _____ advertisements?

W: (Don't worry. It'll only filter out the ads.)

15

M: Eve is a college student who is _____ _____ history. She has been worried about her career path because she's _____ about what to do after she graduates. So, to learn more about her career options, she _____ _____ a career counselor at her college. She feels that it has helped her a lot. One day, Eve finds out that her classmate Tom is also _____ about what to do after he graduates. Eve wants to suggest that Tom _____ _____ the career counselor for advice. In this situation, what would Eve most likely say to Tom?

Eve: (How about getting help from a career counselor?)

16~17

W: Hello, students. As you all know, heavy traffic is a major source of air pollution. To _____ this problem, many European cities are taking various actions. For instance, in Copenhagen, the capital of Denmark, large parts of the city have been _____ _____ _____ for decades, and the city plans to become carbon neutral by 2025. Also, Paris, in _____, _____ cars in many historic districts on weekends and encourages car- and bike-_____ programs. In Belgium, the city of Brussels operates "Mobility Week" to encourage public over _____ _____. And for one day every September, all cars are banned from the entire city center. Lastly, cities in _____ are establishing "green zones" in city centers. If vehicles don't have a sticker showing they have an _____ _____ _____, they can't enter those places. Now, I'll show you some pictures that illustrate this.

05 2019년 11월 학력평가 딕테이션

MP3

2SBL2_A05

녹음을 듣고, 빈칸에 알맞은 말을 쓰시기 바랍니다. 빈칸은 문제풀이에 핵심이 되는 키워드와 헷갈리기 쉬운 발음에 표시되어 있으니 이 점에 유의하여 듣기 바랍니다.

01
고2 2019년 11월 3번

M: Hello, students. I'm Daniel Hopper from the administration office. I'd like to announce the _____ _____ _____ _____ bicycle parking facility. More and more students bike to school and have difficulty finding safe and easy parking spaces. So it's important that we _____ a bicycle parking facility that allows our students to park their bicycles safely and conveniently. Construction on a bicycle parking facility next to the library _____ _____ _____. Starting next Monday, students can leave their bicycles at this facility. It's free and available on a first come, first _____ _____. If you have any further questions, please feel free to contact the administration office.

02
고2 2019년 11월 4번

W: Jack, are you ready for your _____?

M: Yeah. I'm almost done.

W: Great. Did you buy travel insurance?

M: Travel insurance? Do you think I should buy it?

W: Of course. You don't want your trip to be ruined by _____ _____ bills.

M: Does that really happen?

W: Sure it happens. One of my friends _____ _____ during a trip and spent a lot of money at a hospital.

M: In that case, it would be helpful to have insurance.

W: Yeah. For me, last time I traveled, I lost my cell phone and the insurance _____ it.

M: That's amazing. I didn't know insurance covers that kind of stuff, too.

W: See? You'd better buy it before you _____ _____ your trip.

M: Yeah. You're right. I think I should.

03
고2 2019년 11월 5번

W: Hi, James!

M: Hello, Ms. Collins.

W: I've wanted to talk to you about one of your paintings.

M: My paintings? Which one?

W: The work you _____ _____ my art class last week. I was so impressed by your drawing technique, the way you show the objects.

M: Thank you for the _____, Ms. Collins. I tried to make them look realistic, just like a photo.

W: You did an excellent job. _____ _____ _____ _____, I recommended your work for the School Art Festival. The other art teachers agreed.

M: That's amazing. Isn't it next month?

W: Yes. So, why don't you _____ _____ _____ _____ for your painting?

M: Okay. Is that for putting a tag on the painting?

W: Yes. The title will help other students understand your work.

M: Thank you so much, Ms. Collins.

04

M: Lily! I heard that you got your own place to live.

W: Yeah. I finally got a place of my own. I have a picture. Do you want to see it?

M: Sure. *[Pause]* Oh, I like the _____ curtains.

W: Thanks. I got those striped curtains on sale.

M: I see. There is a pair of headphones on the wall _____ _____ _____ piano. What are they for?

W: I use them when playing the piano so I don't disturb my neighbors.

M: How _____ of you. What's the plant under the clock?

W: Isn't it nice? I received the plant as a housewarming gift. I also got the _____ _____ as a gift from my family.

M: How nice! The round table really ties the room together. Oh, the _____ _____ _____ the bed is similar to mine.

W: Really? It's so useful when I read in bed.

M: Right. I wish I had a room like yours.

W: Thanks.

05

W: Peter, the parent-teacher conference is tomorrow. Is there anything left for us to do?

M: I think we're ready for it.

W: Alright. Let's have _____ _____ _____. Did you hang the banner?

M: Yes, I did this morning. What about the hand-outs for parents?

W: I printed them out and _____ them, too.

M: Great. Hmm... last time, the microphone wasn't functioning well.

W: I know. I checked and also prepared spare microphones _____ _____ _____.

M: Good. You're going to use a projector, right?

W: Yes. I need to show some charts on the screen.

M: Then I'll check the projector right away.

W: Thanks. Oh, did you buy _____ to put on the table?

M: Oh, no! I totally forgot about the snacks.

W: Don't worry. _____ _____ _____ on my way home after school.

M: Thanks. It's all set then.

06

W: Welcome to Rock Bowling Center. How may I help you?

M: Hi. We'd like to do some bowling here.

W: Alright. How many _____ _____ _____ _____?

M: We're a group of four.

W: Okay. Since we have a special event today, you can enjoy unlimited bowling all day for $_____ per person.

M: That's amazing. We'll all do that. What about shoes? We didn't bring bowling shoes.

W: You can rent shoes of any size and they're $5 per person.

M: Then, _____ _____ _____ _____ of shoes.

W: Okay. So, that's admission fees and renting shoes for four people.

M: Right. Can I use this coupon for a discount?

W: Sure. You'll get 10% _____ _____ _____ _____.

M: Great. I'll pay by credit card.

M: Hi, Sandy. What are you doing?

W: I'm watching this video on how to make coffee. This is so interesting.

M: Oh, I'm into coffee nowadays.

W: Are you? I like _____ _____ _____ of different coffee beans.

M: Really? I've heard that the Coffee Fair is _____ _____ downtown. Do you want to go there with me?

W: That would be really fun. When are you going?

M: This Saturday. Are you available?

W: Oh, no. I'm not.

M: Why? Do you teach your baking class on Saturdays?

W: No, it's only on weekdays. On Saturday _____ _____ _____ _____ participate in the local flea market.

M: Flea market?

W: Yes. We'll sell cookies and donate the _____ to kids in hospitals.

M: Oh, that's kind of you. We can go next time then.

M: Honey, what are you reading?

W: It's a brochure about the Forest Walk in Elbert Mountain.

M: Is it like a guided walking tour?

W: Exactly. _____ _____ _____ old trees and plants in the forest while walking. Its purpose is to make people feel more _____ _____ nature.

M: Sounds interesting. When is it?

W: Every Saturday the tour _____ at 9 a.m. and lasts for two hours.

M: It'll be wonderful to start a Saturday morning by walking. How much do we have to pay?

W: It's $5 per person and the money will be used to plant more trees.

M: Okay. Let's do it this Saturday. How do we _____?

W: We have to do it through the website by Wednesday.

M: Is there _____ _____ _____ the number of participants?

W: Yeah. It says it's up to twenty people per tour.

M: Let's hurry, then.

W: Hello, listeners. I'm Jessica Norton, manager of Langford Park. We're happy to _____ that the Langford Night Market is coming back. Starting from September 1st for five nights, you can enjoy the event where _____ _____ _____ will be set up. This year's theme is the Global Food Festival. You can try food from all over the world. _____ _____ _____ will be held every night, creating a festive atmosphere. There is also a special _____ for kids where they can have fun playing with toys. The whole family can enjoy this fun festival. If it rains, the market will _____ _____. We hope you enjoy our upcoming event. Thank you.

10

M: Ellen, I think we need a new computer chair. Ours is so old.

W: I think so, too. Let's find one online. [Typing sound] Look, the top five selling models are here.

M: Okay. Which prices look reasonable? I think _____ _____ _____ $100 for a chair is too much.

W: I agree. What about materials? I prefer a fabric chair because leather gets scratch marks more easily.

M: You're right. The fabric also _____ our other furniture.

W: Yeah. Do you want a chair whose height is changeable or _____?

M: The changeable one looks more convenient. I'm quite taller than you. So we need to change the chair's _____.

W: Okay. Do you think a headrest is necessary?

M: Definitely. It supports your _____ _____ _____.

W: Then we've only got one option left. I'll order it now.

M: Perfect.

11

[Cell phone rings.]

M: Hey, Emma. Are you _____ _____ this Friday?

W: Yes, Dad. I've finished my midterms and I want to see you and Mom.

M: That's great. Will you _____ _____ _____ when you come home?

W: (Yes. I've already bought the train ticket.)

12

W: How was the Apple Festival yesterday?

M: It was fantastic. I made _____ _____ _____ from the apples that I picked. I took a lot of pictures, too.

W: Sounds like it was fun. I wish I had been there. _____ _____ _____ the pictures.

M: (Sure. You'll like my pictures of the festival.)

13

[Cell phone rings.]

W: Dad! It's me, Sarah. I just arrived for the computer programming certification test.

M: Good! You _____ _____ early. Are you ready for the test?

W: No. I've got a big problem.

M: A problem? What is it?

W: I just realized that I didn't bring my identification.

M: Oh, do you _____ _____ _____ _____ your student ID now?

W: That's not possible. I lost my student ID last month at school.

M: Oh, no. Did you ask the test administration about what to do?

W: They said I can take the test with my _____ _____. It must be somewhere in my room.

M: Really? Do you remember where you put it?

W: Hmm... oh, I remember! I put it in my desk _____.

M: (Alright. I'll get it and bring it to you right away.)

14

M: Hi, Alice. Is everything okay?

W: Not really, Dr. Johnson. You know my son, Ben?

M: Sure. I saw him at family _____ before.

W: I'm worried about him these days. He wakes up in the middle of the night and won't stop crying.

M: Hmm... he must be _____ _____. Tell me more.

W: He's really mean to his baby brother and always causes trouble.

M: Did it happen to begin after your second child was born?

W: I think so. Is Ben stressed because of his little brother?

M: It's possible. I'm sure you've been busy taking care of the baby and it probably makes Ben feel _____ _____.

W: Right. I don't play with Ben as much as I used to. That might be the reason why he _____ like that.

M: Yes, it's natural for him to feel that way. Now, _____ _____ _____ Ben needs.

W: (Yes. I should make time each day to spend with him.)

15

M: Mike is the leader of a book club and Amy is one of its members. The club members are supposed to read a section of the _____ book before each meeting and have discussions on certain issues. However, Amy _____ _____ _____ the other members lately by not reading the books before the meetings. The group members _____ to Mike about how hard it is to have a discussion about a book when Amy doesn't read it. Mike understands their complaints and wants to _____ Amy to take the club more seriously. Mike wants to tell Amy that she needs to make _____ _____ _____ to reading books. In this situation, what would Mike most likely say to Amy?

Mike: (You should be responsible about reading books for club activities.)

16~17

W: Hello, students. In today's class, we'll learn about some innovative robot designs. Recently, robots have _____ _____ from the natural world. Let's look at the first picture. Notice the snakebot has _____ _____ like a snake. It's able to move on almost any type of _____ just like a snake. Does this second robot resemble anything familiar? That's right, the engineers who designed this robot _____ the complex movements of bat wings when designing this bat-like robot, Bat bot. It can dive like a real bat and is easier to operate thanks to its _____ _____ _____ wings. Now, this third robot's shape may not look familiar, but surely its actions will. This robot is called the BionicANT and it was programmed to behave in a cooperative way, _____ _____ _____ _____.

I'm sure you'll enjoy this last robot called Biscuit, the robot dog. As you can easily see, it was _____ _____ a dog. This robot is friendly and responds to your voice commands. Now let's share our thoughts about these robots.

06 2020년 3월 학력평가
딕 테 이 션

MP3

2SBL2_A06

😊 녹음을 듣고, 빈칸에 알맞은 말을 쓰시기 바랍니다. 빈칸은 문제풀이에 핵심이 되는 키워드와 헷갈리기 쉬운 발음에 표시되어 있으니 이 점에 유의하여 듣기 바랍니다.

01
고2 2020년 3월 3번

M: May I have your _____, please? This is from the management office of Vincent Hospital. The west entrance facing Main Street _____ _____ _____, so it cannot be used. We'd like to remind you all to use the east entrance today. The east entrance is on Wilson Street, and it is _____ _____ _____ visiting hours from 8 a.m. to 6 p.m. And during non-visiting hours, please use the north entrance facing Hyde Street. The west entrance will be _____ _____ from tomorrow. We're sorry for any inconvenience this might cause. Thank you for your cooperation.

02
고2 2020년 3월 4번

W: Jamie, have you decided to join the _____ _____ program?

M: No, Ms. Moore. I haven't decided yet.

W: Come on. I believe you'd be a good peer teacher.

M: Thanks, but I don't think I have _____ _____ to study for myself.

W: I know what you mean. But teaching others can be _____ _____ _____ _____.

M: Do you think so?

W: Yes. The more you explain something to others, the more _____ you can understand its meaning.

M: You mean the more I teach, the more I learn?

W: That's right.

M: Well, then, I'll join the program.

W: Good. I'm sure it'll be a great _____ for you.

03
고2 2020년 3월 5번

W: Excuse me, Mr. Young. I'm Emma Baker.

M: Oh, hi Emma. I've been waiting for you. Nice to meet you.

W: Nice to meet you, too.

M: Is this your first visit to a _____ _____?

W: Yes, it is. I've been looking forward to seeing the news studio myself.

M: I see. You seem to be very interested in broadcasting.

W: Yes, I'm the _____ of my school's broadcasting club.

M: Oh, you are? Today, you'll sit at a news desk and experience what it's like to host a news program.

W: Fantastic! I watch your news program every day. How can you _____ the news so effortlessly?

M: I read my scripts repeatedly before I begin the broadcast.

W: That's impressive. I really _____ _____ _____ a news program like you someday.

M: I hope you will. Shall we go to the news studio now?

04

고2 2020년 3월 6번

M: Joy, I'm excited to be in the _____.

W: I really wanted you to see this play, Daniel.

M: Thanks for bringing me here. By the way, the stage set looks a little strange.

W: This set shows _____ _____ living rooms. One on the left and the other on the right.

M: Oh, now I understand. The left living room has striped wallpaper.

W: Yes. There's a _____ in the left living room, next to the door.

M: Oh, but the right living room has flower-patterned wallpaper.

W: Yeah. Can you see the _____ _____ next to the window?

M: Yes, it matches the room. And there are two telephones, one _____ _____ _____ of the sofa.

W: This play is about a long telephone conversation between the two living rooms. So the title is *On the Line*.

05

고2 2020년 3월 7번

W: Alex, let's go for lunch.

M: Sorry, but I don't have time, Kate.

W: _____ _____ _____ so busy?

M: I'm working on our company's monthly newspaper.

W: When's the deadline?

M: Today. I'm doing the final job of _____ _____ _____ _____.

the photos, but there's a problem.

W: What is it?

M: I don't have any photos of Mr. Williams' retirement ceremony.

W: Really? I've got some photos _____ _____ at the ceremony with my digital camera.

M: Oh, what a relief! Can you send me the _____ _____?

W: Sure. I'll email them right after lunch.

M: Thank you so much, Kate.

06

고2 2020년 3월 9번

M: Welcome to Mary's Gift Shop. How may I help you?

W: Hi. I'd like to _____ a cup for my friend's birthday.

M: How about this pumpkin-shaped cup?

W: It's _____ _____. She'll like the design. How much is it?

M: It's $20.

W: Okay, I'll take it. And I'd also like to buy these teaspoons. How much are they?

M: They're $_____ each.

W: Okay. I'll take two pink ones and two blue ones.

M: Then, one pumpkin-shaped cup and _____ teaspoons, right?

W: Yes. Can I use this coupon that I downloaded from your website?

M: Sure. You'll get a 10% _____ _____ the total price.

W: Great. Here's my credit card.

07

M: Hi, Claire. How did your _____ presentation go?

W: It went better than I expected.

M: Good. You look a little tired, though.

W: I didn't get enough sleep last night, but I'm okay now. You know we have a _____ _____ today, right?

M: Yes, but I don't think I can come.

W: Oh, does your left _____ still hurt?

M: No, I've fully recovered.

W: Then, why?

M: Actually, I got a _____ _____ this morning.

W: I see. I once had a terrible muscle ache after a flu shot.

M: Well, anyway, I'll skip the lesson and

_____ _____ _____

today.

W: Okay, take care.

08

M: Hello, Dr. Peterson. How are you doing these days?

W: Hello, Dr. Collins. Good, I'm _____ _____ the Dream Bio Research Project.

M: You mean the medical research project sponsored by the government?

W: That's right. More than 20 _____ _____ _____ in the project and I'm the head researcher.

M: Wow, you're in charge of a really big job. How big is the _____ for the project?

W: We're allowed to spend one million dollars on the project.

M: That's a really huge amount. It's a project to

_____ _____ _____

_____ for lung cancer, isn't it?

W: That's right.

M: How long will the research project last?

W: It's a 5-year project. I hope we can develop the drug _____ _____

_____.

M: I wish you success, Dr. Peterson.

W: Thank you, Dr. Collins.

09

W: Hello, students. Are you _____ in reading books? Then, join this year's Marathon Reading Program. In this program, students, teachers, and parents will read books

_____ _____ _____

_____ on the 5th of April. It starts at 2 p.m. and ends at 10 p.m. The program will be held at our school library. You can bring your own book or _____ _____ one at the library. After they finish reading their book, all students are required to write a book review.

_____ _____ _____

will be provided. Don't forget to bring some warm clothes in case it gets cold at night. You must sign up for the program by this Friday.

10

M: Ms. Sanders, are you buying something online?

W: Yes. I'm trying to buy a portable speaker and microphone set. Can you help me choose one?

M: Sure. Let's see…. There's a wide range of prices.

W: Well, I want to buy one that's _____ _____ $100.

M: All right. I think running time is also important. What do you think?

W: I agree. I'd like to choose one that can last at least 10 hours _____ _____ _____ _____.

M: I see. What about the color?

W: Well, I don't like the _____ _____.

M: That leaves only two options. Do you want a model with a clip microphone?

W: Of course. It'll _____ _____ _____ _____.

M: Then, this model is the best one for you.

W: Okay. I'll order it. Thanks for your help.

M: You're welcome.

11

W: I enjoyed the _____ here, especially the salad.

M: Thank you. Our restaurant uses only the freshest vegetables. And we make the salad dressing using a special recipe.

W: I see. Can you tell me _____ _____ _____ _____?

M: (Sorry, but our recipe is a secret.)

12

M: Good afternoon. I'd like to _____ these old clothes to this charity.

W: Thank you. Are they all in good condition?

M: Yes, but _____ _____ _____ some shirts have changed a bit.

W: (Let me check if we can accept them.)

13

[Telephone rings.]

M: Hello, Diamond Sports Center. May I help you?

W: Hello. I'm a member of your sports center and I want to know if I can _____ my membership.

M: Okay, would you tell me your name?

W: I'm Katie Walker.

M: [Typing sound] Yes, I see you have an _____ membership for swimming classes. You mean you can't come for a while?

W: That's right. I broke my arm yesterday.

M: Oh, I'm sorry. You can put your membership _____ _____ for up to 60 days.

W: That's good.

M: When do you think you can start taking lessons again?

W: I'll be able to start again _____ _____ _____.

M: (Okay. We'll let you have a one-month break.)

14

고2 2020년 3월 14번

M: Hi, Lucy.

W: Hi, Eric. Look. This is my painting for our art club exhibition next week.

M: Wow, it's really nice. The spring _____ looks so beautiful.

W: I painted it during my family trip last week.

M: You're a really good artist.

W: Thank you. Are you done with your painting?

M: Yes, I _____ _____ _____ it on the wall in the exhibition room.

W: Great. How about the other members? Have they all finished their art work?

M: Not yet. And we _____ _____ _____ to see Jake's painting this time.

W: I know. I heard his whole family is moving to Canada this Friday.

M: So we need to find someone who _____ _____ _____ _____ to fill up his space.

W: (I have another picture that I've almost finished.)

15

고2 2020년 3월 15번

M: Ryan is a high school student. He is _____ _____ president of the student council this year. He needs to come up with some appealing campaign promises. He thinks one of the promises should be _____ _____ _____ the facilities for students. So, Ryan discusses it with one of his campaign staff, Amy. He asks her what school facilities need improvement. Amy suggests promising to _____ all the student lockers. Ryan agrees, but he thinks they should _____ _____ the school can do it. In this situation, what would Ryan most likely say to Amy?

Ryan: (We'd better find out if the school can replace the lockers.)

16~17

고2 2020년 3월 16~17번

W: Hello, everyone. Today, let's learn about some _____ about the Olympic Games. As you all have learned, the first Olympic Games were held in Athens, Greece, in 1896, and there were nine sports events in total. The events in the Olympic Games have been _____ _____ _____ _____ of the IOC members. For example, soccer made its first appearance at the second Olympic Games and was _____ _____ the 10th Olympic Games. The fate of tennis is more interesting. Tennis was one of the nine sports events in the first Athens Olympic Games, but it was excluded from 1928 to 1984 and then _____ at the 1988 Seoul Olympics. The 1936 Berlin Olympics became the first to introduce handball. However, handball _____ _____ the Olympics and later was revived at the 1972 Munich Olympics. Taekwondo made _____ _____ in the relatively recent Sydney Olympic Games in 2000. Overall, the number of sports events in the Olympic Games has gradually increased through some _____ or exclusions.

07 2020년 6월 학력평가
딕테이션

MP3
25BL2_A07

녹음을 듣고, 빈칸에 알맞은 말을 쓰시기 바랍니다. 빈칸은 문제풀이에 핵심이 되는 키워드와 헷갈리기 쉬운 발음에 표시되어 있으니 이 점에 유의하여 듣기 바랍니다.

01

고2 2020년 6월 3번

M: Hello, everyone. This is Ted Williams, the
_____ teacher. As you know, there's a
musical in the school festival every year. And the
_____ _____ _____
are going to be held soon. Even if you don't think
you're talented, that's okay. Most importantly,
I'm looking for students _____
_____. All interested students should
submit an application to me no later than June
23rd. The auditions are going to be held on
June 24th from three to five p.m. in the school
auditorium. If you need more information,
please check the poster on the _____
_____. I'm looking forward to seeing you
at the auditions. Thank you.

02

고2 2020년 6월 4번

M: Hello, Irene. What are you doing?

W: Hi. I'm reading a book for a book _____
assignment.

M: Then, why are you wearing earphones?

W: I'm listening to music. I find it helpful when
_____ a book.

M: Doesn't listening to music hurt your
concentration?

W: Actually, no. I can concentrate on my reading
_____ _____ _____ to
music.

M: Really? I didn't know that was possible.

W: Also, it makes me feel good, and that surely

_____ _____ _____.

M: You mean that you can keep reading when you
feel bored with a book?

W: Right. That's why I listen to music while reading.

M: I see. I'll _____ _____
_____ _____ the next time I
read a book.

W: It'll work for you, too.

03

고2 2020년 6월 5번

M: Good afternoon. How may I help you?

W: I'm looking for an apartment _____
_____ near the downtown area.

M: It is a convenient place to live. When would you
like to move there?

W: I'm thinking next month.

M: Oh, I see. I have some apartments to
_____ _____ _____
_____. What's your budget?

W: I'm afraid I can't afford more than $1,000 a
month.

M: There are some apartments within your budget,
but they have only one bedroom.

W: One bedroom is enough, but I want the kitchen
to be _____ _____ the
bedroom.

M: I see. Anything else?

W: Hmm... it would be better if a refrigerator was
_____.

M: Okay. I have the perfect one for you. Let's go
take a look.

04

M: Lucy, this is a picture of my camping trip last week. Have a look.

W: Hmm, I can see the tent _____

_____ _____ _____.

Did you set it up yourself?

M: Yes, my father taught me how to do it. He is wearing the _____ T-shirt that I bought him for his birthday.

W: Wow! The shirt makes your father look young.

M: I think so, too. And do you see the

_____ on the table?

W: Yes, it looks so delicious. Where did you get it?

M: It was from our family farm. My parents grew it themselves.

W: Really? The woman there must be your mother, right?

M: Yeah. She's _____ _____

_____ behind the pond.

W: Cool! She's awesome. Oh, there's a dog on the chair. Is that your puppy?

M: Of course. We all had a good time there.

05

W: Daniel, let's check our _____ for Ms. Kim's retirement party.

M: Okay, I think we're almost done. How about the thank-you video?

W: Well, I had some _____ _____ the background music, but I finally finished it.

M: Great! I believe it'll be perfect.

W: Thanks. Have you _____ _____ the classroom?

M: I've just done it. It took a long time to blow up all the balloons.

W: Good job. Now, it's time to let the other students know about the party.

M: No worries, I've done that, too. What else should we do then?

W: Hmm, we should write a thank-you letter to Ms. Kim and order a cake for her.

M: Okay. I'll write the thank-you letter.

_____ _____ _____ the cake?

W: No problem. I'll go and order it now.

06

M: Hello, welcome to the Grand Ice Skating Rink. How can I help you?

W: Hi, I'd like to _____ _____ tickets.

M: All right. An adult ticket is $10. A child ticket is $5.

W: Then, two adults and one child. And I need to rent skates, too. How much is that?

M: All skate _____ _____ the same, $5 a person.

W: Okay, I want to rent three pairs of skates.

M: Did you bring gloves?

W: Yes, we did. By the way, can I get _____

_____?

M: If you have a local resident card, you can get a 10% discount off the total.

W: Good! Here's my local resident card.

M: So, _____ adult tickets, one child ticket, and three skate rentals, right?

W: Yes. I'll pay for everything with my credit card.

07

W: Jake. There's going to be a Vincent van Gogh exhibition in the Art Center.

M: Really? He's my _____ _____.

W: Mine, too. How about going to the exhibition together this Sunday?

M: This Sunday? _____ _____ _____ _____, but I'm afraid I can't go.

W: Come on. Do you have to do volunteer work on that day?

M: No, I usually volunteer on Saturdays.

W: Oh, I remember. You said you're going to play soccer?

M: I did, but our game was _____ because of weather.

W: Then, do you have another appointment?

M: Actually, I have to work on a _____ _____. It's due next Monday.

W: You must be busy then.

M: Yeah. I hope you have a good time.

08

M: Hi, Mia. What are you looking at?

W: The student council is holding the _____ Flea Market and I'm going to participate in it as a seller.

M: Oh, really? When is it going to be held?

W: Look. It will be open _____ _____, from 11 a.m. to 6 p.m.

M: I see. Do you remember I participated as a seller last year?

W: I do. You did it in the school auditorium.

M: Right. But the poster says it'll be held in the _____ this year.

W: Why don't you join me? There's no participation fee for sellers.

M: Okay. What are you going to sell at the Flea Market?

W: It says we can sell any of _____ _____ _____. I'm planning to sell my old books.

M: I'm looking forward to it.

09

W: Hello, Highland residents. I'm Jenny Walker, the community center manager. We host the Highland Movie Night every month. This event gives you _____ _____ to enjoy classic movies. It is free for all Highland residents. This month, we will show *The Amazing Wizard Harry*. The movie will _____ at seven p.m. this Saturday. As usual, it'll be held at the Lincoln Library. _____ _____ the limited space, you should register in advance. You can reserve seats on our website until Friday. To keep the library clean, you are _____ _____ _____ _____ any food. For more information, feel free to call us. Thank you.

10
고2 2020년 6월 12번

M: Mom, I _____ _____

_____ for my trip to Hawaii. Look at this

flyer. They are on sale now.

W: Let me see... I think it'd be better if it is

_____ _____ 20 inches, since

your trip is for two weeks.

M: I think so, too. And it's not a good idea to spend

more than _____ dollars on a suitcase.

W: Right. You've already spent a lot for the trip.

M: Okay. There are two colors. Well, the white one

looks nice.

W: That's true, but white things usually get dirty

easily.

M: I agree. The _____ color is the better

choice.

W: Then, we have two options left.

M: Oh, they're giving away free gifts! Hmm... we

already have _____ _____.

W: You'd better choose the other one.

M: You're right. I'll buy this suitcase.

11
고2 2020년 6월 1번

M: Grandmother's birthday is coming up. What

would be a good _____ for her?

W: I think it would be good to give her something

she needs.

M: I agree. I saw that her shoes are old and worn

out. How about _____ _____

some new shoes?

W: (Yeah. Let's go shop for them.)

12
고2 2020년 6월 2번

W: Honey, what a beautiful Sunday! I don't want to

_____ home all day.

M: Neither do I. Why don't we take a walk in a park

or go to watch a movie?

W: We went to the movies last weekend. Let's

_____ _____ _____

_____ this time!

M: (All right! It's perfect for walking outside.)

13
고2 2020년 6월 13번

W: Honey, where is the camera?

M: I put it on the desk. Why do you need it?

W: It's for Kevin's school concert. I want to

_____ _____ _____.

M: Oh, right! It's tomorrow! He has been practicing

so hard for that.

W: Yes, he has. He's excited but also very

_____.

M: It's his first concert. I want to see his

performance, too.

W: That would be nice, but didn't you say you have

an important meeting tomorrow?

M: Sadly, I do. It was _____ _____

_____ it.

W: That's okay. I'll record his performance so you

won't miss a thing.

M: Thanks, if the meeting ends early, I might be

able to be there by four.

W: But unfortunately I think his performance

_____ _____ _____ by

then.

M: (You're right. I'll just watch the video after the

concert.)

14

M: Lisa, I'm looking forward to our _____ _____ in Boston.

W: Me, too. It's only a month away.

M: Yeah, the hotel has been booked. Now we just need to _____ _____ flight schedules.

W: Hmm... why don't we drive instead of flying?

M: Drive ourselves? I don't think that's a good idea.

W: Why not?

M: It would take more than four hours from our office.

W: But I've heard the scenery along the way is really beautiful in October.

M: Then, how about _____ _____ _____ _____?

W: Taking a bus sounds okay.

M: I think we would enjoy the view from the bus as well.

W: You're right. Also, it'd be much safer than driving ourselves.

M: Plus, we can _____ _____ _____ our costs.

W: (Great. Let's check the bus schedule then.)

15

M: Katie and Brian are classmates. They're doing a school project, and they _____ _____ _____ students' eating habits as their topic. Brian says that in order to analyze students' eating habits they need to do a survey. And he _____ they make a pen-and-paper survey. But Katie thinks it would take too much time to _____, _____, _____ _____ hundreds of papers. Then, Katie remembers she once took an online survey that she completed quickly. So Katie wants to suggest that they do a survey _____ _____ _____ rather than on paper. In this situation, what would Katie most likely say to Brian?

Katie: (Why don't we try an online survey instead?)

16~17

W: Welcome back, students. Last time we talked about your favorite numbers. They might come from your birth date or the date of a _____ _____ in your life. Interestingly, some beliefs about numbers seem to _____ _____ one's culture. Today, we're talking about what numbers symbolize in different parts of the world. In Asia, the number four is considered extremely unlucky, but Western people think it is _____. In Islam, the number seven is important. "Seven heavens" is one example of this number's importance. _____ _____ _____ a good number in Japan because it is pronounced "joo", like the Japanese word for "enough." In the Western world, the number _____ _____ _____ to be the unluckiest by millions of people. So, to satisfy anxious customers, _____ and hotels often don't use the number thirteen. Numbers can be _____ _____ _____. Numbers are also just fun to play around with. Let's enjoy learning more about numbers together.

08 2020년 9월 학력평가 딕테이션

🙂 녹음을 듣고, 빈칸에 알맞은 말을 쓰기 바랍니다. 빈칸은 문제풀이에 핵심이 되는 키워드와 헷갈리기 쉬운 발음에 표시되어 있으니 이 점에 유의하여 듣기 바랍니다.

01
고2 2020년 9월 3번

M: Good morning, students! This is your student council _____, William Taylor. As some of you already know, our annual school festival is coming up. We are looking for _____ that want to sign up to share their talents at the festival. Now, I'll tell you _____ _____ _____ _____ for the festival. The application period begins today. If your club wants to register to participate, come to the student council room to _____ _____ the application form. The application deadline is September 28th. Let's make this a festival to remember!

02
고2 2020년 9월 4번

W: Hi, Mike. You look _____. Is something bothering you?

M: Well, my son's preschool teacher told me he's _____ _____ _____ while reading and during conversations. I don't know what I should do.

W: Oh, I see. [Pause] Maybe drawing classes could help.

M: How could they help with his concentration?

W: Children develop their ability to focus as they _____ _____ _____ small details while drawing.

M: That's reasonable. Is that why your daughter takes drawing classes?

W: Exactly. When my daughter was 8 years old, she had a similar problem to your son.

M: Did you _____ a big change when she started drawing?

W: Sure. She concentrates better on reading and conversations now. It might help your son, too.

M: Okay, I'll look for a class right away.

03
고2 2020년 9월 5번

W: Hello, Mr. Stevenson. I'm Rachel Adams from *Entertainment Monthly*. Thank you for meeting with me today.

M: Hello, Ms. Adams. It's my pleasure.

W: Congratulations on gaining more than one million _____ _____ your work, *The Invisible*. Why do you think so many people read your webcomic?

M: I think many people enjoy the comic because my _____ _____ _____ really makes the story come alive.

W: I agree. I especially love Jimmy, the character who wants to be a fashion model.

M: Yes, many of my subscribers like him.

W: I heard you'll finish it soon. The _____ _____ _____ have been asking if you have any plans to publish your work as a book or make it into a movie.

M: If there's a _____, I'd love to.

W: You'll have to let our readers be the first to know if you do.

M: Of course! I hope I can bring you good news soon.

04

M: Honey, I just found a picture of a great living room design. It can give us some ideas for our own living room.

W: Let me see. *[Pause]* Wow! I like the bookshelf behind the _____.

M: Yeah. It's really impressive. I think we should have a bookshelf like that one.

W: I agree. What do you think about how they used the space around the window?

M: The _____ _____ _____ under the window look nice. We should put our plants the same way.

W: Oh, there's a cat lying on a pet cushion.

M: It looks so comfortable. Why don't we buy one for our cat?

W: That's a good idea. Did you notice the _____ _____ between the armchairs?

M: I've always wanted to have a tea table like that one.

W: Look at this floor lamp! The _____ _____ has the same striped pattern as ours.

M: It does! Let's decorate our living room like the one in this picture.

W: I can't wait to see how it turns out.

05

W: I'm so exhausted. I didn't realize _____ was going to be this hard.

M: Me, neither. I think the move is mostly organized. You already called the cleaning company, right?

W: Yes, they should be here soon. What else is left for us to do?

M: We still need to book the appointment to set up our _____ _____.

W: Right. We should also fix the computer.

M: Why? Is it broken?

W: The moving center staff dropped it.

M: Have you asked the staff about _____ _____ it?

W: Yeah. The moving center wants us to fix the computer first and then submit a receipt.

M: My cousin runs an electronics repair shop nearby, so I can take it there today. Can you book the _____ _____ _____ the internet connected?

W: Okay, I'll do that.

06

W: Good afternoon. How can I help you?

M: Hi. I'm looking for a gift for my _____ _____. What would you recommend?

W: These pajama sets and dresses are the best-selling clothes for babies.

M: They're so cute. How much are they?

W: This pajama set is 40 dollars, and this dress is _____ dollars.

M: Hmm.... I'd like to buy the dress you recommended.

W: Okay. Anything else?

M: Do you have any other items that would go well with the dress?

W: How about this hat? It's usually 10 dollars, but it's on sale. You can get 40 percent _____ _____ _____.

M: That sounds great! I'll take it.

W: Wonderful. So, one dress and one hat, right?

M: Yes. I also have this 5 dollar discount coupon. Can I use it?

W: Let me see. *[Pause]* Unfortunately, no. This coupon only _____ _____ _____ over 100 dollars.

M: All right. I'll pay with this credit card.

07
고2 2020년 9월 8번

W: I'm so happy our exams are over.

M: Me, too. They were really _____ this time.

W: I know. Getting a cold made me even more stressed.

M: Are you still sick?

W: No, I feel all right now. What are you doing after school today?

M: Some of our classmates are going to play _____ _____ _____ _____ the end of exams. Do you want to come?

W: I'd love to go, but I can't.

M: Why not?

W: Did I tell you my family is going on a ski trip this weekend?

M: No, you didn't. Why are you _____ _____?

W: It's my dad's birthday, so we planned this trip for him.

M: That sounds like a perfect gift for your dad.

W: I hope so. I need to go shopping for goggles and a ski _____ for myself today.

M: Oh, I see. Have a nice trip.

08
고2 2020년 9월 10번

M: Amy, have you heard about Comedy Allstars?

W: No, I haven't. What is it?

M: It's the biggest comedy show on Broadway. It's _____ _____ _____ the Western Theater this year.

W: Oh, I know that place. When does the show start?

M: It starts on December 15th.

W: _____ _____ _____ in the show?

M: Many famous comedians like Tina Scott, Julia Moore, and James Parker will perform.

W: James Parker? He's my _____ comedian.

M: Do you want to go with me, then? Tickets will go on sale next week.

W: Okay! How can we buy the tickets?

M: We can _____ _____ _____ at the theater's website.

W: Great. I'm so excited for the show.

09
고2 2020년 9월 11번

W: Good evening, listeners. I'm Elizabeth, the hostess of the Organic Fair. This year, the fair will be held at Springfield Park. It'll last three days from October 11th to 13th. It _____ _____ _____ the eco-lifestyle to a wide range of consumers. Various organic products will be displayed such as organic food and natural cosmetics. You can _____ _____ _____ if you buy products at the fair. Furthermore, there will be a class where you can learn how to make organic soap. The class will _____ _____ 9 a.m. to 11 a.m. each day. If you register online in advance, you can enter the fair _____ _____ and join all the activities. For more information, please visit our website at www.springfieldfair.com. I look forward to exploring eco-living with you at the fair.

10

M: Hey, Tiffany. What are you doing?

W: I'm thinking of buying some wireless earbuds. Do you want to help me choose from these five options?

M: Sure. How much can you spend?

W: I don't want to spend more than _____ dollars.

M: These models are within your budget.

W: What do you think would be a good play time from a single charge?

M: Hmm.... I think it should be _____ _____ six hours so you don't have to charge them very often.

W: That's a good point. I'll cross out this one. What is noise canceling?

M: It reduces _____ sound using active noise control.

W: Does that make a big difference?

M: It can really improve the sound quality of what you listen to.

W: I see. Then, I'll _____ _____ _____ _____ noise canceling.

M: Good choice. There are only two models left. Which color do you prefer?

W: I don't want white ones because they'll _____ _____ too easily. So, I'll buy this model.

11

M: Welcome to Alice Bookstore. How may I help you?

W: I _____ this book here yesterday, but I want to exchange it for another copy.

M: Sure. May I ask _____ _____ _____ it?

W: (It's damaged. Several pages are missing.)

12

W: Wow! Josh, this pasta is very _____. I didn't know you cook.

M: Actually, this is the first time I've made pasta by myself.

W: Really? _____ _____ _____ _____ how to cook it?

M: (My aunt recently taught me the recipe.)

13

M: How are you, Rebecca?

W: I'm fine, but you look tired today.

M: That's because my _____ _____ so much last night that I couldn't sleep at all.

W: Your back? Did you injure it while you were exercising?

M: No. I didn't do anything yesterday other than study at the library.

W: Maybe that's the problem. I bet you were sitting for too long _____ _____ _____.

M: You're right. I have a bad habit of hunching my shoulders when I sit.

W: Do you ever take a break and _____ your body?

M: When I'm in the middle of something, it isn't easy to stop.

W: You know what? I recently read an article that said sitting with poor posture can lead to chronic back pain.

M: How _____ _____ _____?

W: (Bad posture can cause increased tension in your back.)

14

W: Andrew, did you _____ _____

_____ for the English essay?

M: I did. The teacher approved it last week.

W: That's great. Have you started writing it?

M: Not yet. I usually have a hard time making

_____ _____ for my essays. Do

you have any suggestions?

W: Well, I read a lot of newspaper articles. I

especially like editorials.

M: Does that really help develop logical thinking?

W: Sure. If you read _____ articles like

editorials, you can see how the arguments are

developed.

M: That makes sense to me. Maybe I should give it

a try.

W: I can _____ _____

_____ _____ I usually use. It

collects editorials from various newspapers.

M: (Thank you. I'll start reading editorials on that

site.)

15

W: Brian and Jennifer are good friends who

_____ _____ _____

_____ together almost every day. When

they're working out, they drink a lot of water.

Brian always brings his own tumbler with him

while Jennifer always buys a bottle of water at

the _____ _____ before going

to the gym. Brian thinks that buying a bottle of

water every day is not only a waste of money

but is also _____ _____ the

environment. One day at the gym, Jennifer

makes a comment about how much she likes

Brian's tumbler. Brian thinks this is a good

chance to suggest that she bring _____

_____ _____ _____ to

the gym. In this situation, what would Brian most

likely say to Jennifer?

Brian: (Why don't you get a tumbler and bring it to

the gym?)

16~17

M: Hello, everyone. I'm Dr. Damon. As parents, we

are all worried about our children starting to

_____ _____ at younger ages.

We surely know using smartphones has negative

effects on their eyes. Today, I will tell you some

_____ _____ _____

_____ protect your children's eyes.

First, carrots are rich in vitamin A, which keeps

the eye _____ healthy by preventing

it from drying out. Cheese is not only rich in

vitamin A, but it also _____ eye fatigue

due to its high levels of iron. Blueberries are rich

in antioxidants, which improve _____

vision as well as maintain general eye health.

Lastly, the omega-3 fatty acids in salmon

lower the chance of eye diseases. I hope you

encourage your children to try the foods I

recommended today.

09 2020년 11월 학력평가
딕테이션

MP3

25BL2_A09

녹음을 듣고, 빈칸에 알맞은 말을 쓰시기 바랍니다. 빈칸은 문제풀이에 핵심이 되는 키워드와 헷갈리기 쉬운 발음에 표시되어 있으니 이 점에 유의하여 듣기 바랍니다.

01

M: Good morning, everyone. I'm your P.E. teacher, Mr. Andrews. Since this is your first class this semester, I'm going to give you some _____ _____ _____ in the P.E. class. First, you are required to wear appropriate clothing such as sportswear and _____ _____ shoes. Second, you must be careful when using sports equipment in the gym. Don't use the equipment _____ _____. Finally, when you hear the whistle, stop what you're doing and pay attention to my instructions. If you keep these rules in your mind, you'll be able to participate _____ in the P.E. class. Now let's do a warm-up exercise.

02

W: Jason, are you going out?

M: Yes. I'm going to take a walk, Mom.

W: Wait! Why are you _____ _____ without socks?

M: I don't want to put them on. They feel uncomfortable.

W: I know you feel that way. But _____ _____ _____, you should wear socks.

M: Really? Why do you say that?

W: Well, your feet will stay dry if you put on socks. And you can avoid _____ _____

_____ on your feet.

M: Hmm.... I hadn't thought about that.

W: And if you don't have socks on, you could get scratched or even get a skin infection.

M: That makes sense, Mom. I'm going to follow your _____.

W: Good. Wearing socks is important for your foot health.

03

W: Hello, Simon. I'm glad that you are here.

M: Hi, Julia. How's it going with recording your new song?

W: Well, it's been tough. _____ _____ _____ the song all the time.

M: I can imagine. How can I help you?

W: The music video for the song will be filmed soon. And I need you to _____ _____ _____ _____ that everyone can follow.

M: No problem. I just need a copy of the song, so I can try to make it as simple and _____ as possible.

W: Okay. Here's a copy of the song.

M: When do you need the dance by?

W: Hmm.... I have a meeting with the music video director next Friday.

M: All right. It'll take a couple of days to make the dance. Then we can _____ it together.

W: Perfect. Thank you so much.

04

M: Hi, Anna. How was your weekend?

W: Hey, Mike! I helped to make the stage for our school play. Here, take a look at the picture I took of the stage.

M: Wow. It's wonderful.

W: Thanks. My favorite is the Christmas tree in the corner.

M: I agree. I also like the picture _____ _____ _____.

W: Do you like it? I painted it myself.

M: It looks so real. Why is there a cup on the round table?

W: The _____ _____ is supposed to have some tea at the table.

M: I see. Look at the toy horse next to the chair. It's so cute.

W: Yeah. And what do you think of the

_____ _____ _____

_____?

M: It really adds to the Christmas atmosphere. You did a great job.

W: Thank you. Will you come to see the play?

M: Sure. I _____ _____ to see it.

05

W: Jake, what are you doing?

M: I'm cleaning the house. Mom and Dad will come back tomorrow from their trip to Hawaii.

W: You're right. We need to _____ _____ to welcome them.

M: Do you know tomorrow is their 25th wedding anniversary?

W: Sure. So I'm going to make a special dinner for them.

M: Oh, what will you make?

W: _____ _____ and cream pasta.

M: That's great! They'll love that.

W: I hope so. How are they coming back home from the airport?

M: They'll take a bus.

W: I'm worried they'll be too tired. Why don't you pick them up at the airport tomorrow?

M: Good idea. Could you please check the

_____ _____ of their airplane?

W: Of course, I can do that now.

M: Thanks. Then I should go to the gas station to

_____ _____ the car.

06

M: Good morning. How may I help you?

W: Hello. I'm looking for a birthday gift for my sister. Can you recommend something?

M: Okay. How about these plates? These are the most popular ones in our store. The plate that has a star-pattern is $_____, and the flower-patterned plate is $15.

W: My sister has star _____ everywhere in her house. So I'll take some star-patterned plates.

M: Great. How many do you want?

W: Four, please.

M: All right. Is there anything else you're looking for?

W: Those _____ _____ are very pretty, too. How much are they?

M: They're $10 each.

W: I'll take two of them.

M: Excellent. You want four star-patterned plates and two coffee cups. Is that right?

W: That's correct.

M: Just to let you know, we're offering a 10 percent discount _____ _____

_____ this month.

W: Great. Here's my credit card.

07

[Cell phone rings.]

W: Hey, Ben. Can I talk to you for a second?

M: Hi, Sarah. I'm sorry _____ _____ _____ the phone this morning. I was in English class.

W: That's okay. I called you to say that our study group meeting _____ _____ _____ this week.

M: Thanks. Did the meeting place change?

W: No, we're still going to meet at the school library. But it'll be at 11 a.m. on Saturday.

M: Saturday? I'm sorry, but I can't make it.

W: Why? You told me that you don't have volunteer work on the weekends.

M: I don't. But I have to go to the hospital.

W: Oh, that's right. I heard you _____ your leg playing soccer. Is that the reason?

M: No, my leg wasn't hurt that badly. Actually I have a _____ _____ this Saturday.

W: I see. I'll call you later to tell you the schedule for next time.

M: Thank you for understanding.

08

M: Honey, what are you doing?

W: I'm looking at this _____ for Lakeville Campground. Why don't we go camping next month?

M: Sounds great. Let's look at the brochure together.

W: Wow. In these photos, the campground is _____ _____ a thick forest. And there's also a huge lake nearby.

M: That's awesome! We can enjoy the beauty of nature.

W: Yeah. And they offer a lot of _____ _____.

M: It says each camping site has a shower room, a barbecue grill, and a place to have a campfire.

W: We're going to have so much fun. How much is it?

M: It's $35 per night.

W: That's reasonable.

M: And it says we should _____ _____ _____ on their website.

W: This campground is really popular. So we need to hurry to reserve a place.

M: Okay. Let's do it right now.

09

W: Hello, ABS radio listeners. I'm Catherine Barton, _____ of Lingston Circus. I'm so happy to tell you that we're hosting this year's Circus Experience Festival. It starts on November 20th and _____ _____ three days. We're offering a variety of hands-on activities including magic tricks and juggling. And qualified instructors will teach you. To ensure your safety, we'll _____ the number of participants to 10 for each activity. You can also enjoy taking pictures with some circus clowns in the photo zone. Additionally, we'll give you _____ _____ as a souvenir of this festival. Are you excited? Come to the Circus Experience Festival and have a great time. Thank you.

10

M: Honey, what are you doing?

W: I'm thinking about buying a _____ _____ set. My throat hurts a lot after giving so many lectures every week.

M: All right. Let me help you. [Typing sound] How long do you think the receiving distance has to be?

W: I'm not sure. I'll be using it in the classroom.

M: Your classroom is not very small. I think 10 meters is _____ _____ for the receiving distance.

W: Okay. That's good advice.

M: And do you want a headset?

W: I'd like to have one so I can use my _____ _____ during the lecture.

M: You're right. What color do you want?

W: It doesn't really matter. But I _____ _____ _____.

M: I see. Now you have only two options left.

W: I'll buy the cheaper one. Thank you for your help.

11

M: Mom, I have to borrow some books from the library today. But it's raining outside.

W: Don't worry. I'll _____ _____ _____ _____. Do you want to leave now?

M: Yes. But I need to look for my library card first. Could you _____ _____ _____ _____?

W: (No problem. Just let me know when you're ready.)

12

[Cell phone rings.]

W: Hi, David. I'm _____ _____ to the restaurant. Where are you?

M: Hi, Amy. I just finished work and got in my car. I'll take the highway, so I'll arrive on time.

W: I heard on the radio that there has been a _____ _____ on the highway. So you're going to get stuck.

M: (I see. I'll take another road then.)

13

M: Ashley, you got a letter from the _____ _____ at Corven University.

W: Oh, it might be my acceptance letter, Dad. I'm so nervous about it. Can you open it for me?

M: Okay. Let's see…. [Pause] You got in, sweetie. Congratulations!

W: Really? Wow, I'm so happy!

M: I'm so proud of you. And you also _____ _____ _____ the mathematics department of the other university.

W: Yeah. I have to make a decision soon. But it's hard for me to choose between the two.

M: Hmm…. What do you really want to study?

W: Actually, I love math. But business is one of the most popular majors.

M: I think you shouldn't choose a major _____ _____ what other people say.

W: Do you mean I have to consider my own interests?

M: Of course. You will be happy doing _____ _____ _____ to do.

W: (I agree. I'd rather major in mathematics.)

14

W: Hi, Steve. I have something to tell you.

M: Hi. What is it, Sophie?

W: We need to _____ _____ a research topic for our science club.

M: Yeah. What topic do you have in mind?

W: I don't have any specific idea. Why don't we ask the other members for their opinions?

M: I'm not sure about that. I think it's our job to _____ a research topic as club leaders.

W: But do you remember last semester? We chose the research topic ourselves, and some members didn't like it.

M: You're right. Then, how can we hear everyone's opinion?

W: Well, we'll have _____ _____ _____ with all of our club members next week.

M: That sounds good. But what if they have too many different ideas?

W: Then we can put the research topic _____ _____ _____ and choose what most members want for the topic.

M: (All right. That way we'll satisfy more members than last time.)

15

M: Melissa and Bob are best friends. Melissa is working for a cyber security company. She _____ _____ the importance of online security, and she's been updating her computer security program with the _____ version. One day, Bob tells Melissa that somebody illegally accessed his personal information and _____ _____ _____ his credit card number. When she checks out his computer, she notices that he's using an old version of the security program. So, she wants to suggest that he _____ _____ _____ the newest version of the security software. In this situation, what would Melissa most likely say to Bob?

Melissa: (Why don't you keep your security program up-to-date?)

16~17

W: Welcome back, listeners. I'm Doris Harrell from Garden Stories. Have you heard that flowers could be sending hidden messages? Today, I'd like to talk about _____ _____ some flowers can convey. First, carnations can send the message, "You are always on my mind, and I _____ _____ you." Therefore, they are widely used as a gift on Parents' Day. Next, people prefer to use _____ in a wedding bouquet since they symbolize "consuming love" as well as "happy years." Did you know that irises _____ _____ the idea of faith and wisdom? So they are frequently used in religious settings and _____ _____ many artists. Last, daisies mean innocence, loyal love, and purity. But at the same time, they imply to friends, "I'll never tell your secret." Now you know flowers say a lot _____ _____ _____ _____.

After the commercial break, I'll talk about how to decorate your home with beautiful flowers. Stay tuned.

10 2021년 3월 학력평가
딕테이션

녹음을 듣고, 빈칸에 알맞은 말을 쓰시기 바랍니다. 빈칸은 문제풀이에 핵심이 되는 키워드와 헷갈리기 쉬운 발음에 표시되어 있으니 이 점에 유의하여 듣기 바랍니다.

01

W: Good morning, parents. I'm Jennifer Lawrence, vice principal of Greenhill Elementary School. Thank you for being here for the Parent-Teacher Meeting. Before we begin, let me tell you about the _____ _____ next month. The students will be visiting the Children's Natural History Museum. They'll have a great opportunity to _____ the different activities there. Today we'll hand out the field trip _____ _____ to each student, which has all the details including the schedule and the fees. Please take a look and _____ _____ _____ to us by next Monday. If you have any questions about the trip, please feel free to call us.

02

W: Hi, Chris. Where are you going?

M: I'm going to the library to _____ _____ some books. Do you want to come along?

W: Well, I don't often read books these days. I'm busy helping with housework, exercising, and so on.

M: Why don't you try audio books then? They're _____ _____ _____ _____ while you're doing other things.

W: I've never tried it. Do you think it'll work for me?

M: Sure. It's an easy way to enjoy books even if you have a busy schedule. I always listen to a _____ _____ when I take a walk.

W: Cool! I guess I could try listening to audio books while I _____ _____.

M: I'm sure you'll enjoy listening to books while dealing with other stuff.

W: Can you recommend some audio books to me?

M: I have a few in mind. I'll text you a list later.

03

[Smartphone rings.]

W: Hello, Liam.

M: Hello, Emily. I'm wondering if we're having our lesson as scheduled.

W: Sure. Why do you ask?

M: The _____ has gone down a lot lately. I'm afraid I can't surf under these weather conditions.

W: Don't worry. The _____ are more important than the temperature in surfing.

M: But I'm still worried. I can't imagine myself going into really cold water.

W: You'll be fine. We have _____ _____ to keep you warm.

M: Okay, I guess I can try. Ah, one more thing.

W: What is it?

M: I'm not a good swimmer. Would it matter?

W: It'll be okay. Good swimming skills are _____ _____ _____ in surfing.

M: I see. Looking forward to your lesson next week.

W: Great! See you then.

04

W: Honey, come and look. I'm decorating Sam's room for his birthday party.

M: Wow. I like what you put on the wall. It's beautiful.

W: Thanks. I made a _____ _____ _____.

M: There's a cake on the table. Is that the one Aunt Mary baked for him?

W: Yeah. Her cakes are the best. I put three candles on it.

M: Good. Where's the gift we prepared?

W: It's under the table. I _____ _____ _____ around the box.

M: Nice. Oh, I love this rug on the floor. It has _____ _____ it.

W: It's cute, right? I bought it online.

M: Did you make the _____ _____ on the bed?

W: Yes, I did. Sam loves dogs.

M: He does. You did a great job.

05

M: Ellie, do you have any idea about our volunteer club's next project?

W: Hmm, last time we _____ _____ for babies and sent them to Africa.

M: Yes, we did.

W: How about making eco-friendly soap this time? It helps the environment and we can give it out to people in need.

M: Good idea. _____ we learned how to make soap in science class.

W: Right. I still have the handout about it.

M: Great. You can bring it to our club meeting. It's next Friday, right?

W: Yeah. We can try making soap then. Shall we do it in our club room?

M: I think it'll be better to use the _____ _____.

W: You're right. Can you go ask Mr. White if we can use it?

M: Sure. I'll do that right away.

W: Thanks. Then, I'll find out where we can _____ _____ _____.

06

W: Honey, we're running out of fine dust masks. Don't we need to order some more?

M: Oh, right. [Typing sound] Let's order them on this website. The masks are $2 each and _____ _____ _____ 10 masks is $15.

W: Then it's cheaper to buy them in packs. Let's get _____ _____.

M: Okay. We also need some hand wash, right?

W: Yes. Is there any special promotion going on?

M: Let me see. [Pause] Oh, there is. We can buy three bottles of hand wash for $10. It was _____ $5 per bottle.

W: That's a good deal. Let's buy three bottles then.

M: All right. Do we need anything else?

W: No, that's all. Oh, hang on. Look here. If we spend more than $_____, we can get a 5-dollar discount.

M: Great. I'll place the order now with my credit card.

07

M: Hi, Jenny. How's your _____ _____ preparation going?

W: It's not going well. It's not easy doing it by myself.

M: Hmm.... Why don't you go to the special lecture on job interviews at the _____ _____?

W: That might help. Do you know when it is?

M: It's this Saturday in the morning, from 10 to 12.

W: Oh, no. I'm afraid I can't make it.

M: Oh, you have a part-time job at the library at that time, don't you?

W: No, I quit last month. Actually, I have to take a _____ _____ _____ on Saturday.

M: I see. Good luck on your test.

W: Thanks. Do you know if another _____ is coming up?

M: I'm not sure. You should check with the career center.

W: Okay, I will.

08

M: Amy, what are you reading?

W: Our school newsletter. It says our school is holding the West Lake Fun Run.

M: Sounds interesting. When is it?

W: _____ _____ _____ _____ April 17th.

M: I see. How long is the course?

W: It's 5km _____. Starting at the school, participants will run through Vincent Park and Central Stadium, and finish at West Lake.

M: Cool!

W: Why don't we sign up together?

M: Good idea. How much is the _____ _____?

W: It's $5 per person. The money raised will be used to _____ the school gym.

M: Great. It's so old. It'll be wonderful to have a new gym.

W: I agree.

09

M: Do you ever wonder what happens in the aquarium at night? Pack your pajamas and join us at Sleep Under the Sea. You'll have the _____ _____ _____ inside the shark tunnel with sharks and giant fish swimming above you. Our staff will give you a guided tour of the aquarium including a special visit to our _____ _____. After the tour, you'll be able to watch a 3D movie about dolphins. To participate in Sleep Under the Sea, children must be _____ _____ _____ _____, and all children under 15 must be accompanied by an adult. Dinner and breakfast will be _____ during the Sleep Under the Sea experience. For more information, visit our website at www.sealifeaquarium.org.

10

M: Honey, what are you looking at on the Internet?

W: I'm looking for a bike helmet for Jason. There's a _____ in his old helmet.

M: Oh, I didn't know that. Let's pick one together then. What's our priority?

W: I guess it's weight. What about you?

M: Same here. Considering Jason's age, it should be _____ _____ grams.

W: I agree. I think this one is too expensive, though. I don't want to spend more than $_____.

M: Okay, let's choose from these three then. Do you think LED lights are necessary?

W: Yes, it'll be safer to have them when riding at night.

M: You're right. Now we have two options left. Do you think our son will like this one?

W: I don't think so. He _____ _____ _____.

M: That's right. Let's order the other one.

11

M: Lydia! You said you were _____ _____ with your family to Mt. Bluestone during the winter vacation. How was it?

W: We couldn't make it because of the heavy snow. We camped indoors at our house instead.

M: That's cool. I wonder _____ _____ _____ was set up.

W: (My father put it up in the living room.)

12

W: Mr. Johnson, do you have a minute? I need your _____ _____ the project I'm doing.

M: I'd love to discuss that with you, but I'm expecting a visitor in 10 minutes. Is 10 minutes enough?

W: I'm afraid it'll take longer than that. _____ _____ _____ _____ later?

M: (Yes. I'll give you a call when I'm available.)

13

W: Dad, I'm home. Where's Max?

M: He's sleeping in his house. I took him to the vet this morning. He _____ _____ _____ well lately.

W: What did the vet say?

M: She said there's nothing wrong with him. He just needs more exercise.

W: More exercise? We take him out for a walk _____.

M: That's true, but we don't walk him every day. The vet said he needs _____ _____ _____ _____ of exercise every day.

W: Oh, I didn't know that.

M: I think we should exercise him every day from now on.

W: I agree. What if we all take turns doing it?

M: Good idea. Your mom and I will do it _____ _____. You're busy with your schoolwork during the weekdays.

W: (Okay. I'll take him out for a walk on weekends then.)

14

M: Hi, Tara. What are you looking at?

W: Hi, Dan. I'm reading a _____ about an online debate competition.

M: Oh, it sounds interesting. Are you going to participate?

W: I want to, but it's a team competition. Why don't we make a team and enter together? You're a great _____.

M: Thanks, I'm flattered. But debating online is new to me. I'm not sure if I can do it well.

W: Don't worry. Everything is _____ _____ _____ _____ it's taking place online. You'll get used to it with a little bit of practice.

M: I see. I'll enter with you then. When's the competition?

W: It's a month away. We have plenty of time to prepare.

M: I guess we need to practice online, right? But my laptop isn't working at the moment.

W: No problem. You can do it _____ _____ _____.

M: (Then I should get used to using it for debating.)

15

W: Lisa and Kevin are _____ for the school newspaper. They decided to interview Mr. Jackson, the new history teacher, for the next issue. Kevin suggests that they take a photo of him to put in their interview article. Lisa knows that Kevin is good at _____ caricatures and that he often draws teachers and students. She has seen the caricature of Mr. Jackson that Kevin drew. So she thinks that it'll be _____ _____ _____ the caricature in the article, instead of a photo, because caricatures can be more appealing than photos. Lisa wants to suggest to Kevin that they _____ _____ _____. In this situation, what would Lisa most likely say to Kevin?

Lisa: (Let's put your caricature of Mr. Jackson in the article.)

16~17

M: Hello, class. Let's continue to talk about different cultures around the world. People _____ the New Year in various ways. In Spain, it's customary to eat 12 grapes at midnight on New Year's Eve. Each grape _____ good luck for one month of the coming year. In Denmark, people _____ the New Year by throwing old plates and glasses against the doors of family and friends. They believe it'll _____ _____ _____ the bad spirits. They also stand on chairs and jump off them together at midnight to "leap" into January. In Mexico, residents carry _____ _____ around the block. Mexicans believe that doing so will bring travel and adventure in the coming year. In _____, an onion is traditionally hung on the front door of homes on New Year's Eve as a _____ _____ _____. On New Year's Day, parents wake their children by tapping them on the head with the onion. Now let's watch some video clips of these _____ traditions.

11 2021년 6월 학력평가 딕테이션

2SBL2_A11

🙂 녹음을 듣고, 빈칸에 알맞은 말을 쓰시기 바랍니다. 빈칸은 문제풀이에 핵심이 되는 키워드와 헷갈리기 쉬운 발음에 표시되어 있으니 이 점에 유의하여 듣기 바랍니다.

01

W: Good morning, Staton High School students! This is Jessica Mcqueen, the vice principal. As you know, tomorrow, two vending machines will be _____ next to the school library. Now, I'd like to inform you of the _____ you have to follow when using them. First, use them only during break times. You can not use them as _____ _____ _____ being late for classes. Second, after eating or drinking, throw trash away in the trash can. No one wants a dirty school. Third, do not _____ _____ _____ the vending machines. If they don't work, just call the number on the machine. Please keep these rules in mind. Thank you.

02

W: Dylan, what are you doing?

M: I'm learning about the history of Rome.

W: Hmm... But you are reading a comic book, aren't you?

M: Yes, it's a comic book about history. It's very helpful.

W: I think reading a _____ history book would be more helpful.

M: Maybe. But learning history through comic books has _____ _____ _____.

W: Why do you think so?

M: Comic books use pictures to convey information, so you can _____ _____ _____ more easily and remember them

for a long time.

W: That makes sense. Anything else?

M: Most importantly, comic books are _____ _____ _____.

W: I see. Then I'll give it a try.

03

W: Hi, Mr. Williams.

M: Hi, Ms. Brown. Thanks for inviting me.

W: _____ _____ to meet you today. I heard that you've been cooking for more than 30 years.

M: Yes. I've studied ways to _____ _____ _____ more delicious since 1990.

W: That's amazing. Actually, many viewers have been asking for pasta _____.

M: Great. I'll teach you how to make tomato bacon pasta today.

W: Isn't that one of the most popular dishes in your restaurant?

M: Right. I'll let you know how to make delicious pasta in an easy way.

W: Fantastic! Also, the recipe will be uploaded to our website _____ _____ _____.

M: That will be helpful for the viewers who miss the show.

W: Great. Can you tell me what to prepare for the dish?

M: All you need is bacon, tomatoes, pasta, and olive oil.

W: Okay. Let's start cooking!

04

W: Tom, I couldn't attend the school club festival last week. How did it go?

M: It went great. Do you want to see a picture of my club's booth?

W: Sure. The _____ _____ on the wall looks good.

M: Thanks. Do you recognize the drawing of the car above the chair?

W: That's Tina's work. I saw her drawing it earlier.

M: You're right. What do you think about the _____ _____ on the table? I made it.

W: You did a great job. By the way, why is there a _____ _____ on the floor?

M: That was for visitors to paint. See, those children are painting it.

W: That must have been a fun experience. Oh, look at the _____ _____ on the shelf! It seems so real!

M: That's Kevin's artwork. He got a prize for it.

W: Everything looks perfect. I wish I could have been there, too.

05

W: Steven, the baseball final is coming up next week. I'm so excited.

M: Me, too. Let's check what we need to prepare to _____ _____ our team.

W: Okay. Did you order small flags to wave?

M: Sure, they were _____ yesterday.

W: Good. Didn't you say you were going to write our team name on the flags?

M: Right, I did it with my brother this morning.

W: Well done. How about songs to cheer on our team?

M: Don't worry. _____ _____ _____ several songs.

W: Wow, you've done a lot. Is there anything I can help with?

M: There is one thing left. We need to _____ _____.

W: I can do that. I'll buy colorful and stylish ones.

M: Great! I hope our team will win the game.

06

W: Hello. May I help you?

M: Yes. I want to buy some toys for my children.

W: We have _____ _____ _____ _____ toys. Come and look around.

M: What kind of robots are popular these days?

W: I'm sure your kids would love this robot. It _____ _____ a TV series recently. It's $100.

M: It's so expensive. Anything else?

W: This toy car is last year's model, but it moves by _____ _____. It costs $60.

M: I like it. Do you have any other good things?

W: The newest speaking doll was released yesterday.

M: It looks cute. How much is it?

W: It's $80, but you can get _____% off on this doll today.

M: Excellent! Then I'll buy one toy car and one speaking doll. I'll pay for them by credit card.

W: Thank you.

07

M: Hi, Jessi. How was the test?

W: It wasn't that difficult. Anyway, I'm glad that it's over.

M: Right, now we need to _____ _____. Why don't we go to the movies?

W: Sure, I'd love to.

M: How about going to a cinema this Saturday? There are a lot of new movies.

W: Sorry, I can't make it that day.

M: Why? Do you have to prepare your

_____ _____ _____ class?

W: No, I finished it yesterday.

M: Ah, you said your mother's birthday is coming up, right?

W: Actually, her birthday is next week.

M: Then, what are you doing on Saturday?

W: I _____ _____ _____ _____ with my family for that day.

M: Oh, I see. Have a good time with your family. We can watch a movie _____ _____ _____.

08

M: Honey, check out this poster. Friday Night Walk is going to be held this month.

W: Friday Night Walk? Is it walking through the city at night?

M: Well, yes. But its _____ _____ _____ _____ money for children's hospitals.

W: That's meaningful. And we can enjoy the

beautiful city _____ at night. Why don't we join it?

M: All right. Let's do it.

W: Great. Look. There are two walking courses _____ _____ _____, a 5km course and a 10km one.

M: Hmm... How about the 10km one? It would be a lot more exercise.

W: Good idea. The _____ _____ is $20 for the 10km course.

M: I see. How can we sign up for the event?

W: It says we must register on their website.

M: Okay. Let's register right away.

09

M: Good afternoon. I'm Michael Lee, the manager of the City Library. We'll be _____ an Advanced English Reading Camp this summer vacation. It will be held for three days from August 6th to August 8th at the City Library. During the camp, you will read _____ _____ _____ by Shakespeare and discuss given issues in English. Two native English-speaking teachers will join the camp and _____ _____ _____.

To take part in the camp, you must register online at our library's website in advance. You can join us for free if you are a member of our library, but if you are not a member, _____ _____ _____ _____ $15. We're limiting the number of participants to a maximum of 20 people, so I recommend you hurry and sign up. Thank you.

10

W: Honey, look at this flyer. This store has bookcases on sale.

M: Great. It may be a good _____ _____ _____ our old bookcase.

W: Let's see. *[Pause]* We should not choose the plastic one. It is likely to break easily.

M: You're right. And, _____ _____ _____ do we need?

W: Not many. We don't have that many books, so three or four would be enough.

M: I agree. Let's choose the color now.

W: I think a red bookcase would be pretty and colorful.

M: Red is good, but it doesn't match our furniture. _____ would be a better choice.

W: Good point. Then, we have only two options left.

M: We've already spent a lot of money decorating the house. Why don't we buy the _____ one?

W: Okay. Then let's buy this one.

11

M: Mom, are you going somewhere?

W: I'm going to buy some _____ for dinner. Can you come with me and help?

M: Sure. But I have to _____ _____ _____. Could you wait for a minute?

W: (No problem. Tell me when you're ready.)

12

W: I have big news. I'm _____ _____ next month.

M: Congratulations! You must be really busy these days.

W: I am. Here, this card is _____ _____ for you. I hope you can come.

M: (Absolutely. I'm excited to see you in your wedding dress.)

13

W: Hello, Jake. How is your job _____ going?

M: I'll have a job interview with the ABC Company in three days. But the interview will be online.

W: Oh, I've done a job interview online before.

M: Really? Can you give me some advice?

W: It's important to make a _____ _____. So, you should have clear video and sound.

M: How can I do that?

W: You need a high-quality camera and a good microphone. I _____ _____ _____ and they were helpful.

M: Sounds good. I want to buy them too, but I don't have much money.

W: You can buy them at a discounted price online, but they will take several days to arrive.

M: Oh, no... Is there _____ _____ _____ to get them?

W: (If you want, you can borrow mine.)

14

M: Kate, you look depressed. What's wrong?

W: I had a medical check-up at the hospital yesterday and got a _____ _____.

M: Sorry to hear that. What did the doctor say?

W: The doctor said I have high cholesterol, so I need to do more exercise.

M: Everyone should exercise. I _____ you take swimming lessons at the sports center near your house.

W: I'd like to, but these days I don't have any extra time for the lessons.

M: Then, how about going to work _____ _____ or by bicycle?

W: Good idea, but my company is too far from home to walk there.

M: If so, why don't you try riding a bicycle?

W: That would be great, but I _____ _____ _____ to do that.

M: (Don't worry. I can teach you how to ride a bicycle.)

15

W: Lucy and Mike are a married couple. Lucy has traveled overseas many times, but Mike has no experience with overseas trips. One day, for their summer vacation, Lucy and Mike decided to _____ _____ _____ to Australia for two weeks. While talking about what to prepare, Mike tells Lucy that he'd like to go there without plans and just do _____ they want in the moment. But Lucy knows the importance of planning _____ _____ _____ with overseas travel. She is worried about having difficulties traveling without

plans. So Lucy wants to suggest to Mike that they _____ _____ for their trip. In this situation, what would Lucy most likely say to Mike?

Lucy: (How about planning out our trip in advance?)

16~17

M: Hello, listeners. I'm Joe Adams from the public health center. Many of you drink tea because you like the taste. But tea can also improve your overall health. Today I will introduce some teas that will _____ _____ _____. First, green tea is good for health. Green tea helps brain function by improving working memory. It can also _____ _____ _____ of bad cells that cause cancer. Second, lemon tea is popular for its _____ _____. With lemon tea, you can get vitamins and minerals without a lot of sugar or calories. Mint tea is another tea which makes you healthier. Mint tea relieves digestive _____ in your body. It can also relieve stomach pain. Next, black tea has _____ been popular. Black tea is well-known for reducing anxiety and stress. Also, a compound in black tea kills bacteria that _____ _____ _____. So did you get some useful information today? I hope you try one of these teas. Thank you.

12
2021년 9월 학력평가
딕테이션

MP3

2SBL2_A12

🙂 녹음을 듣고, 빈칸에 알맞은 말을 쓰시기 바랍니다. 빈칸은 문제풀이에 핵심이 되는 키워드와 헷갈리기 쉬운 발음에 표시되어 있으니 이 점에 유의하여 듣기 바랍니다.

01

M: Hello, students. I'm the school nutritionist, Mr. Jackson. Over the past week, we _____ _____ a survey on the school website about the meals you ate this semester. I want to thank those of you who have _____. Unfortunately, less than 50 percent of students answered the survey. We don't have enough data to make your school meals better. Therefore, we decided to _____ _____ _____ _____ by one week. The meal survey is now open until next Wednesday. We hope that giving you another week to participate in the survey will help _____ _____ _____ of your school meals. Thank you for listening.

02

W: Mike, what are you doing?

M: I'm searching for books to read. My teacher _____ _____ _____ during the vacation.

W: That's a good recommendation.

M: Really? Why do you say that?

W: Reading novels can help you experience _____ _____ _____.

M: I don't get it. What do you mean?

W: While reading a novel, you can understand how the characters feel. You can also imagine the characters' _____ are your own.

M: Oh, now I see what you mean.

W: I bet reading novels will help you improve your empathy, which is your _____ _____ _____ others' emotions.

M: Thanks for explaining. Now I'm really looking forward to reading novels this winter.

03

[Cell phone rings.]

M: Logan Williams speaking.

W: Hello. This is Marion Carver. I'm wondering if I can increase the number of guests for our _____ _____ _____.

M: Let me check. [Pause] Originally, you requested 50 seats for the event. I reserved a middle-sized hall at a local hotel. How many guests would you like to add?

W: I want to add five more guests.

M: That shouldn't be a problem.

W: Great! How about the _____ _____? Were you able to find one?

M: Yes, I was. I think they'll really add to the festive holiday mood.

W: That sounds perfect. Can I ask you one more thing?

M: Absolutely. I always try to _____ _____ _____ _____.

W: There will be kids invited to this party. Is there anything we can do for them?

M: For a children's party I planned last week, I prepared animal-shaped balloons for all the kids. They really liked them.

W: That's a brilliant idea! I'm so pleased with _____ _____ _____ and planned this party. See you next Friday.

04

M: Honey, I've finished decorating the living room for Halloween. Can you come here and take a look?

W: Sure. *[Pause]* Is the _____ on the floor the one you ordered last week?

M: Yeah. I chose the round one because it looks cute. What do you think?

W: It looks really good there. I also love the

_____ _____ _____

that you put on the wall above the piano.

M: Thanks. I thought it would help create the Halloween mood.

W: It definitely does. *[Pause]* Oh! The two carved pumpkins on the bookshelf are so cool.

M: Totally. The _____ _____

_____ into the pumpkins look excellent.

W: Didn't you say you were planning to put flying ghost stickers under the window? Did you change your mind?

M: I did. I think the bat sticker looks better under the window.

W: Good choice. I prefer the bat, too. What's that

_____ _____ on the table for? Is it for trick-or-treating?

M: Right. We can use it when trick-or-treaters visit our house on Halloween.

W: That's a great plan. You did a terrific job decorating the room.

05

W: Henry, the weather's so nice today. We should do some of the _____ _____ Los Angeles has.

M: I agree. Because it's been so hot, we've been going to museums to enjoy the air conditioning.

W: I'm ready to enjoy the real Los Angeles. How should we spend the day?

M: We could go to the beach for lunch first, and I think there's a _____ _____ that we can go to in the evening.

W: That sounds great. I've always wanted to see the local team play.

M: Should we prepare a lunch to take to the beach? The restaurants there might be crowded.

W: I think it would be better to pick up something to eat _____ _____

_____ there.

M: Okay. What about tickets to the baseball game? They might sell out.

W: Oh, you're right. _____ _____

_____ the tickets? I'll search for a place where we can pick up food for our lunch.

M: All right. I'll take care of that now.

06

M: Good morning. Welcome to Happy Bakery. How can I help you?

W: I need to buy a cake for my sister's birthday. Could you recommend one?

M: Sure. These chocolate and strawberry cakes are our best sellers.

W: Oh, they look delicious. How much are they?

M: This chocolate cake is 20 dollars, and the strawberry cake is _____ dollars.

W: Hmm.... I'll buy that strawberry cake.

M: Wonderful. Can I get anything else for you?

W: Well, we're having a small party. It might be nice to be able to give something to _____

_____ _____ _____ home.

M: How about our homemade cookies? They're 4 dollars each.

W: That sounds perfect. Can I get _____ cookies?

M: Absolutely. So, that's one strawberry cake and five cookies, right?

W: Correct. And I think I saw a sign in your window that you're having a sale right now.

M: You're right. If you spend at least 40 dollars, _____ _____ a 10 percent discount on your total purchase.

W: Terrific! Here's my credit card.

07

W: Hi, Joshua. Why didn't you come to the _____ _____ _____ yesterday?

M: I didn't feel well, so I went to the doctor.

W: Oh, I see. Are you feeling better?

M: Yeah, I'm much better now. But I'm sad I _____ the meeting. Did you choose the book for the next meeting?

W: We didn't. How about going to the library to choose the book for the next meeting?

M: That sounds great, but I don't think I can today.

W: Why not? Did the doctor tell you to get more rest?

M: No, it's not that. I need to write my script for the _____ _____.

W: I thought the script is due next week. You have enough time. There's no need to hurry.

M: It is due next week, but the topic is difficult. So, I should write the script today.

W: Okay. Be sure to _____ _____ so you don't get sick again.

M: I will. Thank you for your concern.

08

M: How was your visit to the Electronics Fair, Christine?

W: It was spectacular. You should check it out if you have time.

M: I might. What was there to do at the fair?

W: There were displays for the _____ _____ of electronic devices and new technology.

M: Wow! You must have seen a lot of brand-new electronic devices! Did you participate in any hands-on activities there?

W: Of course I did. _____ _____ _____ _____ including 3-D printing, VR games, and chatting with AI.

M: I want to try talking with AI. Where is the fair held?

W: It _____ _____ _____ Dream Expo Center.

M: That's near here! When does the fair end?

W: It ends on November 30th.

M: Can you tell me what the _____ of a ticket is?

W: It's 5 dollars. But if you purchase it online, you can buy it for 3 dollars.

M: Great! I'll order my ticket now.

09

W: Good afternoon. I'm Julia Harpson, the student body president. I'm glad to have the chance to tell you about Jump and Grow Together, a school _____ _____ _____ _____ by jumping rope together. It's a team competition, and each participating team should _____ _____ 11 freshmen. The goal is to see how many times the team members can jump one rope all together without stopping. Each team will have three _____ to jump. The highest number of team jumps among the three tries will be the team's score. The competition will happen on the first Saturday of October. It'll take place in the school gym. You must register online by September 30th to participate. You cannot register on the _____ _____

_____ _____. Don't miss this

chance to make a precious high school memory!

10

M: Hey, Tiffany. What are you doing?

W: I'm looking at a website where I can buy a monitor stand. Will you help me choose which one I should buy from these five options?

M: I'd be happy to. Have you thought about how much you're _____ _____ _____?

W: I don't want to spend more than 30 dollars.

M: Okay. These models are within your budget. [Pause] The plastic ones look really stylish.

W: They do, but I think plastic is kind of a weak material. I _____ _____ ones.

M: That makes sense. It would be better to have a monitor stand that you can use for a long time. Do you think you would use a _____ drawer?

W: No, I don't need one. I'd rather have more space to store my keyboard.

M: There are only two options left now. How many USB ports do you need?

W: I think I need _____ _____ 3. I'll buy this one. Thanks for your help.

11

M: Kate, look at the time! We've been working for two hours _____.

W: Already? Wow, I didn't realize so much time had passed.

M: Neither did I. Maybe we _____ _____ a break.

W: (Sure. Why don't we go out to get some fresh air?)

12

W: David, how was your driving test yesterday?

M: I _____. I got my driver's license.

W: What a relief! You failed the previous test because you didn't have _____ _____ _____ _____.

M: (That's why I practiced a lot this time.)

13

M: Cathy, can you help me? I'm preparing my science presentation, but it's not easy to _____ my topic.

W: Sure. What can I do to help?

M: I'm having trouble creating a way to visualize what I say in my presentation.

W: How about using an image or a chart? It can help your _____ _____ the topic because they'll be able to clearly see the information.

M: That's a great idea, but I'm not familiar with how to make those things. Do you have any tips?

W: You could use an infographic building program. I've used one to make _____ _____ _____ before. It's easy to use.

M: Really? How did you get the program?

W: I downloaded it from a website last semester. It's a free-share program.

M: That program would help me a lot. Would you _____ _____ the website address?

W: (Of course. I'll send it to you right away.)

14

W: Look at these beautiful snowy branches! It's the perfect day to climb a mountain.

M: Actually, in winter, the weather can cause a lot of problems. Days are short and trails are difficult to climb after it snows.

W: I see, but the views on the way up are stunning. I can't wait to see the amazing view from the _____ _____.

M: I'm afraid we can't reach the top today.

W: Oh, no! I was looking forward to taking photos at the top to prove we made it.

M: Well, it's getting dark. Because of the _____ _____, the climb has taken longer than I expected it would.

W: What about going up faster?

M: That could be very _____. Let's go back down today. We can try reaching the peak another time.

W: That's too bad. We were _____ _____ the view at the top.

M: (The original plan is important, but safety comes first.)

15

W: Amanda and Natalie are roommates who go to the same university. They live in an apartment that is a 30-minute walk to their campus. These days, they _____ _____ electric scooters to commute. Amanda and Natalie both try to be safe while riding the scooters, but Natalie often wears headphones to listen to music _____ _____. Amanda thinks that can put Natalie in danger because Natalie might not hear a car coming or _____ _____ _____ on the road. For the sake of everyone's safety, Amanda wants to tell Natalie to _____ _____ headphones while riding her scooter so she can hear more important sounds from cars, pedestrians, and other riders. In this situation, what would Amanda most likely say to Natalie?

Amanda: (It's dangerous to use headphones while riding a scooter.)

16~17

M: Hello, everyone. I'm Dr. Martin Muller. Do you know that _____ _____ _____ _____ in the animal kingdom? Many biologists have suggested that counting is not unique to humans. For instance, wolves use _____ _____ _____ while hunting. Wolves have optimal group sizes for hunting different prey. In addition, female frogs _____ the number of pulses in a male frog's cry. They can do this for phrases up to 10 notes long. Despite what you may have heard, chickens are _____ _____. Research shows that newly hatched chicks and adult chickens can count and do basic math. Lastly, the real math wizards of the animal kingdom are _____ _____. They are able to find their way back home after leaving their nests for food by _____ _____. Now, we will watch a video about these animals.

13

녹음을 듣고, 빈칸에 알맞은 말을 쓰시기 바랍니다. 빈칸은 문제풀이에 핵심이 되는 키워드와 헷갈리기 쉬운 발음에 표시되어 있으니 이 점에 유의하여 듣기 바랍니다.

01

M: Hello, Edmond High School students! I'm the librarian, Norman Smith. As you know, the school library _____ started last month and the library was supposed to reopen by the end of this month. However, _____ _____ _____ _____ is taking longer than expected because of some problems with the walls. Therefore, the library reopening _____ _____ _____ for a few more days. I'll let you know the date of the reopening as soon as it's decided. Please wait a little more until the library opens again. Thank you for your _____.

02

W: Brian, you look worried. What's the matter?

M: Mom, I'm trying to _____ _____ for vacation, but it's not easy. Could you take a look?

W: Sure. [Pause] Hmm, I think you put too many things in your plan.

M: I know, but there are so many things to do.

W: I understand, but you can't do them all _____ _____ _____ _____.

M: Then can you give me some advice?

W: Okay. First, make a list of things to do and then _____ _____ _____ according to how important they are.

M: You're saying I need to consider their importance first.

W: Right. That way, you'll be able to decide what to include in your plan and what to skip.

M: I understand what you mean.

W: When making a vacation plan, you should consider the _____ _____ _____ _____ you want to include.

M: That makes sense. Thanks for the tip, Mom.

03

M: Welcome. How may I help you?

W: Hi, I'm here to _____ _____ the car that I reserved, but I wonder if I could make a change.

M: Can I have your driver's license, please?

W: Sure, here it is.

M: Okay. [Typing sounds] You reserved a small car for three days.

W: Yes. But can I change the car size from small to medium?

M: Let me check. [Typing sounds] Oh, there's only one medium car _____ _____ _____.

W: That's lucky! I'll take it.

M: Okay. By the way, you chose partial car insurance. But for an additional $20, you can have _____ _____.

W: That's a great deal.

M: Right. Since you changed the size of the car and upgraded the car insurance, the _____ _____ is $50.

W: Okay. Here's my credit card.

M: Thank you. I'll take you to the car.

W: All right. Thanks.

04

W: Honey, look at this. My friend Lisa sent a picture of her newly-opened book cafe.

M: Wow, it looks great. There's a _____ _____ _____ books.

W: Yes. Lisa said she has a variety of genres of books.

M: Great. Look! There's a _____ _____ _____ the wall. That must be for the books on the upper shelf.

W: Right. Also, there are round tables.

M: Yes. Visitors can read books while drinking coffee there.

W: Oh, did you notice the _____ _____ _____ under the clock?

M: Yeah, those must be the gifts you sent Lisa for the grand opening. They look nice.

W: I'm glad that they go so well with the cafe.

M: What's that poster on the wall? It says "Book of the Month."

W: Lisa said she's going to _____ a popular book on that poster every month.

M: That's great. Why don't we go to this cafe together?

W: Good! Let's go this weekend.

05

[Cell phone rings.]

M: Hello, Anna.

W: Hi, David. How was camping at Sunnyside Hill last weekend?

M: I had a wonderful time with my family. The _____ was perfect, and the campsite was fantastic, too.

W: Sounds great. I'm going camping there this weekend.

M: Oh, really? Did you prepare everything you need?

W: I'm _____ _____. Is there anything you think I really need?

M: Sure. Mosquito spray. There are a lot of mosquitoes these days.

W: Oh, I should bring some. And I'm going to have a barbecue. What do I need for that?

M: Don't worry. You can rent everything related to barbecuing there.

W: That's wonderful.

M: And I _____ a portable speaker if you want to listen to music while barbecuing.

W: I'd like to listen to music, but I don't have one.

M: If you want, I'll _____ _____ _____ to you.

W: How nice of you! Thanks, David.

06

W: Hello. How can I help you?

M: Hello, I'm looking for a present for my father's birthday. Can you recommend something?

W: Okay, how about these _____ _____? These are the popular styles.

M: They look nice. How much are they?

W: They're $_____ _____.

M: My father likes blue. I'll take one blue striped necktie.

W: Okay. Anything else?

M: Do you also have men's socks?

W: Of course. Look at these. The _____ _____ of each pair is $6, but if you buy two pairs, you can get them for $10.

M: Good. Then I'll buy _____ _____ of socks. Can you gift-wrap them?

W: Sure. Gift-wrapping usually costs $2, but today gift-wrapping is free.

M: Cool! Thank you. Here's my credit card.

07

M: Hello, Rachel. How was the _____ of the movie, *Blue Sky* last night?

W: Hi, Mike. I had a great time. After the movie, I got an autograph from the main actor, Henry Edward.

M: Amazing! He's your favorite actor.

W: Right. I was so excited to meet him. What did you do last weekend?

M: I wrote a _____ _____ at Steve's Cafe. You know that place.

W: Sure. I like the cookies there.

M: You know what? They're going to have a One-Day Baking Class.

W: Oh, really? _____ _____ _____ _____ that class. When is it?

M: This Saturday, from 1 to 3 p.m. Let's do it together.

W: This Saturday? I'm afraid I can't, then.

M: Why? Are you still taking swimming lessons on Saturdays?

W: No, I quit recently. This Saturday I'm going to _____ _____ _____ _____ with my family.

M: Oh, I see. Have a great time. I'll tell you about the class later.

08

W: Chris, what are you looking at?

M: I'm looking at the website about the Charity Carol Concert. How about going there together?

W: Sounds interesting. Let me see. It's _____ _____ the Lincoln Arts Center on December 20th.

M: Right. The New York Symphony Orchestra will _____ _____ _____ _____ during this concert.

W: Wow! I'm a big fan of the New York Symphony Orchestra.

M: I knew you'd like it.

W: How much is a ticket for the concert?

M: They're $40 each. Since it's a charity concert, all ticket sales will _____ _____ _____ the Dream Children's Hospital.

W: That's amazing. We can enjoy the concert and help the children as well.

M: You're right. Let's hurry to buy the tickets.

W: Okay. *[Pause]* Wait! It says _____ _____ _____ on December 10th.

M: I see. Let's mark the date, so we won't forget.

09

W: Hello, TCN listeners. I'm Kate Dale. I'd like to introduce the Drone Photo Contest to you. This contest first began in 2017, and the number of participants has increased year by year. _____ _____ _____, anyone who loves photography and drones can participate in this contest. There will be _____ _____ for pictures, which are animals, people, and nature. Upload your best drone photo to the website, www.dronephotocontest.com by November 30th. For the winner in each category, an amazing new drone will be _____ _____ _____ _____. And the winners' photos will be posted on the website as well. Don't _____ _____ _____. Stay tuned!

10

M: What are you searching for, Mindy?

W: Dad, I'm searching for a perfume as a gift for Mom to celebrate her promotion. But I don't know which one to buy.

M: You're such a sweet daughter! Do you want me to help?

W: That would be great.

M: I think it's too much for you _____ _____ _____ $100.

W: I agree. Oh, there are different scents to choose from. How about the _____ _____?

M: She already has a floral perfume. I think you'd better pick one she doesn't have.

W: Good idea. Now, let's decide the size.

M: She _____ _____ perfume in her bag, so a portable size would be good.

W: Then, 50 ml would be a little big to carry.

M: Right. Oh, they come with a free gift.

W: I think Mom would like a _____ more than a hand mirror.

M: Yeah, she has a couple of hand mirrors.

W: Then, I'll order this one. Thanks, Dad.

11

W: Honey, what are you making?

M: I'm trying to _____ _____ _____ _____. But there are not enough apples in the refrigerator.

W: Then I'll go and buy some apples. _____ _____ do you need?

M: (I think five apples will be enough.)

12

M: Ms. Thompson, where are we going for _____ _____ _____ on Friday?

W: Hmm, how about the seafood buffet on Huston Street? People can choose their favorite food.

M: I tried to go there a few days ago, but _____ _____ for remodeling.

W: (Really? We need to think of another place.)

13

W: John, what are you doing?

M: Hi, Kelly. I'm taking these cups out of their _____ _____.

W: That looks different from other packaging I've seen.

M: Yeah, I bought the cups from a zero-waste shop, and they packed them using _____ _____.

W: Wow, then there's very little to throw away!

M: Yeah. I'm trying to reduce packaging waste in my daily life.

W: Great. I know the packaging waste problem is getting worse.

M: You can say that again. Zero-waste shops recycle packaging waste to create new products.

W: Then, we can get new things and _____ _____ at the same time.

M: Yes. By shopping at zero-waste shops, we can save the environment.

W: I'd like to join you, but I don't know where the zero-waste shops are _____ _____.

M: (Don't worry. I'll send you the locations of the stores I often use.)

14

M: Hello, Jane. How are you?

W: Hi, Daniel. I'm fine.

M: I haven't seen you _____ _____ _____ lately.

W: Yeah, because of a new project, I've had a lot of work to do these days, so I couldn't go.

M: I see. Even though you don't have time, you need to try _____ _____ to give yourself a boost.

W: I know I need to, but it's hard to make time.

M: Hmm, do you still get to work by bus?

W: Yes. It's about ten stops from my place to work. Why do you ask?

M: Well, you could use the _____ _____ for exercise.

W: How can I use that time to exercise?

M: Normally, I get off two stops in advance and _____ _____ home or to work. That's really effective.

W: (Great. That way, I can exercise even if I have a busy schedule.)

15

M: Amy is a high school student. One day, there is an event called Career Day at her school. Students are _____ _____ _____ a career and listen to a lecture about it, but Amy doesn't have a career that interests her. So Amy just follows one of her friends and _____ the lecture of an architect named Mr. Green. Mr. Green explains how to be an architect and what architects actually do, which makes Amy interested in it. After the lecture, she wants to learn more about the _____ _____ _____. So, Amy wants to ask if she can visit where Mr. Green works and _____ _____ _____ his job. In this situation, what would Amy most likely say to Mr. Green?

Amy: (Is it possible for me to visit you to see what you do at work?)

16~17

W: Hello, students. Last class, we talked about the differences between stars and planets. Today, I'm going to tell you how the planets in the solar system _____ _____ _____. First, Mercury is named after the Roman god of travel who moved quickly delivering messages to other gods. Mercury also _____ _____ around the sun and that's how this planet got its name. Second, Jupiter is the _____ planet in the solar system. Because of its size, it makes sense why ancient Romans named it after their most powerful god, the god of the sky. Third, _____ _____ _____ _____ color which reminded ancient Romans of blood. Therefore, Mars got its name from the god of war who _____ _____ _____ and many people's deaths. Lastly, Neptune is named for the Roman god of the sea. Since the beautiful blue color of the planet looks like the sea, the name is an excellent choice. Isn't it interesting? Now, let's move on to who first _____ these planets. I'll show you a video.

14 2022년 3월 학력평가
딕테이션

녹음을 듣고, 빈칸에 알맞은 말을 쓰시기 바랍니다. 빈칸은 문제풀이에 핵심이 되는 키워드와 헷갈리기 쉬운 발음에 표시되어 있으니 이 점에 유의하여 듣기 바랍니다.

01

M: Hello, students. This is Mr. Watson, your vice principal. I have an important _____ for all of you. As you know, our school has two _____ _____ _____ on each floor. Unfortunately, due to repairs to the water pipes, all the drinking fountains in the school will be _____ _____ _____ starting from tomorrow. It'll take a few days until the water pipes are repaired. Until then, you won't be able to use the school drinking fountains, so make sure you bring your own water. We're very sorry for the _____. Thank you.

02

W: Jason, are you shopping online?

M: Yes, Alice. I'm going to buy some clothes. Look! These are my picks.

W: They look nice, but all of them are dark again this time.

M: I think dark colors _____ _____ _____ and I feel more comfortable with them.

W: I see your point. You always say that you want to be more _____ though. Why don't you try other colors?

M: What colors would you recommend?

W: I think pastel colors would be good. They make the _____ _____ _____ _____.

M: I see. I'm worried they won't look good on me

though.

W: Just give it a try. You won't regret it.

M: All right. I'll _____ _____ the pastel clothes this time.

W: Great. I'm sure you'll look more approachable in them.

M: Thanks for your advice.

03

M: Hi, Miranda.

W: Oh, hi, Henry. I didn't expect you to be here today. I thought you were still traveling around in Switzerland.

M: I came back _____ _____ _____. I just stopped by to see how the preparations for the exhibition are going.

W: They're almost done. Did you take a look at the exhibition hall?

M: Yes, I did. You did a great job _____ all the pictures.

W: Is there anything you want to change?

M: Well, is it still possible to add some more works? I _____ _____ _____ _____ during my trip.

W: Sure. Do you have them with you now?

M: No, but I can send you the photos by email. We can talk after you check them out.

W: Okay. You're such a great artist. I'm so happy to exhibit your works _____ _____ _____.

M: Thanks for saying so. I'm also glad to work with you.

04

W: Hi, David. You look happy.

M: I _____ _____ _____ at the science fair. Look at this photo from the fair.

W: Wow! Congratulations. Oh, the prize ribbon is on the wall _____ _____ _____. Cool!

M: Yeah, I'm so proud.

W: You set up your board on the round table. I see your topic was 'Lemon Battery.' What did you do?

M: I showed how to make a battery using lemons.

W: Interesting. So that's why there is a _____ of lemons next to the battery.

M: That's right.

W: Who is this woman wearing a flower-patterned dress?

M: That's my grandmother. She came to congratulate me.

W: How nice! Oh, you're _____ _____ in your hand. They're so beautiful.

M: Thanks. It was a great day.

05

M: Amy, are you ready for your _____ _____ _____ class this afternoon?

W: Yes, James. I just need to check the file again. *[Clicking sound]* Oh, no. What have I done?

M: What happened?

W: I worked on the presentation file until late last night. I guess I forgot to save the final version.

M: Oh, dear. Do you need to do it all again?

W: Not really. Fortunately, I _____ _____ the final version and brought it with me. It won't take long to update the file.

M: That's good. Do you have a _____ for the class?

W: Yes, I printed it out, but I haven't _____ _____ of it yet.

M: I'll go to the library and do it for you.

W: That's so kind of you. Thanks a lot.

M: No problem.

06

M: Honey, we need to buy swim fins for Ben. He's moving up to the advanced swimming class!

W: Oh, that's right. Let's buy them online. *[Typing sound]* Oh, these fins look good. What do you think?

M: I like them. They're $_____ a pair. Let's get one pair.

W: I think we'd better get two pairs. He often _____ _____ _____.

M: I agree. He also needs new swimming goggles. His goggles are getting too small for him.

W: Okay. Oh, these goggles are _____ _____. They were originally $20 per pair, but they're 10% off right now.

M: Great! Let's get one pair. Anything else?

W: I think that's all. Is there a _____ _____?

M: It's $5, but it's free if we spend more than $50.

W: Good. Let's place an order. I'll pay with my credit card.

07

M: Mom, I'm home.

W: Hi, Ethan. Were you busy preparing for the school festival?

M: Yes. You know I'll be the MC for the school _____ _____. We rehearsed for the show today.

W: How did it go?

M: It went well. I just hope I don't make a mistake on the stage.

W: I'm sure _____ _____ _____. I guess you need to wear a suit for the show. How about going shopping this Saturday?

M: Oh, I wish I could, but I can't.

W: Ah, you go and _____ at the library every Saturday.

M: Not this Saturday. I canceled it because I have to _____ _____ _____ _____ for the festival.

W: I see. Let's go shopping on Sunday then.

M: Okay.

08

M: Emily, come have a look at this leaflet. It's about the Modern Architecture Expo.

W: Oh, it looks interesting.

M: We both have an interest in architecture. Why don't we go there together?

W: Good idea. _____ _____ _____ _____ the Grand Convention Center. It's close to our school.

M: Great! When should we go?

W: It _____ _____ April 1st and ends on April 15th. Can you make it on Saturday, April 9th?

M: Yes, I can. Look here. _____ is $20 for students.

W: Oh, that's quite expensive.

M: I'm sure it'll be worth it. _____ _____ _____ will be giving lectures on their best architectural works. We can attend as many of them as we want.

W: Cool! It'll be great to see them in person.

09

W: Hello, students. This is Ms. Miller, your music teacher. Are you interested in operas? Then, we invite you to 2022 Opera in School. Five _____ _____ _____ will come to our school and present *Romeo and Juliet* to you. They'll bring the classic story to life with opera costumes and sets. The show will be held at the school _____ on March 25th, starting at 6 p.m. It'll last for 45 minutes and be followed by a question and answer session. You can _____ _____ _____ the singers after the question and answer session is finished. There's no admission fee, but to attend, you must _____ _____ _____. I hope to see you there.

10

M: Honey, are you trying to buy a mini oven on the Internet?

W: Yes, we need it to bake cookies or biscuits. What do you think of these five models?

M: Let me have a look. *[Pause]* All of them look nice, but _____ _____ _____ _____ to spend more than $100 for a mini oven.

W: I agree. We should eliminate this one then. I think the _____ should be at least 10 liters.

M: Then let's choose one of these three. What about the weight?

W: I guess the lighter, the better. I don't want it to be _____ _____ _____ kg.

M: All right. Now we're down to these two models. Shall we go for the one with a _____ _____?

W: I don't think so. We can use the pans we already have.

M: I see. Let's buy the other one then.

W: Okay.

11

W: Ian, you're in such _____ _____! Do you still go to the gym every day?

M: Not now. The gym closed down last month, so I just work out alone at home.

W: At home? _____ _____ _____ _____ do you do?

M: (I do push-ups and squats for 30 minutes every day.)

12

M: Jenny, you're planning to _____ the online dance competition, right?

W: Yes, I finished recording a video. I just need to upload it to the website. I hope I'll win a prize.

M: I'm sure you will. You're a great dancer. I wonder _____ _____ _____ the best dancer though.

W: (The person who gets the most votes will be the winner.)

13

M: Sandy, what are you doing with your bike?

W: Oh, hi, Jack. I'm checking it out. It makes strange sounds when I ride it.

M: Let me take a look. *[Pause]* Hmm.... I think the brakes are not _____ _____.

W: Oh, no. I should get them fixed at the bike shop. It'll cost too much.

M: Why don't you try a repair cafe? You can save money.

W: A repair cafe? What's that?

M: It's a place where you can fix your broken stuff on your own. The cafe provides _____ _____ _____.

W: Well, I don't think I can fix my bike by myself.

M: Don't worry. _____ volunteers will be around to help you out there. There are many repair cafes around town.

W: That's great. I'll give it a try. Do you know where the _____ _____ is?

M: (Well, I saw a repair cafe next to the post office.)

14

M: Ellie! Look at this smartphone application.

W: Okay. *[Pause]* Oh, it says that it can help you _____ your blood sugar level.

M: That's right. It shows us how much sugar we eat a day. All we have to do is just click what we ate.

W: Then the app automatically shows _____ _____ _____ sugar in that food?

M: Exactly. It's very easy to use.

W: Interesting! But why do you care about your blood sugar level all of a sudden?

M: Actually, it's for my mom. Recently, she was _____ _____ high blood sugar. She's using the app to control her sugar intake.

W: I'm sorry for your mom. So does she find it useful?

M: Yes, she says it's very helpful. You can _____ _____ _____ _____ who needs it.

W: (My dad has the same problem. I'll tell him about the app.)

15

M: Sandra is the _____ of the student council of her school. Today the student council is having their regular meeting. One of the issues at today's meeting is about how to improve students' _____ _____ _____ health. These days, many students have health problems because they don't get much exercise. The student council agrees that it'd be good to hold a sports competition to _____ the students' health. After the meeting, Sandra goes to the principal's office and tells Mr. Wilson about what they discussed. Now she wants to _____ _____ _____ _____ to host the sports event for the sake of the students. In this situation, what would Sandra most likely say to Mr. Wilson?

Sandra: (Can we hold a sports competition for student health?)

16~17

W: Good morning, class! Today, we'll continue to learn some interesting facts about animals. Did you know that some animals can _____ _____ _____ for months and even years? First, crocodiles, one of the _____ _____ of the planet, can go for a few months without food, and in _____ cases, they can go up to 3 years without food. They save energy by moving slowly and at times by being motionless too. Next, _____ have to wait for their food to come to them, so sometimes the wait could be long. But, no worries. Their body is able to last for 3 to 4 months without food. This can stretch up to 1 year. _____ _____ _____, their metabolism is reduced during cold weather, which can help them sustain themselves without food or water for 2 to 4 months. Lastly, _____ can live without food for 8 to 10 weeks. Interestingly, the longer they live without food, the more _____ _____ _____ become. Now, let's watch some videos of these animals.

15 2022년 6월 학력평가 딕테이션

녹음을 듣고, 빈칸에 알맞은 말을 쓰시기 바랍니다. 빈칸은 문제풀이에 핵심이 되는 키워드와 헷갈리기 쉬운 발음에 표시되어 있으니 이 점에 유의하여 듣기 바랍니다.

01

M: Good morning, Lakeside High School students. This is your principal. As you know, Mrs. Smith _____ a few weeks ago. So, we were without a music teacher for the past few weeks. But today, I'm happy to announce that Cindy White _____ _____ _____ _____ the new music teacher. Ms. White is a passionate teacher and a talented violinist in the local orchestra. She worked at Wellington High School for three years. There, she _____ a school band and led many successful performances. We're excited to have _____ _____ _____ music teacher in our school. Please give her a warm welcome when you see her!

02

W: Jake, you look so nervous today.

M: That's because I have a big test this afternoon.

W: Oh, you must be concerned. Have you studied a lot?

M: Sure. But the problem is, I usually get so nervous that I make _____ _____ on tests.

W: Then, why don't you try eating chocolate before the test?

M: Chocolate? Do you think that will help?

W: Yes, eating chocolate will _____ _____ _____.

M: Really? I always thought that chocolate was just a kind of dessert or snack.

W: Actually, chocolate was originally used as a medicine. It can _____ _____ of anxiety-related hormones.

M: Hmm... But I heard that chocolate can increase one's heart rate.

W: If you eat too much, that's true, but _____ _____ _____ _____ chocolate helps you feel calmer.

M: Sounds interesting. Thanks for the tip.

03

M: Ms. Miller, it's been such a long time since we last met. How have you been?

W: Good. I went abroad on a business trip for 3 months.

M: You must have been very busy. _____ _____ _____ _____ today?

W: I want to make a change to refresh my look.

M: Hmm... What were you thinking of?

W: I want to _____ _____ _____ _____ and cut.

M: Unfortunately, your hair's condition doesn't look good. Why don't you change your hair color next time?

W: Fine. Then, I'll _____ _____ _____ today and visit you again to get my hair colored.

M: Okay. What style of cut do you want?

W: I don't want it too short.

M: Don't worry. I'll _____ _____ _____ it.

04

M: Rebecca, look at this picture.

W: Sure. What is it?

M: This is the garage in my new house. I finally have one.

W: Great. It was your dream to have your own garage, right?

M: Right. Look at this tool board on the wall. It's very _____ _____ _____ tools.

W: Good. And you put a table below the board.

M: Yes, I use it for repairing broken things. Can you see the _____ in the box? I changed its wheels all by myself.

W: Awesome. But isn't it boring to work alone?

M: Yes, that's why I put a big _____ _____ _____ _____ to listen to music.

W: Cool. Is that your new bicycle near the door?

M: Yes, now I can _____ _____ it inside the garage.

W: That's good. You were always worried about your bicycle when it rained. Congratulations.

05

W: Billy, I'm so excited about our first trip to Jeju Island next week.

M: Indeed, honey. We've been waiting so long for it.

W: Yeah. I checked the _____ _____, and it says it will be nice.

M: Good. Is there anything we're forgetting to do before going?

W: Hmm... Oh! I forgot to make a reservation for a rental car.

M: Don't worry. I've already made _____ _____ _____ _____

_____.

W: What a relief! How about our plan to change our room from a city view to an ocean view?

M: I've already called the hotel and changed it to have an ocean view.

W: Great. I heard that the Jeju Tourism Organization is having a special event. They _____ _____ _____ _____ fancy restaurants.

M: Really? How can we get some?

W: We can download them from their website.

M: Okay, _____ _____ _____ right away.

06

M: Welcome to Sky Cable Car. How may I help you?

W: Hi. I want to buy tickets. I see two types of cable cars. What's the difference between the Regular and the Crystal Cable Car?

M: The Crystal Cable Car has a glass floor, so you can _____ _____ you.

W: That must be thrilling! How much is it for an adult?

M: An adult ticket is $20.

W: Is that round-trip?

M: No, this is a one-way ticket. You need to _____ _____ _____ $5 each for round-trip tickets.

W: Then I'll buy round-trip tickets for two adults.

M: So round-trip Crystal Cable Car tickets for two adults, right?

W: Yes, and I have a discount coupon for _____ _____. Can I use it?

M: Let me take a look. [Pause] Yes. You can get a $_____ discount off the total.

W: Very good. Here's my credit card.

07

W: Hi, Jason. I like your T-shirt.

M: Thanks. I bought it for just $3 at the flea market.

W: _____ _____ _____! I want to buy a T-shirt like yours, too.

M: Then, how about going to the flea market together? It'll be held this Saturday.

W: This Saturday? I'd love to, but I can't.

M: Oh, I know you work at Tom's Bakery. Do you work on _____?

W: No, I only work on weekdays.

M: I see. Then is it because of the _____ _____ you reserved last week?

W: I did make an appointment, but I changed the date to next Friday.

M: So, then what's your plan for Saturday?

W: Actually, it's my uncle's wedding that day. I promised to _____ _____ _____ for him at the ceremony.

M: Great! Maybe some other time, then.

08

M: What are you looking at, Hailey?

W: I'm browsing our local community website to check out this month's events. It says the Brantown Community Picnic is coming up.

M: Sounds interesting. It could be a good chance to _____ _____ _____ and talk with them. When is it?

W: It's on June 18th, from 11 a.m. to 3 p.m. Would you like to go with me?

M: Why not? I don't have any plans for that day.

W: Great! _____ _____ it will be held. We've been there several times.

M: Is it going to be in Brantown Park?

W: That's right.

M: I like that place. Let me see... It says they will hand out a tumbler _____ _____ _____ to all of the participants.

W: Terrific! How do we sign up?

M: We just need to _____ _____ _____ _____ by this Friday.

W: Then let's do it right now!

09

W: Good morning, everyone. I'm Olivia Benson, the president of Golden Star Observatory. We'll be hosting Space Science Camp for teenagers this summer vacation. It's _____ _____ camp which goes from August 21st to August 23rd. Our programs will help you learn more about space. A _____ _____, Dr. Michael Russell, will give a special lecture about space travel. Participants will even have a chance to look at stars _____ _____ _____.

If you want to join this camp, you should sign up at our website. The reservation page will _____ _____ _____ _____ the camp. The participation fee is $50 per person. We hope to see you then. Thank you.

10

W: Tom, we have so many dishes to wash after every meal.

M: You're right. Let's buy a dishwasher from this online mall.

W: Well, what's our budget for that?

M: We can't spend more than $_____.
We've already spent too much this month.

W: I agree. Well, dishwashers get dirty easily, so white is _____ _____ _____ _____ for the color.

M: Right. Plus, silver or black would match our kitchen cabinets.

W: Okay. Which would you prefer, a portable or a built-in type?

M: I'd prefer a built-in. We _____ _____ _____ _____ with a built-in.

W: Besides, it would look more stylish.

M: Good point. Then, there are two options left. Which one would be better?

W: Definitely this one. When it comes to _____ _____, the longer, the better.

M: Perfect! Then let's order this one.

11

M: Emily, the plants you gave me are _____.

W: When taking care of plants, giving them enough sunlight and water is very important.

M: I think there's enough sunlight. But _____ _____ should I water the plants?

W: (You need to water them once every three days.)

12

W: Richard, have you chosen a place for Mom's birthday party? It's already next week!

M: I've been trying to make a _____ at Palace Bistro, but the restaurant never answers my calls.

W: Haven't you heard? It's _____ _____ _____ until next month!

M: (Oh, no. I must find another place as soon as possible.)

13

M: Sarah, where did you get those bananas?

W: I just took them _____ _____ _____ _____ box in front of the door.

M: What box? I haven't ordered anything recently.

W: Really? I thought you ordered them, so I ate some.

M: Let's check the address on the box.

W: Oh, no! The package was _____. This is not our address.

M: Umm... The bananas were supposed to be delivered to our next-door neighbor, Mr. Jones.

W: What should I do?

M: I think it would be good to _____ to him why you took them. And we should buy him some new bananas.

W: Okay. I'll tell him what happened right away.

M: Wait! It's too late. Mr. Jones usually goes to bed really early, so I don't think it's a good idea to _____ _____ _____ now.

W: (You're right. I'll take care of it tomorrow.)

14

W: Hi, Tim. Nice to see you.

M: Hi, Christine. You look like you're in good shape. Are you working out these days?

W: Yes, I _____ _____ _____ _____ every morning and take a swimming class some evenings.

M: I want to learn how to swim, but I haven't had a chance to take lessons.

W: How about signing up for the swimming course I'm taking?

M: Good idea. Where are you taking it?

W: At the community center near our apartment. The _____ is quite reasonable and the swimming instructors are kind.

M: That sounds like a perfect place to start.

W: If we _____ _____ together, I'm sure we'll have a great time.

M: Me, too! So, how can I register?

W: You can register online starting this afternoon. But the swimming classes are popular, so _____ _____ _____!

M: (Okay. Then, I need to hurry up and register.)

15

W: Amy and Jerry are close neighbors. They live _____ _____ _____ _____ and their children go to the same kindergarten. One day, when Amy is about to leave work, she's _____ _____ _____ that must be done immediately. Amy looks at her watch and finds that there's only one hour left before the kindergarten classes end. She realizes that _____ _____ _____ _____ she finishes the work, she will never be able to get to her son in time. Amy needs someone to help her and thinks of Jerry. So, she wants to ask Jerry to _____ _____ _____ _____ home from kindergarten. In this situation, what would Amy most likely say to Jerry?

Amy: (Would you pick up my son from kindergarten for me?)

16~17

M: Hello, students. Last time, we talked about the problem of _____ materials. Today, we're going to discuss how used materials are _____ _____ _____ _____ new products. Used paper is usually cut down into small pieces and sent into a machine to _____ any ink or glue on it. Then it can be used for making things such as toilet paper and paper bags. _____ like steel and iron are also valuable as recyclable materials. They are _____ _____ and easily transformed into car parts, frames, foils, and other things. _____ is another special material that can be recycled endlessly. Like metals, glass is also melted down after being crushed, and then it is made into new _____ _____ _____. Plastics are complicated to recycle because there are so many types. After _____ and melting the plastics, they can be turned into new products like bottles and toys through a special process. Now, let's take a look at some video clips and then we'll discuss them in detail.

16 | 2022년 9월 학력평가
딕테이션

MP3

25BL2_A16

녹음을 듣고, 빈칸에 알맞은 말을 쓰시기 바랍니다. 빈칸은 문제풀이에 핵심이 되는 키워드와 헷갈리기 쉬운 발음에 표시되어 있으니 이 점에 유의하여 듣기 바랍니다.

01

W: Hello, Princeton High School students. As you know, our school's website is going to be _____. Our goals are to make our website more accessible to everyone and to strengthen online security. To better prepare our new website, we're _____ _____ _____ to gather your opinions and suggestions. Your participation is strongly _____. The survey must be completed by this Thursday. For more information, please refer to our school bulletin board. Remember that _____ _____ _____ _____ to everyone in our school's community. Thank you!

02

M: Kate, you don't look good. Are you okay?

W: Yes, I'm fine. It's nothing.

M: Are you sure? You seem really stressed.

W: Well, I'm having a hard time _____ _____ _____ of a team project.

M: What's the problem?

W: It's hard handling _____ _____ because my teammates get into arguments easily.

M: I understand, however, arguments can lead people to _____ _____ _____.

W: Do you really think so?

M: Absolutely! Arguments happen all the time. Try to think of arguments as a way to _____ a better decision.

W: That's good advice. I'll try to remember that.

03

W: Hello, Mr. Baker. Thank you for doing this interview.

M: My pleasure. I really like _____ _____ _____ on modern painting in your newspaper.

W: Thank you so much. I'm honored to be interviewing the person who _____ the Modern Asia exhibition at the National Art Museum.

M: Thank you. I'm very surprised it has gotten so much attention.

W: It certainly has. _____ _____ _____ _____ interest in it, too. What was the idea behind it?

M: The idea was to show contemporary Asia to the public.

W: I see. Are you planning to do any other exhibitions?

M: Yes. I'm planning to do one about contemporary Africa. It will _____ _____ _____ people, cities, and homes from around the continent.

W: That sounds great. I look forward to checking it out.

M: You won't be disappointed.

W: Thanks again for your time, Mr. Baker.

04

M: Look at this photo from our family camping trip last year.

W: I remember that trip. We parked our camping van between the two trees.

M: Right. You guys really loved the camping van.

W: Yes, we did. And you set up that _____ _____ for us.

M: That's right. You guys enjoyed playing board games on that table.

W: Yeah, that was so fun! And do you remember the _____ _____ _____ the table?

M: Yes. I played the guitar and we sang songs together while we sat on the blanket.

W: That star-patterned blanket was our dogs' favorite.

M: Look at our _____ dogs, Rex and Rover. They look really happy in the picture.

W: Yeah. They started to _____ _____ _____ _____ while we were singing. That was so funny.

M: Yeah, that was hilarious! We had such a good time.

05

M: Liz, how are you doing with the preparations for our school festival?

W: Well, I've just finished printing out the posters. How about you? Have you found an MC for the ceremony?

M: Yes, I _____ _____ _____ and chose Brian to be the MC.

W: Great. He's a good choice. He's always entertaining.

M: Yes, he is. And the stage is set up for the dance team to rehearse.

W: Sounds good. I'll _____ the dance team's schedule.

M: Thank you for coordinating their schedule. What else do we have to do?

W: Let's see. Well, we invited some graduates this year to come and tell us about their different careers.

M: That's great. _____ _____ _____ are coming?

W: Thirty, but I don't have enough time to call all of them.

M: That's okay. I will _____ _____ _____ _____ for you.

W: Thank you. I'd really appreciate it if you could do that.

06

[Telephone rings.]

M: Good afternoon, Chase Coffee. How may I help you?

W: Hi, I want to have some coffees delivered to my office.

M: Sure. What would you like?

W: Iced latte and hot americano. How much are they?

M: An iced latte is five dollars, and a hot americano is _____ dollars.

W: Then I'd like two iced lattes and one hot americano. And do you charge for delivery?

M: It _____ _____ _____ _____. Delivery is free within three miles of our store, but there's a three-dollar delivery charge if it's beyond that distance. Where is your office located?

W: My office is located at 337 Lincoln Avenue.

M: Hmm... I'm sorry, but that's too far for free delivery. We'd have to apply the three-dollar _____ _____.

W: Okay, I see.

M: Alright, let me confirm your order. It was two iced lattes and one hot americano. Is that _____?

W: Yes, thank you.

07

W: Hey, Jimmy. Have you seen the poster for the rock festival this year?

M: Yeah, a lot of my _____ _____ are part of this year's line-up.

W: I know. The tickets go on sale tomorrow. Do you want to get tickets together?

M: Well, I don't think I can go this year.

W: Why not? Do you have _____ that day?

M: No, but my parents' 20th wedding anniversary is two weeks away, and I'm saving my _____ _____ _____ _____ a special present.

W: That's so nice of you!

M: Thanks. I'm really sorry that I _____ _____ _____, _____.

W: That's okay. Are we still meeting after school for band practice?

M: Of course. See you in the music room.

08

M: Hey, Olivia. Have you heard of Nova's Guide to the Stars?

W: No, I haven't. What is it?

M: It's a program where you _____ _____ _____ _____ and stay overnight at the Nova Observatory on Mt. Crayton.

W: Really? That sounds cool! How much does it cost?

M: It costs $100 _____ _____.

W: That's pretty expensive.

M: Well, it's actually a good deal. A ticket includes _____, _____, _____ _____ such as a guided tour, a science show, and a cable car ride.

W: Alright, that sounds reasonable. Oh, wait a second! I almost forgot about my English camp. When are the _____ for Nova's Guide to the Stars?

M: It runs from September 16th to September 30th.

W: Okay, I need to check my schedule first. I will join you unless it overlaps with my English camp.

09

W: Hello, library visitors! We will soon be holding the 2022 London Public Library Event to _____ _____ _____ of reading. We are going to invite the award-winning children's writer, Bridget George. She's the author of the popular picture book, *It's Mitig!* She will provide answers for parents who are _____ _____ _____ _____ to inspire their children to read. The event will be held on Thursday, October 27th from 9:00 a.m. to 10:00 a.m. If you'd like to join the event, please register in advance through our website. Registration is available _____ _____. A maximum of 50 people will be able to attend the event. If you have any questions for our special guest, please email them to us _____ _____ _____ library@lpl.uk so we can present them to her during the program. We hope to see you on October 27th!

10

W: Hey, Dad. I'm home. What are you doing?

M: Hi, Susan. I'm searching for a new portable folding chair.

W: Oh, okay. Hmm... I like this wooden frame chair.

M: Well, it looks very comfortable, but _____ _____ more than the one we had. It's too heavy. The new chair should be less than three kilograms.

W: I see. What about the color?

M: I _____ any color other than white. It gets dirty too easily.

W: Okay. The gray one and the black one look very nice.

M: I agree. What other features should we consider?

W: I want our new folding chair to have

_____ _____ _____.

M: Isn't one enough?

W: Well, Dad, I'd like to have one holder for my drink and the other for small personal items.

M: I like that idea. And we also _____

_____ _____ _____ for easy storage and for taking it with us on trips.

W: All right. Then this one is your best choice.

M: Okay. I'll order this one.

11

M: That was a great movie! What did you think?

W: The movie was okay, but I _____

_____ _____ it at all.

M: Why not? What happened?

W: (The person sitting behind me kept kicking my seat.)

12

W: Our teacher said we have to make a presentation at the International Exchange Program next week.

M: Next week? We should hurry, then. What should we do first?

W: Let me see. First, I think we'd better

_____ _____ _____

_____ for our presentation.

M: (Okay. Let's find one that is easy and interesting to talk about.)

13

W: Good morning, sir. How can I help you?

M: Hi, this bluetooth speaker I bought here two days ago isn't working anymore. I haven't

_____ _____ _____

_____, but it's just not working.

W: I'm sorry for the inconvenience, sir.

M: This is my favorite brand, but I think something is wrong with this particular one.

W: I understand. You _____ _____

_____.

M: I am. Is there anything you can do for me?

W: We can give you a refund, or you can exchange it for another one.

M: I'd like to exchange it, please. Is there any other model you _____ _____?

W: Well, this model is really popular, but it costs fifty dollars more.

M: Wow, that's too expensive.

W: Then, would you like a new one _____

_____ _____ _____ you bought?

M: (Yes, please. I hope the new speaker works.)

14

M: Emily, is your cellphone working? I've been trying all morning, but I _____ _____ _____ _____.

W: That's strange. Mine is working just fine. Did you try turning the phone off and on again?

M: Yes, I've already done that twice, but it's still not working. I'm really annoyed because I'm expecting an important phone call.

W: Okay. Why don't you try _____ the SIM card?

M: The SIM card? *[Pause]* Uh! I can't get it out!

W: Here, take this paper clip to open the SIM card tray. Insert the clip into the small hole and _____ _____ _____ until it pops out.

M: Okay. I took it out. Now what should I do?

W: Carefully re-position the SIM card and push it gently back into the phone. *[Pause]* Good. Now turn on your phone.

M: Wow! It works! You're a genius! _____ _____ _____ _____!

W: (It's nothing. I'm glad I could help.)

15

W: Amelia and Anna are friends who attend the same school and live in the same neighborhood. A few days ago, they were _____ a presentation. They are now working together on the presentation at Anna's house. Since the presentation is tomorrow, Amelia cannot _____ _____ _____, so she's working hard on it with Anna until they're done with everything. Amelia gets so absorbed in her work that she _____ _____ of time. After completing everything, Amelia looks at the clock and realizes it's too late to catch the bus back to her house. Amelia wants to call and ask her mother to _____ _____ _____ at Anna's house. In this situation, what would Amelia most likely say to her mother?

Amelia: (Could you please pick me up at Anna's house?)

16~17

M: These days, people become vegetarians for different reasons. It may be because of health, personal beliefs, or changes in lifestyle. However, some vegetarians have _____ _____ _____, which means their bodies don't get certain essential nutrients. If you're one of those people, here are some tips to ensure your body doesn't suffer from _____ _____. To start with, if you are not getting enough protein, you can get it from beans, green peas, _____, _____ _____. Next, if you aren't getting enough omega-3, it can be found in foods like walnuts, avocados, and olive oil. Third, if you are in need of _____, good sources include tofu, whole grain bread, peanuts, and raisins. Finally, if _____ _____ is missing from your diet, you can find it in fortified cereals, soy milk, and soy yogurt. By _____ these foods, you'll be getting the essential nutrients you need as a vegetarian.

17 2022년 11월 학력평가
딕테이션

MP3

25BL2_A17

🙂 녹음을 듣고, 빈칸에 알맞은 말을 쓰기 바랍니다. 빈칸은 문제풀이에 핵심이 되는 키워드와 헷갈리기 쉬운 발음에 표시되어 있으니 이 점에 유의하여 듣기 바랍니다.

01

[Chime bell rings.]

W: Hello, Greenville High School students! This is vice principal, Lisa James. Recently, the number of students using the bicycle-sharing system has increased. The shared bicycles are _____ _____ _____.

However, there's one important thing you should remember. If you don't _____ _____ _____ after use, they can block pedestrians' way or cause accidents. Because of _____ shared bicycles in front of the school, students have had trouble commuting. One student even fell over an improperly parked bicycle, and that could have led to a serious accident. So, please be sure to park the shared bicycles in the _____ _____ for the safety of everyone.

Thanks for your cooperation.

02

M: Anna, what are you working on with your computer?

W: Hi, Daniel. I've been writing a history report. My eyes are so tired.

M: You do look a bit tired. Oh, isn't your computer monitor very bright?

W: Yes, it's on the _____ mode. It's better to see clearer than a dark screen, right?

M: It may be so, but if the computer _____ _____ _____ _____, it can be harmful to your eyes.

W: Really? How come?

M: Too bright a screen could cause blurry vision. It makes your eyes get tired easily.

W: Hmm, I think I've often experienced _____ _____.

M: Also bright screens can even make your eyes dry, which has a bad effect on your eyesight.

W: Oh, I see. I should lower the brightness of the screen.

M: Yeah. Don't forget screens that are too bright can _____ _____ _____ _____.

W: Okay. Thanks for the tip.

03

W: Hello. How may I help you?

M: Hi, I wonder if you have _____ _____.

W: Of course. What are you looking for?

M: I want a digital piano for my daughter.

W: Oh, you're in luck. We got a nice one yesterday. Follow me.

M: Wow. It doesn't look like it's ever been played.

W: Yeah. The _____ _____ said her son didn't like playing the piano, so he barely touched it.

M: Really? How much is it?

W: It's $70. That's a pretty good price.

M: Good. I'll take it. By the way, do you buy _____ _____, too? I have many picture books my children don't read any more.

W: We do, but there should be no missing pages or pen marks.

M: Then I'll take a look when I go home.

W: Okay. If you find your books _____ _____ _____, please bring them in.

04

M: Mindy, how did clothing donation day go?

W: Dad, it was such a wonderful event! Do you want to see a picture of it?

M: Sure. Oh, you _____ a T-shirt on the banner.

W: Yeah. My club members came up with the idea.

M: Great. Are the shelves under the clock for the donated items?

W: Right. Do you see the _____ _____ _____ _____ table?

M: Yes. What's that for?

W: We put donation badges in it. We gave hand-made badges to donors.

M: How nice! Oh, I can see _____ _____ _____ _____ the chair.

W: Those were ready for donation to the charity center. We organized the donated clothes and put them in the boxes.

M: I see. What's the picture on the wall?

W: That's the picture _____ _____ _____ the people at the charity center last year.

M: It looks nice. It must have been a fun event.

05

W: Science Lab Day is tomorrow. Let's _____ _____ _____ _____, Kevin.

M: Good idea, Becky. I printed out the list of students who signed up for Science Lab Day.

W: Thank you. A lot more students signed up for it than we expected. There are enough chairs in the science lab, aren't there?

M: Don't worry. I checked the number of chairs and even brought some more yesterday.

W: What a _____ thing to do! And I downloaded the video clip that explains the safety rules.

M: Good. It'll be important to show it before the experiments. How about experimental equipment?

W: I put everything on all the tables. Oh, I forgot to bring _____ _____ from the preparation room.

M: Don't worry. I'll get them.

W: Thank you. Then I'll check the _____ _____ _____.

06

M: Welcome to Extreme Indoor Rock Climbing Center.

W: Hello, I'd like to try indoor rock climbing with my son. It's our first time.

M: Okay. If it's your first time, I recommend that you _____ _____ _____ _____. It takes an hour.

W: Great. How much is it?

M: It's $20 for an adult and $_____ for a child.

W: I see. I'll take an intro session for one adult and one child.

M: Okay, do you have indoor climbing shoes? You need special shoes for climbing.

W: Can we rent the shoes? Both of us need them.

M: Yes. The _____ _____ is $3 per person. Then you want an intro session for one adult and one child and two shoe rentals, right?

W: Yes. Oh, can I use this coupon? I downloaded it online.

M: Sure. You'll get 10% _____ _____ _____ _____.

W: Great. Here's my credit card.

07

[Cell phone rings.]

W: Hello, Anthony. What's up?

M: Hi, Lucy. I'm calling about _____
_____ _____ from the drama
club.

W: Oh, but I'm on my way to my part-time job at the
moment.

M: Okay. Then maybe I can pick them up
tomorrow. Anyway, how was your _____
_____?

W: I had a great time. Oh, my uncle gave me a
coupon for the rail bike at Crystal Riverside. Do
you want to go with me?

M: Sounds great. When do you want to go?

W: How about this Saturday?

M: This Saturday? I'm afraid I can't.

W: Oh, I remember you have your _____
_____ every Saturday.

M: Not this week. It's cancelled.

W: Then why can't you come?

M: I have a _____ _____
_____ on that day.

W: Okay. Good luck on the audition.

08

M: Sarah, what are you doing?

W: Hi, Thomas. I'm looking at a leaflet for the Winter
Robot Camp. How about going with me?

M: Sounds interesting. When is it?

W: It'll be held from _____ _____
to 30th.

M: That's good. The semester will be over by then.

W: Right. And the camp will be at the Watkins Robot
Center. You know where that is.

M: Yes, I've been there several times. Can I see the
leaflet? I wonder what programs _____
_____.

W: Sure. Here it is.

M: Oh, they'll provide daily programs on robot
programming, drone flying, and coding.

W: Yeah. It says _____ _____
_____ _____ with other
students with similar levels of experience.

M: It sounds like fun. How can we register?

W: It's simple. We can scan this QR code and
_____ _____ _____.

M: Great. Let's do it now.

09

M: Hello, listeners! This is Hans Dale with Upcoming
Event News. Do you want to feel _____
_____ for autumn? Then the Go
Greener Festival is a perfect event for you. This
event will be _____ _____
November 11th to 13th in Central Park. Songs
about the environment will be played. Stages will
be built using _____ _____.
You can buy food which is all organic and
served on edible plates. If you bring your own
water bottle, you can get drinks _____
_____ _____ _____.
To reduce the festival's carbon footprint, the
parking lot will not be available. Don't miss the
opportunity to go greener. Stay tuned!

10

M: Honey, since we had fun doing a jigsaw puzzle last time, why don't we order a new one?

W: That's a good idea. What about a _____ _____ again? We can put it in the living room this time.

M: Let's look online. [Typing sounds] Look, these five models are the most popular jigsaw puzzle sets.

W: Great. Which painting do you want this time?

M: _____ _____ Water Lilies last time.

W: Yeah, let's choose something new. What do you think about the number of puzzle pieces?

M: How about doing something more _____ _____ _____ pieces?

W: I agree. And I think spending over $40 for a puzzle set is too much.

M: Right. Oh, we can _____ _____ _____ as well. Which one would be good?

W: How about a wooden frame? I think it'll go better with the living room.

M: Okay. Let's choose this one.

11

W: Paul, what are you writing with that brush? It looks really artistic.

M: Thanks, Clara. I'm _____ calligraphy.

W: It's my first time seeing someone doing calligraphy. _____ _____ _____ _____ it from?

M: (It was my aunt who taught me calligraphy.)

12

[Telephone rings.]

M: Hello, Bluelagoon Scuba Diving. How can I help you?

W: Hi, I'd like to _____ _____ an indoor course on Friday evenings.

M: Let me check. [Typing sounds] We have two courses on Friday. The 7 p.m. is _____ _____, but you can take the 8 o'clock course.

W: (I see. I'll register for the available course.)

13

W: What's that, John? Oh, is that the _____ _____ _____ online?

M: Yes, Kelly. It was delivered today. I'm trying to put it together, but it's _____ _____.

W: Hmm, it doesn't look easy to assemble it.

M: Right, I hardly understand the manual. It's my first time trying to assemble DIY furniture. I'm so confused.

W: That can happen if you're doing something you're not used to.

M: You're right. Oh, didn't you say you had assembled a computer by yourself?

W: Yes, and I also had difficulty understanding the manual.

M: Then how did you do it?

W: I _____ _____ a video and learned how to put it together.

M: I think that would be quite helpful.

W: Yes, it explained every step well. _____ _____ _____ many videos online that can help you, too.

M: (I should find a video for assembling the bookcase.)

14

M: Honey, what are you watching online?

W: It's a documentary about ugly vegetables.

M: Interesting. What does it say?

W: According to the documentary, one-third of all vegetables are _____ _____ at farms just because of their appearance.

M: I can't believe it. That's such a shame.

W: Yeah. They're wasted even though they're as _____ _____ _____ as good-looking vegetables.

M: So, does the farmers' hard work just become useless?

W: Right. I think we should do something for the farmers.

M: I agree. Why don't we search for a way to _____ _____ _____?

W: Great idea! Let's find it on the Internet.

M: Let me do it. *[Typing sounds]* Look. This store is selling ugly vegetables _____ _____ _____ _____.

W: (Good. Let's see if the vegetables we need are for sale.)

15

W: Sofia and Henry _____ _____ in high school. Sofia has worked for ten years, and Henry has just begun teaching. At the beginning of the semester, Henry _____ a book to his students and has them do a presentation about it. However, he notices that many of his students don't show as much interest in the book as he expected, so he asks Sofia for advice. Sofia knows her students are _____ _____ when they pick their own books. So, she wants to suggest to Henry that he allow his students to _____ _____ _____ _____. In this situation, what would Sofia most likely say to Henry?

Sofia: (How about giving students a choice in their books?)

16~17

M: Hello, students. Last class, we learned about different expressions in various languages related to birds. Today, let's talk about what birds _____ _____ _____ _____. First, the eagle was a significant bird in ancient Mexican culture. For ancient Mexicans, the eagle was a symbol of the sun. As a _____, the eagle was also associated with strength and power. Second, in Chinese culture, the _____ _____ _____ _____ and honor. It's admired for its ability to walk, fly, and swim as well as for its graceful appearance. Third, in ancient Greek culture, the owl was a symbol for the Goddess of _____, Athena. The owl's abilities to see, fly, and hunt effectively in the dark often _____ magical powers and mystery. Lastly, in some Native American cultures, the hummingbird is a _____ _____ _____ of love. That's because of its ability to move incredibly fast. The hummingbird is also considered a symbol of joy and good luck. Isn't that interesting? Now, let's watch a video to help you understand better.

18 2023년 3월 학력평가
딕테이션

녹음을 듣고, 빈칸에 알맞은 말을 쓰시기 바랍니다. 빈칸은 문제풀이에 핵심이 되는 키워드와 헷갈리기 쉬운 발음에 표시되어 있으니 이 점에 유의하여 듣기 바랍니다.

01

W: Good morning, students. This is your principal, Ms. Perez. I have an _____ _____ about our indoor gym. Since its opening, it has been a popular destination for students who'd like to stay fit. However, the gym has been _____ _____ for more than 10 years and most sports equipment is now outdated. So, our school has decided to renovate the gym. This means the gym will be _____ _____ until further notice. We apologize for any inconvenience this may cause. Please check our school website for updates on the _____ of the gym. Thank you for your understanding.

02

M: Grace, did you finish preparing for your hiking trip tomorrow?

W: Almost, Dad. I still don't know which jacket I should wear.

M: When you choose your hiking jacket, make sure you _____ the color.

W: How about this brown one? It looks good on me.

M: That _____ _____ _____ _____, but I think you should avoid brown.

W: Why is that?

M: For the sake of your safety, you need to wear a color that _____ _____ the surroundings. It allows you to

be seen easily by others.

W: You mean I should avoid colors that _____ _____ with nature, like browns and greens?

M: Exactly. Safety should always come first.

W: Then I'll go with this bright orange jacket.

03

[Cell phone rings.]

W: Hello. Mia Parsons speaking.

M: Hello. I was told to call you this afternoon.

W: All right. Can I have your name, please?

M: I'm Jonathan Lee.

W: Just a second. *[Pause]* Oh, Mr. Lee. I have good news for you. I was _____ _____ _____ your issue.

M: That's a relief. The photos on my laptop are _____ to me. By the way, what caused the problem?

W: The main board was damaged, so I've _____ _____ _____ a new one.

M: That's great. Can I get my laptop sent via a delivery service?

W: Sure. Please give me your address.

M: It's 11367 White Street, Sandville.

W: Okay. You can get it by Tuesday.

M: Thank you so much. If you _____ _____ _____ _____, I'll pay it right away.

04

M: Hi, Lucia. Welcome back! How was your vacation?

W: Hi, Andrew. It was great. We _____ a guest house.

M: Oh, do you have a picture of it?

W: Yes, look. I chose a sky-themed room for my kids.

M: Wow. The model airplane _____ _____ _____ _____ looks cool.

W: Yeah. And kids never stopped going up and down the slide under the model airplane.

M: I can imagine. This _____ _____ on the table goes well with the theme.

W: Isn't the astronaut doll on the bed cute? It was a gift from the guest house.

M: It is. Your kids must have loved the picture of the _____ _____ beside the bed.

W: They did. I really recommend this place for your next family trip.

M: Thanks. I should visit there next time.

05

W: Dad, our printer is not working again!

M: Really? What do you need to print out?

W: I need a _____ _____ _____ _____ for tomorrow's English class.

M: Okay. Will you pass me the user's manual? Let me take a look.

W: I already _____ _____ _____ _____ _____ in the manual. Nothing helped.

M: Then, I can take the printer to the service center on my way out.

W: It might take more than a day to fix it. We'd better think of another way.

M: Hmm.... Then, how about going to the _____ _____? You can use the printers there.

W: Oh, that'd be great, but I have never been there.

M: Don't worry. I'll _____ _____ _____.

W: Thanks, Dad. Let's go to the library!

06

M: Honey, we need _____ _____ cups for our housewarming party.

W: Okay. Let's buy them online. *[Typing Sound]* Look, I love this floral tea cup.

M: I like it too, and it only costs $8.

W: Hold on. The store's _____ says, "Buy one cup, get one cup free."

M: Fantastic! We only have to pay for two cups. Then, we _____ _____ to buy a new teapot as well.

W: That's a good idea. Let's buy one that matches the tea cups.

M: I like the white one that costs $20.

W: Okay. Let's pay for two tea cups and one teapot. Do we also have to pay for shipping?

M: Yes. The _____ _____ _____ is $3. Do we need anything else?

W: Not really. Let me pay with my credit card.

07

W: Michael, what do you think about doing some volunteer work tomorrow?

M: Well, I thought we're going to join a sports program tomorrow.

W: You haven't heard? It's been cancelled.

M: Oh. Then, tell me more about the volunteer work.

W: We'll _____ _____ _____ at the community center and then deliver them to the elderly in the neighborhood.

M: Hmm.... When does it end? I'm having a family dinner.

W: Before noon. We'll be working for three hours in the morning.

M: Sounds good. Are there any _____ for applicants?

W: Yes. You have to be 16 or older to participate.

M: Then, I'm qualified. I just turned 16 last February.

W: Oh, I almost forgot. You also need a flu _____ _____ since you'll meet the elderly in person.

M: I haven't got a flu shot yet. I'm _____ _____ _____ come.

W: Too bad. Maybe next time then.

08

M: Hi, Jessica. Are you ready for the trip to Nari Island?

W: Not yet. I've been too busy to make a detailed plan.

M: Then, how about booking a package tour? There should be some package tours on the island.

W: Really? Let me check online. [Typing Sound]

This one _____ _____ 5 days, from April 3rd to April 7th. It matches my holiday schedule.

M: It provides a _____ _____ _____ beautiful caves and cliffs.

W: I think I'd enjoy it. I like to explore geological sites.

M: And a minivan will be offered _____ _____.

W: It sounds convenient. What do you think of the price?

M: I think $600 for each person is _____ _____.

W: Perfect. I'll book it right away.

09

M: Good morning, math lovers of Hamington High School. I'm your math teacher, Allen Steward. We have a special announcement for you. The Afterschool Math Festival will be held for _____ _____ _____ next Monday. Nine activities are planned, and you may _____ _____ _____ _____ three different activities. Keep in mind that activities such as the Math Escape Room and the Math Quiz Show will _____ _____ _____ other activities. This year, we are also offering a guest lecture. Our lecturer, Dr. Hilbert will tell us the stories behind famous mathematicians. Students who _____ this special lecture will get a copy of his book for free. Lastly, during the festival, special snacks and drinks will be served at the cafeteria. See you there.

10

M: Honey, why don't we buy a UV toothbrush sanitizer? This online store is offering a good deal.

W: That's great. How about choosing one from these five models?

M: Fine. First, we need to consider the number of slots.

W: For our family, we need _____ _____ _____ slots.

M: Right. Do you think we need one with a built-in battery?

W: Yes. It'd be easier to install.

M: Okay. And I think it's important to _____ _____ _____ _____.

W: I agree. It prevents bacteria from growing on the brushes. We should definitely go with one that has a _____ _____.

M: That leaves us with these two models.

W: How about _____ _____ 50 dollars?

M: Good. Let's order the cheaper one.

11

W: Ben. Would you come take a look at this plant? The leaves are turning brown.

M: Let me see. [Pause] Oh, you _____ _____ _____ it too much.

W: Do you have any idea how I can _____ my plant?

M: (Yes. You should stop watering it for a while.)

12

M: Ouch! I got a paper cut.

W: Are you okay? I know how painful paper cuts are.

M: This is the third time this week. Maybe my _____ _____ _____ _____ that I get paper cuts too easily.

W: (If so, applying hand cream might help.)

13

W: Hey, Pete. What's in the big box?

M: _____ _____ and blankets. I'm taking them to the post office.

W: Where are you sending them?

M: To an animal shelter. The shelter needs them for dogs and cats.

W: I guess it's to _____ _____ _____ _____.

M: Exactly. Without them, the animals have to sleep on the cold floor.

W: Oh, I didn't know that.

M: Many animal shelters are _____ _____ _____ blankets and towels.

W: Then, what about starting a school campaign to collect blankets and towels for the animals?

M: That'd be nice, but how can we do that?

W: We can _____ a campaign at the student council meeting tomorrow.

M: (Good idea. I hope they listen to our suggestion.)

14

M: Hello, Ms. Watson. Did you enjoy the conference?

W: Yes, I did, Dr. Cooper. This year was a _____ _____. Congratulations!

M: Thank you. We had the largest audience ever.

W: I heard some people couldn't come because the number of seats was limited.

M: It was a pity that we couldn't find a larger lecture hall.

W: I think there is a _____ _____ _____ more people next year.

M: Really? How?

W: You can hold the conference on a metaverse platform.

M: What does metaverse mean?

W: It's a virtual world. If you make a lecture hall there, you can _____ _____ a larger audience.

M: That's very interesting. I'd like to try that but I don't know _____ _____ _____.

W: (Don't worry. I can help you create a virtual lecture hall.)

15

W: Jane and David are both violinists in the school orchestra. They have been practicing together for a month for the Spring Concert. Just three days before the concert, Jane _____ _____ _____ and her doctor recommends taking a rest for at least a week. Since Jane cannot play at the concert, David should _____ _____ _____ _____. They have been practicing together and David knows Jane's part.

However, David says that he is _____ _____ _____ play the solo part. Jane knows that David is a skilled violinist. So, Jane wants to _____ David to be more confident. In this situation, what would Jane most likely say to David?

Jane: (I'm sure you can play the solo part beautifully.)

16~17

M: Good afternoon, students. Today we are going to talk about different national flags. There are some colors _____ _____ in national flags. The most common color is red, which _____ _____ about 30 percent of all colors used in national flags. Usually red means life, courage, and _____. For example, the red stripes of the United State's national flag symbolize the _____ _____ _____.

The next is blue, with about a 20 percent share. The color often symbolizes the _____ _____ of water or sky. For example, the blue in Greece's national flag means the seas surrounding the country. The next two most common colors are white and green. In some countries' flags, white means _____ _____ _____, such as in the United Kingdom's flag. Green is often related to nature, such as _____ _____ _____. Can you guess what the green in Brazil's national flag means? Of course, it's the Amazon Rainforest. Now, let's look at the shapes of national flags.

19

🙂 녹음을 듣고, 빈칸에 알맞은 말을 쓰시기 바랍니다. 빈칸은 문제풀이에 핵심이 되는 키워드와 헷갈리기 쉬운 발음에 표시되어 있으니 이 점에 유의하여 듣기 바랍니다.

01

M: Hello, I'm Jason Adams. I'll be teaching chemistry this semester. It's very nice to meet you all. Before we start, let me tell you the most important things to remember _____ _____ _____ your reports. You should use brief sentences to make them clear. If your reports are _____ _____ _____ and complex sentences, they'll be hard to understand. Also, be careful not to use _____ _____ without any explanations. You may think it makes your reports look professional, but the readers may be confused and you won't be able to _____ _____ _____ of your writing. You need to keep these things in mind when you write your reports.

02

W: Hey, Michael. What happened? You look tired.

M: Hi, Claire. I can't sleep well. My daughter has been _____ _____ the past few nights.

W: It must be hard. What do you think is wrong?

M: My wife and I have been trying to get her to sleep alone in her room.

W: Ah, she might feel afraid because she's not used to sleeping alone yet. Why don't you give her _____ _____ when she sleeps?

M: You mean, like blankets or stuffed animals?

W: Exactly! My son had the same problem for a while, but after sleeping with his favorite toy robot, he's come to sleep well on his own.

M: So, do you think it really helped him _____ _____ _____ and sleep better?

W: I believe so. I've heard that young children's favorite items generally give them _____ comfort.

M: Okay, I'll give it a try. Thanks for your advice.

03

M: Sally, welcome to my studio. It's good to see you.

W: Thanks for inviting me, Chris.

M: I hear _____ _____ _____ _____ these days. I like it a lot.

W: Oh, do you? I think it's been popular since it was used in a TV _____.

M: You must be thrilled. Did you listen to the file I sent you?

W: Yes, I did. And I love it. How did you _____ _____ _____ such a sweet and beautiful melody?

M: While taking a walk along the beach, I was so inspired by the sound of the waves.

W: That explains why the melody sounds very refreshing.

M: I thought of you as soon as I wrote it. I think it will go very well with your voice.

W: I like the songs _____ _____ so I've always wanted to sing one of your songs.

M: I'm flattered. Shall we get started?

04

W: Charles, come and look at this photo. My mom took it last weekend.

M: Oh, you went to that park that I really want to visit. The _____ _____ here says Riverside Park.

W: Right. I went there on a picnic with my family. The weather was terrific.

M: That's wonderful! Why are those two balloons _____ _____ the tree?

W: They're in celebration of the second anniversary of the park's opening.

M: How pretty! And you're holding a book.

W: Yes. It's the book that you gave me as a present on my birthday. That book was so interesting.

M: I'm so glad to hear that. Actually, I was worried about whether you would like it.

W: It was a great choice! And look at this _____ _____. The park gave it out for free as a second anniversary souvenir.

M: Cool. By the way, I wonder why that _____ _____ _____ _____ _____.

W: My brother brought it to play soccer.

M: I see. You must've had a good time on the picnic.

05

[Telephone rings.]

M: Hello, this is Sky Print Shop.

W: Hi, this is Lisa Morris. I'm a teacher from Evergreen High School. Could I speak with the manager, Mr. White?

M: Speaking. How may I help you?

W: Well, I checked the _____ _____ of our club activity book and I'd like to change it a bit. I'm afraid it seems too simple.

M: I see. How about adding student pictures or the school mascot?

W: Sounds good. I think putting the school mascot on the cover will make it look better.

M: No problem. Could you send me the image later? Then _____ _____ _____.

W: Okay. Also, I emailed the introduction page of the book to you this morning. Did you get a chance to check it out?

M: Yes, I did. It looks pretty good. Are there any other _____ _____ _____ to make?

W: No, that's all. Do you think I can get the books by next week?

M: Of course. If you _____ _____ _____ _____ of the mascot, we can add it to the cover, and then start printing right away.

W: I'll send it to you now. Thank you!

06

W: Good afternoon, sir. May I help you?

M: Yes, please. I'm looking for swimming goggles for my kids.

W: We have several kinds. Take a look at this display.

M: All right, thank you. *[Pause]* Oh, how much are these? These would be perfect for my children.

W: They're 50 dollars each. They're anti-fog, which _____ _____ _____ for fast swimming.

M: I see. They're a little bit expensive, though.

W: In that case, there are cheaper ones with basically the same function. How about these? They cost _____ dollars each.

M: Sounds better. I'll buy two pairs of these. I also need a swimming cap for myself.

W: I recommend this new cap. It _____

_____ _____ and costs only 20

dollars.

M: Okay. Then I'll buy two pairs of swimming

goggles and one swimming cap.

W: We also have brand-new swimsuits in our store.

Are you interested?

M: No, thanks. These are enough.

W: Sounds good. We have a promotion this

week, so you can get a 10% _____

_____ the total amount.

M: That's great. Here's my credit card.

07

M: Stella, what are you doing?

W: Well, I need to _____ _____

_____ my apartment, so I'm searching

for a moving company.

M: Why? Is your contract almost over?

W: Not yet. I've been here for just five months, and I

still have seven months left.

M: Oh, did you have some problem with your

neighbors?

W: Not at all. They are all kind and I _____

_____ _____ them.

M: I heard you got a new job recently. Is it far from

here?

W: No, it's within five minutes' walking distance.

Actually, the _____ _____

_____ my father is sick.

M: Oh, I'm sorry to hear that.

W: It would be hard for my mother to take care

of him alone, so I decided to move in with

my parents to _____ _____

_____ my father.

M: I hope your father gets better soon.

W: Thank you for your concern.

08

W: Hi, Paul. What's new?

M: Not much. I'm looking at the poster for the

Blueway Spelling Bee Competition.

W: The spelling bee competition? What's that?

M: It's a competition where participants are asked

to spell various words. The Blueway Library

_____ _____ every year.

W: That sounds interesting! Let me have a look.

Oh, it says any Blueway Library member can

_____ _____.

M: Yeah. I'm planning to enter the competition

because I want to test my spelling skills. Do you

want to join, too?

W: Sure, why not? How do we sign up for the

contest?

M: We should email the _____

_____ Thursday. Here's the email

address on the bottom.

W: Got it! Oh, they are _____

_____ 50 people.

M: Then we should hurry!

09

W: Hello, I'm Grace, a manager of Dream Marine

Museum. This year, our museum has a

special program, called Ocean World. The

_____ of the program is deep-sea

exploration. Through this program, children

will become interested in the plants and fish

_____ _____ in the ocean.

It runs from 10 a.m. to 6 p.m. this Saturday,

October 28th. This event will be held on the

first floor. You can watch videos of deep-sea

exploration on a _____ _____

in the central hall. There will be a photo booth

where you can take selfies wearing various

masks of ocean creatures. In addition, you

can make fish-shaped cookies with a chef.

Anyone can participate in Ocean World for free
_____ _____ _____
_____ a reservation. I hope to see you
all there.

10

W: Honey, here's a flyer about smart security
  cameras. They're on sale!
M: Cool! I've been thinking about buying one
  to protect our house before we're away on
  vacation.
W: Same here. Which one do you want to get?
M: Hmm... I don't think we can spend more than
  $_____ on a security camera.
W: You're right. We've already spent a lot for our
  vacation.
M: There are two types of connectivity options,
  wired and wireless.
W: I prefer wireless so that we can _____
  _____ _____ we want.
M: Good idea. We need one that can be installed
  indoors and _____ _____
  _____.
W: I agree. Now we have two options left. Well... The
  one with sound detection looks attractive to me.
M: I heard that sound detection is _____
  _____ _____ _____
  motion detection.
W: Really? Then, we should definitely get one with
  motion detection.
M: Okay. Let's buy this one.

11

M: Jenny, thanks for helping me prepare my speech
  for the graduation ceremony.
W: There was not much to help. You were already
  well-prepared.

M: I'm still worried. Do you really think people will
  _____ _____ _____
  _____ to say?
W: (Definitely! I'm sure your message will be clearly
  delivered.)

12

W: Steve, do you know where my _____
  are? I need them right now but can't find them
  anywhere.
M: I saw Dad taking them this morning for his
  business trip.
W: Oh, no! That means I _____
  _____ _____ _____
  this Saturday!
M: (Don't worry. You can use mine if you want.)

13

M: Hello, is there anything I can do for you?
W: My umbrella is _____. I thought I might
  have left it in the restroom, but when I checked,
  it wasn't there.
M: Which restroom did you use?
W: The one on the third floor.
M: What does your umbrella look like? Could you
  _____ it?
W: It's yellow and it has a wooden handle. There's a
  big picture of a flower on it.
M: Okay, I'll check if it's in the _____
  _____ _____ box right now...
  [Pause] Oh! We have an umbrella that looks like
  yours. Is this it?
W: Wow, that's mine!
M: Wait. Here's a note that says a _____
  _____ _____ and brought it to
  us.
W: (How kind of her! I was worried that I wouldn't
  find it.)

14

W: Fred, I got the blueberry juice we ordered.

M: Thanks, Kathy. Oh, it has a paper straw. Don't they have a plastic one?

W: What's wrong with a paper straw?

M: It can get _____ _____ _____ _____ while drinking. So I prefer a plastic straw.

W: But plastic straws can harm the environment.

M: Protecting the environment is all good, but my drink _____ _____ with paper straws.

W: If so, there are other types of straws to enjoy your drink that _____ less harm to the environment.

M: I didn't know there were other kinds. Can you name some of them?

W: Have you heard of a silicone straw?

M: No, I haven't. It sounds interesting.

W: There are also straws made of glass or metal. They're _____ _____ _____ _____ the taste of your drink.

M: (Thanks for letting me know. I should try using them.)

15

M: Nick and Annie are partners for an art project. They are supposed to make a presentation on the life of Vincent van Gogh. However, while researching and working on their project, they realized that some of the content they found was _____. For example, there was a disagreement about when exactly Van Gogh started painting. Nick _____ his information from the books in the library, while Annie collected hers from the Internet. Nick and Annie are not sure _____ _____ _____ _____. Nick wants their presentation to be as precise as possible, so he thinks that they should _____ _____ _____ for help with deciding which source is more reliable. In this situation, what would Nick most likely say to Annie?

Nick: (We'd better ask our professor about which source to trust.)

16~17

W: Welcome back to Tips for Entrepreneurs. Last time, we talked about this year's trendy colors. Now let's talk about how to use them in _____ _____ _____ _____. Understanding the art of using colors can help create more effective and _____ designs. For example, using red for important elements will make it hard to ignore them. It's _____ _____ that so many fast food logos are red. Orange communicates creativity and youth, which is perfect for a _____ brand. If you're trying to get your customers excited about something, go for orange. Green, on the other hand, can communicate lots of different ideas, like luck, _____, and freshness. Green is also a common choice to communicate environmentalism and sustainability, as well as _____ _____ _____. Lastly, for a cool and calm feel, choose blue. Brands that supply ice or cooling solutions can communicate this _____ _____ through blue logos. So, to design your brand effectively, use colors wisely!

20 2023년 9월 학력평가
딕테이션

MP3

25RL2_A20

🙂 녹음을 듣고, 빈칸에 알맞은 말을 쓰시기 바랍니다. 빈칸은 문제풀이에 핵심이 되는 키워드와 헷갈리기 쉬운 발음에 표시되어 있으니 이 점에 유의하여 듣기 바랍니다.

01

M: Good afternoon. I'm Tom Anderson, the student council president. I'm glad to announce that the student council is _____ _____ for our campus tour event. Next Saturday, our school will be welcoming middle schoolers who are _____ _____ _____ our school. Student volunteers will show the middle schoolers around our campus, and _____ _____ _____ useful information about our school's extracurricular activities and traditions. To sign up to volunteer, please visit our school website. _____ _____ will be a great help to those who wish to attend our school.

02

W: David, the screen on your cell phone looks _____. What happened?

M: I accidentally dropped it on the bathroom floor last week.

W: That's too bad, but why haven't you fixed it yet?

M: It's working perfectly fine, so I don't think I need to fix it.

W: Well, I think it's better to get a phone _____ _____ when the screen is cracked.

M: I don't think a small crack like this is a big deal.

W: It may look okay, but a single crack can _____ _____ _____ screen over time.

M: Really? I didn't know that.

W: Also, tiny pieces of glass from the cracked screen could cut your face or your fingers.

M: Hmm…. That could be dangerous.

W: Exactly. That's why you should fix a cracked phone screen as soon as possible.

M: You're right. I'll _____ _____ today.

03

[Phone rings.]

W: Hello.

M: Hello. Can I speak to Ms. Norton?

W: This is she.

M: Hi, this is Mark Kelly from Polaris Studio. I heard you were a _____ _____ on the movie Space Dynasty.

W: Yes, I helped the writers with the script.

M: I thought the script was well written and had many _____ _____ _____ _____ science.

W: Thank you. It was a lot of fun.

M: I'm actually writing a script for a science fiction movie right now, and I was wondering if you could help me with your _____.

W: Okay. What's the movie about?

M: It's about natural disasters caused by global warming. I need advice from science experts like you to make it more realistic.

W: I'd be interested. I've done a lot of scientific research on global warming in my lab. My _____ _____ _____ _____ for you.

M: Fantastic! I'll send you my script. Thank you so much.

04

M: Hello, Ms. Clark. How's it going with _____ your classroom?

W: Good morning, Mr. Cooper. It's almost done. Do you want to see a picture of what it looks like?

M: Sure. [Pause] Oh, I see a _____ _____ on the wall. It looks nice.

W: Yes. I replaced the old clock with a new one.

M: I also like the bookcase under the window.

W: I put it there to make it easier for students to read books. How do you like the stripe-patterned rug?

M: I like it. It goes well with the classroom. By the way,

what are the _____ _____ on the table for?

W: I'll put some classroom supplies in them. I also put a _____ _____ in the corner.

M: Great idea! I think your students will really like the new classroom.

W: Thank you.

05

M: Mom, I'm home.

W: Hi, Brian. How was your violin lesson?

M: It was fun. I think my violin skills _____ _____ a lot.

W: Good! By the way, did you see the pile of clothes in the living room?

M: Yeah. I wore those clothes when I was a little kid. Are you going to _____ _____ _____?

W: No. I'm going to give them to charity today.

M: Oh, so you want to donate the clothes?

W: Yes. They're all _____ _____ _____ and they've been dry-cleaned.

M: That's great. Is there anything I can help you with?

W: Well, I need some boxes to put the clothes in.

M: No worries. I'll _____ _____ from the garage.

W: Thanks, but be careful. The lights in the garage aren't working.

M: I got it, Mom. I'll be right back.

06

M: Welcome to Platinum Hillside Resort. How can I help you?

W: Hi. I want to reserve an outdoor barbecue table for tonight.

M: Okay, right now we have _____ _____ _____ _____ people and large tables for eight people available.

W: I'd like to reserve two small tables.

M: Sure, it's $_____ per table. Do you also want to try our salad bar?

W: How much is it?

M: It's $30 per table.

W: No, thanks. That _____ _____ _____. I'll just reserve the two tables.

M: Okay. Are you currently a guest at our resort? If you are, you can get a 10% discount.

W: Yes, I'm staying in room 609. My name is May Jones.

M: [Typing sound] Okay, Ms. Jones. _____ _____ you're a guest. How would you like to pay for your tables?

W: I'll pay by credit card.

07

W: Hey, Mike. How was dinner at the French restaurant downtown last weekend? I heard it was _____ _____.

M: Well, I went there, but I didn't get to eat anything.

W: Why? Were there too many people _____ _____ _____?

M: Not really. There were tables available.

W: Did you bring your dog and the restaurant said no?

M: No, I checked their website and it said I could _____ _____ my dog at an outdoor table.

W: Okay, so then why couldn't you eat anything?

M: The restaurant said they _____ _____ _____ _____, so I left.

W: Oh, you must have been disappointed. How about we go there for lunch this Saturday?

M: Sounds great! They don't take reservations on weekends, so we should get there early.

W: Good idea. I look forward to it.

08

M: Honey, check out this advertisement.

W: Okay, let me see. [Pause] Oh, Home Organization Class? That sounds interesting.

M: Yeah, it does. How about we take the class together? We can learn some tips for organizing and cleaning our house.

W: Great idea. Look, the class _____ _____ _____ _____ the community center. It's just a ten-minute walk from here.

M: Right. And it's on Saturday, September 30th, from 2 p.m. to 6 p.m. Is that okay with you?

W: Yes, my schedule is free on that day. _____ _____ is the class?

M: It's $20 per person.

W: That's reasonable. Is there anything we _____ _____ _____ for the class?

M: Yes. We have to bring some pictures of our living room and other rooms in our house.

W: Okay. I'll do that.

M: Great. Let's _____ _____ for the class.

09

W: Hello, viewers. The 2023 Board Game Design Contest is an annual event for designing board games. It's open to board game fans _____ _____ _____ around the world. The contest is split into two rounds. In round one, contestants must _____ a 2-minute video introducing their games. In round two, contestants must hand in a document that explains how to play their game. During round two, contestants get the chance to _____ _____ _____ game designers who will help each contestant with establishing the rules for their game. The final winner of the contest receives $1,000, plus a chance to release his or her game. _____ _____ on Friday, September 15th. Show us your skills as a game designer!

10

W: Sean, look what I found for mom for her birthday.

M: Oh, an electric mug warmer set? What is it?

W: It's a set that includes a mug and a warmer, and the warmer _____ _____ _____.

M: Cool! How much can we spend on this?

W: Well, we didn't buy a cake yet, so _____ _____ _____ spend more than

$50.

M: I see. The mugs come in three different materials. Which one would she like?

W: She already has glass mugs, so let's choose from the other materials.

M: Good idea. How about the _____ of the mug?

W: I think less than 500ml will be appropriate.

M: Yeah, that makes sense. Do you think it's better to buy a set with the LED _____?

W: Yes. I think it's better because it allows you to check the temperature.

M: I like it, too. Let's order this one.

11

M: Clara, I finished designing the poster for our school's musical auditions. Have a look.

W: Wow, it looks fantastic! And _____ _____ _____ _____ a QR code on it for registration? It'll make it easier for students to sign up.

M: Great idea, but I don't know _____ _____ _____ QR codes. Could you help me with that?

W: (Sure. I'll create one and send it to you.)

12

W: Harry, have you decided what school club you will join?

M: Not yet. I'm thinking of joining _____ the poetry club or the history club.

W: I've heard the history club is already full, so they're _____ _____ any more new members.

M: (Then, I'll apply for the poetry club.)

13

W: Dad, did you throw away all the empty plastic bottles?

M: Yes. Why?

W: I need plastic bottle caps for our school's _____ _____ _____.

M: Interesting. So what are you doing with the caps?

W: We'll send them to an upcycling company, and they make _____ like chairs and hairpins from the caps.

M: That's cool.

W: Yeah, and the teacher said if we bring in more than 20 bottle caps, she'll give us a bamboo toothbrush as a prize.

M: Great. How many bottle caps _____ _____ _____ so far?

W: I've collected only eight bottle caps. I need some more.

M: Hmm, I threw the plastic bottles away just an hour ago, so they should be in the _____ _____.

W: (Okay. I'll go there to check if I can find more caps.)

14

[Cell phone rings.]

W: Hi, honey. What's up?

M: Hey, sweetheart! I have good news.

W: What is it?

M: I'm at the mall, and I just saw the hiking shoes you _____ _____ _____ _____.

W: Really? We didn't buy them the other day because they were too expensive.

M: Yeah, but they're 50% off now. Do you want me to buy you _____ _____?

W: Yes, that'd be lovely.

M: You wear a size six for your shoes, right?

W: Yeah, but for hiking shoes, I usually wear a size seven.

M: Hmm.... Wouldn't they be too big for your feet?

W: No, they're fine. My feet _____ _____ _____ while hiking, so I prefer wearing hiking shoes that aren't too tight.

M: Oh, I see.

W: Plus, I usually wear _____ _____ when hiking, so buying a size six wouldn't work for me.

M: (I got it. I'll buy a size seven for your hiking shoes.)

15

M: Kate and Claire are new members of the school orchestra. _____ _____ with the orchestra for the first time next month. Today, they go to a dress shop together and look for a formal dress to wear for their concert. They look around the shop and try on the dresses they like. However, _____ _____ _____ _____ about the prices, they find the dresses are too expensive for their budget. At this moment, Kate realizes that it'd be better to _____ the dresses for their concert at a rental shop. So, Kate wants to suggest to Claire that they _____ _____ _____ _____ spend a lot of money on buying new dresses. In this situation, what would Kate most likely say to Claire?

Kate: (How about renting dresses instead of buying new ones?)

16~17

W: Hello, students. Weddings are held all over the world, but the _____ _____ _____ _____ greatly. Today, we'll learn about unique wedding customs in different countries. In _____, for example, newlyweds cut a log in half using a large saw. By cutting the log together, the couple shows their _____ _____ _____ _____ difficulties in their marriage. Next, in Cuba, wedding guests have to pay to dance with the bride. The money is then used to _____ _____ _____ _____. Thirdly, it's traditional to have a tea ceremony at weddings in China. The couple serves tea to both sides of their families to show their respect and gratitude. Lastly, in _____, guests hold stones during the wedding ceremony. When it's over, they place the stones in a decorated bowl, and it's given to the couple _____ _____ _____ of the support from their family and friends. Now, let's watch a video of these wedding customs.

21

2023년 11월 학력평가
딕테이션

MP3

2SBL2_A21

녹음을 듣고, 빈칸에 알맞은 말을 쓰시기 바랍니다. 빈칸은 문제풀이에 핵심이 되는 키워드와 헷갈리기 쉬운 발음에 표시되어 있으니 이 점에 유의하여 듣기 바랍니다.

01

M: Hello, *City Talk Radio* listeners! This is Tony Moore. As some of you know, the International Motor Show is coming to our city this weekend. I'm here to inform you that the city will

_____ _____ _____

parking lot for visitors' convenience. It's because a huge crowd is _____ _____ visit the motor show. The temporary parking lot is a five-minute walk from the main entrance. Also, parking is free for all visitors. Once again, I announce that a temporary parking lot will be

_____ _____ _____

_____ for visitors. You can enjoy the motor show without parking problems. I'll be back after a short _____ _____. Stay tuned!

02

W: Honey, since you're a fruit lover, I bought some fruits.

M: Wow, they look so fresh and delicious.

W: Yes. Let's have some now.

M: Oh, is it okay to have fruits before lunch?

W: Of course. Actually, _____ _____

_____ a meal can have beneficial effects on your health.

M: What kinds of benefits are you talking about?

W: For example, eating fruits before a meal can

_____ _____ _____

_____ because it helps you feel full.

M: Hmm... That makes sense.

W: Also, nutrients are _____ _____

when fruits are eaten before a meal.

M: I see. I didn't know that when we eat fruit has so much to do with our health.

W: Exactly. Having fruits before a meal can

_____ your health.

M: Okay. Then I'll wash them for us.

03

M: Hello, everyone. Welcome to our environmental lecture, *Love Our Planet*. You've all heard that "Plastic is bad for the environment!," but do you actually know how bad it is? Plastic items take 1,000 years to _____ in landfills. Plus, only a small percentage of plastic items are actually recycled. To overcome the plastic

_____ _____, you can start by taking personal action. As a first step, you ought to _____ _____ _____ tumbler. It helps you work towards reducing plastic waste and make your carbon footprint smaller. Why don't you carry a tumbler to

_____ _____ _____

plastic waste? Let's act now for our planet.

04

W: Hi, Daniel. What are you looking at on your phone?

M: Hello, Jenny. It's a picture I took last Christmas Eve.

W: That's almost a year ago. Oh, I like the _____ _____ _____ of your house. You know, Santa Claus comes in through that.

M: Right. Look at the star-shaped light at the top of the tree. I hung it myself.

W: Great. There's a snowman wearing a _____ _____ .

M: I made him with my younger sisters. What do you think about the ribbon on the door?

W: I think it looks lovely and welcoming.

M: Yes. It really suits the Christmas mood.

W: What are the _____ _____ under the table?

M: They're Christmas presents for my parents. My sisters and I prepared them together.

W: Your parents _____ _____ _____ _____ . Looks like you had a great time.

05

W: Hi, Mr. Williams. How are you doing with making our school promotion video?

M: Hello, Ms. Watson. I've been working on it for two weeks, and I've almost finished.

W: The video will provide _____ _____ _____ _____ who are interested in our school.

M: I hope so. Do you want to watch it?

W: Of course. [Pause] Oh, you included _____ with teachers in the video.

M: Yes. Many teachers participated.

W: That's so kind of them. You know every teacher is busy.

M: Right. I also filmed the science lab.

W: Great! Did you _____ _____ _____ into the video yourself? They're eye-catching.

M: Thank you for mentioning that. I've also been thinking about _____ _____ . Can you choose some?

W: Sure. I'll do that for you. As you know, I have a big music collection.

M: Thank you. That'd be really helpful.

06

W: Welcome to the National Costume Museum. How may I help you?

M: Hi. I'd like to buy admission tickets.

W: They're $_____ _____ _____ and $10 for children under the age of 12.

M: My daughter is 8 years old now, so I'll take two adult tickets and one child ticket, please.

W: Okay. Do you want to see the special exhibition?

M: Oh, special exhibition? What's that about?

W: It's about the _____ _____ from the British royal family. It's open this month only.

M: That sounds interesting. How much is it?

W: It's originally $10 per person. But if you buy an admission ticket, you'll get a 50% _____ _____ the ticket for the special exhibition.

M: Great. Then, I'll get three.

W: So, _____ _____ _____ . Two adults and one child admission tickets. Plus, three special exhibition tickets, right?

M: Yes. Here's my credit card.

07

[Cell phone rings.]

W: Hello, Scott.

M: Hi, Reese. I didn't see you at the guitar club meeting yesterday.

W: I really wanted to go, but I couldn't.

M: _____ _____ _____ _____ with your guitar again?

W: Not at all. My guitar works fine now.

M: Oh, were you working late last night?

W: No. My team _____ the project, so I left the office on time.

M: Is that so? Then why couldn't you come to the club meeting?

W: I've been feeling _____ _____ _____ _____ when I play the guitar.

M: Oh, no. Maybe you should stop practicing for a while.

W: Yeah, but I'm concerned because I can't learn any new techniques.

M: Don't worry. I can _____ _____ _____ if you want.

W: Thanks a lot.

08

M: Sandra, what are you looking at?

W: Dad, I'm looking at the 2023 Laser Light Show website.

M: Oh, it's been a yearly event for the past seven years. What's the _____ of this year?

W: It's 'Fly to the Sky.' Special effects will make the heavens glow.

M: It sounds spectacular. When is the show?

W: It _____ _____ December 22nd to 26th. And my final exams will be over by then.

M: Perfect! _____ _____ _____ _____ at Central Park again?

W: Yes. The park isn't far from home. We can walk to the park.

M: Right. Hmm, do you see how we can book tickets?

W: [Pause] The website says _____ _____ _____ _____ online only.

M: Okay. Let's book tickets now.

09

W: Welcome, shoppers. We're pleased to be hosting the Highville Fashion Pop-up Stores next week. They'll run for three days starting on December 29th. These limited-time pop-up stores will be open on the fifth floor and _____ _____ 10 different brands. You can purchase fashion items including _____ _____ _____ _____ to keep you warm during the winter. The pop-up stores will offer a 60 percent discount _____ _____ fashion items. Also, they'll give away free coffee coupons to all shoppers who make a purchase. The coupon can be used at the cafe on the second floor in the mall. Don't miss this great chance to _____ _____ your style!

10

W: Welcome to Andy's Hiking Equipment Store. What can I do for you?

M: Hi. I'm looking for hiking sticks.

W: These are the five models we have in stock. What's your budget?

M: I'd like to _____ _____ _____ $50.

W: Okay. We have three different materials. Do you have any preference?

M: Well, I _____ _____ _____. It doesn't look strong.

W: I see.

M: And I prefer foldable sticks because they're easier to carry around.

W: Sure. Besides they'll _____ _____ _____ _____ in your backpack. Then there are two options left. Which do you like?

M: I like those _____ ones. They look cool.

W: I agree. This model is the best for you.

M: Right. I'll buy them now.

11

W: Hi, Mr. Smith, how many students signed up for the Green Recipe Contest?

M: Oh, Ms. White, almost 80 students signed up. So I have to _____ _____ _____ for the contest.

W: I think the auditorium has more space. Why don't you _____ that?

M: (Good idea. I'll go check if it's available.)

12

M: Hi, Amy. Have you heard that the central library started their e-book _____ service?

W: Really? I need to borrow some books for my report. Can I try it now?

M: Sure. You can borrow e-books _____ _____ _____ _____.

W: (Great! I'm going to download and try it out.)

13

M: Honey, what are you doing?

W: I'm _____ _____ _____ _____. Look at these clothes.

M: Many of them seem too small for her. Are you going to throw them away?

W: No. I don't want to because some of them still look brand new.

M: You're right. My co-worker says that lately many people buy and sell _____ _____ by using an online platform.

W: Really? We should try that.

M: I think so, too. Some people might want to _____ _____ _____.

W: I agree. Where do we start?

M: We need to take pictures of the clothes we want to sell and then post them on the platform.

W: Then I'm going to take pictures. But I don't know how to _____ _____ _____ the website. Could you do that?

M: (Of course. I'll post them after you're done.)

14

W: Hi, Kevin. How's the preparation going for your concert next week?

M: Oh, Lisa. You haven't heard the news yet. My band ＿＿＿＿＿ ＿＿＿＿＿ ＿＿＿＿＿ the concert until next month.

W: What happened? Is it because of the concert hall? You said the facilities of the hall aren't so good.

M: That's not it. We found a better one.

W: That's good to hear. Do you need ＿＿＿＿＿ ＿＿＿＿＿ ＿＿＿＿＿ ＿＿＿＿＿ with your band?

M: Not really. We've practiced a lot.

W: Then why did you put off the concert? You know a lot of fans are looking forward to it.

M: Of course I do. The problem is the ＿＿＿＿＿ ＿＿＿＿＿ got a bad cold.

W: How awful! Did she lose her voice?

M: Yes. The doctor said she has to ＿＿＿＿＿ ＿＿＿＿＿ for two weeks until she gets better.

W: (Sorry to hear that. I hope she gets well soon.)

15

M: Eric is a high school student. He's been studying hard for the exams next week. Every day he drinks caffeinated beverages ＿＿＿＿＿ ＿＿＿＿＿ water because he thinks they can help increase his concentration. However, caffeinated drinks ＿＿＿＿＿ ＿＿＿＿＿ his sleep at night. One day, he finds that he can't stay awake during class. Eric is worried about it and he decides to ask his teacher, Ms. Parker, for advice. Ms. Parker thinks caffeinated beverages have more disadvantages than advantages. She recalls an article about how drinking water can ＿＿＿＿＿ concentration. It says water carries nutrients to the brain to keep it healthy. So Ms. Parker wants to advise Eric to ＿＿＿＿＿ ＿＿＿＿＿ ＿＿＿＿＿ to enhance his ability to focus. In this situation, what would Ms. Parker most likely say to Eric?

Ms. Parker: (You'd better drink more water to improve concentration.)

16~17

W: Good afternoon, students. Previously, we learned about interesting facilities in airports. Today, we'll talk about city airports ＿＿＿＿＿ ＿＿＿＿＿ ＿＿＿＿＿ figures. First, in February of 1942 during the Second World War, Edward O'Hare was flying a fighter plane. He ＿＿＿＿＿ ＿＿＿＿＿ in the war, and to honor him Chicago renamed an airport after him. Then there's an airport called Jomo Kenyatta Airport in Nairobi. As one of the most important ＿＿＿＿＿ in African history, Jomo Kenyatta played a central role in fighting colonization. Next, Charles de Gaulle Airport is the main airport of Paris, one of the ＿＿＿＿＿ ＿＿＿＿＿ in Europe. It's named after Charles de Gaulle, who was best known as a French army officer and later became the president. Finally, Jorge Newbery Airport ＿＿＿＿＿ ＿＿＿＿＿ the main domestic gateway in Buenos Aires. Jorge Newbery was a great pioneer who made the first ＿＿＿＿＿ ＿＿＿＿＿ the Andes Mountains. Which airport's name interests you the most? Now, I'd like you to think of other examples.

22

녹음을 듣고, 빈칸에 알맞은 말을 쓰기 바랍니다. 빈칸은 문제풀이에 핵심이 되는 키워드와 헷갈리기 쉬운 발음에 표시되어 있으니 이 점에 유의하여 듣기 바랍니다.

01

M: Good morning, students. This is your vice principal, Mr. Gunning. I have an _____ _____ our 'Spring Flower Photo Day' event this afternoon. As you know, we planned to take pictures of beautiful spring flowers as we walk around our neighborhood. I regret to inform you that the event is _____ _____ _____ heavy rain. I understand you've been looking forward to it, but unfortunately it appears we won't be able to get the best photos today. We will _____ the event for a sunny day in the near future. Please understand that this decision was made to _____ that the event will be a success.

02

W: Liam, what's that bunch of paper in your hand?

M: It's a deck of flashcards for _____ new words, but it doesn't work well for me.

W: Really? Why not? I think flashcards are helpful for _____ _____.

M: I thought so, too. But looking at the word on one side of the card and the meaning on the back is too boring.

W: Hmm, how about using them in a more interesting way?

M: A more interesting way to use flashcards? What do you mean?

W: Ask a friend to read the meaning on the back, and you _____ _____ the word as the answer.

M: Oh, you mean like asking and answering questions in a quiz?

W: That's right. By using flashcards for quizzes, you can learn new words _____ _____ _____.

M: I like your idea a lot. I'll give it a try!

03

M: Hello, everyone. I'm Charlie Goodman, your speaker today. I'll be discussing the most effective way to _____ _____ _____ room. Let's start by reflecting on the items in your room. Do you really _____ _____ every day? Probably not. The most important thing to do to keep a clean room is to get rid of things you no longer need. Don't keep your room _____ _____ _____ _____ for more than six months. If you haven't used an item in six months, it likely means you won't use it again! If you _____ unnecessary items, you can keep your room nice and neat.

04

W: I've just finished setting up my booth to sell used items. How does it look?

M: Wow! Everything looks nice, especially the _____ _____ under the roof. People can see it well.

W: I think so, too. I also hope people like this striped dress in the corner.

M: I bet they will. What about the _____ _____ here? Is it a used one, too?

W: Yes. To make it look better, I put some flowers in it.

M: They really catch the eye. Also, the _____ _____ _____ _____ look almost new.

W: I haven't worn them much because they are a bit small for me. So I've decided to sell them. The _____ beside the table is almost new, too.

M: Oh, I like it the most. I hope you can sell everything you prepared!

05

W: We're almost done with our report on climate change. Why don't we check it together to see if everything is okay?

M: That's a good idea. Are you sure we _____ _____ _____ we made?

W: Yes, they are all there in the report. They clearly show the causes of climate change that we've researched.

M: Good to hear that. How about the pictures? We've chosen the five best pictures.

W: They look very _____. What do you think about the part discussing the students' awareness? Many of our friends participated in our survey.

M: The survey _____ _____ that many students know how serious it is. How about the action plans?

W: We have two action plans here, but I think we need more. Could you _____ _____ _____ _____ from our research?

M: Sure. I'll send the data this afternoon.

06

W: Honey, how about getting a pizza from Toby's Place for dinner?

M: Sounds great! Let's try the new _____ _____ that I downloaded recently. [Pause] Hmm... How about a potato pizza?

W: I like that idea. How much is one large potato pizza?

M: It's $_____. Oh, we have to order a minimum of $30 for delivery.

W: Then we can _____ _____ _____. How much is a cola?

M: One small can is $2, and a large one is $3.

W: Then let's order two large cans.

M: Great, one large potato pizza and two large cans of cola. Now we can place the order.

W: Is there a delivery fee?

M: Normally we have to pay $5, but it's _____ _____ because of the app promotion. So I'll pay using the app.

W: Thank you. I'm starving. I hope it gets here quickly.

07

M: Hi, Kathy. How was your drama club's performance last week?

W: It was a _____ _____. Everyone liked it.

M: Good to hear that. Then, can I include your performance video in our school promotion video? Did anyone record it?

W: Yes, Mark _____ _____.

M: Great! Could you send me the video file then?

W: Sorry, I can't send it to you now.

M: Why not? Is it because you don't have the video file?

W: No, that's not it. Mark sent me the file yesterday.

M: Then, you don't _____ _____ _____ _____ the promotion video?

W: I'm okay with it. The problem is, without the club members' _____, I cannot send the file to anyone outside the club.

M: Oh, I see. Can you ask your club members about it?

W: Sure. Once they say it's fine, I'll let you know.

08

[Telephone rings.]

W: Green Forest camping site. How can I help you?

M: Hi, this is Daniel Baker, a teacher from Simon High School. I'm organizing a class camping trip _____ _____ _____. Do you have a camping site available?

W: Certainly, when do you plan on camping?

M: From April 13th to 14th.

W: Let me see. *[Typing]* We have _____ _____ for your students on that day. Do you want to reserve them now?

M: Yes, please. Do you provide a _____ _____ _____ as well?

W: Absolutely. We offer tents that are big enough for six people. We also have sleeping bags for rent.

M: Sounds good. I'll rent five tents and 25 sleeping bags.

W: Alright, the _____ _____ would be $90. You can pay it in advance or onsite.

M: I'll pay onsite. Thanks, and see you then.

09

W: Hello, listeners! Let's dive into the world of _____ _____ at the 2024 AI Expo. It will be held on May 27th and 28th at the city convention center. This year's theme is the use of AI in schools. From language learning to _____ _____, AI is widely used in schools. For just $20, you can experience new AI technologies that have been _____ in more than 50 countries. Come and see the future of AI! And here's the best part. You can get a special portrait drawn by AI used in art classes. If you _____ _____ _____ _____ on our website, you will get a 10% discount. Don't miss this chance to have an unforgettable AI experience!

10

W: Dad, I found a website that provides a service to make photo albums. How about creating one with the photos from our winter holiday?

M: Great! Let me see. *[Pause]* Oh, it says all we need to do is choose a few options and upload our photos.

W: Right. First, let's choose the _____ _____.

M: Umm... Leather might be too heavy.

W: You're right. Let's choose _____ _____ _____ _____.

M: Okay. For the number of pages, is 40 too many?

W: Yes. Let's just _____ _____ _____ or 30 pages. What color would be good for the cover?

M: I want it to reflect our winter holiday. How about white?

W: Perfect. That leaves us with two options.

M: Then, let's choose the _____ one.

W: Sounds great. I'll choose the best pictures and upload them.

11

W: How was your weekend? Did you do anything special?

M: Yes, my older brother and I visited my grandparents who _____ _____ a small island. We had a great time doing lots of outdoor activities together.

W: That sounds lovely! What activity did you _____ _____ _____ there?

M: (Fishing on the boat was the best for me.)

12

M: Hey, Jessica. Have you bought a birthday present for Olivia yet? Her birthday is coming up soon.

W: Oh, not yet. I'm _____ to think of something good for her. What do you think she'll like?

M: I heard her favorite writer _____ _____ _____ _____ recently. How about buying the book as her birthday present?

W: (Good idea. I'll go to the bookstore tomorrow.)

13

M: Hello, welcome to Glow Cosmetics Shop. How can I help you?

W: Hi, I'm looking for sunscreen.

M: Certainly. Is it for you, or someone else?

W: It's for my husband. He asked me to buy one for him.

M: Okay, does your husband _____ _____ _____ _____, playing sports, or working outside?

W: No, not really. He works in an office and usually stays at home after work.

M: In that case, he _____ _____ _____ one with strong sun protection. A mild one is probably best for him.

W: Okay. I'll go with that.

M: We have _____ _____ of sunscreen, spray and cream type. Which one would he prefer?

W: I'm not sure but I guess he is _____ _____ cream type.

M: (I see. Then this one is a perfect choice for him.)

14

M: Ms. Williams! Do you have a minute?

W: Sure. What is it?

M: I have to write an essay to get a scholarship, but I don't know what to write about.

W: Maybe you can start by _____ _____ _____ for learning and school life.

M: I already wrote about that, but it doesn't seem good enough.

W: Umm... How about _____ _____ _____ you've worked on?

M: Weakness? Wouldn't that be a bad idea for an essay?

W: Not necessarily. If you describe how you've been trying to _____ _____ it, your story will show your potential.

M: Well, I used to put my work off until the last minute. But by using a planner, I make my schedule on an hourly basis. Now I no longer have any trouble finishing my work on time.

W: That's perfect! That will be a great story to include in your essay for the scholarship.

M: Thank you for your help! That _____ _____ _____ _____ a lot more confident.

W: (Good luck. Show them who you are, and you'll make it.)

15

W: Lucy is the head of her school's student council. She is concerned about _____ _____ _____ proper recycling practices among students. She notices that many students are not aware of the problem. To address this issue, she decides to create posters to _____ _____ _____ of recycling. However, she lacks confidence in her drawing skills. Lucy wants to seek help from her friend James, as he is _____ _____ _____ and passionate about the environment. Lucy thinks collaborating with him will result in effective poster designs. So, she wants to suggest to James that they _____ _____ _____ the recycling posters. In this situation, what would Lucy most likely say to James?

Lucy: (How about making posters with me about recycling?)

16~17

M: Hello, students. Today, I'd like to talk about four great inventions in history. Throughout history, humans have invented things that _____ _____ how we live. One of the most important inventions is the wheel. This simple yet powerful invention _____ _____. The wheel made it possible to travel far and wide, trade goods, and explore new lands. Another important invention is the _____ _____, which enabled books to be printed much faster. This change affected how knowledge and education spread. Next is the _____ _____. It lengthened our days, allowing for nighttime activities and _____ _____ _____ _____ many other modern technologies. The last invention I'd like to mention is the telephone. With the telephone, people could speak to each other instantly regardless of distance. As a result of this transformation, people are _____ _____ _____ _____, in business and social life. These are just a few examples of the many inventions that have changed the course of human history.

23 2024년 6월 학력평가
딕 테 이 션

MP3

2SBL2_A23

😊 녹음을 듣고, 빈칸에 알맞은 말을 쓰시기 바랍니다. 빈칸은 문제풀이에 핵심이 되는 키워드와 헷갈리기 쉬운 발음에 표시되어 있으니 이 점에 유의하여 듣기 바랍니다.

01

W: Good morning, employees of ABC Company. I'm Tina White, a senior manager. I've noticed that many of you have been _____ _____ at work and are under a lot of stress these days. Your well-being is important to us. Therefore, the _____ _____ a counseling program during lunchtime every day starting next week. Special counselors have been invited to help you _____ _____ your stress. I'm confident that our counseling program will help you feel happier at work. If you are interested in this program, please register for a session. I'm sure _____ _____ _____ your time.

02

M: Jane, are you feeling okay?

W: Well, I exercised at the gym and my _____ _____ _____ a bit now, Dad.

M: Did you stretch after exercising?

W: No. I only stretched before.

M: Oh. You _____ _____ stretch after you finish exercising.

W: Really? I thought stretching after working out would put more pressure on my muscles.

M: That's not true. Stretching _____ helps to loosen your tight muscles and reduce injuries.

W: That makes sense. Are there any other benefits?

M: Absolutely. It allows both your body and mind to slow down and helps you _____ _____.

W: All right. I'll give it a try. Thanks for your tip, Dad.

03

W: Good afternoon, listeners! Do you have a hard time _____ _____ your emotions? Have you suddenly gotten really angry but didn't know exactly what made you feel that way? If so, keeping an emotion diary can be a _____ _____ _____ _____ your feelings. In an emotion diary, you write down in detail how you feel in each situation. This will give you an opportunity to understand why you're feeling _____ _____ _____. Writing an emotion diary won't be easy at first, but you'll soon get used to it. After the break, I'll tell you how to keep an emotion diary _____. Stay tuned!

04

M: Hi, Julia. You were amazing in the play yesterday.

W: Thanks, Mason! Here's a picture from the _____ _____ after the play. Do you want to take a look?

M: Sure. [Pause] I see _____ _____ the flowers I gave you.

W: They're so beautiful. Thanks again.

M: My pleasure. What are those two boxes on the floor?

W: I stored some items for the play in them. I needed many items because I played both a prisoner and the queen.

M: You wore that striped T-shirt _____ _____ _____ as a prisoner, right?

W: Yes. Do you remember that crown on the table?

M: I remember! You wore that as the queen. Wasn't it difficult to change your costume during the play?

W: Not really. But it was hard to see my entire outfit in that _____ _____ on the wall.

M: I understand. Anyway, you did a great job.

05

W: Honey, Mr. and Mrs. Brown are visiting today! What time are they supposed to come?

M: At seven o'clock. We _____ _____ _____ for a long time. I'm so excited.

W: Me, too. Let's check if everything is ready.

M: I'm done cooking tonight's dinner.

W: Thanks for doing that. By the way, do we have _____ _____?

M: Yes, I already checked. There are plenty. Should we prepare some wine?

W: No, they told me they're bringing some. Did we _____ _____ _____ _____?

M: Oh, I forgot. I'll go buy a cake.

W: Then I'll go to the airport to _____ _____ _____.

M: Perfect. Thank you.

06

M: Welcome to the World History Museum. How may I help you?

W: Hi, I'd like to _____ _____ _____ tickets. What's the fee for an adult?

M: An adult ticket is $10.

W: What about for seniors?

M: If you look at the price board, people over 65 years of age _____ _____ $8.

W: Okay, then I'll buy one senior ticket, and two adult tickets.

M: May I see an _____ _____ for the senior?

W: Yeah, just a moment. Here it is.

M: Thank you. And today is National Museum Day, so you can get _____% off the total price.

W: Wow, that's amazing!

M: If you need audio guides, they're $5 each.

W: No, thanks. Only the tickets, please. Here's my credit card.

07

W: Hey, Tim. I didn't see you in Professor Jackson's class yesterday.

M: Hi, Kayla. I had a little _____. Did I miss anything important?

W: As you know, Professor Jackson is retiring next week, so the students have _____ _____ _____ him a farewell party.

M: Sounds great. When is it?

W: It's this Saturday at 12 p.m. in Diamond Hall.

M: Umm... This Saturday? I can't go then.

W: Why not? Ah, you must have your club activity.

M: It's not that. I don't have my club activity that day.

W: Then what is it? Do you need to take care of your brother again?

M: No. Actually, I have to _____ _____ _____ _____ that day.

W: Marathon? Oh, right. I know how hard you've been training for it. Good luck!

M: Thanks. Please _____ the professor for me.

08

W: Honey, I picked up a flyer about the Noodle Cooking Contest.

M: What is it about?

W: It's a competition to cook the most creative dish using noodles.

M: Sounds interesting. Who can participate?

W: _____ _____ _____ can participate. Why don't you give it a try?

M: Let me take a look at the flyer. I should check the date first.

W: Here. It's on the _____ _____ _____. Are you free then?

M: Luckily, I don't have any plans that day. Maybe I can apply for the contest.

W: You should! The _____ _____ _____ $500.

M: Great! It says I have to send a recipe by e-mail to _____ _____ the contest. Any suggestions?

W: Well, do you remember the cold noodle salad you made for my birthday? It was so good. You should use that recipe.

M: That's a great idea. I'll do it.

09

M: Hello, I'm Tony Jones, a librarian at Greenfield Library. We're thrilled to tell you about a brand-new service called Library Plus. Our library _____ _____ _____ books straight to your home. Our book delivery service is here to provide more people with the opportunity to read. All library members can use this service free of charge. In order to get started, use the library's _____ _____ on your phone. You can borrow a maximum of five books at a time. Books may be borrowed for two weeks, but you can _____ the borrowing period simply by giving us a call. You _____ _____ _____ to come to the library to return your books. We'll pick up the books at your place. For more information, visit our website. Thank you.

10

W: Hey Adam, Mom's birthday is coming up. Why don't we buy a gold ring for her present?

M: Good idea. I heard that _____ _____ _____ _____ than in stores. So let's buy one online.

W: Okay. Let me see... Rings are pretty expensive. What's our budget?

M: We spent a lot for Mother's Day last month, so I don't think we can spend more than $_____ on her present this time.

W: You're right. Let's decide on a color now. We have three options: white, yellow, and rose.

M: Mom already has several yellow gold rings. We _____ _____ yellow.

W: Good point. Both the white and rose ones look better anyway.

M: That's true. What about a stone for the ring?

W: How about a ruby? It would go well with Mom's red

earrings.

M: I agree. Oh, this one provides a gift-wrapping service.

W: We don't need that. _____ _____ wrap it myself.

M: Okay, then let's order this one.

11

M: Katie, we have to go to the Modern Art Center sometime this month for our art class project. How about this Sunday?

W: I _____ _____ with my mom that day. Let's go another day.

M: But they have a special artist lecture only this Sunday. Would you _____ _____ your plans?

W: (Yeah, just let me make sure it's okay with my mom first.)

12

W: Jake, are we going to drive to the restaurant for the dinner meeting with our client?

M: Yes. It would be best to go by car. The problem is the place doesn't have a _____ _____.

W: I'm sure we can find a place for the car _____ the restaurant.

M: (Right. I'll check if there's any public parking nearby.)

13

M: Hey Linda, what are you reading?

W: I'm reading Troy Morgan's new book. It's really interesting.

M: You _____ _____ _____ _____ his books.

W: I do! Can you take me to his book signing event next week, Dad?

M: Sure, but didn't he already sign a book for you?

W: Yes, but getting a book signed isn't my _____ _____ for going to the event.

M: Then why do you want to go?

W: It's because of his recent interview. He said he _____ _____ in his writing.

M: Why? What happened?

W: He read some negative reviews about his last work.

M: Oh, really? It sounds like he needs to meet some fans like you to _____ his confidence.

W: (I agree. That's why I want to go to the event to see him.)

14

M: Hi, Sandra. You look excited.

W: Yeah, I just got my driver's license.

M: Congratulations! Are you _____ _____ _____ a car?

W: Actually, I've been browsing cars online. But they're more expensive than I expected.

M: Then, what about a used car? My brother happens to be selling his car.

W: I was considering buying a used car, too. Can I see some pictures of his car?

M: Let me check... Here you go. _____ _____ _____ for about three years.

W: Wow, it looks as shiny as new. Also, it's in my favorite color and design.

M: I'm glad you like it. You'll be even more satisfied when you see it in person.

W: I hope so! Do you know how much he's _____ _____ _____?

M: He wants $10,000 for it.

W: That's within my budget. But I'd need to _____ it first.

M: (No problem. We can schedule a time with my brother.)

15

W: Bill and Susan are second-grade high school students and friends. They are preparing for their final exams at the library after school. It used to be easy for Susan to focus on studying. However, these days she's noticing that she _____ _____ _____ at the library

and doesn't know why she cannot maintain her attention. So, she decides to get some advice from Bill, who gets high scores in school. When Bill hears her problem, he's _____ _____ _____ his own experience of losing focus. He recalls that he changed his study _____ and that really helped him get back his concentration. Therefore, he wants to suggest that Susan try studying in a _____ _____ to find her focus again. In this situation, what would Bill most likely say to Susan?

Bill: (How about changing where you study to regain your focus?)

16~17

M: Good evening, viewers. Last time, I introduced some paintings by well-known Western artists. Today, I'd like to talk about _____ that have symbolic meanings in Western art. Let's begin with mirrors. The reflection seen in mirrors can _____ _____ _____ _____ or expose a lie. As you might imagine, a broken mirror generally represents bad luck. Second, candles. They can _____ the passing of time or show a timeline. This is seen in how much of the candles have burned. Third, let's talk about books. Books often _____ a higher educational status. They're also a symbol of learning or of giving knowledge. Lastly, flowers can be a symbol of life. _____ flowers are used to show power and growth. In a moment, I'll present some paintings with these symbols.

24 2024년 9월 학력평가
딕테이션

녹음을 듣고, 빈칸에 알맞은 말을 쓰시기 바랍니다. 빈칸은 문제풀이에 핵심이 되는 키워드와 헷갈리기 쉬운 발음에 표시되어 있으니 이 점에 유의하여 듣기 바랍니다.

01

W: Hello, community members. I'm Lena Smith, the leader of the Public Relations Team at the San Diego Art Museum. I'm excited to announce that our art museum will offer a _____ _____ event during next week. Our museum has been loved by the community for 50 years, so we're excited to give back to our _____ _____ and welcome new visitors. This event is a great chance for you to explore our _____ _____ of famous artworks free of charge. Don't miss out on this incredible opportunity and _____ _____ _____ to your family and friends.

02

W: Hey, who are you talking to?

M: Hi, Jenny. I'm just talking to my plant.

W: Seriously? I've never heard of doing that.

M: You know what's interesting? _____ _____ _____ _____ can actually help them grow better.

W: No way! How so?

M: When we talk, we breathe out carbon dioxide, and plants love it. It's _____ _____ their growth.

W: That makes sense.

M: And guess what? The vibrations from our voices when we talk can _____ plant growth, too.

W: That's pretty cool!

M: Yeah. We can help our plants _____ _____ by talking to them.

W: I see. I might just say 'hi' to my plants and see how they like it.

03

M: Welcome back to our channel, *Wellness Wisdom*! Are you in the habit of _____ _____ after your meals? Then this video is a must-watch for you. Fruit is packed with essential nutrients such as vitamins and minerals, but eating them _____ _____ a meal might lead to digestive issues. Fruit usually digests faster than other types of foods. So, when you have fruit right after a meal, the fruit may not _____ _____ because other foods stay in the stomach. This increases the pressure on the digestive system and may _____ _____ _____ _____ and discomfort. Remember, choosing fruit as dessert may get your digestive system in trouble. Stay healthy, stay informed.

04

M: Hello, Cindy. What are you looking at on your phone?

W: Hi, Tom. This is my own space in the metaverse.

M: Wow, it's amazing. Oh, there's a _____ _____ in your house. That's unique.

W: Yes. I can enter my home through the door like a real house.

M: Fantastic! Is it possible to _____ _____ _____ next to the tree?

W: Of course. We can do everything in virtual reality.

M: Awesome. I love the two dogs looking at each other.

W: Yeah, they make my place so lovely.

M: I agree. I also like that _____ _____ on the ground.

W: Thanks.

24

24년 9월 딕테이션

M: Oh, there's a girl sitting on the bench. She looks a lot like you.

W: Yes, she's my avatar in the metaverse.

M: That's so cool. I also want to _____ _____ _____ _____ like yours.

05

M: Hey, Sarah, the school's sports day is just a week away. Let's go over our plan for the event.

W: Definitely, Alex. We're _____ _____, a tug-of-war, and soccer, right?

M: Yes. I'll manage the equipment, including whistles and the ropes.

W: Thanks. Can you also check our stock for soccer balls?

M: Sure. I'll look into it. And, Sarah, I think we need some _____ _____ _____ with the event as staff.

W: I already recruited some from the school's sports clubs.

M: Perfect. I think we should make sure they know the _____ _____ of the games.

W: I agree. Let's have a meeting with the volunteers tomorrow. I'll give them a _____ _____ about the meeting.

M: Good idea. Then, I'll make the handout for the games' rules.

W: Deal. Let's make this sports day a success!

06

W: Welcome to Mobile Phone Oasis. How may I help you?

M: Hi, I'd like to get a _____ _____ _____.

W: Okay. What's your phone model?

M: It's a Quantum Plus. Do you have any recommendations?

W: For your model, we have this silicone case and this leather wallet case. The silicone one is _____ dollars and the leather one is 30 dollars.

M: Hmm, I'll _____ _____ the silicone case.

W: Great choice. Is there anything else you need?

M: I'd like to change the _____ _____ on my phone.

W: Certainly. I'd recommend this clear film. It's slim and durable.

M: Fantastic. How much is it?

W: It's _____ 10 dollars, but it's 20 percent off now.

M: That's cool. I'll take it as well. Here's my credit card.

07

M: Hi, Clara. Everybody says that the science camp was a success.

W: Yes. I'm glad the science camp ended well.

M: Me, too. By the way, did you take a picture to submit for the _____ _____ competition? It's due today.

W: Unfortunately, I couldn't take a picture.

M: Oh, no! I thought the weather was _____ _____ _____ a picture last week.

W: Yeah. The weather was really nice.

M: Then what was the problem? Was your camera broken again?

W: No, there was nothing wrong with my camera.

M: Did you not _____ _____ _____ to go out?

W: No, I was fine.

M: Then why couldn't you take a picture?

W: Actually, I searched for some places with beautiful scenery, but I couldn't _____ _____ _____ _____ to take a picture of.

M: Sorry to hear that. I hope you'll have a better chance next time.

08

M: Hi, Alysa. What are you looking at?

W: I'm looking at a website for a _____ _____ event.

M: Sounds interesting. Tell me more about it.

W: It's called "Poetry Magic." Many poets will be

_____ _____ _____ a

reading. The famous poet, Sarah Mitchell, will be

there, too.

M: That's awesome! When will it be?

W: It'll be held at 7 p.m. on _____

_____.

M: Oh, that's next Saturday. I'm available then.

Where's it taking place?

W: At the Bohemian Arts Center downtown. It's the

best place for raising the love of poetry.

M: So how can I _____ _____?

W: You can just click the link here and fill this form out.

M: Good, that's easy. I'll be there to enjoy the beautiful

poetry.

09

W: Hello, listeners. Have you ever _____

_____ _____ your business

with short-form videos? Then how about joining

our Short-form Video Course? It's a free online

course that is _____ _____

_____ interested in using social media

for their business. The course is made up of three

stages that will teach you the art of _____,

_____, _____ _____

videos like a professional. Please visit our website

at www.shortformclass.com to sign up. The best

part of this course is that you can take it at any

time, over and over again. And guess what?

_____ _____ _____

some of the participants and give feedback on

their work. Don't miss this chance to level up your

business!

10

M: Honey, what are you doing now?

W: I'm looking for a white noise machine. The machine

plays white noise to help people _____

_____ _____

quickly.

M: That's what we need. Shall we choose one

together?

W: Okay, how much of the budget can we use?

M: 40 dollars _____ _____ would

be appropriate. How many tracks should the white

noise machine play?

W: I think we'd better choose a model with more than

10 white noise tracks. How about color?

M: I want to put it next to our bed, so I think

_____ _____ _____

_____ than black.

W: I agree. Look at this model. It has an alarm

function.

M: Great. It'll be _____ for us.

W: Let's order this model.

11

W: Honey, you know we often buy from the

Best&Cost Online Shopping Mall, so how about

_____ a membership to it?

M: Sounds good, but there is a five-dollar membership

fee every month. Is it worth it?

W: Absolutely. The membership comes with free

delivery and discounts. We could _____

_____ _____ _____

than the membership fee we pay.

M: (Alright. Let's sign up for the membership.)

12

M: Cathy, this cafe offers a discount when a

_____ _____ _____

_____ tumbler for drinks. So, I brought

mine.

W: Oh, that's a great idea. It'll help reduce the use of

paper and plastic cups.

M: Yeah, it's a small step but can make a big

difference. Would you like to _____

_____ as well?

W: (Sure. I'll bring my tumbler next time.)

13

W: Dad, can you go shopping with me now?

M: Sure, I can. But why, Allie?

W: I need to buy a white shirt today.

M: What do you need it for?

W: It's for the dance performance at the school festival next Friday.

M: I see. But, wouldn't it be more _____ _____ _____ it online?

W: Actually, I ordered a white shirt online a few days ago, but it _____ _____ _____ yet.

M: Sometimes that happens. There's still over a week left until the festival day, though.

W: Right, but all of us _____ _____ _____ white shirts, even for rehearsals.

M: When do you start your rehearsals?

W: The first rehearsal is tomorrow. I'd like to be _____ _____ for it.

M: (Okay. We'd better go buy your shirt right away.)

14

M: Hey, Jessica. How's the preparation for your business trip to Singapore going?

W: It's going well. All the important documents are ready, and I'm _____ _____ for the trip.

M: Glad to hear that.

W: Yeah, but I have a problem.

M: Oh, what is it?

W: You remember Tory, my five-month-old puppy? I need to find _____ _____ _____ _____ him while I'm away.

M: Why don't you leave him at your parents' house?

W: My mother is allergic to pet fur, so I don't think they can take care of him.

M: Ah, got it. _____ _____ _____ a pet hotel?

W: Yes, I have. But I'm not sure about leaving Tory in those places at such a young age.

M: Hmm, fair point. You know what? I could _____ _____ _____ _____ if you're okay with it. Coco, my dog, will welcome a new friend.

W: (I'd really appreciate it if you could take care of him.)

15

M: David and Emily are members of the school musical club. The club has been preparing their creative musical performance for a month. This time, David takes a role as the _____ _____, and Emily as the sound director. Today, David and Emily are _____ _____ _____ that will be used for the performance. After listening to the music, David thinks that the background music for the _____ _____ is not suitable. So, David wants to ask Emily to find other music that _____ _____ _____ the scene. In this situation, what would David most likely say to Emily?

David: (Can you look for different music for the last scene?)

16~17

W: Hello, students. Nowadays, some desserts are very popular and well-known worldwide. Today, we'll learn about _____ _____ _____ those desserts might have originated. First, scones are said to have come from Scotland in the early 1500s. Some _____ _____ that it was named after the Stone of Scone, on which the kings of Scotland sat while being crowned. Secondly, gelato is thought to have been invented in _____ in the 16th century. Historians aren't sure who invented it, but it's generally believed that an Italian architect, Bernardo Buontalenti, _____ _____ _____ _____ the modern-day gelato. Thirdly, the first marshmallows are said to have been produced in _____ around 2000 BC. Marshmallows were offered only to the ancient Egyptian gods and pharaohs as a candy or dessert. Lastly, cinnamon rolls might have _____ _____ Sweden in the 17th century. It's believed that cinnamon spice started arriving in Sweden through _____ _____ and was later used in rolls and desserts. Now, I'd like you to search for more details of these desserts.

정답표

01회
2018년 11월 학력평가   문제편 p.2 해설편 p.1

01 ②	02 ④	03 ②	04 ③	05 ①
06 ③	07 ②	08 ③	09 ④	10 ④
11 ④	12 ①	13 ①	14 ②	15 ⑤
16 ①	17 ⑤			

02회
2019년 3월 학력평가   문제편 p.5 해설편 p.6

01 ③	02 ⑤	03 ①	04 ⑤	05 ②
06 ④	07 ①	08 ⑤	09 ⑤	10 ④
11 ③	12 ⑤	13 ②	14 ①	15 ②
16 ①	17 ④			

03회
2019년 6월 학력평가   문제편 p.8 해설편 p.10

01 ②	02 ④	03 ①	04 ④	05 ①
06 ④	07 ⑤	08 ④	09 ④	10 ②
11 ③	12 ⑤	13 ②	14 ④	15 ③
16 ⑤	17 ④			

04회
2019년 9월 학력평가   문제편 p.11 해설편 p.15

01 ③	02 ⑤	03 ②	04 ③	05 ②
06 ③	07 ①	08 ④	09 ④	10 ④
11 ⑤	12 ①	13 ⑤	14 ①	15 ②
16 ②	17 ④			

05회
2019년 11월 학력평가   문제편 p.14 해설편 p.20

01 ③	02 ②	03 ⑤	04 ④	05 ⑤
06 ②	07 ④	08 ③	09 ⑤	10 ③
11 ①	12 ②	13 ①	14 ③	15 ④
16 ②	17 ⑤			

06회
2020년 3월 학력평가   문제편 p.17 해설편 p.26

01 ⑤	02 ④	03 ⑤	04 ④	05 ②
06 ②	07 ①	08 ④	09 ④	10 ③
11 ①	12 ⑤	13 ①	14 ②	15 ⑤
16 ⑤	17 ③			

07회
2020년 6월 학력평가   문제편 p.20 해설편 p.31

01 ①	02 ②	03 ④	04 ④	05 ①
06 ②	07 ③	08 ④	09 ⑤	10 ④
11 ②	12 ⑤	13 ③	14 ②	15 ③
16 ④	17 ③			

08회
2020년 9월 학력평가   문제편 p.23 해설편 p.36

01 ⑤	02 ②	03 ④	04 ⑤	05 ①
06 ④	07 ⑤	08 ③	09 ④	10 ②
11 ④	12 ④	13 ①	14 ②	15 ⑤
16 ④	17 ④			

09회
2020년 11월 학력평가   문제편 p.26 해설편 p.41

01 ④	02 ②	03 ①	04 ⑤	05 ④
06 ③	07 ⑤	08 ④	09 ⑤	10 ③
11 ①	12 ①	13 ②	14 ④	15 ③
16 ②	17 ④			

10회
2021년 3월 학력평가   문제편 p.29 해설편 p.46

01 ⑤	02 ①	03 ②	04 ④	05 ⑤
06 ②	07 ⑤	08 ③	09 ②	10 ④
11 ②	12 ①	13 ④	14 ④	15 ②
16 ④	17 ④			

11회
2021년 6월 학력평가   문제편 p.32 해설편 p.51

01 ③	02 ⑤	03 ②	04 ④	05 ⑤
06 ②	07 ②	08 ④	09 ④	10 ②
11 ④	12 ⑤	13 ①	14 ⑤	15 ④
16 ①	17 ③			

12회
2021년 9월 학력평가   문제편 p.35 해설편 p.55

01 ③	02 ③	03 ④	04 ⑤	05 ②
06 ③	07 ⑤	08 ④	09 ⑤	10 ③
11 ②	12 ①	13 ②	14 ④	15 ①
16 ①	17 ④			

13회
2021년 11월 학력평가   문제편 p.38 해설편 p.61

01 ③	02 ②	03 ②	04 ④	05 ⑤
06 ②	07 ②	08 ⑤	09 ④	10 ①
11 ②	12 ②	13 ①	14 ⑤	15 ③
16 ③	17 ⑤			

14회
2022년 3월 학력평가   문제편 p.41 해설편 p.66

01 ①	02 ①	03 ②	04 ⑤	05 ③
06 ③	07 ①	08 ②	09 ④	10 ③
11 ④	12 ④	13 ②	14 ①	15 ②
16 ①	17 ④			

15회
2022년 6월 학력평가   문제편 p.44 해설편 p.70

01 ⑤	02 ②	03 ②	04 ④	05 ⑤
06 ④	07 ①	08 ③	09 ④	10 ④
11 ②	12 ②	13 ②	14 ①	15 ③
16 ⑤	17 ③			

16회
2022년 9월 학력평가   문제편 p.47 해설편 p.75

01 ①	02 ④	03 ④	04 ⑤	05 ④
06 ⑤	07 ④	08 ⑤	09 ③	10 ②
11 ①	12 ⑤	13 ③	14 ①	15 ⑤
16 ⑤	17 ③			

17회
2022년 11월 학력평가   문제편 p.50 해설편 p.80

01 ④	02 ②	03 ⑤	04 ④	05 ⑤
06 ④	07 ⑤	08 ②	09 ①	10 ②
11 ②	12 ①	13 ⑤	14 ④	15 ⑤
16 ④	17 ④			

18회
2023년 3월 학력평가   문제편 p.53 해설편 p.85

01 ①	02 ②	03 ④	04 ③	05 ①
06 ②	07 ②	08 ③	09 ③	10 ②
11 ④	12 ④	13 ②	14 ①	15 ①
16 ③	17 ④			

19회
2023년 6월 학력평가   문제편 p.56 해설편 p.90

01 ④	02 ⑤	03 ⑤	04 ⑤	05 ④
06 ②	07 ①	08 ③	09 ⑤	10 ⑤
11 ②	12 ③	13 ①	14 ③	15 ④
16 ⑤	17 ④			

20회
2023년 9월 학력평가   문제편 p.59 해설편 p.95

01 ⑤	02 ⑤	03 ②	04 ④	05 ①
06 ①	07 ⑤	08 ④	09 ④	10 ②
11 ④	12 ①	13 ①	14 ①	15 ⑤
16 ②	17 ④			

21회
2023년 11월 학력평가   문제편 p.62 해설편 p.100

01 ①	02 ②	03 ③	04 ⑤	05 ⑤
06 ③	07 ③	08 ⑤	09 ④	10 ②
11 ②	12 ③	13 ①	14 ④	15 ②
16 ①	17 ④			

22회
2024년 3월 학력평가   문제편 p.65 해설편 p.105

01 ③	02 ①	03 ①	04 ④	05 ⑤
06 ③	07 ②	08 ⑤	09 ⑤	10 ①
11 ④	12 ②	13 ②	14 ①	15 ②
16 ⑤	17 ③			

23회
2024년 6월 학력평가   문제편 p.68 해설편 p.110

01 ④	02 ②	03 ③	04 ①	05 ④
06 ②	07 ③	08 ⑤	09 ⑤	10 ①
11 ④	12 ⑤	13 ④	14 ④	15 ⑤
16 ②	17 ④			

24회
2024년 9월 학력평가   문제편 p.71 해설편 p.115

01 ⑤	02 ③	03 ③	04 ④	05 ⑤
06 ②	07 ⑤	08 ④	09 ⑤	10 ③
11 ④	12 ①	13 ②	14 ③	15 ①
16 ②	17 ④			

정답표

01회
2018년 11월 학력평가   문제편 p.2 해설편 p.1

01 ②	02 ④	03 ②	04 ③	05 ①
06 ③	07 ②	08 ③	09 ④	10 ④
11 ④	12 ①	13 ③	14 ④	15 ⑤
16 ①	17 ⑤			

02회
2019년 3월 학력평가   문제편 p.5 해설편 p.6

01 ③	02 ⑤	03 ①	04 ⑤	05 ②
06 ④	07 ①	08 ③	09 ⑤	10 ④
11 ③	12 ⑤	13 ②	14 ①	15 ②
16 ①	17 ④			

03회
2019년 6월 학력평가   문제편 p.8 해설편 p.10

01 ②	02 ⑤	03 ①	04 ④	05 ①
06 ④	07 ⑤	08 ⑤	09 ⑤	10 ②
11 ③	12 ⑤	13 ③	14 ④	15 ⑤
16 ⑤	17 ④			

04회
2019년 9월 학력평가   문제편 p.11 해설편 p.15

01 ③	02 ⑤	03 ②	04 ④	05 ②
06 ③	07 ①	08 ④	09 ③	10 ④
11 ⑤	12 ④	13 ⑤	14 ①	15 ②
16 ②	17 ④			

05회
2019년 11월 학력평가   문제편 p.14 해설편 p.20

01 ③	02 ②	03 ⑤	04 ④	05 ⑤
06 ②	07 ④	08 ③	09 ⑤	10 ③
11 ①	12 ②	13 ①	14 ③	15 ⑤
16 ②	17 ⑤			

06회
2020년 3월 학력평가   문제편 p.17 해설편 p.26

01 ⑤	02 ④	03 ⑤	04 ④	05 ②
06 ③	07 ①	08 ④	09 ④	10 ③
11 ①	12 ③	13 ①	14 ②	15 ⑤
16 ⑤	17 ③			

07회
2020년 6월 학력평가   문제편 p.20 해설편 p.31

01 ①	02 ⑤	03 ④	04 ④	05 ①
06 ②	07 ④	08 ④	09 ⑤	10 ④
11 ②	12 ①	13 ④	14 ⑤	15 ③
16 ④	17 ⑤			

08회
2020년 9월 학력평가   문제편 p.23 해설편 p.36

01 ⑤	02 ②	03 ④	04 ④	05 ①
06 ④	07 ⑤	08 ③	09 ④	10 ⑤
11 ④	12 ④	13 ①	14 ②	15 ⑤
16 ④	17 ④			

09회
2020년 11월 학력평가   문제편 p.26 해설편 p.41

01 ④	02 ②	03 ①	04 ⑤	05 ④
06 ③	07 ⑤	08 ④	09 ⑤	10 ③
11 ①	12 ①	13 ④	14 ④	15 ③
16 ②	17 ④			

10회
2021년 3월 학력평가   문제편 p.29 해설편 p.46

01 ⑤	02 ①	03 ②	04 ④	05 ⑤
06 ②	07 ⑤	08 ③	09 ②	10 ③
11 ④	12 ④	13 ④	14 ④	15 ②
16 ④	17 ④			

11회
2021년 6월 학력평가   문제편 p.32 해설편 p.51

01 ②	02 ⑤	03 ②	04 ④	05 ①
06 ②	07 ②	08 ④	09 ④	10 ②
11 ④	12 ⑤	13 ①	14 ⑤	15 ④
16 ①	17 ③			

12회
2021년 9월 학력평가   문제편 p.35 해설편 p.55

01 ③	02 ③	03 ④	04 ⑤	05 ②
06 ③	07 ⑤	08 ④	09 ⑤	10 ⑤
11 ④	12 ②	13 ②	14 ④	15 ①
16 ①	17 ④			

13회
2021년 11월 학력평가   문제편 p.38 해설편 p.61

01 ③	02 ②	03 ②	04 ④	05 ⑤
06 ②	07 ②	08 ⑤	09 ④	10 ①
11 ②	12 ②	13 ①	14 ⑤	15 ①
16 ③	17 ⑤			

14회
2022년 3월 학력평가   문제편 p.41 해설편 p.66

01 ①	02 ①	03 ②	04 ⑤	05 ③
06 ③	07 ①	08 ②	09 ④	10 ④
11 ④	12 ④	13 ②	14 ①	15 ②
16 ①	17 ④			

15회
2022년 6월 학력평가   문제편 p.44 해설편 p.70

01 ②	02 ②	03 ③	04 ④	05 ⑤
06 ④	07 ①	08 ③	09 ④	10 ②
11 ②	12 ②	13 ②	14 ①	15 ③
16 ⑤	17 ③			

16회
2022년 9월 학력평가   문제편 p.47 해설편 p.75

01 ①	02 ①	03 ④	04 ⑤	05 ④
06 ⑤	07 ④	08 ⑤	09 ⑤	10 ③
11 ①	12 ⑤	13 ②	14 ①	15 ④
16 ⑤	17 ③			

17회
2022년 11월 학력평가   문제편 p.50 해설편 p.80

01 ④	02 ③	03 ④	04 ④	05 ⑤
06 ④	07 ⑤	08 ⑤	09 ④	10 ②
11 ④	12 ①	13 ③	14 ④	15 ③
16 ④	17 ④			

18회
2023년 3월 학력평가   문제편 p.53 해설편 p.85

01 ②	02 ①	03 ③	04 ③	05 ①
06 ⑤	07 ②	08 ③	09 ③	10 ⑤
11 ①	12 ⑤	13 ②	14 ④	15 ①
16 ③	17 ④			

19회
2023년 6월 학력평가   문제편 p.56 해설편 p.90

01 ④	02 ③	03 ③	04 ⑤	05 ④
06 ⑤	07 ④	08 ③	09 ⑤	10 ⑤
11 ②	12 ②	13 ④	14 ④	15 ②
16 ⑤	17 ②			

20회
2023년 9월 학력평가   문제편 p.59 해설편 p.95

01 ⑤	02 ③	03 ②	04 ④	05 ①
06 ④	07 ⑤	08 ④	09 ③	10 ⑤
11 ②	12 ④	13 ③	14 ④	15 ⑤
16 ②	17 ④			

21회
2023년 11월 학력평가   문제편 p.62 해설편 p.100

01 ①	02 ②	03 ③	04 ⑤	05 ⑤
06 ③	07 ③	08 ⑤	09 ④	10 ②
11 ②	12 ③	13 ④	14 ④	15 ②
16 ④	17 ④			

22회
2024년 3월 학력평가   문제편 p.65 해설편 p.105

01 ③	02 ④	03 ③	04 ④	05 ⑤
06 ③	07 ②	08 ⑤	09 ⑤	10 ①
11 ①	12 ①	13 ②	14 ②	15 ②
16 ⑤	17 ③			

23회
2024년 6월 학력평가   문제편 p.68 해설편 p.110

01 ④	02 ⑥	03 ③	04 ⑤	05 ④
06 ③	07 ③	08 ⑤	09 ⑤	10 ①
11 ④	12 ⑤	13 ④	14 ④	15 ⑤
16 ②	17 ④			

24회
2024년 9월 학력평가   문제편 p.71 해설편 p.115

01 ⑤	02 ③	03 ③	04 ④	05 ⑤
06 ⑤	07 ③	08 ④	09 ⑤	10 ⑤
11 ②	12 ②	13 ②	14 ③	15 ①
16 ②	17 ④			

마더텅 전자책

마음껏 쓰고 지우는 자유로운 필기!
원하는 내용을 손쉽게 검색! 원하는 페이지로 간편하게 이동!

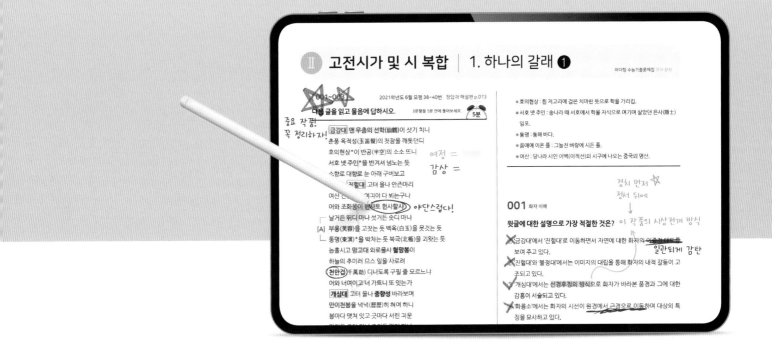

마더텅 전자책 지원 어플리케이션

노팅	스콘	교보eBook	meBOOK
Goodnotes	예스24 eBook	디북	EBS eBook

▶ 구글 플레이스토어 또는 🍎 애플 앱스토어 에서
원하는 **어플리케이션**을 다운로드해 주세요.

MOTHERTONGUE
마더텅출판사
since1999.4.1.

 정답표

2025 마더텅 전국연합 학력평가 기출문제집 고2 영어 듣기

01회
2018년 11월 학력평가　　　문제편 p.2 해설편 p.1

01 ②	02 ④	03 ②	04 ③	05 ①
06 ③	07 ②	08 ⑧	09 ④	10 ④
11 ④	12 ①	13 ④	14 ④	15 ⑤
16 ①	17 ⑤			

02회
2019년 3월 학력평가　　　문제편 p.5 해설편 p.6

01 ③	02 ⑤	03 ①	04 ⑤	05 ②
06 ④	07 ①	08 ③	09 ⑤	10 ④
11 ③	12 ⑤	13 ②	14 ①	15 ②
16 ①	17 ④			

03회
2019년 6월 학력평가　　　문제편 p.8 해설편 p.10

01 ②	02 ⑤	03 ①	04 ④	05 ①
06 ④	07 ⑤	08 ④	09 ⑤	10 ⑤
11 ③	12 ⑤	13 ⑤	14 ④	15 ④
16 ⑤	17 ④			

04회
2019년 9월 학력평가　　　문제편 p.11 해설편 p.15

01 ④	02 ⑤	03 ②	04 ③	05 ②
06 ③	07 ④	08 ④	09 ④	10 ④
11 ⑤	12 ⑤	13 ⑤	14 ①	15 ②
16 ②	17 ④			

05회
2019년 11월 학력평가　　　문제편 p.14 해설편 p.20

01 ③	02 ⑤	03 ④	04 ④	05 ⑤
06 ②	07 ②	08 ⑤	09 ⑤	10 ⑤
11 ①	12 ④	13 ①	14 ⑤	15 ⑤
16 ②	17 ⑤			

06회
2020년 3월 학력평가　　　문제편 p.17 해설편 p.26

01 ⑤	02 ④	03 ⑤	04 ④	05 ②
06 ⑤	07 ④	08 ④	09 ④	10 ④
11 ①	12 ③	13 ⑤	14 ②	15 ⑤
16 ⑤	17 ③			

07회
2020년 6월 학력평가　　　문제편 p.20 해설편 p.31

01 ①	02 ②	03 ④	04 ④	05 ①
06 ②	07 ③	08 ④	09 ⑤	10 ④
11 ①	12 ①	13 ⑤	14 ②	15 ③
16 ①	17 ④			

08회
2020년 9월 학력평가　　　문제편 p.23 해설편 p.36

01 ②	02 ②	03 ④	04 ⑤	05 ①
06 ②	07 ⑤	08 ⑤	09 ④	10 ⑤
11 ④	12 ③	13 ①	14 ②	15 ⑤
16 ④	17 ④			

09회
2020년 11월 학력평가　　　문제편 p.26 해설편 p.41

01 ④	02 ②	03 ①	04 ⑤	05 ④
06 ③	07 ⑤	08 ④	09 ⑤	10 ③
11 ①	12 ①	13 ②	14 ④	15 ⑤
16 ②	17 ④			

10회
2021년 3월 학력평가　　　문제편 p.29 해설편 p.46

01 ⑤	02 ②	03 ②	04 ④	05 ⑤
06 ②	07 ③	08 ⑤	09 ③	10 ⑤
11 ③	12 ①	13 ④	14 ④	15 ②
16 ④	17 ④			

11회
2021년 6월 학력평가　　　문제편 p.32 해설편 p.51

01 ③	02 ③	03 ②	04 ④	05 ①
06 ②	07 ②	08 ④	09 ④	10 ②
11 ④	12 ⑤	13 ①	14 ⑤	15 ④
16 ①	17 ③			

12회
2021년 9월 학력평가　　　문제편 p.35 해설편 p.55

01 ③	02 ③	03 ④	04 ⑤	05 ②
06 ②	07 ⑤	08 ⑤	09 ⑤	10 ③
11 ⑤	12 ②	13 ②	14 ④	15 ①
16 ①	17 ④			

13회
2021년 11월 학력평가　　　문제편 p.38 해설편 p.61

01 ③	02 ②	03 ②	04 ④	05 ⑤
06 ②	07 ②	08 ⑤	09 ④	10 ①
11 ②	12 ①	13 ①	14 ⑤	15 ①
16 ②	17 ⑤			

14회
2022년 3월 학력평가　　　문제편 p.41 해설편 p.66

01 ①	02 ①	03 ②	04 ⑤	05 ③
06 ③	07 ①	08 ②	09 ④	10 ②
11 ④	12 ①	13 ②	14 ①	15 ②
16 ①	17 ④			

15회
2022년 6월 학력평가　　　문제편 p.44 해설편 p.70

01 ⑤	02 ②	03 ②	04 ④	05 ⑤
06 ④	07 ①	08 ③	09 ④	10 ④
11 ②	12 ⑤	13 ②	14 ①	15 ④
16 ⑤	17 ③			

16회
2022년 9월 학력평가　　　문제편 p.47 해설편 p.75

01 ②	02 ①	03 ④	04 ⑤	05 ④
06 ⑤	07 ④	08 ⑤	09 ③	10 ⑤
11 ①	12 ⑤	13 ②	14 ①	15 ④
16 ⑤	17 ③			

17회
2022년 11월 학력평가　　　문제편 p.50 해설편 p.80

01 ④	02 ③	03 ⑤	04 ④	05 ⑤
06 ④	07 ⑤	08 ②	09 ④	10 ②
11 ④	12 ①	13 ④	14 ④	15 ⑤
16 ④	17 ④			

18회
2023년 3월 학력평가　　　문제편 p.53 해설편 p.85

01 ②	02 ①	03 ④	04 ③	05 ①
06 ②	07 ②	08 ③	09 ③	10 ②
11 ④	12 ①	13 ②	14 ①	15 ③
16 ③	17 ④			

19회
2023년 6월 학력평가　　　문제편 p.56 해설편 p.90

01 ②	02 ⑤	03 ①	04 ⑤	05 ④
06 ②	07 ①	08 ⑤	09 ⑤	10 ③
11 ②	12 ④	13 ①	14 ④	15 ②
16 ⑤	17 ④			

20회
2023년 9월 학력평가　　　문제편 p.59 해설편 p.95

01 ⑤	02 ②	03 ②	04 ④	05 ①
06 ⑤	07 ⑤	08 ⑤	09 ④	10 ②
11 ②	12 ①	13 ④	14 ④	15 ⑤
16 ②	17 ④			

21회
2023년 11월 학력평가　　　문제편 p.62 해설편 p.100

01 ②	02 ②	03 ④	04 ⑤	05 ⑤
06 ③	07 ⑤	08 ⑤	09 ④	10 ②
11 ②	12 ①	13 ①	14 ②	15 ②
16 ④	17 ④			

22회
2024년 3월 학력평가　　　문제편 p.65 해설편 p.105

01 ②	02 ①	03 ④	04 ④	05 ⑤
06 ②	07 ⑤	08 ⑤	09 ②	10 ①
11 ④	12 ⑤	13 ②	14 ②	15 ②
16 ⑤	17 ③			

23회
2024년 6월 학력평가　　　문제편 p.68 해설편 p.110

01 ④	02 ②	03 ②	04 ⑤	05 ④
06 ⑤	07 ③	08 ③	09 ⑤	10 ①
11 ②	12 ⑤	13 ②	14 ④	15 ⑤
16 ②	17 ③			

24회
2024년 9월 학력평가　　　문제편 p.71 해설편 p.115

01 ⑤	02 ③	03 ③	04 ④	05 ⑤
06 ②	07 ⑤	08 ④	09 ⑤	10 ③
11 ④	12 ⑤	13 ④	14 ③	15 ①
16 ②	17 ④			

01 2018년 11월 학력평가

01	②	02	④	03	②	04	③	05	①
06	③	07	②	08	③	09	④	10	④
11	④	12	①	13	③	14	②	15	⑤
16	①	17	⑤						

01 남자가 하는 말의 목적

고2 2018년 11월 3번 정답률 95%
▶ 정답 ②

M: Good morning. Welcome to Sunshine Zoo. I'm Mr. Johnson, the
선샤인 동물원
head of the zookeepers. We're working hard to ensure the safety
동물원 사육사 대표   ~의 안전을 보장하다
of tourists and animals. Before the tour, we kindly request that
정중히 요청하다
you keep a few regulations in mind. First, don't feed the animals
몇 가지 규칙들을 명심하다   먹이를 주다
(keep A in mind: A를 명심하다, regulation: 규칙)
or throw things at the cages as it can make them sick or cause
우리들   그들을 아프게 하다
a lot of stress to them. Second, turn off the camera flash while
많은 스트레스를 주다   카메라 플래시를 끄다
taking pictures of the animals because it can startle them. Lastly,
깜짝 놀라게 하다
don't leave young kids unattended. They might get lost and enter
어린 아이들을 혼자 두다   길을 잃다
(leave A unattended: A를 혼자 두다)
prohibited areas. I hope you enjoy your tour.
금지 구역들

해석
남: 안녕하세요. Sunshine Zoo(선샤인 동물원)에 오신 것을 환영합니다. 저는 동물원 사육사
대표인 Johnson입니다. 저희는 관람객들과 동물들의 안전을 보장하기 위해 열심히 일하
고 있습니다. 관람 전에, 몇 가지 규칙들을 명심해 주시기를 정중히 요청드립니다. 첫째,
동물들을 아프게 하거나 그들에게 많은 스트레스를 줄 수 있으므로 먹이를 주거나 우리에
물건을 던지지 마십시오. 둘째, 동물들을 깜짝 놀라게 할 수 있으므로 동물들의 사진을 찍
는 동안에 카메라 플래시를 끄십시오. 마지막으로, 어린 아이들을 혼자 두지 마십시오. 그
들은 길을 잃고 금지 구역에 들어갈지도 모릅니다. 즐거운 관람 되시길 바랍니다.

① 동물 공연 일정을 안내하려고
✓ 동물원 관람 규칙을 설명하려고
③ 동물원에 새로 온 동물들을 소개하려고
④ 변경된 동물원 운영 시간을 공지하려고
⑤ 멸종 위기 동물 보호의 중요성을 강조하려고

02 여자의 의견

고2 2018년 11월 4번 정답률 90%
▶ 정답 ④

W: Honey, you're home early.
M: Hi, sweetie. Where is Cathy?
W: She went shopping with her friends.
쇼핑하러 갔다(go shopping)
M: Hmm.... She's been going shopping a lot lately. She must have
최근에   썼음에 틀림없다
spent all of her allowance.
용돈   (must have p.p.: ~했음에 틀림없다,
spend: (돈을) 쓰다)
W: I think so. She asked me for more money yesterday. I'm worried
나에게 돈을 더 달라고 했다
(ask A for B: A에게 B를 달라고 하다)
that she doesn't think about how she spends her money.
M: I'm worried, too. She'll have to learn how to manage her money on
관리하는 법
her own.
그녀 스스로   (how to V: ~하는 법, manage: 관리하다)
W: Yeah. I think it's the role of the parents to teach their child how to
역할   가르치다
do that.
M: You're right. We should help Cathy to be financially smart.
재정적으로 똑똑한
W: Of course. Home should be the place to gain proper spending
올바른 소비 습관들을 기르다
habits.
M: I agree. Let's talk to her when she comes back home.

해석
여: 여보, 집에 일찍 왔네요.
남: 안녕, 여보. Cathy는 어디 있어요?
여: 친구들과 쇼핑하러 갔어요.

남: 흠.... 그 애가 최근에 쇼핑을 많이 하네요. 용돈을 다 썼음에 틀림없어요.
여: 저도 그렇게 생각해요. 그 애가 어제 저에게 돈을 더 달라고 했어요. 저는 그 애가 돈을 어
떻게 쓰는지에 대해 생각하지 않는 것이 걱정돼요.
남: 저도 걱정되네요. 그 애는 스스로 돈을 관리하는 법을 배워야 할 거예요.
여: 그래요. 저는 아이에게 그렇게 하는 법을 가르치는 것이 부모의 역할이라고 생각해요.
남: 당신 말이 맞아요. 우리는 Cathy가 재정적으로 똑똑해지도록 도와줘야 해요.
여: 물론이죠. 집은 올바른 소비 습관을 기를 수 있는 장소가 되어야 해요.
남: 동의해요. 그 애가 집에 돌아오면 얘기합시다.

① 성인이 되면 경제적으로 독립해야 한다.
② 청소년 시기에 가족 간의 대화가 중요하다.
③ 신문 기사를 통해 경제관념을 기를 수 있다.
✓ 부모가 바람직한 소비 습관을 가르쳐야 한다.
⑤ 구매 목록 작성으로 충동구매를 막을 수 있다.

문제 풀이
남자와 여자는 Cathy의 과소비를 걱정하고 있다. 아이에게 스스로 돈을 관리하는 법을 가르
치는 것이 부모의 역할이라고 생각한다는 말과 집은 올바른 소비 습관을 기를 수 있는 장소가
되어야 한다는 말에서 답을 유추할 수 있다. 따라서 여자의 의견으로 적절한 답은 ④ '부모가
바람직한 소비 습관을 가르쳐야 한다.'이다.

03 두 사람의 관계

고2 2018년 11월 5번 정답률 90%
▶ 정답 ②

W: Hello, sir. Thank you for sitting down with me today.
M: Hello, Erin. Thank you for coming here.
W: No problem. As I mentioned on the phone, I'm writing an article
언급했다(mention)   기사
about you for our school newspaper.
M: Yes, that's right.   우리 학교 신문
W: So, I'd like to know what first attracted you to this job.
당신을 이 직업으로 이끌었다
(attract A to B: A를 B로 이끌다)
M: A documentary about diseases that I saw in a middle school
다큐멘터리   질병들
science class inspired me.
영감을 주었다(inspire)
W: I see. And I heard that you do medical volunteer work every
의료 자원봉사를 하다
summer.
M: I do. Some of the nurses at my hospital help me treat patients
환자들을 치료하다
living in isolated areas.
고립된 지역들
W: That's so impressive. Finally, do you have any advice for students
인상적인   조언
who want to be doctors, like I do?
M: Well, always remember to put others' needs before your own.
다른 사람들의 필요를 너 자신의 것보다 우선시하다
(put A before B: A를 B보다 우선시하다)
W: That's an important point. Can I take pictures of you with the
중요한 점   ~의 사진을 찍다
nurses for our article?
M: Sure. Please come this way.

해석
여: 안녕하세요, 선생님. 오늘 저와 함께 해 주셔서 감사합니다.
남: 안녕, Erin. 여기까지 와 줘서 고맙구나.
여: 천만에요. 전화에서 언급했듯이, 저는 저희 학교 신문에 선생님에 대한 기사를 쓰고 있
어요.
남: 그래, 그렇지.
여: 그래서, 저는 무엇이 처음에 선생님을 이 직업으로 이끌었는지 알고 싶어요.
남: 중학교 과학 수업 시간에 본 질병들에 대한 다큐멘터리가 나에게 영감을 주었단다.
여: 그렇군요. 그리고 선생님께서 매년 여름 의료 자원봉사를 하신다고 들었어요.
남: 그래. 우리 병원의 간호사들 중 일부가 고립된 지역에 사는 환자들을 내가 치료하는 데 도
움을 준단다.
여: 정말 인상적이네요. 마지막으로, 저처럼 의사가 되고 싶어 하는 학생들을 위한 조언이 있
으신가요?
남: 음, 항상 다른 사람들의 필요를 너 자신의 것보다 우선시하는 것을 기억하렴.
여: 그것은 중요한 점이군요. 기사를 위해 간호사들과 함께 선생님의 사진을 찍어도 될까요?
남: 물론이지. 이쪽으로 오렴.

① 환자 ― 간호사
✓ 학생 기자 ― 의사
③ 사진작가 ― 모델
④ 봉사 단체 직원 ― 자원봉사자
⑤ 중학생 ― 보건 교사

04 그림에서 대화의 내용과 일치하지 않는 것

고2 2018년 11월 6번 | 정답률 40%

▶ 정답 ③

M: Hi, Kelly. Have you finished preparing for the skit contest this Friday?
준비하는 것을 끝냈다 (finish V-ing: ~하는 것을 끝내다) / 단막극 대회 (skit: 길이가 짧은 연극)

W: Yes, I almost have. Take a look. The banner with balloons at the back of the stage looks good, doesn't it? 풍선이 달린 현수막

M: Yeah, it looks neat. What's the sofa on the stage for?
멋진 / 무대 / 소파

W: It's for the first skit.

M: Okay. The star-shaped trophy on the table looks cool. Is it for the winning class?
별 모양의 트로피 / 멋진 / 우승 반

W: Exactly. The winning class will also get to perform at the school festival.
공연을 하게 되다 / 학교 축제 (get to V: ~하게 되다, perform: 공연을 하다)

M: That's amazing. And what's the curtain for? I haven't seen it before. 커튼

W: It was set up for the contest yesterday. It'll be used between skits.
설치되었다(be set up) / 사용되다

M: Wonderful! Who is the girl wearing glasses?

W: That's Judy. She's a staff member from another class.
부원

M: I see. The contest will be really fun.

W: You should come and watch.

해석
남: 안녕, Kelly. 이번 주 금요일에 있는 단막극 대회 준비는 끝냈니?
여: 응, 거의 끝냈어. 좀 봐 봐. 무대 뒤쪽에 풍선들이 달린 현수막이 좋아 보이지, 그렇지 않니?
남: 그래, 멋져 보인다. 무대 위의 소파는 무엇을 위한 거야?
여: 그것은 첫 번째 단막극을 위한 거야.
남: 알겠어. 테이블 위에 있는 별 모양의 트로피가 멋져 보이네. 우승 반을 위한 거야?
여: 정확해. 우승 반은 학교 축제에서 공연도 하게 될 거야.
남: 대단한데. 그리고 커튼은 무엇을 위한 거야? 나는 전에 그것을 본 적이 없어.
여: 그것은 어제 대회를 위해 설치되었어. 단막극들 사이에 사용될 거야.
남: 멋지다! 안경을 쓴 여자애는 누구니?
여: 저 애는 Judy야. 그녀는 다른 반에서 온 부원이야.
남: 그렇구나. 대회가 정말 재미있을 거야.
여: 꼭 와서 봐야 해.

05 여자가 남자에게 부탁한 일

고2 2018년 11월 7번 | 정답률 85%

▶ 정답 ①

M: Hello, Alice. How are you?

W: Hi, Chris. I'm doing great. I'm getting used to this new neighborhood.
~에 익숙해지는 중이다 / 동네 (get used to A: A에 익숙해지다)

M: Good. Have you met any of your other neighbors?

W: I met a few. I had dinner with my next door neighbors Tim and Julie last Saturday.
~와 함께 저녁 식사를 했다(have dinner with)

M: That's nice. I know the couple well. I do exercises with them at the community center.
부부 / 운동을 하다 / 주민 센터

W: Community center? Where is it?

M: It's next to the post office. I go there to play table tennis every weekend.
탁구를 치다

W: That sounds interesting. I like playing table tennis, too.
탁구를 치는 것을 좋아하다(like V-ing: ~하는 것을 좋아하다)

M: Then, why don't you join me this Saturday?
~하는 게 어때?

W: I'd like to, but I threw my racket away before moving here. Can you lend me one?
내 탁구채를 버렸다 / 빌려주다 (throw away: 버리다)

M: Sure. I have an extra.
여분을 가지고 있다

W: Thank you.

해석
남: 안녕, Alice. 어떻게 지내?
여: 안녕, Chris. 난 잘 지내고 있어. 나는 이 새로운 동네에 익숙해지는 중이야.
남: 좋네. 다른 이웃들을 만난 적 있니?
여: 몇 명 만났어. 지난주 토요일에는 옆집 이웃인 Tim과 Julie와 함께 저녁 식사를 했어.
남: 그거 멋진데. 나는 그 부부를 잘 알아. 주민 센터에서 그들과 함께 운동을 하거든.
여: 주민 센터? 그게 어디에 있는데?
남: 우체국 옆에 있어. 나는 주말마다 그곳에 가서 탁구를 쳐.
여: 재미있겠다. 나도 탁구를 치는 것을 좋아해.
남: 그럼, 이번 주 토요일에 나와 함께 하는 게 어때?
여: 그러고 싶지만, 여기에 이사 오기 전에 내 탁구채를 버렸어. 나에게 탁구채를 빌려줄 수 있어?
남: 물론이지. 나는 여분을 가지고 있어.
여: 고마워.

✔ 탁구채 빌려주기
② 이삿짐 옮겨 주기
③ 이웃 소개해 주기
④ 저녁 식사 초대하기
⑤ 집 청소 도와주기

06 여자가 지불할 금액

고2 2018년 11월 9번 | 정답률 85%

▶ 정답 ③

M: Hello, how may I help you?

W: I'd like to buy tickets for the next Greenville city bus tour, please.
그린빌 시내 버스 관광

M: There's one departing at 11 a.m. Is that time okay with you?
출발하는(depart)

W: Sounds great. How much is the fare?
요금

M: A ticket for an adult is $30 per person.
한 명당

W: Okay. How much is it for a child?

M: It's $20. How many tickets do you need?

W: Two adults and one child. And I downloaded a coupon from your website. Can I use it?
필요하다 / 쿠폰을 다운받았다

M: Sure, with that you can save 10% off the total fare.
총액에서 10%를 절약하다

W: Sounds good. I'll use the coupon.

M: All right. How would you like to pay?

W: By credit card. 지불하다
신용카드로

해석
남: 안녕하세요, 어떻게 도와드릴까요?
여: 저는 다음 번 Greenville(그린빌) 시내 버스 관광 표를 사고 싶어요.
남: 오전 11시에 출발하는 것이 있어요. 그 시간 괜찮으십니까?
여: 좋아요. 요금은 얼마죠?
남: 성인 표는 한 명당 30달러입니다.
여: 알겠어요. 어린이 표는 얼마인가요?
남: 20달러입니다. 몇 장의 표가 필요하십니까?
여: 성인 표 두 장과 어린이 표 한 장이요. 그리고 웹 사이트에서 쿠폰을 다운받았는데요. 그것을 사용할 수 있나요?
남: 물론이지요, 그것으로 총액에서 10%를 절약하실 수 있습니다.
여: 좋네요. 쿠폰을 사용할게요.
남: 알겠습니다. 어떻게 지불하시겠습니까?
여: 신용카드로 할게요.

① $63 ② $70 ✔ $72
④ $80 ⑤ $88

문제 풀이
성인 표 두 장과 어린이 표 한 장이 필요하므로 60달러와 20달러를 더하면 80달러가 된다. 쿠폰을 사용하면 10퍼센트를 절약할 수 있기 때문에 80달러의 10퍼센트인 8달러를 빼면 총액은 72달러가 된다. 따라서 답은 ③ '$72'이다.

07 남자가 아이스 스케이트를 타러 갈 수 없는 이유

고2 2018년 11월 8번 · 정답률 90% · ▶ 정답 ②

W: Jake, our presentation is finally over. I feel so relieved.
M: So do I. And what will you do now?
W: I'm thinking of going ice skating.
M: That sounds fun. Where can you do that?
W: There's an ice-rink at the mall where I have my part-time job.
M: Really? How is it?
W: It's nice and big! There's also a discount for students. Why don't we go ice skating together today?
M: I wish I could, but I can't go.
W: Why? Do you have something else to do?
M: Yes, I'm going on a trip to Busan with my friends tomorrow. So I have to pack my bag.
W: No problem. We can go ice skating next time. Have a nice trip!
M: Thanks. See you later.

해석
여: Jake, 우리의 발표가 마침내 끝났어. 나는 정말 후련해.
남: 나도 그래. 그래서 너는 이제 무엇을 할 거야?
여: 나는 아이스 스케이트를 타러 갈까 생각 중이야.
남: 재미있겠다. 어디에서 탈 수 있는데?
여: 내가 아르바이트를 하는 쇼핑몰에 아이스링크가 있어.
남: 정말? 그곳은 어때?
여: 멋지고 크지! 학생들을 위한 할인도 있어. 우리 오늘 같이 아이스 스케이트를 타러 가는 게 어때?
남: 나도 그러고 싶지만, 갈 수 없어.
여: 왜? 다른 할 일이 있는 거야?
남: 응, 나는 내일 친구들과 부산으로 여행을 갈 거야. 그래서 가방을 싸야 해.
여: 괜찮아. 우리는 다음에 아이스 스케이트를 타러 가면 돼. 여행 즐겁게 해!
남: 고마워. 나중에 보자.

① 쇼핑몰에 가기로 해서
② 여행 가방을 싸야 해서
③ 발표 준비를 해야 해서
④ 아르바이트를 해야 해서
⑤ 친구를 마중 나가야 해서

08 Global Student Card에 관해 언급되지 않은 것

고2 2018년 11월 10번 · 정답률 90% · ▶ 정답 ③

W: Jim, take a look at this. I got a 'Global Student Card.'
M: Oh, let me see it. Can all students get one?
W: Only students from 16 to 25 years old can get one. It proves that we're students when travelling abroad.
M: It sounds useful. I might get one myself.
W: That's a good idea. Once you have it, it's valid for three years.
M: I see. What do I need to do to get one issued?
W: You need to submit a copy of your student ID card and an application form to the school office.
M: How long does it take to get it issued?
W: It'll take about two weeks, and you'll receive it by mail.
M: Okay. Thank you for the information.
W: You're welcome. You can go right now before the office closes.
M: I might as well try. See you!

해석
여: Jim, 이것 좀 봐. 나는 'Global Student Card(국제 학생 카드)'를 발급받았어.
남: 오, 어디 보자. 모든 학생들이 받을 수 있는 거야?
여: 16세에서 25세까지의 학생들만 받을 수 있어. 그것은 해외 여행을 할 때 우리가 학생이라는 것을 증명하는 거야.
남: 유용할 것 같구나. 내 것도 받아야겠다.
여: 좋은 생각이야. 일단 그것을 받으면, 3년 동안 유효해.
남: 그렇구나. 카드를 발급받기 위해서 무엇을 해야 하니?
여: 교무실에 학생증 사본과 신청서를 제출해야 해.
남: 그것을 발급받는 데 얼마나 걸리니?
여: 2주 정도 걸릴 것이고, 우편으로 받게 될 거야.
남: 알겠어. 정보를 줘서 고마워.
여: 천만에. 교무실이 문을 닫기 전에 지금 당장 가도 돼.
남: 시도해 보는 편이 낫겠다. 다음에 보자!

① 발급 가능 연령
② 유효 기간
③ 발급 비용
④ 발급 필요 서류
⑤ 발급 소요 기간

09 Clearwater University 5km Run에 관한 내용과 일치하지 않는 것

고2 2018년 11월 11번 · 정답률 85% · ▶ 정답 ④

[Chime bell rings.]
W: Hello, everyone. This is Jane Parker from Clearwater University broadcasting center. The Clearwater University 5km Run will be held on November 24th to celebrate the school's 50th anniversary. All students and faculty members can participate in the run. It'll start at 10 a.m. and participants will run a course through the campus. The entry fee is $5 for students and $15 for faculty members. A bottle of water and a small snack will be provided. The run will be finished around noon, and after lunch there will be a music concert in the main hall at 2 p.m. If you're interested, you can sign up through the university website or in the school library in person. Thank you.

해석
[차임벨이 울린다.]
여: 안녕하세요, 여러분. 저는 Clearwater University(클리어워터 대학) 방송 센터의 Jane Parker입니다. 개교 50주년을 기념하기 위해 11월 24일에 Clearwater University 5km Run(클리어워터 대학 5km 달리기)이 개최될 것입니다. 모든 학생들과 교직원들이 달리기에 참가할 수 있습니다. 그것은 오전 10시에 시작하며 참가자들은 캠퍼스를 통과하는 코스를 달릴 것입니다. 참가비는 학생은 5달러이고 교직원은 15달러입니다. 물 한 병과 간단한 간식이 제공될 것입니다. 달리기는 정오쯤에 끝날 것이고, 점심 식사 후에는 오후 2시에 대강당에서 음악회가 있을 것입니다. 관심이 있으시면, 대학 웹 사이트를 통해서 또는 학교 도서관에서 직접 신청하실 수 있습니다. 감사합니다.

① 모든 학생과 교직원이 참가할 수 있다.
② 학생의 경우 참가비는 5달러이다.
③ 물과 간식이 제공될 것이다.
④ 점심 식사 전에 음악회가 있을 것이다.
⑤ 학교 웹 사이트나 도서관에서 신청 가능하다.

10 표에서 두 사람이 관람할 영화

고2 2018년 11월 12번 · 정답률 85% · ▶ 정답 ④

W: Brian, we're off work tomorrow. Do you have any plans?
M: I was thinking of going to see a movie at the Limestone Movie Theater. There're several newly-released movies.
W: Really? Can I come with you?
M: Sure. Let me see. [Pause] We can see the timetable on the mobile app. These are the only tickets left.
W: Why don't we try 'Funny Guys'? I saw the trailer. It looked interesting.
M: Oh, I've already seen it. How about a horror movie?
W: Hmm... I'm not really fond of that kind of movie.
M: Okay. I've never seen a 3D or 4D movie before. Do you want to try out a movie with special features?

W: I'd love to. Then I think that <u>leaves us with two choices</u>.
우리에게 두 가지 선택을 남기다
(leave A with B: A에게 B를 남기다)

M: Okay. Hmm, this movie starts a little late for me. Let's see the one that starts earlier.

W: It must be this one then. What do you think?

M: Great. I <u>look forward to</u> it.
~을 기대하다

해석

여: Brian, 우리 내일 쉬는 날이잖아. 어떤 계획이 있니?

남: Limestone Movie Theater(라임스톤 영화관)에 영화를 보러 갈까 생각 중이었어. 새로 개봉한 영화들이 몇 개 있거든.

여: 정말? 내가 너와 함께 가도 될까?

남: 물론이지. 어디 보자. [잠시 후] 모바일 앱에서 시간표를 볼 수 있어. 남은 표는 이것뿐이네.

여: 우리 'Funny Guys(재미있는 남자들)'를 보는 게 어때? 내가 예고편을 봤어. 재미있어 보이더라.

남: 오, 나는 이미 그것을 봤어. 공포 영화는 어떠니?

여: 흠... 나는 그런 종류의 영화를 별로 좋아하지 않아.

남: 알겠어. 나는 전에 3D나 4D 영화를 본 적이 없어. 특별한 특징들이 있는 영화를 시도해 보고 싶니?

여: 그러고 싶어. 그럼 우리에게 두 가지 선택지가 남는구나.

남: 좋아. 흠, 이 영화는 나에게는 조금 늦게 시작하네. 더 일찍 시작하는 영화를 보자.

여: 그럼 분명 이 영화겠구나. 어떻게 생각해?

남: 좋아. 기대된다.

Limestone 영화관

	제목	장르	특별한 특징	시작 시간
①	Love Really(사랑 정말)	드라마	없음	오전 10시
②	Funny Guys(재미있는 남자들)	코미디	없음	오후 1시
③	Behind You(너의 뒤에)	호러	3D	오후 3시
✔④	Space Wars(우주 전쟁)	액션	4D	오후 6시
⑤	Dinosaurs(공룡)	애니메이션	4D	오후 8시

---

11 남자의 마지막 말에 대한 여자의 응답

▶ 정답 ④

M: Tina, what do you want to have for lunch?
점심 식사로

W: Well, <u>how about</u> the new French restaurant <u>across the street</u>?
~은 어때?　　　　　　　　　길 건너편에

M: Oh, I've heard about it. Have you been to that place?

W: (Yeah, the food was really great.)

해석

남: Tina, 점심 식사로 무엇을 먹고 싶어?

여: 음, 길 건너편에 새로 생긴 프랑스 레스토랑은 어때?

남: 오, 나는 그것에 대해 들어봤어. 너는 그곳에 가 본 적이 있니?

여: (응, 음식이 정말 맛있었어.)

① 아니, 나는 프랑스어를 할 줄 몰라.

② 음, 우리는 길을 건너야 해.

③ 좋아. 나는 직접 요리하는 것을 좋아해.

✔④ 응, 음식이 정말 맛있었어.

⑤ 미안해. 나는 이미 점심을 먹었어.

---

12 여자의 마지막 말에 대한 남자의 응답

▶ 정답 ①

W: Hey, Mike. I <u>got two tickets</u> for the <u>art exhibition</u> this Saturday.
표를 두 장 구했다　　　　　미술 전시회
(get a ticket)

M: Oh, you must be excited. You really like <u>paintings</u>.
그림들

W: Yeah. Let's <u>go together</u> and <u>learn more about</u> paintings.
같이 가다　　　~에 대해 더 배우다

M: (Sure. I'd love to go there with you.)

해석

여: 이봐, Mike. 나는 이번 주 토요일에 있는 미술 전시회 표를 두 장 구했어.

남: 오, 분명 신나겠구나. 너는 그림을 정말 좋아하잖아.

여: 그래. 같이 가서 그림에 대해 더 배우자.

남: (좋아. 나는 너와 함께 그곳에 가고 싶어.)

✔①좋아. 나는 너와 함께 그곳에 가고 싶어.

②글쎄, 우리가 표를 구할 수 있을지 모르겠어.

③그래, 나는 이미 그림을 다 그렸어.

④아니, 너는 전시회에 늦지 않을 거야.

⑤힘내. 너는 그곳에 다음에 갈 수 있어.

---

13 남자의 마지막 말에 대한 여자의 응답

▶ 정답 ③

M: Honey, what are you <u>looking at</u>?
~을 보는(look at)

W: Look at these <u>puppies</u> in this <u>picture</u>.
강아지들　　　　　사진

M: They're so cute. Whose puppies are they?

W: They're my <u>cousin</u> Amy's.
사촌

M: There're five of them! It must be <u>difficult</u> for her to <u>raise</u> all of them.
어려운　　　　　　키우다

W: That's why she asked if we're <u>willing to raise</u> one. She knows I like dogs.
키울 의향이 있는(willing to V: ~할 의향이 있는)

M: Really? That would be a good idea.

W: Yeah, but are you sure we can <u>take good care of</u> it?
~을 잘 돌보다

M: Of course. I raised a dog when I was a kid.

W: Oh, I didn't know that you had a <u>pet</u>. I'll <u>be able to take good care</u> of it with your help.
애완동물　　　　　잘 돌볼 수 있다
(be able to V: ~할 수 있다)

M: Definitely. Our children will also be happy to know that we'll have a puppy.

W: (All right. I'll tell Amy that we'll take one of her puppies.)

해석

남: 여보, 무엇을 보고 있어요?

여: 이 사진 속의 강아지들을 봐요.

남: 너무 귀엽네요. 누구의 강아지들이에요?

여: 제 사촌인 Amy의 강아지들이에요.

남: 다섯 마리네요! 그녀가 그들을 모두 키우는 것은 분명 어려울 거예요.

여: 그래서 그녀가 우리가 강아지를 키울 의향이 있는지 물어본 거예요. 그녀는 제가 개들을 좋아하는 것을 알고 있거든요.

남: 정말이에요? 그거 좋은 생각이네요.

여: 그래요, 하지만 당신은 우리가 강아지를 잘 돌볼 수 있다고 확신해요?

남: 물론이죠. 저는 어렸을 때 개를 키웠어요.

여: 오, 당신에게 애완동물이 있었는지 몰랐네요. 당신의 도움으로 강아지를 잘 돌볼 수 있을 거예요.

남: 당연하죠. 우리 아이들도 강아지를 키우게 될 것을 알면 기뻐할 거예요.

여: (알겠어요. Amy에게 그녀의 강아지들 중 한 마리를 우리가 데려가겠다고 말할게요.)

①알겠어요. 저는 육아에 관한 책을 읽는 것을 좋아해요.

②저는 동의하지 않아요. 우리는 개들을 키울 준비가 되지 않았어요.

✔③알겠어요. Amy에게 그녀의 강아지들 중 한 마리를 우리가 데려가겠다고 말할게요.

④신경 쓰지 마요. 강아지를 키울 수 있는 또 다른 기회가 있을 거예요.

⑤물론이죠. 애완동물 주인들은 그들의 애완동물을 질병으로부터 보호해야 해요.

문제풀이

남자가 애완동물을 키워 본 경험이 있고 강아지를 키우게 되면 아이들도 기뻐할 것이라는 남자의 말을 들은 여자에게서 긍정적인 반응이 예상된다. 따라서 정답은 ③ 'All right. I'll tell Amy that we'll take one of her puppies.(알겠어요. Amy에게 그녀의 강아지들 중 한 마리를 우리가 데려가겠다고 말할게요.)'이다.

---

14 여자의 마지막 말에 대한 남자의 응답

▶ 정답 ②

[Phone rings.]

M: Hello? How can I help you?

W: Hello. I'd like to ask about the <u>library facilities</u>.
도서관 시설들

M: You're talking to the right person. How may I help you?

W: I just <u>checked</u> the <u>public library homepage</u>, but I'm having trouble <u>finding</u> some information.
확인했다　　　공공 도서관 홈페이지　　　찾는 데 어려움을 겪는
(have trouble V-ing:
~하는 데 어려움을 겪다)

M: I apologize. What would you like to know?

W: It says the library <u>is going to reopen</u> after the <u>renovation</u> on the
다시 문을 열다　　　　　보수 공사
15th of November. But what time does it open on that day?

M: It will open at 9 a.m. and close at 6 p.m.

W: Okay. I plan to borrow books on that day. Can I use the library card that I have now?

M: I'm afraid not. We adopted a new system.

W: Oh, how can I get a new card?

M: Come to the check-out desk and we'll give you one.

W: All right. I think putting those details on the website would be helpful.

M: (I agree. I'll update all the information as soon as possible.)

해석

[전화벨이 울린다.]

남: 여보세요? 무엇을 도와드릴까요?

여: 여보세요. 저는 도서관 시설들에 대해 여쭤보고 싶어요.

남: 적임자와 이야기하고 계십니다. 어떻게 도와드릴까요?

여: 제가 방금 공공 도서관 홈페이지를 확인했는데, 정보를 찾는 데 어려움을 겪고 있어요.

남: 죄송합니다. 무엇을 알고 싶으신가요?

여: 도서관이 11월 15일에 보수 공사 후에 다시 문을 열 예정이라고 하더군요. 그런데 그날 몇 시에 문을 여나요?

남: 오전 9시에 문을 열고 오후 6시에 닫을 거예요.

여: 알겠어요. 저는 그날 책들을 빌릴 계획이거든요. 제가 지금 가지고 있는 도서관 카드를 사용할 수 있을까요?

남: 안 될 것 같습니다. 저희가 새 시스템을 도입했거든요.

여: 오, 어떻게 새 카드를 받을 수 있을까요?

남: 대출 창구에 오시면 카드를 드릴 거예요.

여: 알겠어요. 제 생각에는 그런 세부사항들을 웹 사이트에 올리는 것이 도움이 될 것 같아요.

남: (동의해요. 가능한 한 빨리 모든 정보를 업데이트할게요.)

① 네. 도서관으로 가는 길을 찾을 수 없으면 저에게 알려주세요.

✓ 동의해요. 가능한 한 빨리 모든 정보를 업데이트할게요.

③ 유감이네요. 보수 공사가 제가 예상했던 것보다 더 오래 걸리네요.

④ 죄송해요. 한 번에 다섯 권이 넘는 책을 빌리실 수 없어요.

⑤ 맞아요. 모든 도서관 시설들을 무료로 이용하실 수 있어요.

15 다음 상황에서 Peter가 Stella에게 할 말   고2 2018년 11월 15번 정답률 75% ▶ 정답 ⑤

M: Peter and Stella are working in the same office. Their office is packed with computers, copy machines, and other office supplies, so there's always lots of dust in the office. They used to open the windows for some fresh air several times a day, but nowadays they can't because of severe and frequent fine dust. Because of this, Stella suffers from chronic coughing, so Peter tries to think about how to improve air quality in the office. One day, Peter finds out that some plants help purify the air. So, Peter wants to suggest to Stella that they put plant pots in their office. In this situation, what would Peter most likely say to Stella?

Peter: (Why don't we get some plants for fresh air?)

해석

남: Peter와 Stella는 같은 사무실에서 일하고 있다. 그들의 사무실은 컴퓨터들, 복사기들, 그리고 다른 사무용품들로 꽉 차서, 사무실에는 항상 많은 먼지가 있다. 그들은 하루에도 몇 번씩 신선한 공기를 마시기 위해 창문들을 열곤 했지만, 요즘에는 심하고 잦은 미세먼지 때문에 그러지 못한다. 이 때문에, Stella는 만성 기침으로 고통받고 있어서, Peter는 사무실의 공기의 질을 향상시키는 법에 대해 생각해 보려고 한다. 어느 날, Peter는 몇몇 식물들이 공기를 정화하는 데 도움을 준다는 것을 알게 된다. 그래서, Peter는 Stella에게 사무실에 화분들을 놓자고 제안하고 싶다. 이러한 상황에서, Peter는 Stella에게 뭐라고 말하겠는가?

Peter: (우리 신선한 공기를 위해 식물들을 좀 사는 게 어때?)

① 너는 기침약을 좀 먹는 게 좋겠어.

② 새 사무실에 대해 어떻게 생각해?

③ 우리는 최고의 결과를 얻기 위해 협력해야 해.

④ 우리는 복사기를 한 대 더 사야 해.

✓ 우리 신선한 공기를 위해 식물들을 좀 사는 게 어때?

16~17 1지문 2문항

W: Hello, everyone. I'm Wilma Moore from Margaret Medical Center. As the days get shorter during winter, many people find themselves feeling sad. What can we do about it? I'd like to recommend some things to eat that can help you deal with this problem. First, salmon, a popular cold-water fish, can help fight depression. Salmon is rich in omega-3 fatty acids that improve symptoms associated with depression. Second, eating eggs daily can help fight many kinds of mood disorders. Eggs are one of the few foods that contain vitamin D, which can prevent depression. Third, if you eat a few bananas a day, it can keep you happy and relieve the symptoms of depression. Bananas are known to contain a type of protein that helps you relax, improving your mood. Lastly, yogurt also can be effective in beating the winter blues. The protein and calcium in yogurt can ease anxiety. Try these foods and they'll lift you up when you're down. I hope you stay healthy during the cold winter.

해석

여: 안녕하세요, 여러분. 저는 Margaret Medical Center(마가렛 의료 센터)의 Wilma Moore입니다. 겨울 동안 낮이 더 짧아지면서, 많은 사람들은 그들 자신이 슬픔을 느끼고 있음을 알게 됩니다. 우리는 그것에 대해 무엇을 할 수 있을까요? 저는 이 문제를 해결하는 데 도움을 줄 수 있는 몇 가지 먹을거리를 추천하고 싶습니다. 첫째로, 인기 있는 냉수성 어류인 연어는 우울증을 퇴치하는 데 도움을 줄 수 있습니다. 연어는 우울증과 관련된 증상들을 개선하는 오메가3 지방산이 풍부합니다. 둘째로, 매일 계란을 먹는 것은 많은 종류의 기분 장애들을 퇴치하는 데 도움을 줄 수 있습니다. 계란은 비타민D를 함유한 몇 안 되는 식품 중 하나로, 우울증을 예방할 수 있습니다. 셋째로, 하루에 바나나를 몇 개 먹으면, 그것이 기분을 좋게 유지해줘서 우울증의 증상들을 완화할 수 있습니다. 바나나는 기분을 향상시키면서, 진정하는 데 도움을 주는 일종의 단백질을 함유하고 있는 것으로 알려져 있습니다. 마지막으로, 요거트도 겨울 우울증을 물리치는 데 효과가 있을 수 있습니다. 요거트에 들어있는 단백질과 칼슘은 불안감을 완화할 수 있습니다. 이 식품들을 드시면 여러분이 우울할 때 그것들이 여러분을 기운 나게 할 것입니다. 추운 겨울 동안 건강하게 지내시길 바랍니다.

16 여자가 하는 말의 주제   고2 2018년 11월 16번 정답률 80% ▶ 정답 ①

✓ 겨울에 우울증을 감소시키는 식품들

② 추운 겨울 동안 운동하는 것의 필요성

③ 여러 가지 즐길 수 있는 음식을 위한 건강한 요리법들

④ 충분한 영양이 있는 식품을 선택하는 방법들

⑤ 인체 내에서 단백질의 중요한 기능들

17 언급된 식품이 아닌 것   고2 2018년 11월 17번 정답률 90% ▶ 정답 ⑤

① 연어   ② 계란   ③ 바나나

④ 요거트   ✓ 호두

02 2019년 3월 학력평가

01	③	02	⑤	03	①	04	⑤	05	②
06	④	07	①	08	③	09	⑤	10	④
11	③	12	⑤	13	②	14	①	15	②
16	①	17	④						

01 남자가 하는 말의 목적

고2 2019년 3월 3번   정답률 90%   ▶ 정답 ③

M: Hello, everyone. These days, children tend to have vision problems
시력에 문제가 있는 경향이 있다
(tend to V: ~하는 경향이 있다, have a vision problem: 시력에 문제가 있다)
because of too much time spent on digital devices, and many
~ 때문에   디지털 기기들
parents are worried about it. However, there are things you can do
to keep your child's eyes healthy. First of all, set screen time limits
여러분의 아이의 눈을 건강하게 지키다   화면 시간 제한을 설정하다
for your child. Second, provide your child with nutritious foods,
여러분의 아이에게 영양가 있는 음식들을 제공하다
(provide A with B: A에게 B를 제공하다, nutritious: 영양가 있는)
such as vegetables, fruits, nuts, and fish. They contain nutrients
영양소를 함유하다
that are good for your child's eyes. Third, have your child wear
~에 좋은
protective glasses when they play outside in the sun. Last but not
보호 안경   밖에서 놀다
least, have your child's eyes examined regularly. Remember that
아이의 눈을 정기적으로 검사를 받도록 하다
(have+명사+p.p.: (타인에 의해) ~가 …되다)
prevention is better than cure. Thank you.
예방   치료

해석
남: 안녕하세요, 여러분. 요즘에, 아이들은 디지털 기기에 소비되는 너무 많은 시간 때문에 시
력에 문제가 있는 경향이 있고, 많은 부모님들이 그것에 대해 걱정을 합니다. 하지만, 여러
분의 아이의 눈을 건강하게 지키기 위해 할 수 있는 일들이 있습니다. 첫째, 아이를 위한 화
면 시간 제한을 설정하십시오. 둘째, 아이에게 야채, 과일, 견과류, 그리고 생선 같은 영양
가 있는 음식들을 제공하십시오. 그것들은 아이의 눈에 좋은 영양소들을 함유하고 있습니
다. 셋째, 아이가 햇볕을 쬐며 밖에서 놀 때 보호 안경을 쓰게 하십시오. 마지막으로 중요
한 것은, 아이의 눈을 정기적으로 검사를 받도록 하십시오. 예방이 치료보다 더 낫다는 것
을 기억하십시오. 감사합니다.

① 올바른 안경 착용 및 관리 방법에 대해 알려 주려고
② 전자기기를 활용한 효과적인 학습법을 안내하려고
✓③ 어린이의 시력을 보호하는 방법을 소개하려고
④ 어린이의 야외 활동 시 보호자의 동반을 권유하려고
⑤ 성장기에 균형 있는 영양 섭취가 중요함을 강조하려고

02 여자의 의견

고2 2019년 3월 4번   정답률 70%   ▶ 정답 ⑤

W: Are you trying to buy something online, Neil?
사려고 하는(try to V: ~하려고 하다)
M: Yes, Mom. I just found a nice item online.
물건
W: What is it?
M: This black leather jacket. They sell it for only $60.
검은색 가죽 재킷
W: That's very cheap, but did you check if the shop is authorized?
싼   확인하다   인가를 받다(be authorized)
M: No, I didn't. Do I have to?
~해야 하다
W: Well, you need to be cautious. There could be online sellers you
조심해야 한다(need to V: ~해야 하다, cautious: 조심하는) 온라인 판매자들
can't trust.
신뢰하다
M: You mean they could take my money without delivering my order?
배달하지 않고   주문한 물건
(without V-ing: ~하지 않고, deliver: 배달하다)
W: Yeah. That's why you need to buy things only at reliable online
신뢰할 수 있는
shops.
M: Okay, Mom. I'll check that before I buy the jacket.

해석
여: 온라인에서 무언가 사려고 하는 거니, Neil?
남: 네, 엄마. 온라인에서 방금 좋은 물건을 찾았거든요.

여: 그것이 뭔데?
남: 이 검은색 가죽 재킷이요. 겨우 60달러에 팔고 있어요.
여: 매우 싸구나, 그런데 그 가게가 인가를 받았는지 확인했니?
남: 아니요, 안 했어요. 해야 해요?
여: 음, 너는 조심해야 해. 신뢰할 수 없는 온라인 판매자들이 있을 수 있거든.
남: 그들이 제가 주문한 물건을 배달하지 않고 돈을 가져갈 수도 있다는 말씀이세요?
여: 그래. 그런 이유로 신뢰할 수 있는 온라인 상점에서만 물건을 사야 하는 거야.
남: 알겠어요, 엄마. 재킷을 사기 전에 그것을 확인할게요.

① 가격과 품질이 반드시 비례하는 것은 아니다.
② 의류는 매장에서 직접 입어 보고 사는 것이 좋다.
③ 정해진 예산 내에서 소비하는 습관을 가져야 한다.
④ 인터넷에 있는 상품 평가를 그대로 믿어서는 안 된다.
✓⑤ 인터넷을 통한 구매는 신뢰할 수 있는 곳에서 해야 한다.

03 두 사람의 관계

고2 2019년 3월 5번   정답률 65%   ▶ 정답 ①

[Cell phone rings.]
M: Hello, Ms. Johnson.
W: Hello, Mr. Baker. I'd like to talk to you about the commercial for my
이야기하고 싶다   광고
restaurant.
(would like to V: ~하고 싶다)
M: You mean the new menu commercial?
W: Yes. I think there's a problem with it.
문제
M: Really? May I ask what that is?
W: Well, according to our contract, the commercial is supposed to be
~에 따르면   계약   방송되기로 되어 있다
aired before the evening news on your station. (be supposed to V: ~하기로
방송국   되어 있다, be aired: 방송되다)
M: Yes, I remember that.
기억하다
W: But the commercial was not broadcast yesterday.
M: Is that true? 방송되지 않았다(be broadcast: 방송되다)
W: Yes. I checked it myself.
확인했다
M: Okay, Ms. Johnson. I'll talk with our staff about that and fix the
직원   해결하다
problem.
W: Thank you. I want you to do it as soon as possible.
가능한 한 빨리

해석
[휴대전화가 울린다.]
남: 여보세요, Johnson 씨.
여: 안녕하세요, Baker 씨. 제 식당의 광고에 대해 얘기하고 싶어요.
남: 신메뉴 광고를 말씀하시는 거죠?
여: 네. 그것에 문제가 있는 것 같아요.
남: 정말이에요? 그게 뭔지 여쭤봐도 될까요?
여: 음, 우리의 계약에 따르면, 광고는 방송국에서 저녁 뉴스 전에 방송되기로 되어 있잖아요.
남: 네, 기억해요.
여: 하지만 광고가 어제 방송되지 않았어요.
남: 그게 사실이에요?
여: 네. 제가 직접 확인했어요.
남: 알겠어요, Johnson 씨. 저희 직원과 그것에 대해 얘기하고 문제를 해결할게요.
여: 감사합니다. 가능한 한 빨리 그렇게 해 주셨으면 해요.

✓① 광고 방송 담당자 — 의뢰인
② 광고 제작자 — 광고 모델
③ 식당 주인 — 주방장
④ 식당 종업원 — 손님
⑤ 방송 프로듀서 — 뉴스 진행자

04 그림에서 대화의 내용과 일치하지 않는 것

고2 2019년 3월 6번   정답률 85%   ▶ 정답 ⑤

M: Grace, come look at this showcase. These items were donated by
진열장   물건들   기증된
sports stars who graduated from here.
스포츠 스타들   ~을 졸업했다(graduate from)
W: Great! Who is the man in the rectangular picture frame?
직사각형 사진 액자
M: That's Larry Smith, the best player on the national baseball team.
야구 국가 대표 팀
W: There's a baseball bat next to the picture frame. Is it one of his?
야구 방망이
M: Yes. He hit his 100th home run with that bat.
그의 100호 홈런을 쳤다

W: Oh, really? Whose glove is it in front of the uniform?
　　　　　　　　　　　글러브　　　　　　　　　유니폼
M: It's Larry's, too. He used it when he was in high school.
W: I see. The basketball in the middle has a letter K on it. What does
　　　　　　농구공　　　　가운데에　　　　글자
　 it stand for?
　 ~을 의미하다
M: You know the basketball player Kevin Jackson? K is his initial.
　　　　　　　　농구 선수　　　　　　　　　　　　　이름의 머리글자
W: I didn't know he was a graduate of your school.
　　　　　　　　　　　　　　졸업생
M: Look at his trophy beside the ball. That's the very trophy he
　　　　　　　트로피　　　　　　　　　　　　　　바로 그
　 received as MVP.
　 받았다　　MVP로서
W: Wow! You must be very proud of your graduates.
　　　　　　　~을 매우 자랑스러워 하다

해석
남: Grace, 와서 이 진열장을 봐. 이 물건들은 여기를 졸업한 스포츠 스타들이 기증한 것들
　 이야.
여: 멋지다! 직사각형 사진 액자 안에 있는 남자는 누구야?
남: 야구 국가 대표 팀에서 가장 뛰어난 선수인 Larry Smith야.
여: 사진 액자 옆에는 야구 방망이가 있구나. 그의 야구 방망이가 중 하나야?
남: 맞아. 그는 저 방망이로 그의 100호 홈런을 쳤어.
여: 오, 정말? 유니폼 앞에 있는 것은 누구의 글러브야?
남: 그것도 Larry의 것이야. 그는 고등학교 때 그것을 사용했어.
여: 그렇구나. 가운데에 있는 농구공에는 K라는 글자가 있네. 그것은 무엇을 의미하니?
남: 농구 선수 Kevin Jackson을 알지? K는 그의 이름의 머리글자야.
여: 나는 그가 네 학교의 졸업생인 줄 몰랐어.
남: 공 옆에 있는 그의 트로피를 봐. 그것은 그가 MVP로서 받은 바로 그 트로피야.
여: 와! 너는 졸업생들을 매우 자랑스러워 하겠구나.

05 남자가 할 일
고2 2019년 3월 7번 ▶ 정답 ②

W: Honey, I'm so excited that we're finally having a housewarming
　　　　　　　　　　　　　　　　　　　　드디어　　　　　　　집들이
　 party.
M: Me, too.
W: The guests will arrive soon. Is everything ready?
　　　　손님들　　　　도착하다　　　　　　　　　준비된
M: Yes, almost. You've checked the oven, haven't you?
　　　　　　　　　　　　확인한　　　　오븐
W: Yes, I have. The chicken is roasting nicely.
　　　　　　　　　　　　　　　구워지는(roast)
M: Good. The strawberry cake is in the fridge. Hmm.... I think
　　　　　　　딸기 케이크　　　　　　　냉장고
　 everything is all set. I'll take one last look at the bathroom.
　　　　　　　　　　　　　　　　　~을 마지막으로 한 번 더 보다　　　　화장실
W: Oh, I forgot to replace the towels with fresh ones.
　　　　　수건을 새것으로 교체하는 것을 잊었어
　　　　(forget to V: ~하는 것을 잊다, replace A with B: A를 B로 교체하다)
M: No problem. I'll take care of the towels. How about the toilet
　　　　　　　　　　　~을 처리하다　　　　　　　　　　　　　화장지
　 paper?
W: Don't worry. I've already replaced it with a new roll.
　　　　　　　　　　　　　　　　　　　　　　　두루마리
M: Good!

해석
여: 여보, 우리가 드디어 집들이를 하게 되다니 정말 신나요.
남: 저도 그래요.
여: 손님들이 곧 도착할 거에요. 모든 것이 준비되었어요?
남: 네, 거의요. 당신은 오븐을 확인했죠, 그렇지 않아요?
여: 네, 했어요. 닭이 잘 구워지고 있어요.
남: 좋아요. 딸기 케이크는 냉장고에 있어요. 흠.... 모든 것이 준비된 것 같아요. 화장실을 마지

막으로 한 번 더 볼게요.
여: 오, 수건을 새것으로 교체하는 것을 잊었어요.
남: 괜찮아요. 제가 수건을 처리할게요. 화장지는 어때요?
여: 걱정하지 마요. 제가 이미 그것을 새 두루마리로 교체했어요.
남: 잘했네요!

① 손님 명단 확인하기
✓ 수건 교체하기
③ 오븐 속 음식 확인하기
④ 냉장고에 케이크 넣기
⑤ 화장실에 화장지 갖다 놓기

06 여자가 지불할 금액
▶ 정답 ④

M: Emma, we've run out of shampoo.
　　　　　　　~이 다 떨어졌다(run out of: ~이 다 떨어지다)
W: Really? Then I'll order some online now. [Pause]
　　　　　　　　　　주문하다
M: What's the price of the shampoo we usually use?
　　　　　　　가격　　　　　　　　　　　보통
W: It's $15 a bottle at this online store. How many bottles do you want
　　　　　　　　　　　　온라인 상점
　 me to order?
　 내가 주문하기를 원하다
　 (want A to V: A가 ~하기를 원하다)
M: How about two bottles?
W: Okay. Do we have anything else to buy?
M: Hmm, let me think. Oh, didn't you say you need to buy toothbrushes?
　　　　　　　　　　　　　　　　　　　　　　사야 하다　　　칫솔들
　　　　　　　　　　　　　　　　　　　　(need to V: ~해야 하다)
W: That's right. It's $10 for a pack of four toothbrushes.
　　　　　　　　　　　　칫솔 네 개가 든 한 상자
M: Then, let's order two packs.
W: Okay. I have a $2 discount coupon, so I'll use it.
　　　　　　　　　　2달러 할인 쿠폰
M: That's good. Is there a delivery charge?
　　　　　　　　　　　　　배송료
W: No, there's no delivery charge for orders over $20. I'll place the
　　　　　　　　　　　　　　　　　　　　　　　　　　　　주문하다
　 order now.

해석
남: Emma, 샴푸가 다 떨어졌어.
여: 정말? 그럼 지금 온라인으로 주문할게. [잠시 후]
남: 우리가 보통 사용하는 샴푸의 가격은 얼마야?
여: 이 온라인 상점에서는 한 통에 15달러야. 내가 몇 통을 주문하기를 원하니?
남: 두 통은 어때?
여: 좋아. 그 밖에 다른 살 것이 있니?
남: 흠, 생각해 볼게. 오, 네가 칫솔을 사야 한다고 말하지 않았어?
여: 네 말이 맞아. 칫솔 네 개가 든 한 상자에 10달러야.
남: 그럼, 두 상자를 주문하자.
여: 알았어. 나한테 2달러 할인 쿠폰이 있으니까, 그것을 사용할게.
남: 그거 잘됐다. 배송료가 있니?
여: 아니, 20달러 이상의 주문에 대해서는 배송료가 없어. 지금 주문할게.

① $30　　　　　② $38　　　　　③ $42
✓ $48　　　　　⑤ $50

문제풀이
15달러짜리 샴푸 두 통은 30달러, 칫솔 네 개가 들어있는 상자 두 개는 20달러이므로 합치면
총 50달러가 된다. 여자가 2달러 할인 쿠폰을 사용하게 되면 총액이 50달러에서 2달러를 뺀
48달러가 되므로 답은 ④ '$48'이다.

07 남자가 여자와 함께 수리 센터에 갈 수 없는 이유
▶ 정답 ①

W: Hi, Max. Where are you going?
M: I'm going to a print shop. My printer at home is out of order.
　　　　　　　　인쇄소　　　　　프린터　　　　　고장이 난
W: Oh, that must be annoying.
　　　　　　　　　짜증나게 하는
M: You're telling me. I have to fix it right away. Is there any place
　　　　　　　　　　고쳐야 하다(have to V: ~해야 하다, fix: 고치다)
　 nearby that can repair electronics?
　　　　　　　　　　수리하다　전자 제품들
W: There's one near the post office. I'm going there today to have my
　　　　　　　　　　　　우체국
　 laptop fixed.
　 노트북 컴퓨터

M: Really? What time are you going? I'd like to go with you if possible.
  가능하다면
W: I'm going there at around 5 p.m. after Professor Simon's special lecture.
  특별 강연
M: 5 p.m.? I'm afraid I can't go with you then.
W: Oh, you have a tennis lesson today, don't you?
  테니스 강습
M: No, the lesson is tomorrow. Actually I have an appointment with Professor Watson.
  ~와 약속이 있다
W: I see. Then, I'll text you the phone number of the repair shop.
  문자를 보내다   수리점
M: Thank you.

해석
여: 안녕, Max. 어디에 가니?
남: 인쇄소에 가고 있어. 집에 있는 내 프린터가 고장이 났거든.
여: 오, 짜증나겠구나.
남: 정말 그래. 나는 그것을 지금 당장 수리해야 해. 근처에 전자 제품을 수리할 수 있는 곳이 있니?
여: 우체국 근처에 하나 있어. 나는 오늘 내 노트북 컴퓨터를 고치러 그곳에 갈 거야.
남: 정말? 몇 시에 가니? 가능하다면 너와 함께 가고 싶어.
여: 나는 Simon 교수님의 특별 강연 후에 오후 5시쯤 그곳에 갈 거야.
남: 오후 5시? 그럼 나는 너와 함께 갈 수 없을 것 같아.
여: 오, 너는 오늘 테니스 강습이 있지, 그렇지 않니?
남: 아니, 그 강습은 내일이야. 사실, 나는 Watson 교수님과 약속이 있어.
여: 그렇구나. 그럼, 내가 너에게 수리점의 전화번호를 문자로 보내줄게.
남: 고마워.

☑ 교수님과 약속이 있어서
② 우편물을 수령해야 해서
③ 컴퓨터를 사러 가야 해서
④ 특별 강연을 들어야 해서
⑤ 테니스 강습을 받아야 해서

---

08 Romance City에 관해 언급되지 않은 것 ▶ 정답 ③

M: Maria, what are you watching?
W: I'm watching the preview of the new TV drama, *Romance City*.
  예고편
M: *Romance City*? When does it start?
W: The first episode will be aired on March 9th.
  첫 회   방영되다
M: Oh, it's this Saturday!
W: Yes. My favorite actor, Liam Collins, is the main character.
  제일 좋아하는 배우   주인공
M: Oh, he is? I like him, too.
W: The director is Sam Adams. He also directed *Dreamcatcher*.
  감독   감독했다
M: Really? I loved that drama.
W: You know what? *Romance City* is based on the best-selling novel of the same title.
  ~에 기반을 둔   베스트셀러 소설
  제목
M: Have you read the novel?
W: Of course. I enjoyed it very much.

해석
남: Maria, 무엇을 보고 있니?
여: 새 TV 드라마인 〈Romance City〉의 예고편을 보고 있어.
남: 〈Romance City〉? 언제 시작하는데?
여: 첫 회는 3월 9일에 방영될 거야.
남: 오, 이번 주 토요일이구나!
여: 그래. 내가 제일 좋아하는 배우인 Liam Collins가 주인공이야.
남: 오, 그래? 나도 그를 좋아해.
여: 감독은 Sam Adams야. 그는 〈Dreamcatcher〉도 감독했어.
남: 정말? 나는 그 드라마를 정말 좋아했어.
여: 그거 아니? 〈Romance City〉는 같은 제목의 베스트셀러 소설에 기반을 두고 있어.
남: 그 소설을 읽어 봤어?
여: 물론이지. 나는 그것을 매우 재미있게 읽었어.

① 첫 방영 날짜   ② 주연 배우   ☑ 줄거리
④ 감독   ⑤ 원작 소설

---

09 Redland Festival에 관한 내용과 일치하지 않는 것 ▶ 정답 ⑤

W: Hello, listeners. Are you looking for something to do this summer?
  ~을 찾는(look for)
Then, how about going to the Redland Festival? It is a fruit festival
  과일 축제
to promote good health. This festival is an annual event held in
  증진하다   연례 행사
Blue River Park. This year, it will take place on Saturday, July 13th,
  열리다
from 10 a.m. to 8 p.m. During the festival, an unlimited fruit buffet
  무제한 과일 뷔페
will be provided all day long. You can also participate in sports
  제공되다   ~에 참가하다
activities such as soccer and badminton. The $10 admission fee
  ~과 같은   10달러의 입장료
includes sports activities as well as the fruit buffet. Reservations
  과일 뷔페뿐만 아니라 스포츠 활동도   예약들
  (B as well as A: A뿐만 아니라 B도)
are not necessary. Come enjoy this fun festival. Thank you.
  필요한

해석
여: 안녕하세요, 청취자 여러분. 이번 여름에 할 일을 찾고 계시나요? 그렇다면, Redland Festival(레드랜드 축제)에 가는 건 어떠십니까? 그것은 건강을 증진하기 위한 과일 축제입니다. 이 축제는 Blue River Park(블루 리버 파크)에서 열리는 연례 행사입니다. 올해는 7월 13일 토요일에 오전 10시부터 오후 8시까지 열릴 것입니다. 축제 기간 동안, 하루 종일 무제한 과일 뷔페가 제공될 것입니다. 여러분은 축구와 배드민턴 같은 스포츠 활동에도 참가할 수 있습니다. 10달러의 입장료에는 과일 뷔페뿐만 아니라 스포츠 활동들도 포함됩니다. 예약은 필요 없습니다. 오셔서 이 재미있는 축제를 즐겨주십시오. 감사합니다.

① 건강을 증진하기 위한 과일 축제이다.
② Blue River Park에서 열리는 연례행사이다.
③ 과일 뷔페를 무제한 이용할 수 있다.
④ 입장료에 스포츠 활동 비용이 포함된다.
☑ 사전 예약이 필요하다.

---

10 표에서 여자가 주문할 헤어드라이어 ▶ 정답 ④

M: Claire, look at this. Five best-selling hair dryers are on sale at this
                                  헤어드라이어들   할인 판매 중인
online store.
온라인 상점
W: Good. I was going to buy a new one.
M: Why don't you choose one with a higher wattage? The higher the
              선택하다   더 높은 와트 수
wattage, the faster you dry your hair.
              말리다
W: You're right. I'll choose one with 1,500 watts or more.
M: Which material is better, ionic or ceramic?
        재질   이온의   세라믹의
W: The ionic model is good for my hair type. So, I'll get an ionic one.
              ~에 좋은   모발 종류
M: I think the price is also important.
          가격   중요한
W: I agree. I'll buy a model that's under $50.
M: Then, you have only two models to choose from.
W: I think it's better to choose one with a cool shot setting.
M: Yeah, with that function, you can dry your hair with cool air.
          기능   찬 바람
W: Okay, then, I'll order this one.
                주문하다

해석
남: Claire, 이것 좀 봐. 이 온라인 상점에서 가장 잘 팔리는 다섯 개의 헤어드라이어를 할인 판매 중이야.
여: 잘됐다. 나는 새것을 살 예정이었어.
남: 와트 수가 더 높은 것을 선택하는 게 어떠니? 와트 수가 더 높을수록, 머리카락을 더 빨리 말릴 수 있잖아.
여: 네 말이 맞아. 1,500와트 이상인 것을 선택할 거야.
남: 이온과 세라믹 중 어떤 재질이 더 좋니?
여: 이온 모델이 내 모발 종류에 좋아. 그래서, 이온 헤어드라이어를 살 거야.
남: 가격도 중요할 것 같아.
여: 동의해. 나는 50달러 이하인 모델을 살 거야.
남: 그럼, 선택할 수 있는 모델은 두 개뿐이야.
여: 쿨 샷 세팅 기능이 있는 것을 선택하는 게 더 좋을 것 같아.
남: 그래, 그 기능이 있으면, 머리카락을 찬 바람으로 말릴 수 있지.
여: 좋아, 그럼, 이것을 주문할게.

가장 잘 팔리는 헤어드라이어

	모델	전력(와트 수)	재질	가격	쿨 샷 세팅 기능
①	A	1,450	세라믹	30달러	×
②	B	1,600	세라믹	35달러	○
③	C	1,650	이온	40달러	×
✓	D	1,700	이온	45달러	○
⑤	E	1,800	이온	53달러	○

11 남자의 마지막 말에 대한 여자의 응답

고2 2019년 3월 1번 정답률 85%

▶ 정답 ③

M: Esther, I heard from Jack that you had an accident.
<u>사고</u>

W: Yeah, I fell down and twisted my ankle.
<u>넘어졌다(fall down)</u> <u>내 발목을 삐었다(twist one's ankle)</u>

M: That sounds painful. Did you see a doctor?
<u>아픈</u>

W: (Yes. He just told me to relax for a few days.)
<u>쉬다</u> <u>며칠 동안</u>

해석
남: Esther, Jack에게 네가 사고를 당했다고 들었어.
여: 그래, 나는 넘어져서 발목을 삐었어.
남: 그거 아프겠다. 의사에게 가 봤니?
여: (응. 그는 나에게 며칠 동안 쉬라고 말했어.)
① 맞아. 그는 사람들을 돕기 위해 의사가 되었어.
② 말도 안 돼. 나는 그가 발목을 삐었다고 생각하지 않아.
✓ 응. 그는 나에게 며칠 동안 쉬라고 말했어.
④ 물론이지. 너는 더 조심했어야 했어.
⑤ 아니. 나는 네가 병원에 있는 줄 몰랐어.

12 여자의 마지막 말에 대한 남자의 응답

고2 2019년 3월 2번 정답률 85%

▶ 정답 ⑤

W: What are you looking at on your smartphone, Jason?
<u>~을 보는(look at)</u>

M: Oh, I'm looking for a place to have my mother's birthday party.
<u>~을 찾는(look for)</u> <u>엄마의 생신 파티</u> <u>파티를 하다(have a party: 파티를 하다)</u>

W: Really? I know a nice Italian restaurant downtown.
<u>이탈리아 식당</u> <u>시내에</u>

M: (Great. Can you tell me the name of the restaurant?)

해석
여: 스마트폰으로 무엇을 보고 있니, Jason?
남: 오, 엄마의 생신 파티를 할 장소를 찾고 있어.
여: 정말? 내가 시내에 있는 멋진 이탈리아 식당을 알고 있어.
남: (잘됐다. 그 식당의 이름을 나에게 말해줄 수 있니?)
① 문제 없어. 나는 어제 예약을 했어.
② 고마워. 음식이 곧 제공될 거야.
③ 미안해. 나는 파티에 참석할 수 없을 거야.
④ 좋아. 너는 언제 파티를 할 거니?
✓ 잘됐다. 그 식당의 이름을 나에게 말해줄 수 있니?

13 남자의 마지막 말에 대한 여자의 응답

고2 2019년 3월 13번 정답률 75%

▶ 정답 ②

W: Daniel, what are you looking for in the closet?
<u>~을 찾는(look for)</u> <u>옷장</u>

M: I'm looking for my spring pants and shirts. Where are they, Mom?
<u>봄 바지</u> <u>셔츠들</u>

W: All your spring clothes are in the box here.
<u>봄옷들</u>

M: [Pause] Wow, you put all my spring clothes in this box!
<u>넣었다</u>

W: Yeah. Look at what's written on the box.
<u>~을 보다</u>

M: Oh, it says "Daniel's spring clothes."

W: There are many good things about storing off-season clothes in separate boxes.
<u>별도의 상자들</u> <u>보관하는 것</u> <u>철이 지난 옷들</u> <u>(store)</u>

M: I think we can easily find the clothes we need when the seasons change.
<u>쉽게</u> <u>계절이 바뀌다</u>

W: That's right. It also prevents the fading of colors.
<u>방지하다</u> <u>색이 바래는 것</u>

M: I see. Is there any other advantage?
<u>이점</u>

W: (Yes. We can keep clothes from getting dusty.)
<u>옷들에 먼지가 쌓이는 것을 막다</u>
(keep A from V-ing: A가 ~하는 것을 막다, get dusty: 먼지가 쌓이다)

해석
여: Daniel, 옷장에서 무엇을 찾고 있니?
남: 봄 바지와 셔츠를 찾고 있어요. 그것들은 어디에 있어요, 엄마?
여: 네 봄옷은 모두 여기 상자에 있단다.
남: [잠시 후] 와, 제 봄옷을 모두 이 상자에 넣어 놓으셨네요!
여: 그래. 상자에 쓰여 있는 것을 보렴.
남: 오, 'Daniel의 봄옷'이라고 쓰여 있네요.
여: 철이 지난 옷을 별도의 상자에 보관하는 것에는 좋은 점이 많이 있단다.
남: 계절이 바뀔 때 필요한 옷을 쉽게 찾을 수 있을 것 같아요.
여: 맞아. 색이 바래는 것도 방지하지.
남: 그렇군요. 다른 이점도 있나요?
여: (그래. 우리는 옷에 먼지가 쌓이는 것을 막을 수 있어.)
① 전혀 없어. 우리는 먼저 상자들을 비워야 해.
✓ 그래. 우리는 옷에 먼지가 쌓이는 것을 막을 수 있어.
③ 말도 안 돼. 우리는 바지와 셔츠를 따로 보관해야 해.
④ 좋아. 우리는 불필요한 옷을 자선 단체들에 기부할 수 있어.
⑤ 아니. 우리는 절대 옷을 상자에 넣으면 안 돼.

문제 풀이
계절에 따라 별도의 상자에 옷을 보관하는 것에 대한 장점을 이야기하다가 남자가 다른 이점도 있냐고 물었으므로 또 다른 장점을 언급하는 것이 가장 자연스럽다. 따라서 ② 'Yes. We can keep clothes from getting dusty.(그래. 우리는 옷에 먼지가 쌓이는 것을 막을 수 있어.)' 가 대답으로 적절하다.

14 여자의 마지막 말에 대한 남자의 응답

고2 2019년 3월 14번 정답률 80%

▶ 정답 ①

M: Honey, I'm home. What are you doing?

W: I'm doing yoga.
<u>요가를 하는(do yoga)</u>

M: Aren't you going to the yoga center today?
<u>요가 센터</u>

W: No, I'm not going there any longer. It's too far from here.
<u>~에서 너무 먼</u>

M: But don't you think it's better to do yoga at the center?

W: Yes, but I don't want to waste my time on the road.
<u>낭비하고 싶지 않다</u>
<u>(want to V: ~하고 싶다, waste: 낭비하다)</u>

M: If you exercise at home alone, you might lose interest.
<u>운동하다</u> <u>혼자</u> <u>흥미를 잃다</u>

W: Maybe, but I've found a nice fitness app and downloaded it on my smartphone.
<u>피트니스 앱</u> <u>다운로드했다</u>

M: A fitness app? What does it do for you?

W: It helps keep track of my workout schedule, provides personalized information, and so on.
<u>~에게 도움이 되다</u> <u>~을 기록하다</u> <u>운동 일정</u> <u>맞춤형 정보</u>

M: (That's awesome! It'll be very helpful.)

해석
남: 여보, 저 왔어요. 무엇을 하고 있어요?
여: 요가를 하고 있어요.
남: 오늘은 요가 센터에 안 가는 거예요?
여: 네, 더 이상 그곳에 가지 않을 거예요. 여기에서 너무 멀어요.
남: 하지만 센터에서 요가를 하는 것이 더 낫다고 생각하지 않아요?
여: 그래요, 하지만 길에서 제 시간을 낭비하고 싶지 않아요.
남: 집에서 혼자 운동을 하면, 흥미를 잃을 수도 있어요.
여: 그럴지도 모르지만, 저는 좋은 피트니스 앱을 찾아서 스마트폰에 다운로드했어요.
남: 피트니스 앱이요? 그것이 당신에게 무슨 도움이 되죠?
여: 그것은 제 운동 일정을 기록하는 데 도움을 주고, 맞춤형 정보 등을 제공해요.
남: (멋지네요! 그것은 매우 도움이 될 거예요.)
✓ 멋지네요! 그것은 매우 도움이 될 거예요.
② 아니요, 괜찮아요. 이 앱은 저에게 적합하지 않아요.
③ 믿을 수가 없네요! 당신의 운동 일정은 너무 빡빡해요.
④ 걱정하지 마요. 당신은 다른 피트니스 센터를 이용할 수 있어요.
⑤ 알겠어요. 제가 당신이 앱을 다운로드하는 것을 도울 수 있을 거예요.

문제 풀이
여자가 좋은 피트니스 앱을 찾아서 휴대전화에 다운받았고 남자에게 그 기능에 대해 말해주는 상황이다. 많은 장점을 지닌 앱의 기능에 대해 남자가 긍정적인 반응을 보이는 것이 자연스럽다. 따라서 답은 ① 'That's awesome! It'll be very helpful.(멋지네요! 그것은 매우 도움이 될 거예요.)'이 적절하다.

---

15 다음 상황에서 Willy가 수리 기사에게 할 말 고2 2019년 3월 15번 정답률 75% ▶ 정답 ②

M: Willy is a student who lives alone in a house near his university. Returning home after school, he finds that the room temperature of his house is very low. It feels quite chilly. He turns on the heating system, but it doesn't work. Willy calls a repairman and asks him to come and fix it. The repairman comes and fixes the problem. Willy says thanks to him and pays for the repair. After the repairman leaves, Willy finds that one of the repairman's tools is on the floor. Willy calls the repairman again to let him know about this. In this situation, what would Willy most likely say to the repairman?

Willy: (You left one of your tools in my house.)

해석

남: Willy는 그의 대학교 근처에 있는 집에서 혼자 사는 학생이다. 방과 후에 집으로 돌아와서, 그는 집의 실내 온도가 매우 낮다는 것을 알게 된다. 상당히 춥게 느껴지는 것이다. 그는 난방 장치를 켜지만, 작동하지 않는다. Willy는 수리 기사에게 전화를 걸고 그에게 와서 그것을 고쳐달라고 부탁한다. 수리 기사는 와서 문제를 해결한다. Willy는 그에게 고맙다고 말하며 수리비를 지불한다. 수리 기사가 떠난 후에, Willy는 수리 기사의 연장 중 하나가 바닥에 있는 것을 발견한다. Willy는 이것에 대해 알려 주기 위해 수리 기사에게 다시 전화를 건다. 이러한 상황에서, Willy는 수리 기사에게 뭐라고 말하겠는가?

Willy: (당신이 제 집에 연장 중 하나를 두고 갔어요.)

① 수리비로 얼마를 지불해야 하나요?
✓② 당신이 제 집에 연장 중 하나를 두고 갔어요.
③ 난방기가 다시 작동을 멈춘 것 같아요.
④ 나를 위해 온도를 올려 줄래요?
⑤ 와서 난방 장치를 고쳐 줄래요?

16~17 1지문 2문항

W: Hello, everyone. With technologies like Artificial Intelligence, it is possible to digitize homes. Today, I'd like to introduce to you household appliances made smarter with the help of technology. First are smart washing machines. Smart washers with AI techniques can sense the different types of fabric so they regulate the washing strength and detergent. They can even send an alert when detergent is out of stock. Next are smart refrigerators. They allow the user to monitor food items inside. They can even show relevant recipes that can be made with those items. There are also smart speakers. Speakers controlled by voice commands can do various tasks such as creating a play list and searching the Internet. Lastly, robotic vacuum cleaners can automatically clean the tight and usually overlooked spaces that are hard to access in traditional ways. Now, let's watch a video about these smart home appliances.

해석

여: 안녕하세요, 여러분. 인공지능과 같은 기술들로, 집을 디지털화하는 것이 가능합니다. 오늘, 저는 여러분께 기술의 도움으로 더 스마트하게 만들어진 가전제품들을 소개하고 싶습니다. 첫 번째는 스마트 세탁기입니다. AI 기술이 적용된 스마트 세탁기는 다양한 종류의 섬유를 감지해서 세탁 강도와 세제를 조절합니다. 그것들은 심지어 세제가 다 떨어졌을 때 경보를 보낼 수도 있습니다. 다음은 스마트 냉장고입니다. 그것들은 사용자가 내부의 식품을 확인할 수 있도록 해 줍니다. 심지어 그 식품으로 만들 수 있는 관련 요리법을 보여

줄 수도 있습니다. 스마트 스피커도 있습니다. 음성 명령에 의해 제어되는 스피커는 재생 목록 작성과 인터넷 검색과 같은 다양한 작업을 할 수 있습니다. 마지막으로, 로봇 진공 청소기는 전통적인 방법으로는 접근하기 어려운, 비좁으며 보통 간과되는 공간을 자동으로 청소할 수 있습니다. 이제, 이 스마트 가전제품들에 대한 영상을 보겠습니다.

---

16 여자가 하는 말의 주제 고2 2019년 3월 16번 정답률 85% ▶ 정답 ①

✓① 기술로 더 스마트하게 만들어진 가전제품들
② 스마트 가전제품들을 업그레이드하는 방법들
③ 온라인으로 스마트 가전제품들을 구매하는 방법
④ 에너지 효율적인 가전제품들의 이점들
⑤ AI 기술이 인간에게 미치는 부정적인 영향들

---

17 언급된 가전제품이 아닌 것 고2 2019년 3월 17번 정답률 85% ▶ 정답 ④

① 세탁기　　　　　　　　② 냉장고
③ 스피커　　　　　　　✓④ 에어컨
⑤ 진공 청소기

---

03 2019년 6월 학력평가

01	②	02	②	03	①	04	④	05	①
06	④	07	⑤	08	④	09	④	10	②
11	③	12	⑤	13	②	14	④	15	③
16	⑤	17	④						

---

01 여자가 하는 말의 목적 고2 2019년 6월 3번 정답률 80% ▶ 정답 ②

W: Hello, I'm Grace Cooper, the manager of the Dolphin Swimming Center. We always appreciate your love and support for the center. I have a wonderful announcement for all our members. So far, swimming classes have been held only in the mornings and evenings. Since the number of members has increased, many people have asked for new afternoon classes. Finally, we decided to meet your needs. From next month, there will be two classes opening in the afternoons. The instructor will be Mr. Jones. I hope this is good news for our members. For more information about the new afternoon classes, check the center's website. Thank you for listening.

해석

여: 안녕하십니까, 저는 Dolphin Swimming Center(돌고래 수영 센터)의 관리자인 Grace Cooper입니다. 저희는 항상 센터에 대한 여러분의 사랑과 지지에 감사를 드립니다. 모든 저희 회원들을 위한 멋진 소식이 있습니다. 지금까지, 수영 수업은 오전과 저녁에만 열렸습니다. 회원들의 수가 증가했기 때문에, 많은 분들이 새로운 오후 수업을 요청하셨습니다. 마침내, 저희는 여러분의 요구를 충족시키기로 결정했습니다. 다음 달부터, 오후에 열리는 두 개의 수업이 있을 것입니다. 강사는 Jones 씨가 될 것입니다. 이것이 저희 회원들에게 좋은 소식이기를 바랍니다. 새로운 오후 수업에 대한 더 많은 정보를 원하시면, 센터의 웹 사이트를 확인해 주십시오. 들어 주셔서 감사합니다.

① 새로운 수영 강사를 모집하려고
✓② 오후 수영 강좌 개설을 안내하려고
③ 강좌 등록 기간에 대해 공지하려고
④ 수영장 공사에 대한 양해를 구하려고
⑤ 수영 대회에 참가할 것을 권장하려고

---

02 남자의 의견

▶ 정답 ②

M: Hi, Katie. What can I help you with?
W: Hello, Mr. Smith. I want to show you my essay to get your advice.
보여주고 싶다   에세이   당신의 조언을 얻다
(want to V: ~하고 싶다)
M: Let me see. [Pause] You have creative ideas in your writing!
창의적인 아이디어들
W: Thanks, but I think I need to improve my writing skills.
향상시켜야 하다   글쓰기 실력
(need to V: ~해야 하다, improve: 향상시키다)
M: Hmm, that requires a lot of effort. Do you read a lot?
많은 노력을 필요로 하다
W: No, I don't have much time to read.
M: It's the first thing you could do to improve your writing.
W: Why is that? How could reading help my writing?
M: Well, by reading books, you get a sense of how stories flow.
읽음으로써(by V-ing: ~함으로써)   ~을 이해하다   흘러가다
W: Oh, I'd never thought of that.
M: More importantly, you can learn a lot of words to use for your writing!
W: If that's so, I'll make time to read more books.
~할 시간을 내다

해석
남: 안녕, Katie. 무엇을 도와줄까?
여: 안녕하세요, Smith 선생님. 선생님께 제 에세이를 보여드리고 조언을 얻고 싶어요.
남: 어디 보자. [잠시 후] 네 글에는 창의적인 아이디어들이 있구나!
여: 감사해요, 하지만 저는 제 글쓰기 실력을 향상시켜야 한다고 생각해요.
남: 흠, 그것은 많은 노력을 필요로 한다. 너는 독서를 많이 하니?
여: 아니요, 독서를 할 시간이 별로 없어요.
남: 그것은 네 글쓰기를 향상시키기 위해 할 수 있는 첫 번째 일이야.
여: 왜 그렇지요? 어떻게 독서가 제 글쓰기에 도움이 될 수 있나요?
남: 음, 책을 읽음으로써, 이야기가 어떻게 흘러가는지를 이해하는 거지.
여: 오, 저는 그것을 생각해 본 적이 없어요.
남: 더 중요한 것은, 네 글쓰기에 사용할 수 있는 많은 단어들을 배울 수 있다는 거야!
여: 만약 그렇다면, 저는 더 많은 책을 읽을 시간을 낼 거예요.

① 작문 실력은 상상력이 바탕이 되어야 한다.
✔ 글을 잘 쓰기 위해서는 독서를 많이 해야 한다.
③ 독해를 잘 하기 위해서는 속독법을 익혀야 한다.
④ 작가가 되기 위해서는 많은 자료 수집이 필요하다.
⑤ 풍부한 어휘 사용은 글의 내용을 다채롭게 해준다.

03 두 사람의 관계

▶ 정답 ①

W: Hello, what can I do for you?
M: I went to the literature section, but I couldn't find Romeo and Juliet
문학 부문   로미오와 줄리엣
by Shakespeare.
세익스피어
W: Let me check.... [Typing sound] Oh, someone just borrowed it.
확인하다   빌렸다(borrow)
M: Oh, no. I really need it for my school assignment. When can I
필요하다   학교 과제
borrow the book, then?
W: I'm not sure, but it is supposed to be returned in a week.
반납되기로 되어 있다
(be supposed to V: ~하기로 되어 있다, be returned: 반납되다)
M: Then, are there any other books by Shakespeare? My teacher
wants me to write a book review on a work by Shakespeare.
독후감을 쓰다   작품
W: Okay. [Typing sound] We have several books by Shakespeare. How
about Hamlet?
햄릿
M: Oh, I've heard about that story. I'll read that book instead, then.
대신에
W: Hamlet is in literature section H. I can show you where it is if you want.
M: No, that's okay. I can go get it. Thank you so much.
W: You're welcome.

해석
여: 안녕하세요, 무엇을 도와드릴까요?
남: 문학 부문에 갔는데, Shakespeare(셰익스피어)의 〈Romeo and Juliet(로미오와 줄리엣)〉을 찾을 수가 없네요.
여: 제가 확인해 볼게요.... [타자 치는 소리] 오, 누가 방금 그것을 빌렸네요.
남: 오, 이런. 학교 과제를 위해 그것이 정말 필요해요. 그럼 언제 그 책을 빌릴 수 있나요?

여: 확실하진 않지만, 그것은 일주일 후에 반납되기로 되어 있네요.
남: 그럼, Shakespeare의 다른 책들은 있나요? 저희 선생님께서는 제가 Shakespeare의 작품에 대한 독후감을 쓰기를 원하시거든요.
여: 알겠어요. [타자 치는 소리] Shakespeare의 책이 몇 권 있네요. 〈Hamlet(햄릿)〉은 어떠세요?
남: 오, 저는 그 이야기에 대해 들어봤어요. 그럼 대신에 이 책을 읽을게요.
여: 〈Hamlet〉은 문학 부문 H에 있어요. 원하시면 그것이 있는 곳을 안내해 드릴 수 있어요.
남: 아니요, 괜찮아요. 제가 가서 가져올 수 있어요. 정말 감사합니다.
여: 천만에요.

✔ 도서관 사서 — 학생
② 작가 — 출판사 직원
③ 문학 평론가 — 기자
④ 영화 감독 — 신인 배우
⑤ 문학 교사 — 학부모

04 그림에서 대화의 내용과 일치하지 않는 것

▶ 정답 ④

W: Andrew, have a look at this picture.
사진
M: Wow, it is a really nice room. Whose is this?
W: Mine. My family moved into a new house last week, and I
새집으로 이사했다
decorated the room by myself.
꾸몄다(decorate)
M: You did a great job! I especially like the curtains with the striped
특히   줄무늬가 있는
pattern on the window.
W: Thank you. I thought these curtains would make my room stylish.
내 방을 멋지게 만들다
M: Good choice. The teddy bear on the bed is so cute.
곰 인형
W: These days I fall asleep hugging her.
잠이 들다   껴안고 있는(hug)
M: How sweet! What is this lamp for?
전등
W: I put the lamp beside the bed to read before going to sleep.
M: That's a good idea. It also gives the room a nice atmosphere.
좋은 분위기
W: The flower pot on the bookshelf looks beautiful, doesn't it?
화분   책꽂이
M: It really does. And the round clock on the wall goes well with the
둥근 시계   ~과 잘 어울리다
room.
W: I'm happy to hear that you like my room.

해석
여: Andrew, 이 사진을 봐.
남: 와, 정말 멋진 방이다. 누구의 방이니?
여: 내 방이야. 우리 가족이 지난주에 새집으로 이사해서, 내가 혼자서 방을 꾸몄어.
남: 정말 잘했네! 나는 특히 창문에 줄무늬가 있는 커튼이 마음에 들어.
여: 고마워. 나는 이 커튼이 내 방을 멋지게 만들어 줄 것이라고 생각했어.
남: 좋은 선택이야. 침대 위에 있는 곰 인형이 정말 귀엽다.
여: 요즘에 나는 그녀를 껴안고 잠이 들어.
남: 정말 사랑스럽다! 이 전등은 무엇을 위한 거야?
여: 잠을 자기 전에 책을 읽기 위해서 침대 옆에 전등을 놓았어.
남: 그거 좋은 생각이다. 그것은 방에 좋은 분위기를 주기도 해.
여: 책꽂이 위에 있는 화분이 아름다워 보이지, 그렇지 않니?
남: 정말 그래. 그리고 벽에 걸린 둥근 시계는 방과 잘 어울려.
여: 네가 내 방을 마음에 들어 한다는 말을 들으니 기뻐.

05 여자가 할 일

고2 2019년 6월 7번 정답률 85%

▶ 정답 ①

W: Tom, did you pack everything for tomorrow's backpacking trip?
(짐을) 싸다 배낭 여행
M: I'm almost done, Mom. I just need a few more things.
W: Good! Don't forget to pack some extra clothes!
싸는 것을 잊다   여벌의 옷
(forget to V: ~하는 것을 잊다)
M: Sure, I did. Just in case!
만약을 위해서
W: Well done! What about hiking boots? Didn't you say you were going
to borrow Jake's?   등산화들
빌리다
M: Yes, he told me to pick them up in the afternoon.
그것들을 가지러 오다
W: That's so sweet of him. Anything else?
M: There is just one more important thing left. I have to go to the
중요한   남은   식료품점에 가다
grocery store to buy some snacks!
간식들을 좀 사다
W: Snacks are important. I'm going to the grocery store right now. I
could buy them for you if you want.
M: Could you? That would be great!
W: Sure, sweetie. No problem.
M: Then all I have to do is get the boots from Jake!

해석
여: Tom, 내일 배낭 여행을 위한 짐을 다 쌌니?
남: 거의 다 쌌어요, 엄마. 몇 가지만 더 필요해요.
여: 좋아! 여벌의 옷을 좀 싸는 것을 잊지 마라!
남: 물론이죠, 쌌어요. 만약을 위해서요!
여: 잘했어! 등산화는 어쩌니? 네가 Jake의 것을 빌리겠다고 말하지 않았니?
남: 네, 그가 저에게 오후에 그것들을 가지러 오라고 했어요.
여: 그는 정말 친절하구나. 그 밖에 다른 것은 없니?
남: 중요한 것이 하나 더 남았어요. 간식을 좀 사러 식료품점에 가야 해요!
여: 간식은 중요하지. 나는 지금 식료품점에 갈 거야. 네가 원한다면 내가 그것들을 사다 줄
수 있어.
남: 그래요? 그럼 정말 좋겠어요!
여: 그래, 얘야. 문제 없단다.
남: 그럼 제가 해야 할 일은 Jake에게 등산화를 받는 것뿐이에요!

✔ 간식 구매하기   ② 여벌 옷 챙기기
③ 등산화 빌리기   ④ 여행 가방 챙기기
⑤ 친구 집 방문하기

06 여자가 지불할 금액

고2 2019년 6월 9번 정답률 80%

▶ 정답 ④

M: Hi, may I help you?
W: Hello. I'm looking for shampoo.
~을 찾고 있다(look for)
M: Do you have a specific brand in mind?
특정한 브랜드를 염두에 두다
(have A in mind: A를 염두에 두다, specific: 특정한)
W: No, I actually don't. Could you recommend me one?
추천하다
M: Let's see. This brand has just released a new shampoo and it's on
막 출시했다(release)
sale.
할인 판매 중인
W: Great! So how much is it?
M: Originally, it was 20 dollars per bottle, but for this week only, if you
원래   한 통당
buy three, you get 10% off the total price of the shampoo.
총액에서 10% 할인을 받다
W: Awesome. I'll have three then.
M: Alright. Just to let you know, this brand also has another special
promotion only for today!   특별 판촉 행사
W: Oh, really? What's the promotion about?
M: All customers who buy from this brand can get this body cleanser
고객들   바디 클렌저
for 10 dollars.
W: That's great! Then I'll have three bottles of shampoo and one body
cleanser. Here's my credit card.

해석
남: 안녕하세요, 도와드릴까요?
여: 안녕하세요. 저는 샴푸를 찾고 있어요.

남: 염두에 둔 특정한 브랜드가 있으신가요?
여: 아니요, 사실 없어요. 하나 추천해 주시겠어요?
남: 어디 보자. 이 브랜드는 막 새로운 샴푸를 출시했는데 할인 판매 중이에요.
여: 잘됐네요! 그래서 얼마죠?
남: 원래, 한 통당 20달러였는데, 이번 주에 한해서만, 세 통을 사시면, 샴푸 총액에서 10%
할인을 받으세요.
여: 굉장하네요. 그럼 세 통을 살게요.
남: 좋습니다. 알려드리자면, 이 브랜드는 오늘 하루만 다른 특별 판촉 행사도 하고 있어요!
여: 오, 정말이요? 무엇에 대한 판촉 행사인가요?
남: 이 브랜드에서 구매하는 모든 고객들은 이 바디 클렌저를 10달러에 사실 수 있어요.
여: 잘됐네요! 그럼 샴푸 세 통과 바디 클렌저 한 개를 살게요. 여기 제 신용카드가 있어요.

① $46   ② $54   ③ $60
✔ $64   ⑤ $70

문제 풀이
샴푸 한 통은 20달러지만 세 통을 사면 10퍼센트 할인해주는 행사를 진행하고 있으므로 총
60달러에서 6달러를 빼면 54달러가 된다. 이 브랜드에서 구매한 고객들은 바디 클렌저를 10
달러에 살 수 있어서 54달러에 10달러를 합쳐 총액이 64달러가 되므로 답은 ④ '$64'이다.

07 남자가 직장을 옮기려고 하는 이유

고2 2019년 6월 8번 정답률 80%

▶ 정답 ⑤

W: Hey, Mark! You look serious. What's up?
심각해 보이다
M: I'm thinking of leaving my job.
내 직장을 그만두는 것(leave one's job: ~직장을 그만 두다)
W: Why? Did you get a job offer from another company?
취업 제안을 받다   회사
M: Not yet, but I've submitted applications to some other companies.
제출했다(submit) 지원서들
W: I thought you were satisfied with your work and salary.
~에 만족한   급여
M: Well, the pay is good and I'm comfortable with this job.
급여   ~이 편한
W: Then, why do you want to leave?
M: If I don't look for a new challenge, I will get used to doing the same
~을 찾다   도전   하는 것에 익숙해지다
easy job and I won't develop.   (get used to V-ing: ~에 익숙해지다)
발전하다
W: You mean you want to develop your abilities by challenging yourself
네 능력들을 계발하다
with different work, don't you?
M: Exactly. I would be happier with a job that can help me improve my
career.   내 경력을 향상시키다
W: I understand, but you'd better make the decision after considering
결정을 내리다   고려한 후에
the matter carefully.   (consider: 고려하다)
M: Thank you for your advice.

해석
여: 이봐, Mark! 너 심각해 보인다. 무슨 일이니?
남: 나는 직장을 그만둘까 생각 중이야.
여: 왜? 다른 회사에서 취업 제안을 받았니?
남: 아직 아니지만, 다른 몇몇 회사에 지원서를 제출했어.
여: 나는 네가 일과 급여에 만족한다고 생각했어.
남: 글쎄, 급여도 좋고 이 일도 편해.
여: 그럼, 왜 그만두고 싶은 거야?
남: 새로운 도전을 찾지 않는다면, 나는 똑같이 쉬운 일을 하는 것에 익숙해지고 발전하지 않
을 거야.
여: 다른 일에 도전함으로써 네 능력을 계발하고 싶다는 말이네, 그렇지 않아?
남: 바로 그거야. 나는 내 경력을 향상시키는 데 도움을 줄 수 있는 직장에 더 만족할 거야.
여: 이해하지만, 그 문제를 신중하게 고려한 후에 결정을 내리는 게 좋겠어.
남: 조언해줘서 고마워.

① 다른 지방으로 이사를 가게 되어서
② 여가 시간을 더 많이 가지고 싶어서
③ 다른 회사에서 일할 것을 제안 받아서
④ 일에 대한 더 많은 보수를 받기 위해서
✔ 새롭게 도전하여 능력을 개발하고 싶어서

08 Cat Fair에 관해 언급되지 않은 것

고2 2019년 6월 10번 정답률 80%

▶ 정답 ④

M: Rose, I've heard that you have a cat. Will you go to Cat Fair with
me?   고양이 박람회

W: Cat Fair? Sounds interesting.

M: It'll be very useful. You can buy cat food and toys at cheap prices there.

W: Oh, I want to go. Where will it be held?

M: It will be held in Coex Hall.

W: That's not far from here. When is it?

M: It's on the 17th of June. Are you available?

W: Luckily, I'm free that day. I wonder how much the tickets cost.

M: They are 10 dollars per person.

W: I see. Will there be any special events?

M: Yes! A famous cat specialist will be there to answer questions on cat health.

W: That sounds great. I look forward to going!

해석

남: Rose, 나는 네가 고양이를 기른다고 들었어. 나와 함께 Cat Fair(고양이 박람회)에 갈래?

여: Cat Fair(고양이 박람회)? 재미있겠다.

남: 그것은 매우 유용할 거야. 그곳에서 싼 가격에 고양이 먹이와 장난감을 살 수 있어.

여: 오, 가고 싶어. 어디에서 열리니?

남: Coex Hall(코엑스 홀)에서 열릴 거야.

여: 여기에서 멀지 않구나. 언제야?

남: 6월 17일이야. 시간이 있니?

여: 다행히도, 나 그날 한가해. 티켓이 얼마인지 궁금하네.

남: 1인당 10달러야.

여: 그렇구나. 특별한 행사들이 있니?

남: 응! 유명한 고양이 전문가가 와서 고양이 건강에 대한 질문에 답할 거야.

여: 그거 멋진데. 나는 가는 것이 기대돼!

① 행사 장소　　　　　　② 행사 날짜
③ 티켓 가격　　　　　　✔④ 기념품 지급
⑤ 특별 이벤트

---

09 Great Light Festival에 관한 내용과 일치하지 않는 것　▶ 정답 ④

W: Hello, CBC radio listeners! I'm Grace Wilson, the manager of the Great Light Festival. I'm happy to let you know about this event. Famous light artists will join to show their work. The theme of the event is 'Christmas.' There will be a big Christmas tree decorated with beautiful lights, and you can take nice pictures in front of it. The festival will be held for a month from December 1st at Skyline Park. Tickets for the festival are 20 dollars each and can only be purchased at the gate. The lighting hours will be from 6 p.m. to 10 p.m. I hope that many people come and enjoy the festival. Thank you.

해석

여: 안녕하세요, CBC 라디오 청취자 여러분! 저는 Great Light Festival(위대한 조명 축제)의 감독인 Grace Wilson입니다. 여러분께 이 행사에 대해 알려 드리게 되어 기쁩니다. 유명한 조명 예술가들이 자신의 작품을 보여주기 위해 참여할 것입니다. 행사의 주제는 '크리스마스'입니다. 아름다운 조명들로 장식된 큰 크리스마스 트리가 있을 것이고, 여러분은 그 앞에서 멋진 사진을 찍을 수 있습니다. 축제는 12월 1일부터 한 달 동안 Skyline Park(스카이라인 파크)에서 열릴 것입니다. 축제 티켓은 한 장에 20달러이고 입구에서만 구매하실 수 있습니다. 조명이 들어오는 시간은 오후 6시부터 오후 10시까지입니다. 많은 분들께서 오셔서 축제를 즐기길 바랍니다. 감사합니다.

① 유명한 조명 예술가들이 참여한다.
② 큰 크리스마스 트리 앞에서 사진을 찍을 수 있다.
③ 12월 1일부터 한 달 동안 열린다.
✔④ 티켓은 온라인으로만 구매할 수 있다.
⑤ 조명이 들어오는 시간은 오후 6시부터 오후 10시까지이다.

---

10 표에서 두 사람이 구입할 전기 주전자　▶ 정답 ②

M: Amy, look at this flyer. Electric kettles are on sale!

W: Really? That's great! I think it is a good time to buy a new one.

M: Yeah, let's see. [Pause] This one looks cute but maybe it's too small for us.

W: You're right. We drink a lot of tea. It should be at least 1.5 liters.

M: Hmm, this one is too expensive. I don't want to spend more than $30 on a kettle.

W: Me, either. Then we have three options. Which color do you like?

M: I don't think black looks good in our kitchen.

W: I agree. It makes the kitchen too dark.

M: What about the material? There is a plastic one and a glass one.

W: We have used a plastic one before. It's better to try the other material this time.

M: Good point. Then let's buy this one.

해석

남: Amy, 이 전단지를 봐. 전기 주전자를 할인 판매 중이야!

여: 정말? 잘됐다! 새 주전자를 사기에 좋은 시기인 것 같아.

남: 그래, 어디 보자. [잠시 후] 이것은 귀엽게 보이지만 아마도 우리에겐 너무 작을 거야.

여: 네 말이 맞아. 우리는 차를 많이 마시잖아. 최소한 1.5리터는 되어야 해.

남: 흠, 이것은 너무 비싸다. 나는 주전자에 30달러 이상은 쓰고 싶지 않아.

여: 나도 그래. 그럼 세 가지 선택지가 있어. 어떤 색상이 좋니?

남: 우리 부엌에 검은색은 어울리지 않는 것 같아.

여: 동의해. 그것은 부엌을 너무 어둡게 만들어.

남: 재질은 어때? 플라스틱 주전자와 유리 주전자가 있어.

여: 전에 플라스틱을 써 봤잖아. 이번에는 다른 재질을 써 보는 게 더 좋겠어.

남: 좋은 지적이야. 그럼 이것을 사자.

전기 주전자

	모델	용량	가격	색상	재질
①	A	1리터	20달러	분홍색	플라스틱
✔②	B	1.5리터	25달러	하얀색	유리
③	C	1.5리터	27달러	파란색	플라스틱
④	D	2리터	29달러	검은색	유리
⑤	E	2리터	32달러	갈색	유리

---

11 여자의 마지막 말에 대한 남자의 응답　▶ 정답 ③

W: Kevin, have you been to the new shopping mall downtown?

M: Yes, I went there with my family last weekend. It was really nice.

W: Oh, really? What is good about it?

M: (It has various sportswear brands.)

해석

여: Kevin, 시내에 새로 생긴 쇼핑몰에 가 봤니?

남: 그래, 지난 주말에 가족과 함께 갔었어. 정말 좋았어.

여: 오, 정말? 그것에 대해 어떤 점이 좋니?

남: (그것은 다양한 스포츠웨어 브랜드들을 가지고 있어.)

① 그 책은 읽기 쉬워.
② 그것은 주차 공간이 더 필요해.
✔③ 그것은 다양한 스포츠웨어 브랜드들을 가지고 있어.
④ 나는 그 영화의 줄거리에 감동을 받았어.
⑤ 내 친구들은 함께 쇼핑을 가는 것을 정말 좋아해.

---

12 남자의 마지막 말에 대한 여자의 응답　▶ 정답 ⑤

M: Oh, Susan! The light in the bathroom went out.

W: I know, but don't worry. We only have to replace the light bulb. I'll buy one tomorrow.

M: But, it's uncomfortable to use the bathroom.
불편함
W: (Then, I'll go and buy a new one right now.)

해석

남: 오, Susan! 화장실의 전등이 나갔어요.
여: 알아요, 하지만 걱정하지 말아요. 단지 전구를 교체하기만 하면 돼요. 내일 전구를 사올게요.
남: 하지만, 화장실을 사용하는 것이 불편하잖아요.
여: (그럼, 제가 지금 당장 가서 새것을 사 올게요.)
① 맞아요, 방 전체가 너무 밝아요.
② 청소는 곧 끝날 거예요.
③ 좋아요, 화장실에서 머리를 감아요.
④ 목수가 여기에 도착할 예정이에요.
☑ 그럼, 제가 지금 당장 가서 새것을 사 올게요.

---

13 여자의 마지막 말에 대한 남자의 응답

고2 2019년 6월 13번 | 정답률 60% | ▶ 정답 ②

W: Willy, what are you doing?
M: Hi, Kelly! I'm making plans to run for president of student council.
학생회장에 출마하다
(run for: ~에 출마하다, president of student council: 학생회장)
W: Really? I'm guessing there will be strong competition among the
치열한 경쟁   후보자들 사이에
candidates.
(among: ~ 사이에, candidate: 후보자)
M: What do you mean by that?
W: I heard Angela is also going to run for the position. She is popular
자리
among her classmates, you know.
인기가 있는
M: I didn't know she was interested. I thought she was a shy girl.
관심이 있는   수줍음이 많은
W: Her friends are rather enthusiastic about making her student
council president.
상당히 열성적인
M: Good for her! I hope my friends help me, too.
W: I want to assist you in any way I can. Is there anything I can do?
돕고 싶다(want to V: ~하고 싶다, assist: 돕다)
M: You got first prize in the drawing contest, didn't you?
일등상을 탔다(get first prize)   그림 그리기 대회
W: Yeah, but how can that help you?
M: (You can make election campaign posters for me.)
선거 운동 포스터들

해석

여: Willy, 무엇을 하고 있니?
남: 안녕, Kelly! 나는 학생회장에 출마할 계획을 세우고 있어.
여: 정말? 후보자들 사이에 치열한 경쟁이 있을 것 같구나.
남: 그게 무슨 말이야?
여: Angela도 그 자리에 출마할 거라고 들었거든. 그녀가 반 친구들 사이에서 인기가 있는 것을 너도 알잖아.
남: 나는 그녀가 관심이 있는지 몰랐어. 그녀가 수줍음이 많다고 생각했는데.
여: 그녀의 친구들이 그녀를 학생회장으로 만드는 데 상당히 열성적이야.
남: 그녀는 좋겠다! 내 친구들도 나를 도와줬으면 좋겠어.
여: 나는 내가 할 수 있는 어떤 방법으로든 너를 돕고 싶어. 내가 할 수 있는 일이 있을까?
남: 너는 그림 그리기 대회에서 일등상을 탔지, 그렇지 않니?
여: 그래, 하지만 어떻게 그것이 너에게 도움이 될 수 있지?
남: (너는 나를 위해 선거 운동 포스터를 만들 수 있어.)
① 우리 동아리에 다른 회원들을 초대하자.
☑ 너는 나를 위해 선거 운동 포스터를 만들 수 있어.
③ 걱정하지 마, 나는 이번 선거에서 그녀에게 반대투표를 할 거야.
④ 대회가 끝난 후에는 반드시 그림 도구들을 씻어.
⑤ 그녀가 학생회장에 출마하는지 확인해 줘.

문제 풀이

학생회장에 출마하려는 남자를 여자가 돕고 싶어하는 상황에서 남자는 여자가 그림 그리기 대회에서 일등상을 탔다는 점을 언급한다. 여자의 재능을 활용하면서 남자의 선거 활동에 도움을 줄 수 있는 선택지가 어울린다. 따라서 정답은 ② 'You can make election campaign posters for me.(너는 나를 위해 선거 운동 포스터를 만들 수 있어.)'이다.

---

14 남자의 마지막 말에 대한 여자의 응답

고2 2019년 6월 14번 | 정답률 65% | ▶ 정답 ④

M: Katie, how was school today?
W: Great, Dad. We had a special lecture about a new study strategy.
특별 강의   새로운 학습 전략

M: That must have been helpful for you! You have been worried about
도움이 되었음에 틀림없다
(must have p.p.: ~했음에 틀림없다)
your grades these days.
W: Yeah, I have. Now I'm going to make a new study plan based on
성적   새로운 학습 계획을 세우다   ~을 바탕으로
what I learned today.
M: What did you learn? Tell me about it.
W: The lecturer is the author of the book *Just Start Small*. He said we
강사   저자
should start small if we want to get good grades.
좋은 성적을 얻고 싶다(want to V: ~하고 싶다)
M: Start small? That doesn't make sense to me.
이해가 되다
W: Let me give you an example. Memorizing just one simple Spanish
암기하는 것(memorize)   스페인어 문장
sentence after lunch is not difficult, is it?
M: Right, that doesn't seem like much effort.
많은 노력이 필요한 것처럼 보이다
W: But if I do it for a month steadily, I will be able to speak thirty
꾸준히   말할 수 있다
Spanish sentences in total.
(be able to V: ~할 수 있다)
모두 합해서
M: Then that's not so little anymore.
W: (Exactly. Small steps eventually lead to big ones.)
결국   ~으로 이어지다

해석

남: Katie, 오늘 학교 어땠니?
여: 좋았어요, 아빠. 저희는 새로운 학습 전략에 관한 특별 강의를 들었어요.
남: 그것은 너에게 도움이 되었음에 틀림없구나! 너는 요즘에 성적에 대해 걱정을 했잖니.
여: 네, 그랬죠. 이제 저는 오늘 배운 것을 바탕으로 새로운 학습 계획을 세울 거예요.
남: 무엇을 배웠니? 그것에 대해 내게 말해주렴.
여: 강사는 〈Just Start Small(작은 것부터 시작하라)〉이라는 책의 저자예요. 그는 좋은 성적을 얻고 싶다면 작은 것부터 시작해야 한다고 말했어요.
남: 작은 것부터 시작한다고? 나는 이해가 안 되는구나.
여: 예를 들어 볼게요. 점심 식사 후에 간단한 스페인어 문장 하나를 암기하는 것은 어렵지 않아요, 그렇죠?
남: 그래, 그것은 많은 노력이 필요한 것처럼 보이지 않는구나.
여: 하지만 그것을 한 달 동안 꾸준히 한다면, 저는 모두 합해서 30개의 스페인어 문장을 말할 수 있게 되는 거예요.
남: 그럼 그것은 더 이상 그렇게 작은 것이 아니구나.
여: (맞아요. 작은 걸음이 결국 큰 걸음으로 이어지는 거예요.)
① 저는 만화책을 보면서 스페인어를 배우고 있어요.
② 그는 큰 목표를 세우는 것이 먼저 행해져야 한다고 말했어요.
③ 네, 작은 일들은 때때로 성취하기 어려워요.
☑ 맞아요. 작은 걸음이 결국 큰 걸음으로 이어지는 거예요.
⑤ 알아요. 많은 예를 활용하는 것이 학습에 효율적이에요.

문제 풀이

점심 식사 후에 간단한 스페인어 문장을 하나씩 암기하면 한 달 동안 암기하는 문장의 양은 30개가 되므로, 작은 것이 아니라는 남자의 말에서 티끌 모아 태산이라는 의미를 가진 선택지가 답으로 어울린다. 따라서 답은 ④ 'Exactly. Small steps eventually lead to big ones.(맞아요. 작은 걸음이 결국 큰 걸음으로 이어지는 거예요.)'이다.

---

15 다음 상황에서 Sarah가 Peter에게 할 말

고2 2019년 6월 15번 | 정답률 70% | ▶ 정답 ③

W: Sarah and Peter are supposed to act in *Beauty and the Beast*
연기를 하기로 되어 있다   미녀와 야수
(be supposed to V: ~하기로 되어 있다, act: 연기하다)
on stage at the school festival. While practicing together, Peter
연습하는 동안(practice: 연습하다)
looks really nervous. His voice is too small and he even forgets
긴장한   잊어버리다
what he should say from time to time. Sarah is worried about
때때로
Peter, so she asks him to discuss his problem with her. Peter says
그에게 상의하라고 요청하다
(ask A to V: A에게 ~하라고 요청하다, discuss: 상의하다)
that he is afraid of acting in front of many people. Then, Sarah
두려운   ~의 앞에서
remembers her experience from last year. When she felt the same
떠올리다   경험   같은 기분을 느꼈다
way, she used to practice while her family or friends watched, and
연습하곤 했다(used to V: ~하곤 했다)
she found it really helpful. Now, Sarah wants to suggest that he
도움이 되는
practice as she did. In this situation, what would Sarah most likely
그녀가 했던 대로
say to Peter?

Sarah: (Why don't you practice acting in front of your family?)
~하는 게 어떠니?

해석

여: Sarah와 Peter는 학교 축제에서 무대에 올라 〈Beauty and the Beast(미녀와 야수)〉에서 연기를 하기로 되어 있다. 함께 연습하는 동안, Peter는 정말 긴장한 것처럼 보인다. 그의 목소리는 매우 작고 그는 때때로 자신이 말해야 하는 것을 잊어버리기도 한다. Sarah는 Peter가 걱정되어서, 그에게 그의 문제를 자신과 상의하라고 요청한다. Peter는 많은 사람들 앞에서 연기를 하는 것이 두렵다고 말한다. 그때, Sarah는 자신의 작년 경험을 떠올린다. 그녀는 같은 기분을 느꼈을 때, 가족이나 친구들이 지켜보는 동안 연습하곤 했는데, 그것이 정말 도움이 된다는 것을 알게 되었다. 이제, Sarah는 그녀가 했던 대로 그가 연습할 것을 제안하고 싶다. 이러한 상황에서, Sarah는 Peter에게 뭐라고 말하겠는가?

Sarah: (가족들 앞에서 연기를 연습하는 게 어떠니?)

① 아무도 없을 때 무대에서 연습하자.
② 친구들과 연극을 보러 가는 게 어떠니?
✓가족들 앞에서 연기를 연습하는 게 어떠니?
④ 너는 선생님과 의논해서 네 역할을 바꾸는 게 좋겠어.
⑤ 대본을 암기하는 데 많은 시간을 들이는 것이 중요해.

16~17 1지문 2문항

M: Hello, students. Yesterday we looked at movies where robots and ghosts talk and act like human beings. Today we're going to talk about movies where animals play an important role. The 1961 film, *101 Dalmatians*, is a Walt Disney classic. A dog, Pongo, played a lovable role in this memorable film. But animal movies aren't just about dogs. The movie, *Lion King*, tells the story of a young lion, Simba. He becomes the king after overcoming many difficulties. *Jurassic Park* is a 1993 American science fiction film directed by Steven Spielberg. You can feel big thrills while watching many dangerous dinosaurs. In *Babe*, a cute little pig made a strong impression on lots of moviegoers. What's the best animal character movie? If you think your favorite animal film is missing, go ahead and share it with us!

해석

남: 안녕하세요, 학생 여러분. 어제 우리는 로봇들과 유령들이 인간처럼 말하고 행동하는 영화들을 보았습니다. 오늘 우리는 동물들이 중요한 역할을 하는 영화들에 대해 이야기할 것입니다. 1961년 영화 〈101 Dalmatians(101마리의 달마시안)〉은 Walt Disney의 고전입니다. 이 기억할 만한 영화에서는 Pongo라는 개가 사랑스러운 역할을 합니다. 그러나 동물 영화가 개에 관한 것만 있는 것은 아닙니다. 영화 〈Lion King(라이온 킹)〉은 Simba라는 어린 사자의 이야기를 들려줍니다. 그는 많은 어려움을 극복한 후에 왕이 됩니다. 〈Jurassic Park(쥬라기 공원)〉은 Steven Spielberg가 감독한 1993년 미국 공상 과학 영화입니다. 여러분은 많은 위험한 공룡들을 보면서 큰 전율을 느낄 수 있습니다. 〈Babe(베이브)〉에서는, 귀엽고 작은 돼지가 많은 영화 팬들에게 강한 인상을 주었습니다. 최고의 동물 캐릭터 영화는 무엇입니까? 여러분이 가장 좋아하는 동물 영화가 빠졌다고 생각한다면, 어서 그것을 우리와 함께 공유해 주세요!

16 남자가 하는 말의 주제
고2 2019년 6월 16번 | 정답률 80% | ▶ 정답 ⑤

① 인간 생활에 있어서 영화의 중요성
② 인간에게 친근한 동물들
③ 영화 캐릭터 제작 과정
④ 애니메이션이 인기를 얻고 있는 이유들
✓동물들이 주된 초점인 영화들

17 언급된 동물이 아닌 것
고2 2019년 6월 17번 | 정답률 85% | ▶ 정답 ④

① 개
② 사자
③ 공룡
✓토끼
⑤ 돼지

04 2019년 9월 학력평가

01	③	02	⑤	03	②	04	③	05	②
06	③	07	①	08	④	09	④	10	④
11	⑤	12	②	13	⑤	14	①	15	②
16	②	17	④						

01 남자가 하는 말의 목적
고2 2019년 9월 3번 | 정답률 85% | ▶ 정답 ③

M: Good morning, students! I'm Principal Brad Smith. We're pleased to announce the launch of our school's official social media page on U-Channel! For better communication about school news, emergency information, and upcoming events, we've started this social media page as our newest communication tool. We'll continue to use our other notification tools, including the school website, letters home, and emails. The U-Channel page will be an additional method allowing for quick and immediate updates accessible on your computer or mobile phone. As always, if you have any questions, please feel free to ask. Thank you.

해석

남: 안녕하세요, 학생 여러분! 저는 교장인 Brad Smith입니다. U-Channel에 우리 학교의 공식 소셜 미디어 페이지가 개설되었음을 알려드리게 되어 기쁩니다. 학교 소식, 비상 정보, 그리고 다가오는 행사들에 대한 더 나은 의사소통을 위해, 우리의 최신 의사소통 도구로 이 소셜 미디어 페이지를 시작했습니다. 우리는 학교 웹 사이트, 가정 통신문, 그리고 이메일을 포함하여, 다른 알림 도구들을 계속해서 사용할 것입니다. U-Channel 페이지는 여러분의 컴퓨터나 휴대전화에서 접근할 수 있는 빠르고 즉각적인 업데이트를 가능하게 하는 추가적인 방법일 것입니다. 늘 그렇듯이, 문의 사항이 있으면, 언제든지 물어보십시오. 감사합니다.

① 사이버폭력 예방 교육일정을 공지하려고
② 학생들에게 학교 홈페이지 가입을 독려하려고
✓학교 공식 소셜 미디어 페이지 개설을 알리려고
④ 학교 홈페이지 디자인 개선에 대한 의견을 공모하려고
⑤ 소셜 미디어 사용 시 개인 정보 보호 방법을 안내하려고

02 여자의 의견
고2 2019년 9월 4번 | 정답률 85% | ▶ 정답 ⑤

W: Justin, how's your speech coming along?
M: I don't think it's going so well, Ms. Jones.
W: What's wrong? I know you've been working really hard.
M: I think the script and the visual aids are good, but something about my delivery is still awkward.
W: Have you considered recording a video of yourself practicing your speech?

M: No, I haven't. Why?

W: Seeing how you <u>deliver your speech</u> can help you <u>correct</u> your
　　　　　　　　　연설을 하다　　　　　　　　　　고치다
<u>weak points</u>.
약점들

M: How can it help?

W: When you watch a video of yourself giving the speech, you can see
what kinds of <u>gestures</u> you make and hear how you <u>sound</u>.
　　　　　　　몸짓들　　　　　　　　　　　　　　　소리를 내다

M: Oh, you mean that I can <u>fix</u> something <u>strange</u> in my delivery if I
　　　　　　　　　　　　　고치다　　　　　　이상한
see myself do it on video?

W: Exactly! You can <u>improve</u> your delivery through this <u>method</u>.
　　　　　　　　　향상시키다　　　　　　　　　　　방법

M: Thank you. I'll try that now.

해석

여: Justin, 연설은 어떻게 되어 가고 있니?

남: 잘 되고 있는 것 같지 않아요, Jones 선생님.

여: 무슨 일이니? 나는 네가 정말 열심히 노력하고 있는 것으로 아는데.

남: 대본과 시각 자료들은 훌륭한데, 제 전달력에서 뭔가 아직도 어색한 것 같아요.

여: 연설을 연습하는 네 영상을 녹화하는 것을 고려해 본 적이 있니?

남: 아니요, 없어요. 왜요?

여: 네가 어떻게 연설을 하는지 보는 것은 네가 약점들을 고치는 데 도움을 줄 수 있어.

남: 그것이 어떻게 도움을 줄 수 있죠?

여: 연설을 하는 너 자신의 영상을 볼 때, 네가 어떤 종류의 몸짓을 하는지 볼 수 있고 어떻게
소리를 내는지 들을 수 있단다.

남: 오, 영상에서 제가 연설을 하는 것을 보면 제 전달력에서 이상한 부분을 고칠 수 있다는 말
씀이세요?

여: 그렇지! 너는 이 방법을 통해서 전달력을 향상시킬 수 있어.

남: 감사합니다. 지금 그것을 해 볼게요.

① 청중의 특성에 맞는 연설 주제의 선택이 필요하다.

② 시각 자료의 활용은 청중의 집중을 유도할 수 있다.

③ 연설자의 목소리 톤은 연설의 내용에 따라 달라야 한다.

④ 대본을 보지 않고 연설하는 것은 설득력을 높일 수 있다.

☑️ 연설 연습 시 녹화를 활용하면 전달력 향상에 도움이 된다.

03　두 사람의 관계

▶ 정답 ②

M: Excuse me, are you Anna Zimmerman? I can't believe I'm seeing
you here!

W: Oh, hello. Have we met before?

M: No, but I'm a <u>big fan</u> of yours.
　　　　　　　열혈 팬

W: Thank you. I <u>love meeting</u> my fans.
　　　　　　　만나는 것을 정말 좋아하다
　　　　　(love V-ing: ~하는 것을 정말 좋아하다)

M: I just finished your <u>latest book</u>, *The Beautiful Days*. I read the
　　　　　　　　　　　최신 저서
<u>whole</u> thing <u>in a day</u>.
전체의　　　　하루 만에

W: I'm flattered. What did you like most?

M: I really liked the <u>part</u> where Emma and Jason first dance.
　　　　　　　　　　부분

W: That's my favorite <u>moment</u>, too. It took me more than two weeks to
　　가장 좋아하는　순간
<u>write</u> that <u>chapter</u>.
쓰다　　（책의）장

M: Wow! It was <u>worth it</u>. It was so <u>beautifully</u> <u>described</u>. I hope this
　　　　　　　~할 만한 가치가 있는　　　아름답게　　묘사된
book will <u>be made into a movie</u>.
영화로 만들어지다

W: I'm so glad you like it that much.

M: I think you're one of the best <u>novelists</u> in the world. Can I get your
　　　　　　　　　　　　　　　소설가들
<u>autograph</u>, please?
사인

W: Sure.

해석

남: 실례합니다만, Anna Zimmerman 씨세요? 여기에서 당신을 만나다니 믿을 수가 없네요!

여: 오, 안녕하세요. 우리가 전에 만난 적이 있나요?

남: 아니요, 하지만 저는 당신의 열혈 팬이에요.

여: 감사해요. 저는 팬들을 만나는 것을 정말 좋아해요.

남: 저는 당신의 최신 저서인 〈The Beautiful Days(아름다운 날들)〉를 막 다 읽었어요. 전체
를 하루 만에 다 읽었죠.

여: 과찬이세요. 무엇이 가장 좋았나요?

남: 저는 Emma와 Jason이 처음으로 춤을 추는 부분이 정말 좋았어요.

여: 그것은 제가 가장 좋아하는 순간이기도 해요. 그 장을 쓰는 데 2주 이상이 걸렸어요.

남: 와! 그것은 그럴 만한 가치가 있었네요. 그것은 정말 아름답게 묘사되었어요. 저는 이 책이
영화로 만들어졌으면 좋겠어요.

여: 그 정도로 좋아해 주시니 정말 기쁘네요.

남: 저는 당신이 세계 최고의 소설가들 중 한 명이라고 생각해요. 사인을 받을 수 있을까요?

여: 물론이죠.

① 학생 ― 사서교사

☑️ 독자 ― 소설가

③ 출판사 편집자 ― 삽화가

④ 관객 ― 무용가

⑤ 시나리오 작가 ― 영화감독

04　그림에서 대화의 내용과 일치하지 않는 것

▶ 정답 ③

M: Hey, Vicky. Looks like your club's <u>face painting booth</u> is <u>ready for</u>
　　　　　　　　　　　　　　　　　　페이스 페인팅 부스　　　준비가 된
the <u>school festival</u>.
학교 축제

W: I just <u>finished</u> it. Please have a look.
끝냈다(finish)

M: Okay. *[Pause]* You <u>chose</u> the roof with a <u>striped pattern</u>. I love it.
　　　　　　　　　선택했다(choose)　　　　　줄무늬가 있는

W: Thanks. What do you think of the <u>banner</u> between the <u>poles</u>?
　　　　　　　　　　　　　　　　현수막　　　　　　　기둥들

M: The one that says "face painting" on it? It looks really nice.

W: I wanted our booth's <u>activity</u> to be really <u>clear</u>. I <u>designed</u> it myself.
　　　　　　　　　　　활동　　　　　　　분명한　디자인했다(design)

M: Really? You did a great job. Oh, there's one <u>round table</u> in the
　　　　　　　　　　　　　　　　　　　　　　　원형 테이블
booth.

W: Right. That's where we'll do face painting. We also have two <u>stools</u>
next to the table. Do you think it's <u>enough</u>?　　　　　(팔걸이·등받이가 없는)
　　　　　　　　　　　　　　충분한　　　　　　　　　의자들

M: It looks like it'll be enough. That's a nice <u>photo frame</u> outside the
　　　　　　　　　　　　　　　　　　　　　　　사진 액자
booth.

W: Yes. <u>I want visitors to take photos</u> of themselves there.
방문객들이 사진을 찍기를 원하다
(want A to V: A가 ~하기를 원하다)

M: Cool! It'll be a great place to <u>record</u> <u>memories</u> of the festival.
　　　　　　　　　　　　　　　기록하다　추억들

W: I think so, too. I hope many students visit my booth.

해석

남: 이봐, Vicky. 학교 축제를 위한 네 동아리의 페이스 페인팅 부스가 준비가 된 것 같구나.

여: 나는 막 그것을 끝냈어. 좀 봐 줘.

남: 알았어. *[잠시 후]* 줄무늬가 있는 지붕을 선택했구나. 정말 마음에 든다.

여: 고마워. 기둥들 사이에 있는 현수막은 어떠니?

남: 'face painting'이라고 쓰여 있는 것 말이야? 정말 좋아 보여.

여: 나는 우리 부스의 활동이 매우 분명하기를 원했어. 내가 그것을 직접 디자인했어.

남: 정말? 잘했다. 오, 부스 안에 원형 테이블 한 개가 있구나.

여: 맞아. 저기가 우리가 페이스 페인팅을 할 곳이야. 테이블 옆에는 두 개의 의자들도 있어.
충분한 것 같니?

남: 충분할 것 같아. 부스 밖에는 멋진 사진 액자가 있네.

여: 그래. 나는 방문객들이 그곳에서 자신들의 사진을 찍기를 원해.

남: 멋지다! 축제의 추억들을 기록하기에 좋은 장소가 될 거야.

여: 나도 그렇게 생각해. 많은 학생들이 내 부스에 방문하면 좋겠어.

05 남자가 여자에게 부탁한 일

▶ 정답 ②

M: Good morning, Ms. Stevenson.
W: Hi, Minsu, how's your group project going? I heard that you're sending books to Nepal.
그룹 프로젝트
책들을 네팔로 보낼 예정이다
(send A to B: A를 B로 보내다)
M: It's going well. We bought Korean folk tale books, and we're translating them into English.
한국 전래 동화 책들
그것들을 영어로 번역하고 있다
(translate A into B: A를 B로 번역하다)
W: Are you going to remake the books in English?
다시 만들다
M: No. We're planning to put the translations next to the original text.
번역본들
원문
W: That sounds really difficult.
M: It is. But thanks to a translation app, we've been able to finish our first draft.
~ 덕분에
번역 앱
초고
W: That's good! Does that mean you're almost ready to send the books?
준비가 된
M: Actually, that's why I came to see you. We're not sure if our English translation sounds natural. Would you mind checking the first draft of our translation?
사실
자연스러운
검토해 주시겠어요?
(Would you mind V-ing: ~해 주시겠어요?)
W: No problem. I'm happy to help you. When do you need me to finish by?
M: Well, we'll package the books next month.
포장하다
W: If you email me the translation this week, then I'll give you the feedback by the end of this month.
이메일로 보내다
이번 달 말까지
M: Thank you so much.

해석
남: 안녕하세요, Stevenson 선생님.
여: 안녕, Minsu, 그룹 프로젝트는 어떻게 되어 가니? 나는 네가 책들을 네팔로 보낸다고 들었어.
남: 잘 되고 있어요. 저희는 한국 전래 동화 책들을 사서, 그것들을 영어로 번역하고 있어요.
여: 그 책들을 영어로 다시 만들 거니?
남: 아니요. 원문 옆에 번역본을 넣을 계획이에요.
여: 정말 힘들겠구나.
남: 네. 하지만 번역 앱 덕분에, 초고를 마칠 수 있었어요.
여: 잘됐구나! 책들을 보낼 준비가 거의 되었다는 뜻이니?
남: 사실, 그래서 선생님을 뵈러 온 거예요. 저희의 영어 번역본이 자연스럽게 들리는지 잘 모르겠어요. 번역본 초고를 검토해 주시겠어요?
여: 문제 없어. 너희를 돕게 되어 기쁘구나. 언제까지 끝내면 되겠니?
남: 음, 저희는 다음 달에 책들을 포장할 거예요.
여: 네가 이번 주에 번역본을 이메일로 내게 보내면, 이번 달 말까지 피드백을 줄게.
남: 정말 감사합니다.
① 책 구입하기
✓② 번역본 검토하기
③ 책 포장하기
④ 이메일 보내기
⑤ 번역 앱 추천하기

06 남자가 지불할 금액

▶ 정답 ③

W: Hi. How can I help you?
M: I'm looking for vegetable seeds for my garden. Can you recommend some vegetables that are easy to grow?
채소 씨앗들
정원
추천하다
재배하다
W: Sure. How about lettuce or tomatoes?
상추
토마토들
M: How much are they?
W: Lettuce seeds are three dollars for one packet, and tomato seeds are four dollars for one packet.
봉지
M: Sounds good. I'll buy two packets of tomato seeds.
W: Okay. Do you need anything else?
M: I also need fertilizer.
비료
W: I'd recommend this liquid fertilizer. It's one of our best sellers.
액체의
가장 잘 팔리는 상품들
M: How much is it?

W: It was originally ten dollars a bottle, but we're offering a 30 percent discount on this fertilizer.
원래
~을 30% 할인해 주고 있다
(offer a discount on: ~을 할인해 주다)
M: Great! I'll take one bottle. Here's my credit card.

해석
여: 안녕하세요. 어떻게 도와드릴까요?
남: 제 정원에 쓸 채소 씨앗들을 찾고 있어요. 재배하기 쉬운 채소들을 좀 추천해 주시겠어요?
여: 물론이죠. 상추나 토마토는 어떠세요?
남: 그것들은 얼마죠?
여: 상추 씨앗은 한 봉지에 3달러이고, 토마토 씨앗은 한 봉지에 4달러예요.
남: 괜찮네요. 토마토 씨앗 두 봉지를 살게요.
여: 알겠습니다. 다른 필요한 건 없으세요?
남: 비료도 필요해요.
여: 저는 이 액체 비료를 추천해요. 그것은 저희 가게에서 가장 잘 팔리는 상품들 중 하나거든요.
남: 얼마죠?
여: 그것은 원래 한 병에 10달러였는데, 저희는 이 비료를 30% 할인해 주고 있어요.
남: 좋아요! 한 병을 살게요. 여기 제 신용카드가 있어요.
① $11   ② $13   ✓ $15
④ $18   ⑤ $21

문제풀이
한 봉지에 4달러짜리 토마토 씨앗 두 봉지를 사면 8달러이다. 한 병에 10달러짜리 액체 비료는 30% 할인이 들어가기 때문에 7달러가 되어 8달러와 7달러를 합치면 총합 15달러, 즉 ③ '$15'가 답이다.

07 여자가 개를 키울 수 없는 이유

▶ 정답 ①

W: What a cute dog! Is it yours?
M: Yes. I adopted him from an animal rescue center.
입양했다(adopt)
동물 구조 센터
W: I've always wanted a dog. But I can't have one.
M: Why? Are you allergic to animal hair?
~에 알레르기가 있는
동물 털
W: I'm only allergic to cat hair. Dogs are totally fine.
M: What's the problem, then? Your house has a big backyard, so I think it's a perfect place for dogs.
문제
뒷마당
완벽한 장소
W: I think so, too. It's a really dog-friendly environment.
개를 키우기에 좋은
환경
M: Do your parents not like dogs?
W: No, they love dogs. But I'm worried about a dog being alone during the day.
혼자
낮 동안에
M: Is there nobody who can look after a dog?
~을 돌보다
W: There is no one at home during the day. My parents work, and my brother and I go to school.
학교에 가다
M: Oh, I see. That's why you can't get a dog.

해석
여: 정말 귀여운 개구나! 너의 개니?
남: 응. 동물 구조 센터에서 그를 입양했어.
여: 나는 항상 개를 키우고 싶었어. 하지만 키울 수 없어.
남: 왜? 동물 털에 알레르기가 있니?
여: 나는 고양이 털에만 알레르기가 있어. 개는 정말 괜찮아.
남: 그럼 문제가 뭐니? 네 집은 큰 뒷마당이 있어서, 개를 키우기에 완벽한 장소인 것 같은데.
여: 나도 그렇게 생각해. 정말 개를 키우기에 좋은 환경이지.
남: 부모님께서 개를 좋아하지 않으시니?
여: 아니, 그분들은 개를 정말 좋아하셔. 하지만 낮에 혼자 있는 개가 걱정이 돼.
남: 개를 돌봐줄 수 있는 사람이 아무도 없니?
여: 낮 동안에는 집에 아무도 없어. 부모님께서는 일을 하시고, 남동생과 나는 학교에 가.
남: 오, 알겠어. 그런 이유로 네가 개를 키울 수 없는 거구나.
✓① 낮에 개를 돌볼 사람이 없어서
② 부모님이 허락하지 않아서
③ 개를 키울 마당이 없어서
④ 동생이 개를 무서워해서
⑤ 개 알레르기가 있어서

08 World Food Festival에 관해 언급되지 않은 것

▶ 정답 ④

M: Katie, what are you doing?
W: I'm looking at a brochure for the World Food Festival. Do you remember the event I talked about before?
M: Yeah. You said we can enjoy different types of foods from around the world. Where will it be?
W: It'll be held at the central park in Orange County.
M: That's not far from here. Is it on a weekend?
W: Yes. It's on Sunday, September 22nd and starts at 10 a.m.
M: I've never been to a food festival before. What kind of programs does this one have?
W: There are tasting events for foods from all around the world and a variety of folk shows. Would you like to go with me?
M: I'd love to. [Pause] Hmm... we should probably drive there. Will there be parking available?
W: The brochure says there will be a parking lot. It'll cost five dollars to park there for the whole day.
M: Perfect! Let's take my car. I'll pick you up.
W: Okay. I'll see you then.

해석
남: Katie, 무엇을 하고 있니?
여: World Food Festival(세계 음식 축제)에 대한 소책자를 보고 있어. 내가 전에 말했던 그 행사를 기억하니?
남: 그래. 네가 전 세계의 다양한 종류의 음식들을 즐길 수 있다고 말했잖아. 그것이 어디에서 하는데?
여: Orange County(오렌지 카운티)의 중앙 공원에서 개최될 거야.
남: 여기에서 멀지 않구나. 주말에 하는 거야?
여: 그래. 9월 22일 일요일이고 오전 10시에 시작해.
남: 나는 전에 음식 축제에 가 본 적이 없어. 이 축제는 어떤 종류의 프로그램들이 있니?
여: 전 세계의 음식들에 대한 시식 행사들과 다양한 민속 공연들이 있어. 나와 함께 갈래?
남: 그러고 싶어. [잠시 후] 흠... 우리 아마도 그곳에 운전해서 가야 할 것 같아. 이용 가능한 주차 공간이 있을까?
여: 소책자에는 주차장이 있을 것이라고 되어 있어. 하루 종일 그곳에 주차하는 데 5달러래.
남: 완벽해! 내 차를 가지고 가자. 내가 너를 데리러 갈게.
여: 좋아. 그때 보자.

① 개최 장소
② 개최 일시
③ 프로그램 종류
✔ 반입 금지 물품
⑤ 주차 요금

09 Arusha National Park Tour에 관한 내용과 일치하지 않는 것

▶ 정답 ④

W: Hello, everyone. I'm Jessica Parker. Today, I'm here to tell you about the Arusha National Park Tour. It's a one-day tour program. This park is situated between Kilimanjaro and Mount Meru. You can enjoy breathtaking views of lakes and mountains. Also, you can see diverse wildlife such as monkeys, buffalos, and elephants. At 7 a.m., you will be picked up at the East entrance of the park to begin the tour. The drop-off location will be the same as the pick-up location. The tour ends around 9 p.m., but that may change based on weather conditions. I hope you won't miss this tour.

해석
여: 안녕하세요, 여러분. 저는 Jessica Parker입니다. 오늘, 저는 여러분께 Arusha National Park Tour(아루샤 국립 공원 투어)에 대해 말씀드리려고 합니다. 그것은 1일 투어 프로그램입니다. 이 공원은 Kilimanjaro(킬리만자로)와 Mount Meru(메루 산) 사이에 위치해 있습니다. 여러분은 호수와 산의 숨이 막히는 풍경을 즐길 수 있습니다. 또한, 여러분은 원

숭이, 버팔로, 그리고 코끼리와 같은 다양한 야생 동물을 볼 수 있습니다. 오전 7시에, 여러분은 공원의 동쪽 입구에서 승차하여 투어를 시작할 것입니다. 하차 장소는 승차 장소와 같을 것입니다. 투어는 오후 9시쯤에 종료되지만, 기상 상황에 따라 달라질 수도 있습니다. 여러분이 이 투어를 놓치지 않기를 바랍니다.

① 1일 투어 프로그램이다.
② 호수와 산의 풍경을 즐길 수 있다.
③ 다양한 야생 동물을 볼 수 있다.
✔ 승차 장소와 하차 장소가 다르다.
⑤ 종료 시간은 날씨에 따라 달라질 수 있다.

10 표에서 두 사람이 구매할 Air Fryer

▶ 정답 ④

M: Honey, what are you looking at?
W: A website that sells air fryers. I want one so we can cook more healthily.
M: Good idea. We can fry foods using less oil if we buy one. How much do you think we should spend?
W: Well, I don't want to spend more than 100 dollars.
M: Okay. Then how about these models?
W: Hmm... it's safer to buy one that will turn off if it gets too hot.
M: You're right. Let's choose one with the automatic switch off function.
W: What about capacity? My friend bought one that could only hold two liters. She regretted not buying a bigger one.
M: In that case, we should get one with a capacity of at least four liters. Now we have these two to choose from.
W: They both look good. But I think the one with the longer warranty is better.
M: I agree. Let's order this one.

해석
남: 여보, 무엇을 보고 있어요?
여: 에어 프라이어들을 판매하는 웹 사이트예요. 우리가 더 건강하게 요리할 수 있도록 하나 사고 싶어요.
남: 좋은 생각이에요. 그것을 사면 기름을 덜 사용해서 음식들을 튀길 수 있잖아요. 우리가 얼마를 써야 한다고 생각해요?
여: 음, 저는 100달러 이상을 쓰고 싶지는 않아요.
남: 알겠어요. 그럼 이 모델들은 어때요?
여: 흠... 너무 뜨거워지면 꺼지는 제품을 사는 것이 더 안전해요.
남: 당신 말이 맞아요. 자동 스위치 꺼짐 기능이 있는 것으로 선택합시다.
여: 용량은 어때요? 제 친구가 2리터만 담을 수 있는 제품을 샀어요. 그녀는 더 큰 것을 사지 않은 것을 후회했어요.
남: 그렇다면, 우리는 용량이 적어도 4리터인 것을 사야겠네요. 이제 선택할 수 있는 이 두 가지가 남았어요.
여: 그것들은 둘 다 좋아 보여요. 하지만 저는 보증 기간이 더 긴 제품이 더 좋은 것 같아요.
남: 동의해요. 이것을 주문합시다.

에어 프라이어

	모델	가격	자동 스위치 꺼짐 기능	용량(리터)	보증 기간
①	A	59달러	×	2	1년
②	B	68달러	○	2	1년
③	C	84달러	○	4	1년
✔	D	95달러	○	4	2년
⑤	E	109달러	×	5	2년

11 여자의 마지막 말에 대한 남자의 응답

▶ 정답 ⑤

W: What did you do last weekend?
M: I watched the movie The Universe.
W: Oh, really? I'm planning to watch that with my friend tonight. How

did you like it?
M: (Actually, I wouldn't recommend it.)
　　사실　　　　　　추천하다

해석
여: 지난 주말에 무엇을 했니?
남: 〈The Universe(우주)〉라는 영화를 봤어.
여: 오, 정말? 나는 오늘 밤에 친구와 함께 그것을 볼 계획이야. 그것은 어땠어?
남: (사실, 나는 그것을 추천하지 않을 거야.)
① 미안해. 나는 오늘 밤에 계획이 있어.
② 나는 항상 온라인으로 표를 구매해.
③ 너는 다음에 더 잘할 수 있어.
④ 너는 그것을 많이 봤음에 틀림없구나.
☑ 사실, 나는 그것을 추천하지 않을 거야.

12 남자의 마지막 말에 대한 여자의 응답　▶ 정답 ②
고2 2019년 9월 2번　정답률 80%

M: Mom, I'm home. Did my package arrive this afternoon?
　　　　　　　　　　　소포　도착하다
W: No. I've been home all day, but nothing came.
　　　　　　　　하루 종일
M: That's strange. I got a text message that says my package was
　　이상한　　　　　문자 메시지
delivered.
배달되었다(be delivered)
W: (Why don't you call the delivery person?)
　　　　　　　　　　배달 담당자

해석
남: 엄마, 저 왔어요. 오늘 오후에 제 소포가 도착했어요?
여: 아니. 내가 하루 종일 집에 있었는데, 아무것도 안 왔단다.
남: 그거 이상하네요. 저는 제 소포가 배달되었다는 문자 메시지를 받았어요.
여: (배달 담당자에게 전화를 해 보는 게 어떠니?)
① 괜찮아. 너는 내일 그것을 배달할 수 있어.
☑ 배달 담당자에게 전화를 해 보는 게 어떠니?
③ 걱정하지 마. 내가 너를 위해 그것을 반납할게.
④ 내가 포장하는 것을 도와줄 수 있겠니?
⑤ 지금 그 소포를 열어 보자.

13 여자의 마지막 말에 대한 남자의 응답　▶ 정답 ⑤
고2 2019년 9월 13번　정답률 85%

W: Hey, Brian, are you eating chocolate again? You've been eating a
lot of chocolate these days.
많은
M: Yeah, but I can't stop. I eat sweets whenever I'm stressed.
　　　　　　　　　　　단것　～할 때마다　스트레스를 받은
W: What's going on?
M: I've been busy preparing for my final exams, and I have too many
　　　　～을 준비하느라 바쁜　　기말 고사들
(busy V-ing: ~하느라 바쁜)
assignments.
과제들
W: I understand. But eating sweets doesn't really help relieve stress.
　　　　　　　　　　　　　　　　　　　　　스트레스를 해소하다
It does more harm than good.
M: I know. Do you have any idea about what I can do instead?
　　　　　　　　　　　　　　　　　　　　　대신에
W: Maybe you can try walking or stretching. Those have helped me a
　　　　　　걷기나 스트레칭을 해 보다
lot.
M: Really? That sounds like a better way to deal with my stress
　　　　　　　　　　　　　　　방법　～을 다루다
because it's healthier.
더 건강한
W: Definitely. Physical activity will be much more helpful than eating
　　　　　　신체 활동
chocolate.
M: (Okay. I'll exercise when I'm stressed.)
운동하다

해석
여: 이봐, Brian, 너 또 초콜릿 먹니? 요즘에 너무 많은 초콜릿을 먹는구나.
남: 그래, 하지만 멈출 수가 없어. 나는 스트레스를 받을 때마다 단것을 먹거든.
여: 무슨 일이니?
남: 나는 기말 고사를 준비하느라 바쁘고, 과제도 너무 많아.
여: 이해해. 하지만 단것을 먹는 것은 스트레스를 해소하는 데 별로 도움이 되지 않아. 그것은
도움이 되기보다는 더 해가 돼.
남: 알아. 대신에 내가 무엇을 할 수 있는지에 대해 어떤 생각이 있니?
여: 아마도 걷기나 스트레칭을 해 볼 수 있을 거야. 그것들은 나에게 많은 도움을 주었거든.
남: 정말? 그것은 더 건강하기 때문에 내 스트레스를 다루는 더 좋은 방법처럼 들려.

여: 물론이지. 신체 활동은 초콜릿을 먹는 것보다 훨씬 더 도움이 될 거야.
남: (알았어. 나는 스트레스를 받을 때 운동을 할 거야.)
① 네가 회복되기를 바랄게.
② 나는 시험에 떨어진 것 같아.
③ 때때로 스트레스는 도움이 될 수 있어.
④ 물론이지. 내가 너에게 초콜릿을 좀 사 줄게.
☑ 알았어. 나는 스트레스를 받을 때 운동을 할 거야.

14 남자의 마지막 말에 대한 여자의 응답　▶ 정답 ①
고2 2019년 9월 14번　정답률 80%

W: Jay, why do you look so annoyed?
　　　　　　　　　　　짜증 난
M: I've been surfing the Internet, but there are so many ads.
　　　　　서핑을 해왔다(surf)　　　　　　　　광고들
W: What kinds of ads?
M: Pop-up advertisements. Whenever I open a new website, ads pop
　　팝업 광고들　　　　　　　　　　　　　　　　　　나타나다
up. It takes a lot of time for me to close all of them.
많은 시간이 걸리다
W: That used to happen to me, too. Maybe I can help you.
　　　　일어나곤 했다
(used to V: ~하곤 했다, happen: 일어나다)
M: Is there a way to stop them?
　　　　　방법
W: I'm using a program that blocks pop-up advertisements.
　　　　　　　　　　　　　차단하다
M: Is it difficult to use?
W: It's very simple and easy. Just install a pop-up blocker on your
　　　　　　　　　　　　　설치하다　팝업 차단 프로그램
computer, and it'll prevent ads from popping up.
　　　　　　　　　　광고들이 뜨는 것을 막다
(prevent A from V-ing: A가 ~하는 것을 막다)
M: That sounds good. But what if I can't see important pop-up
　　　　　　　　　　　　~하면 어쩌지
messages that are not advertisements?
W: (Don't worry. It'll only filter out the ads.)
　　　　　　　　　　걸러 내다

해석
여: Jay, 너 왜 그렇게 짜증 나 보이니?
남: 인터넷 서핑을 하고 있는데, 광고들이 너무 많아.
여: 어떤 종류의 광고들이니?
남: 팝업 광고들이야. 내가 새로운 웹 사이트를 열 때마다, 광고들이 나타나. 내가 그것들을 모
두 닫는데 많은 시간이 걸려.
여: 나에게도 그런 일이 일어나곤 했어. 아마 내가 너를 도울 수 있을 것 같아.
남: 그것들을 멈출 수 있는 방법이 있니?
여: 나는 팝업 광고들을 차단하는 프로그램을 사용하고 있어.
남: 그것은 사용하기에 어렵니?
여: 매우 간단하고 쉬워. 네 컴퓨터에 팝업 차단 프로그램을 설치해. 그러면 그것이 광고들이
뜨는 것을 막아줄 거야.
남: 좋은 것 같아. 그런데 내가 광고가 아닌 중요한 팝업 메시지를 보지 못하면 어쩌지?
여: (걱정하지 마. 그것은 광고들만 걸러 낼 거야.)
☑ 걱정하지 마. 그것은 광고들만 걸러 낼 거야.
② 조심해. 온라인 광고들을 너무 믿지 마.
③ 네 말이 맞아. 나는 그 프로그램을 사용하는 것을 고려해 볼게.
④ 그것은 네 개인 정보를 위험에 노출시킬 수 있어.
⑤ 그 프로그램을 다운로드하는 것은 네 컴퓨터를 느리게 할 거야.

문제 풀이
팝업 광고들을 차단할 수 있는 프로그램을 알게 된 남자는 그것을 설치하게 되면 광고가 아닌
중요한 팝업 메시지를 보지 못하게 될까 봐 걱정하고 있다. 따라서 광고만 차단한다는 말로 남
자를 안심시키는 선택지인 ① 'Don't worry. It'll only filter out the ads.(걱정하지 마. 그것은
광고들만 걸러 낼 거야.)'가 답이 된다.

15 다음 상황에서 Eve가 Tom에게 할 말　▶ 정답 ②
고2 2019년 9월 15번　정답률 75%

M: Eve is a college student who is majoring in history. She has been
　　　　　　대학생　　　　　~을 전공하고 있다(major in)
worried about her career path because she's uncertain about
　　　　　　　　직업 진로　　　　　　　확신이 없는
what to do after she graduates. So, to learn more about her
무엇을 해야 할지　　졸업하다(graduate)
(what to V: 무엇을 ~해야 할지)
career options, she regularly meets a career counselor at her
직업 선택들　　정기적으로　　　직업 상담사
college. She feels that it has helped her a lot. One day, Eve finds
　　　　　　　　　　　　　　　　　　　　　알게 되다

out that her classmate Tom is also worried about what to do after he graduates. Eve wants to suggest that Tom go see the career
제안하고 싶다
(want to V: ~하고 싶다, suggest: 제안하다)
counselor for advice. In this situation, what would Eve most likely say to Tom?
조언
Eve: (How about getting help from a career counselor?)

해석
남: Eve는 역사를 전공하고 있는 대학생이다. 그녀는 그녀가 졸업한 후에 무엇을 해야 할지에 대해 확신이 없기 때문에 직업 진로에 대해 걱정하고 있다. 그래서, 그녀의 직업 선택에 대해 더 배우기 위해서, 그녀는 정기적으로 그녀의 대학교의 직업 상담자를 만난다. 그녀는 그것이 그녀에게 많은 도움을 주고 있다고 느낀다. 어느 날, Eve는 그녀의 동기인 Tom도 그가 졸업한 후에 무엇을 해야 할지에 대해 걱정하고 있다는 것을 알게 된다. Eve는 Tom이 조언을 구하기 위해 직업 상담사에게 가 볼 것을 제안하고 싶다. 이러한 상황에서, Eve는 Tom에게 뭐라고 말하겠는가?
Eve: (직업 상담사에게 도움을 받는 게 어때?)
① 너는 네 전공 분야와 관련된 직업을 찾아야 해.
✓ ② 직업 상담사에게 도움을 받는 게 어때?
③ 전공을 선택하기 전에 조사를 좀 해 봐.
④ 내가 너라면, 역사를 공부하는 데 집중할 텐데.
⑤ 인턴십에 지원하는 게 어때?

문제 풀이
Eve는 Tom 또한 졸업 후 무엇을 해야 할지 걱정하고 있다는 사실을 알게 된 후 그에게 자신이 도움을 받은 직업 상담사를 찾아갈 것을 제안하고 싶어 한다. 따라서 ② 'How about getting help from a career counselor?(직업 상담사에게 도움을 받는 게 어때?)'가 답이다.

16~17 1지문 2문항

W: Hello, students. As you all know, heavy traffic is a major source
교통 체증   주요 원인
of air pollution. To tackle this problem, many European cities are
대기 오염   해결하다
taking various actions. For instance, in Copenhagen, the capital
다양한 조치들을 취하고 있다   수도
(take action: 조치를 취하다)
of Denmark, large parts of the city have been closed to vehicles
차량 출입이 금지되다(be closed to vehicles)
for decades, and the city plans to become carbon neutral by
수십 년 동안   될 계획이다   탄소 중립적인
(plan to V: ~할 계획이다)
2025. Also, Paris, in France, bans cars in many historic districts
금지하다(ban)   역사적인   지역들
on weekends and encourages car- and bike-sharing programs.
장려하다   자동차와 자전거 공유 프로그램들
In Belgium, the city of Brussels operates "Mobility Week" to
운영하다   교통 주간
encourage public over private transportation. And for one day
민간 교통보다 대중 교통을
every September, all cars are banned from the entire city center.
전체 시내 중심가
Lastly, cities in Germany are establishing "green zones" in city
설치하고 있다(establish) 녹지 지역들
centers. If vehicles don't have a sticker showing they have an
허용 가능한   배출 수준   진입하다
acceptable emission level, they can't enter those places. Now, I'll
show you some pictures that illustrate this.
예시하다

해석
여: 안녕하세요, 학생 여러분. 여러분 모두 알다시피, 교통 체증은 대기 오염의 주요 원인입니다. 이 문제를 해결하기 위해서, 많은 유럽의 도시들이 다양한 조치들을 취하고 있습니다. 예를 들면, 덴마크의 수도인 코펜하겐에서는, 도시의 많은 지역들이 수십 년 동안 차량 출입이 금지되어 왔고, 이 도시는 2025년까지 탄소 중립(이산화탄소를 배출한 만큼 다시 흡수해 실질 배출량을 '0'으로 만드는 것)이 될 계획입니다. 또한, 프랑스의 파리는, 주말에 많은 역사적인 지역들에서 자동차를 금지하고 자동차와 자전거 공유 프로그램들을 장려합니다. 벨기에에서, 브뤼셀 시는 민간 교통보다 대중 교통을 장려하는 'Mobility Week(교통 주간)'를 운영합니다. 그리고 9월마다 하루 동안, 전체 시내 중심가에 모든 자동차가 금지됩니다. 마지막으로, 독일의 도시들은 시내 중심가에 'green zones(녹지 지역들)'를 설치하고 있습니다. 차량들이 허용 가능한 (탄소) 배출 수준을 가지고 있다는 것을 나타내는 스티커를 가지고 있지 않으면, 그것들은 그 장소들에 진입할 수 없습니다. 이제, 저는 여러분께 이것을 예시하는 사진 몇 장을 보여드리겠습니다.

---

16 여자가 하는 말의 주제
① 도시에서 주차 공간을 빠르게 찾을 수 있는 유용한 조언들
✓ ② 교통으로 인한 대기 오염을 처리하기 위한 유럽에서의 노력들
③ 온실 가스가 환경에 미치는 영향들
④ 유럽 수도들에서의 교통 체증의 원인들
⑤ 유럽의 다양한 재생 가능한 에너지원들

17 언급된 나라가 아닌 것
① 덴마크   ② 프랑스   ③ 벨기에
✓ ④ 스위스   ⑤ 독일

---

05 2019년 11월 학력평가

01	③	02	②	03	⑤	04	④	05	⑤
06	②	07	④	08	③	09	⑤	10	③
11	①	12	②	13	①	14	③	15	⑤
16	②	17	⑤						

01 남자가 하는 말의 목적

M: Hello, students. I'm Daniel Hopper from the administration office.
행정실
I'd like to announce the opening of a new bicycle parking facility.
알리다 개관 새로운 자전거 주차 시설
More and more students bike to school and have difficulty finding
점점 더 많은   자전거를 타고 학교에 오다 찾는 데 어려움을 겪다
(have difficulty V-ing: ~하는 데 어려움을 겪다)
safe and easy parking spaces. So it's important that we provide
중요한   제공하다
a bicycle parking facility that allows our students to park their
우리 학생들이 주차할 수 있도록 하다(allow A to V: A가 ~할 수 있도록 하다)
bicycles safely and conveniently. Construction on a bicycle parking
안전하게   편리하게   공사
facility next to the library is now complete. Starting next Monday,
완료된
students can leave their bicycles at this facility. It's free and
놓아두다   무료의
available on a first come, first served basis. If you have any further
이용 가능한   선착순으로
questions, please feel free to contact the administration office.
편하게 연락하다
(feel free to V: 편하게 ~하다, contact: 연락하다)

해석
남: 안녕하세요, 학생 여러분. 저는 행정실의 Daniel Hopper입니다. 새로운 자전거 주차 시설의 개관을 알려드리고자 합니다. 점점 더 많은 학생들이 자전거를 타고 학교에 오는데 안전하고 편리한 주차 공간을 찾는 데 어려움을 겪고 있습니다. 그래서 우리 학생들이 그들의 자전거를 안전하고 편리하게 주차할 수 있도록 하는 자전거 주차 시설을 제공하는 것이 중요합니다. 도서관 옆에 있는 자전거 주차 시설에 대한 공사가 이제 완료되었습니다. 다음 주 월요일부터 시작해서, 학생들은 이 시설에 자전거를 놓아둘 수 있습니다. 그것은 무료이며 선착순으로 이용 가능합니다. 문의 사항이 더 있으면, 행정실로 편하게 연락하세요.

① 행정실 운영 시간 변경을 안내하려고
② 불법 주차 집중 단속 기간을 공지하려고
✓ ③ 신설된 자전거 주차 시설에 대해 알려주려고
④ 도서관 설립을 위한 모금 행사를 홍보하려고
⑤ 자전거 통학 시 보호 장비 착용을 독려하려고

02 여자의 의견

W: Jack, are you ready for your trip?
준비가 된   여행
M: Yeah. I'm almost done.

W: Great. Did you buy travel insurance?
여행자 보험에 가입하다(buy an insurance: 보험에 가입하다)
M: Travel insurance? Do you think I should buy it?
W: Of course. You don't want your trip to be ruined by unexpected
네 여행이 망쳐지기를 바라다   뜻밖의
emergency bills.
응급 비용청구서   (want A to V: A가 ~하기를 바라다, ruin: 망치다)
M: Does that really happen?
일어나다
W: Sure it happens. One of my friends got injured during a trip and
다친
spent a lot of money at a hospital.
(돈을) 썼다(spend)
M: In that case, it would be helpful to have insurance.
도움이 되는
W: Yeah. For me, last time I traveled, I lost my cell phone and the
잃어버렸다(lose)   휴대전화
insurance covered it.
보장했다(cover)
M: That's amazing. I didn't know insurance covers that kind of stuff,
놀라운   그런 종류의 것
too.
W: See? You'd better buy it before you go on your trip.
너는 가입하는 것이 좋겠다   여행을 가다(go on a trip)
(had better V: ~하는 것이 좋겠다)
M: Yeah. You're right. I think I should.

해석
여: Jack, 여행을 위한 준비가 되었니?
남: 응. 거의 다 했어.
여: 좋아. 너는 여행자 보험에 가입했니?
남: 여행자 보험? 내가 그것에 가입해야 한다고 생각하니?
여: 물론이지. 너는 뜻밖의 응급 비용청구서로 인해 네 여행이 망쳐지기를 바라지 않잖아.
남: 그런 일이 정말 일어나니?
여: 물론 일어나지. 내 친구들 중 한 명이 여행하는 동안 다쳐서 병원에서 많은 돈을 썼어.
남: 그런 경우에는, 보험을 가지고 있는 것이 도움이 되겠구나.
여: 그래. 내 경우에는, 지난번에 여행할 때, 휴대전화를 잃어버렸는데 보험이 그것을 보장해줬어.
남: 그거 놀라운데. 나는 보험이 그런 종류의 것도 보장해주는지 몰랐어.
여: 그렇지? 너는 여행을 가기 전에 그것에 가입하는 것이 좋을 거야.
남: 그래. 네 말이 맞아. 그래야겠어.

① 외국 여행을 할 때 현지 문화를 존중해야 한다.
☑ 여행을 가기 전에 여행자 보험에 가입해야 한다.
③ 과소비를 줄이기 위해 지출 계획을 세워야 한다.
④ 관광객 유치를 위해 관광 상품을 다양화해야 한다.
⑤ 응급 처치 방법을 익혀 응급 상황에 대비해야 한다.

03 두 사람의 관계
고2 2019년 11월 5번 정답률 80%
▶ 정답 ⑤

W: Hi, James!
M: Hello, Ms. Collins.
W: I've wanted to talk to you about one of your paintings.
이야기하고 싶었다(want to V: ~하고 싶다)   그림들
M: My paintings? Which one?
W: The work you submitted in my art class last week. I was so impressed
작품   제출했다(submit)   ~에 매우 깊은 인상을 받았다
by your drawing technique, the way you show the objects.
그림 기법   (be impressed by: ~에 깊은 인상을 받다)
대상들
M: Thank you for the compliment, Ms. Collins. I tried to make them
칭찬   만들려고 노력했다
look realistic, just like a photo.
사실적인   (try to V: ~하려고 노력하다)
W: You did an excellent job. As your art teacher, I recommended your
미술 선생님   추천했다(recommend)
work for the School Art Festival. The other art teachers agreed.
학교 예술 축제   동의했다(agree)
M: That's amazing. Isn't it next month?
놀라운
W: Yes. So, why don't you think of a title for your painting?
~하는 게 어떠니?   제목
M: Okay. Is that for putting a tag on the painting?
이름표
W: Yes. The title will help other students understand your work.
이해하다
M: Thank you so much, Ms. Collins.

해석
여: 안녕, James!
남: 안녕하세요, Collins 선생님.
여: 나는 네 그림들 중 하나에 대해 너와 이야기하고 싶었단다.

남: 제 그림들이요? 어떤 것이요?
여: 지난주에 내 미술 수업에서 네가 제출한 작품 말이야. 나는 네 그림 기법, 즉 대상을 나타내는 방식에 매우 깊은 인상을 받았어.
남: 칭찬해 주셔서 감사해요, Collins 선생님. 저는 꼭 사진처럼 그것들이 사실적으로 보이도록 만들려고 노력했어요.
여: 정말 잘했어. 너의 미술 선생님으로서, 나는 School Art Festival(학교 예술 축제)에 네 작품을 추천했어. 다른 미술 선생님들도 동의하셨어.
남: 그거 놀랍네요. 그것은 다음 달 아닌가요?
여: 그래. 그러니까, 네 그림의 제목에 대해서 생각해 보는 게 어떠니?
남: 알겠어요. 그것은 그림에 이름표를 달기 위한 건가요?
여: 그래. 제목은 다른 학생들이 네 작품을 이해하는 데도 도움을 줄 거야.
남: 정말 감사합니다, Collins 선생님.

① 박물관 큐레이터 — 관람객   ② 사진작가 — 비평가
③ 메이크업 아티스트 — 고객   ④ 화가 — 기자
☑ 미술 교사 — 학생

문제 풀이
여자는 자신의 미술 수업에서 남자가 제출한 그림이 매우 인상적이었다고 칭찬하고 있다. 여자가 남자의 미술 선생님으로서 학교 예술 축제에 남자의 그림을 추천했다고 말하고 있으므로 ⑤ '미술 교사 — 학생'이 적절한 답이다.

04 그림에서 대화의 내용과 일치하지 않는 것
고2 2019년 11월 6번 정답률 90%
▶ 정답 ④

M: Lily! I heard that you got your own place to live.
공간   살다
W: Yeah. I finally got a place of my own. I have a picture. Do you want
마침내   사진
to see it?
보고 싶다(want to V: ~하고 싶다)
M: Sure. [Pause] Oh, I like the striped curtains.
줄무늬 커튼
W: Thanks. I got those striped curtains on sale.
세일 중인
M: I see. There is a pair of headphones on the wall above the
헤드폰 한 쌍   ~ 위쪽에
electronic piano. What are they for?
전자 피아노
W: I use them when playing the piano so I don't disturb my neighbors.
사용하다   방해하다   이웃들
M: How considerate of you. What's the plant under the clock?
사려 깊은   식물   ~ 아래에
W: Isn't it nice? I received the plant as a housewarming gift. I also got
받았다(receive)   집들이 선물로
the round table as a gift from my family.
원형 테이블
M: How nice! The round table really ties the room together. Oh, the
방을 함께 묶다
lamp next to the bed is similar to mine.
전등   ~ 옆에   ~과 비슷한
W: Really? It's so useful when I read in bed.
유용한
M: Right. I wish I had a room like yours.
W: Thanks.

해석
남: Lily! 나는 네가 살 너만의 공간을 구했다고 들었어.
여: 그래. 나는 마침내 나만의 공간을 갖게 되었어. 사진이 있어. 그것을 보고 싶니?
남: 물론이지. [잠시 후] 오, 나는 줄무늬 커튼이 마음에 들어.
여: 고마워. 나는 그 줄무늬 커튼을 세일 중일 때 구했어.
남: 그렇구나. 전자 피아노 위쪽 벽에 헤드폰 한 쌍이 있구나. 그것들은 무엇에 쓰는 거니?
여: 피아노를 칠 때 내 이웃들을 방해하지 않도록 그것들을 사용해.
남: 너는 정말 사려 깊구나. 시계 아래에 있는 식물은 무엇이니?
여: 멋지지 않니? 나는 집들이 선물로 그 식물을 받았어. 가족들에게 선물로 원형 테이블도 받았어.
남: 정말 멋지다! 그 원형 테이블이 정말 방을 함께 묶어주는구나(조화롭게 만드는구나). 오, 침대 옆에 있는 전등은 내 것과 비슷해.
여: 정말? 그것은 침대에서 책을 읽을 때 정말 유용해.
남: 맞아. 나도 네 것 같은 방이 있으면 좋겠어.
여: 고마워.

---

05 여자가 할 일

▶ 정답 ⑤

W: Peter, the parent-teacher conference is tomorrow. Is there anything
　　　　　　학부모-교사 회의
　 left for us to do?
　 남은
M: I think we're ready for it.
　　　　　　준비가 된
W: Alright. Let's have one last check. Did you hang the banner?
　　　　　　　　마지막으로 한 번 더 확인하다   걸다   현수막
M: Yes, I did this morning. What about the hand-outs for parents?
　　　　　　　　　　　　　　　　　　　유인물들
W: I printed them out and stapled them, too.
　　　그것들을 출력했다   스테이플러로 고정했다(staple)
　 (print out: ~을 출력하다)
M: Great. Hmm... last time, the microphone wasn't functioning well.
　　　　　　　　　　　　마이크   작동하는(function)
W: I know. I checked and also prepared spare microphones just in
　　　　　　　준비했다(prepare) 여분의   만일의 경우를 대비해서
　 case.
M: Good. You're going to use a projector, right?
　　　　　　　　프로젝터를 사용하다
W: Yes. I need to show some charts on the screen.
　　　　　　보여줘야 하다   도표들   화면
　 (need to V: ~해야 하다)
M: Then I'll check the projector right away.
W: Thanks. Oh, did you buy snacks to put on the table?
　　　　　　　　　　　간식들
M: Oh, no! I totally forgot about the snacks.
　　　　　완전히 잊어버렸다(forget)
W: Don't worry. I'll buy them on my way home after school.
　　　　　　　　　　　　　집에 가는 길에
M: Thanks. It's all set then.
　　　　　준비된

해석
여: Peter, 학부모-교사 회의가 내일이에요. 우리가 해야 할 남은 일이 있나요?
남: 우리는 그것에 대한 준비가 된 것 같아요.
여: 좋아요. 우리 마지막으로 한 번 더 확인해 봐요. 현수막을 걸었나요?
남: 네, 제가 오늘 아침에 했어요. 학부모님들을 위한 유인물은 어때요?
여: 제가 그것들을 출력해서 스테이플러로 고정도 했어요.
남: 좋아요. 흠... 지난번에, 마이크가 잘 작동하지 않았어요.
여: 알아요. 제가 확인했고 만일의 경우를 대비해서 여분의 마이크도 준비했어요.
남: 좋아요. 프로젝터를 사용할 거죠, 그렇죠?
여: 네. 화면에 도표를 좀 보여줘야 하거든요.
남: 그럼 저는 지금 당장 프로젝터를 점검할게요.
여: 고마워요. 오, 테이블에 놓을 간식을 구입했나요?
남: 오, 이런! 간식에 대해서 완전히 잊어버렸어요.
여: 걱정하지 마세요. 제가 방과 후에 집에 가는 길에 그것들을 구입할게요.
남: 고마워요. 그럼 모두 준비되었네요.

① 현수막 걸기　　　　　　　　② 유인물 출력하기
③ 마이크 준비하기　　　　　　④ 프로젝터 점검하기
✔ 간식 구입하기

문제 풀이
내일 있을 학부모-교사 회의에서 테이블에 놓아야 할 간식을 구입했냐는 여자의 질문에 남자는 완전히 잊고 있었다고 대답한다. 여자는 집에 가는 길에 자신이 간식을 구입하겠다고 말한다. 그러므로 여자가 할 일로 가장 적절한 것은 ⑤ '간식 구입하기'이다.

---

06 남자가 지불할 금액

▶ 정답 ②

W: Welcome to Rock Bowling Center. How may I help you?

M: Hi. We'd like to do some bowling here.
　　　　　　　　　볼링을 좀 하다
W: Alright. How many people are you with?
M: We're a group of four.
W: Okay. Since we have a special event today, you can enjoy unlimited
　　　　　~하기 때문에   특별 행사   무제한 볼링을 즐기다
　 bowling all day for $20 per person.
　　　　　　　　　　　　　　1인당
M: That's amazing. We'll all do that. What about shoes? We didn't
　　　　굉장한
　 bring bowling shoes.
　 가져오다 볼링화
W: You can rent shoes of any size and they're $5 per person.
　　　　　　대여하다
M: Then, we'll rent four pairs of shoes.
W: Okay. So, that's admission fees and renting shoes for four people.
　　　　　　　　　　입장료
M: Right. Can I use this coupon for a discount?
　　　　　　　　　　　할인 쿠폰
W: Sure. You'll get 10% off the total price.
　　　　　　　총액에서 10% 할인을 받다
M: Great. I'll pay by credit card.
　　　　　지불하다   신용카드

해석
여: Rock Bowling Center(록 볼링 센터)에 오신 걸 환영합니다. 어떻게 도와드릴까요?
남: 안녕하세요. 저희는 여기에서 볼링을 좀 하고 싶어요.
여: 알겠습니다. 손님과 몇 분이 함께 하시죠?
남: 저희는 네 명입니다.
여: 알겠습니다. 오늘 저희가 특별 행사를 하기 때문에, 1인당 20달러에 하루 종일 무제한 볼링을 즐기실 수 있습니다.
남: 그거 굉장하네요. 저희 모두 그것을 할게요. 신발은요? 저희는 볼링화를 가져오지 않았어요.
여: 어떤 사이즈의 신발이든 대여하실 수 있으며 1인당 5달러입니다.
남: 그럼, 신발 4켤레를 대여할게요.
여: 알겠습니다. 그럼, 그것(비용)은 4명에 대한 입장료와 신발 대여료네요.
남: 네. 저 이 할인 쿠폰을 사용할 수 있을까요?
여: 물론이죠. 총액에서 10% 할인을 받으실 거예요.
남: 좋아요. 신용카드로 지불할게요.

① $80　　　　　　　　✔ $90　　　　　　　　③ $92
④ $98　　　　　　　　⑤ $100

문제 풀이
4명에 대한 무제한 입장료는 총 20달러*4인, 즉 80달러이고, 4명에 대한 신발 대여료는 총 5달러*4인, 즉 20달러로 합치면 모두 100달러이다. 여기에 남자는 총액에서 10퍼센트 할인되는 할인 쿠폰을 사용하므로 총 100달러에서 10달러 할인된 90달러를 지불하면 된다. 따라서 정답은 ② '$90'이다.

---

07 여자가 커피 박람회에 갈 수 없는 이유

▶ 정답 ④

M: Hi, Sandy. What are you doing?
W: I'm watching this video on how to make coffee. This is so
　　　　　　　　　　　　　　　　커피를 만드는 방법(how to V: ~하는 방법)
　 interesting.
　 흥미로운
M: Oh, I'm into coffee nowadays.
　　　　나는 커피에 빠져 있다 요즘에
　 (be into: ~에 빠져 있다)
W: Are you? I like tasting the flavors of different coffee beans.
　　　　　　　맛보는 것을 좋아하다 풍미들   다양한 커피콩들
　 (like V-ing: ~하는 것을 좋아하다, taste: 맛보다)
M: Really? I've heard that the Coffee Fair is being held downtown. Do
　　　　　　　　　　　　　커피 박람회 열리고 있다(be held)
　 you want to go there with me?
W: That would be really fun. When are you going?
　　　　　　　재미있는
M: This Saturday. Are you available?
　　　　　　　　　시간이 있는
W: Oh, no. I'm not.
M: Why? Do you teach your baking class on Saturdays?
　　　　　　　지도하다   제빵 수업
W: No, it's only on weekdays. On Saturday my family plan to
　　　　　　　　　　　　　　　　주중에   ~에 참여할 계획이다
　 participate in the local flea market.
　 ~에 참여할 계획이다 지역 벼룩시장
　 (plan to V: ~할 계획이다, participate in: ~에 참여하다)
M: Flea market?
W: Yes. We'll sell cookies and donate the profits to kids in hospitals.
　　　　　　　팔다   기부하다   수익금
M: Oh, that's kind of you. We can go next time then.

해석
남: 안녕, Sandy. 무엇을 하고 있니?
여: 커피를 만드는 방법에 대해 이 동영상을 보고 있어. 이것은 매우 흥미로워.
남: 오, 나는 요즘에 커피에 빠져 있어.
여: 그러니? 나는 다양한 커피콩의 풍미를 맛보는 것을 좋아해.
남: 정말? 나는 시내에서 Coffee Fair(커피 박람회)가 열리고 있다고 들었어. 나와 함께 그곳에 갈래?
여: 그거 정말 재미있겠다. 언제 갈 거니?
남: 이번 주 토요일에. 너는 시간이 있니?
여: 오, 이런. 나는 안돼.
남: 왜? 토요일마다 제빵 수업을 지도하니?
여: 아니, 그것은 주중에만 해. 토요일에 우리 가족이 지역 벼룩시장에 참여할 계획이거든.
남: 벼룩시장?
여: 그래. 우리는 쿠키를 팔아서 수익금을 병원에 있는 아이들에게 기부할 거야.
남: 오, 너 정말 착하다. 그럼 우리는 다음에 가도 돼.

① 홍보 동영상을 제작해야 해서
② 커피 원두를 사러 가야 해서
③ 제빵 수업을 지도해야 해서
✔④ 벼룩시장에 참여해야 해서
⑤ 병원 진료를 받아야 해서

08 Forest Walk에 관해 언급되지 않은 것 ▶ 정답 ③

M: Honey, what are you reading?
W: It's a brochure about the Forest Walk in Elbert Mountain.
M: Is it like a guided walking tour?
W: Exactly. A guide explains old trees and plants in the forest while walking. Its purpose is to make people feel more connected to nature. (feel connected to: ~과 유대감을 느끼다)
M: Sounds interesting. When is it?
W: Every Saturday the tour starts at 9 a.m. and lasts for two hours.
M: It'll be wonderful to start a Saturday morning by walking. How much do we have to pay? (have to V: ~해야 하다, pay: 지불하다)
W: It's $5 per person and the money will be used to plant more trees.
M: Okay. Let's do it this Saturday. How do we register?
W: We have to do it through the website by Wednesday.
M: Is there a limit on the number of participants?
W: Yeah. It says it's up to twenty people per tour.
M: Let's hurry, then.

해석
남: 여보, 무엇을 읽고 있어요?
여: Elbert Mountain(엘버트 산)에서의 Forest Walk(숲 산책)에 대한 소책자예요.
남: 가이드가 있는 산책 투어 같은 거예요?
여: 맞아요. 산책하면서 가이드가 숲속에 있는 오래된 나무들과 식물들에 대해 설명해요. 그것의 목적은 사람들이 자연과 더 유대감을 느끼도록 만드는 거예요.
남: 흥미롭게 들리네요. 그것이 언제죠?
여: 매주 토요일 오전 9시에 투어가 시작되고 2시간 동안 진행돼요.
남: 토요일 아침을 산책으로 시작하는 것은 멋질 거예요. 얼마를 지불해야 해요?
여: 1인당 5달러이고 그 돈은 더 많은 나무들을 심는 데 사용될 거예요.
남: 좋네요. 이번 주 토요일에 그것을 해요. 어떻게 등록하죠?
여: 수요일까지 웹사이트를 통해서 그것을 해야 해요.
남: 참가자 수에 제한이 있어요?
여: 네. 한 투어당 20명까지라고 적혀 있어요.
남: 그럼, 서두릅시다.

① 목적   ② 시작 시간   ✔③ 준비 물품
④ 신청 방법   ⑤ 최대 참가 인원

문제 풀이
여자는 Forest Walk(숲 산책) 투어의 목적은 사람들로 하여금 자연과 더 유대감을 느끼게 하는 것이며, 투어는 매주 토요일 오전 9시에 시작되는데, 웹사이트를 통해 신청할 수 있고, 참가자 수는 한 투어당 20명으로 제한된다고 말하고 있다. 준비 물품에 대해서는 언급되지 않았으므로, 답은 ③ '준비 물품'이다.

09 Langford Night Market에 관한 내용과 일치하지 않는 것 ▶ 정답 ⑤

W: Hello, listeners. I'm Jessica Norton, manager of Langford Park. We're happy to announce that the Langford Night Market is coming back. Starting from September 1st for five nights, you can enjoy the event where food trucks and booths will be set up. This year's theme is the Global Food Festival. You can try food from all over the world. Live music performances will be held every night, creating a festive atmosphere. There is also a special zone for kids where they can have fun playing with toys. The whole family can (have fun V-ing: ~하면서 즐겁게 보내다, play with: ~을 가지고 놀다) enjoy this fun festival. If it rains, the market will be cancelled. We hope you enjoy our upcoming event. Thank you.

해석
여: 안녕하세요, 청취자 여러분. 저는 Langford Park(랭포드 공원)의 관리자인 Jessica Norton입니다. 저희는 Langford Night Market(랭포드 야시장)이 돌아오는 것을 알려 드리게 되어 기쁩니다. 9월 1일부터 시작해서 5일 동안, 여러분께선 푸드 트럭들과 부스들이 설치되는 행사를 즐기실 수 있습니다. 올해의 주제는 Global Food Festival(세계 음식 축제)입니다. 여러분께선 전 세계의 음식을 먹어보실 수 있습니다. 매일 밤 라이브 음악 공연들이 열려서 축제 분위기를 만들어 낼 것입니다. 또한, 어린이들이 장난감들을 가지고 놀면서 즐겁게 보낼 수 있는 어린이들을 위한 특별 공간도 있습니다. 가족 전체가 이 재미있는 축제를 즐기실 수 있습니다. 만약 비가 오면, 시장은 취소될 것입니다. 저희는 여러분께서 다가오는 행사를 즐기시길 바랍니다. 감사합니다.

① 9월 1일부터 시작한다.
② 올해 주제는 세계 음식 축제이다.
③ 라이브 음악 공연이 매일 밤 열린다.
④ 어린이를 위한 특별 공간이 있다.
✔⑤ 비가 와도 일정대로 진행된다.

10 표에서 여자가 주문할 컴퓨터 의자 ▶ 정답 ③

M: Ellen, I think we need a new computer chair. Ours is so old.
W: I think so, too. Let's find one online. [Typing sound] Look, the top five selling models are here.
M: Okay. Which prices look reasonable? I think spending more than $100 for a chair is too much. (spend)
W: I agree. What about materials? I prefer a fabric chair because leather gets scratch marks more easily.
M: You're right. The fabric also matches our other furniture.
W: Yeah. Do you want a chair whose height is changeable or fixed?
M: The changeable one looks more convenient. I'm quite taller than you. So we need to change the chair's height. (need to V: ~해야 하다, change: 변경하다)
W: Okay. Do you think a headrest is necessary?
M: Definitely. It supports your head and neck.
W: Then we've only got one option left. I'll order it now.
M: Perfect.

해석
남: Ellen, 우리는 새 컴퓨터 의자가 필요할 것 같아. 우리 것은 너무 낡았어.
여: 나도 그렇게 생각해. 온라인에서 하나 찾아보자. [타자 치는 소리] 봐, 가장 잘 팔리는 5개의 모델들이 여기 있어.
남: 좋아. 어떤 가격이 합리적으로 보이니? 나는 의자 하나에 100달러 이상을 쓰는 것은 너무 하다고 생각해.
여: 나도 동의해. 재질은 어때? 나는 가죽은 긁힘 자국이 더 쉽게 생기기 때문에 직물 의자가 더 좋아.
남: 네 말이 맞아. 직물은 또한 우리의 다른 가구와 어울리기도 하잖아.
여: 그래. 너는 높이가 변경 가능한 의자를 원하니 아니면 고정된 의자를 원하니?

남: 변경 가능한 것이 더 편리해 보여. 나는 너보다 꽤 더 크잖아. 그래서 우리는 의자의 높이를 변경해야 해.
여: 알겠어. 너는 머리 받침대가 필요하다고 생각하니?
남: 물론이지. 그것이 네 머리와 목을 지지해주잖아.
여: 그럼 우리에게는 단 하나의 선택만 남았네. 내가 지금 그것을 주문할게.
남: 좋아.

컴퓨터 의자

	모델	가격	재질	높이	머리 받침대
①	A	110달러	가죽	변경 가능	○
②	B	95달러	가죽	고정	X
③	C	80달러	직물	변경 가능	○
④	D	75달러	직물	변경 가능	X
⑤	E	70달러	직물	고정	X

문제 풀이

남자와 여자는 100달러 미만의 직물 의자를 구매하는 데 서로 동의한다. 남자는 높이를 변경할 수 있으며 머리 받침대가 있는 의자를 추천하고 여자는 이에 동의하고 있으므로 여자가 주문할 제품은 ③이다.

11 남자의 마지막 말에 대한 여자의 응답
고2 2019년 11월 1번 정답률 90%
▶ 정답 ①

[Cell phone rings.]
M: Hey, Emma. Are you coming home this Friday?
W: Yes, Dad. I've finished my midterms and I want to see you and Mom.
　　　　　　　끝낸(finish)　　중간고사　　　보고 싶다(want to V: ~하고 싶다)
M: That's great. Will you take a train when you come home?
　　　　　　　　　　　기차를 타다
W: (Yes. I've already bought the train ticket.)
　　　　　　　이미　　　　　　기차표

해석

[휴대전화가 울린다.]
남: 얘야, Emma. 이번 주 금요일에 집에 올 거니?
여: 네, 아빠. 저는 중간고사를 끝냈고 아빠와 엄마가 보고 싶어요.
남: 잘됐구나. 집에 올 때 기차를 탈 거니?
여: (네. 저는 이미 기차표를 샀어요.)
☑ 네. 저는 이미 기차표를 샀어요.
② 아니요. 저는 내일 모임에 갈 수 없어요.
③ 힘내세요. 아빠께선 다음에 더 잘하실 수 있어요.
④ 괜찮아요. 아빠께선 제 집에 머무르셔도 돼요.
⑤ 알겠어요. 저는 엄마께서 빨리 나으셨으면 좋겠어요.

12 여자의 마지막 말에 대한 남자의 응답
고2 2019년 11월 2번 정답률 90%
▶ 정답 ②

W: How was the Apple Festival yesterday?
　　　　　　　　사과 축제
M: It was fantastic. I made pies and jam from the apples that I picked.
　　　　　환상적인　　사과들로 파이와 잼을 만들었다　　　　　　　　　　땄다(pick)
　　　　　　　　　　(make A from B: B로 A를 만들다)
I took a lot of pictures, too.
많은 사진을 찍었다(take a picture)
W: Sounds like it was fun. I wish I had been there. Let me see the pictures.
　　　　　　　재미있는
M: (Sure. You'll like my pictures of the festival.)

해석

여: 어제 Apple Festival(사과 축제)은 어땠니?
남: 환상적이었어. 나는 내가 딴 사과로 파이와 잼을 만들었어. 많은 사진도 찍었어.
여: 그것은 재미있었던 것처럼 들린다. 나도 거기에 갔으면 좋았을 텐데. 사진들 좀 보자.
남: (그래. 너는 내 축제 사진들을 좋아할 거야.)
① 네 말이 맞아. 나는 날씨가 좋았으면 좋겠어.
☑ 그래. 너는 내 축제 사진들을 좋아할 거야.
③ 미안해. 내가 사진 찍는 것이 허락되지 않았어.
④ 더 이상은 안 돼. 너는 이미 사과를 충분히 먹었어.
⑤ 물론이지! 나는 네 파이를 맛보고 싶어.

13 여자의 마지막 말에 대한 남자의 응답
고2 2019년 11월 13번 정답률 85%
▶ 정답 ①

[Cell phone rings.]
W: Dad! It's me, Sarah. I just arrived for the computer programming certification test.
　　　　　　　　　　　도착했다(arrive)　　컴퓨터 프로그래밍 자격 시험
M: Good! You got there early. Are you ready for the test?
　　　　　　　　　　　　　　　　　　준비가 된
W: No. I've got a big problem.
　　　　　　　　큰 문제
M: A problem? What is it?
W: I just realized that I didn't bring my identification.
　　　깨달았다(realize)　　　　　가져오다　　　신분증
M: Oh, do you want me to bring your student ID now?
　　　내가 가져다 주기를 원하다　　　학생증
　　(want A to V: A가 ~하기를 원하다)
W: That's not possible. I lost my student ID last month at school.
　　　　　　가능한　　　잃어버렸다(lose)
M: Oh, no. Did you ask the test administration about what to do?
　　　　　　　　　　　　　　시험 관리실　　　　　　무엇을 해야 할지
　　　　　　　　　　　　　　　　　　　　(what to V: 무엇을 ~할지)
W: They said I can take the test with my passport instead. It must be
　　　　　　　　시험을 보다　　　　　여권　　대신에
somewhere in my room.
M: Really? Do you remember where you put it?
　　　　　　　기억나다　　　　　　두었다(put)
W: Hmm... oh, I remember! I put it in my desk drawer.
　　　　　　　　　　　　　　　　　　책상 서랍
M: (Alright. I'll get it and bring it to you right away.)
　　　　　　　　　　　　　　　　　즉시

해석

[휴대전화가 울린다.]
여: 아빠! 저예요, Sarah. 방금 컴퓨터 프로그래밍 자격 시험을 위해 도착했어요.
남: 좋아! 그곳에 일찍 도착했구나. 시험에 대한 준비가 되었니?
여: 아니요. 큰 문제가 있어요.
남: 문제? 그게 뭔데?
여: 제 신분증을 가져오지 않은 것을 이제 막 깨달았어요.
남: 오, 내가 지금 네 학생증을 가져다 주기를 원하니?
여: 그건 가능하지 않아요. 저는 지난달에 학교에서 학생증을 잃어버렸어요.
남: 오, 이런. 시험 관리실에 무엇을 해야 할지에 대해 물어봤니?
여: 그들은 대신에 제 여권을 가지고 시험을 볼 수 있다고 말했어요. 그것은 분명 제 방 어딘가에 있을 거예요.
남: 정말? 그것을 어디에 두었는지 기억나니?
여: 흠... 오, 기억나요! 제 책상 서랍 안에 두었어요.
남: (알겠어. 내가 그것을 찾아서 너에게 즉시 가져다 줄게.)
☑ 알겠어. 내가 그것을 찾아서 너에게 즉시 가져다 줄게.
② 바로 그거야. 나는 그 서류를 가져왔어야 했어.
③ 미안해. 그날은 우리 중 아무도 시간이 없어.
④ 물론이지. 내 시험을 끝내는 데 30분이 걸릴 거야.
⑤ 걱정하지 마. 그가 시험 전에 그곳에 너를 내려줄 거야.

14 남자의 마지막 말에 대한 여자의 응답
고2 2019년 11월 14번 정답률 80%
▶ 정답 ③

M: Hi, Alice. Is everything okay?
W: Not really, Dr. Johnson. You know my son, Ben?
M: Sure. I saw him at family counseling before.
　　　　　　　　　　가족 상담
W: I'm worried about him these days. He wakes up in the middle of the night and won't stop crying.
　　　　　　　　　　　　　　　　　　　　　　깨다(wake up)　　　한밤중에
　　　　　　　우는 것을 멈추다(stop V-ing: ~하는 것을 멈추다)
M: Hmm... he must be under stress. Tell me more.
　　　　　　　　　스트레스를 받고 있다
W: He's really mean to his baby brother and always causes trouble.
　　　　　　　　못되게 구는　　　　　　　　　　　　　　문제를 일으키다
M: Did it happen to begin after your second child was born?
　　　혹시 시작되다(happen to V: 혹시 ~하다, 우연히 ~하다)
W: I think so. Is Ben stressed because of his little brother?
　　　　　　　　　　스트레스를 받는　　~때문에
M: It's possible. I'm sure you've been busy taking care of the baby and
　　　가능한　　　　　　　　　　　　아기를 돌보느라 바쁜
　　　　　　　　　　　　　　(busy V-ing: ~하느라 바쁜, take care of: ~을 돌보다)
it probably makes Ben feel less special.
　　아마도　　　　　　　　덜 특별한
W: Right. I don't play with Ben as much as I used to. That might be the
　　　　　　　　　　　　　　예전에 그랬던 만큼 많이
reason why he behaves like that.
　이유　　　행동하다(behave)
M: Yes, it's natural for him to feel that way. Now, you know what Ben
　　　　　당연한

needs.
W: (Yes. I should make time each day to spend with him.)
                                          (시간을) 보내다

해석
남: 안녕하세요, Alice. 잘 지내시죠?
여: 별로 그렇지 않아요, Johnson 선생님. 제 아들, Ben 아시죠?
남: 물론이죠. 전에 가족 상담에서 그애를 봤잖아요.
여: 저는 요즘에 이 애 때문에 걱정이에요. 그애는 한밤중에 깨서 우는 것을 멈추지 않아요.
남: 흠... 그애가 스트레스를 받고 있나 보네요. 더 말씀해 주세요.
여: 그애는 어린 남동생에게 정말 못되게 굴고 항상 문제를 일으켜요.
남: 그런 일이 혹시 둘째 아이가 태어난 후에 시작되었나요?
여: 그런 것 같아요. Ben이 남동생 때문에 스트레스를 받는 것일까요?
남: 가능하죠. 당신이 아기를 돌보느라 바빠서 그것이 아마도 Ben을 덜 특별하다는 느낌이 들게끔 만든 거라는 확신이 드네요.
여: 맞아요. 저는 예전에 그랬던 만큼 많이 Ben과 놀아주지 못해요. 그것이 그 애가 그렇게 행동하는 이유일지 모르겠네요.
남: 네, 그 애가 그렇게 느끼는 것은 당연해요. 이제, 당신은 Ben이 무엇을 필요로 하는지 아시죠.
여: (네. 저는 매일 그 애와 함께 보낼 시간을 만들어야겠어요.)
① 맞아요. 당신은 그 애의 이기적이고 무례한 행동을 무시해도 돼요.
② 알겠어요. 저는 학습에서 그 애에게 동기가 더욱 부여되도록 노력할게요.
☑③ 네. 저는 매일 그 애와 함께 보낼 시간을 만들어야겠어요.
④ 물론이죠. 저는 그 애에게 자신의 장난감을 남동생과 같이 가지고 놀라고 할게요.
⑤ 알겠어요. 당신은 그 애가 스스로 잠이 들도록 격려해야 해요.

문제풀이
둘째 아이를 돌보느라 바쁜 엄마 때문에 스트레스를 받은 첫째 아이가 자신을 덜 특별하게 느낀다는 남자의 말에 여자는 예전만큼 첫째 아이와 놀아주지 못한다고 말하고 있다. 첫째 아이에게 필요한 것이 무엇인지 이제 알게 됐다는 말에 이어질 말은 ③ 'Yes. I should make time each day to spend with him.(네. 저는 매일 그 애와 함께 보낼 시간을 만들어야겠어요.)'이 적절하다.

15 다음 상황에서 Mike가 Amy에게 할 말
고2 2019년 11월 15번 | 정답률 80% | ▶ 정답 ⑤

M: Mike is the leader of a book club and Amy is one of its members.
        회장   독서 클럽   회원들
The club members are supposed to read a section of the selected
                    읽도록 되어 있다   부분   선정된
            (be supposed to V: ~하도록 되어 있다)
book before each meeting and have discussions on certain issues.
                                ~에 대해 토론하다   주제들
However, Amy has been annoying the other members lately by
              짜증나게 하고 있다(annoy)   최근에
not reading the books before the meetings. The group members
읽지 않음으로써(by not V-ing: ~하지 않음으로써)
complain to Mike about how hard it is to have a discussion
불평하다   얼마나 힘든지
about a book when Amy doesn't read it. Mike understands their
                                              이해하다
complaints and wants to encourage Amy to take the club more
불평들   Amy가 받아들이도록 권장하고 싶다
            (want to V: ~하고 싶다, encourage A to V: A가 ~하도록 권장하다)
seriously. Mike wants to tell Amy that she needs to make more of
진지하게   책 읽기에 더 헌신해야 하다
            (need to V: ~해야 하다, make a commitment to A: A에 헌신하다)
a commitment to reading books. In this situation, what would Mike
most likely say to Amy?
Mike: (You should be responsible about reading books for club
            activities.) 책임감을 가지다

해석
남: Mike는 독서 클럽의 회장이고 Amy는 클럽의 회원들 중 한 명이다. 클럽 회원들은 매 모임 전에 선정된 책의 한 부분을 읽고 특정한 주제들에 대해 토론하도록 되어 있다. 하지만, Amy가 모임 전에 책을 읽지 않음으로써 최근에 다른 회원들을 짜증나게 하고 있다. 모임 회원들은 Mike에게 Amy가 책을 읽지 않으면 그것(책)에 대해 토론하는 것이 얼마나 힘든지에 대해 불평한다. Mike는 그들의 불평을 이해하고 Amy가 클럽을 더 진지하게 받아들이도록 권장하고 싶다. Mike는 Amy에게 그녀가 책 읽기에 더 헌신해야 한다고 말하고 싶다. 이러한 상황에서, Mike는 Amy에게 뭐라고 말하겠는가?
Mike: (너는 클럽 활동을 위해 책 읽기에 대해 책임감을 가져야 해.)
① 너는 토론을 위해 논리적인 사고력을 개발해야 해.
② 나는 너를 이 독서 클럽의 회장으로 추천하고 싶어.
③ 새로운 클럽 회원들을 찾기 위해서 더 노력해 주겠니?
④ 글쓰기를 향상시키기 위해 신문을 계속 읽는 게 어떠니?
☑⑤ 너는 클럽 활동을 위해 책 읽기에 대해 책임감을 가져야 해.

16~17 1지문 2문항

W: Hello, students. In today's class, we'll learn about some innovative
                                                      혁신적인
robot designs. Recently, robots have taken inspiration from the
로봇 설계들   영감
natural world. Let's look at the first picture. Notice the snakebot
자연계   주목하다
has no legs like a snake. It's able to move on almost any type
                    뱀   이동하다   거의 모든 형태의 표면
of surface just like a snake. Does this second robot resemble
                                                          닮다
anything familiar? That's right, the engineers who designed this
        친숙한   공학자들   설계했다(design)
robot copied the complex movements of bat wings when designing
모방했다(copy)   복잡한 동작들   박쥐 날개들
this bat-like robot, Bat bot. It can dive like a real bat and is easier
박쥐 같은   하강하다
to operate thanks to its soft and flexible wings. Now, this third
작동하다   ~ 덕분에   유연한
robot's shape may not look familiar, but surely its actions will. This
                  모양   움직임들
robot is called the BionicANT and it was programmed to behave in
                                          행동하도록 프로그램 되었다
                (be programmed to V: ~하도록 프로그램 되다, behave: 행동하다)
a cooperative way, similar to an ant. I'm sure you'll enjoy this last
협력적인 방식   ~과 비슷한
robot called Biscuit, the robot dog. As you can easily see, it was
inspired by a dog. This robot is friendly and responds to your voice
개에게서 영감을 받았다   ~에 반응하다(respond to)
(be inspired by A: A에서 영감을 받다)
commands. Now let's share our thoughts about these robots.
음성 명령   나누다

해석
여: 안녕하세요, 학생 여러분. 오늘 수업에서, 우리는 몇몇 혁신적인 로봇 설계들에 대해서 배울 것입니다. 최근에, 로봇들은 자연계에서 영감을 얻고 있습니다. 첫 번째 사진을 봅시다. snakebot(스네이크봇)은 뱀처럼 다리가 없다는 점에 주목해 주세요. 그것은 꼭 뱀처럼 거의 모든 형태의 표면에서 이동할 수 있습니다. 이 두 번째 로봇은 친숙한 어떤 것과 닮았나요? 맞습니다, 이 로봇을 설계한 공학자들은 이러한 박쥐 같은 로봇인 Bat bot(배트봇)을 설계할 때 박쥐 날개의 복잡한 동작들을 모방했습니다. 그것은 진짜 박쥐처럼 하강할 수 있고 그것의 부드럽고 유연한 날개 덕분에 작동하기 더 쉽습니다. 자, 이 세 번째 로봇의 모양은 친숙하게 보이지 않을지도 모르지만, 분명 그것의 움직임들은 그럴(친숙하게 보일) 것입니다. 이 로봇은 BionicANT(바이오닉앤트)라고 불리며 개미와 비슷한 협력적인 방식으로 행동하도록 프로그램 되었습니다. 저는 여러분이 로봇 개인 Biscuit(비스킷)이라 불리는 이 마지막 로봇을 좋아할 거라고 확신합니다. 여러분이 쉽게 알 수 있듯이, 그것은 개에게서 영감을 받았습니다. 이 로봇은 상냥하며 여러분의 음성 명령에 반응합니다. 이제 이 로봇들에 대한 우리의 생각들을 나눠봅시다.

16 여자가 하는 말의 주제
고2 2019년 11월 16번 | 정답률 90% | ▶ 정답 ②

① 동물 구조에서 로봇의 역할들
☑② 실제 세계의 동물들에 의해 영감을 받은 로봇들
③ 좋은 동물 복지를 보장하는 방법들
④ 우리 사회에서 일자리를 얻기 위해 경쟁하는 로봇들
⑤ 의학을 발전시키는 데 도움을 주는 동물들

17 언급된 동물이 아닌 것
고2 2019년 11월 17번 | 정답률 90% | ▶ 정답 ⑤

① 뱀   ② 박쥐   ③ 개미
④ 개   ☑⑤ 개구리

06 2020년 3월 학력평가

01	⑤	02	④	03	⑤	04	④	05	②
06	③	07	①	08	④	09	④	10	③
11	①	12	③	13	①	14	②	15	⑤
16	⑤	17	③						

※2020년 4월 24일에 시행된 3월 전국연합 학력평가는 자율 원격 시험으로 시행되어 성적 발표를 하지 않았습니다. 이에 따라 교재에 기입된 정답률은 실제와 다를 수 있습니다.

01 남자가 하는 말의 목적

고2 2020년 3월 3번 | 정답률 75%

▶ 정답 ⑤

M: May I have your attention, please? This is from the management office of Vincent Hospital. The west entrance facing Main Street is being repaired, so it cannot be used. We'd like to remind you all to use the east entrance today. The east entrance is on Wilson Street, and it is open during regular visiting hours from 8 a.m. to 6 p.m. And during non-visiting hours, please use the north entrance facing Hyde Street. The west entrance will be in use from tomorrow. We're sorry for any inconvenience this might cause. Thank you for your cooperation.

해석
남: 주목해 주시겠습니까? Vincent 병원 관리 사무소에서 알려드립니다. Main Street를 향하는 서쪽 출입구는 수리 중이어서, 이용하실 수 없습니다. 오늘은 여러분 모두에게 동쪽 출입구를 이용하시도록 알려드리고자 합니다. 동쪽 출입구는 Wilson Street에 있으며, 오전 8시에서 오후 6시까지 정기 면회 시간 동안에 개방됩니다. 그리고 비면회 시간 동안에는, Hyde Street를 향하는 북쪽 출입구를 이용해 주십시오. 서쪽 출입구는 내일부터 이용될 것입니다. 이로 인해 야기될 수 있는 불편에 대해 죄송하게 생각합니다. 협조해 주셔서 감사합니다.

① 병실 사용 시 유의 사항을 설명하려고
② 병문안 시 면회 시간 준수를 당부하려고
③ 병원 내 새로운 편의 시설을 소개하려고
④ 병원 주변 도로 통제 구역을 공지하려고
✓ 병원 일부 출입구의 사용 제한을 안내하려고

02 여자의 의견

고2 2020년 3월 4번 | 정답률 85%

▶ 정답 ④

W: Jamie, have you decided to join the peer teaching program?
M: No, Ms. Moore. I haven't decided yet.
W: Come on. I believe you'd be a good peer teacher.
M: Thanks, but I don't think I have enough time to study for myself.
W: I know what you mean. But teaching others can be helpful for your study.
M: Do you think so?
W: Yes. The more you explain something to others, the more deeply you can understand its meaning.
M: You mean the more I teach, the more I learn?
W: That's right.
M: Well, then, I'll join the program.
W: Good. I'm sure it'll be a great experience for you.

해석
여: Jamie, 또래 교습 프로그램에 참가하기로 결정했니?
남: 아니요, Moore 선생님. 아직 결정하지 못했어요.
여: 어서 하렴. 나는 네가 좋은 또래 선생님이 될 거라고 믿어.
남: 감사해요, 그런데 저 자신을 위해 공부할 충분한 시간을 가질 수 없을 것 같아요.
여: 무슨 말인지 알겠어. 하지만 다른 사람들을 가르치는 것은 네 공부에 도움이 될 수 있어.
남: 그렇게 생각하세요?
여: 그래. 네가 무엇인가를 다른 사람들에게 더 많이 설명할수록, 너는 그것의 의미를 더 깊이 이해할 수 있단다.
남: 제가 더 많이 가르칠수록, 더 많이 배운다는 말씀이시죠?
여: 맞아.
남: 음, 그렇다면, 그 프로그램에 참가할게요.
여: 잘했어. 나는 그것이 너에게 좋은 경험이 될 거라고 확신해.

① 꾸준한 봉사 활동은 자아 존중감을 높인다.
② 남을 가르칠 때 자신감을 갖는 것이 중요하다.
③ 학습량과 교과 성적이 정비례하는 것은 아니다.
✓ 남을 가르치는 것은 자신의 학습에 도움이 된다.
⑤ 알고 있는 것과 가르치는 것은 별개의 문제이다.

03 두 사람의 관계

고2 2020년 3월 5번 | 정답률 80%

▶ 정답 ⑤

W: Excuse me, Mr. Young. I'm Emma Baker.
M: Oh, hi Emma. I've been waiting for you. Nice to meet you.
W: Nice to meet you, too.
M: Is this your first visit to a broadcasting station?
W: Yes, it is. I've been looking forward to seeing the news studio myself.
M: I see. You seem to be very interested in broadcasting.
W: Yes, I'm the leader of my school's broadcasting club.
M: Oh, you are? Today, you'll sit at a news desk and experience what it's like to host a news program.
W: Fantastic! I watch your news program every day. How can you deliver the news so effortlessly?
M: I read my scripts repeatedly before I begin the broadcast.
W: That's impressive. I really want to host a news program like you someday.
M: I hope you will. Shall we go to the news studio now?

해석
여: 실례합니다, Young 선생님. 저는 Emma Baker입니다.
남: 오, 안녕하세요 Emma. 당신을 기다리고 있었어요. 만나서 반가워요.
여: 저도 뵙게 되어 반갑습니다.
남: 방송국 방문은 이번이 처음인가요?
여: 네, 그렇습니다. 저는 뉴스 스튜디오를 직접 보기를 고대해 왔어요.
남: 그렇군요. 방송에 매우 관심이 많은 것처럼 보여요.
여: 네, 저는 학교 방송 동아리의 회장이에요.
남: 오, 그래요? 오늘, 당신은 뉴스 진행석에 앉아 뉴스 프로그램을 진행하는 것이 어떤 것인지 체험하게 될 거예요.
여: 환상적이네요! 저는 매일 선생님의 뉴스 프로그램을 시청해요. 어떻게 그렇게 수월하게 뉴스를 전하실 수 있으신 건가요?
남: 저는 방송을 시작하기 전에 대본을 반복해서 읽어요.
여: 인상적이네요. 저는 정말 언젠가 선생님처럼 뉴스 프로그램을 진행하고 싶어요.
남: 그러길 바랄게요. 이제 뉴스 스튜디오로 갈까요?

① 뉴스 제보자 — 기자
② 해외 특파원 — 방송 제작자
③ 동아리 담당 교사 — 방송 작가
④ 방송 광고 의뢰인 — 촬영 감독
✓ 방송국 견학 학생 — 뉴스 진행자

04 그림에서 대화의 내용과 일치하지 않는 것
▶ 정답 ④

M: Joy, I'm excited to be in the theater.
신이 난 극장
W: I really wanted you to see this play, Daniel.
네가 보기를 원했다 연극
(want A to V: A가 ~하기를 원하다)
M: Thanks for bringing me here. By the way, the stage set looks a little
그런데 무대 세트 조금
strange.
이상한
W: This set shows two different living rooms. One on the left and the
보여주다 다른 거실들 (둘 중의) 다른 하나
other on the right.
M: Oh, now I understand. The left living room has striped wallpaper.
알다 줄무늬의 벽지
W: Yes. There's a bookshelf in the left living room, next to the door.
책꽂이 옆에
M: Oh, but the right living room has flower-patterned wallpaper.
꽃무늬의
W: Yeah. Can you see the rectangular mirror next to the window?
직사각형의 거울 창문
M: Yes, it matches the room. And there are two telephones, one at
어울리다 전화기들
each end of the sofa.
~의 양쪽 끝에 소파
W: This play is about a long telephone conversation between the two
전화 통화 ~ 사이의
living rooms. So the title is On the Line.
제목 통화 중인

해석
남: Joy, 나는 극장에 오게 되어 신이 나.
여: 나는 정말 네가 이 연극을 보기를 원했어, Daniel.
남: 나를 여기에 데려와 줘서 고마워. 그런데, 무대 세트가 조금 이상해 보여.
여: 이 세트는 두 개의 다른 거실을 보여줘. 하나는 왼쪽에 그리고 다른 하나는 오른쪽에 있어.
남: 오, 이제 알겠어. 왼쪽 거실에는 줄무늬 벽지가 있구나.
여: 응. 왼쪽 거실에는 책꽂이가 있어, 문 옆에 말이야.
남: 오, 그런데 오른쪽 거실에는 꽃무늬 벽지가 있구나.
여: 그래. 창문 옆에 직사각형 거울이 보이니?
남: 응, 그것은 방과 어울려. 그리고 두 대의 전화기가 있어, 소파의 양쪽 끝에 하나씩 말이야.
여: 이 연극은 두 개의 거실 사이의 긴 전화 통화에 관한 거야. 그래서 제목이 'On the line(통화 중)'이야.

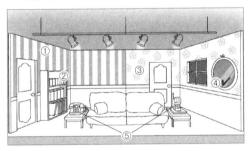

05 남자가 여자에게 부탁한 일
▶ 정답 ②

W: Alex, let's go for lunch.
점심 먹으러 가다
M: Sorry, but I don't have time, Kate.
W: What's keeping you so busy?
~하게 두다(keep) 바쁜
M: I'm working on our company's monthly newspaper.
회사 월간 신문
W: When's the deadline?
마감일
M: Today. I'm doing the final job of matching the articles with the
최종 작업 기사들과 사진들을 일치시키는 것
(match A with B: A와 B를 일치시키다, article: 기사, photo: 사진)
photos, but there's a problem.
문제
W: What is it?
M: I don't have any photos of Mr. Williams' retirement ceremony.
퇴임식
W: Really? I've got some photos I took at the ceremony with my digital
(사진을) 찍었다(take) 디지털 카메라
camera.
M: Oh, what a relief! Can you send me the photo files?
정말 다행이다 보내다 파일들
W: Sure. I'll email them right after lunch.
이메일로 보내다 점심 식사 후에 바로

M: Thank you so much, Kate.

해석
여: Alex, 점심 먹으러 가자.
남: 미안하지만, 나는 시간이 없어, Kate.
여: 무엇 때문에 그렇게 바쁘니?
남: 나는 우리 회사의 월간 신문을 만들고 있어.
여: 마감일이 언제니?
남: 오늘. 기사들과 사진들을 일치시키는 최종 작업을 하고 있는데, 문제가 있어.
여: 뭔데?
남: Williams 씨의 퇴임식 사진이 하나도 없어.
여: 정말? 내가 퇴임식에서 디지털 카메라로 찍은 사진을 몇 장 가지고 있어.
남: 오, 정말 다행이다! 그 사진 파일들을 나에게 보내줄 수 있어?
여: 물론이지. 점심 식사 후에 바로 그것들을 이메일로 보내줄게.
남: 정말 고마워, Kate.

① 퇴임식장 예약하기
✓ ② 사진 파일 보내주기
③ 점심 식사 주문하기
④ 행사 사진 촬영하기
⑤ 신문 기사 작성하기

06 여자가 지불할 금액
▶ 정답 ③

M: Welcome to Mary's Gift Shop. How may I help you?
선물 가게
W: Hi. I'd like to buy a cup for my friend's birthday.
사다 생일
M: How about this pumpkin-shaped cup?
~은 어떠세요? 호박 모양의
W: It's so unique. She'll like the design. How much is it?
독특한 디자인
M: It's $20.
W: Okay, I'll take it. And I'd also like to buy these teaspoons. How
찻숟가락들
much are they?
M: They're $10 each.
각각
W: Okay. I'll take two pink ones and two blue ones.
분홍색의 파란색의
M: Then, one pumpkin-shaped cup and four teaspoons, right?
W: Yes. Can I use this coupon that I downloaded from your website?
사용하다 쿠폰 다운로드했다 웹사이트
M: Sure. You'll get a 10% discount off the total price.
총액에서 10% 할인을 받다
W: Great. Here's my credit card.
신용카드

해석
남: Mary's Gift Shop(Mary의 선물 가게)에 오신 것을 환영합니다. 어떻게 도와드릴까요?
여: 안녕하세요. 친구의 생일을 위한 컵을 사고 싶어요.
남: 이 호박 모양의 컵은 어떠세요?
여: 매우 독특하네요. 그녀가 그 디자인을 좋아할 거예요. 얼마죠?
남: 20달러예요.
여: 좋아요, 그것을 살게요. 그리고 이 찻숟가락들도 사고 싶어요. 얼마죠?
남: 각각 10달러예요.
여: 좋아요. 분홍색 두 개와 파란색 두 개를 살게요.
남: 그럼, 호박 모양의 컵 한 개와 찻숟가락 네 개네요, 맞나요?
여: 네. 제가 웹사이트에서 다운로드한 이 쿠폰을 사용할 수 있을까요?
남: 물론이죠. 총액에서 10% 할인을 받으실 거예요.
여: 잘됐네요. 여기 제 신용카드가 있어요.

① $36 　　② $45 　　✓ $54
④ $63 　　⑤ $72

문제 풀이
여자는 20달러짜리 호박 모양의 컵 한 개와 10달러짜리 분홍 찻숟가락 두 개, 파란 찻숟가락 두 개를 구매하여 총액이 60달러가 된다. 쿠폰을 사용해 10% 할인을 받게 되므로 정답은 ③ '$54'가 된다.

07 남자가 배드민턴 레슨에 갈 수 없는 이유
▶ 정답 ①

M: Hi, Claire. How did your chemistry presentation go?
화학 발표 되다
W: It went better than I expected.
예상했다

M: Good. You look a little tired, though.
조금 피곤한 (문장의 끝에서) 하지만

W: I didn't get enough sleep last night, but I'm okay now. You know we
충분한 수면을 취하다 알다
(get sleep: 수면을 취하다, enough: 충분한)
have a badminton lesson today, right?
배드민턴 수업

M: Yes, but I don't think I can come.

W: Oh, does your left ankle still hurt?
발목 아직도 아프다

M: No, I've fully recovered.
완전히 회복한(recover)

W: Then, why?

M: Actually, I got a flu shot this morning.
사실은 독감 예방 주사

W: I see. I once had a terrible muscle ache after a flu shot.
이전에 심한 근육통

M: Well, anyway, I'll skip the lesson and get some rest today.
어쨌든 빠지다 휴식을 좀 취하다

W: Okay, take care.
몸조심하다

해석

남: 안녕, Claire. 네 화학 발표 어땠니?

여: 내가 예상했던 것보다 더 잘 됐어.

남: 다행이네. 하지만 너는 조금 피곤해 보여.

여: 어젯밤에 충분한 수면을 취하지 못했지만, 지금은 괜찮아. 우리 오늘 배드민턴 수업이 있는 거 알지, 그렇지?

남: 그래, 하지만 나는 갈 수 없을 것 같아.

여: 오, 왼쪽 발목이 아직도 아프니?

남: 아니, 완전히 회복했어.

여: 그럼, 왜?

남: 사실은, 내가 오늘 아침에 독감 예방 주사를 맞았거든.

여: 그렇구나. 나는 이전에 독감 예방 주사를 맞은 후에 심한 근육통을 앓았어.

남: 음, 어쨌든, 나는 오늘 수업에 빠지고 휴식을 좀 취할 거야.

여: 알았어, 몸조심해.

✔️독감 예방 주사를 맞아서
②발표 준비를 해야 해서
③수면 시간이 부족해서
④왼쪽 발목을 다쳐서
⑤진료 예약이 있어서

---

08 Dream Bio Research Project에 관해 언급되지 않은 것
고2 2020년 3월 10번 | 정답률 80% | ▶ 정답 ④

M: Hello, Dr. Peterson. How are you doing these days?
요즘

W: Hello, Dr. Collins. Good, I'm working on the Dream Bio Research
~을 수행하는(work on) 연구
Project.
프로젝트

M: You mean the medical research project sponsored by the
말하다 의학의 ~가 후원하는
government?
정부

W: That's right. More than 20 researchers are involved in the project
~ 이상의 연구원들 ~에 참여하다(be involved in)
and I'm the head researcher.
수석 연구원

M: Wow, you're in charge of a really big job. How big is the budget for
~을 맡은 큰 일 예산
the project?

W: We're allowed to spend one million dollars on the project.
쓰는 것이 허용된다
(be allowed to V: ~하는 것이 허용되다, spend: (돈을) 쓰다)

M: That's a really huge amount. It's a project to develop a new drug
엄청난 금액 개발하다 신약
for lung cancer, isn't it?
폐암

W: That's right.

M: How long will the research project last?
지속되다

W: It's a 5-year project. I hope we can develop the drug within this
바라다 ~ 이내에
period.
기간

M: I wish you success, Dr. Peterson.
빌다, 바라다 성공

W: Thank you, Dr. Collins.

해석

남: 안녕하세요, Peterson 박사님. 요즘 어떻게 지내세요?

여: 안녕하세요, Collins 박사님. 잘 지내요, 저는 Dream Bio Research Project(드림 바이오

연구 프로젝트)를 수행하고 있어요.

남: 정부가 후원하는 의학 연구 프로젝트를 말씀하시는 거죠?

여: 맞아요. 20명 이상의 연구원들이 그 프로젝트에 참여하고 있고 저는 수석 연구원이에요.

남: 와, 정말 큰 일을 맡으셨네요. 그 프로젝트에 대한 예산은 얼마나 크죠?

여: 저희는 그 프로젝트에 백만 달러를 쓰는 것이 허용돼요.

남: 정말 엄청난 금액이네요. 그것은 폐암에 대한 신약을 개발하는 프로젝트죠, 그렇지 않나요?

여: 맞아요.

남: 그 연구 프로젝트는 얼마나 오래 지속되는 거죠?

여: 5년짜리 프로젝트예요. 저는 우리가 이 기간 내에 약을 개발할 수 있기를 바라요.

남: 성공을 빌게요, Peterson 박사님.

여: 감사해요, Collins 박사님.

① 연구원 수   ② 예산 규모   ③ 연구 목적
✔️연구 장소   ⑤ 연구 기간

---

09 Marathon Reading Program에 관한 내용과 일치하지 않는 것
고2 2020년 3월 11번 | 정답률 80% | ▶ 정답 ④

W: Hello, students. Are you interested in reading books? Then, join
학생들 읽는 것에 관심이 있는 책들 참여하다
(interested in V-ing: ~하는 것에 관심이 있는, read: 읽다)
this year's Marathon Reading Program. In this program, students,
마라톤 독서 프로그램
teachers, and parents will read books until late at night on the
선생님들 학부모들 밤늦게까지
5th of April. It starts at 2 p.m. and ends at 10 p.m. The program
시작하다 끝나다
will be held at our school library. You can bring your own book
개최되다(hold: 개최하다) 학교 도서관 가져오다
or check out one at the library. After they finish reading their
~을 빌리다 읽는 것을 끝내다
(finish V-ing: ~하는 것을 끝내다)
book, all students are required to write a book review. Snacks
써야 하다 독서 감상문 간식들
(be required to V: ~해야 하다, write: 쓰다)
and beverages will be provided. Don't forget to bring some warm
음료들 제공되다(provide: 제공하다) 가져오는 것을 잊다 따뜻한
(forget to V: ~하는 것을 잊다)
clothes in case it gets cold at night. You must sign up for the
~한 경우에 대비하여 추운 ~을 신청하다
program by this Friday.

해석

여: 안녕하세요, 학생 여러분. 책을 읽는 것에 관심이 있으십니까? 그렇다면, 올해 Marathon Reading Program(마라톤 독서 프로그램)에 참여하십시오. 이 프로그램에서는, 학생들, 선생님들, 그리고 학부모님들이 4월 5일에 밤늦게까지 책을 읽을 것입니다. 그것은 오후 2시에 시작해서 오후 10시에 끝납니다. 그 프로그램은 우리 학교 도서관에서 개최될 것입니다. 여러분은 자신의 책을 가져오거나 도서관에서 빌릴 수 있습니다. 책을 읽는 것을 끝낸 후에, 모든 학생들은 독서 감상문을 써야 합니다. 간식과 음료가 제공될 것입니다. 밤에 추워지는 경우에 대비하여 따뜻한 옷을 가져오는 것을 잊지 마십시오. 이번 주 금요일까지 프로그램을 신청하셔야 합니다.

① 학생, 교사, 학부모를 대상으로 한다.
② 오후 2시에 시작한다.
③ 학생들은 독서 감상문을 써야 한다.
✔️간식과 음료는 제공되지 않는다.
⑤ 이번 주 금요일까지 신청해야 한다.

---

10 표에서 여자가 주문할 휴대용 스피커와 마이크 세트
고2 2020년 3월 12번 | 정답률 80% | ▶ 정답 ③

M: Ms. Sanders, are you buying something online?
사는(buy) 온라인으로

W: Yes. I'm trying to buy a portable speaker and microphone set. Can
사려고 하는 휴대의 스피커 마이크 세트
(try to V: ~하려고 하다)
you help me choose one?
고르다

M: Sure. Let's see…. There's a wide range of prices.
다양한 가격대

W: Well, I want to buy one that's less than $100.
사고 싶다 ~ 미만의
(want to V: ~하고 싶다)

M: All right. I think running time is also important. What do you think?
지속 시간 중요한

W: I agree. I'd like to choose one that can last at least 10 hours after
동의하다 지속되다 최소한
a full charge.
완전한 충전

M: I see. What about the color?
~은 어때요? 색상

W: Well, I don't like the grey ones.

M: That leaves only two options. Do you want a model with a clip microphone?

W: Of course. It'll keep my hands free.

M: Then, this model is the best one for you.

W: Okay. I'll order it. Thanks for your help.

M: You're welcome.

해석

남: Sanders 씨, 온라인으로 무언가 사실 거예요?

여: 네. 저는 휴대용 스피커와 마이크 세트를 사려고 해요. 제가 하나를 고르는 것을 도와줄 수 있어요?

남: 물론이죠. 어디 보자.... 다양한 가격대가 있군요.

여: 음, 저는 100달러 미만의 것을 사고 싶어요.

남: 좋아요. 저는 지속 시간도 중요한 것 같아요. 어떻게 생각해요?

여: 동의해요. 저는 완전한 충전 후에 최소한 10시간은 지속될 수 있는 것을 고르고 싶어요.

남: 그렇군요. 색상은 어때요?

여: 음, 회색은 마음에 들지 않아요.

남: 그럼 두 가지 선택지만 남네요. 클립형 마이크가 있는 모델을 원하세요?

여: 물론이죠. 그것은 제 손을 자유롭게 해줄 거예요.

남: 그렇다면, 이 모델이 당신에게 가장 잘 맞겠네요.

여: 좋아요. 그것을 주문할게요. 도와줘서 고마워요.

남: 천만에요.

휴대용 스피커와 마이크 세트

	모델	가격	지속 시간	색상	클립형 마이크
①	A	65달러	8시간	흰색	X
②	B	70달러	10시간	회색	○
✓	C	80달러	11시간	흰색	○
④	D	85달러	12시간	빨간색	X
⑤	E	110달러	15시간	회색	○

11 여자의 마지막 말에 대한 남자의 응답 [고2 2020년 3월 1번] [정답률 85%] ▶ 정답 ①

W: I enjoyed the food here, especially the salad.

M: Thank you. Our restaurant uses only the freshest vegetables. And we make the salad dressing using a special recipe.

W: I see. Can you tell me what it's made with?

M: (Sorry, but our recipe is a secret.)

해석

여: 저는 여기 음식, 특히 샐러드를 맛있게 먹었어요.

남: 감사합니다. 저희 식당은 가장 신선한 채소들만 사용합니다. 그리고 저희는 특별한 조리법을 사용해 샐러드 드레싱을 만듭니다.

여: 그렇군요. 그것이 무엇으로 만들어졌는지 말씀해 주실 수 있나요?

남: (죄송하지만, 저희의 조리법은 비밀입니다.)

✓ 죄송하지만, 저희의 조리법은 비밀입니다.

② 물론입니다. 저는 이 드레싱을 사고 싶습니다.

③ 괜찮습니다. 저희는 그 조리법이 필요하지 않습니다.

④ 네, 제가 당신에게 야채 수프를 만들어 드릴 수 있습니다.

⑤ 알겠습니다, 제가 샐러드를 바로 가져다 드리겠습니다.

12 남자의 마지막 말에 대한 여자의 응답 [고2 2020년 3월 2번] [정답률 75%] ▶ 정답 ③

M: Good afternoon. I'd like to donate these old clothes to this charity.

W: Thank you. Are they all in good condition?

M: Yes, but the colors of some shirts have changed a bit.

W: (Let me check if we can accept them.)

해석

남: 안녕하세요. 저는 이 헌 옷들을 이 자선 단체에 기부하고 싶어요.

여: 감사합니다. 그것들은 모두 상태가 좋은가요?

남: 네, 그런데 몇몇 셔츠의 색깔이 조금 변했어요.

여: (저희가 그것들을 받을 수 있는지 확인해 볼게요.)

① 저는 더 이상 기부할 옷들이 없어요.

② 당신은 오늘 오후에 그것들을 찾아가실 수 있어요.

✓ 저희가 그것들을 받을 수 있는지 확인해 볼게요.

④ 저는 흰색 옷들과 색깔 있는 옷들을 구분하는 것을 잊었어요.

⑤ 환불을 받으시려면 영수증을 가져오세요.

13 여자의 마지막 말에 대한 남자의 응답 [고2 2020년 3월 13번] [정답률 85%] ▶ 정답 ①

[Telephone rings.]

M: Hello, Diamond Sports Center. May I help you?

W: Hello. I'm a member of your sports center and I want to know if I can suspend my membership.

M: Okay, would you tell me your name?

W: I'm Katie Walker.

M: [Typing sound] Yes, I see you have an annual membership for swimming classes. You mean you can't come for a while?

W: That's right. I broke my arm yesterday.

M: Oh, I'm sorry. You can put your membership on hold for up to 60 days.

W: That's good.

M: When do you think you can start taking lessons again?

W: I'll be able to start again after a month.

M: (Okay. We'll let you have a one-month break.)

해석

[전화벨이 울린다.]

남: 여보세요, Diamond Sports Center(다이아몬드 스포츠 센터)입니다. 무엇을 도와드릴까요?

여: 안녕하세요. 저는 스포츠 센터의 회원인데 제 회원권을 정지할 수 있는지 알고 싶어요.

남: 알겠습니다, 성함을 말씀해 주시겠어요?

여: Katie Walker예요.

남: [타자 치는 소리] 네, 회원님께서는 수영 강좌에 대한 연간 회원권을 가지고 계시네요. 당분간 오실 수 없다는 말씀이시죠?

여: 맞아요. 제가 어제 팔이 부러졌거든요.

남: 오, 유감이네요. 회원님께서는 회원권을 60일까지 연기하실 수 있어요.

여: 잘됐네요.

남: 언제 다시 강습을 받기 시작할 수 있을 것 같으세요?

여: 한 달 후에 다시 시작할 수 있을 거예요.

남: (알겠습니다. 한 달의 정지 기간을 드릴게요.)

✓ 알겠습니다. 한 달의 정지 기간을 드릴게요.

② 한 달 후에 건강 검진을 받으러 오세요.

③ 죄송합니다. 다른 스포츠 센터를 찾아보시는 게 좋겠네요.

④ 물론이죠. 다음 주에 수영 강습을 받으실 수 있어요.

⑤ 저희는 연간 회원권에 20% 할인을 제공합니다.

문제 풀이

여자가 팔이 부러져 수영 강좌 연간 회원권을 정지하려는 상황에서 그녀는 한 달 후에 다시 강습을 시작할 수 있을 것이라 말하고 있다. 따라서 남자의 답변으로는 한 달의 정지 기간을 주겠다고 말하는 ① 'Okay. We'll let you have a one-month break.(알겠습니다. 한 달의 정지 기간을 드릴게요.)'가 가장 자연스럽다.

14 남자의 마지막 말에 대한 여자의 응답 [고2 2020년 3월 14번] [정답률 65%] ▶ 정답 ②

M: Hi, Lucy.

W: Hi, Eric. Look. This is my painting for our art club exhibition next

20년 3월 학력평가

06회. 2020년 3월 학력평가 정답과 해설 **29**

week.

M: Wow, it's really nice. The spring scenery looks so beautiful.
　　　　　　　　　　　　　　　봄　풍경　　　아름다운

W: I painted it during my family trip last week.
　그렸다　　　~동안에　　　가족 여행

M: You're a really good artist.
　　　　　　　　　예술가

W: Thank you. Are you done with your painting?
　　　　　　　　　　　~을 다 끝낸

M: Yes, I completed and hung it on the wall in the exhibition room.
　　　완성했다(complete)　걸었다(hang)　　　　　　　전시실

W: Great. How about the other members? Have they all finished their
　　　　　~은 어때?　　　　다른　　회원들　　　　　　　　끝냈다
art work?
작품

M: Not yet. And we won't be able to see Jake's painting this time.
　　　　　　　　　　　볼 수 있다
　　　　　　　　　(be able to V: ~할 수 있다)

W: I know. I heard his whole family is moving to Canada this Friday.
　　　들었다(hear)　　　　　~로 이주할 예정이다(move to)

M: So we need to find someone who has an extra painting to fill up his
　　　　　찾아야 하다　　　　　　　여분의　　　　　~을 채우다
　　　(need to V: ~해야 하다, find: 찾다)
space.
공백

W: (I have another picture that I've almost finished.)
　　　다른　　그림　　거의

해석

남: 안녕, Lucy.
여: 안녕, Eric. 봐. 이것은 다음 주에 있을 우리 미술 동아리 전시회에 낼 내 그림이야.
남: 와, 정말 멋지다. 봄 풍경이 매우 아름다워 보여.
여: 나는 지난주 가족 여행 동안에 그것을 그렸어.
남: 너는 정말 훌륭한 예술가야.
여: 고마워. 네 그림은 다 끝냈니?
남: 응, 완성해서 전시실의 벽에 걸어놨어.
여: 좋아. 다른 회원들은 어때? 모두 자신의 작품을 끝냈니?
남: 아직이야. 그리고 우리는 이번에 Jake의 그림을 볼 수 없을 거야.
여: 알아. 그의 가족 전체가 이번 주 금요일에 캐나다로 이주할 예정이라고 들었어.
남: 그래서 우리는 그의 공백을 채울 여분의 그림을 가지고 있는 사람을 찾아야 해.
여: (나는 거의 끝낸 다른 그림을 가지고 있어.)

① 우리는 그를 위해 송별회를 열 수 있어.
✔ 나는 거의 끝낸 다른 그림을 가지고 있어.
③ 나는 이번에 내 그림을 전시할 수 없을 것 같아.
④ 그는 이미 자신의 그림을 전시회에 출품했어.
⑤ 나는 온 가족이 전시회에 올 거라고 믿어.

문제 풀이

미술 동아리 회원인 Jake의 캐나다 이주로 전시회에 걸 그림이 부족해진 상황이다. Jake의 공백을 채울 여분의 그림을 가지고 있는 사람을 찾아야 한다는 남자의 말에 대한 여자의 답변으로 ② 'I have another picture that I've almost finished.(나는 거의 끝낸 다른 그림을 가지고 있어.)'가 가장 어울린다.

15 다음 상황에서 Ryan이 Amy에게 할 말

고2 2020년 3월 15번 | 정답률 75%
▶ 정답 ⑤

M: Ryan is a high school student. He is running for president of
　　　　　　고등학생　　　　　　　　~에 출마할 예정이다(run for)
the student council this year. He needs to come up with some
　　학생회장　　　　　　　　　　　~을 생각해내야 하다
　　　　　　　　　(need to V: ~해야 하다, come up with: ~을 생각해내다)
appealing campaign promises. He thinks one of the promises
호소력 있는　　선거 공약들　　　생각하다
should be related to improving the facilities for students. So, Ryan
　　개선시키는 것과 관계가 있다　　　　시설들
(be related to V-ing: ~하는 것과 관계가 있다, improve: 개선시키다)
discusses it with one of his campaign staff, Amy. He asks her what
　그것을 한 명과 의논하다　　　선거 운동원　　　묻다
(discuss A with B: A를 B와 의논하다)
school facilities need improvement. Amy suggests promising to
　　　　　　개선　　　　　　제안하다　교체하기로 약속하는 것
　　　　　　　　　　　　　　　(promise to V: ~하기로 약속하다, replace: 교체하다)
replace all the student lockers. Ryan agrees, but he thinks they
　　　　　　　사물함들　　　　　동의하다
should check if the school can do it. In this situation, what would
　　　확인하다
Ryan most likely say to Amy?

Ryan: (We'd better find out if the school can replace the lockers.)
　　　　　　　　　　~을 알아보다

해석

남: Ryan은 고등학생이다. 그는 올해 학생회장에 출마할 예정이다. 그는 호소력 있는 선거 공약들을 생각해내야 한다. 그는 공약들 중 하나는 학생들을 위한 시설들을 개선시키는 것

과 관계가 있어야 한다고 생각한다. 그래서, Ryan은 그것을 자신의 선거 운동원들 중 한 명인 Amy와 의논한다. 그는 그녀에게 어떤 학교 시설에 개선이 필요한지 묻는다. Amy는 모든 학생 사물함들을 교체하기로 약속할 것을 제안한다. Ryan은 동의하지만, 학교가 그것을 할 수 있는지 확인해야 한다고 생각한다. 이러한 상황에서, Ryan은 Amy에게 뭐라고 말하겠는가?

Ryan: (우리는 학교가 사물함들을 교체할 수 있는지 알아보는 게 좋겠어.)

① 나는 학생들에게 한 공약을 어기지 않을 거야.
② 우리는 학교 시설들을 더 자주 이용해야 해.
③ 나는 선거에서 이기든 지든 최선을 다할 거야.
④ 너는 지금 사물함에 네 모든 소지품들을 넣어야 해.
✔ 우리는 학교가 사물함들을 교체할 수 있는지 알아보는 게 좋겠어.

16~17 1지문 2문항

W: Hello, everyone. Today, let's learn about some details about
　　　　　　　　　　　　~에 대해 배우다　　　세부 사항들
the Olympic Games. As you all have learned, the first Olympic
　　올림픽 대회
Games were held in Athens, Greece, in 1896, and there were
　　　개최되었다(hold: 개최하다)　아테네　　그리스
nine sports events in total. The events in the Olympic Games have
　　　스포츠 종목들　　통틀어
been changed through the agreement of the IOC members. For
변경되어 왔다(change)　~을 통해　　　합의　　　　위원들
example, soccer made its first appearance at the second Olympic
예를 들어　　축구　　　　　처음으로 등장했다
　　　　　　　　　　　　　(make one's appearance)
Games and was excluded in the 10th Olympic Games. The fate
　　　　　　　제외되었다(exclude)　　　　　　　　　　운명
of tennis is more interesting. Tennis was one of the nine sports
　　테니스　　더 흥미로운
events in the first Athens Olympic Games, but it was excluded
from 1928 to 1984 and then revived at the 1988 Seoul Olympics.
　1928년부터 1984년까지　　　부활된(revive)
　(from A to B: A부터 B까지)
The 1936 Berlin Olympics became the first to introduce handball.
　　　　　베를린　　　　　　　　　　도입하다　　핸드볼
However, handball disappeared from the Olympics and later was
그러나　　　　　~에서 사라졌다　　　　　　　후에
revived at the 1972 Munich Olympics. Taekwondo made its debut
　　　　　　　　　뮌헨　　　　　　태권도　　　데뷔했다
　　　　　　　　　　　　　　　　　　　　　　(make one's debut)
in the relatively recent Sydney Olympic Games in 2000. Overall,
　　　　비교적　　최근의　시드니　　　　　　　　　전체적으로
the number of sports events in the Olympic Games has gradually
　~의 수　　　　　　　　　　　　　　　　　　점차적으로 증가해 왔다
　　　　　　　　　　　　(gradually: 점차적으로, increase: 증가하다)
increased through some additions or exclusions.
　　　　　　　　　추가　　　제외

해석

여: 안녕하세요, 여러분. 오늘은, 올림픽 대회에 관한 몇 가지 세부 사항들에 대해 배워보겠습니다. 여러분 모두가 배웠던 것처럼, 제1회 올림픽 대회는 1896년에 그리스의 아테네에서 개최되었으며, 통틀어 9개의 스포츠 종목들이 있었습니다. 올림픽 대회의 종목들은 IOC(International Olympic Committee 국제 올림픽 위원회) 위원들의 합의를 통해 변경되어 왔습니다. 예를 들어, 축구는 제2회 올림픽 대회에 처음으로 등장했으며 제10회 올림픽 대회에서 제외되었습니다. 테니스의 운명은 더 흥미롭습니다. 테니스는 제1회 아테네 올림픽 대회의 9개 스포츠 종목들 중 하나였지만, 1928년부터 1984년까지는 제외되더니 1988년 서울 올림픽 대회에서 부활되었습니다. 1936년 베를린 올림픽 대회는 핸드볼을 도입한 최초의 올림픽 대회가 되었습니다. 그러나, 핸드볼은 올림픽 대회에서 사라졌으며 후에 1972년 뮌헨 올림픽 대회에서 부활되었습니다. 태권도는 비교적 최근에 열린 2000년 시드니 올림픽 대회에서 데뷔했습니다. 전체적으로, 올림픽 대회의 스포츠 종목들의 수는 일부 종목들의 추가나 제외를 통해 점차적으로 증가해 왔습니다.

16 여자가 하는 말의 주제

고2 2020년 3월 16번 | 정답률 70%
▶ 정답 ⑤

① 고대 올림픽 대회의 기원
② 올림픽 대회의 긍정적인 효과들
③ 올림픽 참가 선수들의 선발 과정
④ 일부 올림픽 대회들이 취소된 이유들
✔ 올림픽 대회의 스포츠 종목들의 변화들

17 언급된 스포츠 종목이 아닌 것

고2 2020년 3월 17번 | 정답률 75%

▶ 정답 ③

① 축구   ② 테니스   ☑레슬링
④ 핸드볼   ⑤ 태권도

---

07 2020년 6월 학력평가

01	①	02	②	03	④	04	④	05	①
06	②	07	③	08	④	09	⑤	10	④
11	②	12	①	13	⑤	14	②	15	③
16	④	17	③						

---

01 남자가 하는 말의 목적

고2 2020년 6월 3번 | 정답률 90%

▶ 정답 ①

M: Hello, everyone. This is Ted Williams, the drama teacher. As you
know, there's a musical in the school festival every year. And the
auditions for actors are going to be held soon. Even if you don't
think you're talented, that's okay. Most importantly, I'm looking
for students with passion. All interested students should submit
an application to me no later than June 23rd. The auditions are
going to be held on June 24th from three to five p.m. in the school
auditorium. If you need more information, please check the poster
on the bulletin board. I'm looking forward to seeing you at the
auditions. Thank you. (look forward to V-ing: ~하기를 기대하다)

해석
남: 안녕하세요, 여러분. 저는 연극 교사인 Ted Williams입니다. 여러분도 알다시피, 매년 학
교 축제에 뮤지컬이 있습니다. 그래서 배우 오디션이 곧 개최될 예정입니다. 여러분이 재
능이 있다고 생각하지 않더라도, 괜찮습니다. 가장 중요한 것은, 제가 열정이 있는 학생들
을 찾고 있다는 것입니다. 관심이 있는 모든 학생들은 늦어도 6월 23일까지 저에게 신청
서를 제출해야 합니다. 오디션은 6월 24일 오후 3시부터 5시까지 학교 강당에서 개최될
예정입니다. 더 많은 정보가 필요하시면, 게시판에 있는 포스터를 확인해 주십시오. 오디
션에서 여러분을 만나기를 기대하고 있습니다. 감사합니다.

① 오디션 개최를 공지하려고 ☑
② 뮤지컬 공연을 홍보하려고
③ 과제 제출 방법을 설명하려고
④ 재능 기부 방법을 안내하려고
⑤ 연극 수업 참여를 독려하려고

---

02 여자의 의견

고2 2020년 6월 4번 | 정답률 90%

▶ 정답 ②

M: Hello, Irene. What are you doing?
W: Hi. I'm reading a book for a book review assignment.
M: Then, why are you wearing earphones?
W: I'm listening to music. I find it helpful when reading a book.
M: Doesn't listening to music hurt your concentration?
W: Actually, no. I can concentrate on my reading better while listening
to music.
M: Really? I didn't know that was possible.
W: Also, it makes me feel good, and that surely keeps me awake.
M: You mean that you can keep reading when you feel bored with a
book? (keep V-ing: 계속 ~하다)
W: Right. That's why I listen to music while reading.

M: I see. I'll give it a try the next time I read a book.
W: It'll work for you, too.

해석
남: 안녕, Irene. 무엇을 하고 있니?
여: 안녕. 독후감 과제를 위해 책을 읽고 있어.
남: 그럼, 왜 이어폰을 착용하고 있니?
여: 음악을 듣고 있어. 책을 읽을 때 그것이 도움이 되거든.
남: 음악을 듣는 것이 네 집중력을 해치지 않니?
여: 사실, 그렇지 않아. 나는 음악을 들으면서 독서에 더 잘 집중할 수 있어.
남: 정말? 나는 그것이 가능한지 몰랐어.
여: 또한, 그것은 기분을 좋게 만들어서, 확실히 나를 깨어 있게 해.
남: 책이 지루한데도 계속 읽을 수 있다는 말이니?
여: 맞아. 그래서 내가 책을 읽으면서 음악을 듣는 거야.
남: 그렇구나. 다음에 내가 책을 읽을 때 시도해 볼게.
여: 너에게도 효과가 있을 거야.

① 기억력은 반복적인 학습을 통해 향상된다.
② 책을 읽을 때 음악을 듣는 것은 도움이 된다. ☑
③ 꾸준한 독서 습관을 형성하는 것이 중요하다.
④ 음악 감상은 아동의 창의력 발달에 효과적이다.
⑤ 청력 보호를 위해 적절한 음량 조절이 필요하다.

---

03 두 사람의 관계

고2 2020년 6월 5번 | 정답률 85%

▶ 정답 ④

M: Good afternoon. How may I help you?
W: I'm looking for an apartment to rent near the downtown area.
M: It is a convenient place to live. When would you like to move there?
W: I'm thinking next month.
M: Oh, I see. I have some apartments to recommend in that area.
What's your budget?
W: I'm afraid I can't afford more than $1,000 a month.
M: There are some apartments within your budget, but they have only
one bedroom.
W: One bedroom is enough, but I want the kitchen to be separate
from the bedroom.
M: I see. Anything else?
W: Hmm... it would be better if a refrigerator was included.
M: Okay. I have the perfect one for you. Let's go take a look.

해석
남: 안녕하세요. 어떻게 도와드릴까요?
여: 도심 지역 근처에 임차할 아파트를 찾고 있어요.
남: 그곳은 살기에 편리한 곳이죠. 언제 그곳으로 이사하고 싶으신가요?
여: 다음 달로 생각하고 있어요.
남: 오, 그렇군요. 그 지역에 추천할 만한 아파트가 몇 군데 있어요. 예산이 어떻게 되시나요?
여: 한 달에 1,000달러 이상을 지불할 여유는 없는 것 같아요.
남: 고객님의 예산 내에 몇 군데의 아파트가 있는데, 그것들은 침실이 하나뿐이에요.
여: 침실 하나면 충분하지만, 주방이 침실과 분리되어 있으면 좋겠어요.
남: 그렇군요. 또 다른 건 없으세요?
여: 흠... 냉장고가 포함된다면 더 좋을 것 같아요.
남: 알겠습니다. 고객님께 딱 맞는 아파트가 있어요. 가서 보시죠.

① 배관공 — 집주인   ② 식당 지배인 — 요리사
③ 관광 안내원 — 관광객   ☑ 부동산 중개인 — 고객
⑤ 인테리어 디자이너 — 의뢰인

---

04 그림에서 대화의 내용과 일치하지 않는 것

고2 2020년 6월 6번 | 정답률 90%

▶ 정답 ④

M: Lucy, this is a picture of my camping trip last week. Have a look.
W: Hmm, I can see the tent between those two trees. Did you set it up
yourself?
M: Yes, my father taught me how to do it. He is wearing the striped

T-shirt that I bought him for his birthday.
사 줬다(buy)

W: Wow! The shirt makes your father look young.
젊어 보이다

M: I think so, too. And do you see the watermelon on the table?
수박

W: Yes, it looks so delicious. Where did you get it?
맛있는

M: It was from our family farm. My parents grew it themselves.
가족 농장   키웠다(grow)

W: Really? The woman there must be your mother, right?

M: Yeah. She's playing the flute behind the pond.
연주하는(play) 플루트   연못

W: Cool! She's awesome. Oh, there's a dog on the chair. Is that your
멋진   강아지
puppy?

M: Of course. We all had a good time there.

해석

남: Lucy, 이것은 지난주 내가 다녀온 캠핑 여행의 사진이야. 봐봐.

여: 흠, 저 두 나무 사이에 텐트가 보이네. 그것을 네가 직접 설치했니?

남: 응, 아버지께서 그것을 하는 방법을 가르쳐 주셨어. 아버지께선 내가 생신 선물로 사 드린 줄무늬 티셔츠를 입고 계셔.

여: 와! 그 셔츠는 네 아버지를 젊어 보이게 만들어.

남: 나도 그렇게 생각해. 그리고 테이블 위에 있는 수박이 보이니?

여: 그래, 정말 맛있어 보인다. 그것을 어디에서 샀어?

남: 우리 가족 농장에서 가져온 거야. 우리 부모님께서 직접 키우셨어.

여: 정말? 저기 있는 여자분이 네 어머니시구나, 그렇지?

남: 그래. 어머니께서는 연못 뒤에서 플루트를 연주하고 계셔.

여: 대단하다! 어머니 멋지시다. 오, 의자 위에 개가 있네! 네 강아지니?

남: 물론이지. 우리 모두는 그곳에서 즐거운 시간을 보냈어.

05 여자가 할 일

고2 2020년 6월 7번 정답률 90%
▶ 정답 ①

W: Daniel, let's check our preparations for Ms. Kim's retirement party.
확인하다   준비 사항들   퇴임 파티

M: Okay, I think we're almost done. How about the thank-you video?
거의   감사 영상

W: Well, I had some difficulties inserting the background music, but I
삽입하는 데 어려움을 좀 겪었다   배경 음악
(have difficulty V-ing: ~하는 데 어려움을 겪다, insert: 삽입하다)
finally finished it.

M: Great! I believe it'll be perfect.
완벽한

W: Thanks. Have you finished decorating the classroom?
장식하는 것을 끝낸   교실
(finish V-ing: ~하는 것을 끝내다, decorate: 장식하다)

M: I've just done it. It took a long time to blow up all the balloons.
(시간이) 걸렸다(take)   ~을 불다   풍선들

W: Good job. Now, it's time to let the other students know about the
하게 할 시간이다   ~에 대해 알다
party.
(it's time to V: ~할 시간이다)

M: No worries, I've done that, too. What else should we do then?

W: Hmm, we should write a thank-you letter to Ms. Kim and order a
쓰다   감사 편지   주문하다
cake for her.

M: Okay. I'll write the thank-you letter. Can you order the cake?

W: No problem. I'll go and order it now.

해석

여: Daniel, 김 선생님의 퇴임 파티를 위한 준비 사항들을 확인해 보자.

남: 그래, 거의 다 된 것 같아. 감사 영상은 어때?

여: 음, 배경 음악을 삽입하는 데 어려움을 좀 겪었는데, 결국 그것을 끝냈어.

남: 좋아! 그것은 완벽할 거라고 믿어.

여: 고마워. 교실을 장식하는 것은 끝냈니?

남: 방금 끝냈어. 모든 풍선들을 부는 데 오랜 시간이 걸렸어.

여: 잘했어. 이제, 다른 학생들에게 파티에 대해 알려줘야 할 시간이야.

남: 걱정하지 마, 내가 그것도 했어. 그럼 우린 그 외에 또 무엇을 해야 하지?

여: 흠, 김 선생님께 감사 편지를 쓰고 그분을 위한 케이크를 주문해야 해.

남: 알겠어. 내가 감사 편지를 쓸게. 네가 케이크를 주문해 주겠니?

여: 문제없어. 내가 지금 가서 주문할게.

✔ 케이크 주문하기
② 감사 편지 쓰기
③ 영상 편집하기
④ 파티 공지하기
⑤ 교실 꾸미기

문제 풀이

김 선생님의 퇴임 파티를 준비하는 두 사람은 감사 편지 쓰기와 케이크 주문이 남았다는 것을 알게 된다. 남자는 여자에게 자신이 감사 편지를 쓸 테니 케이크를 주문해 달라고 부탁하고 여자는 이를 수락한다. 따라서 여자가 할 일은 ① '케이크 주문하기'이다.

06 여자가 지불할 금액

고2 2020년 6월 9번 정답률 80%
▶ 정답 ②

M: Hello, welcome to the Grand Ice Skating Rink. How can I help you?

W: Hi, I'd like to buy admission tickets.
입장권들

M: All right. An adult ticket is $10. A child ticket is $5.

W: Then, two adults and one child. And I need to rent skates, too. How
빌려야 하다   스케이트들
much is that?
(need to V: ~해야 하다, rent: 빌리다)

M: All skate rentals cost the same, $5 a person.
대여   (비용이) ~이다   한 사람당

W: Okay, I want to rent three pairs of skates.
빌리고 싶다(want to V: ~하고 싶다, rent: 빌리다)

M: Did you bring gloves?
가져오다 장갑들

W: Yes, we did. By the way, can I get any discounts?
할인을 좀 받다

M: If you have a local resident card, you can get a 10% discount off
지역 주민 카드
the total.
총액

W: Good! Here's my local resident card.

M: So, two adult tickets, one child ticket, and three skate rentals,
right?

W: Yes. I'll pay for everything with my credit card.
지불하다   신용카드

해석

남: 안녕하세요, Grand Ice Skating Rink에 오신 것을 환영합니다. 어떻게 도와드릴까요?

여: 안녕하세요, 저는 입장권을 사고 싶어요.

남: 알겠습니다. 성인 입장권은 10달러입니다. 어린이 입장권은 5달러입니다.

여: 그럼, 성인 두 장과 어린이 한 장이요. 그리고 스케이트도 빌려야 해요. 그것은 얼마죠?

남: 모든 스케이트 대여료는 똑같은데, 한 사람당 5달러입니다.

여: 알겠어요, 저는 스케이트 세 켤레를 빌리고 싶어요.

남: 장갑은 가져오셨나요?

여: 네, 가져왔어요. 그런데, 할인을 좀 받을 수 있을까요?

남: 지역 주민 카드를 가지고 계시면, 총액에서 10% 할인을 받으실 수 있습니다.

여: 잘됐네요! 여기 제 지역 주민 카드가 있어요.

남: 그럼, 성인 입장권 두 장, 어린이 입장권 한 장, 그리고 스케이트 대여 세 켤레, 맞으시죠?

여: 네, 모두 신용카드로 지불할게요.

① $30   ✔ $36   ③ $40
④ $45   ⑤ $50

문제 풀이

스케이트를 타러 온 여자는 10달러짜리 성인 입장권 두 장과 5달러짜리 어린이 입장권 한 장을 사고, 스케이트 세 켤레를 빌리려 하는데 대여료는 한 사람당 5달러이다. 여자가 지불할 금액은 총 40달러인데 지역 주민 카드를 이용해 총액에서 10% 할인을 받을 수 있으므로 40달러에서 10%가 할인된 36달러를 지불해야 한다. 따라서 답은 ② '$36'이다.

07 남자가 전시회에 갈 수 없는 이유

고2 2020년 6월 8번 정답률 85%
▶ 정답 ③

W: Jake. There's going to be a Vincent van Gogh exhibition in the Art
전시회
Center.

M: Really? He's my favorite artist.
가장 좋아하는 화가

W: Mine, too. How about going to the exhibition together this Sunday?

M: This Sunday? I'd really love to, but I'm afraid I can't go.

W: Come on. Do you have to do volunteer work on that day?

M: No, I usually volunteer on Saturdays.

W: Oh, I remember. You said you're going to play soccer?

M: I did, but our game was delayed because of weather.

W: Then, do you have another appointment?

M: Actually, I have to work on a science assignment. It's due next Monday.

W: You must be busy then.

M: Yeah. I hope you have a good time.

해석

여: Jake. Art Center에서 Vincent van Gogh(빈센트 반 고흐) 전시회가 열릴 거야.

남: 정말? 그는 내가 가장 좋아하는 화가야.

여: 나도 그래. 이번 주 일요일에 전시회에 함께 가는 게 어때?

남: 이번 주 일요일? 정말 가고 싶지만, 난 갈 수 없을 것 같아.

여: 제발. 그날 자원봉사를 해야 하니?

남: 아니, 나는 보통 토요일에 자원봉사를 해.

여: 오, 기억난다. 축구를 할 거라고 말했지?

남: 그랬는데, 날씨 때문에 경기가 연기되었어.

여: 그럼, 다른 약속이 있니?

남: 사실, 과학 과제를 해야 해. 다음 주 월요일까지가 기한이거든.

여: 그럼 바쁘겠구나.

남: 그래. 즐거운 시간을 보내기를 바랄게.

① 봉사활동을 해야 해서
② 축구 경기를 해야 해서
✓③ 과학 과제를 해야 해서
④ 아르바이트를 해야 해서
⑤ 기말고사 준비를 해야 해서

---

08 Flea Market에 관해 언급되지 않은 것 ▶ 정답 ④

고2 2020년 6월 10번 | 정답률 75%

M: Hi, Mia. What are you looking at?

W: The student council is holding the annual Flea Market and I'm going to participate in it as a seller.

M: Oh, really? When is it going to be held?

W: Look. It will be open next Friday, from 11 a.m. to 6 p.m.

M: I see. Do you remember I participated as a seller last year?

W: I do. You did it in the school auditorium.

M: Right. But the poster says it'll be held in the playground this year.

W: Why don't you join me? There's no participation fee for sellers.

M: Okay. What are you going to sell at the Flea Market?

W: It says we can sell any of our old stuff. I'm planning to sell my old books.

M: I'm looking forward to it.

해석

남: 안녕, Mia. 무엇을 보고 있니?

여: 학생회에서 연례 벼룩 시장을 개최할 건데 나는 판매자로 참가할 거야.

남: 오, 정말? 언제 개최되니?

여: 봐. 다음 주 금요일 오전 11시부터 오후 6시까지 열릴 거야.

남: 그렇구나. 내가 작년에 판매자로 참가했던 것을 기억하니?

여: 기억해. 학교 강당에서 했잖아.

남: 맞아. 하지만 포스터에 올해에는 운동장에서 열릴 것이라고 쓰여 있네.

여: 나와 함께 하는 게 어떠니? 판매자에 대한 참가비는 없어.

남: 좋아. 벼룩 시장에서 무엇을 판매할 거니?

여: 오래된 물건이라면 어떤 것이나 판매할 수 있대. 나는 내 오래된 책들을 판매할 계획이야.

남: 기대된다.

① 개최 일시　　② 행사 장소　　③ 판매자 참가비
✓④ 신청 방법　　⑤ 판매 가능 물품

---

09 Highland Movie Night에 관한 내용과 일치하지 않는 것 ▶ 정답 ⑤

고2 2020년 6월 11번 | 정답률 80%

W: Hello, Highland residents. I'm Jenny Walker, the community center manager. We host the Highland Movie Night every month. This event gives you a chance to enjoy classic movies. It is free for all Highland residents. This month, we will show *The Amazing Wizard Harry*. The movie will start at seven p.m. this Saturday. As usual, it'll be held at the Lincoln Library. Due to the limited space, you should register in advance. You can reserve seats on our website until Friday. To keep the library clean, you are not allowed to bring any food. For more information, feel free to call us. Thank you.

해석

여: 안녕하세요, Highland 주민 여러분. 저는 지역 주민 센터 관리자 Jenny Walker입니다. 저희는 매월 Highland Movie Night(Highland 영화의 밤)를 개최합니다. 이 행사는 여러분에게 고전 영화들을 즐길 수 있는 기회를 줍니다. 그것은 모든 Highland 주민에게 무료입니다. 이번 달에, 저희는 '놀라운 마법사 Harry'를 상영할 것입니다. 영화는 이번 주 토요일 오후 7시에 시작될 것입니다. 늘 그렇듯이, 그것은 Lincoln 도서관에서 열릴 것입니다. 제한된 공간 때문에, 여러분은 사전에 등록하셔야 합니다. 금요일까지 저희 웹사이트에서 좌석을 예약하실 수 있습니다. 도서관을 청결하게 유지하기 위해서, 어떤 음식물도 가져오는 것이 허용되지 않습니다. 더 많은 정보를 원하시면, 언제든지 저희에게 전화해 주십시오. 감사합니다.

① 매월 개최하는 행사이다.
② Highland 주민에게는 무료이다.
③ Lincoln 도서관에서 열린다.
④ 사전에 등록해야 한다.
✓⑤ 음식물 반입이 허용된다.

---

10 표에서 남자가 구매할 여행 가방 ▶ 정답 ④

고2 2020년 6월 12번 | 정답률 75%

M: Mom, I need a suitcase for my trip to Hawaii. Look at this flyer. They are on sale now.

W: Let me see... I think it'd be better if it is at least 20 inches, since your trip is for two weeks.

M: I think so, too. And it's not a good idea to spend more than 200 dollars on a suitcase.

W: Right. You've already spent a lot for the trip.

M: Okay. There are two colors. Well, the white one looks nice.

W: That's true, but white things usually get dirty easily.

M: I agree. The darker color is the better choice.

W: Then, we have two options left.

M: Oh, they're giving away free gifts! Hmm... we already have several umbrellas.

W: You'd better choose the other one.

M: You're right. I'll buy this suitcase.

해석

남: 엄마, 저는 하와이로의 여행을 위해 여행 가방이 필요해요. 이 전단지를 보세요. 그것들은 지금 할인 판매 중이에요.

여: 어디 보자... 내 생각에는 그것이 최소한 20인치라면 더 나을 것 같아, 네 여행이 2주 동안이니까 말이야.

남: 저도 그렇게 생각해요. 그리고 여행 가방에 200달러 이상을 쓰는 것은 좋은 생각이 아니에요.

여: 맞아. 너는 이미 여행을 위해 많은 돈을 썼잖니.

남: 알겠어요. 두 가지 색상이 있어요. 음, 흰색이 좋아 보여요.

여: 그건 사실인데, 흰색 물건들은 보통 쉽게 더러워지잖니.

남: 동의해요. 더 어두운 색상이 더 나은 선택이에요.

여: 그럼, 두 가지 선택지가 남았구나.

남: 오, 사은품을 나누어 주고 있어요! 흠... 우리는 이미 몇 개의 우산이 있잖아요.

여: 너는 다른 것을 선택하는 게 좋겠구나.

남: 맞아요. 이 여행 가방을 살게요.

여행 가방들

	모델	크기(인치)	가격	색상	사은품
①	A	18	80달러	흰색	여행용 베개
②	B	24	100달러	흰색	우산
③	C	26	130달러	검은색	우산
✓④	D	28	160달러	검은색	여행용 베개
⑤	E	30	210달러	흰색	우산

---

11 남자의 마지막 말에 대한 여자의 응답

고2 2020년 6월 1번 | 정답률 85% | ▶ 정답 ②

M: Grandmother's birthday is coming up. What would be a good present for her?
선물 다가오고 있다(come up)

W: I think it would be good to give her something she needs.
주다 필요로 하다

M: I agree. I saw that her shoes are old and worn out. How about buying her some new shoes?
동의하다 신발들 낡은 ~하는 게 어때?

W: (Yeah. Let's go shop for them.)
~을 사러 가다

해석

남: 할머니의 생신이 다가오고 있어. 어떤 선물이 좋을까?
여: 할머니께서 필요로 하시는 것을 드리는 게 좋을 것 같아.
남: 동의해. 나는 할머니의 신발이 오래되고 낡은 것을 보았어. 할머니께 새 신발을 좀 사드리는 게 어때?
여: (그래. 그것들을 사러 가자.)

① 응. 그것들은 너에게 잘 어울려.
✓② 그래. 그것들을 사러 가자.
③ 맞아. 나를 초대해줘서 고마워.
④ 미안해. 나는 파티에 갈 수 없어.
⑤ 아니. 나는 아직 그 신발을 사지 않았어.

---

12 여자의 마지막 말에 대한 남자의 응답

고2 2020년 6월 2번 | 정답률 85% | ▶ 정답 ①

W: Honey, what a beautiful Sunday! I don't want to stay home all day.
아름다운 집에 있고 싶지 않다 하루 종일
(want to V: ~하고 싶다, stay home: 집에 있다)

M: Neither do I. Why don't we take a walk in a park or go to watch a movie?
산책하다 공원 영화를 보러 가다

W: We went to the movies last weekend. Let's enjoy the nice weather this time!
영화를 보러 갔다(go to the movies) 즐기다 날씨

M: (All right! It's perfect for walking outside.)
~에 딱 좋은

해석

여: 여보, 정말 아름다운 일요일이네요! 저는 하루 종일 집에 있고 싶지 않아요.
남: 나도 그래요. 우리 공원에서 산책하거나 영화를 보러 가는 게 어때요?
여: 우리 지난 주말에 영화를 보러 갔어요. 이번에는 좋은 날씨를 즐겨요!
남: (알겠어요! 밖에서 산책하기에 딱 좋네요.)

✓① 알겠어요! 밖에서 산책하기에 딱 좋네요.
② 멋지네요! 그 영화는 꼭 봐야 해요.
③ 고마워요. 제가 혼자서 차를 주차할게요.
④ 미안해요. 제가 날씨를 확인하지 않았어요.
⑤ 휴! 저는 더 이상 걸을 수 없어요.

---

13 여자의 마지막 말에 대한 남자의 응답

고2 2020년 6월 13번 | 정답률 70% | ▶ 정답 ⑤

W: Honey, where is the camera?

M: I put it on the desk. Why do you need it?
놓았다(put) 필요하다

W: It's for Kevin's school concert. I want to record his performance.
학교 콘서트 녹화하고 싶다 공연
(want to V: ~하고 싶다, record: 녹화하다)

M: Oh, right! It's tomorrow! He has been practicing so hard for that.
연습해왔다(practice) 열심히

W: Yes, he has. He's excited but also very nervous.
흥분한 긴장한

M: It's his first concert. I want to see his performance, too.

W: That would be nice, but didn't you say you have an important meeting tomorrow?
중요한 회의

M: Sadly, I do. It was impossible to reschedule it.
슬프게도 불가능한 일정을 변경하다

W: That's okay. I'll record his performance so you won't miss a thing.
놓치다

M: Thanks, if the meeting ends early, I might be able to be there by four.
끝나다 일찍 그곳에 갈 수 있다
(be able to V: ~할 수 있다)

W: But unfortunately I think his performance will be over by then.
불행히도 끝나다 그때쯤이면

M: (You're right. I'll just watch the video after the concert.)

해석

여: 여보, 카메라 어디 있어요?
남: 책상 위에 올려 놓았어요. 그것이 왜 필요해요?
여: Kevin의 학교 콘서트를 위해서요. 저는 그 애의 공연을 녹화하고 싶어요.
남: 오, 맞다! 내일이네요! 그 애는 그것을 위해 매우 열심히 연습해왔잖아요.
여: 네, 그랬죠. 그 애는 흥분했지만 또한 매우 긴장하고 있어요.
남: 그것은 그 애의 첫 번째 콘서트예요. 저도 그 애의 공연을 보고 싶어요.
여: 그러면 좋겠지만, 당신은 내일 중요한 회의가 있다고 말하지 않았어요?
남: 슬프게도, 그래요. 회의 일정을 변경하는 것은 불가능했어요.
여: 괜찮아요. 당신이 하나도 놓치지 않도록 제가 그 애의 공연을 녹화할게요.
남: 고마워요, 회의가 일찍 끝나면, 4시까지 그곳에 갈 수 있을 거예요.
여: 그런데 불행히도 그때쯤이면 그 애의 공연이 끝나 있을 것 같아요.
남: (당신 말이 맞아요. 저는 그냥 콘서트 후에 동영상을 볼게요.)

① 사실이에요. 저는 다음 주에 새 카메라를 살 거예요.
② 유감이에요. 당신이 올 수 없다면 저는 실망할 거예요.
③ 정말이에요? 당신은 상사에게 콘서트에 대해 말해야 해요.
④ 신경 쓰지 마요. 어쨌든 콘서트는 일정이 변경될 거예요.
✓⑤ 당신 말이 맞아요. 저는 그냥 콘서트 후에 동영상을 볼게요.

문제 풀이

회의가 일찍 끝난다고 해도 남자가 Kevin의 공연을 보는 것이 불가능한 상황이다. 따라서 여자의 말에 수긍하며 다른 대안을 택하는 ⑤ 'You're right. I'll just watch the video after the concert.(당신 말이 맞아요. 저는 그냥 콘서트 후에 동영상을 볼게요.)'가 답이 된다.

---

14 남자의 마지막 말에 대한 여자의 응답

고2 2020년 6월 14번 | 정답률 85% | ▶ 정답 ②

M: Lisa, I'm looking forward to our team workshop in Boston.
~을 기대하는(look forward to)

W: Me, too. It's only a month away.

M: Yeah, the hotel has been booked. Now we just need to look up flight schedules.
예약되었다(book) 알아봐야 하다
항공편 일정들 (need to V: ~해야 하다, look up: ~을 알아보다)

W: Hmm... why don't we drive instead of flying?
운전해서 가다 비행기를 타는 대신에
(instead of V-ing: ~하는 대신에, fly: 비행기를 타다)

M: Drive ourselves? I don't think that's a good idea.

W: Why not?

M: It would take more than four hours from our office.
(시간이) 걸리다 사무실

W: But I've heard the scenery along the way is really beautiful in October.
풍경 길을 따라서 아름다운

M: Then, how about taking a bus instead?
버스를 타는 게 어때?
(how about V-ing: ~하는 게 어때?, take a bus: 버스를 타다)

W: Taking a bus sounds okay.

M: I think we would enjoy the view from the bus as well.
즐기다 풍경

W: You're right. Also, it'd be much safer than driving ourselves.
훨씬 더 안전한

M: Plus, we can cut down on our costs.
~을 줄이다 비용들

W: (Great. Let's check the bus schedule then.)
확인하다

해석

남: Lisa, 나는 보스턴에서 있을 우리의 팀 워크숍을 기대하고 있어.
여: 나도 그래. 한 달밖에 안 남았네.
남: 그래, 호텔은 예약되었어. 이제 우리는 항공편 일정만 알아보면 돼.
여: 흠... 우리 비행기를 타는 대신에 운전해서 가는 게 어때?
남: 직접 운전해서 가자고? 그것은 좋은 생각이 아닌 것 같아.
여: 왜 안 돼?
남: 우리 사무실에서 4시간 이상 걸릴 거야.

여: 하지만 10월에 길을 따라서 펼쳐진 풍경이 정말 아름답다고 들었어.
남: 그럼, 대신에 버스를 타는 게 어때?
여: 버스를 타는 것은 괜찮을 것 같아.
남: 우리는 버스에서도 풍경을 즐길 수 있을 것 같아.
여: 네 말이 맞아. 또한, 그것은 우리가 직접 운전하는 것보다 훨씬 더 안전할 거야.
남: 게다가, 우리는 비용들을 줄일 수 있어.
여: (좋아. 그럼 버스 일정을 확인해 보자.)

① 물론이지! 너는 최고의 드라이버야.
✓② 좋아. 그럼 버스 일정을 확인해 보자.
③ 걱정하지 마. 우리에게 최고의 계절이 될 거야.
④ 당연하지. 버스 요금은 너무 비싸.
⑤ 문제없어. 우리는 항공편을 변경할 수 있을 거야.

문제 풀이

보스턴에 버스를 타고 가자는 남자의 제안에 여자는 긍정적인 반응을 보인다. 버스를 타면 바깥 풍경을 즐길 수 있고 비용도 줄일 수 있다는 남자의 의견에 동의하는 응답이 적절하므로 답은 ② 'Great. Let's check the bus schedule then.(좋아. 그럼 버스 일정을 확인해 보자.)'이다.

---

15 다음 상황에서 Katie가 Brian에게 할 말

고2 2020년 6월 15번 | 정답률 80%
▶ 정답 ③

M: Katie and Brian are classmates. They're doing a school project, and they decide to research students' eating habits as their topic.
(decide to V: ~하기로 결정하다, research: 연구하다)
Brian says that in order to analyze students' eating habits they need to do a survey. And he proposes they make a pen-and-paper survey.
(need to V: ~해야 하다, do a survey: 설문 조사를 하다)
But Katie thinks it would take too much time to distribute, collect, and count hundreds of papers. Then, Katie remembers she once took an online survey that she completed quickly. So Katie wants to suggest that they do a survey using the Internet rather than on paper. In this situation, what would Katie most likely say to Brian?
Katie: (Why don't we try an online survey instead?)

해석

남: Katie와 Brian은 반 친구이다. 그들은 학교 프로젝트를 하고 있으며, 학생들의 식습관을 그들의 주제로 연구하기로 결정한다. Brian은 학생들의 식습관을 분석하기 위해서 설문 조사를 해야 한다고 말한다. 그리고 그는 지필 설문 조사를 할 것을 제안한다. 그러나 Katie는 수백 장의 종이를 배부하고, 수집하고, 세는 것은 너무 많은 시간이 걸릴 것이라고 생각한다. 그때, Katie는 언젠가 온라인 설문 조사를 했었는데, 그것을 그녀가 빠르게 작성했던 것을 떠올린다. 그래서 Katie는 종이보다는 인터넷을 이용하여 설문 조사를 할 것을 제안하고 싶다. 이러한 상황에서, Katie는 Brian에게 뭐라고 말하겠는가?
Katie: (대신에 우리 온라인 설문 조사를 시도해 보는 게 어떠니?)

① 너는 식습관을 바꾸는 것이 좋겠어.
② 우리는 프로젝트의 주제를 선택해야 해.
✓③ 대신에 우리 온라인 설문 조사를 시도해 보는 게 어떠니?
④ 설문 조사를 위해 복사본들을 수집해 주겠니?
⑤ 나는 이미 설문 조사를 위한 질문들을 만들었어.

문제 풀이

Katie는 Brian이 하려고 하는 지필 설문 조사가 시간이 너무 많이 걸릴 것이라고 생각하며 인터넷을 이용한 온라인 설문 조사를 하자고 제안하고 싶어 한다. 따라서 Katie가 Brian에게 할 말로 가장 적절한 것은 ③ 'Why don't we try an online survey instead?(대신에 우리 온라인 설문 조사를 시도해 보는 게 어떠니?)'이다.

16~17 1지문 2문항

W: Welcome back, students. Last time we talked about your favorite numbers. They might come from your birth date or the date of a special occasion in your life. Interestingly, some beliefs about numbers seem to depend on one's culture. Today, we're talking
(seem to V: ~하는 것처럼 보이다, depend on: ~에 의존하다)
about what numbers symbolize in different parts of the world.
In Asia, the number four is considered extremely unlucky, but Western people think it is promising. In Islam, the number seven is important. "Seven heavens" is one example of this number's importance. Ten is considered a good number in Japan because it is pronounced "joo", like the Japanese word for "enough." In
(pronounce: 발음하다)
the Western world, the number thirteen is believed to be the unluckiest by millions of people. So, to satisfy anxious customers, airlines and hotels often don't use the number thirteen. Numbers can be captivating and mystical. Numbers are also just fun to play around with. Let's enjoy learning more about numbers together.
(enjoy V-ing: 재미있게 ~하다, learn: 배우다)

해석

여: 다시 만나서 반가워요, 학생 여러분. 지난 시간에 우리는 여러분이 가장 좋아하는 숫자들에 대해서 이야기했어요. 그것들은 여러분의 생년월일 또는 여러분의 인생에서 특별한 날의 날짜에서 비롯될 수도 있어요. 흥미롭게도, 숫자들에 대한 몇몇 믿음들은 문화에 의존하는 것처럼 보여요. 오늘, 우리는 세계의 여러 지역에서 숫자들이 무엇을 상징하는지에 대해 이야기할 거예요. 아시아에서, 숫자 4는 매우 불길하게 여겨지지만, 서양 사람들은 그것이 조짐이 좋다고 생각해요. 이슬람 세계에서는, 숫자 7이 중요해요. '7개의 천국'은 이 숫자의 중요성을 보여주는 하나의 예예요. 일본에서는 10이 좋은 숫자로 여겨지는데 왜냐하면 그것이 '충분한'에 해당하는 일본어처럼 'joo'로 발음되기 때문이에요. 서양에서, 숫자 13은 수많은 사람들에 의해 가장 불길하다고 여겨져요. 그래서, 불안한 고객들을 만족시키기 위해, 항공사들과 호텔들은 종종 숫자 13을 사용하지 않아요. 숫자들은 매혹적이고 신비로울 수 있어요. 숫자들은 또한 그냥 가지고 놀기에도 재미있어요. 우리 함께 숫자들에 대해 더 많은 것을 재미있게 배워봅시다.

---

16 여자가 하는 말의 주제

고2 2020년 6월 16번 | 정답률 85%
▶ 정답 ④

① 고대의 행운의 숫자들
② 사람들에게 부를 가져다 주는 숫자들
③ 숫자와 종교 사이의 관계
✓④ 여러 문화에 걸친 숫자들의 상징적 의미들
⑤ 비밀번호에 가장 좋아하는 숫자를 사용하는 것의 위험성

---

17 언급된 숫자가 아닌 것

고2 2020년 6월 17번 | 정답률 85%
▶ 정답 ③

① 4
② 7
✓③ 9
④ 10
⑤ 13

08 2020년 9월 학력평가

01	⑤	02	②	03	④	04	⑤	05	①
06	④	07	⑤	08	③	09	④	10	④
11	④	12	③	13	①	14	②	15	⑤
16	④	17	④						

01 남자가 하는 말의 목적

고2 2020년 9월 3번 | 정답률 85% ▶ 정답 ⑤

M: Good morning, students! This is your student council president, William Taylor. As some of you already know, our annual school festival is coming up. We are looking for clubs that want to sign up to share their talents at the festival. Now, I'll tell you how to sign up for the festival. The application period begins today. If your club wants to register to participate, come to the student council room to fill out the application form. The application deadline is September 28th. Let's make this a festival to remember!

해석
남: 좋은 아침입니다, 학생 여러분! 저는 여러분의 학생회장인 William Taylor입니다. 여러분 중 몇 분은 이미 알고 계시듯이, 연례 학교 축제가 다가오고 있습니다. 저희는 축제에서 재능을 나누기 위해 참가하기를 원하는 동아리들을 찾고 있습니다. 이제, 축제에 참가 신청을 하는 방법을 알려드리겠습니다. 신청 기간은 오늘부터 시작됩니다. 여러분의 동아리가 참가하기 위해 등록하기를 원하시면, 학생회실로 오셔서 신청서를 작성하십시오. 신청 마감일은 9월 28일입니다. 이것을 기억에 남는 축제로 만듭시다!

① 축제 장소 변경을 공지하려고
② 교내 동아리 부원을 모집하려고
③ 교내 축제 홍보문구를 공모하려고
④ 동아리 전시회 관람을 독려하려고
✓ 축제 참가신청 방법을 안내하려고

02 여자의 의견

고2 2020년 9월 4번 | 정답률 90% ▶ 정답 ②

W: Hi, Mike. You look distracted. Is something bothering you?
M: Well, my son's preschool teacher told me he's having trouble focusing while reading and during conversations. I don't know what I should do.
W: Oh, I see. [Pause] Maybe drawing classes could help.
M: How could they help with his concentration?
W: Children develop their ability to focus as they pay attention to small details while drawing.
M: That's reasonable. Is that why your daughter takes drawing classes?
W: Exactly. When my daughter was 8 years old, she had a similar problem to your son.
M: Did you notice a big change when she started drawing?
W: Sure. She concentrates better on reading and conversations now. It might help your son, too.
M: Okay, I'll look for a class right away.

해석
여: 안녕, Mike. 너 심란해 보인다. 무슨 걱정거리가 있니?
남: 음, 내 아들의 유치원 선생님이 그 애가 책을 읽고 대화를 하는 동안에 집중하는 데 어려움을 겪고 있다고 말했어. 어떻게 해야 할지 모르겠어.
여: 오, 그렇구나. [잠시 후] 그림 그리기 수업들이 도움이 될 수도 있어.
남: 어떻게 그것들이 그의 집중력에 도움을 줄 수 있지?

여: 아이들은 그림을 그리는 동안에 작은 세부 사항들에 주의를 기울이면서 집중하는 능력을 발달시켜.
남: 그거 일리가 있네. 그런 이유로 네 딸이 그림 그리기 수업을 듣는 거야?
여: 맞아. 내 딸이 8살이었을 때, 네 아들과 비슷한 문제가 있었어.
남: 그 애가 그림 그리기를 시작했을 때 큰 변화를 느꼈니?
여: 물론이지. 그 애는 이제 독서와 대화에 더 잘 집중해. 그것은 네 아들에게도 도움이 될지도 몰라.
남: 알았어, 지금 당장 수업을 찾아볼게.

① 다양한 신체활동은 어린이의 창의력 신장에 필수적이다.
✓ 그림 그리기는 어린이의 집중력 향상에 도움이 된다.
③ 그림책을 읽어 주는 것은 자녀의 정서 안정에 좋다.
④ 부모와의 많은 대화는 자녀의 언어발달을 촉진한다.
⑤ 독서는 어린이의 상상력을 키우는 데 효과가 있다.

03 두 사람의 관계

고2 2020년 9월 5번 | 정답률 90% ▶ 정답 ④

W: Hello, Mr. Stevenson. I'm Rachel Adams from *Entertainment Monthly*. Thank you for meeting with me today.
M: Hello, Ms. Adams. It's my pleasure.
W: Congratulations on gaining more than one million subscribers on your work, *The Invisible*. Why do you think so many people read your webcomic?
M: I think many people enjoy the comic because my style of drawing really makes the story come alive.
W: I agree. I especially love Jimmy, the character who wants to be a fashion model.
M: Yes, many of my subscribers like him.
W: I heard you'll finish it soon. The readers of our magazine have been asking if you have any plans to publish your work as a book or make it into a movie.
M: If there's a chance, I'd love to.
W: You'll have to let our readers be the first to know if you do.
M: Of course! I hope I can bring you good news soon.

해석
여: 안녕하세요, Stevenson 씨. 'Entertainment Monthly(월간 연예)'의 Rachel Adams입니다. 오늘 저와 만나주셔서 감사해요.
남: 안녕하세요, Adams 씨. 별말씀을요.
여: 당신의 작품인 'The Invisible(보이지 않는 사람들)'이 100만 명 이상의 구독자들을 얻게 된 것을 축하해요. 왜 그렇게 많은 사람들이 당신의 웹툰을 읽는다고 생각하세요?
남: 제 그림체가 정말로 이야기를 흥미롭게 만들기 때문에 많은 사람들이 이 만화를 즐기는 것 같아요.
여: 동의해요. 저는 특히 패션 모델이 되고 싶어 하는 등장인물인 Jimmy를 정말 좋아해요.
남: 네, 제 구독자들 중 많은 분들이 그를 좋아하죠.
여: 당신이 그것을 곧 완결할 거라고 들었어요. 저희 잡지의 독자들은 당신의 작품을 책으로 출판하거나 영화로 만들 계획이 있는지 묻고 있어요.
남: 기회가 있다면, 정말 그렇게 하고 싶어요.
여: 만약 그렇게 한다면 저희 독자들에게 가장 먼저 알려주셔야 해요.
남: 물론이죠! 곧 좋은 소식을 전해드릴 수 있으면 좋겠네요.

① 디자이너 ― 패션모델
② 영화감독 ― 영화배우
③ 출판사 직원 ― 소설가
✓ 잡지사 기자 ― 웹툰 작가
⑤ 미술관 큐레이터 ― 화가

04 그림에서 대화의 내용과 일치하지 않는 것

고2 2020년 9월 6번 | 정답률 85% ▶ 정답 ⑤

M: Honey, I just found a picture of a great living room design. It can give us some ideas for our own living room.
W: Let me see. [Pause] Wow! I like the bookshelf behind the armchairs.

M: Yeah. It's really impressive. I think we should have a bookshelf like that one.
인상적인
W: I agree. What do you think about how they used the space around the window?
활용했다   공간
M: The two flower pots under the window look nice. We should put our plants the same way.
화분들
식물들
W: Oh, there's a cat lying on a pet cushion.
누워 있는(lie)
M: It looks so comfortable. Why don't we buy one for our cat?
편안한   우리 ~하는 게 어때?
W: That's a good idea. Did you notice the round table between the armchairs?
보다   둥근 탁자
M: I've always wanted to have a tea table like that one.
W: Look at this floor lamp! The lamp shade has the same striped pattern as ours.
(바닥에 세우는) 전등   전등갓   줄무늬
M: It does! Let's decorate our living room like the one in this picture.
꾸미다
W: I can't wait to see how it turns out.
빨리 보고 싶다(can't wait to V: 빨리 ~하고 싶다)

해석
남: 여보, 내가 방금 멋진 거실 디자인의 사진을 찾았어요. 그것이 우리의 거실을 위한 몇 가지 아이디어들을 우리에게 줄 수 있어요.
여: 어디 봐요. [잠시 후] 와! 저는 안락의자들 뒤에 있는 책장이 마음에 들어요.
남: 그래요. 정말 인상적이네요. 우리도 저것과 같은 책장이 있어야 할 것 같아요.
여: 동의해요. 그들이 창문 주위의 공간을 활용한 방식에 대해 어떻게 생각해요?
남: 창문 아래에 있는 두 개의 화분들이 좋아 보여요. 우리의 식물들도 같은 방식으로 놓아야 겠어요.
여: 오, 애완동물 쿠션 위에 누워 있는 고양이가 있네요.
남: 그것은 매우 편안해 보여요. 우리 고양이를 위해 하나 사는 게 어때요?
여: 좋은 생각이에요. 안락의자들 사이에 있는 둥근 탁자를 봤어요?
남: 저는 항상 저것과 같은 차 탁자를 가지고 싶었어요.
여: 이 전등을 봐요! 전등갓이 우리의 것과 같은 줄무늬를 가지고 있어요.
남: 그렇네요! 이 사진 속의 거실처럼 우리의 거실을 꾸밉시다.
여: 어떻게 될지 빨리 보고 싶어요.

고2 2020년 9월 7번   정답률 85%

05 남자가 여자에게 부탁한 일   ▶ 정답 ①

W: I'm so exhausted. I didn't realize moving was going to be this hard.
지친   알다   이사하는 것(move)   힘든
M: Me, neither. I think the move is mostly organized. You already called the cleaning company, right?
거의 정리되다
청소업체
W: Yes, they should be here soon. What else is left for us to do?
남았다(leave)
M: We still need to book the appointment to set up our internet connection.
예약을 하다   설정하다   인터넷 연결
W: Right. We should also fix the computer.
수리하다
M: Why? Is it broken?
고장이 난
W: The moving center staff dropped it.
직원   떨어뜨렸다(drop)
M: Have you asked the staff about compensation for it?
보상
W: Yeah. The moving center wants us to fix the computer first and then submit a receipt.
제출하다   영수증
M: My cousin runs an electronics repair shop nearby, so I can take it there today. Can you book the appointment to get the internet connected?
운영하다   전자제품 수리점
W: Okay, I'll do that.

해석
여: 나는 너무 지쳤어. 이사하는 것이 이렇게 힘들 줄은 몰랐어.
남: 나도 그래. 이사는 거의 정리된 것 같아. 네가 이미 청소업체에 전화했지, 그렇지?
여: 응, 그들이 곧 여기에 올 거야. 우리가 해야 할 일이 또 뭐가 남았지?
남: 우리는 아직 인터넷을 연결하기 위한 예약을 해야 해.
여: 맞아. 우리 컴퓨터도 수리해야 해.
남: 왜? 고장이 났어?
여: 이사업체 직원이 그것을 떨어뜨렸어.
남: 그 직원에게 그것에 대한 보상에 대해서 물어봤어?
여: 그래. 이사업체는 우리가 먼저 컴퓨터를 수리하고 나서 영수증을 제출하기를 원해.
남: 내 사촌이 근처에서 전자제품 수리점을 운영하고 있으니까, 내가 오늘 거기에 그것을 가져갈 수 있어. 네가 인터넷 연결을 위한 예약을 해 줄래?
여: 알았어, 내가 그것을 할게.

✔ ① 인터넷 연결 예약하기
② 컴퓨터 수리 맡기기
③ 영수증 재발급 받기
④ 가전제품 교환하기
⑤ 청소업체 연락하기

고2 2020년 9월 9번   정답률 75%

06 남자가 지불할 금액   ▶ 정답 ④

W: Good afternoon. How can I help you?
M: Hi. I'm looking for a gift for my newborn niece. What would you recommend?
선물   새로 태어난 (여자) 조카
추천하다
W: These pajama sets and dresses are the best-selling clothes for babies.
잠옷 세트들   가장 잘 팔리는
M: They're so cute. How much are they?
W: This pajama set is 40 dollars, and this dress is 50 dollars.
M: Hmm.... I'd like to buy the dress you recommended.
W: Okay. Anything else?
M: Do you have any other items that would go well with the dress?
상품들   ~과 잘 어울리다
W: How about this hat? It's usually 10 dollars, but it's on sale. You can get 40 percent off that price.
~은 어때요?   할인 판매 중인
40% 할인을 받다
M: That sounds great! I'll take it.
W: Wonderful. So, one dress and one hat, right?
M: Yes. I also have this 5 dollar discount coupon. Can I use it?
할인 쿠폰
W: Let me see. [Pause] Unfortunately, no. This coupon only applies to purchases over 100 dollars.
유감스럽게도   ~에 적용되다
M: All right. I'll pay with this credit card.
지불하다   신용카드

해석
여: 안녕하세요. 어떻게 도와드릴까요?
남: 안녕하세요. 새로 태어난 제 조카를 위한 선물을 찾고 있어요. 어떤 것을 추천하시겠어요?
여: 이 잠옷 세트들과 드레스들은 가장 잘 팔리는 아기 옷이에요.
남: 너무 귀엽네요. 얼마인가요?
여: 이 잠옷 세트는 40달러이고, 이 드레스는 50달러예요.
남: 흠.... 추천하신 드레스를 사고 싶어요.
여: 알겠습니다. 다른 필요하신 건 없으세요?
남: 그 드레스와 잘 어울리는 다른 상품들이 있나요?
여: 이 모자는 어떠세요? 그것은 보통 10달러인데, 할인 판매 중이에요. 그 가격에서 40% 할인을 받으실 수 있어요.
남: 그거 괜찮네요! 그것을 살게요.
여: 좋습니다. 그럼, 드레스 한 벌과 모자 한 개네요, 맞으시죠?
남: 네. 저는 5달러 할인 쿠폰도 있어요. 그것을 사용할 수 있나요?
여: 어디 볼게요. [잠시 후] 유감스럽게도, 안 되네요. 이 쿠폰은 100달러 이상 구매 시에만 적용돼요.
남: 알겠습니다. 이 신용카드로 지불할게요.

① $41   ② $46   ③ $51
✔ ④ $56   ⑤ $60

문제 풀이
50달러인 드레스 한 벌과 10달러에서 40% 할인을 받은 모자 한 개를 사면 총액은 56달러이다. 구매액이 100달러를 넘지 않으므로 5달러 할인 쿠폰은 사용할 수 없다. 따라서 정답은 ④ '$56'이다.

07 여자가 보드게임을 하러 갈 수 없는 이유

고2 2020년 9월 8번 | 정답률 90% ▶ 정답 ⑤

W: I'm so happy our exams are over.
시험들

M: Me, too. They were really tough this time.
힘든

W: I know. Getting a cold made me even more stressed.
감기   훨씬 더 스트레스를 받은

M: Are you still sick?
아직도 아픈

W: No, I feel all right now. What are you doing after school today?

M: Some of our classmates are going to play board games to
보드게임을 하다
celebrate the end of exams. Do you want to come?
기념하다

W: I'd love to go, but I can't.

M: Why not?

W: Did I tell you my family is going on a ski trip this weekend?
스키 여행을 갈 예정이다   주말
(go on a ski trip)

M: No, you didn't. Why are you going skiing?

W: It's my dad's birthday, so we planned this trip for him.
계획했다(plan)

M: That sounds like a perfect gift for your dad.
선물

W: I hope so. I need to go shopping for goggles and a ski suit for
~을 사러 가야 하다   스키복
myself today. (need to V: ~해야 하다, go shopping for: ~을 사러 가다)

M: Oh, I see. Have a nice trip.

해석
여: 시험들이 끝나서 정말 행복해.
남: 나도 그래. 이번에는 정말 힘들었어.
여: 알아. 감기에 걸린 것이 나를 훨씬 더 스트레스를 받게 했어.
남: 너 아직도 아프니?
여: 아니, 지금은 괜찮아. 오늘 방과 후에 무엇을 할 거야?
남: 우리 반 친구들 중 몇 명이 시험 종료를 기념하기 위해 보드게임을 할 거야. 너도 올래?
여: 가고 싶지만, 그럴 수 없어.
남: 왜 안 돼?
여: 내가 이번 주말에 우리 가족이 스키 여행을 갈 예정이라고 말했니?
남: 아니, 안 했어. 왜 스키를 타러 가는 거야?
여: 아빠의 생신이라서, 아빠를 위해 이 여행을 계획했어.
남: 네 아빠를 위한 완벽한 선물인 것 같아.
여: 그랬으면 좋겠어. 오늘 내 고글과 스키복을 사러 가야 해.
남: 오, 그렇구나. 여행 잘 다녀와.

① 병문안을 가야 해서
② 시험공부를 해야 해서
③ 방과 후 수업이 있어서
④ 생일 파티에 참석해야 해서
✓ 스키용품을 사러 가야 해서

08 Comedy Allstars에 관해 언급되지 않은 것

고2 2020년 9월 10번 | 정답률 90% ▶ 정답 ③

M: Amy, have you heard about Comedy Allstars?

W: No, I haven't. What is it?
코미디

M: It's the biggest comedy show on Broadway. It's being held at the
Western Theater this year.
극장   열린(hold: 열다)

W: Oh, I know that place. When does the show start?
장소

M: It starts on December 15th.

W: Who will perform in the show?
공연하다

M: Many famous comedians like Tina Scott, Julia Moore, and James
유명한   코미디언들   ~와 같은
Parker will perform.

W: James Parker? He's my favorite comedian.
가장 좋아하는

M: Do you want to go with me, then? Tickets will go on sale next week.
판매되다

W: Okay! How can we buy the tickets?

M: We can book them online at the theater's website.
예매하다   온라인으로

W: Great. I'm so excited for the show.

해석
남: Amy, Comedy Allstars에 대해 들어본 적이 있니?

여: 아니, 없어. 그게 뭔데?
남: Broadway에서 가장 큰 코미디 쇼야. 올해는 Western Theater(Western 극장)에서 열릴 거야.
여: 오, 나는 그 장소를 알아. 그 쇼는 언제 시작하니?
남: 12월 15일에 시작해.
여: 그 쇼에서 누가 공연을 하니?
남: Tina Scott, Julia Moore, 그리고 James Parker와 같은 많은 유명한 코미디언들이 공연할 거야.
여: James Parker? 그는 내가 가장 좋아하는 코미디언이야.
남: 그럼, 나와 같이 갈래? 티켓들은 다음 주에 판매될 거야.
여: 좋아! 어떻게 티켓들을 살 수 있어?
남: 극장의 웹사이트에서 온라인으로 그것들을 예매할 수 있어.
여: 좋아. 나는 그 쇼가 너무 기대돼.

① 공연 장소   ② 공연 시작일   ✓ 관람료
④ 출연자   ⑤ 티켓 예매 방법

09 Organic Fair에 관한 내용과 일치하지 않는 것

고2 2020년 9월 11번 | 정답률 80% ▶ 정답 ④

W: Good evening, listeners. I'm Elizabeth, the hostess of the Organic
(여성) 주최자   유기농 박람회
Fair. This year, the fair will be held at Springfield Park. It'll last
열리다(hold)   계속되다
three days from October 11th to 13th. It aims to promote the
홍보하는 것을 목표로 하다
(aim to V: ~하는 것을 목표로 하다, promote: 홍보하다)
eco-lifestyle to a wide range of consumers. Various organic
친환경 생활양식   다양한
products will be displayed such as organic food and natural
제품들   전시되다
cosmetics. You can get a discount if you buy products at the fair.
천연 화장품   할인을 받다
Furthermore, there will be a class where you can learn how to
또한   수업   만드는 방법
(how to V: ~하는 방법)
make organic soap. The class will run from 9 a.m. to 11 a.m. each
진행되다
day. If you register online in advance, you can enter the fair for
등록하다   사전에
free and join all the activities. For more information, please visit
무료로
our website at www.springfieldfair.com. I look forward to exploring
탐험하기를 기대하다
eco-living with you at the fair.
(look forward to V-ing: ~하기를 기대하다,
explore: 탐험하다)

해석
여: 안녕하세요, 청취자 여러분. 저는 Organic Fair(유기농 박람회)의 주최자인 Elizabeth입니다. 올해에는, 박람회가 Springfield Park에서 열릴 것입니다. 그것은 10월 11일부터 13일까지 3일 동안 계속될 것입니다. 그것은 다양한 소비자들에게 친환경 생활양식을 홍보하는 것을 목표로 합니다. 유기농 식품과 천연 화장품과 같은 다양한 유기농 제품들이 전시될 것입니다. 박람회에서 제품들을 구매하시면 할인을 받으실 수 있습니다. 또한, 유기농 비누를 만드는 방법을 배울 수 있는 수업이 있을 것입니다. 수업은 매일 오전 9시부터 11시까지 진행될 것입니다. 사전에 온라인으로 등록하시면, 박람회에 무료로 입장하여 모든 활동들에 참가하실 수 있습니다. 더 많은 정보를 원하시면, 저희 웹사이트 www.springfieldfair.com을 방문해 주십시오. 박람회에서 여러분과 함께 친환경 생활을 탐험하기를 기대합니다.

① 3일 동안 열린다.
② 다양한 유기농 제품이 전시된다.
③ 현장에서 제품 구매 시 할인을 받을 수 있다.
✓ 유기농 비누 만들기 수업은 오후에 진행된다.
⑤ 온라인 사전 등록 시 무료로 입장할 수 있다.

문제풀이
유기농 비누 만들기 수업은 매일 오전 9시부터 11시까지 진행된다고 했으므로 ④ '유기농 비누 만들기 수업은 오후에 진행된다.'는 박람회에 관한 내용과 일치하지 않는다.

10 표에서 여자가 구입할 무선 이어폰

고2 2020년 9월 12번 | 정답률 90% ▶ 정답 ④

M: Hey, Tiffany. What are you doing?

W: I'm thinking of buying some wireless earbuds. Do you want to help
무선 이어폰
me choose from these five options?
고르다

M: Sure. How much can you spend?
(돈을) 쓰다

W: I don't want to spend more than 200 dollars.

M: These models are within your budget.
예산

W: What do you think would be a good play time from a single charge?
재생 시간 / 1회 충전

M: Hmm.... I think it should be longer than six hours so you don't have to charge them very often.
충전할 필요가 없다 / (don't have to V: ~할 필요가 없다)

W: That's a good point. I'll cross out this one. What is noise canceling?
(선을 그어) 지우다 / 소음 제거

M: It reduces unwanted sound using active noise control.
줄이다 / 원치 않는 / 능동 소음 제어

W: Does that make a big difference?
큰 차이를 만들다

M: It can really improve the sound quality of what you listen to.
향상시키다 / 음질

W: I see. Then, I'll go with ones with noise canceling.

M: Good choice. There are only two models left. Which color do you prefer?

W: I don't want white ones because they'll get dirty too easily. So, I'll buy this model.
더러워지다

해석

남: 안녕, Tiffany. 무엇을 하고 있니?
여: 무선 이어폰을 살까 생각 중이야. 이 다섯 가지 옵션들에서 고르는 것을 도와줄래?
남: 물론이지. 얼마를 쓸 수 있어?
여: 200달러 이상을 쓰고 싶지는 않아.
남: 이 모델들은 네 예산 내에 있어.
여: 1회 충전 시 재생 시간은 어떤 게 좋을 것 같아?
남: 흠.... 너무 자주 그것들을 충전할 필요가 없도록 6시간보다 길어야 할 것 같아.
여: 좋은 지적이야. 이것은 지울게. 소음 제거는 뭐야?
남: 능동 소음 제어를 이용해 원치 않는 소리를 줄이는 거야.
여: 그것이 큰 차이를 만들까?
남: 그것은 네가 듣는 것의 음질을 정말로 향상시킬 수 있어.
여: 그렇구나. 그럼, 소음 제거가 있는 것을 살게.
남: 좋은 선택이야. 두 개의 모델만 남았네. 어떤 색상이 더 좋니?
여: 흰색은 너무 쉽게 더러워지니까 흰색 제품은 원하지 않아. 그러니까, 이 모델을 살게.

무선 이어폰

	모델	가격	재생 시간 (1회 충전 시)	소음 제거	색상
①	A	135달러	5시간	X	은색
②	B	145달러	8시간	X	은색
③	C	160달러	8시간	O	흰색
✔④	D	180달러	10시간	O	검은색
⑤	E	205달러	10시간	O	검은색

11 남자의 마지막 말에 대한 여자의 응답

고2 2020년 9월 1번 / 정답률 80% / ▶ 정답 ④

M: Welcome to Alice Bookstore. How may I help you?
서점

W: I bought this book here yesterday, but I want to exchange it for another copy.
샀다(buy) / 그것을 (같은 제목의) 다른 책으로 교환하다 / (exchange A for B: A를 B로 교환하다)

M: Sure. May I ask what's wrong with it?

W: (It's damaged. Several pages are missing.)
손상된 / 빠진

해석

남: Alice Bookstore(Alice 서점)에 오신 것을 환영합니다. 어떻게 도와드릴까요?
여: 제가 어제 여기에서 이 책을 샀는데, 그것을 (같은 제목의) 다른 책으로 교환하고 싶어요.
남: 알겠습니다. 그것에 무슨 문제가 있는지 여쭤봐도 될까요?
여: (그것은 손상됐어요. 몇 페이지가 빠져 있거든요.)
① 그것은 잘못된 주소로 발송되었어요.
② 제가 직접 그 책을 가져오고 싶어요.
③ 그 구획에서 그 책을 찾을 수 없었거든요.
✔④ 그것은 손상됐어요. 몇 페이지가 빠져 있거든요.
⑤ 문제없어요. 이 신용카드로 지불할게요.

12 여자의 마지막 말에 대한 남자의 응답

고2 2020년 9월 2번 / 정답률 90% / ▶ 정답 ③

W: Wow! Josh, this pasta is very delicious. I didn't know you cook.
파스타 / 맛있는 / 요리하다

M: Actually, this is the first time I've made pasta by myself.
사실 / 혼자서(by oneself)

W: Really? Where did you learn how to cook it?
배우다 / 요리하는 방법 / (how to V: ~하는 방법)

M: (My aunt recently taught me the recipe.)
최근에 / 요리법

해석

여: 와! Josh, 이 파스타 아주 맛있다. 나는 네가 요리하는 줄 몰랐어.
남: 사실, 내가 혼자서 파스타를 만든 것은 이번이 처음이야.
여: 정말? 어디에서 그것을 요리하는 방법을 배웠니?
남: (최근에 이모께서 요리법을 가르쳐 주셨어.)
① 나는 이탈리아 음식이 건강에 좋다고 생각하지 않아.
② 나는 보기 좋은 음식이 맛도 좋다고 믿어.
✔③ 최근에 이모께서 요리법을 가르쳐 주셨어.
④ 너무 많은 요리사들이 수프를 망친다는 것을 기억해.
⑤ 너는 내가 준 요리법을 따라야 했어.

13 남자의 마지막 말에 대한 여자의 응답

고2 2020년 9월 13번 / 정답률 60% / ▶ 정답 ①

M: How are you, Rebecca?

W: I'm fine, but you look tired today.
피곤한

M: That's because my back hurt so much last night that I couldn't sleep at all.
아팠다 / 잠을 자다

W: Your back? Did you injure it while you were exercising?
다치게 하다 / 운동하고 있었다(exercise)

M: No. I didn't do anything yesterday other than study at the library.
도서관

W: Maybe that's the problem. I bet you were sitting for too long with bad posture.
(~이) 틀림없다 / 나쁜 자세로

M: You're right. I have a bad habit of hunching my shoulders when I sit.
구부리는 나쁜 습관이 있다 / (have a bad habit of V-ing: ~하는 나쁜 습관이 있다, hunch: 구부리다)

W: Do you ever take a break and stretch your body?
휴식을 취하다 / 스트레칭하다

M: When I'm in the middle of something, it isn't easy to stop.

W: You know what? I recently read an article that said sitting with poor posture can lead to chronic back pain.
최근에 / 기사 / 만성 요통

M: How can that happen?

W: (Bad posture can cause increased tension in your back.)
~의 원인이 되다 / 긴장

해석

남: 잘 지내니, Rebecca?
여: 난 좋아, 그런데 너 오늘 피곤해 보인다.
남: 그건 내가 어젯밤에 허리가 너무 아파서 잠을 전혀 잘 수 없었기 때문이야.
여: 허리? 운동하다가 다친 거니?
남: 아니. 도서관에서 공부하는 것 말고는 어제 아무것도 안 했어.
여: 아마도 그것이 문제일 수 있어. 네가 나쁜 자세로 너무 오랫동안 앉아 있었음이 틀림없어.
남: 네 말이 맞아. 나는 앉아 있을 때 어깨를 구부리는 나쁜 습관이 있어.
여: 휴식을 취하고 몸을 스트레칭한 적은 있니?
남: 나는 무언가에 빠져 있을 때, 멈추는 것이 쉽지 않아.
여: 그거 알아? 내가 최근에 나쁜 자세로 앉아 있는 것이 만성 요통으로 이어질 수 있다는 기사를 읽었어.
남: 어떻게 그럴 수 있는 거지?
여: (나쁜 자세는 허리에 증가되는 긴장의 원인이 될 수 있어.)
✔① 나쁜 자세는 허리에 증가되는 긴장의 원인이 될 수 있어.
② 무거운 것을 들어 올릴 때 조심해.
③ 여기 수면 문제들에 대한 몇 가지 조언들이 있어.
④ 지나친 운동은 근육통으로 이어질 수 있어.
⑤ 공부하는 동안 규칙적인 휴식을 취하는 것은 네가 집중하는 데 도움을 줄 거야.

문제 풀이

나쁜 자세가 만성 요통의 원인이 될 수 있다는 기사의 내용을 전한 여자에게 남자는 나쁜 자세가 어떻게 만성 요통으로 이어질 수 있는지 묻고 있다. 따라서 여자의 답변으로는 ① 'Bad posture can cause increased tension in your back.(나쁜 자세는 허리에 증가되는 긴장의 원인이 될 수 있어.)'이 가장 적절하다.

14 여자의 마지막 말에 대한 남자의 응답

고2 2020년 9월 14번 | 정답률 85% | ▶ 정답 ②

W: Andrew, did you choose a topic for the English essay?
  (선택하다) (주제) (영어 에세이)
M: I did. The teacher approved it last week.
  (승인했다(approve))
W: That's great. Have you started writing it?
  (쓰기 시작한(start V-ing: ~하기 시작하다))
M: Not yet. I usually have a hard time making logical arguments for my
  (논리적인 주장들을 하는 데 어려움을 겪다)
  (have a hard time V-ing: ~하는 데 어려움을 겪다, make an argument: 주장을 하다)
  essays. Do you have any suggestions?
  (제안들)
W: Well, I read a lot of newspaper articles. I especially like editorials.
  (많은) (기사들) (특히) (사설들)
M: Does that really help develop logical thinking?
  (발달시키다)
W: Sure. If you read persuasive articles like editorials, you can see
  (설득력 있는)
  how the arguments are developed.
M: That makes sense to me. Maybe I should give it a try.
  (일리가 있다) (한번 해 보다)
W: I can send you the website I usually use. It collects editorials from
  (수집하다)
  various newspapers.
  (다양한)
M: (Thank you. I'll start reading editorials on that site.)

해석
여: Andrew, 영어 에세이 주제를 선택했니?
남: 했어. 선생님께서 지난주에 그것을 승인하셨어.
여: 잘됐구나. 그것을 쓰기 시작했니?
남: 아직은 아니야. 나는 보통 에세이들에서 논리적인 주장들을 하는 데 어려움을 겪어. 너는 혹시 어떤 제안이라도 있니?
여: 음, 나는 많은 신문 기사들을 읽어. 나는 특히 사설들을 좋아해.
남: 그것이 정말 논리적인 사고를 발달시키는 데 도움이 되니?
여: 물론이지. 사설들과 같은 설득력 있는 기사들을 읽으면, 주장들이 어떻게 전개되는지 알 수 있어.
남: 그거 일리가 있구나. 한번 해 봐야 할 것 같아.
여: 내가 보통 사용하는 웹사이트를 너에게 보내줄 수 있어. 그것은 다양한 신문들의 사설들을 수집하거든.
남: (고마워. 그 사이트에서 사설들을 읽기 시작할게.)
① 물론이지. 인용문들을 잊지 않도록 주의할게.
☑ 고마워. 그 사이트에서 사설들을 읽기 시작할게.
③ 기사들을 요약하는 것은 쉽지 않지만, 그것은 나에게 효과가 있어.
④ 네 말이 맞아. 자기 스스로 쓰는 것보다 더 좋은 것은 없어.
⑤ 동의해. 웹상의 모든 정보가 신뢰할 만한 것은 아니야.

15 다음 상황에서 Brian이 Jennifer에게 할 말

고2 2020년 9월 15번 | 정답률 85% | ▶ 정답 ⑤

W: Brian and Jennifer are good friends who go to the gym together
  (체육관에 가다)
  almost every day. When they're working out, they drink a lot of
  (거의) (운동을 하는(work out)) (많은)
  water. Brian always brings his own tumbler with him while Jennifer
  (텀블러) (반면에)
  always buys a bottle of water at the convenience store before
  (편의점)
  going to the gym. Brian thinks that buying a bottle of water
  every day is not only a waste of money but is also harmful to the
  (낭비) (해로운)
  environment. One day at the gym, Jennifer makes a comment
  (환경) (언급하다)
  about how much she likes Brian's tumbler. Brian thinks this is a
  good chance to suggest that she bring her own reusable bottle
  (기회) (제안하다) (재사용 가능한)
  to the gym. In this situation, what would Brian most likely say to
  Jennifer?
Brian: (Why don't you get a tumbler and bring it to the gym?)
  (~하는 게 어때?)

해석
여: Brian과 Jennifer는 거의 매일 체육관에 함께 가는 좋은 친구다. 운동을 할 때, 그들은 많은 물을 마신다. Brian은 항상 자신의 텀블러를 가지고 다니는 반면에 Jennifer는 항상 체육관에 가기 전에 편의점에서 물 한 병을 산다. Brian은 매일 물 한 병을 사는 것은 돈 낭비일 뿐만 아니라 환경에도 해롭다고 생각한다. 어느 날 체육관에서, Jennifer는 자신이 Brian의 텀블러를 얼마나 마음에 들어 하는지에 대해 언급한다. Brian은 이것이 그녀에게 자신의 재사용 가능한 병을 체육관에 가져오라고 제안할 수 있는 좋은 기회라고 생각한다. 이러한 상황에서, Brian은 Jennifer에게 뭐라고 말하겠는가?

Brian: (텀블러를 사서 체육관에 가져오는 게 어때?)
① 우리는 더 자주 함께 운동해야 해.
② 그렇게 많은 텀블러들을 사느라 돈을 낭비하지 마.
③ 우리는 운동하는 동안 물을 더 마시는 게 좋겠어.
④ 체육관 근처의 편의점은 언제 문을 닫니?
☑ 텀블러를 사서 체육관에 가져오는 게 어때?

16~17 1지문 2문항

M: Hello, everyone. I'm Dr. Damon. As parents, we are all worried
  about our children starting to wear glasses at younger ages. We
  (쓰기 시작하는 것(start to V: ~하기 시작하다))
  surely know using smartphones has negative effects on their
  (확실히) (~에 부정적인 영향을 미치다)
  (have an effect on: ~에 영향을 미치다, negative: 부정적인)
  eyes. Today, I will tell you some foods that can help protect your
  (보호하다)
  children's eyes. First, carrots are rich in vitamin A, which keeps
  (당근들) (~이 풍부한)
  the eye surface healthy by preventing it from drying out. Cheese
  (표면) (그것이 건조해지는 것을 막음으로써) (치즈)
  (by V-ing: ~함으로써, dry out: 건조해지다)
  (prevent A from V-ing: A가 ~하는 것을 막다)
  is not only rich in vitamin A, but it also prevents eye fatigue due
  (피로) (~ 때문에)
  to its high levels of iron. Blueberries are rich in antioxidants,
  (철분) (블루베리들) (항산화제들)
  which improve night vision as well as maintain general eye health.
  (향상시키다) (야간 시력) (유지하다)
  Lastly, the omega-3 fatty acids in salmon lower the chance of eye
  (오메가-3 지방산들) (낮추다) (가능성)
  diseases. I hope you encourage your children to try the foods I
  (여러분의 아이들이 먹어 보도록 격려하다)
  recommended today.
  (encourage A to V: A가 ~하도록 격려하다, try: 먹어 보다)

해석
남: 안녕하세요, 여러분. 저는 Damon 박사입니다. 부모로서, 우리는 모두 우리 아이들이 더 어린 나이에 안경을 쓰기 시작하는 것에 대해 걱정합니다. 우리는 스마트폰을 사용하는 것이 그들의 눈에 부정적인 영향들을 미친다는 것을 확실히 알고 있습니다. 오늘, 저는 여러분의 자녀들의 눈을 보호하는 데 도움을 줄 수 있는 몇 가지 식품들을 알려드릴 것입니다. 첫째, 당근은 비타민 A가 풍부한데, 그것은 눈의 표면이 건조해지는 것을 막음으로써 건강하게 유지해 줍니다. 치즈는 비타민 A가 풍부할 뿐만 아니라, 높은 함량의 철분 때문에 눈의 피로를 막아줍니다. 블루베리는 항산화제가 풍부한데, 그것은 전반적인 눈 건강을 유지해 줄 뿐만 아니라 야간 시력을 향상시킵니다. 마지막으로, 연어에 들어 있는 오메가-3 지방산은 눈 질환의 가능성을 낮춥니다. 여러분께서 여러분의 아이들이 오늘 제가 추천한 식품들을 먹어 보도록 격려해 주시기를 바랍니다.

16 남자가 하는 말의 주제

고2 2020년 9월 16번 | 정답률 90% | ▶ 정답 ④

① 노화 방지를 위한 슈퍼푸드들
② 아이들의 성장을 위한 핵심 영양소들
③ 비타민이 신체에 미치는 영향들
☑ 아이들의 눈 건강을 보호하는 식품들
⑤ 균형 잡힌 식사의 중요성

17 언급된 식품이 아닌 것

고2 2020년 9월 17번 | 정답률 85% | ▶ 정답 ④

① 당근   ② 치즈   ③ 블루베리
☑ 아몬드   ⑤ 연어

09 2020년 11월 학력평가

01	④	02	②	03	①	04	⑤	05	④
06	③	07	⑤	08	④	09	⑤	10	③
11	①	12	①	13	②	14	④	15	③
16	②	17	④							

01 남자가 하는 말의 목적

정답률 90%
▶ 정답 ④

M: Good morning, everyone. I'm your P.E. teacher, Mr. Andrews.
Since this is your first class this semester, I'm going to give you
some rules to follow in the P.E. class. First, you are required to
wear appropriate clothing such as sportswear and proper athletic
shoes. Second, you must be careful when using sports equipment
in the gym. Don't use the equipment without permission. Finally,
when you hear the whistle, stop what you're doing and pay
attention to my instructions. If you keep these rules in your mind,
(keep A in one's mind: A를 명심하다)
you'll be able to participate safely in the P.E. class. Now let's do a
warm-up exercise.

해석
남: 안녕하세요, 여러분. 저는 체육 교사인 Andrews 선생님입니다. 이것은 이번 학기 여러분
의 첫 수업이기 때문에, 체육 수업 시간에 여러분이 따라야 할 몇 가지 규칙들을 알려드릴
게요. 첫째, 운동복과 같은 적절한 옷과 적합한 운동화를 착용해야 해요. 둘째, 체육관에
서 운동 기구를 사용할 때 조심해야 해요. 허락 없이 기구를 사용하지 마세요. 마지막으
로, 호루라기 소리를 들으면, 하던 일을 멈추고 제 지시에 주의를 기울이세요. 이 규칙들
을 명심한다면, 여러분은 체육 수업 시간에 안전하게 참여할 수 있을 거예요. 이제 준비 운
동을 합시다.

① 기초 체력 향상을 위한 운동법을 설명하려고
② 체육 대회 참가 시 필요한 준비물을 공지하려고
③ 체육관 공사로 인한 수업 장소 변경을 알리려고
✓④ 체육 수업 시간에 준수해야 할 규칙을 안내하려고
⑤ 무리한 운동으로 인한 부상의 위험성을 경고하려고

02 여자의 의견

정답률 90%
▶ 정답 ②

W: Jason, are you going out?
M: Yes. I'm going to take a walk, Mom.
W: Wait! Why are you wearing shoes without socks?
M: I don't want to put them on. They feel uncomfortable.
(put A on: A를 착용하다)
W: I know you feel that way. But for your foot health, you should wear
socks.
M: Really? Why do you say that?
W: Well, your feet will stay dry if you put on socks. And you can avoid
germs and bacteria on your feet.
M: Hmm.... I hadn't thought about that.
W: And if you don't have socks on, you could get scratched or even get
a skin infection.
M: That makes sense, Mom. I'm going to follow your advice.
W: Good. Wearing socks is important for your foot health.

해석
여: Jason, 나갈 거니?
남: 네. 산책할 거예요, 엄마.
여: 잠깐! 왜 양말 없이 신발을 신고 있니?

남: 저는 그것들을 착용하고 싶지 않아요. 불편하게 느껴지거든요.
여: 네가 그렇게 느끼는 것을 알아. 하지만 발 건강을 위해서, 양말을 신어야 해.
남: 정말이에요? 왜 그런 말씀을 하세요?
여: 음, 양말을 착용하면 발이 건조한 상태로 있을 거야. 그리고 발의 세균과 박테리아를 피
할 수 있지.
남: 흠.... 저는 그것에 대해 생각해 본 적이 없어요.
여: 그리고 양말을 신지 않으면, 긁히거나 심지어 피부 감염이 될 수도 있어.
남: 그거 일리가 있네요, 엄마. 엄마의 충고를 따를게요.
여: 좋아. 양말을 신는 것은 발 건강에 중요하단다.

① 족욕을 하는 것은 건강에 도움이 된다.
✓② 발 건강을 위해서 양말을 신어야 한다.
③ 운동 종목에 적합한 신발을 선택해야 한다.
④ 계절에 맞는 소재의 양말을 구입해야 한다.
⑤ 높은 굽의 신발은 척추에 무리를 줄 수 있다.

03 두 사람의 관계

정답률 85%
▶ 정답 ①

W: Hello, Simon. I'm glad that you are here.
M: Hi, Julia. How's it going with recording your new song?
W: Well, it's been tough. I've been singing the song all the time.
M: I can imagine. How can I help you?
W: The music video for the song will be filmed soon. And I need you to
make an easy dance that everyone can follow.
M: No problem. I just need a copy of the song, so I can try to make it
as simple and memorable as possible.
(as A as possible: 가능한 한 A만큼, memorable: 기억할 만한)
W: Okay. Here's a copy of the song.
M: When do you need the dance by?
W: Hmm.... I have a meeting with the music video director next Friday.
M: All right. It'll take a couple of days to make the dance. Then we can
practice it together.
W: Perfect. Thank you so much.

해석
여: 안녕하세요, Simon. 와주셔서 기뻐요.
남: 안녕하세요, Julia. 당신의 신곡 녹음은 잘 되고 있나요?
여: 음, 힘들었어요. 저는 줄곧 그 노래를 부르고 있어요.
남: 상상이 돼요. 제가 어떻게 도와줄까요?
여: 노래의 뮤직 비디오가 곧 촬영될 거예요. 그리고 저는 당신이 모두가 따라 할 수 있는 쉬운
춤을 만들어 주었으면 해요.
남: 문제 없어요. 저는 단지 그 곡의 복사본이 필요해요, 그러면 그것을 가능한 한 단순하고 기
억할 만하게 만들도록 노력할 수 있어요.
여: 좋아요. 여기 그 곡의 복사본이 있어요.
남: 춤이 언제까지 필요해요?
여: 흠.... 다음 주 금요일에 뮤직 비디오 감독과 회의를 해요.
남: 알겠어요. 춤을 만드는 데 이틀 정도 걸릴 거예요. 그런 다음 우리는 그것을 함께 연습할
수 있어요.
여: 완벽해요. 정말 고마워요.

✓① 가수 — 안무가
② 작곡가 — 작사가
③ 성우 — 녹음 기사
④ 방송 작가 — 프로듀서
⑤ 뮤지컬 배우 — 음향 감독

04 그림에서 대화의 내용과 일치하지 않는 것

정답률 85%
▶ 정답 ⑤

M: Hi, Anna. How was your weekend?
W: Hey, Mike! I helped to make the stage for our school play. Here,
take a look at the picture I took of the stage.
M: Wow. It's wonderful.

W: Thanks. My favorite is the Christmas tree in the corner.
　　　　　　　가장 좋아하는 것　　　　　　　　　　　구석
M: I agree. I also like the picture above the fireplace.
　　　　　　　　　　　　　그림　　　　　벽난로
W: Do you like it? I painted it myself.
　　　　　　　　　(그림물감으로) 그렸다
M: It looks so real. Why is there a cup on the round table?
　　　　　　　　　　　　　　　　　　　　　둥근 탁자
W: The main character is supposed to have some tea at the table.
　　　　주인공　　　　차를 마시기로 되어 있다
　　　　　　(be supposed to V: ~하기로 되어 있다)
M: I see. Look at the toy horse next to the chair. It's so cute.
　　　　　　　　　　장난감 말
W: Yeah. And what do you think of the bell on the door?
　　　　　　　　　　　　　　　　　　　종
M: It really adds to the Christmas atmosphere. You did a great job.
　　　　　~을 더하다　　　　　　분위기
W: Thank you. Will you come to see the play?
M: Sure. I can't wait to see it.
　　　　빨리 보고 싶다(can't wait to V: 빨리 ~하고 싶다)

해석
남: 안녕, Anna. 주말 잘 보냈니?
여: 안녕, Mike! 나는 학교 연극을 위한 무대를 만드는 것을 도왔어. 여기, 내가 무대를 찍은 사진을 봐.
남: 와, 멋지다.
여: 고마워. 내가 가장 좋아하는 것은 구석에 있는 크리스마스 트리야.
남: 동의해. 나는 벽난로 위의 그림도 마음에 들어.
여: 마음에 드니? 내가 그것을 직접 그렸어.
남: 정말 진짜처럼 보여. 왜 둥근 탁자 위에 컵이 있는 거니?
여: 주인공이 탁자에서 차를 마시기로 되어 있거든.
남: 그렇구나. 의자 옆에 있는 장난감 말을 봐. 너무 귀여워.
여: 그래. 그리고 문에 달린 종에 대해 어떻게 생각하니?
남: 그것은 정말 크리스마스 분위기를 더해줘. 너 정말 잘했다.
여: 고마워. 연극을 보러 올 거니?
남: 물론이지. 그것을 빨리 보고 싶어.

05　남자가 여자에게 부탁한 일

정답률 85%

▶ 정답 ④

W: Jake, what are you doing?
M: I'm cleaning the house. Mom and Dad will come back tomorrow
　　　청소하는(clean)　　　　　　　　　　　　돌아오다
　　from their trip to Hawaii.
　　　　　　여행
W: You're right. We need to get ready to welcome them.
　　　　　　　　　　　　준비를 하다　　맞이하다
M: Do you know tomorrow is their 25th wedding anniversary?
　　　　　　　　　　　　　　　　　결혼기념일
W: Sure. So I'm going to make a special dinner for them.
　　　　　　　　　　　　특별한　　저녁 식사
M: Oh, what will you make?
W: Roast chicken and cream pasta.
M: That's great! They'll love that.
W: I hope so. How are they coming back home from the airport?
M: They'll take a bus.　　　　　　　　　　　　　　공항
　　　버스를 타다
W: I'm worried they'll be too tired. Why don't you pick them up at the
　　　　　　　　　　　　피곤한　　　　　　그들을 태우러 가다
　　airport tomorrow?
M: Good idea. Could you please check the arrival time of their
　　　　　　　　　　　　　　　　확인하다　도착 시간
　　airplane?
W: Of course, I can do that now.
M: Thanks. Then I should go to the gas station to fill up the car.
　　　　　　　　　　　　　　　주유소　기름을 가득 채우다

해석
여: Jake, 무엇을 하고 있니?
남: 집을 청소하고 있어. 엄마와 아빠께서 내일 하와이 여행에서 돌아오실 거야.
여: 네 말이 맞아. 우리는 그분들을 맞이할 준비를 해야 해.

남: 내일이 그분들의 25번째 결혼기념일인 거 아니?
여: 물론이지. 그래서 나는 그분들을 위해 특별한 저녁 식사를 만들 거야.
남: 오, 무엇을 만들 거야?
여: 구운 닭고기와 크림 파스타를 만들 거야.
남: 잘됐다! 그분들께서 정말 좋아하실 거야.
여: 그랬으면 좋겠어. 그분들께서 공항에서 집으로 어떻게 돌아오시는 거야?
남: 버스를 타실 거야.
여: 너무 피곤하실까 봐 걱정돼. 내일 공항에 그분들을 태우러 가는 게 어떠니?
남: 좋은 생각이야. 그분들의 비행기 도착 시간을 확인해 주겠니?
여: 물론이지, 지금 할 수 있어.
남: 고마워. 그럼 나는 주유소에 가서 차에 기름을 가득 채워야겠다.

① 집안 청소하기
② 저녁 식사 준비하기
③ 부모님 마중 나가기
✔④ 비행기 도착 시간 확인하기
⑤ 자동차에 주유하기

06　여자가 지불할 금액

정답률 80%

▶ 정답 ③

M: Good morning. How may I help you?
W: Hello. I'm looking for a birthday gift for my sister. Can you
　　　　　　　　　　　　　생일 선물
　　recommend something?
　　추천하다
M: Okay. How about these plates? These are the most popular ones
　　　　　　　　　　　접시들　　　　　　　　　　인기 있는
　　in our store. The plate that has a star-pattern is $20, and the
　　　　가게　　　　　　　　　　　별무늬
　　flower-patterned plate is $15.
　　　꽃무늬의
W: My sister has star decoration everywhere in her house. So I'll take
　　　　　　　　　　　장식
　　some star-patterned plates.
M: Great. How many do you want?
W: Four, please.
M: All right. Is there anything else you're looking for?
W: Those coffee cups are very pretty, too. How much are they?
　　　　　커피잔들　　　　　예쁜
M: They're $10 each.
W: I'll take two of them.
M: Excellent. You want four star-patterned plates and two coffee cups.
　　Is that right?
W: That's correct.
M: Just to let you know, we're offering a 10 percent discount on all
　　　　　　　　　　　　　제공하는(offer)　10% 할인
　　items this month.
　　품목들
W: Great. Here's my credit card.
　　　　　　　　신용카드

해석
남: 안녕하세요. 어떻게 도와드릴까요?
여: 안녕하세요. 저는 언니를 위한 생일 선물을 찾고 있어요. 추천을 좀 해주시겠어요?
남: 알겠습니다. 이 접시들은 어떠세요? 이것들은 저희 가게에서 가장 인기 있는 것들이에요. 별무늬가 있는 접시는 20달러, 꽃무늬 접시는 15달러예요.
여: 제 언니는 집안 곳곳에 별 장식을 해요. 그러니까 저는 별무늬 접시를 살게요.
남: 좋습니다. 몇 개를 원하시나요?
여: 4개 주세요.
남: 알겠습니다. 더 찾으시는 건 없으세요?
여: 저 커피잔들도 매우 예쁘네요. 얼마죠?
남: 개당 10달러예요.
여: 2개를 살게요.
남: 좋습니다. 별무늬 접시 4개와 커피잔 2개를 원하시죠? 맞아요?
여: 맞아요.
남: 참고로 말씀드리면, 저희는 이번 달에 모든 품목들에 대해 10% 할인을 제공하고 있어요.
여: 잘됐네요. 여기 제 신용카드가 있어요.

① $72　　　　　　　② $80　　　　　　✔③ $90
④ $100　　　　　　⑤ $108

문제 풀이
20달러인 별무늬 접시 4개와 10달러인 커피잔 2개를 사면 총액은 100달러이다. 모든 품목들에 대해 10% 할인을 받을 수 있으므로 여자는 100달러에서 10%가 할인된 금액인 90달러를 지불해야 한다. 따라서 답은 ③ '$90'이다.

07 남자가 스터디 모임에 참여할 수 없는 이유

▶ 정답 ⑤

[Cell phone rings.]

W: Hey, Ben. Can I talk to you for a second?
잠깐

M: Hi, Sarah. I'm sorry for not answering the phone this morning. I was in English class.
영어 수업

W: That's okay. I called you to say that our study group meeting made some changes this week.
전화했다 / 스터디 그룹 모임

M: Thanks. Did the meeting place change?
장소

W: No, we're still going to meet at the school library. But it'll be at 11 a.m. on Saturday.
여전히 / 학교 도서관

M: Saturday? I'm sorry, but I can't make it.
(모임에) 가다

W: Why? You told me that you don't have volunteer work on the weekends.
봉사 활동

M: I don't. But I have to go to the hospital.
병원에 가다

W: Oh, that's right. I heard you injured your leg playing soccer. Is that the reason?
다쳤다 / 이유

M: No, my leg wasn't hurt that badly. Actually I have a medical check-up this Saturday.
다치지 않았다(hurt) / 사실 / 건강 검진

W: I see. I'll call you later to tell you the schedule for next time.
나중에 / 일정

M: Thank you for understanding.

해석

[휴대전화가 울린다.]

여: 안녕, Ben. 잠깐 얘기 좀 할 수 있을까?
남: 안녕, Sarah. 오늘 아침에 전화를 받지 못해서 미안해. 나는 영어 수업 중이었어.
여: 괜찮아. 이번 주에 우리 스터디 그룹 모임에 약간 변화가 있다는 것을 알려주려고 전화했어.
남: 고마워. 모임 장소가 바뀌었어?
여: 아니, 우리는 여전히 학교 도서관에서 만날 거야. 하지만 토요일 오전 11시가 될 거야.
남: 토요일? 미안하지만, 나는 갈 수 없어.
여: 왜? 너는 주말에 봉사 활동이 없다고 말했잖아.
남: 그래. 하지만 병원에 가야 해.
여: 오, 맞아. 네가 축구를 하다가 다리를 다쳤다고 들었어. 그게 이유니?
남: 아니, 내 다리는 그렇게 심하게 다치지 않았어. 사실 나는 이번 주 토요일에 건강 검진을 받아.
여: 그렇구나. 내가 나중에 전화해서 다음 일정을 알려줄게.
남: 이해해 줘서 고마워.

① 영어 수업을 들어야 해서
② 학교 도서관에 가야 해서
③ 봉사 활동에 참여해야 해서
④ 다친 다리를 치료해야 해서
☑ 건강 검진을 받아야 해서

08 Lakeville Campground에 관해 언급되지 않은 것

▶ 정답 ④

M: Honey, what are you doing?

W: I'm looking at this brochure for Lakeville Campground. Why don't we go camping next month?
안내 책자 / 캠프장 / 캠핑을 가다

M: Sounds great. Let's look at the brochure together.

W: Wow. In these photos, the campground is surrounded by a thick forest. And there's also a huge lake nearby.
둘러싸여 있다(surround) / 울창한 숲 / 거대한 / 근처에

M: That's awesome! We can enjoy the beauty of nature.
아름다움 / 자연

W: Yeah. And they offer a lot of convenient facilities.
제공하다 / 편의 시설

M: It says each camping site has a shower room, a barbecue grill, and a place to have a campfire.
캠프장 / 샤워실 / 바비큐 그릴 / 캠프파이어를 하다

W: We're going to have so much fun. How much is it?

M: It's $35 per night.
1박에

W: That's reasonable.
합리적인

M: And it says we should make a reservation on their website.
예약하다

W: This campground is really popular. So we need to hurry to reserve a place.
인기 있는 / 서둘러야 하다 / 예약하다
(need to V: ~해야 하다, hurry: 서두르다)

M: Okay. Let's do it right now.

해석

남: 여보, 무엇을 하고 있어요?
여: Lakeville Campground(Lakeville 캠프장)에 대한 안내 책자를 보고 있어요. 우리 다음 달에 캠핑을 가는 게 어때요?
남: 좋아요. 안내 책자를 같이 봐요.
여: 와. 이 사진들 속에서, 캠프장은 울창한 숲으로 둘러싸여 있어요. 그리고 근처에 거대한 호수도 있네요.
남: 멋지네요! 우리는 자연의 아름다움을 즐길 수 있어요.
여: 그래요. 그리고 그들은 많은 편의 시설을 제공해요.
남: 각 캠프장에는 샤워실, 바비큐 그릴, 그리고 캠프파이어를 할 수 있는 장소가 있다고 쓰여 있어요.
여: 정말 재미있을 거예요. 얼마예요?
남: 1박에 35달러예요.
여: 합리적이네요.
남: 그리고 그들의 웹사이트에서 예약해야 한다고 쓰여 있어요.
여: 이 캠프장은 정말 인기가 있어요. 그러니까 우리는 서둘러서 장소를 예약해야 해요.
남: 알겠어요. 지금 당장 합시다.

① 주변 자연환경　　② 편의 시설　　③ 이용료
☑ 이용 시간　　⑤ 예약 방법

09 Circus Experience Festival에 관한 내용과 일치하지 않는 것

▶ 정답 ⑤

W: Hello, ABS radio listeners. I'm Catherine Barton, director of Lingston Circus. I'm so happy to tell you that we're hosting this year's Circus Experience Festival. It starts on November 20th and lasts for three days. We're offering a variety of hands-on activities including magic tricks and juggling. And qualified instructors will teach you. To ensure your safety, we'll limit the number of participants to 10 for each activity. You can also enjoy taking pictures with some circus clowns in the photo zone. Additionally, we'll give you free postcards as a souvenir of this festival. Are you excited? Come to the Circus Experience Festival and have a great time. Thank you.
감독 / 개최하는(host) / 서커스 체험 축제 / 지속되다 / 다양한 / 체험 활동들 / 마술 / 저글링 / 자격을 갖춘 / 강사들 / 보장하다 / 안전 / 제한하다 / 참가자들 / 광대들 / 또한 / 무료 / 엽서들 / 기념품으로

해석

여: 안녕하세요, ABS 라디오 청취자 여러분. 저는 Lingston 서커스의 감독인 Catherine Barton입니다. 저희가 올해의 Circus Experience Festival(서커스 체험 축제)을 개최한다는 것을 알려드리게 되어 매우 기쁩니다. 그것은 11월 20일에 시작해서 3일 동안 지속됩니다. 저희는 마술과 저글링을 포함한 다양한 체험 활동들을 제공할 것입니다. 그리고 자격을 갖춘 강사들이 여러분을 가르칠 것입니다. 여러분의 안전을 보장하기 위해, 저희는 각 활동의 참가자들의 수를 10명으로 제한할 것입니다. 여러분은 포토존에서 몇몇 서커스 광대들과 사진을 찍는 것도 즐길 수 있습니다. 또한, 저희는 이 축제의 기념품으로 무료 엽서를 증정할 것입니다. 흥분되시나요? Circus Experience Festival에 오셔서 즐거운 시간을 보내세요. 감사합니다.

① 11월 20일에 시작해서 3일 동안 지속된다.
② 마술과 저글링을 포함한 다양한 체험 활동을 제공할 것이다.
③ 각 활동의 참가자 수를 10명으로 제한할 것이다.
④ 포토존에서 서커스 광대들과 함께 사진을 찍을 수 있다.
☑ 기념품으로 무료 티셔츠를 증정할 것이다.

10 표에서 여자가 구입할 무선 마이크 세트

▶ 정답 ③

M: Honey, what are you doing?

W: I'm thinking about buying a wireless microphone set. My throat hurts a lot after giving so many lectures every week.
무선 마이크 세트 / 아프다 / 강의들 / 매주

M: All right. Let me help you. *[Typing sound]* How long do you think the receiving distance has to be?
<u>receiving distance</u>
수신 거리

W: I'm not sure. I'll be using it in the <u>classroom</u>.
교실

M: Your classroom is not very small. I think 10 meters is not <u>enough</u> for the receiving distance.
충분한

W: Okay. That's good <u>advice</u>.
조언

M: And do you want a <u>headset</u>?
(마이크가 부착된) 헤드폰

W: I'd like to have one so I can use my hands freely during the lecture.
자유롭게

M: You're right. What color do you want?

W: It doesn't really <u>matter</u>. But I don't want silver.
중요하다

M: I see. Now you have only two <u>options</u> <u>left</u>.
선택들 남은(leave: 남기다)

W: I'll buy the cheaper one. Thank you for your help.

해석

남: 여보, 무엇을 하고 있어요?

여: 무선 마이크 세트를 살까 생각 중이에요. 매주 너무 많은 강의를 한 후에 목이 많이 아파서요.

남: 알겠어요. 내가 도와줄게요. *[타자 치는 소리]* 수신 거리는 얼마나 길어야 한다고 생각해요?

여: 잘 모르겠어요. 저는 그것을 교실에서 사용할 거예요.

남: 당신의 교실은 그렇게 작지 않잖아요. 10미터는 수신 거리로 충분하지 않을 것 같아요.

여: 알겠어요. 좋은 조언이네요.

남: 그리고 헤드폰을 사고 싶어요?

여: 강의 중에 손을 자유롭게 사용할 수 있도록 하나 갖고 싶어요.

남: 당신 말이 맞아요. 어떤 색상을 원해요?

여: 그것은 별로 중요하지 않아요. 하지만 은색은 원하지 않아요.

남: 그렇군요. 이제 두 가지 선택지가 남았어요.

여: 더 저렴한 것을 살게요. 도와줘서 고마워요.

무선 마이크 세트

	제품	수신 거리	헤드폰	색상	가격
①	A	10m	불포함	흰색	50달러
②	B	20m	포함	은색	65달러
✔③	C	30m	포함	빨간색	80달러
④	D	40m	포함	금색	90달러
⑤	E	50m	불포함	검은색	100달러

11 남자의 마지막 말에 대한 여자의 응답
정답률 80%
▶ 정답 ①

M: Mom, I have to <u>borrow</u> some books from the <u>library</u> today. But it's <u>raining</u> outside.
빌리다 도서관 비가 오는(rain)

W: Don't worry. I'll <u>give you a ride</u>. Do you want to <u>leave</u> now?
(give A a ride: A를 태워 주다) 출발하다

M: Yes. But I <u>need to</u> <u>look for</u> my library card first. Could you wait for a <u>second</u>?
(need to V: ~해야 하다, look for: ~을 찾다) 잠깐

W: (No problem. Just let me know when you're <u>ready</u>.)
준비가 된

해석

남: 엄마, 저는 오늘 도서관에서 책을 좀 빌려야 해요. 그런데 밖에 비가 오고 있어요.

여: 걱정하지 마. 내가 너를 태워다 줄게. 지금 출발하고 싶니?

남: 네. 그런데 도서관 카드를 먼저 찾아야 해요. 잠깐 기다려 주시겠어요?

여: (그럼. 네가 준비가 되면 나에게 알려줘.)

✔① 그럼. 네가 준비가 되면 나에게 알려줘.

② 미안하지만 안 될 것 같아. 나는 어제 도서관 카드를 잃어버렸어.

③ 물론이지. 너는 네가 원할 때는 언제든지 내 책을 빌릴 수 있어.

④ 미안해. 햇빛이 너무 강해서 밖에 나갈 수 없어.

⑤ 당연하지. 나는 도서관까지 걸어갈 거야.

12 여자의 마지막 말에 대한 남자의 응답
정답률 75%
▶ 정답 ①

[Cell phone rings.]

W: Hi, David. I'm <u>almost</u> halfway to the restaurant. Where are you?
거의

M: Hi, Amy. I just <u>finished</u> work and <u>got in</u> my car. I'll take the <u>highway</u>, so I'll <u>arrive</u> <u>on time</u>.
끝냈다 ~에 탔다(get in) 고속도로 도착하다 제시간에

W: I heard on the radio that there has been a <u>car accident</u> on the highway. So you're going to <u>get stuck</u>.
교통 사고 꼼짝 못하게 되다

M: (I see. I'll take another road then.)

해석

[휴대전화가 울린다.]

여: 안녕, David. 나는 식당까지 거의 절반 정도 왔어. 너는 어디에 있니?

남: 안녕, Amy. 나는 방금 일을 끝내고 차에 탔어. 고속도로를 이용할 테니까, 제시간에 도착할 거야.

여: 고속도로에서 교통 사고가 났다고 라디오에서 들었어. 그래서 너는 꼼짝 못하게 될 거야.

남: (그렇구나. 그럼 다른 길로 갈게.)

✔① 그렇구나. 그럼 다른 길로 갈게.

② 정말? 지금 당장 병원으로 가.

③ 정말 안됐다. 너는 더 일찍 떠났어야 했는데.

④ 미안해. 나는 고속도로에서 속도 위반 딱지를 떼었어.

⑤ 좋아. 내가 식당을 예약할게.

13 남자의 마지막 말에 대한 여자의 응답
정답률 80%
▶ 정답 ②

M: Ashley, you got a letter from the <u>business department</u> at Corven University.
경영학과

W: Oh, it might be my <u>acceptance letter</u>, Dad. I'm so <u>nervous</u> about it. Can you open it for me?
합격 통지서 긴장되는

M: Okay. Let's see.... *[pause]* You got in, sweetie. Congratulations!

W: Really? Wow, I'm so happy!

M: I'm so <u>proud of</u> you. And you also <u>got accepted to</u> the <u>mathematics department</u> of the other university.
자랑스러운 ~에 합격했다 수학과

W: Yeah. I have to <u>make a decision</u> soon. But it's <u>hard</u> for me to <u>choose</u> between the two.
결정을 하다 어려운 선택하다

M: Hmm.... What do you really want to study?

W: Actually, I love <u>math</u>. But <u>business</u> is one of the most <u>popular</u> <u>majors</u>.
수학 경영학 인기 있는 전공들

M: I think you shouldn't choose a major <u>based on</u> what other people say.
~에 근거하여

W: Do you mean I have to <u>consider</u> my own <u>interests</u>?
고려하다 관심사들

M: Of course. You will be happy doing what you love to do.

W: (I agree. I'd rather major in mathematics.)

해석

남: Ashley, Corven 대학교의 경영학과에서 네게 편지가 왔구나.

여: 오, 제 합격 통지서일지도 몰라요, 아빠. 저는 너무 긴장돼요. 그것을 열어주시겠어요?

남: 그래. 어디 보자.... *[잠시 후]* 합격했구나, 얘야. 축하한다!

여: 정말이에요? 와, 정말 기뻐요!

남: 네가 정말 자랑스럽구나. 그리고 너는 다른 대학교의 수학과에도 합격을 했잖니.

여: 네. 저는 곧 결정을 해야 해요. 하지만 둘 중에서 선택하는 것은 저에게 어려워요.

남: 흠.... 네가 정말 공부하고 싶은 게 뭐니?

여: 사실, 저는 수학을 정말 좋아해요. 하지만 경영학은 가장 인기 있는 전공들 중 하나잖아요.

남: 나는 네가 다른 사람들이 말하는 것에 근거하여 전공을 선택해서는 안 된다고 생각해.

여: 제 자신의 관심사들을 고려해야 한다는 말씀이세요?

남: 물론이지. 너는 네가 정말 하고 싶은 일을 하면서 행복할 거야.

여: (동의해요. 저는 수학을 전공하고 싶어요.)

① 그렇지 않아요. 저는 전공을 바꿔야겠어요.

✔② 동의해요. 저는 수학을 전공하고 싶어요.

③ 오, 이런. 제가 그들에게 전화해서 다시 확인해 볼게요.

④ 알겠어요. 전공의 인기는 중요해요.

⑤ 멋져요! 저는 성공적인 사업가가 될 수 있어요.

문제 풀이

경영학과 수학 중 어떤 전공을 선택해야 할지 고민하는 여자에게 남자는 자신이 정말 하고 싶은 일을 해야 행복할 것이라고 말한다. 수학을 좋아하는 여자가 남자의 말에 동의하는 응답이 적절하므로 답은 ② 'I agree. I'd rather major in mathematics.(동의해요. 저는 수학을 전공하고 싶어요.)'이다.

14 여자의 마지막 말에 대한 남자의 응답

정답률 65%
▶ 정답 ④

W: Hi, Steve. I have something to tell you.
M: Hi. What is it, Sophie?
W: We need to decide on a research topic for our science club.
　　　　결정해야 하다　　　　　연구 주제　　　　과학 동아리
　(need to V: ~해야 하다, decide: 결정하다)
M: Yeah. What topic do you have in mind?
　　　　　　　　　　　　　염두에 두다
W: I don't have any specific idea. Why don't we ask the other
　　　　　　　　　　구체적인　　　우리 ~하는 게 어때?
　members for their opinions?
　　　　　　　　의견들
M: I'm not sure about that. I think it's our job to determine a research
　　　　　　　　　　　　　　　　　　　　　　　결정하다
　topic as club leaders.
W: But do you remember last semester? We chose the research topic
　　　　　　　　　　　　학기　　　선택했다(choose)
　ourselves, and some members didn't like it.
M: You're right. Then, how can we hear everyone's opinion?
W: Well, we'll have time to discuss with all of our club members next
　　　　　　　　　　　　　논의하다
　week.
M: That sounds good. But what if they have too many different ideas?
　　　　　　　　　　　　　~이라면 어쩌지?　　　　　다른
W: Then we can put the research topic to the vote and choose what
　　　　　　　　　연구 주제를 표결에 부치다
　　　　　　　(put A to the vote: A를 표결에 부치다)
　most members want for the topic.
M: (All right. That way we'll satisfy more members than last time.)
　　　　　　　　　　　　　　만족시키다

해석
여: 안녕, Steve. 너에게 할 말이 있어.
남: 안녕. 뭐, Sophie?
여: 우리는 우리 과학 동아리의 연구 주제를 결정해야 해.
남: 그래. 너는 어떤 주제를 염두에 두고 있니?
여: 구체적인 생각은 없어. 우리 다른 회원들한테 의견을 물어보는 게 어때?
남: 그것은 잘 모르겠어. 나는 동아리 회장들로서 연구 주제를 결정하는 것이 우리의 일이라고 생각해.
여: 하지만 지난 학기를 기억하니? 우리가 직접 연구 주제를 선택했는데, 일부 회원들이 그것을 좋아하지 않았잖아.
남: 네 말이 맞아. 그럼, 우리는 어떻게 모든 사람들의 의견을 들을 수 있을까?
여: 음, 다음 주에 모든 우리 동아리 회원들과 의논할 시간이 있을 거야.
남: 좋은 생각이야. 그런데 그들이 너무 많은 다른 생각들을 가지고 있으면 어쩌지?
여: 그럼 우리는 연구 주제를 표결에 부치고 가장 많은 회원들이 주제로 원하는 것을 선택할 수 있어.
남: (좋아. 그런 방식으로 우리는 지난번보다 더 많은 회원들을 만족시킬 거야.)
① 걱정하지 마. 나는 그들이 분명히 네 의견을 지지할 것을 알고 있어.
② 물론 아니야. 우리는 지금 동아리 회장들을 바꿀 수 없어.
③ 이해해. 그럼 내가 다른 연구 주제를 찾아볼게.
✔④ 좋아. 그런 방식으로 우리는 지난번보다 더 많은 회원들을 만족시킬 거야.
⑤ 신경 쓰지 마. 우리는 그룹 토론을 위한 시간을 재조정할 수 있어.

문제 풀이
남자와 여자는 지난 학기에 자신들이 선택한 연구 주제를 일부 동아리 회원들이 좋아하지 않았기 때문에 이번에는 모든 동아리 회원들에게 의견을 묻기로 한다. 회원들의 생각이 다를 경우에 투표를 통해 연구 주제를 다수결로 결정할 수 있다는 여자의 말에 대한 남자의 응답으로 ④ 'All right. That way we'll satisfy more members than last time.(좋아. 그런 방식으로 우리는 지난번보다 더 많은 회원들을 만족시킬 거야.)'가 적절하다.

15 다음 상황에서 Melissa가 Bob에게 할 말

정답률 70%
▶ 정답 ③

M: Melissa and Bob are best friends. Melissa is working for a cyber
　　　　　　　　　　　　　　　　　　　　　　　　　사이버 보안 회사
　security company. She fully understands the importance of online
　　　　　　　　　　　충분히　　　　　　　중요성
　security, and she's been updating her computer security program
　　　　　　　　　　　업데이트하는(update)
　with the latest version. One day, Bob tells Melissa that somebody
　　　　최신의
　illegally accessed his personal information and tried to steal
　불법적으로　접근했다　　개인 정보　　　　　훔치려고 했다
　　　　　　　　　　　　　　　　　　(try to V: ~하려고 하다, steal: 훔치다)
　his credit card number. When she checks out his computer, she
　　　　　　　　　　　　　　　　점검하다
　notices that he's using an old version of the security program. So,
　알아차리다
　she wants to suggest that he keep up with the newest version of
　　　　　　　　　　　　　　　~을 계속 유지하다
　the security software. In this situation, what would Melissa most
　likely say to Bob?
Melissa: (Why don't you keep your security program up-to-date?)
　　　　　　　　　　　　　　　　　　　　　　　　　　최신의

해석
남: Melissa와 Bob은 가장 친한 친구이다. Melissa는 사이버 보안 회사에서 일하고 있다. 그녀는 온라인 보안의 중요성을 충분히 이해하고 있으며, 자신의 컴퓨터 보안 프로그램을 최신 버전으로 업데이트해오고 있다. 어느 날, Bob은 Melissa에게 누군가가 그의 개인 정보에 불법적으로 접근해서 그의 신용카드 번호를 훔치려고 했다고 말한다. 그의 컴퓨터를 점검했을 때, 그녀는 그가 오래된 버전의 보안 프로그램을 사용하고 있다는 것을 알아차린다. 그래서, 그녀는 그가 최신 버전의 보안 소프트웨어를 계속 유지할 것을 제안하고 싶다. 이러한 상황에서, Melissa는 Bob에게 뭐라고 말하겠는가?
Melissa: (보안 프로그램을 최신 상태로 유지하는 게 어떠니?)
① 반드시 네 신용카드의 비밀번호를 설정해.
② 너는 인터넷 연결이 안정적인지 확인해야 해.
✔③ 보안 프로그램을 최신 상태로 유지하는 게 어떠니?
④ 다른 사람들의 개인 정보에 불법적으로 접근하지 마.
⑤ 온라인 장바구니에 물품들을 추가하는 게 어떠니?

16~17 1지문 2문항

W: Welcome back, listeners. I'm Doris Harrell from Garden Stories. Have you heard that flowers could be sending hidden messages?
　　　　　　　　　　　　　　　　　　　　　　　　　　　　　숨겨진(hide: 숨기다)
　Today, I'd like to talk about secret meanings some flowers can
　　　　　　　　　　　　　　비밀스러운　의미들
　convey. First, carnations can send the message, "You are always
　전달하다　　카네이션들
　on my mind, and I deeply admire you." Therefore, they are widely
　　　　　　　　진심으로　존경하다　　　　　　　　　　　널리
　used as a gift on Parents' Day. Next, people prefer to use tulips in
　선물로　　　어버이날　　　　　　　　사용하는 것을 선호하다　튤립들
　　　　　　　　　　　　　　　　　　　　(prefer to V: ~하는 것을 선호하다)
　a wedding bouquet since they symbolize "consuming love" as well
　　결혼식 부케　　　　　상징하다　　　열렬한
　as "happy years." Did you know that irises generally represent the
　　　행복한 세월　　　　　　　　　아이리스들　　　나타내다
　idea of faith and wisdom? So they are frequently used in religious
　　　　　믿음　　지혜　　　　　　자주　　　　　　종교적인
　settings and have inspired many artists. Last, daisies mean
　　장소들　　　영감을 주었다(inspire)　　　　데이지들
　innocence, loyal love, and purity. But at the same time, they imply
　　순결　　충실한　　순수　　　　동시에　　　암시하다
　to friends, "I'll never tell your secret." Now you know flowers say a
　　　　　　　　　　　　비밀
　lot more than you think. After the commercial break, I'll talk about
　　　　　　　　　　　　　　광고 시간
　how to decorate your home with beautiful flowers. Stay tuned.
　　　장식하는 방법
　(how to V: ~하는 방법, decorate: 장식하다)

해석
여: 어서 오세요, 청취자 여러분. 저는 Garden Stories의 Doris Harrell입니다. 여러분은 꽃들이 숨겨진 메시지를 보낼 수 있다는 것을 들어본 적이 있나요? 오늘, 저는 몇몇 꽃들이 전달할 수 있는 비밀스러운 의미에 대해 이야기하고자 합니다. 먼저, 카네이션은 "당신은 항상 내 마음속에 있고, 나는 당신을 진심으로 존경합니다."라는 메시지를 보낼 수 있습니다. 그러므로, 그것들은 어버이날에 선물로 널리 사용됩니다. 다음으로, 사람들은 결혼식 부케에 튤립을 사용하는 것을 선호하는데 그것들이 '행복한 세월'뿐만 아니라 '열렬한 사랑'을 상징하기 때문입니다. 여러분은 아이리스가 일반적으로 믿음과 지혜에 대한 생각을 나타낸다는 것을 알고 있었나요? 그래서 그것들은 종교적인 장소에서 자주 사용되며 많은 예술가들에게 영감을 주었습니다. 마지막으로, 데이지는 순결, 충실한 사랑, 그리고 순수를 의미합니다. 하지만 동시에, 그것들은 친구들에게 "나는 절대 네 비밀을 말하지 않을 거야."라고 암시합니다. 이제 여러분은 여러분이 생각하는 것보다 꽃들이 훨씬 더 많은 것을 말한다는 것을 아시겠지요. 광고 시간 후에, 여러분의 집을 아름다운 꽃으로 장식하는 방법에 대해 말씀드릴 것입니다. 채널을 고정해 주세요.

16 여자가 하는 말의 주제

정답률 90%
▶ 정답 ②

① 꽃의 개화기
✔② 꽃의 함축된 의미
③ 화단을 만드는 방법
④ 국화의 기원
⑤ 꽃을 심는 단계

17 언급된 꽃이 아닌 것

정답률 85%
▶ 정답 ④

① 카네이션   ② 튤립   ③ 아이리스
☑ 장미   ⑤ 데이지

10 2021년 3월 학력평가

01	⑤	02	①	03	②	04	④	05	⑤
06	②	07	⑤	08	③	09	②	10	③
11	③	12	①	13	④	14	④	15	②
16	④	17	④						

01 여자가 하는 말의 목적

정답률 80%
▶ 정답 ⑤

W: Good morning, parents. I'm Jennifer Lawrence, vice principal of
Greenhill Elementary School. Thank you for being here for the
Parent-Teacher Meeting. Before we begin, let me tell you about the
field trip next month. The students will be visiting the Children's
Natural History Museum. They'll have a great opportunity to
explore the different activities there. Today we'll hand out the field
trip permission form to each student, which has all the details
including the schedule and the fees. Please take a look and send
it back to us by next Monday. If you have any questions about the
trip, please feel free to call us.
(feel free to V: 언제든지 ~하다)

해석

여: 안녕하세요, 학부모님 여러분. 저는 Greenhill 초등학교의 교감인 Jennifer Lawrence입니다. 학부모-교사 간담회에 와 주셔서 감사합니다. 시작하기 전에, 다음 달에 있는 현장 학습에 대해 알려드리겠습니다. 학생들은 어린이 자연사 박물관에 방문할 것입니다. 그들은 그곳의 다양한 활동을 탐구할 좋은 기회를 갖게 될 것입니다. 오늘 저희는 학생들에게 현장 학습 동의서를 나눠줄 것이며, 그것에는 일정과 비용을 포함한 모든 세부사항이 있습니다. 그것을 보시고 다음 주 월요일까지 다시 보내주십시오. 현장 학습에 대해 문의 사항이 있으시면, 언제든지 저희에게 전화해 주십시오.

① 학부모 간담회 일정 변경을 공지하려고
② 현장 학습에 동행해 줄 것을 부탁하려고
③ 학부모 동의서 온라인 제출 방법을 안내하려고
④ 현장 학습 장소에 관한 학부모의 의견을 구하려고
☑ 현장 학습 학부모 동의서 확인 및 제출을 요청하려고

02 남자의 의견

정답률 85%
▶ 정답 ①

W: Hi, Chris. Where are you going?
M: I'm going to the library to check out some books. Do you want to
come along?
W: Well, I don't often read books these days. I'm busy helping with
housework, exercising, and so on.
(busy V-ing: ~하느라 바쁜)
M: Why don't you try audio books then? They're convenient to listen to
while you're doing other things.
W: I've never tried it. Do you think it'll work for me?
M: Sure. It's an easy way to enjoy books even if you have a busy
schedule. I always listen to a short story when I take a walk.

W: Cool! I guess I could try listening to audio books while I do chores.
(try V-ing: ~해 보다)
M: I'm sure you'll enjoy listening to books while dealing with other
stuff.
(deal with: ~을 처리하다)
W: Can you recommend some audio books to me?
M: I have a few in mind. I'll text you a list later.

해석

여: 안녕, Chris. 어디에 가니?
남: 책 몇 권을 대출하기 위해 도서관에 가는 중이야. 함께 갈래?
여: 음, 나는 요즘에 책을 자주 읽지 않아. 집안일을 돕고, 운동 등을 하느라 바쁘거든.
남: 그럼 오디오 북을 써 보는 게 어떠니? 그것들은 네가 다른 일들을 하면서 듣기에 편리해.
여: 나는 그것을 써 본 적이 없어. 그것이 내게 효과가 있을 거라고 생각하니?
남: 물론이지. 그것은 비록 네가 바쁜 일정을 가지고 있다 할지라도 책을 즐길 수 있는 쉬운 방법이야. 나는 산책을 할 때 항상 짧은 이야기를 들어.
여: 멋지다! 나는 집안일을 하면서 오디오 북을 들어 볼 수 있을 것 같아.
남: 나는 네가 다른 일을 처리하면서 책을 듣는 것을 즐길 거라고 확신해.
여: 내게 오디오 북을 좀 추천해 주겠니?
남: 내가 생각하는 게 몇 개 있어. 나중에 목록을 문자로 보내줄게.

☑ 오디오 북은 다른 활동을 하면서 듣기에 편리하다.
② 오디오 북은 책의 내용을 깊이 이해하는 데 도움이 된다.
③ 운동을 할 때는 오디오 북보다 음악을 듣는 것이 더 낫다.
④ 도서관은 다양한 장르의 오디오 북을 구비해야 한다.
⑤ 오디오 북은 조용한 장소에서 들을 필요가 있다.

03 두 사람의 관계

정답률 85%
▶ 정답 ②

[Smartphone rings.]
W: Hello, Liam.
M: Hello, Emily. I'm wondering if we're having our lesson as scheduled.
W: Sure. Why do you ask?
M: The temperature has gone down a lot lately. I'm afraid I can't surf
under these weather conditions.
W: Don't worry. The waves are more important than the temperature
in surfing.
M: But I'm still worried. I can't imagine myself going into really cold
water.
W: You'll be fine. We have thick wetsuits to keep you warm.
M: Okay, I guess I can try. Ah, one more thing.
W: What is it?
M: I'm not a good swimmer. Would it matter?
W: It'll be okay. Good swimming skills are not really necessary in
surfing.
M: I see. Looking forward to your lesson next week.
(look forward to)
W: Great! See you then.

해석

[스마트폰이 울린다.]
여: 안녕하세요, Liam.
남: 안녕하세요, Emily. 우리 강습을 예정대로 하는지 궁금해요.
여: 물론이조. 왜 물어보시는 거예요?
남: 최근에 기온이 많이 내려갔잖아요. 이런 기상 조건에서는 서핑을 할 수 없을 것 같아요.
여: 걱정하지 마세요. 서핑에서는 기온보다 파도가 더 중요해요.
남: 하지만 여전히 걱정돼요. 저는 저 자신이 정말 차가운 물에 들어가는 것을 상상할 수가 없어요.
여: 괜찮을 거예요. 당신을 따뜻하게 해 줄 두꺼운 서핑복이 있잖아요.
남: 좋아요, 해 볼 수 있을 것 같아요. 아, 한 가지 더 있어요.
여: 뭔데요?
남: 저는 수영을 잘 못해요. 그게 문제가 될까요?
여: 괜찮을 거예요. 좋은 수영 실력이 서핑에 꼭 필요한 것은 아니거든요.
남: 그렇군요. 다음 주 당신의 강습을 기대할게요.
여: 좋아요! 그때 봐요.

① 수영 코치 — 선수
☑ 서핑 강사 — 강습생

③ 인명 구조 요원 — 관광객
④ 기상청 직원 — 기상 캐스터
⑤ 서핑용품점 주인 — 거래처 직원

04 그림에서 대화의 내용과 일치하지 않는 것

정답률 85%

▶ 정답 ④

W: Honey, come and look. I'm decorating Sam's room for his birthday
   꾸미는(decorate) 생일 파티
   party.
M: Wow. I like what you put on the wall. It's beautiful.
W: Thanks. I made a heart with flowers.
   아름다운
   하트 모양
M: There's a cake on the table. Is that the one Aunt Mary baked for
   구웠다
   him?
W: Yeah. Her cakes are the best. I put three candles on it.
   초들
M: Good. Where's the gift we prepared?
   선물 준비했다
W: It's under the table. I tied a ribbon around the box.
   리본을 묶었다
M: Nice. Oh, I love this rug on the floor. It has stars on it.
   깔개 바닥 별들
W: It's cute, right? I bought it online.
M: Did you make the balloon dog on the bed?
   풍선 개
W: Yes, I did. Sam loves dogs.
M: He does. You did a great job.

해석
여: 여보, 와서 봐요. 저는 Sam의 생일 파티를 위해 그 애의 방을 꾸미고 있어요.
남: 와. 저는 당신이 벽에 붙인 것이 마음에 들어요. 아름답네요.
여: 고마워요. 저는 꽃으로 하트 모양을 만들었어요.
남: 테이블 위에 케이크가 있네요. Mary 이모가 그 애를 위해 구워주신 것이에요?
여: 네. 그분의 케이크는 최고죠. 제가 그 위에 세 개의 초를 꽂았어요.
남: 잘했어요. 우리가 준비한 선물은 어디에 있어요?
여: 테이블 아래에 있어요. 제가 상자에 리본을 묶었어요.
남: 멋지네요. 오, 저는 바닥의 이 깔개가 정말 마음에 들어요. 별들이 그려져 있네요.
여: 귀엽죠, 그렇죠? 온라인으로 그것을 샀어요.
남: 당신이 침대 위의 풍선 개를 만들었어요?
여: 네, 그랬어요. Sam이 개를 정말 좋아하잖아요.
남: 그렇죠. 정말 잘했네요.

05 여자가 남자에게 부탁한 일

정답률 85%

▶ 정답 ⑤

M: Ellie, do you have any idea about our volunteer club's next project?
   자원봉사 동아리의
W: Hmm, last time we knitted hats for babies and sent them to Africa.
   모자들을 떴다 보냈다(send)
   (knit: 뜨다)
M: Yes, we did.
W: How about making eco-friendly soap this time? It helps the
   친환경 비누
   environment and we can give it out to people in need.
   환경 그것을 나눠주다 어려움에 처한
M: Good idea. Luckily we learned how to make soap in science class.
   다행히도 만드는 방법 과학 수업 시간
   (how to V: ~하는 방법)
W: Right. I still have the handout about it.
   유인물
M: Great. You can bring it to our club meeting. It's next Friday, right?
   가져오다 모임
W: Yeah. We can try making soap then. Shall we do it in our club
   만들어 보다
   room?
   (try V-ing: ~해 보다)
M: I think it'll be better to use the science lab.
   사용하다 과학 실험실

W: You're right. Can you go ask Mr. White if we can use it?
M: Sure. I'll do that right away.
   당장
W: Thanks. Then, I'll find out where we can get the ingredients.
   알아보다 재료들

해석
남: Ellie, 우리 자원봉사 동아리의 다음 프로젝트에 대해 좋은 생각이 있니?
여: 흠, 지난번에 우리는 아기들을 위한 모자들을 떠서 아프리카에 보냈잖아.
남: 응, 그랬지.
여: 이번에는 친환경 비누를 만드는 게 어떠니? 그것은 환경에 도움을 주고 우리는 그것을 어려움에 처한 사람들에게 나눠줄 수 있어.
남: 좋은 생각이야. 다행히도 우리는 과학 수업 시간에 비누 만드는 방법을 배웠잖아.
여: 맞아. 나는 아직도 그것에 대한 유인물을 가지고 있어.
남: 잘됐다. 동아리 모임에 그것을 가져오면 돼. 다음 주 금요일이지, 그렇지?
여: 그래. 우리는 그때 비누를 만들어 볼 수 있어. 우리 동아리 방에서 그것을 할까?
남: 내 생각에는 과학 실험실을 사용하는 게 나을 것 같아.
여: 네 말이 맞아. 우리가 그곳을 사용할 수 있는지 네가 White 선생님께 가서 여쭤볼래?
남: 물론이지. 당장 그렇게 할게.
여: 고마워. 그럼, 나는 어디에서 재료들을 구할 수 있는지 알아볼게.

① 아기 모자 뜨기
② 유인물 가져오기
③ 동아리 모임 날짜 정하기
④ 비누 만들기 재료 구입하기
✔ 과학 실험실 사용 허락받기

문제 풀이
과학 실험실에서 비누를 만들자는 남자의 말에 여자는 담당 선생님에게 가서 과학 실험실 사용이 가능한지 물어볼 것을 부탁하고 있다. 따라서 답은 ⑤ '과학 실험실 사용 허락받기'이다.

06 남자가 지불할 금액

정답률 60%

▶ 정답 ②

W: Honey, we're running out of fine dust masks. Don't we need to
   ~이 떨어지는 미세먼지 마스크들 주문해야 하다
   (run out of) (need to V: ~해야 하다, order: 주문하다)
   order some more?
M: Oh, right. [Typing sound] Let's order them on this website. The
   masks are $2 each and a pack of 10 masks is $15.
W: Then it's cheaper to buy them in packs. Let's get four packs.
   더 싼
M: Okay. We also need some hand wash, right?
   손 세정제
W: Yes. Is there any special promotion going on?
   특별 할인 행사
M: Let me see. [Pause] Oh, there is. We can buy three bottles of hand
   wash for $10. It was originally $5 per bottle.
   원래 한 병에
W: That's a good deal. Let's buy three bottles then.
M: All right. Do we need anything else?
W: No, that's all. Oh, hang on. Look here. If we spend more than $50,
   we can get a 5-dollar discount. (돈을) 쓰다
   5달러 할인을 받다
M: Great. I'll place the order now with my credit card.
   주문하다 신용카드

해석
여: 여보, 우리 미세먼지 마스크가 떨어져가고 있어요. 좀 더 주문해야 하지 않아요?
남: 오, 맞아요. [타자 치는 소리] 이 웹사이트에서 주문합시다. 마스크는 개당 2달러이고 10개들이 한 꾸러미는 15달러예요.
여: 그럼 꾸러미로 사는 것이 더 싸네요. 네 꾸러미를 사요.
남: 알았어요. 우리 손 세정제도 좀 필요하죠, 맞죠?
여: 네. 진행 중인 특별 할인 행사가 있나요?
남: 어디 보자. [잠시 후] 오, 있어요. 손 세정제 세 병을 10달러에 살 수 있네요. 그것은 원래 한 병에 5달러였어요.
여: 좋은 거래네요. 그럼 세 병을 사요.
남: 좋아요. 그밖에 필요한 게 있어요?
여: 아니요, 그게 다예요. 오, 잠시만요. 여기 봐요. 50달러 이상을 쓰면, 5달러 할인을 받을 수 있어요.
남: 잘됐네요. 지금 제 신용카드로 주문할게요.

① $60 ✔ $65 ③ $70
④ $75 ⑤ $80

문제 풀이
한 꾸러미에 15달러인 마스크 네 꾸러미와 세 병에 10달러인 손 세정제 세 병을 사면 총액은 70달러이다. 50달러 이상의 제품을 구매하면 5달러 할인을 받을 수 있다고 했으므로 남자가

지불할 금액은 65달러이다. 따라서 답은 ② '$65'이다.

07 여자가 취업 면접 특강에 갈 수 없는 이유
정답률 85%
▶ 정답 ⑤

M: Hi, Jenny. How's your job interview preparation going?
취업 면접 ／ 준비
W: It's not going well. It's not easy doing it by myself.
쉬운 ／ 혼자서(by oneself)
M: Hmm.... Why don't you go to the special lecture on job interviews at
특강
the career center?
진로 센터
W: That might help. Do you know when it is?
M: It's this Saturday in the morning, from 10 to 12.
W: Oh, no. I'm afraid I can't make it.
(모임 등에) 가다
M: Oh, you have a part-time job at the library at that time, don't you?
아르바이트 ／ 도서관 ／ 그때
W: No, I quit last month. Actually, I have to take a computer skill test
그만뒀다(quit) 컴퓨터 능력 시험을 보다
on Saturday. (take a test: 시험을 보다)
M: I see. Good luck on your test.
W: Thanks. Do you know if another lecture is coming up?
M: I'm not sure. You should check with the career center.
확인하다
W: Okay, I will.

해석
남: 안녕, Jenny. 취업 면접 준비는 어떻게 되어 가니?
여: 잘 안 되고 있어. 혼자서 그것을 하는 것이 쉽지 않아.
남: 흠.... 진로 센터의 취업 면접 특강에 가 보는 건 어떠니?
여: 그거 도움이 될 수 있겠다. 언제인지 알고 있니?
남: 이번 주 토요일 오전 10시부터 12시까지야.
여: 아, 이런. 나는 갈 수 없을 것 같아.
남: 아, 너는 그때 도서관에서 아르바이트를 하지, 그렇지 않니?
여: 아니, 지난달에 그만뒀어. 사실, 토요일에 컴퓨터 능력 시험을 봐야 해.
남: 그렇구나. 네 시험에 행운을 빌게.
여: 고마워. 또 다른 강의가 있는지 알고 있니?
남: 잘 모르겠어. 진로 센터에 확인해 봐.
여: 알았어, 그렇게.

① 전공 강의를 들어야 해서
② 진로 센터를 방문해야 해서
③ 취업 면접을 보러 가야 해서
④ 도서관 아르바이트를 해야 해서
☑ 컴퓨터 능력 시험에 응시해야 해서

08 West Lake Fun Run에 관해 언급되지 않은 것
정답률 85%
▶ 정답 ③

M: Amy, what are you reading?
W: Our school newsletter. It says our school is holding the West Lake
소식지 개최할 예정이다(hold)
Fun Run.
M: Sounds interesting. When is it?
W: It'll be held on April 17th.
M: I see. How long is the course?
코스
W: It's 5km long. Starting at the school, participants will run through
참가자들 ~을 통과해서 달리다
Vincent Park and Central Stadium, and finish at West Lake.
M: Cool!
W: Why don't we sign up together?
참가하다
M: Good idea. How much is the entry fee?
참가비
W: It's $5 per person. The money raised will be used to renovate the
1인당 모금된(raise: 모금하다, 모으다) 개조하다
school gym.
체육관
M: Great. It's so old. It'll be wonderful to have a new gym.
멋진
W: I agree.

해석
남: Amy, 무엇을 읽고 있니?
여: 우리 학교 소식지야. 우리 학교에서 West Lake Fun Run을 개최할 예정이라고 쓰여 있어.
남: 재미있겠다. 그게 언제니?
여: 4월 17일에 개최될 거야.

남: 그렇구나. 코스는 얼마나 길어?
여: 5km야. 학교에서 시작해서, 참가자들은 Vincent Park와 Central Stadium을 통과해서 달리고 West Lake에서 마칠 거야.
남: 멋지다!
여: 우리 함께 참가하는 게 어떠니?
남: 좋은 생각이야. 참가비는 얼마니?
여: 1인당 5달러야. 모금된 돈은 학교 체육관을 개조하기 위해 사용될 거야.
남: 잘됐다. 그것은 너무 오래됐어. 새로운 체육관이 생긴다면 멋질 거야.
여: 동의해.

① 개최 날짜　　　　　② 코스 길이　　　　　☑ 출발 시간
④ 참가비　　　　　⑤ 모금액 용도

09 Sleep Under the Sea에 관한 내용과 일치하지 않는 것
정답률 75%
▶ 정답 ②

M: Do you ever wonder what happens in the aquarium at night? Pack
수족관 챙기다
your pajamas and join us at Sleep Under the Sea. You'll have the
잠옷
opportunity to sleep inside the shark tunnel with sharks and giant
기회 상어 터널
fish swimming above you. Our staff will give you a guided tour of
헤엄치는(swim) 직원들
the aquarium including a special visit to our staff-only areas. After
~을 포함하여 특별 방문 직원 전용 구역
the tour, you'll be able to watch a 3D movie about dolphins. To
볼 수 있다
(be able to V: ~할 수 있다)
participate in Sleep Under the Sea, children must be aged 5 and
~에 참여하다
up, and all children under 15 must be accompanied by an adult.
~와 동반하다(accompany)
Dinner and breakfast will be provided during the Sleep Under the
저녁 식사 아침 식사 제공되다(provide: 제공하다)
Sea experience. For more information, visit our website at www.
체험
sealifeaquarium.org.

해석
남: 여러분은 밤에 수족관에서 무슨 일이 일어나는지 궁금해한 적이 있나요? 잠옷을 챙겨서 Sleep Under the Sea에서 저희와 함께 하세요. 여러분은 여러분 위에서 헤엄치는 상어들과 거대한 물고기들과 함께 상어 터널 안에서 잘 기회를 갖게 될 것입니다. 저희 직원들이 직원 전용 구역 특별 방문을 포함하여 수족관을 안내해 드릴 것입니다. 안내 후에는, 돌고래에 관한 3D 영화를 볼 수 있을 것입니다. Sleep Under the Sea에 참여하기 위해서는, 어린이는 5세 이상이어야 하며, 15세 미만 어린이는 모두 성인과 동반해야 합니다. Sleep Under the Sea 체험 기간 동안에 저녁 식사와 아침 식사가 제공될 것입니다. 더 많은 정보를 원하시면, 저희 웹사이트 www.sealifeaquarium.org를 방문해 주세요.

① 상어 터널 안에서 잘 기회가 있을 것이다.
☑ 직원 전용 구역 방문은 포함되지 않는다.
③ 돌고래에 관한 3D 영화를 볼 수 있을 것이다.
④ 15세 미만 어린이는 성인과 동반해야 한다.
⑤ 저녁 식사와 아침 식사가 제공될 것이다.

10 표에서 두 사람이 주문할 자전거 헬멧
정답률 85%
▶ 정답 ③

M: Honey, what are you looking at on the Internet?
W: I'm looking for a bike helmet for Jason. There's a crack in his old
자전거 헬멧 금
helmet.
M: Oh, I didn't know that. Let's pick one together then. What's our
고르다
priority?
우선 순위
W: I guess it's weight. What about you?
무게
M: Same here. Considering Jason's age, it should be under 600
~을 고려하면
grams.
W: I agree. I think this one is too expensive, though. I don't want to
비싼
spend more than $70.
(돈을) 쓰다
M: Okay, let's choose from these three then. Do you think LED lights
선택하다 조명들
are necessary?
필요한
W: Yes, it'll be safer to have them when riding at night.
더 안전한 타는(ride)
M: You're right. Now we have two options left. Do you think our son
선택들 남은(leave: 남기다)
will like this one?

W: I don't think so. He doesn't like yellow.
M: That's right. Let's order the other one.
주문하다

해석
남: 여보, 인터넷에서 무엇을 보고 있어요?
여: Jason을 위한 자전거 헬멧을 찾고 있어요. 그 애의 낡은 헬멧에 금이 갔어요.
남: 오, 저는 몰랐어요. 그럼 같이 하나 고릅시다. 우리의 우선 순위는 뭐예요?
여: 무게인 것 같아요. 당신은 어때요?
남: 저도 그래요. Jason의 나이를 고려하면, 600그램 미만이어야 해요.
여: 동의해요. 하지만 이것은 너무 비싼 것 같아요. 저는 70달러 이상을 쓰고 싶지 않아요.
남: 좋아요, 그럼 이 세 가지 중에서 선택합시다. LED 조명이 필요하다고 생각해요?
여: 네, 밤에 자전거를 탈 때 그것들을 가지고 있는 게 더 안전할 거예요.
남: 당신 말이 맞아요. 이제 두 가지 선택지가 남았어요. 우리 아들이 이것을 좋아할 것 같아요?
여: 저는 그렇게 생각하지 않아요. 그 애는 노란색을 좋아하지 않잖아요.
남: 맞아요. 다른 것을 주문합시다.

자전거 헬멧

	모델	무게(그램)	가격	LED 조명	색상
①	A	620	25달러	X	파란색
②	B	550	30달러	X	노란색
✔	C	420	45달러	O	파란색
④	D	310	55달러	O	노란색
⑤	E	240	75달러	O	흰색

11 남자의 마지막 말에 대한 여자의 응답
정답률 50% ▶ 정답 ③

M: Lydia! You said you were going camping with your family to Mt.
캠핑을 가는(go camping)
   Bluestone during the winter vacation. How was it?
   겨울방학
W: We couldn't make it because of the heavy snow. We camped
   ~ 때문에   폭설
   indoors at our house instead.
   실내에서   대신에
M: That's cool. I wonder where the tent was set up.
   설치되었는지(set up: 설치하다)
W: (My father put it up in the living room.)
   그것을 세웠다(put up)

해석
남: Lydia! 너는 겨울방학 동안에 가족과 함께 Bluestone 산에 캠핑을 갈 거라고 했잖아. 어땠어?
여: 우리는 폭설 때문에 갈 수 없었어. 대신에 우리 집 실내에서 캠핑을 했어.
남: 멋지다. 나는 텐트가 어디에 설치되었는지 궁금해.
여: (아버지께서 거실에 그것을 세우셨어.)
① 그것은 3일간의 캠핑 여행이었어.
② 우리는 집에서 캠핑을 할 수 없었어.
✔ 아버지께서 거실에 그것을 세우셨어.
④ 나는 근처의 캠핑 용품 가게에서 그것을 샀어.
⑤ 텐트에서 자기에 매우 좋은 날씨였어.

12 여자의 마지막 말에 대한 남자의 응답
정답률 55% ▶ 정답 ①

W: Mr. Johnson, do you have a minute? I need your opinion on the
   의견
   project I'm doing.
   프로젝트
M: I'd love to discuss that with you, but I'm expecting a visitor in 10
   의논하다   기다리는(expect) 손님
   minutes. Is 10 minutes enough?
   충분한
W: I'm afraid it'll take longer than that. Shall I come back later?
   (시간이) 걸리다   나중에
M: (Yes. I'll give you a call when I'm available.)
   시간이 있는

해석
여: Johnson 씨, 잠깐 시간 좀 내줄 수 있어요? 제가 하고 있는 프로젝트에 대한 당신의 의견이 필요해요.
남: 그것을 당신과 의논하고 싶지만, 저는 10분 후에 올 손님을 기다리고 있어요. 10분이면 충분한가요?
여: 그것보다 더 오래 걸릴 것 같아요. 나중에 다시 올까요?
남: (네. 제가 시간이 있을 때 당신에게 전화할게요.)

✔ 네. 제가 시간이 있을 때 당신에게 전화할게요.
② 음, 당신은 지금 어떤 프로젝트도 하고 있지 않군요.
③ 좋아요. 손님이 방금 가셨기 때문에 우리는 이제 얘기할 수 있어요.
④ 왜 안 되겠어요? 당신은 언제든지 프로젝트에 참여할 수 있어요.
⑤ 물론이죠. 저는 지금 30분이 있어요.

13 남자의 마지막 말에 대한 여자의 응답
정답률 85% ▶ 정답 ④

W: Dad, I'm home. Where's Max?
M: He's sleeping in his house. I took him to the vet this morning. He
   수의사
   hasn't been eating well lately.
   최근에
W: What did the vet say?
M: She said there's nothing wrong with him. He just needs more
   exercise.
   운동
W: More exercise? We take him out for a walk regularly.
   산책시키다   규칙적으로
M: That's true, but we don't walk him every day. The vet said he needs
   at least an hour of exercise every day.
   적어도
W: Oh, I didn't know that.
M: I think we should exercise him every day from now on.
   운동시키다   이제부터
W: I agree. What if we all take turns doing it?
   교대로 하다
   (take turns V-ing: 교대로 ~하다)
M: Good idea. Your mom and I will do it on weekdays. You're busy with
   평일에
   your schoolwork during the weekdays.   ~으로 바쁜
   학교 공부
W: (Okay. I'll take him out for a walk on weekends then.)
   주말에

해석
여: 아빠, 저 왔어요. Max는 어디에 있어요?
남: 그의 집에서 자고 있어. 나는 오늘 아침에 그를 수의사에게 데려갔어. 그가 최근에 잘 먹지 못하고 있었잖아.
여: 수의사가 뭐라고 했어요?
남: 그에게 아무런 문제가 없다고 했어. 단지 더 많은 운동이 필요한 거야.
여: 더 많은 운동이요? 우리는 규칙적으로 그를 산책시키잖아요.
남: 맞아, 하지만 우리는 매일 그를 산책시키지는 않잖아. 수의사는 그가 매일 적어도 한 시간의 운동이 필요하다고 말했어.
여: 오, 저는 몰랐어요.
남: 우리는 이제부터 매일 그를 운동시켜야 할 것 같구나.
여: 동의해요. 우리 모두 그것을 교대로 하면 어때요?
남: 좋은 생각이야. 네 엄마와 나는 평일에 그것을 할 거야. 너는 평일에 학교 공부로 바쁘잖아.
여: (좋아요. 그럼 저는 주말에 그를 산책시킬게요.)
① 맞아요. 그는 최근에 너무 많이 먹고 있었어요.
② 그건 불공평해요. 저는 일주일 내내 그를 산책시키고 싶지 않아요.
③ 죄송해요. 저는 지금 그를 수의사에게 데려갈 시간이 없어요.
✔ 좋아요. 그럼 저는 주말에 그를 산책시킬게요.
⑤ 그렇지 않아요. 지나친 운동은 그의 건강에 좋지 않아요.

문제풀이
모든 가족이 교대로 매일 애완동물을 운동시키자는 딸의 제안에 아빠는 학교 공부로 바쁜 딸을 위해 평일에 엄마와 함께 애완동물을 산책시키겠다고 대답한다. 이에 대한 딸의 응답으로는 ④ 'Okay. I'll take him out for a walk on weekends then.(좋아요. 그럼 저는 주말에 그를 산책시킬게요.)'가 가장 적절하다.

14 여자의 마지막 말에 대한 남자의 응답
정답률 70% ▶ 정답 ④

M: Hi, Tara. What are you looking at?
W: Hi, Dan. I'm reading a post about an online debate competition.
   게시물   온라인 토론 대회
M: Oh, it sounds interesting. Are you going to participate?
   참가하다
W: I want to, but it's a team competition. Why don't we make a team
   단체전
   and enter together? You're a great debater.
   참가하다   토론자
M: Thanks, I'm flattered. But debating online is new to me. I'm not
   sure if I can do it well.

W: Don't worry. Everything is basically the same except it's taking
기본적으로 ~을 제외하고는
place online. You'll get used to it with a little bit of practice.
열리는(take place) ~에 익숙해지다 연습
M: I see. I'll enter with you then. When's the competition?
W: It's a month away. We have plenty of time to prepare.
충분한 준비하다
M: I guess we need to practice online, right? But my laptop isn't
working at the moment.
작동하는(work) 지금
W: No problem. You can do it on your smartphone.
M: (Then I should get used to using it for debating.)

해석
남: 안녕, Tara. 무엇을 보고 있니?
여: 안녕, Dan. 나는 온라인 토론 대회에 관한 게시물을 읽고 있어.
남: 오, 재미있을 것 같아. 너 참가할 거야?
여: 하고 싶은데, 단체전이야. 우리 팀을 만들어서 함께 참가하는 게 어때? 너는 훌륭한 토론
   자잖아.
남: 고마워, 과찬이야. 하지만 온라인으로 토론하는 것은 나에게 생소해. 내가 그것을 잘 할 수
   있을지 모르겠어.
여: 걱정하지 마. 온라인에서 열린다는 점을 제외하고는 모든 것이 기본적으로 똑같아. 너는
   조금만 연습하면 익숙해질 거야.
남: 그렇구나. 그럼 너와 함께 참가할게. 대회는 언제야?
여: 한 달 남았어. 우리는 준비할 충분한 시간이 있어.
남: 우리는 온라인으로 연습해야 할 것 같아, 그렇지? 그런데 지금 내 노트북 컴퓨터가 작동
   하지 않아.
여: 문제 없어. 네 스마트폰으로 그것을 할 수 있거든.
남: (그럼 나는 토론을 위해 그것을 사용하는 데 익숙해져야겠구나.)
① 나는 그렇게 생각하지 않아. 대회는 겨우 일주일 남았어.
② 물론이지. 우리는 시험을 준비하는 데 집중하는 게 좋겠어.
③ 그래서 나는 지난 온라인 토론 대회에서 그것을 사용했어.
☑ 그럼 나는 토론을 위해 그것을 사용하는 데 익숙해져야겠구나.
⑤ 걱정하지 마. 나는 이미 내 노트북 컴퓨터를 수리했어.

15 다음 상황에서 Lisa가 Kevin에게 할 말
정답률 75% ▶ 정답 ②

W: Lisa and Kevin are reporters for the school newspaper. They
기자들
decided to interview Mr. Jackson, the new history teacher, for the
인터뷰하기로 결정했다 역사 교사
(decide to V: ~하기로 결정하다, interview: 인터뷰하다)
next issue. Kevin suggests that they take a photo of him to put in
(정기 간행물의) 호 제안하다 ~의 사진을 찍다
their interview article. Lisa knows that Kevin is good at drawing
기사 잘 그리다
(be good at V-ing: ~을 잘하다, draw: 그리다)
caricatures and that he often draws teachers and students. She
캐리커처들
has seen the caricature of Mr. Jackson that Kevin drew. So she
thinks that it'll be better to put the caricature in the article, instead
of a photo, because caricatures can be more appealing than
~ 대신에 더 매력적인
photos. Lisa wants to suggest to Kevin that they use his work. In
this situation, what would Lisa most likely say to Kevin?
작품
Lisa: (Let's put your caricature of Mr. Jackson in the article.)

해석
여: Lisa와 Kevin은 학교 신문의 기자이다. 그들은 다음 호를 위해 새로 온 역사 교사인
   Jackson 선생님을 인터뷰하기로 결정했다. Kevin은 인터뷰 기사에 넣을 그의 사진을 찍
   을 것을 제안한다. Lisa는 Kevin이 캐리커처를 잘 그리고 그가 종종 선생님들과 학생들을
   그린다는 것을 알고 있다. 그녀는 Kevin이 그린 Jackson 선생님의 캐리커처를 본 적이 있
   다. 그래서 그녀는 사진 대신에 기사에 캐리커처를 넣는 것이 더 나을 것이라고 생각하는
   데, 캐리커처가 사진보다 더 매력적일 수 있기 때문이다. Lisa는 Kevin에게 그들이 그의 작
   품을 사용할 것을 제안하고 싶다. 이러한 상황에서, Lisa는 Kevin에게 뭐라고 말하겠는가?
Lisa: (기사에 네가 그린 Jackson 선생님의 캐리커처를 넣자.)
① 우리 새로 온 역사 선생님을 인터뷰하는 게 어때?
☑ 기사에 네가 그린 Jackson 선생님의 캐리커처를 넣자.
③ 우리는 캐리커처 대회에 대한 기사를 써야 해.
④ 나는 네가 학생들의 캐리커처를 더 그릴 수 있는지 궁금해.
⑤ 인터뷰하는 동안에 Jackson 선생님의 사진을 찍는 게 어때?

16~17 1지문 2문항

M: Hello, class. Let's continue to talk about different cultures around
계속 이야기하다 문화들
(continue to V: 계속 ~하다)
the world. People celebrate the New Year in various ways. In Spain,
기념하다 다양한
it's customary to eat 12 grapes at midnight on New Year's Eve.
관례의 자정에
Each grape represents good luck for one month of the coming
나타내다 행운
year. In Denmark, people greet the New Year by throwing old plates
맞이하다 던짐으로써 접시들
(by V-ing: ~함으로써, throw: 던지다)
and glasses against the doors of family and friends. They believe
유리잔들
it'll get rid of the bad spirits. They also stand on chairs and jump
~을 없애다 나쁜 기운들 ~위에 서다 ~에서 뛰어내리다
off them together at midnight to "leap" into January. In Mexico,
도약하다
residents carry empty suitcases around the block. Mexicans
주민들 빈 여행가방들
believe that doing so will bring travel and adventure in the coming
여행 모험
year. In Greece, an onion is traditionally hung on the front door of
전통적으로 걸리다
(traditionally: 전통적으로, hang: 걸다)
homes on New Year's Eve as a symbol of rebirth. On New Year's
상징으로 부활
Day, parents wake their children by tapping them on the head
깨우다 가볍게 두드림으로써
(tap: 가볍게 두드리다)
with the onion. Now let's watch some video clips of these unique
동영상들 독특한
traditions.
전통들

해석
남: 안녕하세요, 학생 여러분. 전 세계의 다른 문화들에 대해 계속 이야기해 봅시다. 사람들은
   다양한 방법들로 새해를 기념합니다. 스페인에서는, 새해 전야의 자정에 12알의 포도를
   먹는 것이 관례입니다. 각각의 포도알은 다가오는 해의 한 달에 대한 행운을 나타냅니다.
   덴마크에서는, 사람들이 가족과 친구들의 문에 오래된 접시와 유리잔을 던짐으로써 새해
   를 맞이합니다. 그들은 그것이 나쁜 기운을 없앨 것이라고 믿습니다. 그들은 또한 1월로
   '도약하기' 위해서 자정에 함께 의자 위에 서 있다가 의자에서 뛰어내립니다. 멕시코에서
   는, 주민들이 빈 여행가방을 가지고 동네를 돌아다닙니다. 멕시코 사람들은 그렇게 하는
   것이 다가오는 해에 여행과 모험을 가져올 것이라고 믿습니다. 그리스에서는, 양파가 전
   통적으로 새해 전야에 부활의 상징으로 집의 현관에 걸립니다. 새해 첫날에, 부모들은 그
   양파로 아이들의 머리를 가볍게 두드림으로써 그들을 깨웁니다. 이제 이러한 독특한 전통
   들에 대한 몇몇 동영상을 봅시다.

16 남자가 하는 말의 주제
정답률 85% ▶ 정답 ④

① 세계적으로 인기 있는 독특한 현지 음식들
② 새해 첫날 가족 모임의 중요성
③ 여러 문화에 걸쳐 가장 흔한 새해 결심들
☑ 전 세계의 새해를 기념하는 다양한 방법들
⑤ 여러 나라의 전통 요리법을 보존하기 위한 노력들

17 언급된 나라가 아닌 것
정답률 85% ▶ 정답 ④

① 스페인 ② 덴마크 ③ 멕시코
☑ 프랑스 ⑤ 그리스

11 2021년 6월 학력평가

01	③	02	③	03	②	04	④	05	①
06	②	07	②	08	④	09	④	10	②
11	④	12	⑤	13	①	14	⑤	15	④
16	①	17	③						

01 여자가 하는 말의 목적

정답률 90%
▶ 정답 ③

W: Good morning, Staton High School students! This is Jessica McQueen, the vice principal. As you know, tomorrow, two vending machines will be installed next to the school library. Now, I'd like to inform you of the rules you have to follow when using them. First, use them only during break times. You can not use them as an excuse for being late for classes. Second, after eating or drinking, throw trash away in the trash can. No one wants a dirty school. Third, do not kick or push the vending machines. If they don't work, just call the number on the machine. Please keep these rules in mind. Thank you.

해석
여: 안녕하세요, Staton 고등학교 학생 여러분! 저는 교감인 Jessica McQueen입니다. 여러분도 알다시피, 내일 학교 도서관 옆에 두 대의 자판기가 설치될 것입니다. 이제, 여러분께 그것들을 사용할 때 따라야 하는 규칙들을 알려드리고자 합니다. 첫째, 쉬는 시간에만 그것들을 사용하십시오. 수업에 늦었다는 핑계로 그것들을 사용할 수 없습니다. 둘째, 먹거나 마신 후에, 쓰레기통에 쓰레기를 버리십시오. 아무도 더러운 학교를 원하지 않습니다. 셋째, 자판기를 발로 차거나 밀지 마십시오. 그것들이 작동하지 않으면, 자판기 위에 있는 번호로 전화하십시오. 이 규칙들을 명심하십시오. 감사합니다.

① 도서관의 새로운 행사를 홍보하려고
② 자판기 관리 도우미 학생을 모집하려고
③ 자판기 사용 시 규칙에 대해 안내하려고
④ 자판기 설치 일정이 연기된 것을 알리려고
⑤ 학교 식당을 깨끗이 사용할 것을 당부하려고

02 남자의 의견

정답률 90%
▶ 정답 ③

W: Dylan, what are you doing?
M: I'm learning about the history of Rome.
W: Hmm... But you are reading a comic book, aren't you?
M: Yes, it's a comic book about history. It's very helpful.
W: I think reading a general history book would be more helpful.
M: Maybe. But learning history through comic books has many good points.
W: Why do you think so?
M: Comic books use pictures to convey information, so you can understand historical events more easily and remember them for a long time.
W: That makes sense. Anything else?
M: Most importantly, comic books are interesting to read.
W: I see. Then I'll give it a try.

해석
여: Dylan, 무엇을 하고 있니?
남: 로마 역사에 대해 배우고 있어.
여: 흠... 그런데 너는 만화책을 읽고 있구나, 그렇지 않니?
남: 그래, 역사에 관한 만화책이야. 그것은 매우 도움이 돼.
여: 내 생각에는 일반적인 역사책을 읽는 것이 더 도움이 될 것 같아.
남: 그럴지도 모르지. 하지만 만화책을 통해 역사를 배우는 것은 좋은 점이 많아.
여: 왜 그렇게 생각하니?
남: 만화책은 정보를 전달하기 위해 그림들을 이용해서, 역사적인 사건들을 더 쉽게 이해할 수 있고 그것들을 오랫동안 기억할 수 있어.
여: 그거 일리가 있네. 또 다른 건 없니?
남: 가장 중요한 것은, 만화책은 읽기에 재미있다는 거야.
여: 그렇구나. 그럼 나도 한번 해 볼게.

① 올바른 역사관을 가지는 것이 중요하다.
② 암기력은 학습 효과를 높이는 데 중요한 요인이다.
③ 역사 만화책을 읽는 것이 역사 공부에 도움이 된다.
④ 다양한 주제의 독서를 통해 창의력을 키울 수 있다.
⑤ 만화 그리기는 아이들의 상상력을 풍부하게 해 준다.

03 두 사람의 관계

정답률 85%
▶ 정답 ②

W: Hi, Mr. Williams.
M: Hi, Ms. Brown. Thanks for inviting me.
W: We're honored to meet you today. I heard that you've been cooking for more than 30 years.
M: Yes. I've studied ways to make Italian dishes more delicious since 1990.
W: That's amazing. Actually, many viewers have been asking for pasta recipes.
M: Great. I'll teach you how to make tomato bacon pasta today.
W: Isn't that one of the most popular dishes in your restaurant?
M: Right. I'll let you know how to make delicious pasta in an easy way.
W: Fantastic! Also, the recipe will be uploaded to our website after the show.
M: That will be helpful for the viewers who miss the show.
W: Great. Can you tell me what to prepare for the dish?
M: All you need is bacon, tomatoes, pasta, and olive oil.
W: Okay. Let's start cooking!

해석
여: 안녕하세요, Williams 씨.
남: 안녕하세요, Brown 씨. 초대해 주셔서 감사해요.
여: 오늘 만나 뵙게 되어 영광이에요. 당신은 30년 이상 요리를 해 오시고 있다고 들었어요.
남: 네. 1990년 이후로 이탈리아 요리를 더 맛있게 만드는 방법을 연구해 왔어요.
여: 놀랍네요. 사실, 많은 시청자들이 파스타 조리법을 요청해 오고 있어요.
남: 좋아요. 제가 오늘 토마토 베이컨 피스타를 만드는 방법을 가르쳐 드릴게요.
여: 그것은 당신의 식당에서 가장 인기 있는 요리 중 하나가 아닌가요?
남: 맞아요. 제가 맛있는 파스타를 쉽게 만드는 방법을 알려드릴게요.
여: 멋지네요! 또한, 조리법은 쇼가 끝난 후에 저희 웹사이트에 업로드될 거예요.
남: 그것은 쇼를 놓친 시청자들에게 도움이 될 거예요.
여: 좋아요. 요리를 위해 무엇을 준비해야 할지 알려주시겠어요?
남: 필요한 것은 베이컨, 토마토, 파스타, 그리고 올리브 오일뿐이에요.
여: 알겠어요. 요리를 시작합시다!

① 신문 기자 — 화가
② 방송 진행자 — 요리사
③ 식료품점 직원 — 농부
④ 촬영 감독 — 배우
⑤ 식당 주인 — 손님

04 그림에서 대화의 내용과 일치하지 않는 것

정답률 85%
▶ 정답 ④

W: Tom, I couldn't attend the school club festival last week. How did it go?
M: It went great. Do you want to see a picture of my club's booth?
W: Sure. The banner hanging on the wall looks good.
M: Thanks. Do you recognize the drawing of the car above the chair?

W: That's Tina's work. I saw her drawing it earlier.
<u>작품</u>
M: You're right. What do you think about the <u>flower vase</u> on the table? I made it.
<u>꽃병</u>
W: You did a great job. By the way, why is there a <u>soccer ball</u> on the floor?
<u>축구공</u> <u>바닥</u>
M: That was for <u>visitors</u> to paint. See, those children are painting it.
<u>방문객들</u>
W: That must have been a fun <u>experience</u>. Oh, look at the <u>bird sculpture</u> on the shelf! It seems so real!
<u>경험</u> <u>새 조각상</u> <u>선반</u>
M: That's Kevin's <u>artwork</u>. He got a prize for it.
<u>예술 작품</u>
W: Everything looks perfect. I wish I could have been there, too.

해석

여: Tom, 나는 지난주에 학교 동아리 축제에 참석하지 못했어. 그것은 어떻게 됐니?
남: 아주 잘 됐어. 우리 동아리 부스의 사진을 보고 싶니?
여: 물론이지. 벽에 걸린 현수막이 좋아 보인다.
남: 고마워. 의자의 위쪽에 있는 자동차 그림을 알아보겠니?
여: 그것은 Tina의 작품이잖아. 전에 그녀가 그것을 그리는 것을 봤어.
남: 네 말이 맞아. 테이블 위에 있는 꽃병에 대해 어떻게 생각해? 내가 만들었어.
여: 정말 잘 만들었다. 그런데, 왜 축구공이 바닥에 있니?
남: 그것은 방문객이 그리도록 하기 위한 거야. 봐, 저 아이들이 그것을 그리고 있잖아.
여: 분명 재미있는 경험이었겠다. 오, 선반 위에 있는 새 조각상을 봐! 정말 진짜 같아!
남: 그것은 Kevin의 예술 작품이야. 그는 그것으로 상을 받았어.
여: 모든 것이 완벽해 보여. 나도 거기에 갔으면 좋았을 텐데.

05   여자가 할 일
정답률 85%
▶ 정답 ①

W: Steven, the <u>baseball final</u> is coming up next week. I'm so excited.
<u>야구 결승전</u>
M: Me, too. Let's check what we need to prepare to <u>cheer for</u> our team.
<u>~를 응원하다</u>
W: Okay. Did you <u>order</u> small <u>flags</u> to <u>wave</u>?
<u>주문하다</u> <u>깃발들</u> <u>흔들다</u>
M: Sure, they were <u>delivered</u> yesterday.
<u>배송되었다(deliver: 배송하다)</u>
W: Good. Didn't you say you were going to write our team name on the flags?
M: Right, I did it with my brother this morning.
W: Well done. How about songs to cheer on our team?
M: Don't worry. I've <u>already</u> chosen <u>several</u> songs.
<u>이미</u> <u>몇 개의</u>
W: Wow, you've done a lot. Is there anything I can help with?
M: There is one thing <u>left</u>. We need to buy <u>hairbands</u>.
<u>남은(leave: 남기다)</u> <u>머리띠들</u>
W: I can do that. I'll buy <u>colorful</u> and <u>stylish</u> ones.
<u>화려한</u> <u>멋진</u>
M: Great! I hope our team will win the game.

해석

여: Steven, 야구 결승전이 다음 주에 열릴 거야. 나는 너무 흥분돼.
남: 나도 그래. 우리 팀을 응원하기 위해 무엇을 준비해야 하는지 확인해 보자.
여: 알았어. 흔들기 위한 작은 깃발들을 주문했니?
남: 물론이지, 그것들은 어제 배송되었어.
여: 좋아. 너는 깃발에 우리 팀 이름을 쓸 거라고 말하지 않았니?
남: 맞아, 오늘 아침에 남동생이랑 했어.
여: 잘했어. 우리 팀을 응원할 노래는 어때?
남: 걱정하지 마. 내가 이미 몇 곡을 골랐어.

여: 와, 너는 정말 많은 일을 했구나. 내가 도울 수 있는 일이 있을까?
남: 한 가지가 남아 있어. 우리는 머리띠를 사야 해.
여: 내가 할 수 있어. 화려하고 멋진 것들로 살게.
남: 좋아! 나는 우리 팀이 경기에서 이겼으면 좋겠어.

✔️ 머리띠 사기
② 깃발 주문하기
③ 응원가 고르기
④ 깃발에 팀 이름 쓰기
⑤ 남동생에게 도움 요청하기

06   남자가 지불할 금액
정답률 70%
▶ 정답 ②

W: Hello. May I help you?
M: Yes. I want to buy some toys for my children.
W: We have a <u>wide selection</u> of toys. Come and look around.
<u>다양하게 엄선해 놓은</u>
M: What kind of robots are popular <u>these days</u>?
<u>요즘</u>
W: I'm sure your kids would love this robot. It <u>appeared in</u> a TV series <u>recently</u>. It's $100.
<u>~에 나왔다</u> <u>최근에</u>
M: It's so <u>expensive</u>. Anything else?
<u>비싼</u>
W: This toy car is last year's model, but it moves by <u>remote control</u>. It <u>costs</u> $60.
<u>리모컨</u> <u>(값·비용이) ~이다</u>
M: I like it. Do you have any other good things?
W: The newest speaking doll <u>was released</u> yesterday.
<u>출시되었다(release: 출시하다)</u>
M: It looks cute. How much is it?
W: It's $80, but you can <u>get 50% off</u> on this doll today.
<u>~에 50% 할인을 받다</u>
M: Excellent! Then I'll buy one toy car and one speaking doll. I'll <u>pay</u> for them by credit card.
<u>지불하다</u>
W: Thank you.

해석

여: 안녕하세요. 도와드릴까요?
남: 네. 제 아이들을 위한 장난감을 좀 사고 싶어요.
여: 다양하게 엄선해 놓은 장난감이 있어요. 오셔서 둘러보세요.
남: 요즘 어떤 종류의 로봇이 인기가 있나요?
여: 저는 고객님의 자녀들이 이 로봇을 좋아할 거라고 확신해요. 그것은 최근에 한 TV 시리즈에 나왔거든요. 100달러예요.
남: 너무 비싸네요. 다른 건 없나요?
여: 이 장난감 자동차는 작년 모델이지만, 리모컨으로 움직여요. 60달러예요.
남: 마음에 드네요. 다른 좋은 상품들이 있나요?
여: 최신형 말하는 인형이 어제 출시되었어요.
남: 귀여워 보이네요. 얼마죠?
여: 80달러인데, 오늘 이 인형에 50% 할인을 받으실 수 있어요.
남: 잘됐네요! 그럼 장난감 자동차 한 개와 말하는 인형 한 개를 살게요. 신용카드로 지불할게요.
여: 감사합니다.

① $70   ✔️ $100   ③ $140
④ $160   ⑤ $180

문제 풀이

남자는 60달러인 장난감 자동차 한 개와 80달러인 말하는 인형 한 개를 사기로 했는데, 말하는 인형은 50% 할인을 받을 수 있다고 했으므로 40달러이다. 따라서 남자가 지불할 금액은 60달러 + 40달러로 답은 ② '$100'이다.

07   여자가 영화관에 갈 수 없는 이유
정답률 90%
▶ 정답 ②

M: Hi, Jessi. How was the <u>test</u>?
<u>시험</u>
W: It wasn't that <u>difficult</u>. <u>Anyway</u>, I'm glad that it's over.
<u>어려운</u> <u>어쨌든</u>
M: Right, now we need to <u>reward</u> ourselves. Why don't we <u>go to the movies</u>?
<u>보상을 하다</u> <u>영화를 보러 가다</u>
W: Sure, I'd love to.
M: How about going to a <u>cinema</u> this Saturday? There are a lot of new movies.
<u>영화관</u>

W: Sorry, I can't make it that day.

M: Why? Do you have to prepare your presentation for biology class?
발표 / 생물학 수업

W: No, I finished it yesterday.

M: Ah, you said your mother's birthday is coming up, right?

W: Actually, her birthday is next week.

M: Then, what are you doing on Saturday?

W: I planned a camping trip with my family for that day.
계획했다(plan) / 캠핑 여행

M: Oh, I see. Have a good time with your family. We can watch a movie some other time.

해석

남: 안녕, Jessi. 시험은 어땠니?

여: 그렇게 어렵지는 않았어. 어쨌든, 시험이 끝나서 기뻐.

남: 맞아, 이제 우리는 우리 자신에게 보상을 해야 해. 우리 영화를 보러 가는 게 어때?

여: 물론, 가고 싶어.

남: 이번 주 토요일에 영화관에 가는 게 어때? 새로운 영화들이 많이 있어.

여: 미안해, 나는 그날 갈 수 없어.

남: 왜? 생물학 수업을 위한 발표를 준비해야 하니?

여: 아니, 그것은 어제 끝냈어.

남: 아, 네 어머니 생신이 다가오고 있다고 했잖아, 그렇지?

여: 사실, 어머니 생신은 다음 주야.

남: 그럼, 토요일에 무엇을 할 거야?

여: 그날 가족과 함께 캠핑 여행을 계획했어.

남: 오, 그렇구나. 가족과 즐거운 시간을 보내. 우리는 다음에 영화를 보면 돼.

① 시험이 끝나지 않아서
✓② 가족들과 캠핑을 가야 해서
③ 어머니 생일 파티가 있어서
④ 프레젠테이션을 준비해야 해서
⑤ 영화 티켓을 구할 수가 없어서

---

08 Friday Night Walk에 관해 언급되지 않은 것

정답률 85% ▶ 정답 ④

M: Honey, check out this poster. Friday Night Walk is going to be held this month.
금요일 밤 걷기 / 열리다(hold: 열다)

W: Friday Night Walk? Is it walking through the city at night?

M: Well, yes. But its purpose is to raise money for children's hospitals.
목적 / 기금을 모으다 / 아동 병원들

W: That's meaningful. And we can enjoy the beautiful city views at night. Why don't we join it?
의미가 있는

M: All right. Let's do it.

W: Great. Look. There are two walking courses we can choose from, a 5km course and a 10km one.
걷기 코스들

M: Hmm... How about the 10km one? It would be a lot more exercise.
훨씬 더 많은 운동이 되다

W: Good idea. The participation fee is $20 for the 10km course.
참가비

M: I see. How can we sign up for the event?
~에 참가 신청을 하다 / 행사

W: It says we must register on their website.
등록하다

M: Okay. Let's register right away.

해석

남: 여보, 이 포스터를 봐요. Friday Night Walk(금요일 밤 걷기)가 이번 달에 열릴 예정이에요.

여: Friday Night Walk? 밤에 시내를 걷는 거예요?

남: 음, 네. 하지만 그것의 목적은 아동 병원을 위한 기금을 모으는 거예요.

여: 의미가 있네요. 그리고 밤에 아름다운 도시 경치를 즐길 수 있잖아요. 우리 참가하는 게 어때요?

남: 알았어요. 그렇게 합시다.

여: 좋아요. 봐요. 우리가 선택할 수 있는 두 개의 걷기 코스가 있는데, 5km 코스와 10km 코스네요.

남: 흠... 10km 코스는 어때요? 그것이 훨씬 더 많은 운동이 될 거예요.

여: 좋은 생각이에요. 참가비는 10km 코스가 20달러예요.

남: 그렇군요. 어떻게 그 행사에 참가 신청을 할 수 있나요?

여: 웹사이트에서 등록해야 한다고 되어 있어요.

남: 알았어요. 당장 등록합시다.

① 행사 목적   ② 코스 종류   ③ 참가비
✓④ 기념품   ⑤ 신청 방법

---

09 Advanced English Reading Camp에 관한 내용과 일치하지 않는 것

정답률 80% ▶ 정답 ④

M: Good afternoon. I'm Michael Lee, the manager of the City Library.
관리자

We'll be hosting an Advanced English Reading Camp this summer
주최하는(host) / 고급 영어 독서 캠프

vacation. It will be held for three days from August 6th to August
개최되다(hold: 개최하다)

8th at the City Library. During the camp, you will read original
원작들

written works by Shakespeare and discuss given issues in English.
토론하다 / 주제들

Two native English-speaking teachers will join the camp and lead
영어 원어민 교사들 / 이끌다

the discussions. To take part in the camp, you must register online
토론들 / ~에 참가하다 / 등록하다

at our library's website in advance. You can join us for free if you
사전에 / 무료로

are a member of our library, but if you are not a member, you'll
회원

have to pay $15. We're limiting the number of participants to a
제한하는(limit) / 참가자들

maximum of 20 people, so I recommend you hurry and sign up.
서두르다 / 신청하다

Thank you.

해석

남: 안녕하세요. 저는 시립 도서관의 관리자인 Michael Lee입니다. 저희는 이번 여름 방학에 Advanced English Reading Camp(고급 영어 독서 캠프)를 주최할 예정입니다. 그것은 8월 6일부터 8월 8일까지 3일 동안 시립 도서관에서 개최될 것입니다. 캠프 기간 동안, 여러분은 셰익스피어의 원작들을 읽고 주어진 주제들에 대해 영어로 토론할 것입니다. 영어 원어민 교사 2명이 캠프에 참석하여 토론을 이끌 것입니다. 캠프에 참가하기 위해서는, 저희 도서관 웹사이트에서 사전에 온라인으로 등록하셔야 합니다. 저희 도서관 회원이시면 무료로 저희와 함께 하실 수 있지만, 회원이 아니면 15달러를 지불하셔야 합니다. 참가자의 수를 최대 20명으로 제한하고 있으니, 서둘러서 신청하실 것을 추천합니다. 감사합니다.

① 8월 6일부터 8일까지 개최된다.
② 영어 원어민 교사 2명이 참석한다.
③ 온라인으로 사전 등록을 해야 한다.
✓④ 누구나 무료로 참가할 수 있다.
⑤ 참가 인원은 최대 20명으로 제한된다.

문제풀이

시립 도서관의 회원이라면 도서관이 주최하는 고급 영어 독서 캠프에 무료로 참가할 수 있지만, 회원이 아닌 사람은 참가비 15달러를 지불해야 한다고 했으므로 일치하지 않는 내용은 ④ '누구나 무료로 참가할 수 있다.'이다.

---

10 표에서 두 사람이 구입할 책장

정답률 80% ▶ 정답 ②

W: Honey, look at this flyer. This store has bookcases on sale.
전단지 / 책장들 / 할인 판매 중인

M: Great. It may be a good chance to replace our old bookcase.
기회 / 교체하다

W: Let's see. [Pause] We should not choose the plastic one. It is likely to break easily.
부서질 것 같다
(be likely to V: ~할 것 같다, break: 부서지다)

M: You're right. And, how many shelves do we need?
선반들

W: Not many. We don't have that many books, so three or four would be enough.
충분한

M: I agree. Let's choose the color now.

W: I think a red bookcase would be pretty and colorful.
예쁜

M: Red is good, but it doesn't match our furniture. White would be a better choice.
어울리다 / 가구

W: Good point. Then, we have only two options left.

M: We've already spent a lot of money decorating the house. Why
이미 꾸미는 데 많은 돈을 썼다
(spend A V-ing: ~하는 데 A를 쓰다, decorate: 꾸미다)

don't we buy the cheaper one?

W: Okay. Then let's buy this one.

해석

여: 여보, 이 전단지를 봐요. 이 가게에서 책장을 할인 판매 중이에요.

남: 잘됐네요. 우리의 오래된 책장을 교체할 좋은 기회일지도 몰라요.

여: 어디 봐요. [잠시 후] 플라스틱 책장을 선택하면 안 돼요. 그것은 쉽게 부서질 것 같아요.

남: 당신 말이 맞아요. 그리고 우리 몇 개의 선반이 필요하죠?

여: 많이 필요하지는 않아요. 그렇게 많은 책이 있지 않아서, 3개나 4개면 충분할 거예요.
남: 동의해요. 이제 색상을 골라 봐요.
여: 빨간색 책장이 예쁘고 화려할 것 같아요.
남: 빨간색은 좋지만, 우리 가구와 어울리지 않아요. 흰색이 더 나은 선택일 것 같아요.
여: 좋은 지적이에요. 그럼, 두 개의 선택지만 남았네요.
남: 우리는 이미 집을 꾸미는 데 많은 돈을 썼어요. 우리 더 싼 것을 사는 게 어때요?
여: 좋아요. 그럼 이것을 사요.

책장

모델	재질	선반의 수	색상	가격
① A	플라스틱	3	흰색	40달러
✔ B	금속	3	흰색	50달러
③ C	금속	4	빨간색	60달러
④ D	나무	4	흰색	80달러
⑤ E	나무	5	빨간색	100달러

11 남자의 마지막 말에 대한 여자의 응답

정답률 85%
▶ 정답 ④

M: Mom, are you going somewhere?
W: I'm going to buy some groceries for dinner. Can you come with me
   식료품들
   and help?
M: Sure. But I have to change my clothes. Could you wait for a minute?
   옷을 갈아입다   기다리다
W: (No problem. Tell me when you're ready.)
                                준비된

해석
남: 엄마, 어디 가세요?
여: 저녁 식사를 위해 식료품을 좀 살 거야. 나와 같이 가서 도와 줄래?
남: 물론이죠. 하지만 옷을 갈아입어야 해요. 잠시만 기다려 주시겠어요?
여: (그래. 네가 준비되면 내게 말해줘.)
① 당연하지. 나는 그녀를 도울 것을 약속해.
② 아니. 나는 근처에서 옷 가게를 찾을 수 없어.
③ 미안해. 나는 지금 저녁 식사를 준비하느라 바빠.
✔ 그래. 네가 준비되면 내게 말해줘.
⑤ 좋아. 내가 내일 네가 부탁한 것을 살게.

12 여자의 마지막 말에 대한 남자의 응답

정답률 80%
▶ 정답 ⑤

W: I have big news. I'm getting married next month.
                         결혼하는(get married)
M: Congratulations! You must be really busy these days.
                                     바쁜
W: I am. Here, this card is an invitation for you. I hope you can come.
                              초대장
M: (Absolutely. I'm excited to see you in your wedding dress.)
                                            웨딩드레스

해석
여: 큰 뉴스가 있어. 나 다음 달에 결혼해.
남: 축하해! 요즘에 정말 바쁘겠구나.
여: 그래. 여기, 이 카드는 너를 위한 초대장이야. 네가 올 수 있으면 좋겠어.
남: (당연하지. 웨딩드레스를 입은 너를 보게 되어 흥분돼.)
① 와! 신혼여행에서 돌아온 걸 환영해.
② 좋아. 내 친구들이 내게 이 생일 카드를 줬어.
③ 미안해. 나는 네가 지난달에 결혼했다는 것을 잊을 뻔했어.
④ 유감이야. 네 감기가 나았으면 좋겠다.
✔ 당연하지. 웨딩드레스를 입은 너를 보게 되어 흥분돼.

13 남자의 마지막 말에 대한 여자의 응답

정답률 80%
▶ 정답 ①

W: Hello, Jake. How is your job search going?
                            구직 활동
M: I'll have a job interview with the ABC Company in three days. But
                취업 면접
   the interview will be online.
W: Oh, I've done a job interview online before.
M: Really? Can you give me some advice?
                                  조언
W: It's important to make a good impression. So, you should have
                        좋은 인상을 주다

clear video and sound.
       영상   음향
M: How can I do that?
W: You need a high-quality camera and a good microphone. I bought
              고품질의   카메라   마이크
   those things and they were helpful.
                           도움이 되는
M: Sounds good. I want to buy them too, but I don't have much money.
W: You can buy them at a discounted price online, but they will take
                        할인된 가격
   several days to arrive.
               도착하다
M: Oh, no... Is there any other way to get them?
W: (If you want, you can borrow mine.)
                          빌리다

해석
여: 안녕, Jake. 구직 활동은 어떻게 되어 가니?
남: 3일 후에 ABC사에서 취업 면접을 볼 거야. 그런데 그 면접은 온라인으로 진행될 거야.
여: 오, 나는 전에 온라인으로 취업 면접을 본 적이 있어.
남: 정말? 나에게 조언을 좀 해줄래?
여: 좋은 인상을 주는 것이 중요해. 그러니까, 깨끗한 영상과 음향을 갖추어야 해.
남: 그것을 어떻게 할 수 있어?
여: 고품질의 카메라와 좋은 마이크가 필요해. 나는 그 물건들을 샀는데 그것들이 도움이 되었어.
남: 좋은 생각이야. 나도 그것들을 사고 싶지만, 돈이 별로 없어.
여: 온라인에서 할인된 가격으로 살 수 있지만, 도착하는 데 며칠이 걸릴 거야.
남: 오, 이런... 그것들을 구할 다른 방법이 있을까?
여: (네가 원한다면, 내 것을 빌릴 수 있어.)
✔ 네가 원한다면, 내 것을 빌릴 수 있어.
② 내 마이크는 네 것과 달라.
③ 음, 네 소포는 이미 도착했어.
④ 좋은 첫인상을 주는 것이 중요해.
⑤ 말도 안 돼. 이것은 내가 제안할 수 있는 최저 가격이야.

14 여자의 마지막 말에 대한 남자의 응답

정답률 85%
▶ 정답 ⑤

M: Kate, you look depressed. What's wrong?
                    우울한
W: I had a medical check-up at the hospital yesterday and got a bad
          건강 검진
   result.
   결과
M: Sorry to hear that. What did the doctor say?
W: The doctor said I have high cholesterol, so I need to do more
                              콜레스테롤   운동을 더 하다
   exercise.
M: Everyone should exercise. I recommend you take swimming
                              추천하다   수영 강습을 받다
   lessons at the sports center near your house.
W: I'd like to, but these days I don't have any extra time for the lessons.
                                            여분의
M: Then, how about going to work on foot or by bicycle?
W: Good idea, but my company is too far from home to walk there.
                              집에서 너무 멀어서 걸어갈 수 없는
                              (too A to V: 너무 A해서 ~할 수 없는)
M: If so, why don't you try riding a bicycle?
                              타보다
                    (try V-ing: ~해보다, ride: (탈것에) 타다)
W: That would be great, but I don't know how to do that.
                                        하는 방법
                              (how to V: ~하는 방법)
M: (Don't worry. I can teach you how to ride a bicycle.)

해석
남: Kate, 너 우울해 보여. 무슨 일 있니?
여: 어제 병원에서 건강 검진을 받았는데 결과가 안 좋아.
남: 안됐구나. 의사 선생님이 뭐라고 했어?
여: 의사 선생님이 내가 콜레스테롤이 높아서 운동을 더 해야 한다고 말씀하셨어.
남: 누구나 운동을 해야 해. 나는 네가 너희 집 근처에 있는 스포츠 센터에서 수영 강습을 받을 것을 추천해.
여: 그러고 싶지만, 요즘에 나는 강습을 받을 여분의 시간이 없어.
남: 그럼, 도보나 자전거로 출근하는 건 어떠니?
여: 좋은 생각이지만, 내 회사는 집에서 너무 멀어서 그곳까지 걸어갈 수 없어.
남: 그렇다면, 자전거를 타보는 건 어떠니?
여: 그렇게 하면 좋겠지만, 그것을 하는 방법을 모르겠어.
남: (걱정하지 마. 내가 너에게 자전거를 타는 방법을 가르쳐 줄 수 있어.)
① 늦었어. 너는 대신 택시를 타야 해.

② 잘됐다. 수영은 너를 더 건강하게 만들어 줄 거야.
③ 네 말이 맞아. 걷는 것이 자전거를 타는 것보다 더 나아.
④ 그렇다면, 너는 수리점에 가서 그것을 고쳐야 해.
✔ 걱정하지 마. 내가 너에게 자전거를 타는 방법을 가르쳐 줄 수 있어.

문제 풀이
회사와 집의 거리가 멀어서 도보로 출근하는 것은 불가능하다는 여자의 말에 남자는 자전거를 탈 것을 권유했다. 여자가 자전거로 출근하고 싶지만 탈 줄 모른다고 했으므로 이에 대한 남자의 응답으로는 ⑤ 'Don't worry. I can teach you how to ride a bicycle.(걱정하지 마. 내가 너에게 자전거를 타는 방법을 가르쳐 줄 수 있어.)'가 가장 적절하다.

15 다음 상황에서 Lucy가 Mike에게 할 말
정답률 80% ▶ 정답 ④

W: Lucy and Mike are a <u>married couple</u>. Lucy has traveled <u>overseas</u>
부부   해외로
many times, but Mike has no <u>experience</u> with <u>overseas</u> trips.
경험   해외
One day, for their <u>summer vacation</u>, Lucy and Mike <u>decided to</u>
여름 휴가   여행을 가기로 결정했다
(decide to V: ~하기로 결정하다, take a trip: 여행을 가다)
<u>take a trip</u> to Australia for two weeks. While talking about <u>what to</u>
무엇을 준비해야 할지
(what to V: 무엇을 ~해야 할지, prepare: 준비하다)
<u>prepare</u>, Mike tells Lucy that he'd like to go there without <u>plans</u>
계획들
and just do whatever they want <u>in the moment</u>. But Lucy knows
그 순간에
the <u>importance</u> of planning based on her experience with overseas
중요성   ~을 바탕으로
travel. She is worried about <u>having difficulties traveling</u> without
여행하는 데 어려움을 겪는 것
(have difficulty V-ing: ~하는 데 어려움을 겪다)
plans. So Lucy wants to suggest to Mike that they make plans for
their trip. In this situation, what would Lucy most likely say to Mike?
Lucy: (How about planning out our trip <u>in advance</u>?)
미리

해석
여: Lucy와 Mike는 부부이다. Lucy는 여러 번 해외로 여행을 갔지만, Mike는 해외 여행에 대한 경험이 없다. 어느 날, 여름 휴가를 위해, Lucy와 Mike는 2주 동안 호주로 여행을 가기로 결정했다. 무엇을 준비해야 할지에 대해 이야기하면서, Mike는 Lucy에게 계획 없이 그 곳에 가서 그 순간에 그들이 원하는 것을 그냥 하고 싶다고 말한다. 하지만 Lucy는 그녀의 해외 여행 경험을 바탕으로 계획의 중요성을 알고 있다. 그녀는 계획 없이 여행하는 데 어려움을 겪는 것에 대해 걱정한다. 그래서 Lucy는 Mike에게 여행을 위한 계획을 세울 것을 제안하고 싶다. 이러한 상황에서 Lucy는 Mike에게 뭐라고 말하겠는가?
Lucy: (우리의 여행 계획을 미리 세우는 게 어때요?)

① 우리는 해외 여행을 갈 형편이 안 돼요.
② 우리 휴가 때 집에 있는 게 어때요?
③ 그곳에 도착하면 제게 전화하는 것을 잊지 마세요.
✔ 우리의 여행 계획을 미리 세우는 게 어때요?
⑤ 당신은 마감일 전에 일을 끝내야 해요.

16~17 1지문 2문항

M: Hello, listeners. I'm Joe Adams from the <u>public health center</u>.
보건소
Many of you drink tea because you like the <u>taste</u>. But tea can also
만
improve your <u>overall</u> health. Today I will <u>introduce</u> some teas that
향상시키다   전반적인   소개하다
will <u>benefit</u> your health. First, <u>green tea</u> is good for health. Green
이롭게 하다   녹차
tea helps <u>brain function</u> by improving <u>working memory</u>. It can also
뇌 기능   작동 기억
<u>reduce</u> the growth of bad <u>cells</u> that cause <u>cancer</u>. Second, <u>lemon</u>
감소시키다   세포들   유발하다   레몬차
tea is popular for its <u>positive</u> <u>effects</u>. With lemon tea, you can get
긍정적인   효과들
vitamins and minerals without a lot of sugar or calories. <u>Mint tea</u> is
민트차
another tea which makes you healthier. Mint tea <u>relieves</u> <u>digestive</u>
완화시키다 소화불량
<u>discomfort</u> in your body. It can also relieve <u>stomach pain</u>. Next,
복통
<u>black tea</u> has <u>traditionally</u> been popular. Black tea is <u>well-known</u>
홍차   전통적으로   잘 알려진
for reducing <u>anxiety</u> and <u>stress</u>. Also, a <u>compound</u> in black tea
불안감   스트레스   화합물

kills <u>bacteria</u> that cause <u>tooth decay</u>. So did you get some useful
박테리아   충치
information today? I hope you try one of these teas. Thank you.

해석
남: 안녕하세요, 청취자 여러분. 저는 보건소의 Joe Adams입니다. 여러분 중 많은 분들이 차를 마시는데 왜냐하면 그 맛을 좋아하기 때문입니다. 하지만 차는 또한 여러분의 전반적인 건강도 향상시킬 수 있습니다. 오늘 저는 여러분의 건강을 이롭게 할 몇 가지 차를 소개하겠습니다. 첫째, 녹차는 건강에 좋습니다. 녹차는 작동 기억을 향상시킴으로써 뇌 기능을 돕습니다. 그것은 또한 암을 유발하는 나쁜 세포의 성장도 감소시킬 수 있습니다. 둘째, 레몬차는 그것의 긍정적인 효과로 인기가 높습니다. 레몬차로, 여러분은 많은 설탕이나 칼로리 없이 비타민과 미네랄을 섭취할 수 있습니다. 민트차는 여러분을 더 건강하게 만드는 또 다른 차입니다. 민트차는 몸의 소화불량을 완화시킵니다. 그것은 또한 복통도 완화시킬 수 있습니다. 다음으로, 홍차는 전통적으로 인기가 있었습니다. 홍차는 불안감과 스트레스를 감소시키는 것으로 잘 알려져 있습니다. 게다가, 홍차 속의 화합물은 충치를 유발하는 박테리아를 죽입니다. 그럼 여러분은 오늘 유용한 정보를 얻었나요? 이 차들 중 하나를 드셔보기 바랍니다. 감사합니다.

16 남자가 하는 말의 주제
정답률 90% ▶ 정답 ①

✔ 건강에 좋은 차들
② 차와 잘 어울리는 간식들
③ 차나무를 재배하는 다양한 방법들
④ 전 세계의 다양한 차 예절
⑤ 많은 차를 소비하는 나라들의 목록

17 언급된 차가 아닌 것
정답률 90% ▶ 정답 ③

① 녹차   ② 레몬차   ✔ 장미차
④ 민트차   ⑤ 홍차

12 2021년 9월 학력평가

01	③	02	③	03	④	04	⑤	05	②
06	③	07	⑤	08	④	09	⑤	10	③
11	⑤	12	③	13	②	14	④	15	①
16	①	17	④						

01 남자가 하는 말의 목적
정답률 85% ▶ 정답 ③

M: Hello, students. I'm the school <u>nutritionist</u>, Mr. Jackson. Over the
영양사
past week, we have <u>conducted</u> a <u>survey</u> on the school website
실시했다(conduct)   설문 조사
about the meals you ate this semester. I want to thank those of
급식들   학기
you who have <u>responded</u>. <u>Unfortunately</u>, less than 50 percent
응답했다(respond)   안타깝게도
of students answered the survey. We don't have <u>enough</u> <u>data</u> to
충분한   자료
make your school meals better. Therefore, we <u>decided to extend</u>
연장하기로 결정했다
(decide to V: ~하기로 결정하다, extend: 연장하다)
the survey <u>period</u> by one week. The meal survey is now open
기간
until next Wednesday. We hope that giving you another week to
<u>participate</u> in the survey will help <u>improve</u> the <u>quality</u> of your school
~에 참여하다   향상시키다   품질
meals. Thank you for listening.

해석
남: 안녕하세요, 학생 여러분. 저는 학교 영양사인 Jackson 선생님입니다. 지난 한 주 동안, 저희는 여러분이 이번 학기에 먹은 급식에 대해 학교 웹사이트에서 설문 조사를 실시했습니다. 응답해주신 분들께 감사드리고 싶습니다. 안타깝게도, 50퍼센트 미만의 학생들이 이

설문 조사에 답했습니다. 저희는 학교 급식을 더 좋게 만들 수 있는 충분한 자료가 없습니다. 그러므로, 저희는 설문 조사 기간을 일주일 연장하기로 결정했습니다. 급식 설문 조사는 이제 다음 주 수요일까지 진행됩니다. 여러분들에게 설문 조사에 참여할 수 있는 일주일의 시간을 더 드리는 것이 학교 급식의 품질을 향상시키는 데 도움이 되기를 바랍니다. 들어주셔서 감사합니다.

① 학교 급식 일정 변경을 알리려고
② 학교 식당 이용 시 주의 사항을 안내하려고
✓③ 학교 급식 설문 조사 기간 연장을 공지하려고
④ 설문 조사로 선정된 학교 급식 메뉴를 소개하려고
⑤ 학교 급식 개선을 위한 토론회 참석을 요청하려고

02 여자의 의견

정답률 90%
▶ 정답 ③

W: Mike, what are you doing?
M: I'm searching for books to read. My teacher recommended reading
~을 찾고 있는(search for) / 추천했다
novels during the vacation.
소설들 / 방학
W: That's a good recommendation.
추천
M: Really? Why do you say that?
W: Reading novels can help you experience another person's feelings.
경험하다 / 기분들
M: I don't get it. What do you mean?
W: While reading a novel, you can understand how the characters
~하면서, ~하는 동안 / 등장인물들
feel. You can also imagine the characters' emotions are your own.
상상하다 / 감정들
M: Oh, now I see what you mean.
W: I bet reading novels will help you improve your empathy, which is
확신하다 / 공감 능력
your ability to share others' emotions.
능력 / 공유하다
M: Thanks for explaining. Now I'm really looking forward to reading
읽는 것을 기대하는
novels this winter.
(look forward to V-ing: ~하는 것을 기대하다)

해 석

여: Mike, 무엇을 하고 있니?
남: 읽을 책을 찾고 있어. 선생님께서 방학 동안에 소설을 읽는 것을 추천하셨거든.
여: 그거 훌륭한 추천이네.
남: 정말? 왜 그런 말을 하니?
여: 소설을 읽는 것은 다른 사람의 기분을 경험하는 데 도움을 줄 수 있어.
남: 나는 이해가 안 되는데. 무슨 말이야?
여: 소설을 읽으면서, 등장인물들이 어떻게 느끼는지 이해할 수 있어. 또한 등장인물들의 감정이 너 자신의 감정이라고 상상할 수도 있지.
남: 오, 이제 무슨 말인지 알겠어.
여: 나는 소설을 읽는 것이 다른 사람들의 감정을 공유하는 능력인 공감 능력을 향상시키는 데 도움이 될 거라고 확신해.
남: 설명해줘서 고마워. 이제 나는 이번 겨울에 소설을 읽는 것이 정말 기대가 돼.

① 꾸준한 독서는 집중력 향상에 효과적이다.
② 학생의 연령에 맞는 도서 추천이 중요하다.
✓③ 소설을 읽는 것은 공감 능력 향상에 도움이 된다.
④ 학생의 흥미를 유발할 수 있는 독서 교육이 필요하다.
⑤ 창의적인 글쓰기를 위해 다양한 주제의 소설을 읽어야 한다.

03 두 사람의 관계

정답률 90%
▶ 정답 ④

[Cell phone rings.]
M: Logan Williams speaking.
W: Hello. This is Marion Carver. I'm wondering if I can increase the
~할지 궁금해하는(wonder if) / 늘리다
number of guests for our company holiday party.
손님들 / 회사 연휴 파티
M: Let me check. [Pause] Originally, you requested 50 seats for the
원래 / 요청했다
event. I reserved a middle-sized hall at a local hotel. How many
예약했다 / 지역 호텔
guests would you like to add?
추가하다
W: I want to add five more guests.
M: That shouldn't be a problem.
W: Great! How about the live band? Were you able to find one?
라이브 밴드

M: Yes, I was. I think they'll really add to the festive holiday mood.
~에 더하다, 보태다 / 즐거운 / 분위기
W: That sounds perfect. Can I ask you one more thing?
M: Absolutely. I always try to meet my clients' needs.
충족시키려고 노력하다
(try to V: ~하려고 노력하다, meet: 충족시키다)
W: There will be kids invited to this party. Is there anything we can do
~에 초대된
for them?
M: For a children's party I planned last week, I prepared animal-
계획했다 / 동물 모양의
shaped balloons for all the kids. They really liked them.
풍선들
W: That's a brilliant idea! I'm so pleased with how you've coordinated
~에 만족한 / 조직했다(coordinate)
and planned this party. See you next Friday.

해 석

[휴대전화가 울린다.]
남: Logan Williams입니다.
여: 안녕하세요. Marion Carver예요. 저희 회사 연휴 파티를 위한 손님의 수를 늘릴 수 있는지 궁금해요.
남: 확인해 볼게요. [잠시 후] 원래, 그 행사를 위해 50석을 요청하셨죠. 제가 지역 호텔에 중간 크기의 홀을 예약했어요. 얼마나 많은 손님을 추가하고 싶으신가요?
여: 다섯 명의 손님을 더 추가하고 싶어요.
남: 그건 문제가 안 될 거예요.
여: 잘됐네요! 라이브 밴드는 어때요? 밴드를 찾을 수 있었나요?
남: 네, 그랬죠. 그들이 정말 즐거운 연휴 분위기를 더해줄 것 같아요.
여: 완벽할 것 같아요. 하나만 더 여쭤봐도 될까요?
남: 물론이죠. 저는 항상 제 의뢰인들의 요구를 충족시키려고 노력한답니다.
여: 이 파티에 초대된 아이들이 있을 거예요. 저희가 그들을 위해 할 수 있는 일이 있나요?
남: 제가 지난주에 계획했던 어린이 파티의 경우에는, 모든 아이들을 위해 동물 모양의 풍선을 준비했어요. 그들은 그것들을 정말 좋아했어요.
여: 정말 좋은 생각이네요! 저는 당신이 이 파티를 조직하고 계획한 것에 매우 만족해요. 다음 주 금요일에 봬요.

① 호텔 직원 ― 투숙객
② 음반 제작자 ― 밴드 연주자
③ 유치원 교사 ― 학부모
✓④ 파티 플래너 ― 의뢰인
⑤ 레크리에이션 강사 ― 수강생

04 그림에서 대화의 내용과 일치하지 않는 것

정답률 65%
▶ 정답 ⑤

M: Honey, I've finished decorating the living room for Halloween. Can
장식하는 것을 끝냈다
(finish V-ing: ~하는 것을 끝내다, decorate: 장식하다)
you come here and take a look?
W: Sure. [Pause] Is the carpet on the floor the one you ordered last
카펫 / 바닥 / 주문했다
week?
M: Yeah. I chose the round one because it looks cute. What do you
원형의
think?
W: It looks really good there. I also love the spider web decoration that
거미줄 장식
you put on the wall above the piano.
M: Thanks. I thought it would help create the Halloween mood.
W: It definitely does. [Pause] Oh! The two carved pumpkins on the
조각된 호박들
bookshelf are so cool.
책장
M: Totally. The faces we carved into the pumpkins look excellent.
W: Didn't you say you were planning to put flying ghost stickers under
날아다니는 유령 스티커들
the window? Did you change your mind?
M: I did. I think the bat sticker looks better under the window.
박쥐 스티커
W: Good choice. I prefer the bat, too. What's that empty basket on the
빈 / 바구니
table for? Is it for trick-or-treating?
사탕 받기
M: Right. We can use it when trick-or-treaters visit our house on
Halloween.
W: That's a great plan. You did a terrific job decorating the room.

해 석

남: 여보, 핼러윈을 위해 거실을 장식하는 것을 끝냈어요. 여기 와서 좀 봐줄래요?
여: 물론이죠. [잠시 후] 바닥에 있는 카펫은 당신이 지난주에 주문한 건가요?
남: 네. 귀여워 보여서 원형 카펫을 골랐어요. 어때요?
여: 거기 있으니 정말 좋아 보이네요. 당신이 피아노 위쪽의 벽에 걸어놓은 거미줄 장식도 정

말 마음에 들어요.

남: 고마워요. 핼러윈 분위기를 내는 데 도움이 될 것 같았어요.

여: 확실히 그러네요. [잠시 후] 오! 책장 위에 있는 조각된 호박 두 개가 너무 멋져요.

남: 그렇죠. 우리가 호박에 조각한 얼굴들이 훌륭해 보여요.

여: 창문 아래에 날아다니는 유령 스티커들을 붙일 계획이라고 말하지 않았어요? 마음을 바꿨어요?

남: 네. 창문 아래에 박쥐 스티커가 더 나아 보여요.

여: 좋은 선택이에요. 저도 박쥐가 더 좋아요. 테이블 위에 있는 빈 바구니는 어디에 쓰는 거예요? 사탕 받기를 위한 거예요?

남: 맞아요. 핼러윈에 사탕 받기를 하는 아이들이 우리 집을 방문할 때 그것을 사용할 수 있어요.

여: 멋진 계획이에요. 당신은 거실을 정말 잘 꾸몄네요.

05 여자가 남자에게 부탁한 일

정답률 75% ▶ 정답 ②

W: Henry, the weather's so nice today. We should do some of the outdoor activities Los Angeles has.
  야외 활동들

M: I agree. Because it's been so hot, we've been going to museums to
  박물관들
  enjoy the air conditioning.
  에어컨을 쐬다

W: I'm ready to enjoy the real Los Angeles. How should we spend the
  즐길 준비가 되어 있다   (시간을) 보내다
  (be ready to V: ~할 준비가 되다)
  day?

M: We could go to the beach for lunch first, and I think there's a
  해변
  baseball game that we can go to in the evening.
  야구 경기

W: That sounds great. I've always wanted to see the local team play.
  지역 팀

M: Should we prepare a lunch to take to the beach? The restaurants
  there might be crowded.
  붐비다

W: I think it would be better to pick up something to eat on the way
  사가다   그곳으로 가는 길에
  there.

M: Okay. What about tickets to the baseball game? They might sell
  out.   다 팔리다

W: Oh, you're right. Will you buy the tickets? I'll search for a place
  장소
  where we can pick up food for our lunch.

M: All right. I'll take care of that now.
  ~을 처리하다

해석

여: Henry, 오늘 날씨가 정말 좋아. Los Angeles에서 할 수 있는 야외 활동을 좀 해야겠어.

남: 동의해. 너무 더웠기 때문에, 우리는 에어컨을 쐬기 위해서 박물관에 갔잖아.

여: 나는 진짜 Los Angeles를 즐길 준비가 되어 있어. 하루를 어떻게 보낼까?

남: 우선 점심을 먹으러 해변에 갈 수도 있고, 저녁에 우리가 보러 갈 수 있는 야구 경기가 있는 것 같아.

여: 그거 괜찮을 것 같아. 나는 항상 지역 팀이 경기하는 것을 보고 싶었어.

남: 해변에 가져갈 점심을 준비해야 할까? 그곳의 식당들은 붐빌지도 몰라.

여: 그곳으로 가는 길에 먹을 것을 사는 게 더 좋을 것 같아.

남: 알았어. 야구 경기 티켓은 어때? 그것들은 다 팔릴지도 몰라.

여: 오, 네 말이 맞아. 네가 티켓을 구매할래? 나는 점심에 먹을 음식을 사갈 수 있는 장소를 찾아볼게.

남: 알았어. 내가 지금 그것을 처리할게.

① 에어컨 수리 요청하기
✓ 야구 경기 티켓 구매하기
③ 주문한 음식 찾아오기
④ 박물관 투어 취소하기
⑤ 식사 장소 예약하기

문제 풀이

저녁에 있는 야구 경기의 티켓이 다 팔릴 수도 있다는 남자의 말에 여자는 남자에게 티켓을 구매해 줄 것을 부탁했으며 남자는 자신이 그 일을 처리하겠다고 대답했다. 따라서 정답은 ② '야구 경기 티켓 구매하기'이다.

06 여자가 지불할 금액

정답률 80% ▶ 정답 ③

M: Good morning. Welcome to Happy Bakery. How can I help you?

W: I need to buy a cake for my sister's birthday. Could you recommend
  사야 하다   추천하다
  (need to V: ~해야 하다)
  one?

M: Sure. These chocolate and strawberry cakes are our best sellers.
                                                        잘 나가는 제품들

W: Oh, they look delicious. How much are they?
            맛있는

M: This chocolate cake is 20 dollars, and the strawberry cake is 30 dollars.

W: Hmm…. I'll buy that strawberry cake.

M: Wonderful. Can I get anything else for you?

W: Well, we're having a small party. It might be nice to be able to give
                                                        줄 수 있다
  something to our guests to take home.
                                        (be able to V: ~할 수 있다)

M: How about our homemade cookies? They're 4 dollars each.
              수제 쿠키들   각각

W: That sounds perfect. Can I get five cookies?

M: Absolutely. So, that's one strawberry cake and five cookies, right?

W: Correct. And I think I saw a sign in your window that you're having a
                              간판   세일하고 있다(have a sale)
  sale right now.

M: You're right. If you spend at least 40 dollars, you'll receive a 10
                    (돈을) 쓰다   10퍼센트 할인을 받다
  percent discount on your total purchase.
                        총 구매 금액

W: Terrific! Here's my credit card.

해석

남: 안녕하세요. Happy Bakery에 오신 것을 환영합니다. 어떻게 도와드릴까요?

여: 여동생 생일을 위해 케이크를 사야 해요. 하나 추천해주시겠어요?

남: 그럼요. 이 초콜릿과 딸기 케이크가 잘 나가는 제품들이에요.

여: 오, 맛있어 보이네요. 얼마죠?

남: 이 초콜릿 케이크는 20달러이고, 딸기 케이크는 30달러예요.

여: 흠…. 저 딸기 케이크를 살게요.

남: 좋아요. 더 필요하신 건 없으세요?

여: 음, 저희는 작은 파티를 열 거예요. 손님들에게 집으로 가져갈 뭔가를 줄 수 있다면 좋을 것 같아요.

남: 수제 쿠키는 어떠세요? 그것들은 각각 4달러예요.

여: 완벽할 것 같네요. 쿠키 다섯 개 주시겠어요?

남: 물론이죠. 그럼, 딸기 케이크 한 개와 쿠키 다섯 개네요, 맞죠?

여: 정확해요. 그리고 창문에 지금 세일하고 있다는 간판을 본 것 같아요.

남: 맞아요. 최소한 40달러를 쓰시면, 총 구매 금액에 10퍼센트 할인을 받으실 거예요.

여: 잘됐네요! 여기 제 신용카드가 있어요.

① $36   ② $40   ✓ $45
④ $50   ⑤ $63

문제 풀이

30달러인 딸기 케이크 1개와 4달러인 수제 쿠키 5개를 사면 총 구매 금액은 50달러이다. 40달러 이상을 쓰면 총 구매 금액에서 10퍼센트 할인을 받을 수 있다고 했으므로 여자가 지불할 금액은 50달러에서 5달러가 할인된 45달러이다. 따라서 정답은 ③ '$45'이다.

07 남자가 도서관에 갈 수 없는 이유

정답률 90% ▶ 정답 ⑤

W: Hi, Joshua. Why didn't you come to the book club meeting yesterday?
                                              독서 동아리 모임

M: I didn't feel well, so I went to the doctor.

W: Oh, I see. Are you feeling better?

M: Yeah, I'm much better now. But I'm sad I missed the meeting. Did
                                              빠졌다
  you choose the book for the next meeting?

W: We didn't. How about going to the library to choose the book for
                                        도서관
  the next meeting?

M: That sounds great, but I don't think I can today.

W: Why not? Did the doctor tell you to get more rest?
                                        더 쉬다

12

21년 9월 학력평가

M: No, it's not that. I need to write my script for the speech contest.
　　　　　　　　　　　　　　　　　　　　대본　　　　　말하기 대회
W: I thought the script is due next week. You have enough time.
　　　　　　　　　　　예정인, ~하기로 되어 있는
There's no need to hurry.
　　　　　　　　서두르다
M: It is due next week, but the topic is difficult. So, I should write the
script today.　　　　　　　　주제
W: Okay. Be sure to take breaks so you don't get sick again.
　　　　　반드시 ~하다　　휴식을 취하다　　　　　　　　아프다
M: I will. Thank you for your concern.
　　　　　　　　　　　　　　　　걱정

해석
여: 안녕, Joshua. 어제 독서 동아리 모임에 왜 안 왔니?
남: 몸이 안 좋아서, 병원에 갔었어.
여: 오, 그렇구나. 좀 나아졌니?
남: 그래, 지금은 훨씬 좋아졌어. 하지만 모임에 빠져서 아쉬워. 다음 모임을 위한 책을 골랐니?
여: 아니. 다음 모임을 위한 책을 고르기 위해 도서관에 가는 게 어떠니?
남: 좋긴 한데, 오늘은 안 될 것 같아.
여: 왜 안 돼? 의사가 더 쉬라고 했어?
남: 아니, 그런 거 아니야. 말하기 대회를 위한 대본을 써야 해.
여: 나는 대본 마감이 다음 주까지라고 생각했어. 충분한 시간이 있잖아. 서두를 필요 없어.
남: 마감이 다음 주까지인데, 주제가 어려워. 그래서 오늘 대본을 써야 해.
여: 알았어. 또 아프지 않도록 반드시 휴식을 취해야 해.
남: 그렇게. 걱정해줘서 고마워.
① 독서 토론을 위해 책을 읽어야 해서
② 학생회 회의에 참석해야 해서
③ 병원 진료를 받아야 해서
④ 동아리 면접을 준비해야 해서
☑ 말하기 대회 대본을 작성해야 해서

08 Electronics Fair에 관해 언급되지 않은 것

정답률 90%
▶ 정답 ④

M: How was your visit to the Electronics Fair, Christine?
　　　　　　　　　　　　　　　전자제품 박람회
W: It was spectacular. You should check it out if you have time.
　　　　　장관의
M: I might. What was there to do at the fair?
W: There were displays for the latest models of electronic devices and
　　　　　　　　전시들　　　　　최신의　　　　　　　전자 기기들
new technology.
신기술
M: Wow! You must have seen a lot of brand-new electronic devices!
　　　　　　봤음이 틀림없다　　　　　　아주 새로운
(must have p.p.: ~했음이 틀림없다)
Did you participate in any hands-on activities there?
　　　~에 참여하다　　　　체험 활동들
W: Of course I did. Various programs were available including 3-D
　　　　　　　　　다양한　　　　　　　　이용 가능한　~을 포함하여
printing, VR games, and chatting with AI.
M: I want to try talking with AI. Where is the fair held?
W: It takes place at Dream Expo Center. 개최된(hold: 개최하다; 쥐다)
　　개최되다　　드림 엑스포 센터
M: That's near here! When does the fair end?
W: It ends on November 30th. 끝나다
M: Can you tell me what the price of a ticket is?
　　　　　　　　　　　　가격
W: It's 5 dollars. But if you purchase it online, you can buy it for 3 dollars.
　　　　　　　　　　　구매하다
M: Great! I'll order my ticket now.

해석
남: Electronics Fair(전자제품 박람회) 방문은 어땠어, Christine?
여: 장관이었어. 시간이 있으면 너도 확인해 봐.
남: 그래야겠다. 박람회에 뭐가 있었어?
여: 최신 모델의 전자 기기와 신기술에 대한 전시가 있었어.
남: 와! 너는 아주 새로운 전자 기기를 많이 봤음이 틀림없구나! 그곳에서 체험 활동에 참여했니?
여: 물론 했지. 3-D 프린팅, VR 게임, 그리고 AI와의 채팅을 포함하여 다양한 프로그램들이 이용 가능했어.
남: 나는 AI와 이야기를 해보고 싶어. 박람회는 어디에서 개최되니?
여: Dream Expo Center(드림 엑스포 센터)에서 개최돼.
남: 이 근처구나! 박람회는 언제 끝나니?
여: 11월 30일에 끝나.
남: 티켓의 가격이 얼마인지 알려줄래?

여: 5달러야. 하지만 온라인으로 구매하면, 3달러에 살 수 있어.
남: 잘됐다! 지금 티켓을 주문할게.

① 프로그램　　　② 장소　　　③ 종료일
☑ 참가 업체　　　⑤ 티켓 가격

09 Jump and Grow Together에 관한 내용과 일치하지 않는 것

정답률 90%
▶ 정답 ⑤

W: Good afternoon. I'm Julia Harpson, the student body president.
　　　　　　　　　　　　　　　　　　　　　　　　학생회장
I'm glad to have the chance to tell you about Jump and Grow
　　　　　　　　　　기회　　　　　　　　　　함께 뛰고 자라다
Together, a school tradition where freshmen compete by jumping
　　　　　　　　　　　전통　　　　　신입생들　겨루다　줄넘기를 함으로써
rope together. It's a team competition, and each participating (by V-ing: ~함으로써)
　　　　　　　　　　단체전　　　　　　　　　참가팀
team should consist of 11 freshmen. The goal is to see how
　　　　　~으로 구성되다　　　　　　　　　목표
many times the team members can jump one rope all together
　　　　　　　　　팀원들
without stopping. Each team will have three chances to jump. The
멈추지 않고
(without V-ing: ~하지 않고, stop: 멈추다)
highest number of team jumps among the three tries will be the
　　　　　　　　　　　　　　　　　　　　　　　시도들
team's score. The competition will happen on the first Saturday
　　　　점수
of October. It'll take place in the school gym. You must register
　　　　　　　　　　　　　　　학교 체육관　　　　　　신청하다
online by September 30th to participate. You cannot register on
the day of the event. Don't miss this chance to make a precious
행사 당일에　　　　　놓치다　　　　　　　　　　　소중한
high school memory!

해석
여: 안녕하세요. 저는 학생회장인 Julia Harpson입니다. 신입생들이 같이 줄넘기를 함으로써 겨루는 학교 전통인 Jump and Grow Together(함께 뛰고 자라다)에 대해 알려드릴 기회를 갖게 되어 기쁩니다. 그것은 단체전이고, 각 참가팀은 신입생 11명으로 구성되어야 합니다. 목표는 팀원들이 멈추지 않고 모두 함께 한 줄을 얼마나 많이 넘을 수 있는지 보는 것입니다. 각 팀은 점프할 수 있는 세 번의 기회를 갖습니다. 세 번의 시도 중에서 가장 많은 팀 점프 횟수가 그 팀의 점수입니다. 대회는 10월 첫 번째 토요일에 열릴 것입니다. 그것은 학교 체육관에서 개최될 것입니다. 참가하기 위해서는 9월 30일까지 온라인으로 신청해야 합니다. 행사 당일에는 신청할 수 없습니다. 소중한 고등학교 추억을 만들 수 있는 이번 기회를 놓치지 마십시오!
① 신입생 11명으로 팀을 구성해야 한다.
② 각 팀은 세 번의 점프 기회를 갖는다.
③ 10월 첫 번째 토요일에 열린다.
④ 학교 체육관에서 개최된다.
☑ 행사 당일에 참가 신청이 가능하다.

10 표에서 여자가 구입할 Monitor Stand

정답률 80%
▶ 정답 ③

M: Hey, Tiffany. What are you doing?
W: I'm looking at a website where I can buy a monitor stand. Will you
　　　　　　　　　　　　　　　　　　　　　　　모니터 스탠드
help me choose which one I should buy from these five options?
M: I'd be happy to. Have you thought about how much you're willing to
spend?　　　　　　　　　　　　　　　　　　　　　기꺼이[흔쾌히] ~하다
W: I don't want to spend more than 30 dollars.
M: Okay. These models are within your budget. [Pause] The plastic
　　　　　　　　　　　　　네 예산의 범위 내에
ones look really stylish.
　　　　　　멋진
W: They do, but I think plastic is kind of a weak material. I prefer metal
ones.　　　　　　　　　　　약간　　　재질
M: That makes sense. It would be better to have a monitor stand that
you can use for a long time. Do you think you would use a storage
　　　　　오랫동안　　　　　　　　　　　보관용 서랍
drawer?
W: No, I don't need one. I'd rather have more space to store my keyboard.
　　　　　　　　　　　　　　　　　　공간　보관하다
M: There are only two options left now. How many USB ports do you
need?　　　　　　　　　　　　　　　　　　　USB 포트들
W: I think I need at least 3. I'll buy this one. Thanks for your help.
　　　　　　최소한

해석

남: 안녕, Tiffany. 무엇을 하고 있니?

여: 모니터 스탠드를 살 수 있는 웹 사이트를 보고 있어. 이 다섯 가지의 선택 중에서 어떤 것을 사야 할지 고르는 것을 도와줄래?

남: 기꺼이 도와줄게. 돈을 얼마나 쓸지에 대해서 생각해 봤어?

여: 나는 30달러 이상을 쓰고 싶지는 않아.

남: 알았어. 이 모델들이 네 예산의 범위 내에 있어. [잠시 후] 플라스틱 제품이 정말 멋져 보여.

여: 그렇긴 한데, 플라스틱은 약간 약한 재질인 것 같아. 나는 금속 제품이 더 좋아.

남: 일리가 있네. 오랫동안 사용할 수 있는 모니터 스탠드를 사는 게 더 좋을 거야. 너는 보관용 서랍을 사용할 것 같니?

여: 아니, 필요 없어. 차라리 키보드를 보관할 수 있는 공간이 더 있었으면 좋겠어.

남: 이제 두 가지 선택만 남았어. 몇 개의 USB 포트가 필요하니?

여: 최소한 3개는 필요할 것 같아. 나는 이것을 살게. 도와줘서 고마워.

모니터 스탠드

모델	가격	재질	보관용 서랍	USB 포트
① A	20달러	플라스틱	O	2
② B	23달러	금속	X	2
✔ C	25달러	금속	X	3
④ D	28달러	금속	O	3
⑤ E	35달러	플라스틱	O	4

11 남자의 마지막 말에 대한 여자의 응답

정답률 80%
▶ 정답 ⑤

M: Kate, look at the time! We've been working for two hours straight.

W: Already? Wow, I didn't realize so much time had passed.

M: Neither did I. Maybe we should take a break.

W: (Sure. Why don't we go out to get some fresh air?)

해석

남: Kate, 시간 좀 봐! 우리는 두 시간 동안 연속으로 일하고 있어.

여: 벌써? 와, 나는 그렇게 많은 시간이 흘렀는지 깨닫지 못했어.

남: 나도 마찬가지야. 우리는 휴식을 취해야 할 것 같아.

여: (물론이지. 우리 나가서 바람을 쐬는 게 어때?)

① 안타깝네. 언제 시계를 고장 낸 거야?

② 미안해. 나는 어제 회의에 참석하지 못했어.

③ 맞아. 우리 지금 당장 다시 일하러 갈까?

④ 고마워. 그것은 더 배울 수 있는 좋은 기회였어.

✔ 물론이지. 우리 나가서 바람을 쐬는 게 어때?

12 여자의 마지막 말에 대한 남자의 응답

정답률 75%
▶ 정답 ②

W: David, how was your driving test yesterday?

M: I passed. I got my driver's license.

W: What a relief! You failed the previous test because you didn't have enough time to prepare.

M: (That's why I practiced a lot this time.)

해석

여: David, 어제 운전면허 시험 어땠어?

남: 통과했어. 운전면허증을 땄지.

여: 다행이다! 너는 준비할 충분한 시간이 없어서 이전 시험에서 떨어졌잖아.

남: (그래서 이번에는 연습을 많이 했어.)

① 우리는 여행하기 위해 항상 차가 필요한 건 아니야.

✔ 그래서 이번에는 연습을 많이 했어.

③ 네가 교통 체증에 갇히지 않았다니 기쁘네.

④ 시험을 위해 반드시 제시간에 도착하도록 해.

⑤ 나는 시험용 신분증을 잊어버렸어.

13 남자의 마지막 말에 대한 여자의 응답

정답률 90%
▶ 정답 ②

M: Cathy, can you help me? I'm preparing my science presentation, but it's not easy to explain my topic.

W: Sure. What can I do to help?

M: I'm having trouble creating a way to visualize what I say in my presentation.

W: How about using an image or a chart? It can help your audience understand the topic because they'll be able to clearly see the information.

M: That's a great idea, but I'm not familiar with how to make those things. Do you have any tips?

W: You could use an infographic building program. I've used one to make proper graphs and tables before. It's easy to use.

M: Really? How did you get the program?

W: I downloaded it from a website last semester. It's a free-share program.

M: That program would help me a lot. Would you give me the website address?

W: (Of course. I'll send it to you right away.)

해석

남: Cathy, 나 좀 도와줄래? 과학 발표를 준비하고 있는데, 내 주제를 설명하기가 쉽지 않아.

여: 그래. 내가 뭘 도와줄까?

남: 나는 발표에서 내가 말하는 것을 시각화하는 방법을 만드는 데 어려움을 겪고 있어.

여: 이미지나 도표를 이용하는 게 어때? 그것은 청중이 주제를 이해하는 데 도움을 줄 수 있는 데 왜냐하면 그들이 정보를 명확히 볼 수 있기 때문이야.

남: 좋은 생각이긴 하지만, 나는 그런 것들을 만드는 방법에 익숙하지 않아. 비법이 있니?

여: 인포그래픽 제작 프로그램을 이용하면 돼. 나는 전에 적절한 그래프와 표를 만드는 데 사용한 적이 있어. 그것은 사용하기 쉬워.

남: 정말? 그 프로그램을 어떻게 구했어?

여: 지난 학기에 한 웹 사이트에서 그것을 다운로드했어. 그것은 무료 공유 프로그램이거든.

남: 그 프로그램이 나에게 많은 도움이 되겠어. 그 웹 사이트 주소를 알려줄래?

여: (물론이지. 지금 바로 그것을 보내줄게.)

① 괜찮아. 나는 나만의 인포그래픽을 만들 수 있어.

✔ 물론이지. 지금 바로 그것을 보내줄게.

③ 미안해. 어제 그것을 다운로드하는 것을 잊었어.

④ 알겠어. 너는 짧으면 짧을수록 더 좋다는 말이구나.

⑤ 좋아. 나는 그래프를 이 페이지에 넣을 거야.

14 여자의 마지막 말에 대한 남자의 응답

정답률 80%
▶ 정답 ④

W: Look at these beautiful snowy branches! It's the perfect day to climb a mountain.

M: Actually, in winter, the weather can cause a lot of problems. Days are short and trails are difficult to climb after it snows.

W: I see, but the views on the way up are stunning. I can't wait to see the amazing view from the mountain peak.

M: I'm afraid we can't reach the top today.

W: Oh, no! I was looking forward to taking photos at the top to prove we made it.

M: Well, it's getting dark. Because of the icy trails, the climb has taken longer than I expected it would.

W: What about going up faster?

M: That could be very dangerous. Let's go back down today. We can try reaching the peak another time.

W: That's too bad. We were planning to see the view at the top.
보려고 계획하고 있었다
(plan to V: ~하려고 계획하다)
M: (The original plan is important, but safety comes first.)
원래의 안전

해석
여: 이 아름다운 눈에 덮인 나뭇가지들을 봐! 산에 오르기에 딱 좋은 날씨야.
남: 사실, 겨울에는, 날씨가 많은 문제를 일으킬 수 있어. 눈이 내린 후에는 낮이 짧고 산길은 오르기에 어려워.
여: 그렇구나, 하지만 올라가는 길에 보이는 경치는 놀랄 만큼 아름다워. 나는 산꼭대기에서 멋진 경치를 빨리 보고 싶어.
남: 오늘은 정상에 도달하지 못할 것 같아.
여: 오, 안 돼! 나는 우리가 해냈다는 것을 증명하기 위해 정상에서 사진을 찍는 것을 기대하고 있었단 말이야.
남: 음, 날이 어두워지고 있어. 얼음에 뒤덮인 산길 때문에, 내가 예상했던 것보다 등반 시간이 더 오래 걸렸어.
여: 더 빠르게 올라가는 게 어떠니?
남: 그것은 매우 위험할 수 있어. 오늘은 다시 내려가자. 우리는 다음에 정상에 도달하는 것을 시도할 수 있어.
여: 정말 아쉽다. 우리는 정상에서 경치를 보려고 계획하고 있었잖아.
남: (원래 계획도 중요하지만, 안전이 우선이야.)

① 너는 정상에서 사진을 더 찍었어야 했어.
② 이 광경을 놓쳤다면 나는 그것을 후회했을 거야.
③ 산길은 장비 없이 등산할 수 있을 만큼 충분히 평탄해.
✓④ 원래 계획도 중요하지만, 안전이 우선이야.
⑤ 나는 전에도 이런 등산을 해봐서, 그것이 위험하지 않다는 것을 알아.

문제 풀이
겨울에 등산을 하던 중 남자는 위험하기 때문에 산의 정상까지 오르지 않고 다시 내려갈 것을 제안한다. 이에 대해 여자는 정상에서 경치를 보려던 계획이 좌절된 것에 아쉬워한다. 따라서 여자의 말에 대한 남자의 응답으로 가장 적절한 것은 ④ 'The original plan is important, but safety comes first.(원래 계획도 중요하지만, 안전이 우선이야.)'이다.

15 다음 상황에서 Amanda가 Natalie에게 할 말
정답률 90% ▶ 정답 ①

W: Amanda and Natalie are roommates who go to the same university.
룸메이트들
They live in an apartment that is a 30-minute walk to their campus.
~에 살다   걸어서 30분 거리
These days, they frequently use electric scooters to commute.
자주   전동 스쿠터들   통학하다
Amanda and Natalie both try to be safe while riding the scooters,
but Natalie often wears headphones to listen to music while riding.
헤드폰을 착용하다   음악을 듣다
Amanda thinks that can put Natalie in danger because Natalie
Natalie를 위험에 빠뜨리다
(put A in danger: A를 위험에 빠뜨리다)
might not hear a car coming or notice emergency situations on
알아차리다   비상 상황들
the road. For the sake of everyone's safety, Amanda wants to tell
~을 위해서
Natalie to stop wearing headphones while riding her scooter so
착용하는 것을 그만두다
(stop V-ing: ~하는 것을 그만두다)
she can hear more important sounds from cars, pedestrians, and
소리들   보행자들
other riders. In this situation, what would Amanda most likely say
탑승자들
to Natalie?
Amanda: (It's dangerous to use headphones while riding a scooter.)

해석
여: Amanda와 Natalie는 같은 대학교에 다니는 룸메이트이다. 그들은 캠퍼스까지 걸어서 30분 거리에 있는 아파트에 살고 있다. 요즘에, 그들은 통학하기 위해 전동 스쿠터를 자주 이용한다. Amanda와 Natalie는 둘 다 스쿠터를 탈 때 조심하려고 노력하지만, Natalie는 종종 스쿠터를 타면서 음악을 듣기 위해 헤드폰을 착용한다. Amanda는 그것이 Natalie를 위험에 빠뜨릴 수 있다고 생각하는데 왜냐하면 Natalie가 자동차가 오는 소리를 듣지 못하거나 도로에서 비상 상황을 알아차리지 못할 수도 있기 때문이다. 모두의 안전을 위해서, Amanda는 Natalie에게 그녀가 자동차, 보행자, 그리고 다른 탑승자로부터 더 중요한 소리를 들을 수 있도록 스쿠터를 타면서 헤드폰을 착용하는 것을 그만두라고 말하고 싶다. 이러한 상황에서, Amanda는 Natalie에게 뭐라고 말하겠는가?
Amanda: (스쿠터를 타면서 헤드폰을 사용하는 것은 위험해.)

✓① 스쿠터를 타면서 헤드폰을 사용하는 것은 위험해.
② 나는 네가 스쿠터를 정기적으로 점검해야 한다고 생각해.
③ 걸어서 등교하는 것이 네 건강에 더 좋아.

④ 전동 스쿠터를 타려면 면허증이 필요해.
⑤ 음악을 크게 트는 것은 네가 공부에 집중할 수 없게 할지도 몰라.

16~17 1지문 2문항

M: Hello, everyone. I'm Dr. Martin Muller. Do you know that mathematical
수학적 능력
ability is widespread in the animal kingdom? Many biologists have
널리 퍼진   생물학자들
suggested that counting is not unique to humans. For instance,
수를 세는 것 ~에 고유한
wolves use strength in numbers while hunting. Wolves have optimal
늑대들   힘   최적의
group sizes for hunting different prey. In addition, female frogs
먹잇감   암컷의 개구리들
count the number of pulses in a male frog's cry. They can do this
진동들   수컷의
for phrases up to 10 notes long. Despite what you may have heard,
악구들   음   ~에도 불구하고
chickens are quite smart. Research shows that newly hatched
닭들   연구   새로 부화한
chicks and adult chickens can count and do basic math. Lastly, the
병아리들   기본적인 수학을 하다
real math wizards of the animal kingdom are desert ants. They are
마법사들   사막 개미들
able to find their way back home after leaving their nests for food
찾을 수 있다   둥지들
(be able to V: ~할 수 있다, find: 찾다)
by counting steps. Now, we will watch a video about these animals.
수를 셈으로써 걸음들
(by V-ing: ~함으로써)

해석
남: 안녕하세요. 여러분. 저는 Martin Muller 박사입니다. 여러분은 동물의 왕국에 수학적 능력이 널리 퍼져 있다는 것을 알고 있나요? 많은 생물학자들은 수를 세는 것이 인간에 고유한 것이 아니라고 주장해왔습니다. 예를 들어, 늑대는 사냥할 때 수적으로 힘을 사용합니다. 늑대는 다른 먹잇감을 사냥하기 위한 최적의 집단 크기를 가지고 있습니다. 이외에도, 암컷 개구리는 수컷 개구리의 울음소리에 있는 진동의 수를 셉니다. 그들은 10개 정도의 음이 있는 길이의 악구에 대해 이것을 할 수 있습니다. 여러분이 들어봤을지도 모르는 사실에도 불구하고, 닭은 꽤 똑똑합니다. 연구는 새로 부화한 병아리와 다 자란 닭이 수를 세고 기본적인 수학을 할 수 있다는 것을 보여줍니다. 마지막으로, 동물의 왕국의 진정한 수학 마법사는 사막 개미입니다. 그들은 먹이를 찾아 둥지를 떠난 후에 걸음의 수를 셈으로써 집으로 돌아가는 길을 찾을 수 있습니다. 이제, 우리는 이 동물들에 대한 영상을 시청할 것입니다.

16 남자가 하는 말의 주제
정답률 65% ▶ 정답 ①

✓① 동물들의 수를 세는 능력
② 동물들이 이주하는 이유
③ 야생동물들의 사냥 습관
④ 동물 권리 보호의 필요성
⑤ 멸종 위기 동물들을 보존하는 방법

17 언급된 동물이 아닌 것
정답률 90% ▶ 정답 ④

① 늑대　　　　　② 개구리　　　　　③ 닭
✓④ 뱀　　　　　⑤ 사막 개미

13 2021년 11월 학력평가

01	③	02	②	03	②	04	④	05	⑤
06	②	07	②	08	⑤	09	④	10	①
11	②	12	②	13	①	14	⑤	15	①
16	③	17	⑤

01 남자가 하는 말의 목적

정답률 85%

▶ 정답 ③

M: Hello, Edmond High School students! I'm the librarian, Norman
Smith. As you know, the school library renovation started last
month and the library was supposed to reopen by the end of
this month. However, making wider reading spaces is taking
longer than expected because of some problems with the walls.
Therefore, the library reopening will be delayed for a few more
days. I'll let you know the date of the reopening as soon as it's
decided. Please wait a little more until the library opens again.
Thank you for your patience.

해석

남: 안녕하세요, Edmond 고등학교 학생 여러분! 저는 도서관 사서인 Norman Smith입니다. 아시다시피, 학교 도서관 보수 공사가 지난달에 시작되었고 도서관은 이번 달 말까지 재개관하기로 되어 있었습니다. 하지만, 벽의 몇 가지 문제 때문에 더 넓은 독서 공간을 만드는 것이 예상보다 더 오래 걸리고 있습니다. 그러므로, 도서관 재개관이 며칠 더 연기될 것입니다. 재개관 날짜가 결정되는 대로 알려드리겠습니다. 도서관이 다시 문을 열 때까지 조금만 더 기다려 주십시오. 양해해 주셔서 감사합니다.

① 도서관 홈페이지 개설을 홍보하려고
② 도서관 운영 시간 연장을 공지하려고
✓ 도서관 재개관 날짜 연기를 안내하려고
④ 도서관 환경 조성 아이디어를 공모하려고
⑤ 도서관 벽 공사로 인한 소음에 대해 사과하려고

02 여자의 의견

정답률 85%

▶ 정답 ②

W: Brian, you look worried. What's the matter?
M: Mom, I'm trying to make plans for vacation, but it's not easy. Could
you take a look?
W: Sure. [Pause] Hmm, I think you put too many things in your plan.
M: I know, but there are so many things to do.
W: I understand, but you can't do them all in a limited time.
M: Then can you give me some advice?
W: Okay. First, make a list of things to do and then put them in order
according to how important they are. (put A in order: A에 순서를 부여하다, 정돈하다)
M: You're saying I need to consider their importance first.
W: Right. That way, you'll be able to decide what to include in your
plan and what to skip.
M: I understand what you mean.
W: When making a vacation plan, you should consider the importance
of the things you want to include.
M: That makes sense. Thanks for the tip, Mom.

해석

여: Brian, 걱정스러워 보이는구나. 무슨 일이니?
남: 엄마, 방학 계획을 세우려고 하는데, 쉽지 않아요. 한번 봐 주시겠어요?

여: 물론이지. [잠시 후] 흠, 네 계획에 너무 많은 것을 넣은 것 같구나.
남: 알아요, 하지만 할 일이 너무 많거든요.
여: 이해해, 그런데 한정된 시간 안에 그것들을 다 할 수는 없어.
남: 그럼 조언을 좀 해주실래요?
여: 좋아. 우선, 해야 할 일들의 목록을 만든 다음 그것들이 얼마나 중요한지에 따라 그것들에 순서를 부여하렴.
남: 그것들의 중요도를 먼저 고려해야 한다는 말씀이시죠.
여: 맞아. 그렇게 하면, 네 계획에 무엇을 포함시키고 무엇을 건너뛰어야 할지 결정할 수 있을 거야.
남: 무슨 말씀인지 알겠어요.
여: 방학 계획을 세울 때는, 포함시키고 싶은 일들의 중요도를 고려해야 해.
남: 일리가 있네요. 조언해 주셔서 감사해요, 엄마.

① 방학 계획표에는 매일 해야 할 일을 포함해야 한다.
✓ 방학 계획을 세울 때는 일의 중요도를 고려해야 한다.
③ 규칙적인 생활 습관이 시간 활용의 효율성을 높여준다.
④ 학생들의 시간 관리 방법에 대한 교육을 강화해야 한다.
⑤ 방학 중에는 다양한 체험 활동을 해보는 것이 필요하다.

03 두 사람의 관계

정답률 90%

▶ 정답 ②

M: Welcome. How may I help you?
W: Hi, I'm here to pick up the car that I reserved, but I wonder if I could
make a change.
M: Can I have your driver's license, please?
W: Sure, here it is.
M: Okay. [Typing sounds] You reserved a small car for three days.
W: Yes. But can I change the car size from small to medium?
M: Let me check. [Typing sounds] Oh, there's only one medium car
you can rent.
W: That's lucky! I'll take it.
M: Okay. By the way, you chose partial car insurance. But for an
additional $20, you can have full coverage.
W: That's a great deal.
M: Right. Since you changed the size of the car and upgraded the car
insurance, the additional fee is $50.
W: Okay. Here's my credit card.
M: Thank you. I'll take you to the car.
W: All right. Thanks.

해석

남: 어서 오세요. 어떻게 도와드릴까요?
여: 안녕하세요, 제가 예약한 차를 가지러 왔는데, 바꿀 수 있는지 궁금해요.
남: 운전면허증을 주시겠어요?
여: 물론이죠, 여기 있어요.
남: 알겠습니다. [타자 치는 소리] 소형차를 3일 동안 예약하셨네요.
여: 네. 그런데 차 크기를 소형에서 중형으로 바꿀 수 있을까요?
남: 확인해 볼게요. [타자 치는 소리] 오, 고객님께서 빌리실 수 있는 중형차가 딱 한 대 있네요.
여: 운이 좋네요! 그것으로 할게요.
남: 알겠습니다. 그런데, 부분 자동차 보험을 선택하셨네요. 하지만 20달러를 추가하시면, 전액 보장을 받으실 수 있어요.
여: 그거 정말 좋은데요.
남: 그렇죠. 차의 크기를 바꾸고 자동차 보험을 업그레이드하셨기 때문에, 추가 요금은 50달러예요.
여: 알겠어요. 여기 제 신용카드가 있어요.
남: 감사합니다. 차로 모셔다 드릴게요.
여: 네. 감사해요.

① 자동차 정비사 — 운전자
✓ 렌터카 회사 직원 — 고객
③ 운전면허 강사 — 수강생
④ 공항 주차 요원 — 여행객
⑤ 보험 설계사 — 보험 계약자

04 그림에서 대화의 내용과 일치하지 않는 것

정답률 80%

▶ 정답 ④

W: Honey, look at this. My friend Lisa sent a picture of her newly-opened book cafe.
새로 문을 연

M: Wow, it looks great. There's a bookshelf full of books.
~으로 가득 찬

W: Yes. Lisa said she has a variety of genres of books.
다양한 장르의

M: Great. Look! There's a ladder leaning against the wall. That must be for the books on the upper shelf.
벽에 기대어 있는(lean against: ~에 기대다)
위쪽의 선반

W: Right. Also, there are round tables.

M: Yes. Visitors can read books while drinking coffee there.

W: Oh, did you notice the two flower pots under the clock?
보다   화분

M: Yeah, those must be the gifts you sent Lisa for the grand opening. They look nice.
선물들   개업

W: I'm glad that they go so well with the cafe.
~과 잘 어울리다

M: What's that poster on the wall? It says "Book of the Month."

W: Lisa said she's going to introduce a popular book on that poster every month.
소개하다   인기 있는

M: That's great. Why don't we go to this cafe together?

W: Good! Let's go this weekend.

해석

여: 여보, 이것 좀 봐요. 내 친구 Lisa가 새로 문을 연 북카페의 사진을 보냈어요.

남: 와, 좋아 보여요. 책들로 가득 찬 책장이 있네요.

여: 네. Lisa가 다양한 장르의 책들을 가지고 있다고 했어요.

남: 멋지네요. 봐요! 벽에 기대어 있는 사다리가 있어요. 그것은 분명 위쪽의 선반에 있는 책들을 위한 것이겠네요.

여: 맞아요. 또한, 원형 테이블들도 있어요.

남: 네. 방문객들이 그곳에서 커피를 마시면서 책을 읽을 수 있어요.

여: 오, 시계 아래에 있는 두 개의 화분을 봤어요?

남: 네, 그것들은 당신이 Lisa에게 개업 기념으로 보낸 선물이 틀림없어요. 좋아 보이네요.

여: 그것들이 카페와 잘 어울려서 기뻐요.

남: 벽에 있는 저 포스터는 뭐죠? '이달의 책'이라고 써 있어요.

여: Lisa가 매달 그 포스터에 인기 있는 책을 소개할 거라고 했어요.

남: 멋지네요. 우리 카페에 같이 가는 게 어때요?

여: 좋아요! 이번 주말에 가요.

05 남자가 여자를 위해 할 일

정답률 90%

▶ 정답 ⑤

[Cell phone rings.]

M: Hello, Anna.

W: Hi, David. How was camping at Sunnyside Hill last weekend?

M: I had a wonderful time with my family. The weather was perfect, and the campsite was fantastic, too.
날씨
캠핑장

W: Sounds great. I'm going camping there this weekend.

M: Oh, really? Did you prepare everything you need?
준비하다

W: I'm still packing. Is there anything you think I really need?
짐을 싸는(pack)

M: Sure. Mosquito spray. There are a lot of mosquitoes these days.
모기 퇴치제

W: Oh, I should bring some. And I'm going to have a barbecue. What do I need for that?
바비큐를 하다

M: Don't worry. You can rent everything related to barbecuing there.
~과 관련된

W: That's wonderful.

M: And I recommend a portable speaker if you want to listen to music while barbecuing.
추천하다   휴대용 스피커

W: I'd like to listen to music, but I don't have one.

M: If you want, I'll lend my speaker to you.
내 스피커를 너에게 빌려주다
(lend A to B: A를 B에게 빌려주다)

W: How nice of you! Thanks, David.

해석

[휴대전화가 울린다.]

남: 안녕, Anna.

여: 안녕, David. 지난 주말에 Sunnyside Hill에서 캠핑은 어땠니?

남: 나는 가족과 함께 멋진 시간을 보냈어. 날씨는 완벽했고, 캠핑장도 환상적이었어.

여: 좋았겠다. 나도 이번 주말에 그곳에 캠핑하러 갈 거야.

남: 오, 정말? 필요한 건 다 준비했니?

여: 아직 짐을 싸고 있는 중이야. 네가 생각하기에 내게 정말 필요한 게 있을까?

남: 물론이지. 모기 퇴치제. 요즘 모기가 많거든.

여: 오, 좀 가져가야겠다. 그리고 나는 바비큐를 할 거야. 그것을 위해 무엇이 필요할까?

남: 걱정하지 마. 그곳에서 바비큐와 관련된 모든 것을 빌릴 수 있어.

여: 잘됐다.

남: 그리고 바비큐를 하면서 음악을 듣고 싶다면 휴대용 스피커를 추천해.

여: 나는 음악을 듣고 싶은데, 스피커가 없어.

남: 네가 원한다면, 내 스피커를 너에게 빌려줄게.

여: 정말 친절하구나! 고마워, David.

① 캠핑장 예약하기
② 일기 예보 확인하기
③ 모기 퇴치제 가져오기
④ 바비큐 물품 구매하기
✓⑤ 휴대용 스피커 빌려주기

문제 풀이

캠핑을 가서 음악을 들으며 바비큐를 하고 싶다면 휴대용 스피커를 추천한다는 남자의 말에 여자는 스피커가 없다고 대답한다. 이에 대해 남자는 자신의 스피커를 빌려주겠다고 말하고 있으므로 남자가 여자를 위해 할 일은 ⑤ '휴대용 스피커 빌려주기'이다.

06 남자가 지불할 금액

정답률 80%

▶ 정답 ②

W: Hello. How can I help you?

M: Hello, I'm looking for a present for my father's birthday. Can you recommend something?
선물

W: Okay, how about these striped neckties? These are the popular styles.
줄무늬 넥타이들

M: They look nice. How much are they?

W: They're $30 each.

M: My father likes blue. I'll take one blue striped necktie.

W: Okay. Anything else?

M: Do you also have men's socks?
남자 양말

W: Of course. Look at these. The original price of each pair is $6, but if you buy two pairs, you can get them for $10.
원래 가격

M: Good. Then I'll buy two pairs of socks. Can you gift-wrap them?
선물용으로 포장하다

W: Sure. Gift-wrapping usually costs $2, but today gift-wrapping is free.
보통   (값·비용이) ~이다
무료의

M: Cool! Thank you. Here's my credit card.

해석

여: 안녕하세요. 어떻게 도와드릴까요?

남: 안녕하세요. 아버지의 생신을 위한 선물을 찾고 있어요. 추천 좀 해주시겠어요?

여: 알겠습니다. 이 줄무늬 넥타이들은 어떠세요? 이것들은 인기 있는 스타일이에요.

남: 좋아 보이네요. 얼마죠?

여: 한 개에 30달러예요.

남: 저희 아버지는 파란색을 좋아하세요. 파란색 줄무늬 넥타이 하나를 살게요.

여: 알겠습니다. 또 다른 건 없으신가요?

남: 남자 양말도 있나요?

여: 물론이죠. 이것들을 보세요. 한 켤레의 원래 가격은 6달러이지만, 두 켤레를 사시면, 10달러에 사실 수 있어요.

남: 좋아요. 그럼 양말 두 켤레를 살게요. 선물용으로 포장해 주시겠어요?

여: 네. 선물용 포장은 보통 2달러인데, 오늘 선물용 포장은 무료예요.
남: 좋네요! 감사해요. 여기 제 신용카드가 있어요.

① $38　　　　　② $40　　　　　③ $42
④ $44　　　　　⑤ $50

문제 풀이

줄무늬 넥타이 한 개의 가격은 30달러이다. 남자 양말은 한 컬레에 6달러, 두 컬레에 10달러이다. 파란색 줄무늬 넥타이 한 개와 남자 양말 두 컬레를 사면 총액은 40달러이다. 원래 2달러인 선물용 포장은 오늘 무료라고 했으므로 남자가 지불할 금액은 40달러이다. 따라서 답은 ②'$40'이다.

07　여자가 One-Day Baking Class에 참여할 수 없는 이유

정답률 90%　▶ 정답 ②

M: Hello, Rachel. How was the preview of the movie, *Blue Sky* last night?
　　　　　　　　　　　　　시사회　　　　　영화
W: Hi, Mike. I had a great time. After the movie, I got an autograph from the main actor, Henry Edward.
　　　　　　　　　　　　　　　　　　　사인　　　　주연배우
M: Amazing! He's your favorite actor.
W: Right. I was so excited to meet him. What did you do last weekend?
M: I wrote a book report at Steve's Cafe. You know that place.
　　　　　　　독후감
W: Sure. I like the cookies there.
M: You know what? They're going to have a One-Day Baking Class.
　　　　　　　　　　　　　　　　　　　　　　일일 제빵 수업
W: Oh, really? I'd like to join that class. When is it?
　　　　　　　　　　참여하다
M: This Saturday, from 1 to 3 p.m. Let's do it together.
W: This Saturday? I'm afraid I can't, then.
M: Why? Are you still taking swimming lessons on Saturdays?
　　　　　　　　　　　　　　수영 수업들
W: No, I quit recently. This Saturday I'm going to my cousin's
　　　　그만뒀다(quit: 그만두다)
housewarming party with my family.
집들이
M: Oh, I see. Have a great time. I'll tell you about the class later.
　　　　　　　　　　　　　　　　　　　　　　　　　나중에

해석

남: 안녕, Rachel. 어젯밤에 영화 'Blue Sky'의 시사회는 어땠어?
여: 안녕, Mike. 정말 즐거웠어. 영화가 끝난 후에, 주연배우인 Henry Edward에게 사인을 받았어.
남: 굉장하다! 그는 네가 가장 좋아하는 배우잖아.
여: 맞아. 나는 그를 만나서 매우 신났어. 너는 지난 주말에 무엇을 했니?
남: Steve's Cafe에서 독후감을 썼어. 너는 그 장소를 알잖아.
여: 물론이지. 나는 그곳의 쿠키를 좋아해.
남: 그거 알아? 그들은 One-Day Baking Class(일일 제빵 수업)를 할 거야.
여: 오, 정말? 나는 그 수업에 참여하고 싶어. 언제야?
남: 이번 주 토요일 오후 1시부터 3시까지야. 같이 하자.
여: 이번 주 토요일? 그럼 나는 못 갈 것 같아.
남: 왜? 너는 아직도 토요일에 수영 수업을 수강하고 있니?
여: 아니, 최근에 그만뒀어. 이번 주 토요일에 가족과 함께 사촌의 집들이에 갈 거야.
남: 오, 그렇구나. 즐거운 시간 보내. 내가 나중에 수업에 대해 말해 줄게.

① 독후감을 작성해야 해서
✓② 사촌 집들이에 가야 해서
③ 영화 시사회에 초대받아서
④ 배우 사인회에 가기로 해서
⑤ 수영 수업을 수강해야 해서

08　Charity Carol Concert에 관해 언급되지 않은 것

정답률 90%　▶ 정답 ⑤

W: Chris, what are you looking at?
M: I'm looking at the website about the Charity Carol Concert. How about going there together?
　　　　　　　　　　　　　　　　　　자선 캐럴 콘서트
W: Sounds interesting. Let me see. It's held in the Lincoln Arts Center
　　　　　　　　　　　　　　　　열리다(hold: 열다, 개최하다)　　링컨 아트 센터
on December 20th.
M: Right. The New York Symphony Orchestra will play popular carols
　　　　　뉴욕 심포니 오케스트라　　　　　연주하다
during this concert.
W: Wow! I'm a big fan of the New York Symphony Orchestra.
　　　　　　　열혈 팬
M: I knew you'd like it.

W: How much is a ticket for the concert?
M: They're $40 each. Since it's a charity concert, all ticket sales will be donated to the Dream Children's Hospital.
　　　　　　　~에 기부되다(donate: 기부하다)　　드림 아동 병원
W: That's amazing. We can enjoy the concert and help the children as well.
M: You're right. Let's hurry to buy the tickets.
　　　　　　　　　　　　서두르다
W: Okay. *[Pause]* Wait! It says ticket sales start on December 10th.
M: I see. Let's mark the date, so we won't forget.
　　　　　　　　표시하다　　　　　　　　　　잊어버리다

해석

여: Chris, 무엇을 보고 있니?
남: Charity Carol Concert(자선 캐럴 콘서트)에 관한 웹사이트를 보고 있어. 그곳에 같이 가는 게 어때?
여: 재미있겠다. 어디 보자. 12월 20일에 Lincoln Arts Center(링컨 아트 센터)에서 열리는구나.
남: 맞아. 이 콘서트 동안 New York Symphony Orchestra(뉴욕 심포니 오케스트라)가 인기 있는 캐럴을 연주할 거야.
여: 와! 나는 New York Symphony Orchestra의 열혈 팬이야.
남: 네가 좋아할 줄 알았어.
여: 콘서트 티켓은 얼마니?
남: 한 장에 40달러야. 자선 콘서트이기 때문에, 티켓 판매금은 모두 Dream Children's Hospital(드림 아동 병원)에 기부될 거야.
여: 멋지다. 우리는 콘서트를 즐기고 아이들도 도울 수 있구나.
남: 네 말이 맞아. 티켓을 사려면 서두르자.
여: 알았어. *[잠시 후]* 잠깐만! 티켓 판매는 12월 10일에 시작한다고 쓰여 있어.
남: 그렇구나. 날짜를 표시해 두자, 그러면 잊어버리지 않을 거야.

① 공연 장소　　　② 공연 팀　　　③ 티켓 판매금 기부처
④ 티켓 판매 시작일　　✓⑤ 최대 관람 인원

09　Drone Photo Contest에 관한 내용과 일치하지 않는 것

정답률 90%　▶ 정답 ④

W: Hello, TCN listeners. I'm Kate Dale. I'd like to introduce the Drone Photo Contest to you. This contest first began in 2017, and the
　　　　　드론 사진 대회
number of participants has increased year by year. Regardless of
　　　　　참가자들　　　　　　　　　　　해마다　　　~에 상관없이
age, anyone who loves photography and drones can participate in
　　　　　　　　　　　　　　　　　　　　　　　~에 참가하다
this contest. There will be three categories for pictures, which are
　　　　　　　　　　　　　　　　분야들
animals, people, and nature. Upload your best drone photo to the
　　　　　　　　　　　　자연　　업로드하다
website, www.dronephotocontest.com by November 30th. For the
winner in each category, an amazing new drone will be given as
　우승자　　　　　　　　　놀라운
a prize. And the winners' photos will be posted on the website as
　상으로　　　　　　　　　　　　　　　　　게시되다(post: 게시하다)
well. Don't miss this opportunity. Stay tuned!
　　　　　놓치다　　　　기회

해석

여: 안녕하세요, TCN 청취자 여러분. 저는 Kate Dale입니다. 여러분에게 Drone Photo Contest(드론 사진 대회)를 소개하고 싶습니다. 이 대회는 2017년에 처음 시작되었으며, 참가자의 수가 해마다 증가해 왔습니다. 연령에 상관없이, 사진과 드론을 좋아하는 누구나 이 대회에 참가할 수 있습니다. 3개의 사진 분야가 있을 것이며, 그것은 동물, 사람, 그리고 자연입니다. 여러분의 최고의 드론 사진을 11월 30일까지 웹 사이트 www.dronephotocontest.com에 업로드하십시오. 각 분야의 우승자에게 상으로 놀라운 새 드론이 주어질 것입니다. 그리고 우승자의 사진은 웹 사이트에도 게시될 것입니다. 이 기회를 놓치지 마세요. 채널을 고정해 주세요!

① 2017년에 처음 시작된 대회이다.
② 사진과 드론을 좋아하는 누구나 참가할 수 있다.
③ 3개의 사진 분야가 있을 것이다.
✓④ 우승자에게 최신형 컴퓨터를 줄 것이다.
⑤ 우승 사진은 웹 사이트에 게시될 것이다.

10　표에서 여자가 주문할 향수

정답률 80%　▶ 정답 ①

M: What are you searching for, Mindy?
W: Dad, I'm searching for a perfume as a gift for Mom to celebrate her
　　　　　　　　　　　　　향수　　　　　　　　　　　　　　　축하하다

promotion. But I don't know which one to buy.

M: You're such a sweet daughter! Do you want me to help?

W: That would be great.

M: I think it's too much for you to spend over $100.

W: I agree. Oh, there are different scents to choose from. How about the floral scent?

M: She already has a floral perfume. I think you'd better pick one she doesn't have.

W: Good idea. Now, let's decide the size.

M: She usually carries perfume in her bag, so a portable size would be good.

W: Then, 50 ml would be a little big to carry.

M: Right. Oh, they come with a free gift.

W: I think Mom would like a pouch more than a hand mirror.

M: Yeah, she has a couple of hand mirrors.

W: Then, I'll order this one. Thanks, Dad.

해석

남: 무엇을 찾고 있니, Mindy?

여: 아빠, 엄마의 승진을 축하하기 위해서 선물로 향수를 찾고 있어요. 그런데 어떤 것을 사야 할지 모르겠어요

남: 너는 정말 착한 딸이구나! 내가 도와줄까?

여: 그럼 좋죠.

남: 네가 100달러 이상 쓰는 것은 지나친 것 같아.

여: 동의해요. 오, 선택할 수 있는 여러가지의 향들이 있어요. 꽃 향은 어때요?

남: 엄마는 이미 꽃 향수를 가지고 있어. 엄마가 가지고 있지 않은 것을 고르는 게 좋을 것 같아.

여: 좋은 생각이에요. 이제, 크기를 결정해요.

남: 엄마는 보통 가방에 향수를 가지고 다니니까, 휴대용 크기가 좋을 거야.

여: 그럼, 50ml는 가지고 다니기에 조금 크겠네요.

남: 그래. 오, 그것들은 사은품이 딸려 있구나.

여: 엄마는 손거울보다 파우치(작은 주머니)를 더 좋아할 것 같아요.

남: 그래, 엄마는 손거울이 몇 개 있거든.

여: 그럼, 이것을 주문할게요. 감사해요, 아빠.

여자 향수

	제품	가격	향	크기 (ml)	사은품
✔	A	60달러	감귤의	30	파우치
②	B	70달러	나무의	30	손거울
③	C	80달러	흙의	50	파우치
④	D	90달러	꽃의	50	파우치
⑤	E	110달러	과일의	70	손거울

11 여자의 마지막 말에 대한 남자의 응답　정답률 90%　▶ 정답 ②

W: Honey, what are you making?

M: I'm trying to bake some apple pies. But there are not enough apples in the refrigerator.

W: Then I'll go and buy some apples. How many do you need?

M: (I think five apples will be enough.)

해석

여: 여보, 무엇을 만들고 있어요?

남: 사과 파이를 좀 구우려고 해요. 그런데 냉장고에 사과가 충분하지 않네요.

여: 그럼 제가 가서 사과를 좀 사올게요. 몇 개나 필요해요?

남: (사과 다섯 개면 충분할 것 같아요.)

① 저는 이미 사과 파이 두 개를 샀어요.

✔사과 다섯 개면 충분할 것 같아요.

③ 그 요리법은 너무 어려워서 따라 할 수 없어요.

④ 당신은 그것들을 슈퍼마켓에서 살 수 있어요.

⑤ 그것들을 냉장고에 넣는 것이 안전해요.

12 남자의 마지막 말에 대한 여자의 응답　정답률 85%　▶ 정답 ②

M: Ms. Thompson, where are we going for dinner after the conference on Friday?

W: Hmm, how about the seafood buffet on Huston Street? People can choose their favorite food.

M: I tried to go there a few days ago, but it's closed for remodeling.

W: (Really? We need to think of another place.)

해석

남: Thompson 씨, 금요일에 회의 끝나고 저녁 먹으러 어디로 갈까요?

여: 흠, Huston Street에 있는 해산물 뷔페는 어때요? 사람들이 자신이 가장 좋아하는 음식을 고를 수 있잖아요.

남: 제가 며칠 전에 그곳에 가려고 했는데, 보수 공사 때문에 문을 닫았어요.

여: (정말이에요? 우리는 다른 장소를 생각해 봐야겠네요.)

① 죄송해요. 제가 해산물 알레르기가 있어요.

✔정말이에요? 우리는 다른 장소를 생각해 봐야겠네요.

③ 신경 쓰지 마세요. 회의는 취소되었어요.

④ 왜 안 되겠어요? 당신은 보수 공사를 시작하는 게 좋겠어요.

⑤ 감사해요. 저는 당신이 요리한 저녁을 정말 맛있게 먹었어요.

13 여자의 마지막 말에 대한 남자의 응답　정답률 95%　▶ 정답 ①

W: John, what are you doing?

M: Hi, Kelly. I'm taking these cups out of their recyclable packaging.

W: That looks different from other packaging I've seen.

M: Yeah, I bought the cups from a zero-waste shop, and they packed them using reusable materials.

W: Wow, then there's very little to throw away!

M: Yeah. I'm trying to reduce packaging waste in my daily life.

W: Great. I know the packaging waste problem is getting worse.

M: You can say that again. Zero-waste shops recycle packaging waste to create new products.

W: Then, we can get new things and reduce waste at the same time.

M: Yes. By shopping at zero-waste shops, we can save the environment.

W: I'd like to join you, but I don't know where the zero-waste shops are around us.

M: (Don't worry. I'll send you the locations of the stores I often use.)

해석

여: John, 무엇을 하고 있니?

남: 안녕, Kelly. 이 컵들을 재활용 가능한 포장재에서 꺼내고 있어.

여: 그것은 내가 본 다른 포장재와 다르게 보이는데.

남: 그래, 내가 제로 웨이스트 숍(폐기물 배출 없는 가게)에서 컵을 샀는데, 재사용할 수 있는 재료를 이용해서 포장해 줬거든.

여: 와, 그럼 버릴 게 거의 없겠구나!

남: 그래. 나는 일상 생활에서 포장재 쓰레기를 줄이려고 노력하고 있어.

여: 멋지다. 나는 포장재 쓰레기 문제가 악화되고 있다는 것을 알고 있어.

남: 네 말이 맞아. 제로 웨이스트 숍은 포장재 쓰레기를 재활용하여 새로운 제품을 만들어.

여: 그러면, 우리는 새로운 것을 얻으면서 동시에 쓰레기를 줄일 수 있겠다.

남: 그래. 제로 웨이스트 숍에서 쇼핑을 함으로써, 우리는 환경을 지킬 수 있어.

여: 너와 함께 하고 싶지만, 나는 우리 주위에 제로 웨이스트 숍이 어디에 있는지 모르겠어.

남: (걱정하지 마. 내가 자주 이용하는 가게들의 위치를 너에게 보내줄게.)

✔걱정하지 마. 내가 자주 이용하는 가게들의 위치를 너에게 보내줄게.

② 고마워. 나는 네가 제로 웨이스트 숍에서 산 컵이 마음에 들었어.

③ 당연하지. 우리는 네 노력 덕분에 쓰레기를 줄이기 시작했어.

④ 괜찮아. 내가 너에게 이 포장재를 재활용하는 방법을 보여줄게.

⑤ 내가 낼게. 네가 정말 원하는 것을 마음대로 사.

문제 풀이

포장재 쓰레기를 줄이기 위해서 제로 웨이스트 숍을 이용한다는 남자의 말에 공감하며 여자

는 자신도 제로 웨이스트 숍을 이용하고 싶지만 어디에 있는지 모르겠다고 말한다. 이에 대한 남자의 응답으로는 ① 'Don't worry. I'll send you the locations of the stores I often use.(걱정하지 마. 내가 자주 이용하는 가게들의 위치를 너에게 보내줄게.)'가 적절하다.

14 남자의 마지막 말에 대한 여자의 응답

정답률 85%
▶ 정답 ⑤

M: Hello, Jane. How are you?
W: Hi, Daniel. I'm fine.
M: I haven't seen you at the gym lately.
　　　　　　　　　　　　　체육관 최근에
W: Yeah, because of a new project, I've had a lot of work to do these days, so I couldn't go.
M: I see. Even though you don't have time, you need to try exercising regularly to give yourself a boost.
　　　　　　　　　　　　　　　　　　　　운동하는 것을 시도하다
　스스로에게 활력을 불어넣다　　　　(try V-ing: ~하는 것을 시도하다, exercise: 운동하다)
W: I know I need to, but it's hard to make time.
　　　　　　　　　　　　　　　　시간을 내다
M: Hmm, do you still get to work by bus?
　　　　　　　　　출근하다
W: Yes. It's about ten stops from my place to work. Why do you ask?
　　　　　　　열 정거장
M: Well, you could use the commuting time for exercise.
　　　　　　　　　　　　　통근 시간
W: How can I use that time to exercise?
M: Normally, I get off two stops in advance and walk either home or to
　보통　　　내리다　　　　　전에　　　걸어서 집에 가거나 회사에 가다
work. That's really effective.　(either A or B: A이거나 B인)
　　　　　　효과적인
W: (Great. That way, I can exercise even if I have a busy schedule.)

해석
남: 안녕, Jane. 어떻게 지내니?
여: 안녕, Daniel. 나는 잘 지내.
남: 최근에 체육관에서 너를 못 봤어.
여: 그래, 새로운 프로젝트 때문에 요즘 해야 할 일이 많아서 갈 수 없었어.
남: 그렇구나. 시간이 없다 하더라도, 스스로에게 활력을 불어넣기 위해 규칙적으로 운동하는 것을 시도해야 해.
여: 그래야 하는 것을 알지만, 시간을 내기가 힘들어.
남: 흠, 너는 아직도 버스로 출근하니?
여: 응. 우리 집에서 회사까지 열 정거장 정도 되지. 왜 묻는 거야?
남: 음, 너는 통근 시간을 운동을 위해 사용할 수 있어.
여: 어떻게 그 시간을 운동하는 데 사용할 수 있을까?
남: 보통, 나는 두 정거장 전에 내려서 걸어서 집에 가거나 회사에 가. 그것은 정말 효과적이야.
여: (좋아. 그렇게 하면, 나는 바쁜 일정이 있어도 운동할 수 있겠어.)

① 미안해. 나는 버스보다 지하철을 타는 것이 더 좋아.
② 걱정하지 마. 나는 네가 그 프로젝트를 잘 해낼 것이라고 확신해.
③ 유감이야. 우리는 그 걷기 프로그램을 취소했어야 했어.
④ 동의해. 충분한 휴식을 취함으로써 삶을 건강하게 유지할 수 있어.
✓ 좋아. 그렇게 하면, 나는 바쁜 일정이 있어도 운동할 수 있겠어.

15 다음 상황에서 Amy가 Mr. Green에게 할 말

정답률 70%
▶ 정답 ①

M: Amy is a high school student. One day, there is an event called
Career Day at her school. Students are supposed to choose a
　직업 체험의 날　　　　　　　　　　선택하기로 되어 있다
　　　　　　　　　　　　(be supposed to V: ~하기로 되어 있다, choose: 선택하다)
career and listen to a lecture about it, but Amy doesn't have a
　　　　　　　　　　　강의
career that interests her. So Amy just follows one of her friends
　　　　　　　관심을 끌다
and attends the lecture of an architect named Mr. Green. Mr.
　참석하다　　　　　　　　　건축가
Green explains how to be an architect and what architects actually
　　　　　건축가가 되는 방법(how to V: ~하는 방법)　　　실제로
do, which makes Amy interested in it. After the lecture, she wants
to learn more about the field of architecture. So, Amy wants to ask
　　　　　　　　　　　분야　　　건축
if she can visit where Mr. Green works and watch him do his job. In
this situation, what would Amy most likely say to Mr. Green?
Amy: (Is it possible for me to visit you to see what you do at work?)
　　　　　　가능한

해석
남: Amy는 고등학생이다. 어느 날, 그녀의 학교에서 Career Day(직업 체험의 날)라고 불리는 행사가 열린다. 학생들은 직업을 선택하고 그것에 대한 강의를 듣기로 되어 있지만, Amy

에게는 그녀의 관심을 끄는 직업이 없다. 그래서 Amy는 그저 그녀의 친구들 중 한 명을 따라가서 Mr. Green이라는 이름의 건축가의 강의에 참석한다. Mr. Green은 건축가가 되는 방법과 건축가가 실제로 하는 일을 설명해 주는데, 그것은 Amy가 그것에 관심을 갖게 만든다. 강의 후에, 그녀는 건축 분야에 대해 더 배우고 싶어 한다. 그래서 Amy는 Mr. Green이 일하는 곳을 방문해서 그가 일하는 것을 볼 수 있는지 물어보고 싶다. 이러한 상황에서, Amy는 Mr. Green에게 뭐라고 말하겠는가?
Amy: (당신이 직장에서 무엇을 하는지 보기 위해 제가 당신을 방문하는 것이 가능할까요?)

✓ 당신이 직장에서 무엇을 하는지 보기 위해 제가 당신을 방문하는 것이 가능할까요?
② 제가 건축가에 대한 발표를 준비하는 것을 도와주실 수 있을까요?
③ 제가 건물을 설계하는 데 참여하도록 허락해 주시겠어요?
④ 당신은 건축 분야에서 일자리를 찾으려고 하나요?
⑤ 직업 체험의 날에 학교에서 강의를 하는 게 어때요?

16~17 1지문 2문항

W: Hello, students. Last class, we talked about the differences
　　　　　　　　　　　　　　　　　　　　　　　　차이점들
between stars and planets. Today, I'm going to tell you how the
　　　　　별들　　　행성들
planets in the solar system got their names. First, Mercury is
　　　　　　　태양계　　　　　　　　　　　　　　　수성
named after the Roman god of travel who moved quickly delivering
~을 따라 명명되다(be named after)　　　　　　　　전달하면서(deliver)
messages to other gods. Mercury also moves rapidly around the
sun and that's how this planet got its name. Second, Jupiter is the
　　　　　　　　　　　　　　　　　　　　　　　　　　　목성
largest planet in the solar system. Because of its size, it makes
　　　　　　　　　　　　　　　　　　　　　　　　　　　　　이해가 되다
sense why ancient Romans named it after their most powerful
　　　　　고대의
god, the god of the sky. Third, Mars has a reddish color which
　　　　　　　　　　　　　　화성　　　　붉은
reminded ancient Romans of blood. Therefore, Mars got its name
　고대 로마인들에게 피를 떠올리게 했다
　(remind A of B: A에게 B를 떠올리게 하다)
from the god of war who caused many battles and many people's
　　　　　　　　　　　　　　야기했다　　　전투들
deaths. Lastly, Neptune is named for the Roman god of the sea.
　　　　　　　해왕성
Since the beautiful blue color of the planet looks like the sea, the
name is an excellent choice. Isn't it interesting? Now, let's move on
to who first discovered these planets. I'll show you a video.
　　　　　　발견했다

해석
여: 안녕하세요, 학생 여러분. 지난 수업 시간에, 우리는 별과 행성의 차이점에 대해 이야기했습니다. 오늘, 저는 여러분에게 태양계의 행성들이 어떻게 그 이름을 갖게 되었는지 말해 줄 것입니다. 첫째, 수성(Mercury)은 다른 신들에게 메시지를 전달하면서 빠르게 움직였던 로마 여행의 신을 따라 명명되었습니다. 수성은 또한 태양 주위를 빠르게 돌며 그렇게 해서 이 행성은 그 이름을 갖게 된 것입니다. 둘째, 목성(Jupiter)은 태양계에서 가장 큰 행성입니다. 그 크기 때문에, 고대 로마인들이 왜 그들의 가장 강력한 신인 하늘의 신을 따라 그것을 명명했는지 이해가 됩니다. 셋째, 화성(Mars)은 고대 로마인들에게 피를 떠올리게 했던 붉은 색을 가지고 있습니다. 그러므로, 화성은 많은 전투와 많은 사람들의 죽음을 야기했던 전쟁의 신에서 그 이름을 얻었습니다. 마지막으로, 해왕성(Neptune)은 로마 바다의 신에서 이름을 따왔습니다. 이 행성의 아름다운 파란색이 바다처럼 보이기 때문에, 그 이름은 훌륭한 선택입니다. 흥미롭지 않나요? 이제, 누가 이 행성들을 처음 발견했는지 알아봅시다. 영상을 보여드리겠습니다.

16 여자가 하는 말의 주제

정답률 80%
▶ 정답 ③

① 별과 행성의 차이점
② 밤에 행성을 관측하는 효과적인 방법
✓ 로마 신에서 유래한 행성 이름의 기원
④ 행성을 처음 발견한 고대 사람들
⑤ 행성의 환경과 기상 조건

17 언급된 행성이 아닌 것

정답률 90%
▶ 정답 ⑤

① 수성　　　　② 목성　　　　③ 화성
④ 해왕성　　　✓ 토성

14 2022년 3월 학력평가

01	①	02	①	03	②	04	⑤	05	③
06	③	07	①	08	②	09	④	10	③
11	④	12	①	13	②	14	①	15	②
16	①	17	④						

01 남자가 하는 말의 목적

정답률 90%
▶ 정답 ①

M: Hello, students. This is Mr. Watson, your vice principal. I have an
important announcement for all of you. As you know, our school
has two drinking fountains installed on each floor. Unfortunately,
due to repairs to the water pipes, all the drinking fountains in the
school will be out of service starting from tomorrow. It'll take a few
days until the water pipes are repaired. Until then, you won't be
able to use the school drinking fountains, so make sure you bring
your own water. We're very sorry for the inconvenience. Thank you.

해석

남: 안녕하세요, 학생 여러분. 저는 교감인 Watson 선생님입니다. 여러분 모두에게 중요한
안내 사항이 있습니다. 아시다시피, 우리 학교에는 각 층마다 설치된 두 개의 음수대가 있
습니다. 유감스럽게도, 수도관 수리 때문에, 내일부터 학교 내 모든 음수대는 이용이 중단
될 것입니다. 수도관이 수리되기까지는 며칠이 걸릴 것입니다. 그때까지, 여러분은 학교
음수대를 사용할 수 없을 것이므로, 반드시 자신의 물을 가져오도록 하세요. 불편을 드려
대단히 죄송합니다. 감사합니다.

✓ 수도관 수리로 음수대를 이용할 수 없다는 것을 알리려고
② 수도관 수리 일정이 변경되는 것을 공지하려고
③ 음수대 이용 시 질서를 지킬 것을 당부하려고
④ 물을 자주 마시는 것의 중요성을 강조하려고
⑤ 음수대가 추가로 설치된 장소를 안내하려고

02 여자의 의견

정답률 90%
▶ 정답 ①

W: Jason, are you shopping online?
M: Yes, Alice. I'm going to buy some clothes. Look! These are my
picks.
W: They look nice, but all of them are dark again this time.
M: I think dark colors suit me well and I feel more comfortable with
them.
W: I see your point. You always say that you want to be more
approachable though. Why don't you try other colors?
M: What colors would you recommend?
W: I think pastel colors would be good. They make the wearer appear
more friendly.
M: I see. I'm worried they won't look good on me though.
W: Just give it a try. You won't regret it.
M: All right. I'll go for the pastel clothes this time.
W: Great. I'm sure you'll look more approachable in them.
M: Thanks for your advice.

해석

여: Jason, 온라인으로 쇼핑을 하고 있니?
남: 그래, Alice. 옷을 좀 살 거야. 봐! 이것들이 내가 고른 거야.
여: 좋아 보이는데, 이번에도 모두 어두운 색이구나.
남: 어두운 색상이 나에게 잘 어울리는 것 같고 더 편하게 느껴져.
여: 무슨 말인지 알겠어. 하지만 너는 항상 더 가까이 하기 쉬운 사람이 되고 싶다고 말하잖아.

다른 색상을 입어보는 게 어때?
남: 너는 어떤 색상을 추천할 거니?
여: 파스텔 색상이 좋을 것 같아. 그것들은 착용자를 더 친근해 보이게 만들거든.
남: 그렇구나. 하지만 그것들이 나에게 어울리지 않을까 봐 걱정돼.
여: 그냥 한번 해봐. 후회하지 않을 거야.
남: 알았어. 이번에는 파스텔 색상의 옷을 선택하게.
여: 좋아. 네가 그것들을 입으면 분명 더 가까이 하기 쉬워 보일 거야.
남: 조언해 줘서 고마워.

✓ 파스텔 색상의 옷을 입으면 더 친근해 보인다.
② 공식적인 자리에는 어두운 색상의 옷이 어울린다.
③ 밝은 표정으로 인사하면 친근한 인상을 줄 수 있다.
④ 다양한 디자인의 옷을 통해 개성을 표현할 수 있다.
⑤ 기분이 우울할 때는 파스텔 색상의 옷을 입는 것이 좋다.

03 두 사람의 관계

정답률 85%
▶ 정답 ②

M: Hi, Miranda.
W: Oh, hi, Henry. I didn't expect you to be here today. I thought you
were still traveling around in Switzerland.
M: I came back earlier than scheduled. I just stopped by to see how
the preparations for the exhibition are going.
W: They're almost done. Did you take a look at the exhibition hall?
M: Yes, I did. You did a great job arranging all the pictures.
W: Is there anything you want to change?
M: Well, is it still possible to add some more works? I took some nice
photos during my trip.
W: Sure. Do you have them with you now?
M: No, but I can send you the photos by email. We can talk after you
check them out.
W: Okay. You're such a great artist. I'm so happy to exhibit your works
at our gallery.
M: Thanks for saying so. I'm also glad to work with you.

해석

남: 안녕하세요, Miranda.
여: 오, 안녕하세요, Henry. 오늘 여기에 오실 줄 몰랐어요. 여전히 스위스를 여행하고 계실 거
라고 생각했어요.
남: 예정보다 더 일찍 돌아왔어요. 전시회 준비가 어떻게 되어 가는지 보려고 잠깐 들렀어요.
여: 거의 다 됐어요. 전시장을 보셨어요?
남: 네, 봤어요. 모든 사진들을 정리하는 것을 잘 하셨더군요.
여: 바꾸고 싶으신 것이 있나요?
남: 음, 작품을 좀 더 추가하는 것이 아직 가능할까요? 여행 중에 멋진 사진을 몇 장 찍었거든
요.
여: 물론이죠. 지금 가지고 계신가요?
남: 아니요, 하지만 이메일로 사진을 보내드릴 수 있어요. 당신이 그것들을 확인한 후에 이야
기하면 되겠네요.
여: 알겠어요. 당신은 정말 훌륭한 예술가예요. 저희 미술관에서 당신의 작품을 전시하게 되
어 정말 행복해요.
남: 그렇게 말씀해주셔서 감사해요. 저도 당신과 함께 일하게 되어 기쁘네요.

① 관광객 — 관광 안내원
✓ 사진작가 — 미술관 큐레이터
③ 화가 — 화가 지망생
④ 관람객 — 박물관 관장
⑤ 촬영 감독 — 배우

04 그림에서 대화의 내용과 일치하지 않는 것

정답률 85%
▶ 정답 ⑤

W: Hi, David. You look happy.
M: I won a prize at the science fair. Look at this photo from the fair.
W: Wow! Congratulations. Oh, the prize ribbon is on the wall above the
board. Cool!

M: Yeah, I'm so proud.
자랑스러운
W: You set up your board on the round table. I see your topic was
세워 놓았다(set up)   주제
'Lemon Battery.' What did you do?
M: I showed how to make a battery using lemons.
만드는 방법
(how to V: ~하는 방법)
W: Interesting. So that's why there is a basket of lemons next to the
레몬 한 바구니
battery.
M: That's right.
W: Who is this woman wearing a flower-patterned dress?
꽃무늬 드레스
M: That's my grandmother. She came to congratulate me.
축하하다
W: How nice! Oh, you're holding flowers in your hand. They're so
들고 있는(hold)
beautiful.
M: Thanks. It was a great day.

해석
여: 안녕, David. 너 행복해 보인다.
남: 과학 박람회에서 상을 탔거든. 박람회에서 찍은 이 사진을 봐.
여: 와! 축하해. 오, 상품인 리본은 게시판 위쪽의 벽에 있구나. 멋지다!
남: 그래, 나는 정말 자랑스러워.
여: 원형 테이블 위에 네 게시판을 세워 놓았구나. 네 주제는 '레몬 배터리'였네. 너는 무엇을 했니?
남: 레몬을 이용해 배터리를 만드는 방법을 보여줬어.
여: 흥미로운데. 그래서 배터리 옆에 레몬 한 바구니가 있는 거구나.
남: 맞아.
여: 꽃무늬 드레스를 입고 있는 이 여자는 누구니?
남: 우리 할머니야. 나를 축하해주러 오셨어.
여: 정말 멋지다! 오, 너는 손에 꽃을 들고 있구나. 너무 예쁘다.
남: 고마워. 정말 좋은 날이었어.

05 남자가 여자를 위해 할 일
정답률 65%
▶ 정답 ③

M: Amy, are you ready for your presentation for history class this
발표   역사 수업
afternoon?
W: Yes, James. I just need to check the file again. [Clicking sound] Oh,
파일
no. What have I done?
M: What happened?
W: I worked on the presentation file until late last night. I guess I
forgot to save the final version.
저장하는 것을 잊었다   최종본
(forget to V: ~하는 것을 잊다, save: 저장하다)
M: Oh, dear. Do you need to do it all again?
W: Not really. Fortunately, I printed out the final version and brought it
다행히도   출력했다(print out)
with me. It won't take long to update the file.
업데이트하다
M: That's good. Do you have a handout for the class?
유인물
W: Yes, I printed it out, but I haven't made copies of it yet.
~을 복사하지 못했다
(make a copy of: ~을 복사하다)
M: I'll go to the library and do it for you.
W: That's so kind of you. Thanks a lot.
M: No problem.

해석
남: Amy, 오늘 오후에 있을 역사 수업을 위한 발표 준비가 됐니?

여: 그래, James. 파일을 다시 확인하기만 하면 돼. [클릭하는 소리] 오, 이런. 내가 뭘 한 거지?
남: 무슨 일이야?
여: 나는 어젯밤 늦게까지 발표 파일 작업을 했어. 최종본을 저장하는 것을 잊었나 봐.
남: 오, 맙소사. 그것을 다 다시 해야 하는 거야?
여: 그렇진 않아. 다행히도, 최종본을 출력해서 가지고 왔거든. 파일을 업데이트하는 데 오래 걸리지 않을 거야.
남: 잘됐다. 수업을 위한 유인물을 가지고 있니?
여: 그래, 출력했는데, 아직 복사하지 못했어.
남: 내가 도서관에 가서 너를 위해 그것을 해줄게.
여: 너는 정말 친절하구나. 고마워.
남: 별 거 아니야.

① 파일 수정하기
② 파일 출력하기
✓③ 유인물 복사하기
④ 유인물 검토하기
⑤ 발표 일정 확인하기

문제 풀이
역사 수업에 쓸 유인물이 있는지 묻는 남자의 질문에 여자는 출력은 했지만 아직 복사하지 못했다고 대답한다. 이에 대해 남자는 자신이 도서관에 가서 대신 그 일을 해주겠다고 말하고 있다. 따라서 남자가 여자를 위해 할 일은 ③ '유인물 복사하기'이다.

06 여자가 지불할 금액
정답률 75%
▶ 정답 ③

M: Honey, we need to buy swim fins for Ben. He's moving up to the
수영용 오리발
advanced swimming class!
수영 고급반
W: Oh, that's right. Let's buy them online. [Typing sound] Oh, these
fins look good. What do you think?
M: I like them. They're $30 a pair. Let's get one pair.
W: I think we'd better get two pairs. He often loses his stuff.
잃어버리다   물건
M: I agree. He also needs new swimming goggles. His goggles are
물안경
getting too small for him.
W: Okay. Oh, these goggles are on sale. They were originally $20 per
할인 판매 중인   원래
pair, but they're 10% off right now.
M: Great! Let's get one pair. Anything else?
W: I think that's all. Is there a shipping fee?
배송비
M: It's $5, but it's free if we spend more than $50.
무료의
W: Good. Let's place an order. I'll pay with my credit card.
주문하다

해석
남: 여보, 우리는 Ben을 위한 수영용 오리발을 사야 해요. 그는 수영 고급반으로 올라갈 거예요!
여: 오, 맞아요. 온라인으로 삽시다. [타자 치는 소리] 오, 이 오리발이 괜찮아 보이네요. 당신은 어떻게 생각해요?
남: 마음에 들어요. 한 켤레에 30달러네요. 한 켤레 사요.
여: 두 켤레를 사는 게 좋을 것 같아요. 그는 자주 물건을 잃어버리잖아요.
남: 동의해요. 그는 새로운 물안경도 필요해요. 그의 물안경은 그에게 너무 작아지고 있잖아요.
여: 알겠어요. 오, 이 물안경은 할인 판매 중이에요. 원래 한 개에 20달러였는데, 지금은 10% 할인하고 있어요.
남: 잘됐네요! 한 개 삽시다. 또 다른 건 없어요?
여: 그게 다인 것 같아요. 배송비가 있어요?
남: 5달러인데, 우리가 50달러 이상을 쓰면 무료예요.
여: 좋아요. 주문해요. 제 신용카드로 결제할게요.

① $48   ② $55   ✓③ $78
④ $80   ⑤ $83

문제 풀이
한 켤레에 30달러인 수영용 오리발 두 켤레와 원래 20달러이지만 현재 10% 할인된 가격으로 판매되는 물안경을 한 개 사면 총액은 78달러이다. 구매 물품의 가격이 50달러를 초과했기 때문에 배송비는 지불하지 않아도 된다. 따라서 답은 ③ '$78'이다.

07 남자가 이번 토요일에 쇼핑하러 갈 수 없는 이유
정답률 90% ▶ 정답 ①

M: Mom, I'm home.
W: Hi, Ethan. Were you busy preparing for the school festival?
~을 준비하느라 바쁜
(busy V-ing: ~하느라 바쁜, prepare for: ~을 준비하다)
M: Yes. You know I'll be the MC for the school talent show. We
사회
장기 자랑 대회
rehearsed for the show today.
예행연습을 했다
W: How did it go?
M: It went well. I just hope I don't make a mistake on the stage.
실수를 하다　무대
W: I'm sure you'll do great. I guess you need to wear a suit for the
정장을 입다
show. How about going shopping this Saturday?
M: Oh, I wish I could, but I can't.
W: Ah, you go and volunteer at the library every Saturday.
자원봉사를 하다
M: Not this Saturday. I canceled it because I have to help make a
video for the festival. 취소했다　동영상을 제작하다
W: I see. Let's go shopping on Sunday then.
M: Okay.

해석
남: 엄마, 저 왔어요.
여: 안녕, Ethan. 학교 축제를 준비하느라 바빴니?
남: 네. 제가 학교 장기 자랑 대회의 사회를 맡은 것을 아시잖아요. 오늘 대회를 위한 예행연습을 했어요.
여: 어떻게 됐니?
남: 잘 됐어요. 제가 무대에서 실수만 하지 않았으면 좋겠어요.
여: 너는 분명 잘할 거야. 대회를 위해 정장을 입어야 할 것 같구나. 이번 주 토요일에 쇼핑하러 가는 게 어떠니?
남: 오, 저도 그러고 싶지만, 안 되겠어요.
여: 아, 너는 매주 토요일마다 도서관에 가서 자원봉사를 하는구나.
남: 이번 주 토요일은 아니에요. 축제를 위한 동영상을 제작하는 것을 도와야 하기 때문에 취소했어요.
여: 그렇구나. 그럼 일요일에 쇼핑하러 가자.
남: 좋아요.

✔️학교 축제에 쓸 동영상 제작을 도와야 해서
② 도서관에 봉사 활동을 하러 가야 해서
③ 장기 자랑 대회 예행연습을 해야 해서
④ 장기 자랑 대회 사회를 맡아야 해서
⑤ 무대 의상을 제작해야 해서

08 Modern Architecture Expo에 관해 언급되지 않은 것
정답률 70% ▶ 정답 ②

M: Emily, come have a look at this leaflet. It's about the Modern
전단
Architecture Expo.
현대 건축 박람회
W: Oh, it looks interesting.
M: We both have an interest in architecture. Why don't we go there
~에 관심이 있다
together?
W: Good idea. It'll be held at the Grand Convention Center. It's close
to our school. 개최되다(hold: 개최하다)
M: Great! When should we go?
W: It starts on April 1st and ends on April 15th. Can you make it on
Saturday, April 9th? (모임 등에) 가다
M: Yes, I can. Look here. Admission is $20 for students.
입장료
W: Oh, that's quite expensive.
꽤 비싼
M: I'm sure it'll be worth it. Ten great architects will be giving lectures
가치가 있다　건축가들　강연들
on their best architectural works. We can attend as many of them
건축 작품들　참석하다
as we want.
W: Cool! It'll be great to see them in person.
직접

해석
남: Emily, 와서 이 전단을 봐. Modern Architecture Expo(현대 건축 박람회)에 관한 거야.
여: 오, 재미있어 보이네.
남: 우리 둘 다 건축에 관심이 있잖아. 같이 그곳에 가는 게 어떠니?
여: 좋은 생각이야. 그것은 Grand Convention Center에서 개최될 거야. 우리 학교에서 가까워.

남: 잘됐다! 우리 언제 갈까?
여: 그것은 4월 1일에 시작해서 4월 15일에 끝나. 4월 9일 토요일에 갈 수 있겠니?
남: 응, 그래. 여기 봐. 학생 입장료는 20달러야.
여: 오, 꽤 비싸구나.
남: 분명 그만한 가치가 있을 거야. 10명의 대단한 건축가들이 그들의 최고의 건축 작품들에 대한 강연을 할 거야. 우리가 원하는 만큼 강연에 참석할 수 있어.
여: 멋지다! 그들을 직접 보면 정말 좋을 거야.

① 개최 장소　　✔️주최 기관　　③ 개최 기간
④ 입장료　　　⑤ 강연자 수

09 2022 Opera in School에 관한 내용과 일치하지 않는 것
정답률 75% ▶ 정답 ④

W: Hello, students. This is Ms. Miller, your music teacher. Are you
interested in operas? Then, we invite you to 2022 Opera in School.
~에 관심이 있는　　초대하다
Five professional opera singers will come to our school and
전문 오페라 가수들
present Romeo and Juliet to you. They'll bring the classic story to
공연하다　　고전 이야기에 생명을 불어넣다
(bring A to life: A에 생명을 불어넣다, classic: 고전의)
life with opera costumes and sets. The show will be held at the
의상들　무대 장치들
school auditorium on March 25th, starting at 6 p.m. It'll last for 45
학교 강당　　진행되다
minutes and be followed by a question and answer session. You
질의응답 시간
can take photos with the singers after the question and answer
~와 사진을 찍다
session is finished. There's no admission fee, but to attend, you
must register in advance. I hope to see you there.
등록하다　사전에

해석
여: 안녕하세요, 학생 여러분. 저는 음악 교사인 Miller 선생님입니다. 여러분은 오페라에 관심이 있나요? 그렇다면, 2022 Opera in School에 여러분을 초대합니다. 5명의 전문 오페라 가수들이 우리 학교에 와서 여러분에게 'Romeo and Juliet'을 공연할 것입니다. 그들은 오페라 의상과 무대 장치로 고전 이야기에 생명을 불어넣을 것입니다. 그 공연은 3월 25일 오후 6시부터 학교 강당에서 열릴 것입니다. 45분 동안 진행되며 질의응답 시간이 이어질 것입니다. 질의응답 시간이 끝난 후에는 가수들과 사진을 찍을 수 있습니다. 입장료는 없지만, 참석하기 위해서는, 사전에 등록하셔야 합니다. 그곳에서 뵙기를 바랍니다.

① Romeo and Juliet을 공연할 것이다.
② 3월 25일 학교 강당에서 열릴 것이다.
③ 공연은 45분간 진행될 것이다.
✔️질의응답 시간 전에 가수들과 사진을 찍을 수 있다.
⑤ 참석하려면 사전에 등록해야 한다.

10 표에서 두 사람이 구입할 미니 오븐
정답률 75% ▶ 정답 ③

M: Honey, are you trying to buy a mini oven on the Internet?
미니 오븐
W: Yes, we need it to bake cookies or biscuits. What do you think of
these five models? 굽다
M: Let me have a look. [Pause] All of them look nice, but it seems too
much to spend more than $100 for a mini oven.
W: I agree. We should eliminate this one then. I think the capacity
제외하다　용량
should be at least 10 liters.
최소한
M: Then let's choose one of these three. What about the weight?
무게
W: I guess the lighter, the better. I don't want it to be more than 6 kg.
더 가벼울수록, 더 좋다
M: All right. Now we're down to these two models. Shall we go for the
one with a baking pan?
베이킹 팬
W: I don't think so. We can use the pans we already have.
M: I see. Let's buy the other one then.
W: Okay.

해석
남: 여보, 인터넷에서 미니 오븐을 사려고 하는 거예요?
여: 네, 우리는 쿠키나 비스킷을 굽기 위해서 그것이 필요해요. 이 다섯 가지 모델에 대해 어떻게 생각해요?
남: 한번 볼게요. [잠시 후] 모두 좋아 보이지만, 미니 오븐에 100달러 이상을 쓰는 것은 너무 많은 것 같아요.

여: 동의해요. 그럼 이것은 제외해야겠어요. 용량은 최소한 10리터는 되어야 할 것 같아요.
남: 그럼 이 세 가지 중에 하나를 골라봐요. 무게는 어때요?
여: 더 가벼울수록, 더 좋을 것 같아요. 6kg 이상 되는 것은 원하지 않아요.
남: 알겠어요. 이제 이 두 가지 모델로 좁혀졌네요. 베이킹 팬이 있는 것을 선택해야 할까요?
여: 저는 그렇게 생각하지 않아요. 우리가 이미 가지고 있는 팬을 사용할 수 있잖아요.
남: 알겠어요. 그럼 다른 것을 삽시다.
여: 좋아요.

미니 오븐

	모델	가격	용량(리터)	무게(킬로그램)	베이킹 팬
①	A	92달러	9	6.0	X
②	B	93달러	10	6.5	O
✓③	C	95달러	12	5.5	X
④	D	98달러	13	5.0	O
⑤	E	110달러	13	4.5	O

11 여자의 마지막 말에 대한 남자의 응답

정답률 85% ▶ 정답 ④

W: Ian, you're in such good shape! Do you still go to the gym every day?
M: Not now. The gym closed down last month, so I just work out alone at home.
W: At home? What kind of exercises do you do?
M: (I do push-ups and squats for 30 minutes every day.)

해석

여: Ian, 몸 상태가 정말 좋구나! 아직도 매일 체육관에 가니?
남: 지금은 아니야. 지난달에 체육관이 문을 닫아서, 그냥 집에서 혼자 운동해.
여: 집에서? 어떤 종류의 운동을 하니?
남: (나는 매일 30분 동안 팔굽혀펴기와 스쿼트를 해.)

① 나는 너와 함께 체육관에 가서 운동할 수 있어.
② 나는 일주일에 세 번 체육관에서 역기를 들어.
③ 팀 스포츠에 참여하는 것은 활동적으로 지낼 수 있는 좋은 방법이야.
✓④ 나는 매일 30분 동안 팔굽혀펴기와 스쿼트를 해.
⑤ 식이요법은 건강을 유지하기 위해 운동만큼 중요해.

12 남자의 마지막 말에 대한 여자의 응답

정답률 60% ▶ 정답 ①

M: Jenny, you're planning to enter the online dance competition, right?
W: Yes, I finished recording a video. I just need to upload it to the website. I hope I'll win a prize.
M: I'm sure you will. You're a great dancer. I wonder how they will choose the best dancer though.
W: (The person who gets the most votes will be the winner.)

해석

남: Jenny, 너는 온라인 댄스 대회에 참가할 계획이지, 그렇지?
여: 그래, 나는 영상을 녹화하는 것을 끝냈어. 그것을 웹사이트에 업로드하기만 하면 돼. 상을 받으면 좋겠어.
남: 분명 그럴 거야. 너는 춤을 잘 추잖아. 그런데 어떻게 최고의 댄서를 뽑을지 궁금해.
여: (가장 많은 표를 얻은 사람이 우승자가 될 거야.)

✓① 가장 많은 표를 얻은 사람이 우승자가 될 거야.
② 나는 최고의 댄서로 뽑혀서 정말 행복해.
③ 나는 댄스 영상을 만드는 게 힘들어.
④ 나는 네가 영상을 웹사이트에 업로드하는 것을 도와줄 수 있어.
⑤ 나는 참가하기에 좋은 댄스 대회를 찾고 있어.

13 여자의 마지막 말에 대한 남자의 응답

정답률 75% ▶ 정답 ②

M: Sandy, what are you doing with your bike?
W: Oh, hi, Jack. I'm checking it out. It makes strange sounds when I ride it.
M: Let me take a look. [Pause] Hmm.... I think the brakes are not working properly.
W: Oh, no. I should get them fixed at the bike shop. It'll cost too much.
M: Why don't you try a repair cafe? You can save money.
W: A repair cafe? What's that?
M: It's a place where you can fix your broken stuff on your own. The cafe provides tools and materials.
W: Well, I don't think I can fix my bike by myself.
M: Don't worry. Expert volunteers will be around to help you out there. There are many repair cafes around town.
W: That's great. I'll give it a try. Do you know where the nearest place is?
M: (Well, I saw a repair cafe next to the post office.)

해석

남: Sandy, 자전거로 무엇을 하고 있니?
여: 오, 안녕, Jack. 살펴보고 있는 중이야. 내가 그것을 탈 때 이상한 소리가 나거든.
남: 내가 좀 볼게. [잠시 후] 흠.... 브레이크가 제대로 작동하지 않는 것 같아.
여: 오, 이런. 자전거 가게에서 고쳐야겠네. 비용이 너무 많이 들 거야.
남: 무료 수리점에 가보는 건 어때? 돈을 절약할 수 있잖아.
여: 무료 수리점? 그게 뭐야?
남: 고장이 난 물건을 스스로 고칠 수 있는 곳이야. 그 수리점은 도구와 재료를 제공해.
여: 음, 나 혼자서 자전거를 고칠 수 없을 것 같아.
남: 걱정하지 마. 전문 자원봉사자들이 그곳에서 너를 도와주기 위해 주위에 있을 거야. 동네에 무료 수리점이 많이 있어.
여: 잘됐다. 한번 해볼게. 가장 가까운 곳이 어디에 있는지 알고 있니?
남: (음, 나는 우체국 옆에 있는 무료 수리점을 봤어.)

① 좋아, 네가 전에 추천했던 무료 수리점에 가볼게.
✓② 음, 나는 우체국 옆에 있는 무료 수리점을 봤어.
③ 물론이지, 너는 자원봉사를 할 수 있는 곳을 쉽게 찾을 수 있어.
④ 그래, 새로 생긴 자전거 가게는 물건을 싸게 팔아.
⑤ 미안하지만, 내가 너무 바빠서 네 자전거를 고칠 수가 없어.

문제 풀이

고장이 난 자전거를 고치기 위해 남자가 말한 무료 수리점에 가기로 한 여자는 남자에게 가장 가까운 무료 수리점이 있는 위치를 묻고 있다. 이에 대한 남자의 응답으로는 ② 'Well, I saw a repair cafe next to the post office.(음, 나는 우체국 옆에 있는 무료 수리점을 봤어.)'가 적절하다.

14 남자의 마지막 말에 대한 여자의 응답

정답률 75% ▶ 정답 ①

M: Ellie! Look at this smartphone application.
W: Okay. [Pause] Oh, it says that it can help you track your blood sugar level.
M: That's right. It shows us how much sugar we eat a day. All we have to do is just click what we ate.
W: Then the app automatically shows the amount of sugar in that food?
M: Exactly. It's very easy to use.
W: Interesting! But why do you care about your blood sugar level all of a sudden?
M: Actually, it's for my mom. Recently, she was diagnosed with high blood sugar. She's using the app to control her sugar intake.
W: I'm sorry for your mom. So does she find it useful?
M: Yes, she says it's very helpful. You can recommend it to anyone who needs it.
W: (My dad has the same problem. I'll tell him about the app.)

해석

남: Ellie! 이 스마트폰 앱을 봐.
여: 알겠어. [잠시 후] 오, 혈당 수치를 추적하는 데 도움을 줄 수 있다고 써있네.
남: 맞아. 그것은 우리가 하루에 얼마나 많은 설탕을 먹는지 보여줘. 우리는 먹은 것을 클릭하기만 하면 돼.

14 22년 3월 학력평가

여: 그럼 그 앱이 자동으로 그 음식에 들어있는 설탕의 양을 보여주는 거야?
남: 바로 그거야. 그것은 사용하기에 매우 쉬워.
여: 흥미롭다! 그런데 너는 왜 갑자기 혈당 수치에 관심을 가지는 거야?
남: 사실, 우리 엄마를 위한 거야. 최근에, 엄마는 고혈당으로 진단을 받으셨거든. 설탕 섭취량을 조절하기 위해서 그 앱을 사용하고 계셔.
여: 엄마 일은 유감이야. 그래서 엄마께서는 그것이 유용하다고 생각하시니?
남: 그래, 매우 도움이 된다고 말씀하셔. 너는 그것을 필요로 하는 누구에게나 추천할 수 있어.
여: (우리 아빠도 같은 문제를 가지고 계셔. 나는 그 앱에 대해 알려드릴 거야.)
☑ 우리 아빠도 같은 문제를 가지고 계셔. 나는 그 앱에 대해 알려드릴 거야.
② 과일을 너무 많이 먹지 마. 그것은 혈당 수치를 올라가게 해.
③ 맞아. 운동은 혈당 수치를 낮추는 데 도움을 줘.
④ 왜 안 돼? 나는 이 앱을 몇 달 동안 사용해 오고 있어.
⑤ 네 말이 맞아. 나는 스마트폰 사용 시간을 조절해야 해.

15 다음 상황에서 Sandra가 Mr. Wilson에게 할 말
정답률 70% ▶ 정답 ②

M: Sandra is the president of the student council of her school.
회장   학생회
Today the student council is having their regular meeting.
정기 회의
One of the issues at today's meeting is about how to improve
안건들   향상시키는 방법
(how to V: ~하는 방법, improve: 향상시키다)
students' mental and physical health. These days, many students
정신적인   신체적인
have health problems because they don't get much exercise.
운동을 많이 하지 않다(get exercise: 운동을 하다)
The student council agrees that it'd be good to hold a sports
competition to improve the students' health. After the meeting,
체육 대회
Sandra goes to the principal's office and tells Mr. Wilson about
교장실
what they discussed. Now she wants to ask him for permission to
논의했다   그에게 허락을 구하다
(ask A for permission: A에게 허락을 구하다)
host the sports event for the sake of the students. In this situation,
주최하다   ~을 위해
what would Sandra most likely say to Mr. Wilson?
Sandra: (Can we hold a sports competition for student health?)

해석
남: Sandra는 학교 학생회의 회장이다. 오늘 학생회는 정기 회의를 가질 예정이다. 오늘 회의의 안건들 중 하나는 학생들의 정신적 및 신체적 건강을 향상시키는 방법에 관한 것이다. 요즘, 많은 학생들이 운동을 많이 하지 않기 때문에 건강 문제를 가지고 있다. 학생회는 학생들의 건강을 향상시키기 위해 체육 대회를 개최하는 것이 좋을 것이라는 데 동의한다. 회의가 끝난 후에, Sandra는 교장실로 가서 Wilson 선생님에게 그들이 논의했던 것에 대해 이야기한다. 이제 그녀는 학생들을 위해 체육 대회를 주최할 수 있도록 그에게 허락을 구하고 싶어 한다. 이러한 상황에서, Sandra는 Wilson 선생님에게 뭐라고 말하겠는가?
Sandra: (학생들의 건강을 위해 체육 대회를 개최할 수 있을까요?)
① 학생회 회의를 주관하는 방법을 알려주시겠어요?
☑ 학생들의 건강을 위해 체육 대회를 개최할 수 있을까요?
③ 학생들에게 새로운 스포츠 장비를 제공해 주세요.
④ 저희의 정기 회의에 참석하실 수 있을까요?
⑤ 우리 학교를 대표해서 스포츠 리그에 참가합시다.

16~17 1지문 2문항

W: Good morning, class! Today, we'll continue to learn some
계속해서 배우다
(continue to V: 계속해서 ~하다, learn: 배우다)
interesting facts about animals. Did you know that some animals
can live without food for months and even years? First, crocodiles,
~ 없이 살다   악어들
one of the oldest reptiles of the planet, can go for a few months
파충류들
without food, and in extreme cases, they can go up to 3 years
극단적인 경우에는
without food. They save energy by moving slowly and at times by
움직임으로써   때로는
(by V-ing: ~함으로써, move: 움직이다)
being motionless too. Next, spiders have to wait for their food
움직이지 않음으로써   거미들   그들의 먹이가 오기를 기다리다
(motionless: 움직이지 않는)   (wait for A to V: A가 ~하기를 기다리다)
to come to them, so sometimes the wait could be long. But, no

worries. Their body is able to last for 3 to 4 months without food.
견딜 수 있다
(be able to V: ~할 수 있다, last: 견디다)
This can stretch up to 1 year. As for penguins, their metabolism
늘어나다   펭귄들   신진대사
is reduced during cold weather, which can help them sustain
지탱하다
themselves without food or water for 2 to 4 months. Lastly, sharks
상어들
can live without food for 8 to 10 weeks. Interestingly, the longer
흥미롭게도
they live without food, the more deadly their hunting skills become.
사냥 기술들
Now, let's watch some videos of these animals.

해석
여: 좋은 아침이에요, 학생 여러분! 오늘, 우리는 계속해서 동물들에 대한 몇 가지 흥미로운 사실들을 배울 것입니다. 여러분은 일부 동물들이 몇 달 그리고 심지어 몇 년 동안 먹이 없이 살 수 있다는 것을 알고 있었나요? 먼저, 지구에서 가장 오래된 파충류들 중 하나인 악어는 먹이 없이 몇 달 동안 지낼 수 있고, 극단적인 경우에는, 먹이 없이 3년까지 지낼 수 있습니다. 그들은 천천히 움직임으로써 그리고 때로는 움직이지 않음으로써 에너지를 절약합니다. 다음으로, 거미는 그들의 먹이가 그들에게 오기를 기다려야 하기 때문에, 때때로 그 기다림이 길어질 수 있습니다. 하지만, 걱정하지 마세요. 그들의 몸은 먹이 없이 3~4개월 동안 견딜 수 있습니다. 이것은 1년까지 늘어날 수 있습니다. 펭귄의 경우에, 그들의 신진대사는 추운 날씨 동안 감소하는데, 이것은 그들이 2~4개월 동안 먹이나 물 없이 스스로를 지탱하는 데 도움을 줄 수 있습니다. 마지막으로, 상어는 8~10주 동안 먹이 없이 살 수 있습니다. 흥미롭게도, 그들이 먹이 없이 더 오래 살수록, 그들의 사냥 기술은 더 치명적이게 됩니다. 이제, 이 동물들의 영상을 좀 보겠습니다.

16 여자가 하는 말의 주제
정답률 85% ▶ 정답 ①

☑ 먹이가 없이 오랫동안 생존할 수 있는 동물들
② 동물이 극심한 날씨에 적응해 내는 방법들
③ 기후 변화가 동물의 서식지에 미치는 영향들
④ 포식자를 피하기 위해 동물이 사용하는 기술들
⑤ 다양한 동물들의 독특한 사냥 기술들

17 언급된 동물이 아닌 것
정답률 90% ▶ 정답 ④

① 악어   ② 거미   ③ 펭귄
☑ 돌고래   ⑤ 상어

15 2022년 6월 학력평가

01	⑤	02	②	03	②	04	④	05	⑤
06	④	07	①	08	③	09	④	10	④
11	②	12	②	13	②	14	①	15	③
16	②	17	③						

01 남자가 하는 말의 목적
정답률 90% ▶ 정답 ⑤

M: Good morning, Lakeside High School students. This is your
principal. As you know, Mrs. Smith retired a few weeks ago. So, we
교장   퇴직했다
were without a music teacher for the past few weeks. But today,
음악 선생님
I'm happy to announce that Cindy White joined our school as
알리다   지난
the new music teacher. Ms. White is a passionate teacher and a
열정적인
talented violinist in the local orchestra. She worked at Wellington
재능 있는   지역 오케스트라
High School for three years. There, she organized a school band
조직했다

and led many successful underline{performances}. We're excited to have such an underline{enthusiastic} music teacher in our school. Please give her a warm welcome when you see her!
공연들 / 열성적인

해석

남: 안녕하세요, Lakeside 고등학교 학생 여러분. 저는 교장입니다. 아시다시피, Smith 선생님께서 몇 주 전에 퇴직하셨습니다. 그래서, 우리는 지난 몇 주 동안 음악 선생님 없이 지냈습니다. 하지만 오늘, Cindy White 선생님이 새로운 음악 선생님으로 우리 학교에 오셨다는 것을 알려드리게 되어 기쁩니다. White 선생님은 열정적인 선생님이자 지역 오케스트라의 재능 있는 바이올린 연주자입니다. 그녀는 Wellington 고등학교에서 3년 동안 근무했습니다. 그곳에서, 그녀는 학교 밴드를 조직했고 많은 성공적인 공연들을 이끌었습니다. 우리 학교에 이렇게 열성적인 음악 선생님을 모시게 되어 기쁩니다. 그녀를 보면 따뜻하게 환영해 주십시오!

① 교내 밴드 공연을 홍보하려고
② 교장 선생님의 퇴임을 축하하려고
③ 변경된 음악 수업 장소를 안내하려고
④ 지역 오케스트라의 단원을 모집하려고
☑ 새로운 음악 선생님의 부임을 알리려고

02 여자의 의견
정답률 90%
▶ 정답 ②

W: Jake, you look so underline{nervous} today.
긴장한

M: That's because I have a big underline{test} this afternoon.
시험

W: Oh, you must underline{be concerned}. Have you studied a lot?
걱정되다(concern: 걱정스럽게 만들다, ~에 영향을 미치다)

M: Sure. But the problem is, I usually get so nervous that I underline{make stupid mistakes} on tests.
어리석은 실수를 하다 (make a mistake: 실수를 하다, stupid: 어리석은)

W: Then, why don't you underline{try eating} chocolate before the test?
먹어 보다 (try V-ing: ~해 보다)

M: Chocolate? Do you think that will help?

W: Yes, eating chocolate will underline{relieve} your underline{anxiety}.
완화시키다 / 불안감

M: Really? I always thought that chocolate was just a kind of underline{dessert} or underline{snack}.
후식 / 간식

W: Actually, chocolate was underline{originally} used underline{as a medicine}. It can underline{lower} levels of underline{anxiety-related} hormones.
원래 / 약으로 / 낮추다 / 불안감과 관련된

M: Hmm... But I heard that chocolate can underline{increase} one's underline{heart rate}.
증가시키다 / 심장 박동수

W: If you eat too much, that's true, but a underline{proper amount} of chocolate helps you feel underline{calmer}.
적당한 양 / 더 차분한

M: Sounds interesting. Thanks for the underline{tip}.
조언

해석

여: Jake, 너 오늘 너무 긴장한 것처럼 보여.
남: 오늘 오후에 중요한 시험이 있어서 그래.
여: 오, 걱정되겠다. 공부는 많이 했니?
남: 물론이지. 그런데 문제는, 나는 보통 너무 긴장해서 시험에서 어리석은 실수를 한다는 거야.
여: 그렇다면, 시험 전에 초콜릿을 먹어 보는 건 어떠니?
남: 초콜릿? 그것이 도움이 될 것 같니?
여: 응, 초콜릿을 먹는 것은 네 불안감을 완화시킬 거야.
남: 정말? 나는 항상 초콜릿이 단지 일종의 후식이나 간식이라고 생각했어.
여: 사실, 초콜릿은 원래 약으로 사용됐어. 그것은 불안감과 관련된 호르몬의 수치를 낮출 수 있어.
남: 흠... 하지만 나는 초콜릿이 심장 박동수를 증가시킬 수 있다고 들었어.
여: 너무 많이 먹는 경우에는 그것이 맞지만, 적당한 양의 초콜릿은 네가 더 차분하게 느끼도록 도움을 줘.
남: 흥미롭게 들린다. 조언해 줘서 고마워.

① 반복적인 학습을 통해 시험에서의 실수를 줄일 수 있다.
☑ 적당량의 초콜릿 섭취는 불안감 완화에 도움이 된다.
③ 단 음식을 많이 먹으면 호르몬의 균형이 깨진다.
④ 초콜릿의 효능에 대한 과학적 연구가 필요하다.
⑤ 의약품 남용에 대한 규제를 강화해야 한다.

문제 풀이

시험 때문에 긴장하는 남자에게 여자는 초콜릿을 먹어 보라고 권한다. 여자는 초콜릿이 불안감을 완화시키며 적당량의 초콜릿을 먹게 되면 차분해지는 데 도움이 된다고 말한다. 따라서 여자의 의견으로 적절한 것은 ② '적당량의 초콜릿 섭취는 불안감 완화에 도움이 된다.'이다.

03 두 사람의 관계
정답률 90%
▶ 정답 ②

M: Ms. Miller, it's been such a long time since we last met. How have you been?

W: Good. I went underline{abroad on a business trip} for 3 months.
해외 출장을 다녀왔다(go on a business trip)

M: You must have been very underline{busy}. What brings you here today?
바쁜

W: I want to make a change to underline{refresh} my underline{look}.
새롭게 하다 / 외모

M: Hmm... What were you thinking of?

W: I want to get my hair colored and cut.

M: underline{Unfortunately}, your hair's underline{condition} doesn't look good. Why don't you change your hair color next time?
안타깝게도 / 상태

W: Fine. Then, I'll underline{get a haircut} today and visit you again to get my hair colored.
머리카락을 자르다

M: Okay. What style of cut do you want?

W: I don't want it too short.

M: Don't worry. I'll underline{take care of} it.
~에 신경을 쓰다

해석

남: Miller 씨, 우리가 지난번에 만난 이후에 정말 오래됐어요. 어떻게 지냈어요?
여: 잘 지냈어요. 저는 3개월 동안 해외 출장을 다녀왔어요.
남: 매우 바쁘셨겠네요. 오늘 무슨 일로 오셨어요?
여: 제 외모를 새롭게 하기 위해서 변화를 주고 싶어요.
남: 흠... 어떤 생각을 하셨어요?
여: 머리카락을 염색하고 자르고 싶어요.
남: 안타깝게도, 머리카락의 상태가 좋아 보이지 않네요. 머리카락 색깔은 다음에 바꾸시는 게 어때요?
여: 좋아요. 그럼, 오늘은 머리카락을 자르고 염색하러 다시 올게요.
남: 알겠어요. 어떤 스타일로 자르기를 원하세요?
여: 너무 짧지 않으면 좋겠어요.
남: 걱정하지 마세요. 제가 그것에 신경을 쓸게요.

① 여행사 직원 — 여행객
☑ 헤어 디자이너 — 고객
③ 가구 제작자 — 의뢰인
④ 화가 — 모델
⑤ 영화감독 — 배우

04 그림에서 대화의 내용과 일치하지 않는 것
정답률 85%
▶ 정답 ④

M: Rebecca, look at this picture.

W: Sure. What is it?

M: This is the underline{garage} in my new house. I underline{finally} have one.
차고 / 드디어

W: Great. It was your dream to have your own garage, right?
자신의

M: Right. Look at this underline{tool board} on the wall. It's very underline{convenient} for underline{hanging} tools.
연장 정리판 / 편리한 / 걸어 놓는 것(hang)

W: Good. And you put a table below the board.

M: Yes, I use it for underline{repairing broken} things. Can you see the underline{skateboard} in the box? I changed its underline{wheels} all by myself.
수리하는 것(repair) 고장 난 / 스케이트보드 / 바퀴들

W: Awesome. But isn't it underline{boring} to work alone?
지루한

M: Yes, that's why I put a big underline{speaker} in the underline{corner} to listen to music.
스피커 / 구석

W: Cool. Is that your new bicycle near the door?

M: Yes, now I can underline{safely store} it inside the garage.
안전하게 보관하다

W: That's good. You were always worried about your bicycle when it rained. Congratulations.

해석

남: Rebecca, 이 사진을 봐.

여: 그래. 그게 뭐니?
남: 나의 새 집에 있는 차고야. 드디어 하나 갖게 되었어.
여: 잘됐다. 네 자신의 차고를 갖는 것이 네 꿈이었잖아, 그렇지?
남: 맞아. 벽에 있는 이 연장 정리판을 봐. 그것은 연장들을 걸어 놓기에 매우 편리해.
여: 좋다. 그리고 정리판 아래에 테이블을 놓았구나.
남: 그래, 고장 난 물건들을 수리하는 데 그것을 사용해. 상자 안에 있는 스케이트보드가 보이니? 나는 혼자서 그것의 바퀴를 교체했어.
여: 멋지다. 그런데 혼자 작업하는 것은 지루하지 않니?
남: 맞아, 그런 이유로 음악을 듣기 위해 구석에 큰 스피커를 놓은 거야.
여: 멋지다. 문 근처에 있는 것은 너의 새 자전거니?
남: 응, 이제 차고 안에 그것을 안전하게 보관할 수 있어.
여: 잘됐다. 너는 비가 올 때 항상 자전거에 대해 걱정했잖아. 축하해.

05 남자가 할 일

▶ 정답 ⑤

W: Billy, I'm so excited about our first trip to Jeju Island next week.
M: Indeed, honey. We've been waiting so long for it.
W: Yeah. I checked the weather forecast, and it says it will be nice.
　　　　　　　　　　　　　　　일기 예보
M: Good. Is there anything we're forgetting to do before going?
　　　　　　　　　　　　　해야 하는 것을 잊어버리는
　　　　　　　　　　　(forget to V: ~해야 하는 것을 잊어버리다)
W: Hmm... Oh! I forgot to make a reservation for a rental car.
　　　　　　　　　　　　　　예약하다　　　　　　　　렌트카
M: Don't worry. I've already made one at a reasonable price.
　　　　　　　　　　　　　　　　　　　　　적정한
W: What a relief! How about our plan to change our room from a city
　　　　　　　　　　　　　　　계획　　　　　　　　　　도시 전망
view to an ocean view?
　　　바다 전망
M: I've already called the hotel and changed it to have an ocean view.
W: Great. I heard that the Jeju Tourism Organization is having a
　　　　　　　　　　　　　　　　　관광 공사
special event. They provide discount coupons to fancy restaurants.
　　　　　　　　　　　　　　할인 쿠폰들　　　　고급의
M: Really? How can we get some?
W: We can download them from their website.
　　　　　다운로드하다
M: Okay, I'll do that right away.

해석
여: Billy, 다음 주에 갈 우리의 첫 제주도 여행이 정말 기대돼요.
남: 그래요, 여보. 우리는 그것을 정말 오래 기다려 왔어요.
여: 네. 일기 예보를 확인했는데, 날씨가 좋을 거라고 해요.
남: 잘됐네요. 가기 전에 우리가 해야 하는 것을 잊어버린 일이 있나요?
여: 흠... 오! 렌트카를 예약해야 하는 것을 잊어버렸어요.
남: 걱정하지 마요. 제가 이미 적정한 가격으로 예약했어요.
여: 정말 다행이에요! 방을 도시 전망에서 바다 전망으로 변경하는 계획은 어때요?
남: 제가 이미 호텔에 전화해서 바다 전망으로 변경했어요.
여: 잘됐네요. 저는 제주 관광 공사에서 특별 행사를 한다고 들었어요. 고급 식당의 할인 쿠폰을 제공한대요.
남: 정말이에요? 어떻게 얻을 수 있어요?
여: 웹사이트에서 다운로드할 수 있어요.
남: 알겠어요, 제가 바로 할게요.

① 날씨 확인하기
② 렌트카 예약하기
③ 호텔 방 변경하기
④ 비행기표 예매하기
✔ 할인 쿠폰 다운받기

06 여자가 지불할 금액

▶ 정답 ④

M: Welcome to Sky Cable Car. How may I help you?
W: Hi. I want to buy tickets. I see two types of cable cars. What's the
difference between the Regular and the Crystal Cable Car?
　차이점
M: The Crystal Cable Car has a glass floor, so you can see below you.
　　　　　　　　　　　　　　유리 바닥
W: That must be thrilling! How much is it for an adult?
　　　　　　　　짜릿한
M: An adult ticket is $20.
W: Is that round-trip?
　　　　왕복의
M: No, this is a one-way ticket. You need to pay an additional $5 each
　　　　　　편도의　　　　　　　　　　　　　추가의
for round-trip tickets.
W: Then I'll buy round-trip tickets for two adults.
M: So round-trip Crystal Cable Car tickets for two adults, right?
W: Yes, and I have a discount coupon for local residents. Can I use it?
　　　　　　　　　　　　　　　　　지역 주민들
M: Let me take a look. [Pause] Yes. You can get a $5 discount off the
total.　　　　　　　　　　　　　　　총액에서 5달러 할인을 받다
W: Very good. Here's my credit card.

해석
남: Sky Cable Car(Sky 케이블카)에 오신 것을 환영합니다. 어떻게 도와드릴까요?
여: 안녕하세요. 저는 티켓을 사고 싶어요. 두 종류의 케이블카가 보이네요. 일반 케이블카와 크리스털 케이블카의 차이점이 뭐죠?
남: 크리스털 케이블카는 유리 바닥으로 되어 있어서, 아래를 보실 수 있어요.
여: 짜릿하겠네요! 성인은 얼마인가요?
남: 성인 티켓은 20달러예요.
여: 왕복인가요?
남: 아니요, 이것은 편도 티켓이에요. 왕복 티켓은 각각 5달러를 추가로 지불하셔야 해요.
여: 그렇다면 성인 두 명의 왕복 티켓을 살게요.
남: 그럼 성인 두 명의 크리스털 케이블카 왕복 티켓이죠, 맞나요?
여: 네, 그리고 저는 지역 주민을 위한 할인 쿠폰이 있어요. 그것을 사용할 수 있나요?
남: 한번 볼게요. [잠시 후] 네. 총액에서 5달러 할인을 받으실 수 있어요.
여: 아주 좋네요. 여기 제 신용카드가 있어요.

① $30　　　　　　　② $35　　　　　　　③ $40
✔ $45　　　　　　　⑤ $50

문제 풀이
크리스털 케이블카의 성인 편도 티켓은 20달러, 왕복 티켓은 5달러가 추가된 25달러이다. 성인 두 명의 왕복 티켓을 사면 총액은 50달러이다. 여자가 가지고 있는 할인 쿠폰으로 총액에서 5달러 할인을 받을 수 있다고 했으므로 지불할 금액은 45달러이다. 따라서 답은 ④ '$45'이다.

07 여자가 벼룩시장에 갈 수 없는 이유

▶ 정답 ①

W: Hi, Jason. I like your T-shirt.
M: Thanks. I bought it for just $3 at the flea market.
　　　　　　　　　　　　　　　　　　　벼룩시장
W: What a bargain! I want to buy a T-shirt like yours, too.
M: Then, how about going to the flea market together? It'll be held
this Saturday.　　　　　　　　　　　　　　　　　열리다(hold: 열다)
W: This Saturday? I'd love to, but I can't.
M: Oh, I know you work at Tom's Bakery. Do you work on Saturdays?
W: No, I only work on weekdays.
　　　　　　　　　　평일에
M: I see. Then is it because of the medical check-up you reserved last
　　　　　　　　　　　　　　　　　건강 검진　　　　　　예약했다
week?
W: I did make an appointment, but I changed the date to next Friday.
　　　　　　예약하다　　　　　　　　　　　날짜
M: So, then what's your plan for Saturday?
W: Actually, it's my uncle's wedding that day. I promised to play the
piano for him at the ceremony.　　　　　　　연주하기로 약속했다
　　　　　　　　　　　결혼식　　　　(promise to V: ~하기로 약속하다, play: 연주하다)
M: Great! Maybe some other time, then.

해석
여: 안녕, Jason. 나는 네 티셔츠가 마음에 들어.
남: 고마워. 나는 그것을 벼룩시장에서 단돈 3달러에 샀어.
여: 정말 싸다! 나도 네 것과 같은 티셔츠를 사고 싶어.

남: 그럼, 함께 벼룩시장에 가는 건 어때? 그것은 이번 주 토요일에 열릴 거야.
여: 이번 주 토요일? 가고 싶지만, 안 되겠어.
남: 오, 네가 Tom's Bakery에서 일하는 거 알아. 토요일마다 일하니?
여: 아니, 나는 평일에만 일해.
남: 그렇구나. 그럼 지난주에 예약했던 건강 검진 때문이니?
여: 예약했지만, 다음 주 금요일로 날짜를 바꿨어.
남: 그럼, 토요일 계획이 뭐야?
여: 사실, 그날 삼촌의 결혼식이 있거든. 나는 결혼식에서 그를 위해 피아노를 연주하기로 약속했어.
남: 잘됐다! 그럼, 다음에 가자.

✓ 결혼식에서 피아노를 연주해야 해서
② 빵집에서 아르바이트를 해야 해서
③ 티셔츠를 교환하러 가야 해서
④ 건강 검진을 받아야 해서
⑤ 과제를 제출해야 해서

08 Brantown Community Picnic에 관해 언급되지 않은 것 ▶ 정답 ③
정답률 90%

M: What are you looking at, Hailey?
W: I'm browsing our local community website to check out this month's events. It says the Brantown Community Picnic is coming up.
M: Sounds interesting. It could be a good chance to meet our neighbors and talk with them. When is it?
W: It's on June 18th, from 11 a.m. to 3 p.m. Would you like to go with me?
M: Why not? I don't have any plans for that day.
W: Great! Guess where it will be held. We've been there several times.
M: Is it going to be in Brantown Park?
W: That's right.
M: I like that place. Let me see... It says they will hand out a tumbler as a gift to all of the participants.
W: Terrific! How do we sign up?
M: We just need to call the community center by this Friday.
W: Then let's do it right now!

해석
남: 무엇을 보고 있니, Hailey?
여: 이번 달 행사를 확인하기 위해 지역 사회 웹사이트를 둘러보고 있어. Brantown Community Picnic(Brantown 주민 소풍)이 다가오고 있어.
남: 재미있겠다. 그것은 이웃들을 만나서 이야기를 나눌 수 있는 좋은 기회가 될 수 있어. 언제야?
여: 6월 18일 오전 11시에서 오후 3시까지지. 나와 함께 가겠니?
남: 왜 안 되겠어? 나는 그날 아무런 계획이 없거든.
여: 잘됐다! 어디에서 열릴지 맞춰봐. 우리는 그곳에 몇 번 갔어.
남: Brantown Park(Brantown 공원)에서 열릴 예정이야?
여: 맞아.
남: 나는 그곳이 좋아. 어디 보자... 참가자 모두에게 선물로 텀블러를 나눠 줄 거라고 해.
여: 잘됐다! 어떻게 신청하지?
남: 이번 주 금요일까지 주민 센터에 전화하기만 하면 돼.
여: 그럼 지금 바로 하자!

① 일시 ② 장소 ✓ 참가비
④ 증정품 ⑤ 신청 방법

09 Space Science Camp에 관한 내용과 일치하지 않는 것 ▶ 정답 ④
정답률 90%

W: Good morning, everyone. I'm Olivia Benson, the president of Golden Star Observatory. We'll be hosting Space Science Camp for teenagers this summer vacation. It's a 3-day camp which goes from August 21st to August 23rd. Our programs will help you learn more about space. A former astronaut, Dr. Michael Russell, will give a special lecture about space travel. Participants will

---

even have a chance to look at stars through our telescopes. If you want to join this camp, you should sign up at our website. The reservation page will open two weeks before the camp. The participation fee is $50 per person. We hope to see you then. Thank you.

해석
여: 안녕하세요, 여러분. 저는 Golden Star Observatory(Golden Star 천문대)의 대표인 Olivia Benson입니다. 저희는 이번 여름 방학에 십 대들을 위한 Space Science Camp(우주 과학 캠프)를 개최할 것입니다. 그것은 8월 21일부터 8월 23일까지 3일간 진행되는 캠프입니다. 저희의 프로그램은 여러분이 우주에 대해 더 많이 배우도록 도와줄 것입니다. 전직 우주 비행사인 Michael Russell 박사가 우주 여행에 관한 특별 강연을 할 것입니다. 참가자들은 저희의 망원경을 통해 별을 볼 수 있는 기회도 갖게 될 것입니다. 이 캠프에 참여하고 싶다면, 저희 웹 사이트에서 신청해야 합니다. 예약 페이지는 캠프 2주 전에 열릴 것입니다. 참가비는 1인당 50달러입니다. 그때 뵙기를 바랍니다. 감사합니다.

① 8월 21일부터 8월 23일까지 진행된다.
② 우주 여행에 관한 특별 강연이 있다.
③ 참가자에게는 별을 관측할 기회가 있다.
✓ 예약 페이지는 캠프 3주 전에 열린다.
⑤ 참가비는 1인당 50달러이다.

10 표에서 두 사람이 구매할 식기세척기 ▶ 정답 ④
정답률 85%

W: Tom, we have so many dishes to wash after every meal.
M: You're right. Let's buy a dishwasher from this online mall.
W: Well, what's our budget for that?
M: We can't spend more than $800. We've already spent too much this month.
W: I agree. Well, dishwashers get dirty easily, so white is not a good choice for the color.
M: Right. Plus, silver or black would match our kitchen cabinets.
W: Okay. Which would you prefer, a portable or a built-in type?
M: I'd prefer a built-in. We would have more space with a built-in.
W: Besides, it would look more stylish.
M: Good point. Then, there are two options left. Which one would be better?
W: Definitely this one. When it comes to warranty periods, the longer, the better.
M: Perfect! Then let's order this one.

해석
여: Tom, 매 식사 후에 씻어야 할 그릇들이 너무 많아요.
남: 당신 말이 맞아요. 이 온라인 몰에서 식기세척기를 삽시다.
여: 음, 우리 예산이 얼마나 되죠?
남: 800달러 이상은 쓸 수 없어요. 우리는 이번 달에 이미 너무 많이 썼어요.
여: 동의해요. 음, 식기세척기는 쉽게 더러워지니까, 흰색은 색상에 있어 좋은 선택이 아니에요.
남: 맞아요. 게다가, 은색이나 검은색이 우리 주방 수납장과 어울릴 거예요.
여: 알았어요. 휴대용 유형과 붙박이 유형 중 어느 것이 더 좋아요?
남: 붙박이면 더 좋겠어요. 붙박이로 되어 있으면 우리는 더 많은 공간을 가질 수 있잖아요.
여: 뿐만 아니라, 더 멋져 보일 거예요.
남: 좋은 지적이에요. 그럼, 두 가지 선택지가 남았네요. 어떤 것이 더 나을까요?
여: 확실히 이것이네요. 보증 기간에 관한 한, 더 길수록 더 좋잖아요.
남: 완벽해요! 그럼 이것을 주문합시다.

식기세척기

	모델	가격	색상	유형	보증 기간
①	A	650달러	검은색	휴대용	6개월
②	B	680달러	검은색	붙박이	6개월
③	C	720달러	흰색	휴대용	1년
✓	D	760달러	은색	붙박이	1년
⑤	E	850달러	은색	붙박이	2년

문제편 45

15
22년 6월 학력평가

15회. 2022년 6월 학력평가 정답과 해설 73

11 남자의 마지막 말에 대한 여자의 응답

정답률 80%

▶ 정답 ②

M: Emily, the plants you gave me are dying.
W: When taking care of plants, giving them enough sunlight and water is very important.
M: I think there's enough sunlight. But how often should I water the plants?
W: (You need to water them once every three days.)

해석
남: Emily, 네가 내게 준 식물들이 죽어가고 있어.
여: 식물들을 돌볼 때, 충분한 햇빛과 물을 주는 것이 아주 중요해.
남: 햇빛은 충분한 것 같아. 그런데 얼마나 자주 식물들에게 물을 줘야 하니?
여: (너는 3일에 한 번 그것들에게 물을 줘야 해.)
① 지구를 위해 많은 식물들을 기르는 것이 중요해.
✓ 너는 3일에 한 번 그것들에게 물을 줘야 해.
③ 너무 많은 햇빛은 식물들에게 해로울 수 있어.
④ 나는 환경을 위해 물을 절약해야겠어.
⑤ 우리는 하루에 1리터의 물을 마셔야 해.

12 여자의 마지막 말에 대한 남자의 응답

정답률 70%

▶ 정답 ②

W: Richard, have you chosen a place for Mom's birthday party? It's already next week!
M: I've been trying to make a reservation at Palace Bistro, but the restaurant never answers my calls.
W: Haven't you heard? It's closed for repairs until next month!
M: (Oh, no. I must find another place as soon as possible.)

해석
여: Richard, 엄마의 생신 파티를 위한 장소를 골랐니? 벌써 다음 주잖아!
남: Palace Bistro에 예약하려고 했는데, 그 식당에서 내 전화를 받지 않아.
여: 너 못 들었니? 그곳은 보수 공사를 위해 다음 달까지 문을 닫아!
남: (오, 이런. 나는 가능한 한 빨리 다른 장소를 찾아야 해.)
① 미안해. 나는 이미 그 식당에 예약을 했어.
✓ 오, 이런. 나는 가능한 한 빨리 다른 장소를 찾아야 해.
③ 잘됐다. 지금 당장 전화기를 수리하자.
④ 말도 안 돼! 너무 멀어서 그곳에 갈 수 없어.
⑤ 고마워. 네 파티에 꼭 갈게.

13 남자의 마지막 말에 대한 여자의 응답

정답률 80%

▶ 정답 ②

M: Sarah, where did you get those bananas?
W: I just took them out of the parcel box in front of the door.
M: What box? I haven't ordered anything recently.
W: Really? I thought you ordered them, so I ate some.
M: Let's check the address on the box.
W: Oh, no! The package was misdelivered. This is not our address.
M: Umm… The bananas were supposed to be delivered to our next-door neighbor, Mr. Jones.
W: What should I do?
M: I think it would be good to explain to him why you took them. And we should buy him some new bananas.
W: Okay. I'll tell him what happened right away.
M: Wait! It's too late. Mr. Jones usually goes to bed really early, so I don't think it's a good idea to wake him up now.
W: (You're right. I'll take care of it tomorrow.)

해석
남: Sarah, 그 바나나들을 어디에서 가져왔어?
여: 문 앞에 있는 택배 상자에서 방금 꺼냈어.
남: 무슨 상자? 나는 최근에 아무것도 주문하지 않았어.
여: 정말? 나는 네가 주문한 줄 알고, 좀 먹었어.
남: 상자에 있는 주소를 확인해 보자.
여: 오, 이런! 택배가 잘못 배달되었어. 이것은 우리 주소가 아니야.
남: 음… 바나나는 우리 옆집 이웃인 Jones 씨에게 배달될 예정이었어.
여: 어떻게 해야 하지?
남: 네가 왜 그것들을 가져갔는지 그에게 설명하는 게 좋을 것 같아. 그리고 우리는 그에게 새 바나나를 좀 사줘야 해.
여: 알았어. 내가 그에게 무슨 일이 있었는지 바로 말할게.
남: 잠깐! 너무 늦었어. Jones 씨는 보통 매우 일찍 잠자리에 드니까, 지금 그를 깨우는 것은 좋은 생각이 아닌 것 같아.
여: (네 말이 맞아. 내가 내일 그 일을 처리할게.)
① 걱정하지 마. 내가 이미 그것을 주문했어.
✓ 네 말이 맞아. 내가 내일 그 일을 처리할게.
③ 내 잘못이야! 내가 거기에 주소를 잘못 적었어.
④ 미안해. 다음에는 내가 너를 일찍 깨워줄게.
⑤ 물론이지. 너는 빌린 물건을 지금 돌려주는 게 좋을 거야.

문제 풀이
잘못 배달된 택배의 원래 주인인 Jones 씨에게 가서 상황 설명을 하려는 여자에게 남자는 이미 잠자리에 들었을 그를 깨우지 않는 게 좋을 것 같다고 말한다. 이에 대한 여자의 응답으로 적절한 것은 ② 'You're right. I'll take care of it tomorrow.(네 말이 맞아. 내가 내일 그 일을 처리할게.)'이다.

14 여자의 마지막 말에 대한 남자의 응답

정답률 90%

▶ 정답 ①

W: Hi, Tim. Nice to see you.
M: Hi, Christine. You look like you're in good shape. Are you working out these days?
W: Yes, I go to the gym every morning and take a swimming class some evenings.
M: I want to learn how to swim, but I haven't had a chance to take lessons.
W: How about signing up for the swimming course I'm taking?
M: Good idea. Where are you taking it?
W: At the community center near our apartment. The fee is quite reasonable and the swimming instructors are kind.
M: That sounds like a perfect place to start.
W: If we work out together, I'm sure we'll have a great time.
M: Me, too! So, how can I register?
W: You can register online starting this afternoon. But the swimming classes are popular, so sign up soon!
M: (Okay. Then, I need to hurry up and register.)

해석
여: 안녕하세요, Tim. 만나서 반가워요.
남: 안녕하세요, Christine. 몸이 건강해 보이네요. 요즘 운동하고 있어요?
여: 네, 매일 아침 체육관에 가고 어떤 저녁에는 수영 수업을 들어요.
남: 저는 수영하는 방법을 배우고 싶지만, 수업을 들을 기회가 없었어요.
여: 제가 듣는 수영 수업에 등록하시는 건 어떠세요?
남: 좋은 생각이네요. 어디에서 들으세요?
여: 우리 아파트 근처에 있는 주민 센터에서요. 요금이 꽤 합리적이고 수영 강사들이 친절해요.
남: 시작하기에 완벽한 장소인 것 같아요.
여: 우리가 함께 운동하면, 즐거운 시간을 보낼 거라고 확신해요.
남: 저도 그래요! 그럼, 어떻게 등록할 수 있나요?
여: 오늘 오후부터 온라인으로 등록할 수 있어요. 하지만 수영 수업은 인기가 있으니까, 빨리 등록하세요!
남: (알겠어요. 그럼, 서둘러서 등록해야겠네요.)
✓ 알겠어요. 그럼, 서둘러서 등록해야겠네요.
② 죄송해요. 당신은 직접 그것에 등록해야만 해요.
③ 고마워요. 저는 친구에게 그것들을 추천했어요.

④ 걱정하지 마세요. 당신은 물에 대한 두려움을 극복할 수 있어요.
⑤ 환상적이네요! 그 수영 강사는 전문적이에요.

15 다음 상황에서 Amy가 Jerry에게 할 말

정답률 80% ▶ 정답 ③

W: Amy and Jerry are close neighbors. They live next to each other and their children go to the same kindergarten. One day, when Amy is
유치원
about to leave work, she's given some tasks that must be done
막 퇴근하려고 하다   업무들
(be about to V: 막 ~하려고 하다, leave work: 퇴근하다)
immediately. Amy looks at her watch and finds that there's only
즉시
one hour left before the kindergarten classes end. She realizes
깨닫다
that no matter how fast she finishes the work, she will never be
아무리 ~해도   ~에게 갈 수 없다
able to get to her son in time. Amy needs someone to help her and
~에게 갈 수 없다   제시간에
(be able to V: ~할 수 있다,
get to: ~에게 가다)
thinks of Jerry. So, she wants to ask Jerry to bring her son back home from kindergarten. In this situation, what would Amy most likely say to Jerry?
Amy: (Would you pick up my son from kindergarten for me?)
데려오다

해석
여: Amy와 Jerry는 가까운 이웃이다. 그들은 서로의 옆집에 살고 있고 그들의 아이들은 같은 유치원에 다닌다. 어느 날, Amy가 막 퇴근하려고 할 때, 그녀에게 즉시 끝내야 하는 몇 가지 업무들이 주어졌다. Amy는 시계를 보고 유치원 수업이 끝나려면 한 시간 밖에 남지 않았다는 것을 알게 된다. 그녀는 아무리 빨리 일을 끝내도 제시간에 아들에게 갈 수 없을 것이라는 것을 깨닫는다. Amy에게는 그녀를 도와줄 누군가가 필요한데 Jerry를 생각해낸다. 그래서, 그녀는 Jerry에게 자신의 아들을 유치원에서 집으로 데려와 달라고 부탁하고 싶다. 이러한 상황에서, Amy는 Jerry에게 뭐라고 말하겠는가?
Amy: (저를 위해 제 아들을 유치원에서 데려와 주시겠어요?)
① 당신이 오늘까지 그것들을 끝낼 수 있을 것 같아요.
② 그곳에 제시간에 도착할 수 있는 방법을 아시나요?
✓③ 저를 위해 제 아들을 유치원에서 데려와 주시겠어요?
④ 유치원 장기자랑에서 빨리 당신을 봤으면 좋겠어요.
⑤ 집들이에 아무것도 가져올 필요가 없어요.

16~17 1지문 2문항

M: Hello, students. Last time, we talked about the problem of wasting materials. Today, we're going to discuss how used materials are
소재들   논의하다
recycled and turned into new products. Used paper is usually cut
재활용되다(recycle: 재활용하다)   제품들   종이
down into small pieces and sent into a machine to remove any
조각들   기계
ink or glue on it. Then it can be used for making things such as
잉크   접착제
toilet paper and paper bags. Metals like steel and iron are also
금속들
valuable as recyclable materials. They are melted down and easily
가치가 있는   재활용 가능한   녹여지다(melt down: 녹다)
transformed into car parts, frames, foils, and other things. Glass
자동차 부품들 뼈대들 포장지들   유리
is another special material that can be recycled endlessly. Like
끊임없이
metals, glass is also melted down after being crushed, and then
분쇄된 후에(crush: 분쇄하다)
it is made into new bottles and jars. Plastics are complicated to
플라스틱들   복잡한
recycle because there are so many types. After sorting and melting
분류한 후에(sort)
the plastics, they can be turned into new products like bottles and toys through a special process. Now, let's take a look at some
과정
video clips and then we'll discuss them in detail.
동영상들   자세히

해석
남: 안녕하세요, 학생 여러분. 지난 시간에, 우리는 소재를 낭비하는 것의 문제에 대해 이야기했습니다. 오늘, 우리는 사용된 소재들이 어떻게 재활용되고 새로운 제품들로 바뀌는지에 대해 논의할 것입니다. 사용된 종이는 보통 작은 조각으로 잘라져서 그것에 있는 잉크나 접착제를 제거하기 위해 기계로 보내집니다. 그리고 나서 그것은 화장지와 종이 가방 같

은 것을 만드는 데 사용될 수 있습니다. 강철과 철 같은 금속도 재활용 가능한 소재로 가치가 있습니다. 그것들은 녹여져서 자동차 부품, 뼈대, 포장지, 그리고 다른 것들로 쉽게 변형됩니다. 유리는 끊임없이 재활용될 수 있는 또 다른 특별한 소재입니다. 금속처럼, 유리도 분쇄된 후에 녹여져서, 새로운 병과 항아리로 만들어집니다. 플라스틱은 매우 많은 종류가 있기 때문에 재활용하기가 복잡합니다. 플라스틱을 분류하고 녹인 후에, 그것들은 특별한 과정을 통해 병과 장난감 같은 새로운 제품들로 바뀔 수 있습니다. 이제, 몇 편의 동영상들을 본 다음 그것들에 대해 자세히 논의하겠습니다.

16 남자가 하는 말의 주제

정답률 80% ▶ 정답 ②

① 재활용 제품에 대한 오해
✓② 재활용의 과정과 산출물
③ 폐기물 오염으로 인한 문제
④ 재활용 시스템의 역사
⑤ 쓰레기를 줄이기 위한 조언

17 언급된 소재가 아닌 것

정답률 90% ▶ 정답 ③

① 종이   ② 금속   ✓③ 직물
④ 유리   ⑤ 플라스틱

16 2022년 9월 학력평가

01	①	02	①	03	④	04	⑤	05	④
06	⑤	07	④	08	⑤	09	③	10	③
11	①	12	⑤	13	②	14	①	15	④
16	⑤	17	③						

01 여자가 하는 말의 목적

정답률 80% ▶ 정답 ①

W: Hello, Princeton High School students. As you know, our school's website is going to be redesigned. Our goals are to make our
다시 디자인되다   목표들
(redesign: 다시 디자인하다)
website more accessible to everyone and to strengthen online
이용할 수 있는   강화하다
security. To better prepare our new website, we're conducting a
보안   준비하다   실시하고 있는(conduct)
survey to gather your opinions and suggestions. Your participation
설문조사   모으다 의견들   제안들   참여
is strongly encouraged. The survey must be completed by this
강력히 독려되다   완료되다
(encourage: 독려하다)   (complete: 완료하다)
Thursday. For more information, please refer to our school bulletin
~을 참고하다   게시판
board. Remember that your input is valuable to everyone in our
조언   소중한
school's community. Thank you!

해석
여: 안녕하세요, Princeton 고등학교 학생 여러분. 알다시피, 우리 학교 웹사이트가 다시 디자인될 것입니다. 우리의 목표는 웹사이트를 모두가 더 쉽게 이용할 수 있게 만들고 온라인 보안을 강화하는 것입니다. 새로운 웹사이트를 더 잘 준비하기 위해서, 여러분의 의견과 제안을 모으는 설문조사를 실시하고 있습니다. 여러분의 참여가 강력히 독려됩니다. 설문조사는 이번 주 목요일까지 완료되어야 합니다. 더 많은 정보를 원하시면, 학교 게시판을 참고하세요. 여러분의 조언은 학교 공동체의 모든 사람들에게 소중하다는 것을 기억하세요. 감사합니다!
✓① 설문조사 참여를 독려하려고
② 설문조사 결과를 공유하려고
③ 설문조사 기간 변경을 공지하려고
④ 학교 홈페이지 가입을 요청하려고
⑤ 학교 홈페이지 점검 시간을 안내하려고

02 남자의 의견
정답률 80%
▶ 정답 ①

M: Kate, you don't look good. Are you okay?
W: Yes, I'm fine. It's nothing.
M: Are you sure? You seem really stressed.
W: Well, I'm having a hard time being the leader of a team project.
스트레스를 받는
리더가 되는 데 힘든 시간을 보내는
(have a hard time V-ing: ~하는 데 힘든 시간을 보내다)
M: What's the problem?
W: It's hard handling different opinions because my teammates get into arguments easily.
다루는(handle)   의견들
논쟁을 벌이다(argument: 논쟁)
M: I understand, however, arguments can lead people to make better decisions.
이끌다   더 나은 결정을 하다
W: Do you really think so?
M: Absolutely! Arguments happen all the time. Try to think of
항상   생각하도록 노력하다
arguments as a way to reach a better decision. (try to V: ~하도록 노력하다)
도달하다
W: That's good advice. I'll try to remember that.
조언

해석
남: Kate, 너 안 좋아 보여. 괜찮아?
여: 응, 괜찮아. 아무 일도 아니야.
남: 확실해? 너 정말 스트레스를 받는 것처럼 보여.
여: 음, 나는 팀 프로젝트의 리더가 되는 데 힘든 시간을 보내고 있어.
남: 문제가 뭐야?
여: 내 팀원들이 쉽게 논쟁을 벌이기 때문에 다양한 의견들을 다루는 것이 힘들어.
남: 이해해, 하지만 논쟁은 사람들이 더 나은 결정을 하도록 이끌 수 있어.
여: 정말 그렇게 생각해?
남: 당연하지! 논쟁은 항상 일어나. 논쟁을 더 나은 결정에 도달하기 위한 방법으로 생각하도록 노력해 봐.
여: 좋은 조언이야. 그것을 기억하도록 노력할게.
✔ 논쟁은 더 나은 결정을 위한 기회가 된다.
② 의사 결정에 있어서 전원의 합의가 필수적이다.
③ 고민이 있을 때는 전문가에게 조언을 구해야 한다.
④ 리더로서 팀원들과 수평적 관계를 유지하는 것이 중요하다.
⑤ 팀 프로젝트의 성공을 위해서는 리더의 결단력이 필요하다.

03 두 사람의 관계
정답률 85%
▶ 정답 ④

W: Hello, Mr. Baker. Thank you for doing this interview.
M: My pleasure. I really like reading your articles on modern painting in your newspaper.
기사들   현대 회화
W: Thank you so much. I'm honored to be interviewing the person who
~하게 되어 영광이다(be honored to V)
organized the Modern Asia exhibition at the National Art Museum.
기획했다   근대 아시아   전시   국립 미술관
M: Thank you. I'm very surprised it has gotten so much attention.
놀란   관심
W: It certainly has. Our readers have expressed interest in it, too.
확실히, 분명히   독자들   표현했다(express) 관심
What was the idea behind it?
M: The idea was to show contemporary Asia to the public.
현대의   대중
W: I see. Are you planning to do any other exhibitions?
M: Yes. I'm planning to do one about contemporary Africa. It will contain paintings featuring people, cities, and homes from around
포함하다   특징으로 하는(feature)
the continent.
대륙
W: That sounds great. I look forward to checking it out.
그것을 확인하기를 기대하다
(look forward to V-ing: ~하기를 기대하다, check out: 확인하다)
M: You won't be disappointed.
실망한
W: Thanks again for your time, Mr. Baker.

해석
여: 안녕하세요, Baker 씨. 이 인터뷰를 해 주셔서 감사합니다.
남: 천만에요. 저는 신문에서 현대 회화에 관한 당신의 기사를 읽는 것을 정말 좋아해요.
여: 정말 감사합니다. National Art Museum(국립 미술관)에서 Modern Asia(근대 아시아) 전시를 기획한 분과 인터뷰하게 되어 영광이에요.
남: 감사해요. 저는 그것이 그렇게 많은 관심을 받아서 매우 놀랐어요.

여: 확실히 그랬죠. 저희 독자들도 그것에 관심을 표현했어요. 그 이면에 있는 아이디어는 무엇이었나요?
남: 그 아이디어는 대중에게 현대의 아시아를 보여주는 것이었어요.
여: 그렇군요. 다른 전시를 할 계획이 있으신가요?
남: 네. 현대 아프리카에 대한 전시를 할 계획이에요. 그것은 그 대륙의 사람들, 도시들, 그리고 집들을 특징으로 하는 회화를 포함할 거예요.
여: 멋질 것 같네요. 그것을 확인하기를 기대하겠습니다.
남: 실망하지 않으실 거예요.
여: 시간을 내주셔서 다시 한번 감사드립니다, Baker 씨.

① 학생 ─ 문화 인류학 교수
② 미술관 관장 ─ 건축가
③ 여행 작가 ─ 삽화가
✔ 신문 기자 ─ 전시 기획자
⑤ 구호 활동가 ─ 후원자

04 그림에서 대화의 내용과 일치하지 않는 것
정답률 80%
▶ 정답 ⑤

M: Look at this photo from our family camping trip last year.
W: I remember that trip. We parked our camping van between the two trees.
주차했다
M: Right. You guys really loved the camping van.
W: Yes, we did. And you set up that square table for us.
설치했다(set up) 네모난 테이블
M: That's right. You guys enjoyed playing board games on that table.
보드게임들
W: Yeah, that was so fun! And do you remember the guitar next to the table?
M: Yes. I played the guitar and we sang songs together while we sat
연주했다   불렀다(sing)
on the blanket.
담요
W: That star-patterned blanket was our dogs' favorite.
별무늬의
M: Look at our two dogs, Rex and Rover. They look really happy in the picture.
W: Yeah. They started to run around and bark while we were singing.
짖다   ~하는 동안
That was so funny.
M: Yeah, that was hilarious! We had such a good time.
아주 재미있는

해석
남: 작년에 우리 가족 캠핑 여행에서 찍은 이 사진을 봐.
여: 그 여행이 기억나. 우리는 두 나무 사이에 캠핑카를 주차했잖아.
남: 맞아. 너희는 그 캠핑카를 정말 좋아했어.
여: 응, 그랬어. 그리고 네가 우리를 위해 저 네모난 테이블을 설치했잖아.
남: 맞아. 너희는 저 테이블에서 보드게임을 즐겼지.
여: 그래, 정말 재미있었어! 그리고 테이블 옆에 있는 기타를 기억해?
남: 응. 내가 기타를 연주하고 우리는 담요 위에 앉아서 함께 노래를 불렀지.
여: 저 별무늬 담요는 우리 개들이 가장 좋아하는 것이었어.
남: 우리 개 두 마리 Rex와 Rover를 봐. 그들은 사진 속에서 정말 행복해 보여.
여: 그래, 그들은 우리가 노래를 부르는 동안 뛰어다니고 짖기 시작했어. 너무 웃겼어.
남: 그래, 아주 재미있었어! 우리는 정말 즐거운 시간을 보냈어.

05 남자가 할 일
정답률 85%
▶ 정답 ④

M: Liz, how are you doing with the preparations for our school festival?
준비들
W: Well, I've just finished printing out the posters. How about you?
끝냈다 인쇄하는 것(print out)

Have you found an MC for the <u>ceremony</u>?
기념식
M: Yes, I reviewed the <u>candidates</u> and chose Brian to be the MC.
검토했다(review)　　후보들
W: Great. He's a good choice. He's always <u>entertaining</u>.
즐거움을 주는
M: Yes, he is. And the <u>stage</u> is set up for the dance team to <u>rehearse</u>.
무대　　　　　　　　　　　리허설을 하다
W: Sounds good. I'll <u>arrange</u> the dance team's schedule.
정리하다
M: Thank you for <u>coordinating</u> their schedule. What else do we have to do?
조정하는 것(coordinate: 조정하다)
W: Let's see. Well, we <u>invited</u> some <u>graduates</u> this year to come and
초청했다　　　졸업생들
tell us about their <u>different careers</u>.
다양한, 다른　직업들
M: That's great. How many graduates are coming?
W: Thirty, but I don't have enough time to call all of them.
M: That's okay. I will <u>take care of</u> that for you.
~을 처리하다
W: Thank you. I'd really <u>appreciate</u> it if you could do that.
고마워하다

해석
남: Liz, 우리 학교 축제를 위한 준비는 어떻게 하고 있니?
여: 음, 포스터 인쇄하는 것을 막 끝냈어. 너는 어때? 기념식을 위한 사회자를 찾았니?
남: 응, 후보들을 검토했고 Brian을 사회자로 선발했어.
여: 좋아. 그는 훌륭한 선택이야. 항상 즐거움을 주잖아.
남: 응, 맞아. 그리고 댄스팀이 리허설을 할 수 있도록 무대가 설치되었어.
여: 좋아. 내가 댄스팀의 일정을 정리할게.
남: 그들의 일정을 조정해 줘서 고마워. 우리가 또 무엇을 해야 하지?
여: 어디 보자. 음, 우리는 올해 몇 명의 졸업생에게 와서 그들의 다양한 직업에 대해 이야기해 달라고 초청했어.
남: 그거 멋지다. 몇 명의 졸업생이 오는 거야?
여: 30명인데, 나는 그들 모두에게 전화를 할 충분한 시간이 없어.
남: 괜찮아. 내가 너를 위해 그 일을 처리할게.
여: 고마워. 네가 그렇게 해 줄 수 있다면 정말 고맙겠어.
① 포스터 인쇄하기
② MC 선발하기
③ 무대 설치하기
✔졸업생에게 전화하기
⑤ 댄스팀 스케줄 정하기

문제 풀이
학교 축제에 초청한 졸업생 30명 모두에게 전화를 할 수 있는 시간이 충분하지 않다는 여자의 말에 남자는 자신이 그 일을 처리하겠다고 말한다. 따라서 남자가 할 일은 ④ '졸업생에게 전화하기'이다.

06 여자가 지불할 금액　　정답률 80%　▶ 정답 ⑤

[Telephone rings.]
M: Good afternoon, Chase Coffee. How may I help you?
W: Hi, I want to have some coffees delivered to my <u>office</u>.
사무실
M: Sure. What would you like?
W: Iced latte and hot americano. How much are they?
M: An iced latte is five dollars, and a hot americano is four dollars.
W: Then I'd like two iced lattes and one hot americano. And do you <u>charge for delivery</u>?
배달료를 받다
(charge: 청구하다, delivery: 배달)
M: It depends on the <u>distance</u>. Delivery is <u>free within</u> three miles of
~에 따라 다르다　거리　　　　　　무료의　~ 이내
our store, but there's a three-dollar delivery <u>charge</u> if it's <u>beyond</u>
요금　　　　　~ 이상
that distance. Where is your office located?
W: My office is located at 337 Lincoln Avenue.
M: Hmm... I'm sorry, but that's too <u>far</u> for free delivery. We'd have to
먼
<u>apply</u> the three-dollar delivery charge.
적용하다
W: Okay, I see.
M: Alright, let me <u>confirm</u> your <u>order</u>. It was two iced lattes and one
확인하다　　주문
hot americano. Is that <u>correct</u>?
맞는
W: Yes, thank you.

해석
[전화벨이 울린다.]

남: 안녕하세요, Chase Coffee입니다. 어떻게 도와드릴까요?
여: 안녕하세요, 제 사무실로 커피를 배달시키고 싶은데요.
남: 네. 무엇으로 하시겠어요?
여: 아이스 라떼와 따뜻한 아메리카노요. 얼마인가요?
남: 아이스 라떼는 5달러이고, 따뜻한 아메리카노는 4달러예요.
여: 그럼 아이스 라떼 두 잔과 따뜻한 아메리카노 한 잔 주세요. 그리고 배달료를 받으시나요?
남: 거리에 따라 달라요. 저희 가게에서 3마일 이내라면 배달이 무료이지만, 그 거리 이상이면 3달러의 배달료가 있어요. 사무실이 어디에 있으신가요?
여: 제 사무실은 Lincoln Avenue 337번지에 있어요.
남: 흠... 죄송하지만, 무료 배달을 하기에는 너무 머네요. 3달러의 배달료를 적용해야겠어요.
여: 네, 알겠어요.
남: 네, 주문을 확인하겠습니다. 아이스 라떼 두 잔과 따뜻한 아메리카노 한 잔이었네요. 맞나요?
여: 네, 감사해요.

① $13　②$14　③ $15
④$16　✔$17

문제 풀이
5달러인 아이스 라떼 두 잔과 4달러인 따뜻한 아메리카노 한 잔을 주문하면 총액은 14달러인데, 여자의 사무실은 무료 배달이 가능한 거리에 있지 않으므로 3달러의 배달료를 추가로 지불해야 한다. 따라서 답은 ⑤ '$17'이다.

07 남자가 락 페스티벌에 가지 않는 이유　　정답률 85%　▶ 정답 ④

W: Hey, Jimmy. Have you seen the poster for the rock festival this year?
M: Yeah, a lot of my favorite musicians <u>are part of</u> this year's line-up.
~에 포함되다(be part of)
W: I know. The tickets <u>go on sale</u> tomorrow. Do you want to get tickets
판매되다
together?
M: Well, I don't think I can go this year.
W: Why not? Do you have <u>plans</u> that day?
계획들
M: No, but my parents' <u>20th wedding anniversary</u> is two weeks away,
20주년 결혼 기념일
and I'm <u>saving</u> my money to buy them a special <u>present</u>.
모으는(save)　　　　　　　　　　선물
W: That's so nice of you!
M: Thanks. I'm really sorry that I can't <u>join</u> you, though.
함께 하다
W: That's okay. Are we still meeting after school for <u>band practice</u>?
밴드 연습
M: Of course. See you in the <u>music room</u>.
음악실

해석
여: 안녕, Jimmy. 올해 락 페스티벌 포스터 봤니?
남: 응, 내가 가장 좋아하는 많은 뮤지션들이 올해의 라인업에 포함되어 있어.
여: 알아. 티켓은 내일부터 판매돼. 함께 티켓을 살까?
남: 음, 나는 올해에는 못 갈 것 같아.
여: 왜? 그날 계획이 있니?
남: 아니, 하지만 부모님의 20주년 결혼 기념일이 2주 남아서, 특별한 선물을 사드리려고 돈을 모으고 있어.
여: 너 정말 멋지다!
남: 고마워. 그래도 너와 함께 할 수 없어서 정말 미안해.
여: 괜찮아. 우리 아직도 밴드 연습을 위해 방과 후에 만나는 거지?
남: 물론이지. 음악실에서 보자.
① 밴드 연습을 해야 해서
② 결혼식에 참석해야 해서
③ 할인 티켓이 매진되어서
✔선물 살 돈을 모아야 해서
⑤ 라인업이 마음에 들지 않아서

08 Nova's Guide to the Stars에 관해 언급되지 않은 것　　정답률 85%　▶ 정답 ⑤

M: Hey, Olivia. <u>Have you heard of</u> Nova's Guide to the Stars?
~에 대해 들어본 적 있니(hear of: ~에 대해 듣다)
W: No, I haven't. What is it?
M: It's a program where you <u>view</u> thousands of stars and <u>stay</u>
보다
<u>overnight</u> at the Nova <u>Observatory</u> on Mt. Crayton.
하룻밤 머무르다　　　　　전문대

16

22년 9월 학력평가

W: Really? That sounds cool! How much does it cost?
M: It costs $100 per person.
  1인당(per: ~당)   (비용이) 들다
W: That's pretty expensive.
  꽤 비싼
M: Well, it's actually a good deal. A ticket includes lodging, meals, and
  사실 거래 포함하다 숙박
  activities such as a guided tour, a science show, and a cable car
  활동들   케이블카 타기
  ride.
W: Alright, that sounds reasonable. Oh, wait a second! I almost forgot
  합리적인   거의 잊었다
                                (forget)
  about my English camp. When are the dates for Nova's Guide to
                              날짜
  the Stars?
M: It runs from September 16th to September 30th.
  진행되다
W: Okay, I need to check my schedule first. I will join you unless it
                                              ~하지 않는다면
  overlaps with my English camp.
  ~과 겹치다

해석

남: 안녕, Olivia. Nova's Guide to the Stars(Nova의 별 안내)에 대해 들어본 적이 있니?
여: 아니, 없어. 그게 뭐야?
남: Crayton 산에 있는 Nova Observatory(Nova 천문대)에서 수천 개의 별을 보고 하룻밤을 머무르는 프로그램이야.
여: 정말? 멋질 것 같아! 비용이 얼마나 드니?
남: 1인당 100달러야.
여: 꽤 비싸구나.
남: 음, 사실 좋은 거래야. 티켓에 숙박, 식사, 그리고 가이드 투어, 과학 쇼, 그리고 케이블카 타기와 같은 활동들이 포함되어 있어.
여: 알겠어, 합리적인 것 같아. 오, 잠깐만! 내 영어 캠프에 대해 거의 잊을 뻔 했어. Nova's Guide to the Stars의 날짜는 언제니?
남: 9월 16일부터 9월 30일까지 진행돼.
여: 알겠어, 우선 내 일정을 확인해야겠어. 영어 캠프와 겹치지 않는다면 너와 함께 할게.

① 장소   ② 참가 비용   ③ 활동 내용
④ 운영 기간   ☑ 신청 방법

09

정답률 90%

2022 London Public Library Event에 관한 내용과 일치하지 않는 것 ▶ 정답 ③

W: Hello, library visitors! We will soon be holding the 2022 London
                                          개최하는(hold)
  Public Library Event to promote the importance of reading. We
  공공 도서관 행사   홍보하다 중요성
  are going to invite the award-winning children's writer, Bridget
              초청하다 상을 받은 아동 작가
  George. She's the author of the popular picture book, It's Mitig!
              작가   그림책
  She will provide answers for parents who are eager to find ways to
          제공하다   찾고 싶어 하다
                                (be eager to V: ~하고 싶어 하다)
  inspire their children to read. The event will be held on Thursday,
  자녀들에게 독서를 하도록 영감을 주다
  (inspire A to V: A에게 ~하도록 영감을 주다)
  October 27th from 9:00 a.m. to 10:00 a.m. If you'd like to join the
                                              참여하다
  event, please register in advance through our website. Registration
          접수하다 미리   접수
  is available online only. A maximum of 50 people will be able to
  가능한   할 수 있다
  attend the event. If you have any questions for our special guest,
  참여하다   특별 초청 손님
  please email them to us in advance at library@lpl.uk so we can
        이메일로 보내다
  present them to her during the program. We hope to see you on
  제시하다
  October 27th!

해석

여: 안녕하세요, 도서관 방문객 여러분! 저희는 곧 독서의 중요성을 홍보하기 위해서 2022 London Public Library Event(2022 런던 공공 도서관 행사)를 개최할 것입니다. 저희는 상을 받은 아동 작가인 Bridget George를 초청할 예정입니다. 그녀는 인기 있는 그림책인 'It's Mitig!'의 작가입니다. 그녀는 자녀들에게 독서를 하도록 영감을 줄 방법을 찾고 싶어 하는 부모님들에게 답을 제공할 것입니다. 행사는 10월 27일 목요일 오전 9시부터 10시까지 열릴 것입니다. 행사에 참여하시려면, 저희 웹사이트를 통해 미리 접수하시기 바랍니다. 접수는 온라인으로만 가능합니다. 최대 50명까지 행사에 참여할 수 있을 것입니다. 우리의 특별 초청 손님에게 질문이 있으시면, 저희가 프로그램 동안에 그녀에게 제시할 수 있도록 library@lpl.uk로 이메일로 미리 보내주세요. 10월 27일에 뵙기를 바랍니다!

① 작가를 초청한다.
② 10월 27일에 열린다.

☑ 현장 접수가 가능하다.
④ 참여 가능 인원은 최대 50명이다.
⑤ 질문을 이메일로 미리 보낼 수 있다.

10

정답률 85%

표에서 남자가 구입할 휴대용 접이식 의자 ▶ 정답 ③

W: Hey, Dad. I'm home. What are you doing?
M: Hi, Susan. I'm searching for a new portable folding chair.
              검색하고 있는(search for) 휴대용 접이식 의자
W: Oh, okay. Hmm... I like this wooden frame chair.
                          나무 뼈대
M: Well, it looks very comfortable, but it weighs more than the one
                  편한   무게가 나가다
  we had. It's too heavy. The new chair should be less than three
          무거운
  kilograms.
W: I see. What about the color?
M: I prefer any color other than white. It gets dirty too easily.
  더 좋다   더러워지다
W: Okay. The gray one and the black one look very nice.
          회색의
M: I agree. What other features should we consider?
  동의하다   기능들   고려하다
W: I want our new folding chair to have two cup holders.
                                    컵 거치대들
M: Isn't one enough?
W: Well, Dad, I'd like to have one holder for my drink and the other for
  small personal items.
        개인적인
M: I like that idea. And we also need a carry bag for easy storage and
                                  운반용 가방   보관
  for taking it with us on trips.
W: All right. Then this one is your best choice.
M: Okay. I'll order this one.
        주문하다

해석

여: 안녕하세요, 아빠. 저 집에 왔어요. 무엇을 하고 계세요?
남: 안녕, Susan. 새 휴대용 접이식 의자를 검색하고 있단다.
여: 오, 알겠어요. 흠... 저는 이 나무 뼈대 의자가 마음에 들어요.
남: 음, 그것은 매우 편해 보이지만, 우리가 가지고 있던 것보다 무게가 더 나가. 너무 무거워. 새 의자는 3킬로그램 이하여야 해.
여: 그렇군요. 색상은 어때요?
남: 나는 흰색이 아닌 다른 색상이 더 좋구나. 그것은 너무 쉽게 더러워지거든.
여: 알겠어요. 회색과 검은색이 매우 멋져 보여요.
남: 동의해. 우리가 다른 어떤 기능들을 고려해야 할까?
여: 우리의 새 접이식 의자에는 두 개의 컵 거치대가 있으면 좋겠어요.
남: 한 개면 충분하지 않니?
여: 음, 아빠, 저는 음료수를 위한 거치대 한 개와 작은 개인적인 물품을 위한 다른 거치대 한 개를 가지고 싶어요.
남: 그 생각이 마음에 드는구나. 그리고 쉽게 보관하고 여행 시에 가지고 다니기 위한 운반용 가방도 필요해.
여: 맞아요. 그럼 이것이 가장 좋은 선택이에요.
남: 알겠어. 이것을 주문할게.

휴대용 접이식 의자

	모델	무게(kg)	색상	컵 거치대 수	운반용 가방
①	A	3.2	흰색	1	O
②	B	2.3	흰색	2	O
☑	C	2.1	회색	2	O
④	D	1.8	회색	2	X
⑤	E	1.6	검은색	1	X

11

정답률 85%

남자의 마지막 말에 대한 여자의 응답 ▶ 정답 ①

M: That was a great movie! What did you think?
                  영화
W: The movie was okay, but I couldn't concentrate on it at all.
                                  ~에 집중하다
M: Why not? What happened?
W: (The person sitting behind me kept kicking my seat.)
                              계속해서 발로 찼다
                          (keep V-ing: 계속해서 ~하다, kick: 발로 차다)

해석

남: 그것은 정말 좋은 영화였어! 너는 어떻게 생각해?
여: 영화는 괜찮았지만, 나는 전혀 그것에 집중할 수 없었어.

남: 왜? 무슨 일이 있었어?
여: (내 뒤에 앉은 사람이 계속해서 내 좌석을 발로 찼어.)
✓내 뒤에 앉은 사람이 계속해서 내 좌석을 발로 찼어.
② 너는 너를 도와줄 직원을 불렀어야 했어.
③ 내가 그것에 너무 빠져서 그것이 너무 빨리 지나갔어.
④ 네가 그것을 즐기지 못했다니 유감이야.
⑤ 나는 빨리 그 영화를 보고 싶어.

12 여자의 마지막 말에 대한 남자의 응답 　정답률 75%　▶ 정답 ⑤

W: Our teacher said we have to make a presentation at the
　　　　　　　　　　　　　　　　　　　발표를 하다
International Exchange Program next week.
　국제 교류 프로그램
M: Next week? We should hurry, then. What should we do first?
　　　　　　　　　서두르다
W: Let me see. First, I think we'd better decide on the topic for our
　　　　　　　　　　　　　　　　　　　~을 정하다　　주제
presentation.
M: (Okay. Let's find one that is easy and interesting to talk about.)

해석
여: 우리 선생님께서 우리가 다음 주에 International Exchange Program(국제 교류 프로그램)에서 발표를 해야 한다고 말씀하셨어.
남: 다음 주에? 그럼 서둘러야겠네. 먼저 무엇을 해야 하지?
여: 어디 보자. 우선, 우리의 발표 주제를 정하는 게 좋을 것 같아.
남: (알겠어. 이야기하기 쉽고 재미있는 것을 찾아보자.)
① 말도 안 돼. 우리는 국제 프로그램이 필요해.
② 걱정하지 마. 내 책과 네 책을 교환해 줄 수 있어.
③ 나쁘지 않아. 그것은 주제문의 좋은 예시야.
④ 이해해. 나는 발표를 하는 동안 정말 긴장했어.
✓알겠어. 이야기하기 쉽고 재미있는 것을 찾아보자.

13 여자의 마지막 말에 대한 남자의 응답 　정답률 75%　▶ 정답 ②

W: Good morning, sir. How can I help you?
M: Hi, this bluetooth speaker I bought here two days ago isn't working
　　　블루투스 스피커　　　　　　　　　　　　　작동하지 않다(work)
anymore. I haven't dropped it or anything, but it's just not working.
　　　　　　　　　떨어뜨리지 않았다(drop)
W: I'm sorry for the inconvenience, sir.
　　　　　　　　　　불편
M: This is my favorite brand, but I think something is wrong with this
　　　　　　　　　가장 좋아하는
particular one.
　특정한
W: I understand. You must be frustrated.
　　　　　　　　　　　　실망한
M: I am. Is there anything you can do for me?
W: We can give you a refund, or you can exchange it for another one.
　　　　　　　　　　환불　　　　　　　교환하다
M: I'd like to exchange it, please. Is there any other model you would
recommend?
추천하다
W: Well, this model is really popular, but it costs fifty dollars more.
　　　　　　　　　　　　　인기가 있는　　(비용이) 들다
M: Wow, that's too expensive.
W: Then, would you like a new one from the same model you bought?
M: (Yes, please. I hope the new speaker works.)

해석
여: 안녕하세요, 손님. 어떻게 도와드릴까요?
남: 안녕하세요, 이틀 전에 여기서 산 이 블루투스 스피커가 더 이상 작동하지 않아요. 떨어뜨리거나 그런 건 하지 않았는데, 그냥 작동하지 않아요.
여: 불편을 드려 죄송합니다, 손님.
남: 이것은 제가 가장 좋아하는 브랜드인데, 이 특정한 스피커에 뭔가 문제가 있는 것 같아요.
여: 이해해요. 분명 실망하셨겠네요.
남: 네. 저를 위해 해 줄 수 있는 일이 있나요?
여: 저희가 환불을 해 드릴 수도 있고, 그것을 다른 것으로 교환하실 수도 있어요.
남: 저는 교환하고 싶어요. 추천하고 싶은 다른 모델이 있나요?
여: 음, 이 모델이 정말 인기가 있는데, 50달러 더 비싸요.
남: 와, 너무 비싸네요.
여: 그럼, 구매하신 것과 같은 모델로 새 것을 드릴까요?
남: (네, 부탁해요. 새 스피커는 작동했으면 좋겠네요.)

① 죄송해요. 대신 10% 할인해 드릴 수 있어요.
✓네, 부탁해요. 새 스피커는 작동했으면 좋겠네요.
③ 괜찮아요. 하지만 당신은 영수증이 필요할 거예요.
④ 신경 쓰지 마세요. 저는 방금 전액 환불을 받았어요.
⑤ 감사해요. 하지만 저는 그것을 이미 수리했어요.

문제 풀이
남자는 작동하지 않는 블루투스 스피커를 환불하는 대신 다른 제품과 교환하고 싶어 한다. 여자는 자신이 추천한 모델은 너무 비싸다고 말하는 남자에게 구매한 것과 같은 모델의 새 제품을 원하는지 묻는다. 이에 대한 남자의 응답으로는 ② 'Yes, please. I hope the new speaker works.(네, 부탁해요. 새 스피커는 작동했으면 좋겠네요.)'가 가장 적절하다.

14 남자의 마지막 말에 대한 여자의 응답 　정답률 85%　▶ 정답 ①

M: Emily, is your cellphone working? I've been trying all morning, but I
can't get a connection.
　전화가 연결되다
W: That's strange. Mine is working just fine. Did you try turning the
　　　　이상한　　　　　　　　　　　　　　　　　전화기를 껐다가 켜 보다
phone off and on again? (try V-ing: ~해 보다, turn A off and on: A를 껐다가 켜다)
M: Yes, I've already done that twice, but it's still not working. I'm really
　　　　　아직도
annoyed because I'm expecting an important phone call.
짜증 난　　　　　기다리는(expect)
W: Okay. Why don't you try reinserting the SIM card?
　　　　　　　　　다시 삽입해 보다
　　　　　　　　　(reinsert: 다시 삽입하다)
M: The SIM card? [Pause] Uh! I can't get it out!
　　　　　　　　　　　　　　그것을 빼다
W: Here, take this paper clip to open the SIM card tray. Insert the clip
　　　　　　　종이 클립　　열다　　　　　　　　　삽입하다
into the small hole and push it slightly until it pops out.
　　　　구멍　　　밀다　　살짝　　　　튀어나오다
M: Okay. I took it out. Now what should I do?
W: Carefully re-position the SIM card and push it gently back into the
　조심스럽게　원위치에 놓다　　　　　　　　부드럽게
phone. [Pause] Good. Now turn on your phone.
M: Wow! It works! You're a genius! You made my day!
　　　　　　　　　　　천재　　　나를 행복하게 했다
　　　　　　　　　　　　　　(make one's day: ~를 행복하게 하다)
W: (It's nothing. I'm glad I could help.)

해석
남: Emily, 네 휴대폰은 작동하니? 내가 오전 내내 시도하고 있는데, 전화가 연결되지 않아.
여: 이상하네. 내 것은 잘 작동하고 있어. 전화기를 껐다가 다시 켜 봤니?
남: 응, 이미 두 번이나 해 봤는데, 아직도 작동하지 않아. 중요한 전화를 기다리고 있어서 정말 짜증 나.
여: 알겠어. SIM 카드를 다시 삽입해 보는 게 어때?
남: SIM 카드? [잠시 후] 어! 그것을 뺄 수가 없어!
여: 여기, 이 종이 클립을 가지고 SIM 카드 트레이를 열어. 클립을 작은 구멍에 삽입하고 그것이 튀어나올 때까지 살짝 밀어.
남: 알겠어. 그것을 꺼냈어. 이제 무엇을 해야 해?
여: SIM 카드를 조심스럽게 원위치에 놓고 전화기에 다시 부드럽게 밀어 넣어. [잠시 후] 좋아. 이제 전화기를 켜.
남: 와! 작동한다! 너는 천재야! 네가 나를 행복하게 했어!
여: (별거 아니야. 내가 도울 수 있어서 기뻐.)
✓별거 아니야. 내가 도울 수 있어서 기뻐.
② 미안해. 하지만 나는 그것을 고칠 수 없을 것 같아.
③ 미안해. 나는 중요한 전화를 받지 못했어.
④ 물론이지. 나는 네가 예약을 하도록 도와줄 수 있어.
⑤ 네 말이 맞아. 우리는 자원을 낭비하면 안 돼.

15 다음 상황에서 Amelia가 엄마에게 할 말 　정답률 80%　▶ 정답 ④

W: Amelia and Anna are friends who attend the same school and live
　　　　　　　　　　　　　　　　　　　다니다
in the same neighborhood. A few days ago, they were assigned a
　　　　　　　　　　　~에 살다　　　　　　　　　배정받았다(assign: 배정하다)
presentation. They are now working together on the presentation
발표
at Anna's house. Since the presentation is tomorrow, Amelia
　　　　　　　~ 때문에
cannot leave anything unfinished, so she's working hard on it
　　　　　두다　　　　완료되지 않은　　　　　　　열심히
with Anna until they're done with everything. Amelia gets so

absorbed in her work that she loses track of time. After completing
~에 열중한 / 시간 가는 줄 모르다 / 끝마친(complete)
everything, Amelia looks at the clock and realizes it's too late to
깨닫다
catch the bus back to her house. Amelia wants to call and ask
버스를 타다
her mother to pick her up at Anna's house. In this situation, what
그녀를 데리러 오다(pick up)
would Amelia most likely say to her mother?
Amelia: (Could you please pick me up at Anna's house?)

해석

여: Amelia와 Anna는 같은 학교에 다니고 같은 동네에 사는 친구이다. 며칠 전에, 그들은 발표를 배정받았다. 그들은 지금 Anna의 집에서 같이 발표 준비를 하고 있다. 발표가 내일이기 때문에, Amelia는 어떤 것도 완료되지 않은 상태로 둘 수 없어서 모든 것을 끝낼 때까지 Anna와 함께 열심히 발표 준비를 하고 있다. Amelia는 자신의 일에 너무 열중해서 시간 가는 줄 모른다. 모든 것을 끝마친 후, Amelia는 시계를 보고 자신의 집으로 돌아가는 버스를 타기에는 너무 늦었다는 것을 깨닫는다. Amelia는 엄마에게 전화해서 Anna의 집으로 자신을 데리러 오라고 부탁하고 싶다. 이러한 상황에서, Amelia는 엄마에게 뭐라고 말하겠는가?

Amelia: (Anna의 집으로 저를 데리러 오실 수 있어요?)

① 발표와 관련하여 어떤 좋은 생각이 있으세요?
② 너무 늦기 전에 Anna를 집에 데려가는 게 어때요?
③ 우리는 내일 나머지 일을 끝낼 수 있을 것 같아요.
✔Anna의 집으로 저를 데리러 오실 수 있어요?
⑤ Anna와 놀고 싶다면 저에게 말해주세요.

16~17 1지문 2문항

M: These days, people become vegetarians for different reasons.
채식주의자들
It may be because of health, personal beliefs, or changes in
개인적인 / 신념
lifestyle. However, some vegetarians have poorly planned diets,
생활 방식 / 엉성하게 / 식단들
which means their bodies don't get certain essential nutrients. If
특정한 / 필수 영양소들
you're one of those people, here are some tips to ensure your body
~하게 하다
doesn't suffer from nutrient deficiency. To start with, if you are not
~으로 고통받다 / 결핍 / 우선
getting enough protein, you can get it from beans, green peas,
단백질 / 완두콩
nuts, and seeds. Next, if you aren't getting enough omega-3, it can
견과류 / 씨앗 / 오메가3
be found in foods like walnuts, avocados, and olive oil. Third, if you
호두
are in need of iron, good sources include tofu, whole grain bread,
~을 필요로 하는 / 철분 / 공급원 / 포함하다 / 두부 / 통곡물 빵
peanuts, and raisins. Finally, if vitamin B12 is missing from your
땅콩 / 건포도 / 비타민 B12
diet, you can find it in fortified cereals, soy milk, and soy yogurt. By
강화 시리얼
consuming these foods, you'll be getting the essential nutrients
섭취함으로써
(by V-ing: ~함으로써, consume: 섭취하다)
you need as a vegetarian.

해석

남: 요즘, 사람들은 다양한 이유로 채식주의자가 됩니다. 그것은 건강, 개인적 신념, 또는 생활 방식의 변화 때문일지도 모릅니다. 하지만, 일부 채식주의자들은 엉성하게 계획된 식단을 가지고 있는데, 그것은 그들의 몸이 특정한 필수 영양소를 얻지 못한다는 것을 의미합니다. 여러분이 그러한 사람들 중 한 명이라면, 여러분의 몸이 영양소 결핍으로 고통받지 않도록 하기 위한 몇 가지 조언들이 여기에 있습니다. 우선, 여러분이 충분한 단백질을 섭취하지 않고 있다면, 콩, 완두콩, 견과류, 그리고 씨앗에서 그것을 얻을 수 있습니다. 다음으로, 여러분이 충분한 오메가3를 섭취하지 않고 있다면, 그것은 호두, 아보카도, 그리고 올리브 오일과 같은 음식에서 찾을 수 있습니다. 셋째, 여러분이 철분을 필요로 한다면, 좋은 공급원에는 두부, 통곡물 빵, 땅콩, 그리고 건포도가 포함되어 있습니다. 마지막으로, 여러분의 식단에서 비타민 B12가 빠져있다면, 강화 시리얼, 두유, 그리고 두유 요거트에서 그것을 찾을 수 있습니다. 이러한 음식들을 섭취함으로써, 여러분은 채식주의자로서 여러분이 필요로 하는 필수 영양소를 얻게 될 것입니다.

16 남자가 하는 말의 주제
정답률 70% ▶ 정답 ⑤

① 사람들이 채식주의자가 되도록 장려하는 방법들

② 엉성하게 계획된 식단과 관련된 건강상의 위험들
③ 사람들이 채식주의자가 되는 다양한 이유들
④ 필수 영양소의 일일 권장량
✔채식주의자가 영양소 결핍을 예방하도록 하는 음식 공급원

17 언급된 영양소가 아닌 것
정답률 85% ▶ 정답 ③

① 단백질　　② 오메가3　　✔칼슘
④ 철분　　⑤ 비타민 B12

17 2022년 11월 학력평가

01	④	02	③	03	⑤	04	④	05	⑤
06	③	07	⑤	08	③	09	④	10	②
11	②	12	①	13	⑤	14	③	15	③
16	④	17	④						

01 여자가 하는 말의 목적
정답률 85% ▶ 정답 ④

[Chime bell rings.]

W: Hello, Greenville High School students! This is vice principal, Lisa
교감
James. Recently, the number of students using the bicycle-sharing
자전거 공유 시스템
system has increased. The shared bicycles are convenient and
공유 자전거들 / 편리한
eco-friendly. However, there's one important thing you should
친환경적인
remember. If you don't park them properly after use, they can
주차하다 / 제대로
block pedestrians' way or cause accidents. Because of misplaced
보행자들 / 야기하다 / 잘못 둔
(misplace: 잘못 두다)
shared bicycles in front of the school, students have had trouble
통학하는 데 어려움을 겪어왔다
(have trouble V-ing: ~하는 데 어려움을 겪다, commute: 통학하다)
commuting. One student even fell over an improperly parked
~에 걸려 넘어졌다 / 부적절하게
(fall over)
bicycle, and that could have led to a serious accident. So, please
~로 이어질 수 있었다
(could have p.p.: ~할 수 있었다, lead to: ~로 이어지다)
be sure to park the shared bicycles in the designated areas for the
반드시 주차하다 / 지정된 / 장소들
(be sure to V: 반드시 ~하다) / (designate: 지정하다, 지명하다)
safety of everyone. Thanks for your cooperation.
안전 / 협조

해석

[차임벨이 울린다.]

여: 안녕하세요, Greenville 고등학교 학생 여러분! 저는 교감인 Lisa James입니다. 최근, 자전거 공유 시스템을 이용하는 학생들의 수가 증가했습니다. 공유 자전거는 편리하고 친환경적입니다. 하지만, 여러분이 기억해야 할 한 가지 중요한 사항이 있습니다. 사용 후에 제대로 주차하지 않는다면, 그것들이 보행자의 길을 막거나 사고를 야기할 수 있습니다. 학교 앞에 잘못 둔 공유 자전거 때문에, 학생들이 통학하는 데 어려움을 겪어왔습니다. 한 학생은 심지어 제대로 주차되지 않은 자전거에 걸려 넘어졌고, 그것은 심각한 사고로 이어질 수도 있었습니다. 그러므로, 모두의 안전을 위해 공유 자전거를 반드시 지정된 장소에 주차해 주십시오. 협조해 주셔서 감사합니다.

① 자전거 전용 도로의 정비 일정을 공지하려고
② 자전거 안전 장비 착용의 중요성을 강조하려고
③ 공유 자전거 주차장의 설치 장소를 안내하려고
✔공유 자전거를 지정된 장소에 주차할 것을 당부하려고
⑤ 친환경적인 교통수단을 이용해 등교할 것을 권장하려고

02 남자의 의견

▶ 정답 ③

M: Anna, what are you working on with your computer?
W: Hi, Daniel. I've been writing a history report. My eyes are so tired.
M: You do look a bit tired. Oh, isn't your computer monitor very bright?
W: Yes, it's on the brightest mode. It's better to see clearer than a dark screen, right?
M: It may be so, but if the computer screen is too bright, it can be harmful to your eyes.
W: Really? How come?
M: Too bright a screen could cause blurry vision. It makes your eyes get tired easily.
W: Hmm, I think I've often experienced similar symptoms.
M: Also bright screens can even make your eyes dry, which has a bad effect on your eyesight.
W: Oh, I see. I should lower the brightness of the screen.
M: Yeah. Don't forget screens that are too bright can damage your eye health.
W: Okay. Thanks for the tip.

해석
남: Anna, 컴퓨터로 무엇을 하고 있니?
여: 안녕, Daniel. 나는 역사 보고서를 쓰고 있어. 눈이 너무 피곤해.
남: 정말 조금 피곤해 보인다. 오, 컴퓨터 모니터가 매우 밝지 않니?
여: 응, 가장 밝은 모드거든. 어두운 화면보다 더 선명하게 보는 게 좋잖아, 그렇지?
남: 그럴지도 모르지만, 컴퓨터 화면이 지나치게 밝으면, 눈에 해로울 수 있어.
여: 정말? 어째서?
남: 화면이 지나치게 밝으면 흐릿한 시야를 야기할 수 있어. 그것은 눈을 쉽게 피곤하게 만들어.
여: 흠, 나도 비슷한 증상을 자주 경험한 것 같아.
남: 또한 밝은 화면은 심지어 눈을 건조하게 만들 수 있는데, 그것은 시력에 나쁜 영향을 미쳐.
여: 오, 그렇구나. 화면의 밝기를 낮춰야겠어.
남: 그래. 지나치게 밝은 화면은 눈 건강을 해칠 수 있다는 것을 잊지 마.
여: 알겠어. 알려줘서 고마워.

① 눈병 예방을 위해 정기적인 안과 검진을 받아야 한다.
② 적절한 휴식은 작업의 집중도를 높이는 데 도움이 된다.
✓ 지나치게 밝은 컴퓨터 화면은 눈 건강에 해로울 수 있다.
④ 너무 작은 글씨를 읽는 것은 눈의 피로를 유발할 수 있다.
⑤ 시력 보호를 위해 화면과의 적당한 거리 유지가 필요하다.

03 두 사람의 관계

▶ 정답 ⑤

W: Hello. How may I help you?
M: Hi, I wonder if you have musical instruments.
W: Of course. What are you looking for?
M: I want a digital piano for my daughter.
W: Oh, you're in luck. We got a nice one yesterday. Follow me.
M: Wow. It doesn't look like it's ever been played.
W: Yeah. The previous owner said her son didn't like playing the piano, so he barely touched it.
M: Really? How much is it?
W: It's $70. That's a pretty good price.
M: Good. I'll take it. By the way, do you buy used books, too? I have many picture books my children don't read any more.
W: We do, but there should be no missing pages or pen marks.
M: Then I'll take a look when I go home.
W: Okay. If you find your books in a good condition, please bring them in.

해석
여: 안녕하세요. 어떻게 도와드릴까요?
남: 안녕하세요, 악기가 있는지 궁금해요.
여: 물론이죠. 무엇을 찾으시나요?
남: 제 딸을 위한 디지털 피아노를 사고 싶어요.
여: 오, 운이 좋으시네요. 저희가 어제 좋은 것을 구했거든요. 저를 따라오세요.
남: 와. 그것은 한 번도 연주된 적이 없는 것처럼 보이네요.
여: 네. 이전 소유자가 자신의 아들은 피아노 치는 것을 좋아하지 않아서, 그것을 거의 손대지 않았다고 하더군요.
남: 정말이에요? 얼마인가요?
여: 70달러예요. 꽤 괜찮은 가격이죠.
남: 좋네요. 그것을 살게요. 그런데, 중고책도 구매하시나요? 저희 아이들이 더 이상 읽지 않는 그림책이 많거든요.
여: 그렇긴 한데, 누락된 페이지나 펜 자국이 있으면 안 돼요.
남: 그럼 제가 집에 가서 한번 볼게요.
여: 알겠습니다. 책의 상태가 좋다면, 그것들을 가지고 오세요.

① 동화 작가 — 삽화가
② 악기 조율사 — 연주가
③ 학부모 — 유치원 교사
④ 피아노 강사 — 수강생
✓ 중고 용품점 직원 — 손님

04 그림에서 대화의 내용과 일치하지 않는 것

▶ 정답 ④

M: Mindy, how did clothing donation day go?
W: Dad, it was such a wonderful event! Do you want to see a picture of it?
M: Sure. Oh, you drew a T-shirt on the banner.
W: Yeah. My club members came up with the idea.
M: Great. Are the shelves under the clock for the donated items?
W: Right. Do you see the basket on the round table?
M: Yes. What's that for?
W: We put donation badges in it. We gave hand-made badges to donors.
M: How nice! Oh, I can see three boxes next to the chair.
W: Those were ready for donation to the charity center. We organized the donated clothes and put them in the boxes.
M: I see. What's the picture on the wall?
W: That's the picture we took with the people at the charity center last year.
M: It looks nice. It must have been a fun event.

해석
남: Mindy, 옷 기부의 날은 어땠니?
여: 아빠, 정말 멋진 행사였어요! 그것의 사진을 보고 싶으세요?
남: 물론이지. 오, 현수막에 티셔츠를 그렸구나.
여: 네. 동아리 회원들이 그 아이디어를 생각해 냈어요.
남: 멋지구나. 시계 아래에 있는 선반은 기부된 물품들을 위한 거니?
여: 맞아요. 원형 테이블 위에 있는 바구니가 보이세요?
남: 그래. 어떤 용도니?
여: 그 안에 기부 배지를 넣었어요. 저희는 기부자들에게 손으로 만든 배지를 줬어요.
남: 정말 멋지다! 오, 의자 옆에 세 개의 상자가 보이는구나.
여: 그것들은 자선 센터에 기부할 수 있도록 준비되었던 거예요. 저희는 기부된 옷을 정리해서 그 상자에 넣었어요.
남: 그렇구나. 벽에 있는 사진은 무엇이니?
여: 작년에 자선 센터에서 사람들과 찍은 사진이에요.
남: 멋져 보이는구나. 틀림없이 재미있는 행사였을 거야.

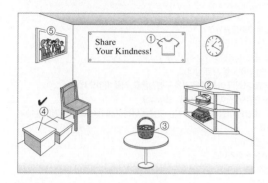

05 남자가 할 일

정답률 85%
▶ 정답 ⑤

W: Science Lab Day is tomorrow. Let's do a final check, Kevin.
　　　　　　과학 실험의 날　　　　　　최종 점검을 하다
M: Good idea, Becky. I printed out the list of students who signed up
　　　　　　　　　　　　출력했다(print out)　　　명단　　　　　~에 참가 신청을 했다(sign up for)
　 for Science Lab Day.
W: Thank you. A lot more students signed up for it than we expected.
　　　　　　　　　 훨씬　　　　　　　　　　　　　　　　　　　　　　예상했다
　 There are enough chairs in the science lab, aren't there?
　　　　　　　　 충분한
M: Don't worry. I checked the number of chairs and even brought
　　　　　　　　　　　　　　　　　　　　　　　　　　　　 심지어
　 some more yesterday.
W: What a considerate thing to do! And I downloaded the video clip
　　　　　 사려 깊은　　　　　　　　　　　　　　 내려받았다
　 that explains the safety rules.
　　　　　 설명하다　 안전 수칙
M: Good. It'll be important to show it before the experiments. How
　　　　　　　　　　　　　　　　　　　　　　　　　　실험들
　 about experimental equipment?
　　　　　 실험 장비
W: I put everything on all the tables. Oh, I forgot to bring laboratory
　　　　　　　　　　　　　　　　　　　　　　　 가져오는 것을 잊었다　실험용 장갑들
　 gloves from the preparation room.　　　(forget to V: ~하는 것을 잊다)
M: Don't worry. I'll get them.
W: Thank you. Then I'll check the first aid kit.
　　　　　　　　　　　　　　　　 구급상자

해석

여: Science Lab Day(과학 실험의 날)이 내일이야. 최종 점검을 하자, Kevin.
남: 좋은 생각이야, Becky. 나는 Science Lab Day에 참가 신청을 한 학생들의 명단을 출력했어.
여: 고마워. 우리가 예상했던 것보다 훨씬 더 많은 학생들이 참가 신청을 했어. 과학 실험실에는 충분한 의자가 있지, 그렇지 않니?
남: 걱정하지 마. 내가 어제 의자의 개수를 확인하고 심지어 몇 개 더 가져왔어.
여: 정말 사려 깊은 행동이구나! 그리고 나는 안전 수칙을 설명하는 동영상을 내려받았어.
남: 좋아. 실험 전에 그것을 보여주는 것이 중요할 거야. 실험 장비는 어때?
여: 모든 테이블 위에 전부 올려 놓았어. 오, 준비실에서 실험용 장갑을 가져오는 것을 잊었어.
남: 걱정하지 마. 내가 그것들을 가져올게.
여: 고마워. 그럼 나는 구급상자를 확인할게.

① 명단 출력하기
② 의자 가져오기
③ 동영상 내려받기
④ 구급상자 확인하기
✔ 실험용 장갑 가져오기

문제 풀이

준비실에서 실험용 장갑을 가져오지 않았다는 여자의 말에 남자는 자신이 가져오겠다고 대답한다. 따라서 남자가 할 일은 ⑤ '실험용 장갑 가져오기'이다.

06 여자가 지불할 금액

정답률 80%
▶ 정답 ③

M: Welcome to Extreme Indoor Rock Climbing Center.
　　　　　　　 익스트림 실내 암벽 등반 센터
W: Hello, I'd like to try indoor rock climbing with my son. It's our first
　 time.
M: Okay. If it's your first time, I recommend that you take an intro session.
　　　　　　　　　　　　　　　　 추천하다　　　　　　　　　 입문 과정
　 It takes an hour.
W: Great. How much is it?
M: It's $20 for an adult and $14 for a child.
W: I see. I'll take an intro session for one adult and one child.
M: Okay, do you have indoor climbing shoes? You need special shoes

for climbing.
W: Can we rent the shoes? Both of us need them.
　　　　　 빌리다
M: Yes. The rental fee is $3 per person. Then you want an intro
　　　　　　 대여료　　　　　 1인당
　 session for one adult and one child and two shoe rentals, right?
W: Yes. Oh, can I use this coupon? I downloaded it online.
M: Sure. You'll get 10% off the total price.
　　　　　　　　　　　　총액에서 10% 할인을 받다
W: Great. Here's my credit card.

해석

남: Extreme Indoor Rock Climbing Center(익스트림 실내 암벽 등반 센터)에 오신 것을 환영합니다.
여: 안녕하세요, 아들과 함께 실내 암벽 등반을 해보고 싶은데요. 처음이에요.
남: 알겠습니다. 처음이시라면, 입문 과정을 수강하시는 것을 추천해요. 그것은 한 시간이 걸려요.
여: 좋아요. 얼마죠?
남: 성인은 20달러이고 어린이는 14달러예요.
여: 그렇군요. 성인 한 명과 어린이 한 명을 위한 입문 과정을 수강할게요.
남: 알겠습니다. 실내 등반화는 있으신가요? 등반을 위한 특별한 신발이 필요해요.
여: 신발을 빌릴 수 있을까요? 저희 둘 다 필요하거든요.
남: 네. 대여료는 1인당 3달러예요. 그럼 성인 한 명과 어린이 한 명을 위한 입문 과정과 신발 두 켤레 대여를 원하시는 거네요, 맞나요?
여: 네. 오, 이 쿠폰을 사용할 수 있나요? 온라인으로 다운로드했어요.
남: 물론이죠. 총액에서 10% 할인을 받으실 거예요.
여: 잘됐네요. 여기 제 신용카드가 있어요.

① $27　　　　　② $34　　　　　✔ $36
④ $37　　　　　⑤ $40

문제 풀이

입문 과정 수강 비용은 성인이 20달러이고 어린이는 14달러이다. 실내 등반화 대여료는 1인당 3달러이다. 여자가 자신과 아들을 위해 지불해야 할 총액은 40달러이지만, 쿠폰을 사용해 10% 할인을 받는다고 했으므로 4달러가 할인된 36달러를 지불하면 된다. 따라서 답은 ③ '$36'이다.

07 남자가 레일 바이크를 타러 갈 수 없는 이유

정답률 90%
▶ 정답 ⑤

[Cell phone rings.]
W: Hello, Anthony. What's up?
M: Hi, Lucy. I'm calling about borrowing some costumes from the
　　　　　　　　　　　　　　　　　　　　　　　　 의상들
　 drama club.
　 연극 동아리
W: Oh, but I'm on my way to my part-time job at the moment.
　　　　　　　　　　　　　　　 아르바이트　　　　지금
M: Okay. Then maybe I can pick them up tomorrow. Anyway, how was
　　　　　　　　　　　　　　 그것들을 가지러 가다
　 your family gathering?
　　　　 가족 모임
W: I had a great time. Oh, my uncle gave me a coupon for the rail bike
　　　　　　　　　　　　　　　　　　　　　　　　　　　　　　　　 레일 바이크
　 at Crystal Riverside. Do you want to go with me?
M: Sounds great. When do you want to go?
W: How about this Saturday?
M: This Saturday? I'm afraid I can't.
W: Oh, I remember you have your soccer practice every Saturday.
　　　　　　　　　　　　　　　　　 축구 연습
M: Not this week. It's cancelled.
　　　　　　　　 취소되었다(cancel: 취소하다)
W: Then why can't you come?
M: I have a musical audition scheduled on that day.
　　　　　 뮤지컬 오디션　 예정된(schedule: 예정하다; 일정)
W: Okay. Good luck on the audition.

해석

[휴대전화가 울린다.]
여: 안녕, Anthony. 무슨 일이야?
남: 안녕, Lucy. 연극 동아리에서 의상들을 빌리는 일 때문에 전화했어.
여: 오, 그런데 나는 지금 아르바이트를 하러 가는 길이야.
남: 알겠어. 그럼 아마도 내일 그것들을 가지러 갈 수 있겠구나. 그나저나, 가족 모임은 어땠니?
여: 정말 즐거웠어. 오, 삼촌께서 Crystal Riverside에 있는 레일 바이크 쿠폰을 주셨어. 나와 함께 갈래?
남: 좋아. 언제 가고 싶어?
여: 이번 주 토요일은 어때?
남: 이번 주 토요일? 나는 못 갈 것 같아.

여: 오, 나는 네가 토요일마다 축구 연습을 하는 것을 기억해.
남: 이번 주는 아니야. 취소되었거든.
여: 그럼 왜 못 가는 거야?
남: 그날 예정된 뮤지컬 오디션이 있어.
여: 알겠어. 오디션에 행운을 빌게.

① 가족 모임에 가야 해서
② 축구 연습을 해야 해서
③ 아르바이트를 해야 해서
④ 연극 의상을 제작해야 해서
☑ 뮤지컬 오디션이 예정되어 있어서

08 Winter Robot Camp에 관해 언급되지 않은 것

정답률 85% ▶ 정답 ③

M: Sarah, what are you doing?
W: Hi, Thomas. I'm looking at a leaflet for the Winter Robot Camp.
　　　　　　　　　　　　　　　　　　 전단　　　　　 겨울 로봇 캠프
　 How about going with me?
M: Sounds interesting. When is it?
W: It'll be held from December 28th to 30th.
　　 열리다(hold: 열다, 개최하다)
M: That's good. The semester will be over by then.
　　　　　　　　　 학기　　　　 끝나다
W: Right. And the camp will be at the Watkins Robot Center. You know
　 where that is.
M: Yes, I've been there several times. Can I see the leaflet? I wonder
　　　　　　　　　　　 몇 번
　 what programs they'll offer.
　　　　　　　　　　　 제공하다
W: Sure. Here it is.
M: Oh, they'll provide daily programs on robot programming, drone
　　　　　　　　　　　　　　　　　　　　　　　　　　　　　 드론 비행
　 flying, and coding.
　　　　 코딩
W: Yeah. It says participants will work together with other students
　　　　　　　　 참가자들
　 with similar levels of experience.
　　　　 비슷한 수준의
M: It sounds like fun. How can we register?
　　　　　　　　　　　　　　　　 등록하다
W: It's simple. We can scan this QR code and complete the form.
　　　　　　　　　 스캔하다　　　　　　　　 신청서를 작성하다
M: Great. Let's do it now.

해석
남: Sarah, 무엇을 하고 있니?
여: 안녕, Thomas. Winter Robot Camp(겨울 로봇 캠프)에 대한 전단을 보고 있어. 나와 함께 가는 게 어때?
남: 흥미로울 것 같아. 언제야?
여: 12월 28일부터 30일까지 열릴 거야.
남: 잘됐네. 그때쯤에는 학기가 끝날 거야.
여: 맞아. 그리고 캠프는 Watkins Robot Center(Watkins 로봇 센터)에 있을 거야. 그것이 어디에 있는지 알잖아.
남: 응, 그곳에 몇 번 가 봤어. 전단지를 볼 수 있을까? 그들이 어떤 프로그램을 제공할지 궁금해.
여: 물론이지. 여기 있어.
남: 오, 로봇 프로그래밍, 드론 비행, 코딩에 관한 일일 프로그램을 제공하는구나.
여: 그래. 참가자들은 비슷한 수준의 경험을 가진 다른 학생들과 함께 작업을 할 것이라고 되어 있어.
남: 재미있을 것 같아. 어떻게 등록할 수 있어?
여: 간단해. 이 QR 코드를 스캔해서 신청서를 작성할 수 있어.
남: 좋아. 지금 하자.

① 기간　　　　　　　② 장소　　　　　　☑ 준비물
④ 운영 프로그램　　 ⑤ 등록 방법

09 Go Greener Festival에 관한 내용과 일치하지 않는 것

정답률 80% ▶ 정답 ④

M: Hello, listeners! This is Hans Dale with Upcoming Event News.
　　　　　　　　　　　　　　　　　　　　　　　 다가오는　　 행사 뉴스
　 Do you want to feel festive vibes for autumn? Then the Go
　　　　　　　　　　　　 축제의　 분위기　　　　　　　　　　　　 Go
　 Greener Festival is a perfect event for you. This event will be held
　 친환경 축제(go greener: 더 친환경적이게 되다)
　 from November 11th to 13th in Central Park. Songs about the
　 environment will be played. Stages will be built using recycled
　 환경　　　　　　　　　　　　　 무대들　　　　　　　　　　 재활용된

materials. You can buy food which is all organic and served on
재료들　　　　　　　　　　　　　　　　　　 유기농의　　 제공되는
edible plates. If you bring your own water bottle, you can get drinks
먹을 수 있는　　　　　　　　　　　　 물병
at a discounted price. To reduce the festival's carbon footprint, the
　 할인된 가격에　　　 줄이다　　　　　　　　　 탄소 발자국
parking lot will not be available. Don't miss the opportunity to go
주차장　　　　　　　　 이용이 가능한
greener. Stay tuned!

해석
남: 안녕하세요, 청취자 여러분! 저는 Upcoming Event News(다가오는 행사 뉴스)의 Hans Dale입니다. 가을에 축제 분위기를 느끼고 싶으신가요? 그렇다면 Go Greener Festival(친환경 축제)이 여러분에게 완벽한 행사입니다. 이 행사는 11월 11일부터 13일까지 Central Park에서 열릴 것입니다. 환경에 관한 노래가 연주될 것입니다. 무대는 재활용된 재료를 사용하여 만들어질 것입니다. 모두 유기농이고 먹을 수 있는 접시에 제공되는 음식을 구매하실 수 있습니다. 여러분 자신의 물병을 가져오시면, 음료를 할인된 가격에 사실 수 있습니다. 축제의 탄소 발자국을 줄이기 위해, 주차장은 이용이 가능하지 않을 것입니다. 더 친환경적으로 될 수 있는 기회를 놓치지 마세요. 채널 고정해 주세요!

① 11월 11일부터 13일까지 진행된다.
② 환경에 관한 노래가 연주된다.
③ 무대는 재활용된 재료로 제작된다.
☑ 물병을 가져오면 음료를 무료로 받을 수 있다.
⑤ 주차장 이용이 불가능하다.

문제 풀이
친환경 축제에서 자신 소유의 물병을 가져오는 사람들은 음료를 할인된 가격에 살 수 있다고 했으므로 ④ '물병을 가져오면 음료를 무료로 받을 수 있다.'는 내용과 일치하지 않는다.

10 표에서 두 사람이 주문할 직소 퍼즐 세트

정답률 75% ▶ 정답 ②

M: Honey, since we had fun doing a jigsaw puzzle last time, why don't
　　　　　　　　　　　　　　　　　　　 직소 퍼즐
　 we order a new one?
　　　 주문하다
W: That's a good idea. What about a famous painting again? We can
　　　　　　　　　　　　　　　　　　 유명한　　 그림
　 put it in the living room this time.
　　　　　　　 거실
M: Let's look online. [Typing sounds] Look, these five models are the
　 most popular jigsaw puzzle sets.
　 가장 인기 있는
W: Great. Which painting do you want this time?
M: We did Water Lilies last time.
　　　　　 수련
W: Yeah, let's choose something new. What do you think about the
　 number of puzzle pieces?
　 개수　　　　　 조각들
M: How about doing something more challenging than 400 pieces?
　　　　　　　　　　　　　　　 더 어려운
W: I agree. And I think spending over $40 for a puzzle set is too much.
　　　　　　　　　　　 쓰는 것(spend)
M: Right. Oh, we can choose the frame as well. Which one would be
　　　　　　　　　　　　　　　　 액자
　 good?
W: How about a wooden frame? I think it'll go better with the living
　　　　　　　 나무의　　　　　　　　　　　 ~과 더 잘 어울리다
　 room.
M: Okay. Let's choose this one.

해석
남: 여보, 지난번에 직소 퍼즐을 재미있게 했으니까, 새로운 것을 주문하는 게 어때요?
여: 좋은 생각이에요. 또 유명한 그림은 어때요? 이번에는 그것을 거실에 놓을 수 있잖아요.
남: 온라인으로 찾아봅시다. [타자 치는 소리] 봐요, 이 다섯 가지 모델이 가장 인기 있는 직소 퍼즐 세트예요.
여: 좋아요. 이번에는 어떤 그림을 원해요?
남: 우리는 지난번에 '수련'을 했잖아요.
여: 그래요, 새로운 것을 골라봐요. 퍼즐 조각의 개수에 대해서는 어떻게 생각해요?
남: 400조각보다 더 어려운 것을 하는 게 어때요?
여: 동의해요. 그리고 퍼즐 세트에 40달러 이상을 쓰는 것은 너무 많은 것 같아요.
남: 맞아요. 오, 액자도 선택할 수 있어요. 어떤 게 좋을까요?
여: 나무 액자는 어때요? 그것이 거실과 더 잘 어울릴 것 같아요.
남: 알겠어요. 이것을 선택합시다.

직소 퍼즐 세트

	세트	그림 제목	퍼즐 조각 개수	가격	액자
①	A	모나리자	1,000	44달러	나무
☑	B	별이 빛나는 밤	800	38달러	나무
③	C	수련	700	35달러	나무

| ④ | D | 비너스의 탄생 | 600 | 33달러 | 금속 |
| ⑤ | E | 해바라기 | 400 | 30달러 | 금속 |

11 여자의 마지막 말에 대한 남자의 응답

정답률 85% ▶ 정답 ②

W: Paul, what are you writing with that brush? It looks really artistic.

붓 / 예술적인

M: Thanks, Clara. I'm practicing calligraphy.

연습하는(practice) / 서예

W: It's my first time seeing someone doing calligraphy. Who did you learn it from?

배우다

M: (It was my aunt who taught me calligraphy.)

이모

해석

여: Paul, 그 붓으로 무엇을 쓰고 있는 거니? 정말 예술적으로 보여.
남: 고마워, Clara. 나는 서예를 연습하고 있어.
여: 누군가가 서예를 하는 걸 보는 것은 처음이야. 그것을 누구한테 배웠니?
남: (나에게 서예를 가르쳐주신 분은 이모님이었어.)

① 새로운 것을 배우기에는 너무 늦었어.
✔② 나에게 서예를 가르쳐주신 분은 이모님이었어.
③ 나는 남동생에게 글씨 쓰는 법을 가르치곤 했어.
④ 나는 네가 나와 같은 취미를 가지고 있는지 몰랐어.
⑤ 나는 온라인에서 서예를 위한 특별한 붓을 샀어.

12 남자의 마지막 말에 대한 여자의 응답

정답률 75% ▶ 정답 ①

[Telephone rings.]

M: Hello, Bluelagoon Scuba Diving. How can I help you?

스쿠버 다이빙

W: Hi, I'd like to register for an indoor course on Friday evenings.

~에 등록하다 / 실내 강습

M: Let me check. [Typing sounds] We have two courses on Friday. The 7 p.m. is fully booked, but you can take the 8 o'clock course.

예약이 모두 차다(book: 예약하다)

W: (I see. I'll register for the available course.)

수강이 가능한, 이용 가능한

해석

[전화벨이 울린다.]

남: 안녕하세요, Bluelagoon Scuba Diving(Bluelagoon 스쿠버 다이빙)입니다. 어떻게 도와드릴까요?
여: 안녕하세요, 금요일 저녁의 실내 강습에 등록하고 싶은데요.
남: 확인해 볼게요. [타자 치는 소리] 금요일에 두 개의 강습이 있네요. 오후 7시는 예약이 모두 찼지만, 8시 강습은 수강하실 수 있어요.
여: (그렇군요. 저는 수강이 가능한 강습에 등록할게요.)

✔① 그렇군요. 저는 수강이 가능한 강습에 등록할게요.
② 말도 안 돼요. 저는 수상 활동에 관심이 없어요.
③ 문제없어요. 오후 7시 수업을 선택할 수 있게 해드릴게요.
④ 멋지네요. 스쿠버 다이빙을 가르칠 수 있어서 기뻐요.
⑤ 정말이에요? 저는 이미 금요일 강습에 등록했어요.

13 여자의 마지막 말에 대한 남자의 응답

정답률 80% ▶ 정답 ⑤

W: What's that, John? Oh, is that the bookcase you ordered online?

책장

M: Yes, Kelly. It was delivered today. I'm trying to put it together, but it's quite complicated.

그것을 조립하다 / 복잡한 / (put A together: A를 조립하다)

W: Hmm, it doesn't look easy to assemble it.

조립하다

M: Right, I hardly understand the manual. It's my first time trying to assemble DIY furniture. I'm so confused.

거의 ~하지 못하다 / 설명서 / 가구 / 혼란스러운

W: That can happen if you're doing something you're not used to.

~에 익숙하지 않다(be used to: ~에 익숙하다)

M: You're right. Oh, didn't you say you had assembled a computer by yourself?

W: Yes, and I also had difficulty understanding the manual.

이해하는 데 어려움을 겪었다 / (have difficulty V-ing: ~하는 데 어려움을 겪다)

M: Then how did you do it?

W: I searched for a video and learned how to put it together.

~을 검색했다(search for)

M: I think that would be quite helpful.

W: Yes, it explained every step well. There will be many videos online that can help you, too.

단계

M: (I should find a video for assembling the bookcase.)

해석

여: 그게 뭐야, John? 오, 온라인으로 주문한 책장이니?
남: 응, Kelly. 오늘 배달됐어. 나는 그것을 조립하려고 노력 중인데, 꽤 복잡해.
여: 흠, 조립하기가 쉽지 않아 보여.
남: 맞아, 나는 설명서를 거의 이해하지 못하겠어. DIY 가구를 조립해 보는 건 처음이야. 너무 혼란스러워.
여: 익숙하지 않은 일을 하고 있다면 그럴 수도 있어.
남: 네 말이 맞아. 오, 너는 컴퓨터를 혼자 조립했다고 하지 않았어?
여: 그래, 그리고 나 또한 설명서를 이해하는 데 어려움을 겪었어.
남: 그럼 너는 어떻게 했어?
여: 동영상을 검색해서 조립하는 방법을 배웠지.
남: 그게 꽤 도움이 될 것 같아.
여: 그래, 그것은 모든 단계를 잘 설명해줬어. 온라인에 너에게 도움을 줄 수 있는 동영상들도 많이 있을 거야.
남: (나는 책장 조립을 위한 동영상을 찾아봐야겠어.)

① DIY 가구를 배달하는 것이 도움이 될 거야.
② 내가 설명서를 사용해서 네 컴퓨터를 고쳐줄게.
③ 나는 이미 그것을 조립하는 방법을 완전히 익혔어.
④ 나는 네가 온라인에서 새 책장을 샀으면 좋겠어.
✔⑤ 나는 책장 조립을 위한 동영상을 찾아봐야겠어.

문제 풀이

주문한 책장을 조립하는 데 어려움을 겪고 있는 남자에게 여자는 동영상을 통해 컴퓨터 조립 방법을 배운 자신의 경험을 얘기하며 온라인에 남자에게 도움이 되는 동영상도 많을 거라고 말한다. 이에 대한 남자의 응답으로 가장 적절한 것은 ⑤ 'I should find a video for assembling the bookcase.(나는 책장 조립을 위한 동영상을 찾아봐야겠어.)'이다.

14 남자의 마지막 말에 대한 여자의 응답

정답률 75% ▶ 정답 ③

M: Honey, what are you watching online?

W: It's a documentary about ugly vegetables.

못생긴 / 채소들

M: Interesting. What does it say?

W: According to the documentary, one-third of all vegetables are thrown away at farms just because of their appearance.

~에 의하면 / 버려지다(throw away: 버리다) / 겉모양

M: I can't believe it. That's such a shame.

W: Yeah. They're wasted even though they're as delicious and nutritious as good-looking vegetables.

맛있는 / 영양분이 많은 / 잘생긴

M: So, does the farmers' hard work just become useless?

노력 / 소용없는

W: Right. I think we should do something for the farmers.

M: I agree. Why don't we search for a way to buy ugly produce?

~을 찾다 / 농산물

W: Great idea! Let's find it on the Internet.

M: Let me do it. [Typing sounds] Look. This store is selling ugly vegetables at a reasonable price.

합리적인

W: (Good. Let's see if the vegetables we need are for sale.)

판매 중인

해석

남: 여보, 온라인으로 무엇을 보고 있어요?
여: 못생긴 채소에 대한 다큐멘터리예요.
남: 흥미롭네요. 뭐라고 해요?
여: 다큐멘터리에 의하면, 모든 채소의 3분의 1이 단지 겉모양 때문에 농장에서 버려진다고 해요.
남: 믿을 수가 없네요. 그거 참 안타깝네요.
여: 네. 그것들은 잘생긴 채소만큼 맛있고 영양분이 많다고 할지라도 버려지는 거예요.
남: 그럼, 농부들의 노력은 소용없게 되는 건가요?
여: 맞아요. 우리가 농부들을 위해 무언가를 해야 할 것 같아요.
남: 동의해요. 우리 못생긴 농산물을 구매할 수 있는 방법을 찾아보는 게 어때요?
여: 좋은 생각이에요! 인터넷에서 찾아봐요.

남: 제가 할게요. *[타자 치는 소리]* 봐요. 이 가게는 못생긴 채소를 합리적인 가격에 팔고 있어요.

여: (잘됐네요. 우리에게 필요한 채소가 판매 중인지 알아봐요.)

① 물론이죠. 우리는 채소만 먹는 것을 피해야 해요.
② 미안해요. 저는 못생긴 채소보다 잘생긴 채소를 더 좋아해요.
☑ 잘됐네요. 우리에게 필요한 채소가 판매 중인지 알아봐요.
④ 맞아요. 못생긴 채소는 먹기에 적합하지 않아요.
⑤ 아주 좋아요. 저는 당신이 사준 못생긴 채소가 마음에 들어요.

15 다음 상황에서 Sofia가 Henry에게 할 말
정답률 70% ▶ 정답 ③

W: Sofia and Henry teach literature in high school. Sofia has worked for ten years, and Henry has just begun teaching. At the beginning of the semester, Henry assigns a book to his students and has them do a presentation about it. However, he notices that many of his students don't show as much interest in the book as he expected, so he asks Sofia for advice. Sofia knows her students are highly motivated when they pick their own books. So, she wants to suggest to Henry that he allow his students to choose books for themselves. In this situation, what would Sofia most likely say to Henry?

Sofia: (How about giving students a choice in their books?)

해석

여: Sofia와 Henry는 고등학교에서 문학을 가르친다. Sofia는 10년 동안 일했고, Henry는 이제 막 가르치기 시작했다. 학기 초반에, Henry는 자신의 학생들에게 책을 지정해주고 그것에 대한 발표를 하도록 한다. 하지만, 그는 많은 학생들이 그가 기대했던 것만큼 책에 관심을 보이지 않는다는 것을 알아채고, Sofia에게 조언을 구한다. Sofia는 학생들이 자신만의 책을 고를 때 매우 의욕적이라는 것을 알고 있다. 그래서, 그녀는 Henry에게 그의 학생들이 스스로 책을 선택하도록 허용할 것을 제안하고 싶다. 이러한 상황에서, Sofia는 Henry에게 뭐라고 말하겠는가?

Sofia: (학생들에게 책에 대한 선택권을 주는 게 어때요?)

① 당신은 책을 고를 때 후기를 봐야 해요.
② 발표의 예시를 보여주는 게 어때요?
☑ 학생들에게 책에 대한 선택권을 주는 게 어때요?
④ 학생들에게 독후감을 할당하는 것을 추천해요.
⑤ 학생들에게 다른 사람들과 작업할 시간을 줘야 해요.

16~17 1지문 2문항

M: Hello, students. Last class, we learned about different expressions in various languages related to birds. Today, let's talk about what birds represent in different cultures. First, the eagle was a significant bird in ancient Mexican culture. For ancient Mexicans, the eagle was a symbol of the sun. As a predator, the eagle was also associated with strength and power. Second, in Chinese culture, the crane stands for intelligence and honor. It's admired for its ability to walk, fly, and swim as well as for its graceful appearance. Third, in ancient Greek culture, the owl was a symbol for the Goddess of wisdom, Athena. The owl's abilities to see, fly, and hunt effectively in the dark often implied magical powers and mystery. Lastly, in some Native American cultures, the hummingbird is a healer and deliverer of love. That's because of its ability to move incredibly fast. The hummingbird is also considered a symbol of joy and good luck. Isn't that interesting? Now, let's watch a video to help you understand better.

해석

남: 안녕하세요, 학생 여러분. 지난 수업에서, 우리는 새와 관련된 다양한 언어의 다른 표현들에 대해서 배웠습니다. 오늘은, 다른 문화에서 새가 무엇을 나타내는지에 대해 이야기해 봅시다. 첫째, 독수리는 고대 멕시코 문화에서 중요한 새였습니다. 고대 멕시코 사람들에게, 독수리는 태양의 상징이었습니다. 포식자로서, 독수리는 힘과 권력과도 연관이 있었습니다. 둘째, 중국 문화에서, 학은 지성과 명예를 상징합니다. 그것은 우아한 외모뿐만 아니라 걷고, 날고, 헤엄치는 능력으로 찬사를 받습니다. 셋째, 고대 그리스 문화에서, 부엉이는 지혜의 여신인 Athena(아테나)의 상징이었습니다. 어둠 속에서 효과적으로 보고, 날고, 사냥하는 부엉이의 능력은 종종 마법의 힘과 신비로움을 의미했습니다. 마지막으로, 일부 아메리카 원주민 문화에서, 벌새는 사랑의 치유자이자 전달자입니다. 그것은 믿을 수 없을 정도로 빠르게 움직이는 그것의 능력 때문입니다. 벌새는 또한 기쁨과 행운의 상징으로 여겨집니다. 흥미롭지 않습니까? 이제, 여러분이 더 잘 이해할 수 있도록 도움을 주는 동영상을 봅시다.

16 남자가 하는 말의 주제
정답률 85% ▶ 정답 ④

① 다양한 새의 이동 패턴
② 도시 성장에 의해 영향 받는 새의 다양성
③ 새와 관련된 일상적인 표현
☑ 다른 문화에서 사용되는 새의 상징적 의미
⑤ 농업 발전에 미치는 새의 영향

17 언급된 새가 아닌 것
정답률 85% ▶ 정답 ④

① 독수리　　　② 학　　　③ 부엉이
☑ 참새　　　⑤ 벌새

18 2023년 3월 학력평가

01	①	02	①	03	④	04	③	05	①
06	②	07	②	08	③	09	③	10	②
11	①	12	②	13	②	14	①	15	①
16	③	17	④								

01 여자가 하는 말의 목적
정답률 80% ▶ 정답 ①

W: Good morning, students. This is your principal, Ms. Perez. I have an important announcement about our indoor gym. Since its opening, it has been a popular destination for students who'd like to stay fit. However, the gym has been in use for more than 10 years and most sports equipment is now outdated. So, our school has decided to renovate the gym. This means the gym will be temporarily closed until further notice. We apologize for any inconvenience this may cause. Please check our school website for updates on the reopening of the gym. Thank you for your understanding.

해석

여: 안녕하세요, 학생 여러분. 저는 교장인 Perez 선생님입니다. 실내 체육관에 관한 중요한 공지 사항이 있습니다. 개관 이래로, 그곳은 건강을 유지하고자 하는 학생들에게 인기 있

는 장소였습니다. 하지만, 체육관은 10년 이상 사용되어 왔고 대부분의 스포츠 장비는 이제 구식입니다. 그래서, 우리 학교는 체육관을 보수하기로 결정했습니다. 이것은 추후 안내가 있을 때까지 체육관이 일시적으로 폐쇄된다는 것을 의미합니다. 이것이 초래할 불편에 대해 사과드립니다. 체육관의 재개관에 대한 업데이트는 학교 웹사이트에서 확인해 주시기 바랍니다. 이해해 주셔서 감사합니다.

☑① 학교 실내 체육관의 임시 폐쇄를 안내하려고
② 학교 실내 체육관의 방과 후 이용을 권장하려고
③ 학교 실내 체육관 개관 10주년 기념식에 초대하려고
④ 학교 실내 체육관 시설 보수를 위한 의견을 모으려고
⑤ 학교 실내 체육관 이용 후 운동 기구 정리를 당부하려고

02 남자의 의견

정답률 95% ▶ 정답 ①

M: Grace, did you finish preparing for your hiking trip tomorrow?

W: Almost, Dad. I still don't know which jacket I should wear.

M: When you choose your hiking jacket, make sure you consider the color.
_{입다 / 등산복 / 고려하다}

W: How about this brown one? It looks good on me.

M: That does suit you well, but I think you should avoid brown.
_{~에게 어울리다 / 어울리다 / 피하다}

W: Why is that?

M: For the sake of your safety, you need to wear a color that stands out from the surroundings. It allows you to be seen easily by others.
_{~을 위해서 / 안전 / ~과 대비되다 / 주위 환경 / ~하게 해주다}

W: You mean I should avoid colors that blend in with nature, like browns and greens?
_{~과 섞이다}

M: Exactly. Safety should always come first.
_{우선하다}

W: Then I'll go with this bright orange jacket.
_{~을 선택하다}

해석

남: Grace, 내일 등산을 위한 준비를 끝냈니?
여: 거의 다 했어요, 아빠. 저는 아직도 어떤 겉옷을 입어야 할지 모르겠어요.
남: 등산복을 고를 때는, 반드시 색을 고려해야 해.
여: 이 갈색은 어때요? 저에게 어울려요.
남: 확실히 잘 어울리기는 하지만 갈색은 피해야 할 것 같구나.
여: 왜 그렇죠?
남: 네 안전을 위해서, 주위 환경과 대비되는 색을 입어야 해. 그것은 네가 다른 사람들에게 쉽게 보일 수 있게 해주거든.
여: 갈색과 녹색처럼 자연과 섞이는 색은 피해야 한다는 말씀이세요?
남: 바로 그거야. 안전이 항상 우선이 되어야 해.
여: 그럼 이 밝은 주황색 옷을 선택할게요.

☑① 주위 환경과 대비되는 색의 등산복을 입는 것이 안전하다.
② 얇은 옷을 여러 겹 입으면 기온 변화에 대비할 수 있다.
③ 등산로를 벗어나 산행하면 자연을 훼손할 위험이 있다.
④ 등산복을 고를 때 방수 기능이 있는지 확인해야 한다.
⑤ 등산 전에 하는 준비 운동은 부상의 위험을 줄인다.

03 두 사람의 관계

정답률 85% ▶ 정답 ④

[Cell phone rings.]

W: Hello. Mia Parsons speaking.

M: Hello. I was told to call you this afternoon.

W: All right. Can I have your name, please?

M: I'm Jonathan Lee.

W: Just a second. [Pause] Oh, Mr. Lee. I have good news for you. I was able to fix your issue.
_{해결하다 / 문제}

M: That's a relief. The photos on my laptop are precious to me. By the way, what caused the problem?
_{노트북 컴퓨터 / 소중한 / ~을 일으켰다(cause)}

W: The main board was damaged, so I've replaced it with a new one.
_{손상되었다 / 그것을 새것으로 교체했다 / (damage: 손상시키다) / (replace A with B: A를 B로 교체하다)}

M: That's great. Can I get my laptop sent via a delivery service?

W: Sure. Please give me your address.
_{~을 통해 / 배달 서비스 / 주소}

M: It's 11367 White Street, Sandville.

W: Okay. You can get it by Tuesday.

M: Thank you so much. If you send me the bill, I'll pay it right away.
_{청구서}

해석

[휴대전화가 울린다.]
여: 안녕하세요. Mia Parsons입니다.
남: 안녕하세요. 저는 오늘 오후에 당신에게 전화하라고 들었어요.
여: 알겠어요. 성함을 알려주시겠어요?
남: 저는 Jonathan Lee입니다.
여: 잠깐만 기다려 주세요. [잠시 후] 오, Lee 씨. 좋은 소식이 있어요. 저는 당신의 문제를 해결할 수 있었어요.
남: 다행이네요. 제 노트북 컴퓨터에 있는 사진들은 제게 소중하거든요. 그런데, 무엇이 문제를 일으켰나요?
여: 메인보드가 손상되어서, 그것을 새것으로 교체했어요.
남: 잘됐네요. 제 노트북 컴퓨터를 배달 서비스를 통해 보내주실 수 있나요?
여: 물론이죠. 주소를 알려주세요.
남: Sandville, White Street 11367번지예요.
여: 알겠습니다. 화요일까지 받으실 수 있어요.
남: 정말 감사해요. 청구서를 보내주시면, 바로 지불할게요.

① 사진작가 — 모델
② 휴대 전화 판매원 — 손님
③ 제품 디자이너 — 제조업자
☑④ 노트북 수리 기사 — 의뢰인
⑤ 택배 배달원 — 고객 센터 직원

04 그림에서 대화의 내용과 일치하지 않는 것

정답률 75% ▶ 정답 ③

M: Hi, Lucia. Welcome back! How was your vacation?
_{휴가}

W: Hi, Andrew. It was great. We rented a guest house.
_{빌렸다}

M: Oh, do you have a picture of it?

W: Yes, look. I chose a sky-themed room for my kids.
_{하늘을 주제로 한}

M: Wow. The model airplane hanging from the ceiling looks cool.
_{매달린(hang) / 천장}

W: Yeah. And kids never stopped going up and down the slide under the model airplane.
_{미끄럼틀}

M: I can imagine. This star-shaped lamp on the table goes well with the theme.
_{별 모양의 / 전등 / ~과 잘 어울리다}

W: Isn't the astronaut doll on the bed cute? It was a gift from the guest house.
_{우주 비행사 인형 / 선물}

M: It is. Your kids must have loved the picture of the space shuttle beside the bed.
_{정말 좋아했음이 틀림없다 / 우주 왕복선 / (must have p.p.: ~했음이 틀림없다)}

W: They did. I really recommend this place for your next family trip.
_{추천하다}

M: Thanks. I should visit there next time.

해석

남: 안녕하세요, Lucia. 돌아온 것을 환영해요! 휴가는 어땠어요?
여: 안녕하세요, Andrew. 정말 좋았어요. 우리는 게스트 하우스를 빌렸어요.
남: 오, 그것의 사진이 있나요?
여: 네, 보세요. 저는 아이들을 위해 하늘을 주제로 한 방을 선택했어요.
남: 와. 천장에 매달린 모형 비행기가 멋져 보여요.
여: 네. 그리고 아이들은 모형 비행기 아래에 있는 미끄럼틀을 계속 오르내렸어요.
남: 상상이 되네요. 테이블 위에 있는 이 별 모양의 전등은 주제와 잘 어울리네요.
여: 침대 위에 있는 우주 비행사 인형이 귀엽지 않나요? 그것은 게스트 하우스의 선물이에요.
남: 그렇네요. 당신의 아이들은 침대 옆에 있는 우주 왕복선 그림을 틀림없이 정말 좋아했겠어요.
여: 그랬어요. 저는 당신의 다음 가족 여행을 위해 이 장소를 정말 추천해요.
남: 고마워요. 다음에 그곳을 방문해야겠어요.

05 남자가 여자를 위해 할 일

정답률 90%   ▶ 정답 ①

W: Dad, our printer is not working again!
M: Really? What do you need to print out?
W: I need a copy of my essay for tomorrow's English class.
M: Okay. Will you pass me the user's manual? Let me take a look.
W: I already did everything it says in the manual. Nothing helped.
M: Then, I can take the printer to the service center on my way out.
W: It might take more than a day to fix it. We'd better think of another way.
M: Hmm.... Then, how about going to the city library? You can use the printers there.
W: Oh, that'd be great, but I have never been there.
M: Don't worry. I'll take you there.
W: Thanks, Dad. Let's go to the library!

해석
여: 아빠, 프린터가 또 작동하지 않아요!
남: 정말? 무엇을 출력해야 하니?
여: 내일 영어 수업을 위해 제 에세이 한 부가 필요해요.
남: 알겠어. 사용 설명서를 건네주겠니? 내가 좀 볼게.
여: 제가 이미 설명서에 나와 있는 모든 것을 했어요. 아무것도 도움이 되지 않았어요.
남: 그럼, 내가 나가는 길에 프린터를 서비스 센터에 가져가면 돼.
여: 그것을 수리하는 데 하루 이상 걸릴지도 몰라요. 다른 방법을 생각해 보는 게 좋겠어요.
남: 흠.... 그럼, 시립 도서관에 가는 게 어때? 그곳에서 프린터를 사용할 수 있어.
여: 오, 그게 좋을 것 같은데, 저는 그곳에 가본 적이 없어요.
남: 걱정하지 마. 내가 너를 그곳에 데려다줄게.
여: 고마워요, 아빠. 도서관에 가요!

✔ 도서관에 데려다주기
② 에세이 검토해 주기
③ 프린터 설치해 주기
④ 출력물 가져다주기
⑤ 수리 센터에 연락해 주기

문제 풀이
남자는 여자에게 프린터를 사용할 수 있는 시립 도서관에 갈 것을 제안한다. 여자가 도서관에 가본 적이 없다고 대답하자 남자는 자신이 데려다주겠다고 말한다. 따라서 답은 ① '도서관에 데려다주기'이다.

06 여자가 지불할 금액

정답률 65%   ▶ 정답 ②

M: Honey, we need four extra cups for our housewarming party.
W: Okay. Let's buy them online. [Typing Sound] Look, I love this floral tea cup.
M: I like it too, and it only costs $8.
W: Hold on. The store's promotion says, "Buy one cup, get one cup free."
M: Fantastic! We only have to pay for two cups. Then, we can afford to buy a new teapot as well.
(can afford to V: ~할 수 있다)

W: That's a good idea. Let's buy one that matches the tea cups.
M: I like the white one that costs $20.
W: Okay. Let's pay for two tea cups and one teapot. Do we also have to pay for shipping?
M: Yes. The total shipping fee is $3. Do we need anything else?
W: Not really. Let me pay with my credit card.

해석
남: 여보, 집들이를 위해 우리는 네 개의 잔이 더 필요해요.
여: 알겠어요. 온라인으로 사요. [타자 치는 소리] 봐요, 저는 이 꽃무늬 찻잔이 정말 마음에 들어요.
남: 저도 마음에 드는데, 8달러밖에 안 하네요.
여: 잠깐만요. 그 상점의 판촉물에 "한 잔 사면, 한 잔 무료"라고 쓰여 있어요.
남: 환상적이네요! 우리는 두 잔에 대해서만 지불하면 돼요. 그럼, 새 찻주전자도 살 수 있어요.
여: 좋은 생각이에요. 찻잔에 어울리는 것을 사요.
남: 저는 20달러인 흰색이 마음에 들어요.
여: 좋아요. 찻잔 두 개와 찻주전자 한 개에 대해서 지불해요. 배송에 대해서도 지불해야 해요?
남: 네. 총 배송비가 3달러예요. 다른 필요한 건 없어요?
여: 네. 제 신용카드로 지불할게요.

① $36   ✔ $39   ③ $47
④ $52   ⑤ $55

문제 풀이
두 사람은 네 개의 찻잔과 한 개의 찻주전자를 사기로 했다. 한 개에 8달러인 찻잔은 한 개를 사면 한 개가 무료라고 했으므로 두 개에 대한 비용인 16달러만 계산하면 된다. 여기에 찻주전자는 20달러이고, 배송비는 3달러라고 했으므로 지불해야 할 총액은 39달러이다. 따라서 답은 ② '$39'이다.

07 남자가 내일 봉사 활동에 같이 갈 수 없는 이유

정답률 70%   ▶ 정답 ②

W: Michael, what do you think about doing some volunteer work tomorrow?
M: Well, I thought we're going to join a sports program tomorrow.
W: You haven't heard? It's been cancelled. (cancel: 취소하다)
M: Oh. Then, tell me more about the volunteer work.
W: We'll pick up meals at the community center and then deliver them to the elderly in the neighborhood.
M: Hmm.... When does it end? I'm having a family dinner.
W: Before noon. We'll be working for three hours in the morning.
M: Sounds good. Are there any restrictions for applicants?
W: Yes. You have to be 16 or older to participate.
M: Then, I'm qualified. I just turned 16 last February.
W: Oh, I almost forgot. You also need a flu vaccination record since you'll meet the elderly in person.
M: I haven't got a flu shot yet. I'm afraid I can't come.
W: Too bad. Maybe next time then.

해석
여: Michael, 내일 봉사 활동을 하는 것에 대해 어떻게 생각해?
남: 음, 나는 우리가 내일 스포츠 프로그램에 참여할 거라고 생각했어.
여: 못 들었니? 그것은 취소되었어.
남: 오. 그럼, 봉사 활동에 대해 좀 더 말해줘.
여: 우리는 지역 복지관에서 식사를 가져가서 동네의 어르신들에게 전달할 거야.
남: 흠.... 그것이 언제 끝나니? 나는 가족과 저녁 식사를 할 거야.
여: 정오 전에. 우리는 오전에 세 시간 동안 활동을 할 거야.
남: 괜찮은 것 같아. 지원자에게 어떤 제한 사항이 있니?
여: 응. 참가하려면 16세 이상이어야 해.
남: 그럼, 나는 자격이 있어. 지난 2월에 막 16세가 되었거든.
여: 오, 잊어버릴 뻔했네. 어르신들을 직접 만날 것이기 때문에 독감 예방 접종 기록도 필요해.
남: 아직 독감 예방 주사를 맞지 않았어. 나는 갈 수 없을 것 같아.
여: 유감이다. 그럼 다음에 가면 되지.

① 봉사 활동 장소가 너무 멀어서
✔ 독감 예방 주사를 맞지 않아서
③ 가족과 저녁 식사를 해야 해서

④ 참여 가능한 나이가 되지 않아서
⑤ 스포츠 프로그램에 참여해야 해서

08 Nari Island 패키지 여행에 관해 언급되지 않은 것
정답률 85% ▶ 정답 ③

M: Hi, Jessica. Are you ready for the trip to Nari Island?
W: Not yet. I've been too busy to make a detailed plan.
　　　　　　　　　　　　　　세부적인 계획을 세우다
　　　　　　　(make a plan: 계획을 세우다, detailed: 세부적인)
M: Then, how about booking a package tour? There should be some
　　　　　　　　예약하는 것(book)　패키지 여행
　package tours on the island.
W: Really? Let me check online. [Typing Sound] This one runs for 5
　days, from April 3rd to April 7th. It matches my holiday schedule.
　　　　　　　　　　　　　　　　일치하다　　　휴가 일정
M: It provides a guided tour to beautiful caves and cliffs.
　　　　　　　　　가이드가 안내하는　　　　동굴들　　절벽들
W: I think I'd enjoy it. I like to explore geological sites.
　　　　　　　　　　　　　　탐험하다　지질학적인
M: And a minivan will be offered for transportation.
　　　　미니밴　　　　　　　　　　　이동 수단
W: It sounds convenient. What do you think of the price?
　　　　　　편리한
M: I think $600 for each person is quite reasonable.
　　　　　　　　　　　　　　　　　합리적인
W: Perfect. I'll book it right away.

해석
남: 안녕, Jessica. Nari Island(Nari 섬) 여행을 위한 준비는 다 됐니?
여: 아직이야. 너무 바빠서 세부적인 계획을 세우지 못했어.
남: 그럼, 패키지 여행을 예약하는 게 어떠니? 그 섬에 대한 패키지 여행이 있을 거야.
여: 정말? 온라인으로 확인해 볼게. [타자 치는 소리] 이것은 4월 3일부터 4월 7일까지 5일 동
　안 진행돼. 내 휴가 일정과 일치해.
남: 그것은 아름다운 동굴과 절벽으로 가는 가이드가 안내하는 여행을 제공해.
여: 나는 그것을 즐길 것 같아. 지질학적인 장소를 탐험하는 것을 좋아하거든.
남: 그리고 미니밴이 이동 수단으로 제공될 거야.
여: 편리할 것 같아. 가격은 어떻게 생각해?
남: 한 사람당 600달러는 꽤 합리적인 것 같아.
여: 완벽해. 바로 그것을 예약할게.
① 여행 기간　　　　②방문 장소　　　✓최소 출발 인원
④ 이동 수단　　　　⑤가격

09 Afterschool Math Festival에 관한 내용과 일치하지 않는 것
정답률 85% ▶ 정답 ③

M: Good morning, math lovers of Hamington High School. I'm your
　math teacher, Allen Steward. We have a special announcement
　　　　　　　　　　　　　　　　　　　특별 공지 사항
　for you. The Afterschool Math Festival will be held for three days
　　　　　　방과 후 수학 축제　　　　　열리다
　starting next Monday. Nine activities are planned, and you may
　　　　　　　　　　　　(hold: 열다, 개최하다)
　participate in up to three different activities. Keep in mind that
　~에 참가하다　~까지　　　　　　　　　　　　　　~을 명심하다
　activities such as the Math Escape Room and the Math Quiz
　　　　　　　　　　수학 방탈출　　　　　　수학 퀴즈 쇼
　Show will take longer than other activities. This year, we are also
　　　　시간이 더 오래 걸리다
　offering a guest lecture. Our lecturer, Dr. Hilbert will tell us the
　　　　초청 강연　　　　강연자
　stories behind famous mathematicians. Students who attend this
　　　　　　　　　　　수학자들　　　　　　　　　참석하다
　special lecture will get a copy of his book for free. Lastly, during the
　　　　　　　　　　　　　　　　　　무료로
　festival, special snacks and drinks will be served at the cafeteria.
　　　　　　간식들　　　　　제공되다(serve: 제공하다)　구내식당
　See you there.

해석
남: 안녕하세요, Hamington 고등학교의 수학 애호가 여러분. 저는 수학 선생님인 Allen
　Steward입니다. 여러분을 위한 특별 공지 사항이 있습니다. 다음 주 월요일부터 3일 동안
　Afterschool Math Festival(방과 후 수학 축제)이 열릴 것입니다. 9개의 활동이 계획되어
　있으며, 3개까지 다른 활동에 참가할 수 있습니다. Math Escape Room(수학 방탈출)과
　Math Quiz Show(수학 퀴즈 쇼)와 같은 활동은 다른 활동보다 시간이 더 오래 걸릴 것이
　라는 점을 명심하십시오. 올해, 저희는 초청 강연도 제공할 것입니다. 강연자인 Hilbert 박
　사님은 유명한 수학자들의 이면에 있는 이야기를 들려줄 것입니다. 이 특별 강연에 참석
　하는 학생들은 그의 책 한 권을 무료로 받을 것입니다. 마지막으로, 축제 기간 동안에, 구
　내식당에서 특별한 간식과 음료가 제공될 것입니다. 그곳에서 뵙겠습니다.

① 다음 주 월요일부터 3일간 진행된다.
② 9개의 활동 중 3개까지 참가할 수 있다.
✓모든 활동의 예상 소요 시간은 같다.
④ 강연에 참석한 학생에게 강연자의 책이 무료로 제공된다.
⑤ 구내식당에서 특별한 간식과 음료가 제공된다.

10 표에서 두 사람이 구매할 자외선 칫솔 소독기
정답률 85% ▶ 정답 ②

M: Honey, why don't we buy a UV toothbrush sanitizer? This online
　　　　　　　　　　　　　　자외선 칫솔 소독기
　store is offering a good deal.　온라인 상점
W: That's great. How about choosing one from these five models?
M: Fine. First, we need to consider the number of slots.
　　　　　　　　　　　　고려하다　　　　슬롯들
W: For our family, we need four or more slots.
M: Right. Do you think we need one with a built-in battery?
　　　　　　　　　　　　　　　　　　내장 배터리
W: Yes. It'd be easier to install.
　　　　　　　　　설치하다
M: Okay. And I think it's important to keep the brushes dry.
　　　　　　　　중요한　　　　　　　　　건조한
W: I agree. It prevents bacteria from growing on the brushes. We
　　　　　박테리아가 자라는 것을 방지하다
　　(prevent A from V-ing: A가 ~하는 것을 방지하다,
　　bacteria: 박테리아, grow: 자라다)
　should definitely go with one that has a drying function.
　　　　반드시　　　　　　　　　　　　　건조 기능
M: That leaves us with these two models.
　　　　남기다
W: How about staying under 50 dollars?
M: Good. Let's order the cheaper one.
　　　　　　주문하다

해석
남: 여보, 자외선 칫솔 소독기를 사는 게 어때요? 이 온라인 상점에서 싸게 팔고 있어요.
여: 잘됐네요. 이 다섯 가지 모델 중에서 하나를 고르는 게 어때요?
남: 좋아요. 먼저, 슬롯의 개수를 고려해야 해요.
여: 우리 가족을 위해서는, 4개 이상의 슬롯이 필요해요.
남: 맞아요. 내장 배터리가 있는 제품이 필요할까요?
여: 네. 설치하기가 더 쉬울 거예요.
남: 알겠어요. 그리고 칫솔을 건조하게 유지하는 것이 중요한 것 같아요.
여: 동의해요. 그것은 칫솔에서 박테리아가 자라는 것을 방지해요. 반드시 건조 기능이 있는
　제품을 선택해야 해요.
남: 그럼 이 두 가지 모델이 남네요.
여: 50달러 이하로 하는 게 어때요?
남: 좋아요. 더 싼 제품을 주문합시다.

자외선 칫솔 소독기

	모델	슬롯 개수	내장 배터리	건조 기능	가격
①	A	3	X	X	39달러
✓	B	4	O	O	48달러
③	C	4	X	X	40달러
④	D	5	O	X	50달러
⑤	E	6	O	O	54달러

11 여자의 마지막 말에 대한 남자의 응답
정답률 80% ▶ 정답 ①

W: Ben. Would you come take a look at this plant? The leaves are
　　　　　　　　　　　　~을 보다　　　식물　　　잎들
　turning brown.
M: Let me see. [Pause] Oh, you might have watered it too much.
　　　　　　　　　　　　　　　물을 줬을지도 모른다
　　　　　(might have p.p.: ~했을지도 모른다, water: 물을 주다)
W: Do you have any idea how I can fix my plant?
　　　　　　　　　　　　　　　치료하다
M: (Yes. You should stop watering it for a while.)
　　　　　　　　　　　　　　　　　당분간

해석
여: Ben. 와서 이 식물을 봐주겠니? 잎들이 갈색으로 변하고 있어.
남: 어디 보자. [잠시 후] 오, 네가 물을 너무 많이 줬을지도 몰라.
여: 내 식물을 어떻게 치료할 수 있는지 알고 있니?
남: (응. 당분간 그것에 물을 주는 것을 중단해야 해.)
✓응. 당분간 그것에 물을 주는 것을 중단해야 해.
②아니, 괜찮아. 나는 집에서 식물을 키울 수 없어.
③동의해. 저 다채로운 나뭇잎은 멋져 보여.

④ 물론이지. 정원 가꾸기는 좋은 취미인 것 같아.
⑤ 아니. 실내에서 식물을 기르는 것은 쉬워.

12 남자의 마지막 말에 대한 여자의 응답
정답률 65% ▶ 정답 ②

M: Ouch! I got a paper cut.
　　　　　　종이에 베었다
　　　　　　(get a paper cut)
W: Are you okay? I know how painful paper cuts are.
　　　　　　　　　　　　　　고통스러운
M: This is the third time this week. Maybe my hands are so dry that I
　　　　　　　　　　　　　　　　　　아마도
　　get paper cuts too easily.
　　　　　　　　　　쉽게
W: (If so, applying hand cream might help.)
　　　　　　바르는 것(apply)

해석
남: 아야! 종이에 베었어.
여: 괜찮아? 종이에 베인 상처가 얼마나 고통스러운지 알지.
남: 이번 주에만 세 번째야. 아마도 내 손이 매우 건조해서 너무 쉽게 종이에 베이는 것 같아.
여: (그렇다면, 핸드크림을 바르는 것이 도움이 될지도 몰라.)

① 내가 논문을 늦게 제출한 것 같아.
✔ 그렇다면, 핸드크림을 바르는 것이 도움이 될지도 몰라.
③ 원단 가위를 사용할 때는 조심해.
④ 음, 그 장갑은 내 아들에게 너무 커.
⑤ 이번에는 종이 장바구니를 가지고 가자.

13 여자의 마지막 말에 대한 남자의 응답
정답률 80% ▶ 정답 ②

W: Hey, Pete. What's in the big box?
M: Old towels and blankets. I'm taking them to the post office.
　　　　수건들　　담요들　　　　　　　　　　　　　우체국
W: Where are you sending them?
M: To an animal shelter. The shelter needs them for dogs and cats.
　　　　동물 보호소
W: I guess it's to keep the animals warm.
　　　　　　　　　　　　　　　　　따뜻한
M: Exactly. Without them, the animals have to sleep on the cold floor.
　　　　　　　　　　　　　　　　　　　　　　　　　차가운　바닥
W: Oh, I didn't know that.
M: Many animal shelters are in need of blankets and towels.
　　　　　　　　　　　　　~을 필요로 하는
W: Then, what about starting a school campaign to collect blankets
　　　　　　　　　　　　　　학교 캠페인　　　　모으다
　　and towels for the animals?
M: That'd be nice, but how can we do that?
W: We can propose a campaign at the student council meeting
　　　　　제안하다　　　　　　　　　학생회의
　　tomorrow.
M: (Good idea. I hope they listen to our suggestion.)
　　　　　　　　　　　　　　　　　　　제안

해석
여: 얘, Pete. 그 큰 상자 안에 무엇이 있니?
남: 오래된 수건과 담요야. 그것들을 우체국에 가져갈 거야.
여: 어디로 보낼 거니?
남: 동물 보호소로. 보호소는 개와 고양이를 위해 그것들이 필요하거든.
여: 동물들을 따뜻하게 하기 위한 거구나.
남: 맞아. 그것들이 없다면, 동물들은 차가운 바닥에서 자야 해.
여: 오, 나는 그것은 몰랐어.
남: 많은 동물 보호소들이 담요와 수건을 필요로 해.
여: 그렇다면, 동물들을 위한 담요와 수건을 모으기 위해 학교 캠페인을 시작하는 건 어때니?
남: 좋을 것 같은데, 그것을 어떻게 할 수 있을까?
여: 우리는 내일 학생회에서 캠페인을 제안할 수 있어.
남: (좋은 생각이야. 그들이 우리의 제안을 들어줬으면 좋겠다.)

① 알겠어. 내가 그 상자들을 수거하러 갈게.
✔ 좋은 생각이야. 그들이 우리의 제안을 들어줬으면 좋겠다.
③ 내 견해는 달라. 그 수건들은 재사용될 수 있어.
④ 신경 쓰지 마. 나는 우체국에 혼자 갈 수 있어.
⑤ 그렇지는 않아. 학생들은 그들 자신의 침실을 청소해야 해.

14 남자의 마지막 말에 대한 여자의 응답
정답률 85% ▶ 정답 ①

M: Hello, Ms. Watson. Did you enjoy the conference?
　　　　　　　　　　　　　　　　　　　학회

W: Yes, I did, Dr. Cooper. This year was a huge success. Congratulations!
　　　　　　　　　　　　　　　　　　　　대성공
M: Thank you. We had the largest audience ever.
　　　　　　　　　　　　　　　　청중
W: I heard some people couldn't come because the number of seats
　　　　　　　　　　　　　　　　　　　　　　　　　　　　　좌석들
　　was limited.
　　　　제한된
M: It was a pity that we couldn't find a larger lecture hall.
　　　　　　　　　　　　　　　　　　　　　　강의실
W: I think there is a way to accommodate more people next year.
　　　　　　　　　　방법　　수용하다
M: Really? How?
W: You can hold the conference on a metaverse platform.
　　　　개최하다　　　　　　　　　　메타버스 플랫폼
M: What does metaverse mean?
W: It's a virtual world. If you make a lecture hall there, you can interact
　　　　　가상 세계　　　　　　　　　　　　　　　　　　　　~와 상호 작용하다
　　with a larger audience.
M: That's very interesting. I'd like to try that but I don't know how to
　　　　　　　　　　　　　　　　시도하다　　　　　　　　시작하는 방법
　　start.
　　　　　　　　　　　　　　　　　　　(how to V: ~하는 방법)
W: (Don't worry. I can help you create a virtual lecture hall.)

해석
남: 안녕하세요, Watson 씨. 학회는 즐거우셨나요?
여: 네, 즐거웠어요, Cooper 박사님. 올해는 대성공이었어요. 축하해요!
남: 고마워요. 역대 가장 많은 청중이 왔어요.
여: 좌석의 수가 제한되어 있어서 일부 사람들은 오지 못했다고 들었어요.
남: 더 큰 강의실을 찾지 못해서 아쉬웠어요.
여: 내년에는 더 많은 사람들을 수용할 수 있는 방법이 있을 것 같아요.
남: 정말이에요? 어떻게요?
여: 메타버스 플랫폼에서 학회를 개최할 수 있어요.
남: 메타버스가 무슨 뜻이죠?
여: 그것은 가상 세계예요. 그곳에 강의실을 만들면, 더 많은 청중과 상호 작용할 수 있어요.
남: 매우 흥미롭네요. 저는 그것을 시도해 보고 싶은데 시작하는 방법을 모르겠어요.
여: (걱정하지 마세요. 제가 가상 강의실을 만드는 것을 도와드릴 수 있어요.)

✔ 걱정하지 마세요. 제가 가상 강의실을 만드는 것을 도와드릴 수 있어요.
② 기억나지 않으세요? 우리가 같은 장소를 빌린 적이 있어요.
③ 아직 아니에요. 저는 곧 학회에 참가 신청을 해야 해요.
④ 말도 안 돼요. 메타버스는 온라인 게임만을 위한 것이 아니에요.
⑤ 왜 안 되겠어요? 청중은 당신의 발표를 정말 좋아했어요.

문제풀이
여자는 가상 세계인 메타버스를 활용해 강의실을 만들어서 학회를 개최할 수 있다고 말한다. 남자는 여자가 제시한 방법을 시도하고 싶지만 어떻게 하는지 모르겠다고 말한다. 이에 대한 여자의 응답으로 가장 적절한 것은 ① 'Don't worry. I can help you create a virtual lecture hall.(걱정하지 마세요. 제가 가상 강의실을 만드는 것을 도와드릴 수 있어요.)'이다.

15 다음 상황에서 Jane이 David에게 할 말
정답률 75% ▶ 정답 ①

W: Jane and David are both violinists in the school orchestra. They
　　　　　　　　　　　　바이올린 연주자들
　　have been practicing together for a month for the Spring Concert.
　　연습해 오고 있다(practice)
　　Just three days before the concert, Jane sprains her wrist and
　　　　　　　　　　　　　　　　　　그녀의 손목을 삐다
　　her doctor recommends taking a rest for at least a week. Since
　　　　　　　권하다　　　　　　　휴식
　　Jane cannot play at the concert, David should take her solo part.
　　　　　연주하다　　　　　　　　　　　　　　　독주 부분
　　They have been practicing together and David knows Jane's part.
　　However, David says that he is too nervous to play the solo part.
　　　　　　　　　　　　　　너무 긴장해서 연주할 수 없는
　　　　　　　　　　　(too A to V: 너무 A해서 ~할 수 없는, nervous: 긴장한)
　　Jane knows that David is a skilled violinist. So, Jane wants to
　　　　　　　　　　　　　　　숙련된
　　encourage David to be more confident. In this situation, what
　　David가 더 자신감을 가지도록 격려하다
　　(encourage A to V: A가 ~하도록 격려하다, confident: 자신감을 가진)
　　would Jane most likely say to David?
Jane: (I'm sure you can play the solo part beautifully.)
　　　　　　　　　　　　　　　　　　멋지게

해석
여: Jane과 David는 둘 다 학교 오케스트라의 바이올린 연주자이다. 그들은 Spring Concert(봄 콘서트)를 위해 한 달 동안 함께 연습해 오고 있다. 콘서트가 있기 불과 3일 전에, Jane은 손목을 삐었고 의사는 적어도 일주일 동안 휴식을 취할 것을 권한다. Jane이 콘서트에서 연주할 수 없기 때문에, David가 그녀의 독주 부분을 맡아야 한다. 그들은 함께 연습해 와서 David는 Jane의 부분을 알고 있다. 하지만, David는 자신이 너무 긴장해서 독주 부분

을 연주할 수 없다고 말한다. Jane은 David가 숙련된 바이올린 연주자라는 것을 알고 있다. 그래서, Jane은 David가 더 자신감을 가지도록 격려하고 싶다. 이러한 상황에서, Jane은 David에게 뭐라고 말하겠는가?

Jane: (나는 네가 독주 부분을 멋지게 연주할 수 있을 거라고 확신해.)

✓① 나는 네가 독주 부분을 멋지게 연주할 수 있을 거라고 확신해.
② 모두 내 잘못이야. 내가 더 조심했어야 했어.
③ 네 독주 부분을 다른 사람에게 맡기는 게 어때?
④ 유감이야. 우리는 콘서트를 일주일 연기해야 해.
⑤ 나는 '봄 콘서트'에 참여하기 위해 최선을 다할 거야.

16~17 1지문 2문항

M: Good afternoon, students. Today we are going to talk about different national flags. There are some colors commonly used in national flags. The most common color is red, which makes up about 30 percent of all colors used in national flags. Usually red means life, courage, and revolution. For example, the red stripes of the United State's national flag symbolize the struggle for independence. The next is blue, with about a 20 percent share. The color often symbolizes the natural element of water or sky. For example, the blue in Greece's national flag means the seas surrounding the country. The next two most common colors are white and green. In some countries' flags, white means peace and honesty, such as in the United Kingdom's flag. Green is often related to nature, such as grasslands and forests. Can you guess what the green in Brazil's national flag means? Of course, it's the Amazon Rainforest. Now, let's look at the shapes of national flags.

해석

남: 안녕하세요, 학생 여러분. 오늘 우리는 다양한 국기에 대해 이야기할 것입니다. 국기에 흔히 사용되는 몇 가지 색이 있습니다. 가장 흔한 색은 빨간색인데, 그것은 국기에 사용되는 모든 색 중에서 약 30퍼센트를 차지합니다. 일반적으로 빨간색은 생명, 용기, 그리고 혁명을 의미합니다. 예를 들면, 미국 국기의 빨간색 줄무늬는 독립을 위한 투쟁을 상징합니다. 다음은 파란색으로, 약 20퍼센트의 점유율을 가지고 있습니다. 이 색은 종종 물이나 하늘의 자연적인 요소를 상징합니다. 예를 들면, 그리스 국기의 파란색은 그 나라를 둘러싸고 있는 바다를 의미합니다. 다음으로 가장 흔한 두 가지 색은 흰색과 녹색입니다. 일부 국가의 국기에서, 흰색은 영국 국기에서와 같이 평화와 정직을 의미합니다. 녹색은 종종 초원이나 숲과 같은 자연과 관련이 있습니다. 여러분은 브라질 국기에 있는 녹색이 무엇을 의미하는지 추측할 수 있나요? 물론, 그것은 아마존 열대 우림입니다. 이제, 국기의 모양을 살펴보겠습니다.

16 남자가 하는 말의 주제
정답률 80%
▶ 정답 ③

① 국기가 단순한 디자인과 색을 가지고 있는 이유
② 국가 정체성에 영향을 미치는 지리적 특징
✓③ 국기에 있어서의 흔한 색과 그 의미
④ 국기에서 가장 자주 사용되는 상징
⑤ 문화 간의 색 선호도의 차이

17 언급된 색이 아닌 것
정답률 90%
▶ 정답 ④

① 빨간색   ② 파란색   ③ 흰색
✓④ 검은색   ⑤ 녹색

19 2023년 6월 학력평가

01	①	02	⑤	03	①	04	⑤	05	④
06	②	07	①	08	③	09	⑤	10	③
11	②	12	⑤	13	①	14	①	15	②
16	⑤	17	②						

01 남자가 하는 말의 목적
정답률 90%
▶ 정답 ①

M: Hello, I'm Jason Adams. I'll be teaching chemistry this semester. It's very nice to meet you all. Before we start, let me tell you the most important things to remember when you write your reports. You should use brief sentences to make them clear. If your reports are full of long and complex sentences, they'll be hard to understand. Also, be careful not to use difficult words without any explanations. You may think it makes your reports look professional, but the readers may be confused and you won't be able to convey the intention of your writing. You need to keep these things in mind when you write your reports.

해석

남: 안녕하세요, Jason Adams입니다. 저는 이번 학기에 화학을 가르칠 것입니다. 여러분 모두를 만나게 되어 매우 반갑습니다. 시작하기 전에, 여러분이 보고서를 작성할 때 기억해야 할 가장 중요한 사항들을 알려드리겠습니다. 여러분은 보고서를 명확하게 하기 위해 간결한 문장을 사용해야 합니다. 보고서가 길고 복잡한 문장으로 가득 차 있다면, 이해하기 힘들 것입니다. 또한, 어떠한 설명도 없이 어려운 단어를 사용하지 않도록 조심하십시오. 여러분은 그것이 보고서를 전문적으로 보이게 한다고 생각할지도 모르지만, 읽는 사람은 혼란스러울 수 있고 여러분은 글의 의도를 전달할 수 없을 것입니다. 여러분은 보고서를 작성할 때 이러한 사항들을 명심해야 합니다.

✓① 보고서 작성 시 유의 사항을 안내하려고
② 화학 실험의 중요성을 강조하려고
③ 과제 제출 마감일을 공지하려고
④ 과학 보고서 주제를 소개하려고
⑤ 수강 신청 방법을 설명하려고

02 여자의 의견
정답률 90%
▶ 정답 ⑤

W: Hey, Michael. What happened? You look tired.
M: Hi, Claire. I can't sleep well. My daughter has been up crying the past few nights.
W: It must be hard. What do you think is wrong?
M: My wife and I have been trying to get her to sleep alone in her room.
W: Ah, she might feel afraid because she's not used to sleeping alone yet. Why don't you give her something she likes when she sleeps?
M: You mean, like blankets or stuffed animals?
W: Exactly! My son had the same problem for a while, but after sleeping with his favorite toy robot, he's come to sleep well on his own.
M: So, do you think it really helped him feel more comfortable and sleep better?
W: I believe so. I've heard that young children's favorite items generally give them psychological comfort.
M: Okay, I'll give it a try. Thanks for your advice.

해석

여: 안녕하세요, Michael. 무슨 일 있어요? 피곤해 보이네요.

남: 안녕하세요, Claire. 제가 잠을 잘 자지 못해요. 딸이 지난 며칠 밤 내내 울면서 깨어 있거든요.

여: 힘들겠군요. 무엇이 잘못되었다고 생각하나요?

남: 제 아내와 저는 그 애가 자신의 방에서 혼자 잠을 자게 하려고 노력해 왔어요.

여: 아, 그녀는 아직 혼자 잠을 자는 데 익숙하지 않기 때문에 무서움을 느낄지도 몰라요. 그녀가 잠을 잘 때 좋아하는 것을 주는 게 어때요?

남: 담요나 동물 인형 같은 것을 말씀하시는 거예요?

여: 맞아요! 제 아들도 한동안 같은 문제를 겪었는데, 가장 좋아하는 장난감 로봇과 함께 잠을 잔 후에 혼자서 잠을 잘 수 있게 되었어요.

남: 그럼, 당신은 그것이 정말로 그가 더 편안하게 느끼고 잠을 더 잘 자는 데 도움을 주었다고 생각하나요?

여: 그렇게 생각해요. 어린 아이들이 좋아하는 물건은 대체로 그들에게 심리적인 위안을 준다고 들었어요.

남: 알겠어요, 시도해 볼게요. 조언해 줘서 고마워요.

① 아이를 안아주는 것은 아이의 불안감을 덜어준다.

② 수면 시간에 아이에게 우유를 주는 것은 피해야 한다.

③ 아이에게 장난감을 주는 것은 인지 발달을 촉진한다.

④ 올바른 수면 습관 형성을 위해 부모와 아이는 함께 자야 한다.

☑ 좋아하는 물건을 주는 것은 아이가 혼자 자는 데 도움이 된다.

03 두 사람의 관계
▶ 정답 ①
정답률 85%

M: Sally, welcome to my studio. It's good to see you.
（작업실）

W: Thanks for inviting me, Chris.

M: I hear your new song everywhere these days. I like it a lot.
（어디에서나）

W: Oh, do you? I think it's been popular since it was used in a TV commercial.
（인기가 있는） （광고）

M: You must be thrilled. Did you listen to the file I sent you?
（정말 기쁘다） （파일）

W: Yes, I did. And I love it. How did you come up with such a sweet and beautiful melody?
（~을 생각해 내다） （멜로디）

M: While taking a walk along the beach, I was so inspired by the sound of the waves.
（해변을 따라） （~에 매우 영감을 받았다）（inspire: 영감을 주다）

W: That explains why the melody sounds very refreshing.
（설명해 주다） （상쾌한）

M: I thought of you as soon as I wrote it. I think it will go very well with your voice.
（~하자 마자） （~과 매우 잘 어울리다）（목소리）

W: I like the songs you've composed so I've always wanted to sing one of your songs.
（작곡했다）（compose）

M: I'm flattered. Shall we get started?

해석

남: Sally, 제 작업실에 오신 것을 환영해요. 만나서 반가워요.

여: 초대해 주셔서 감사해요, Chris.

남: 요즘 어디에서나 당신의 새 노래를 들어요. 저는 그것을 매우 좋아해요.

여: 오, 그래요? TV 광고에 사용된 이후로 인기가 있었던 것 같아요.

남: 정말 기쁘시겠어요. 제가 보내드린 파일을 들으셨나요?

여: 네, 그랬죠. 그리고 저는 그것이 정말 마음에 들어요. 어떻게 그렇게 달콤하고 아름다운 멜로디를 생각해 냈어요?

남: 해변을 따라 산책하면서, 파도 소리에 매우 영감을 받았어요.

여: 그것은 멜로디가 아주 상쾌하게 들리는 이유를 설명해 주는군요.

남: 저는 그것을 쓰자마자 당신을 생각했어요. 당신의 목소리와 매우 잘 어울릴 것 같아요.

여: 저는 당신이 작곡한 노래들을 좋아해서 항상 당신의 노래들 중 하나를 부르고 싶었어요.

남: 영광스럽네요. 시작해 볼까요?

☑ 작곡가 — 가수

② 지휘자 — 피아니스트

③ 프로듀서 — 방송 작가

④ 광고 기획자 — 뮤지컬 배우

⑤ 영화 감독 — 음향 기사

04 그림에서 대화의 내용과 일치하지 않는 것
▶ 정답 ⑤
정답률 85%

W: Charles, come and look at this photo. My mom took it last weekend.

M: Oh, you went to that park that I really want to visit. The square sign here says Riverside Park.
（공원） （네모난 표지판）

W: Right. I went there on a picnic with my family. The weather was terrific.
（그곳으로 소풍을 갔다）（go on a picnic） （날씨）
（아주 좋은）

M: That's wonderful! Why are those two balloons tied to the tree?
（풍선들）（~에 묶인）

W: They're in celebration of the second anniversary of the park's opening.
（~을 축하하여） （2주년）

M: How pretty! And you're holding a book.

W: Yes. It's the book that you gave me as a present on my birthday. That book was so interesting.
（선물로）

M: I'm so glad to hear that. Actually, I was worried about whether you would like it.

W: It was a great choice! And look at this star-patterned mat. The park gave it out for free as a second anniversary souvenir.
（별무늬의） （무료로） （기념품）

M: Cool. By the way, I wonder why that ball is on the table.
（공）

W: My brother brought it to play soccer.
（축구를 하다）

M: I see. You must've had a good time on the picnic.

해석

여: Charles, 와서 이 사진을 봐. 지난 주말에 엄마께서 찍어주셨어.

남: 오, 너는 내가 정말 방문하고 싶어 하는 그 공원에 갔구나. 여기 네모난 표지판에 Riverside Park라고 쓰여 있어.

여: 맞아. 나는 가족과 함께 그곳으로 소풍을 갔어. 날씨가 아주 좋았어.

남: 정말 멋지구나! 저 두 개의 풍선은 왜 나무에 묶여 있니?

여: 그것들은 공원의 개장 2주년을 축하하는 거야.

남: 정말 예쁘다! 그리고 너는 책을 들고 있구나.

여: 그래. 그것은 내 생일에 네가 선물로 준 책이야. 그 책은 매우 재미있었어.

남: 그 말을 들으니 정말 기뻐. 사실, 나는 네가 그것을 좋아할지 걱정했어.

여: 훌륭한 선택이었어! 그리고 이 별무늬 매트를 봐. 공원에서 2주년 기념품으로 그것을 무료로 나눠주었어.

남: 멋지다. 그런데, 나는 저 공이 왜 테이블 위에 있는지 궁금해.

여: 남동생이 축구를 하기 위해서 그것을 가져왔어.

남: 그렇구나. 너는 소풍에서 즐거운 시간을 보냈음에 틀림없어.

05 여자가 할 일
▶ 정답 ④
정답률 85%

[Telephone rings.]

M: Hello, this is Sky Print Shop.

W: Hi, this is Lisa Morris. I'm a teacher from Evergreen High School. Could I speak with the manager, Mr. White?
（관리자）

M: Speaking. How may I help you?

W: Well, I checked the cover design of our club activity book and I'd like to change it a bit. I'm afraid it seems too simple.
（표지 디자인） （동아리 활동집） （단순한）

M: I see. How about adding student pictures or the school mascot?
（추가하는 것）（add: 추가하다） （학교 마스코트）

W: Sounds good. I think putting the school mascot on the cover will make it look better.

M: No problem. Could you send me the <u>image later</u>? Then I'll add it.
　　　　　　　　　　　　　　　　이미지　나중에

W: Okay. Also, I emailed the <u>introduction page</u> of the book to you this
　　　　　　　　　　　　　　소개 글
　　morning. Did you get a <u>chance</u> to check it out?
　　　　　　　　　　　　기회

M: Yes, I did. It looks pretty good. Are there any other changes you
　　want to make?

W: No, that's all. Do you think I can get the books by next week?

M: Of course. If you send the image file of the mascot, we can add it to
　　the cover, and then start printing right away.

W: I'll send it to you now. Thank you!

해석

[전화벨이 울린다.]

남: 여보세요, Sky Print Shop입니다.

여: 안녕하세요, 저는 Lisa Morris입니다. Evergreen 고등학교의 선생님이에요. 관리자인 White 씨와 통화할 수 있을까요?

남: 저입니다. 어떻게 도와드릴까요?

여: 음, 저희 동아리 활동집의 표지 디자인을 확인했는데 조금 변경하고 싶어요. 아무래도 너무 단순해 보이는 것 같아요.

남: 그렇군요. 학생 사진이나 학교 마스코트를 추가하는 것은 어떠세요?

여: 좋은 것 같아요. 표지에 학교 마스코트를 넣는 것이 그것을 더 멋져 보이게 할 것 같네요.

남: 문제없어요. 나중에 이미지를 보내주실 수 있나요? 그럼 제가 그것을 추가할게요.

여: 알겠어요. 또한, 제가 오늘 아침에 활동집의 소개 글을 이메일로 보냈어요. 그것을 확인할 기회가 있으셨어요?

남: 네, 그럼요. 꽤 괜찮아 보여요. 변경하고 싶은 다른 사항이 있으세요?

여: 아니요, 그게 다예요. 다음 주까지 활동집을 받을 수 있을까요?

남: 물론이죠. 마스코트의 이미지 파일을 보내주시면, 표지에 추가해서 곧바로 인쇄를 시작할 수 있어요.

여: 지금 그것을 보내드릴게요. 감사해요!

① 학생 사진 찍기
② 동아리 이름 바꾸기
③ 소개 글 작성하기
✓ 마스코트 이미지 보내기
⑤ 동아리 활동집 인쇄하기

---

06 남자가 지불할 금액
정답률 75%
▶ 정답 ②

W: Good afternoon, sir. May I help you?

M: Yes, please. I'm looking for <u>swimming goggles</u> for my kids.
　　　　　　　　　　　　　　　물안경

W: We have several kinds. Take a look at this <u>display</u>.
　　　　　　　　　　　　　　　　　　진열 상품

M: All right, thank you. *[Pause]* Oh, how much are these? These would
　　be perfect for my children.

W: They're 50 dollars each. They're <u>anti-fog</u>, which <u>guarantees</u> clear
　　　　　　　　　　　　　　　　김 서림 방지의　　보장하다
　　<u>vision</u> for fast swimming.
　　시야

M: I see. They're a little bit <u>expensive</u>, though.
　　　　　　　　　　　　　비싼

W: <u>In that case</u>, there are cheaper ones with <u>basically</u> the same
　　그렇다면　　　　　　　　　　　　기본적으로
　　<u>function</u>. How about these? They cost 40 dollars each.
　　기능

M: Sounds better. I'll buy two pairs of these. I also need a <u>swimming</u>
　　<u>cap</u> for myself.　　　　　　　　　　　　　　　　　　　수영 모자

W: I <u>recommend</u> this new cap. It uses <u>high-quality</u> <u>materials</u> and costs
　　추천하다　　　　　　　　　　고품질의　　소재들
　　only 20 dollars.

M: Okay. Then I'll buy two pairs of swimming goggles and one
　　swimming cap.

W: We also have <u>brand-new</u> <u>swimsuits</u> in our store. Are you
　　　　　　　　새로 나온　수영복들
　　interested?

M: No, thanks. These are enough.

W: Sounds good. We <u>have a promotion</u> this week, so you can get a
　　　　　　　　　　판촉 행사를 하다
　　10% discount on the <u>total amount</u>.
　　　　　　　　　　　총액

M: That's great. Here's my credit card.

해석

여: 안녕하세요, 고객님. 도와드릴까요?

남: 네, 부탁드려요. 제 아이들을 위한 물안경을 찾고 있어요.

여: 몇 가지 종류가 있습니다. 이 진열 상품을 보세요.

남: 알겠어요, 감사합니다. *[잠시 후]* 오, 이것들은 얼마인가요? 제 아이들에게 꼭 알맞을 것 같아요.

여: 각각 50달러입니다. 그것들은 김 서림 방지 기능이 있는데, 그것은 빠른 수영을 위한 선명한 시야를 보장합니다.

남: 그렇군요. 하지만, 조금 비싸네요.

여: 그렇다면, 기본적으로 같은 기능을 가진 더 저렴한 제품들이 있습니다. 이것들은 어떠신가요? 각각 40달러입니다.

남: 더 나은 것 같네요. 이것들로 두 개를 살게요. 제가 쓸 수영 모자도 필요해요.

여: 이 새로운 모자를 추천합니다. 그것은 고품질의 소재를 사용하고 가격은 20달러에 불과합니다.

남: 좋네요. 그럼 물안경 두 개와 수영 모자 한 개를 살게요.

여: 저희 매장에는 새로 나온 수영복도 있습니다. 관심이 있으신가요?

남: 아니요, 괜찮아요. 이것들로 충분해요.

여: 좋습니다. 저희가 이번 주에 판촉 행사를 해서, 총액에서 10% 할인을 받으실 수 있습니다.

남: 잘됐네요. 여기 제 신용카드가 있어요.

① $80　　　　　✓ $90　　　　　③ $100
④ $108　　　　⑤ $120

문제 풀이

한 개에 40달러인 물안경 두 개와 20달러인 수영 모자 한 개를 사면 총액은 100달러이다. 판촉 행사를 통해 10% 할인을 받을 수 있다고 했으므로 남자가 지불할 금액은 10달러가 할인된 90달러이다. 따라서 답은 ② '$90'이다.

---

07 여자가 이사를 가려는 이유
정답률 95%
▶ 정답 ①

M: Stella, what are you doing?

W: Well, I need to <u>move out of</u> my apartment, so I'm searching for a
　　　　　　　　　~에서 이사를 나가다
　　<u>moving company</u>.
　　이삿짐 운송 회사

M: Why? Is your <u>contract</u> almost over?
　　　　　　　계약

W: Not yet. I've been here for just five months, and I still have seven
　　months left.

M: Oh, did you have some problem with your <u>neighbors</u>?
　　　　　　　　　　　　　　　　　　　이웃들

W: Not at all. They are all kind and I <u>get along with</u> them.
　　　　　　　　　　　　　　　　　~와 잘 지내다

M: I heard you got a new job recently. Is it far from here?

W: No, it's <u>within five minutes' walking distance</u>. Actually, the <u>issue</u> is
　　　　　걸어서 5분 거리에　　　　　~에서 거리가 먼　　　　　　문제
　　that my father is <u>sick</u>.
　　　　　　　　아픈

M: Oh, I'm sorry to hear that.

W: It would be hard for my mother to <u>take care of</u> him alone, so
　　　　　　　　　　　　　　　　　　　　~을 보살피다
　　I decided to <u>move in with my parents</u> to help <u>look after</u> my father.
　　　　　　　　~의 집으로 이사하다　　　　　　~을 돌보다

M: I hope your father gets better soon.

W: Thank you for your <u>concern</u>.
　　　　　　　　　　걱정

해석

남: Stella, 무엇을 하고 있니?

여: 음, 아파트에서 이사를 나가야 해서, 이삿짐 운송 회사를 찾고 있어.

남: 왜? 계약이 거의 끝났니?

여: 아직이야. 여기에 불과 5개월 동안 있었고, 아직도 7개월이나 남았어.

남: 오, 이웃들과 무슨 문제라도 있었니?

여: 전혀 아니야. 그들은 모두 친절하고 나는 그들과 잘 지내.

남: 나는 네가 최근에 새 직장을 구했다고 들었어. 여기에서 거리가 머니?

여: 아니야, 걸어서 5분 거리에 있어. 사실, 문제는 아버지께서 아프시다는 거야.

남: 오, 그 말을 들으니 유감이야.

여: 어머니께서 혼자 아버지를 보살피는 것은 힘들 거야, 그래서 나는 아버지를 돌보는 것을 돕기 위해 부모님의 집으로 이사하기로 결정했어.

남: 아버지께서 빨리 회복되시기를 바랄게.

여: 걱정해 줘서 고마워.

✓ 아픈 아버지를 돌보기 위해서
② 회사와 가까운 곳으로 가려고
③ 이웃과 사이가 좋지 않아서
④ 부모님으로부터 독립하려고
⑤ 집 계약 기간이 만료되어서

08

Blueway Spelling Bee Competition에 관해 언급되지 않은 것 ▶ 정답 ③

W: Hi, Paul. What's new?
M: Not much. I'm looking at the poster for the Blueway Spelling Bee Competition.
　　　　　　　　　　　　포스터　　　　　　　　　철자 맞히기 대회
W: The spelling bee competition? What's that?
M: It's a competition where participants are asked to spell various
　　　　　　　　　　　　　참가자들　　　　　　　　　　　　다양한
words. The Blueway Library hosts it every year.
　　　　　　　　　　　주최하다
W: That sounds interesting! Let me have a look. Oh, it says any Blueway Library member can take part.
　　　　　　　　　　회원　　　참가하다
M: Yeah. I'm planning to enter the competition because I want to test
　　　　　　　　　　　참가하다　　　　　　　　　　　　　　시험하다
my spelling skills. Do you want to join, too?
W: Sure, why not? How do we sign up for the contest?
　　　　　　　　　　　　　~에 참가 신청을 하다　대회
M: We should email the application by Thursday. Here's the email
　　　　　　　　　　신청서
address on the bottom.
주소
W: Got it! Oh, they are only accepting 50 people.
M: Then we should hurry!
　　　　　　　　　서두르다

해석
여: 안녕, Paul. 잘 지내니?
남: 별일 없어. 나는 Blueway Spelling Bee Competition(Blueway 철자 맞히기 대회)의 포스터를 보고 있어.
여: 철자 맞히기 대회? 그게 뭐니?
남: 참가자들이 다양한 단어들의 철자를 말하도록 요청을 받는 대회야. Blueway Library(Blueway 도서관)가 매년 그것을 주최해.
여: 흥미롭게 들린다! 내가 한번 볼게. 오, Blueway Library 회원이라면 누구나 참가할 수 있다고 쓰여 있어.
남: 그래. 나는 내 철자 실력을 시험해 보고 싶기 때문에 대회에 참가할 계획이야. 너도 참가하고 싶니?
여: 물론이지, 왜 아니겠어? 어떻게 대회에 참가 신청을 하니?
남: 목요일까지 신청서를 이메일로 보내야 해. 하단에 이메일 주소가 있어.
여: 알겠어! 오, 그들은 50명만 모집하고 있어.
남: 그럼 서둘러야겠어!

① 주최 기관　　　② 참가 대상　　　✔③ 참가 비용
④ 신청 방법　　　⑤ 모집 인원

09

Ocean World에 관한 내용과 일치하지 않는 것 ▶ 정답 ⑤

W: Hello, I'm Grace, a manager of Dream Marine Museum. This year,
　　　　　　　　　　　소장　　　　　　해양 박물관
our museum has a special program, called Ocean World. The topic
　　　　　　　　　　　　　　　　　　　　　　　　　　　　주제
of the program is deep-sea exploration. Through this program,
　　　　　　　　심해 탐험
children will become interested in the plants and fish living deep
　　　　　　~에 관심을 가지게 되다
in the ocean. It runs from 10 a.m. to 6 p.m. this Saturday, October
　　　　　　　운영되다
28th. This event will be held on the first floor. You can watch videos
　　　　　　　　　열리다(hold: 열다, 개최하다)
of deep-sea exploration on a huge screen in the central hall. There
　　　　　　　　　　　　　　　　　　　　　　　중앙 홀
will be a photo booth where you can take selfies wearing various
　　　　즉석 사진 촬영 부스　　　　　셀카를 찍다
masks of ocean creatures. In addition, you can make fish-shaped
　　　　　　　　　　　　게다가　　　　　　　　물고기 모양의
cookies with a chef. Anyone can participate in Ocean World for free
　　　　　요리사　　　　　　~에 참여하다
without having to make a reservation. I hope to see you all there.
　　　　　　　　예약을 하다

해석
여: 안녕하세요, 저는 Dream Marine Museum(Dream 해양 박물관)의 소장인 Grace입니다. 올해, 저희 박물관은 Ocean World라고 불리는 특별한 프로그램을 엽니다. 프로그램의 주제는 심해 탐험입니다. 이 프로그램을 통해서, 어린이들은 바다 깊은 곳에 사는 식물과 물고기에 관심을 가지게 될 것입니다. 그것은 10월 28일 이번 주 토요일 오전 10시부터 오후 6시까지 운영됩니다. 이 행사는 1층에서 열릴 것입니다. 중앙 홀에 있는 거대한 화면에서 심해 탐험 영상을 시청할 수 있습니다. 바다 생물의 다양한 가면을 쓰고 셀카를 찍을 수 있는 즉석 사진 촬영 부스가 있을 것입니다. 게다가, 요리사와 함께 물고기 모양의 쿠키를 만들 수 있습니다. 누구나 예약을 할 필요 없이 무료로 Ocean World에 참여할 수 있습니다. 그곳에서 여러분 모두를 뵙기를 바랍니다.

① 주제는 심해 탐험이다.
② 오전 10시부터 오후 6시까지 운영된다.
③ 중앙 홀에서 영상을 시청할 수 있다.
④ 물고기 모양의 쿠키를 만들 수 있다.
✔⑤ 사전 예약제로 운영된다.

문제 풀이
박물관 방문객들은 Ocean World 프로그램에 무료로 참여할 수 있으며 예약을 하지 않아도 된다고 했으므로 ⑤ '사전 예약제로 운영된다.'는 내용과 일치하지 않는다.

10

표에서 두 사람이 구매할 보안 카메라 ▶ 정답 ③

W: Honey, here's a flyer about smart security cameras. They're on sale!
　　　　　　　　　　전단지　　　　　스마트 보안 카메라들　　　　할인 판매 중인
M: Cool! I've been thinking about buying one to protect our house
　　　　　　　　　　　　　　　　　　　　　　　　　　지키다
before we're away on vacation.
　　　　휴가로 떠나다
W: Same here. Which one do you want to get?
M: Hmm... I don't think we can spend more than $500 on a security camera.
W: You're right. We've already spent a lot for our vacation.
M: There are two types of connectivity options, wired and wireless.
　　　　　　　　　　　　연결　　　　　　유선의　　　무선의
W: I prefer wireless so that we can install it anywhere we want.
　　　　　　　　　　　　　　　　설치하다
M: Good idea. We need one that can be installed indoors and
　　　　　　　　　　　　　　　　　　　　　　실내에
outdoors as well.
실외에
W: I agree. Now we have two options left. Well... The one with sound
detection looks attractive to me.
소리 감지
　　　매력적인
M: I heard that sound detection is not as accurate as motion
　　　　　　　　　　　　　　　　　　정확한　　　동작 감지
detection.
W: Really? Then, we should definitely get one with motion detection.
M: Okay. Let's buy this one.

해석
여: 여보, 여기 스마트 보안 카메라에 관한 전단이 있어요. 할인 판매 중이에요!
남: 멋지네요! 저는 우리가 휴가로 떠나기 전에 집을 지키기 위해 하나 살까 생각 중이었어요.
여: 저도 그래요. 어떤 것을 사고 싶어요?
남: 흠... 보안 카메라에 500달러 이상을 쓸 수는 없을 것 같아요.
여: 당신 말이 맞아요. 우리는 이미 휴가를 위해 많은 돈을 썼어요.
남: 연결 선택에는 유선과 무선의 두 가지 유형이 있어요.
여: 저는 우리가 원하는 곳 어디든 그것을 설치할 수 있도록 무선이 더 좋아요.
남: 좋은 생각이에요. 실내 및 실외에도 설치될 수 있는 것이 필요해요.
여: 동의해요. 이제 두 가지 선택지가 남았어요. 음... 제게는 소리 감지 기능이 있는 것이 매력적으로 보여요.
남: 소리 감지는 동작 감지만큼 정확하지 않다고 들었어요.
여: 정말이에요? 그럼, 동작 감지 기능이 있는 것을 꼭 사야겠네요.
남: 알겠어요. 이것을 삽시다.

보안 카메라

	모델	가격	연결	설치	특수 기능
①	A	270달러	유선	실내	동작 감지
②	B	300달러	무선	실내	소리 감지
✔	C	400달러	무선	실내 및 실외	동작 감지
④	D	470달러	무선	실내 및 실외	소리 감지
⑤	E	520달러	유선	실내 및 실외	동작 감지

11

남자의 마지막 말에 대한 여자의 응답 ▶ 정답 ②

M: Jenny, thanks for helping me prepare my speech for the graduation
　　　　　　　　　　　　　　　　　　　　　연설　　　　　졸업식
ceremony.
W: There was not much to help. You were already well-prepared.
　　　　　　　　　　　　　　　　　　　만반의 준비가 된
M: I'm still worried. Do you really think people will understand what
　　　　　　　　　　　　　　　　　　　　　　　　　이해하다
I'm trying to say?
W: (Definitely! I'm sure your message will be clearly delivered.)
　　　　　　　　　　　　　　　　　　　분명하게 전달되다
　　　　　　　　　　　　　　　　　(deliver: 전달하다, clearly: 분명하게)

해석

남: Jenny, 졸업식 연설을 준비하는 데도 움을 줘서 고마워.

여: 별로 도와줄 게 없었어. 너는 이미 만반의 준비가 되어 있었잖아.

남: 나는 아직도 걱정이 돼. 너는 정말 사람들이 내가 말하고자 하는 바를 이해할 것이라고 생각하니?

여: (당연하지! 나는 네 메시지가 분명하게 전달될 것이라고 확신해.)

① 신경 쓰지 마. 나는 그들이 대회에서 말하는 것을 빨리 보고 싶어.

✓ 당연하지! 나는 네 메시지가 분명하게 전달될 것이라고 확신해.

③ 물론이지. 나는 주장으로서 연설을 하게 되어 영광스러워.

④ 오, 이런! 나는 네 졸업식에 갈 수 없어.

⑤ 물론이지. 내 대본에 네 훌륭한 생각을 추가할게.

12 여자의 마지막 말에 대한 남자의 응답

정답률 80% ▶ 정답 ③

W: Steve, do you know where my <u>earphones</u> are? I need them right now but can't <u>find</u> them anywhere.
이어폰들 / 찾다

M: I saw Dad taking them this morning for his <u>business trip</u>.
출장

W: Oh, no! That means I can't use them until this Saturday!

M: (Don't worry. You can use mine if you want.)

해석

여: Steve, 내 이어폰이 어디에 있는지 알고 있니? 지금 당장 필요한데 어디에서도 찾을 수가 없구나.

남: 아빠께서 출장을 위해 오늘 아침에 그것들을 가지고 가시는 것을 봤어.

여: 오, 이런! 그것은 내가 이번 주 토요일까지 그것들을 사용할 수 없다는 의미잖아!

남: (걱정하지 마세요. 원하신다면 제 것을 사용하실 수 있어요.)

① 왜 안되겠어요? 저는 꼭 당신과 함께 갈 거예요.

② 죄송해요. 저는 어디에서도 그것들을 찾을 수 없어요.

✓ 걱정하지 마세요. 원하신다면 제 것을 사용하실 수 있어요.

④ 꼭 그렇지는 않아요. 저는 지금 당장 그것들을 사용할 필요가 없어요.

⑤ 잊어버리세요. 그는 어차피 제 이어폰을 사용할 거예요.

13 남자의 마지막 말에 대한 여자의 응답

정답률 65% ▶ 정답 ①

M: Hello, is there anything I can do for you?

W: My umbrella is <u>missing</u>. I thought I <u>might have left</u> it in the
없어진 / 놓고 왔을지도 모른다
(might have p.p.: ~했을지도 모른다, leave: 놓고 오다)
<u>restroom</u>, but when I checked, it wasn't there.
화장실

M: Which restroom did you use?

W: The one on the third floor.

M: What does your umbrella look like? Could you <u>describe</u> it?
설명하다

W: It's yellow and it has a <u>wooden handle</u>. There's <u>a big picture of a flower</u> on it.
나무 손잡이 / 커다란 꽃 그림

M: Okay, I'll check if it's in the <u>Lost and Found box</u> right now... [Pause]
분실물 보관함
Oh! We have an umbrella that looks like yours. Is this it?

W: Wow, that's mine!

M: Wait. Here's a <u>note</u> that says a lady found it and brought it to us.
쪽지

W: (How kind of her! I was worried that I wouldn't find it.)

해석

남: 안녕하세요, 제가 도와드릴 일이 있나요?

여: 제 우산이 없어졌어요. 화장실에 놓고 왔을지도 모른다고 생각했는데, 확인했을 때 그곳에 없었어요.

남: 어느 화장실을 사용하셨나요?

여: 3층에 있는 화장실이에요.

남: 우산이 어떻게 생겼나요? 설명해 주시겠나요?

여: 노란색이고 나무 손잡이가 있어요. 커다란 꽃 그림이 그려져 있어요.

남: 알겠습니다, 그것이 지금 분실물 보관함에 있는지 확인해 볼게요... [잠시 후] 오! 고객님의 것처럼 보이는 우산이 있네요. 이것인가요?

여: 와, 그것은 제 것이에요!

남: 잠시만요. 어떤 여성분이 그것을 발견해서 저희에게 가져다 주었다는 쪽지가 있네요.

여: (정말 친절하시네요! 저는 그것을 찾지 못할까 봐 걱정했어요.)

✓ 정말 친절하시네요! 저는 그것을 찾지 못할까 봐 걱정했어요.

② 그럼, 제가 그녀에게 그것은 당신 잘못이 아니라 제 잘못이라고 말할게요.

③ 비가 올 때 다시 들러주시겠어요?

④ 제게 당신의 새 우산을 빌려주셔서 감사해요.

⑤ 그녀에게 다음에 무엇을 하고 싶은지 물어보는 게 어때요?

14 여자의 마지막 말에 대한 남자의 응답

정답률 75% ▶ 정답 ①

W: Fred, I got the blueberry juice we ordered.

M: Thanks, Kathy. Oh, it has a <u>paper straw</u>. Don't they have a plastic one?
종이 빨대

W: What's wrong with a paper straw?

M: It can <u>get soaked</u> and <u>fall apart</u> while drinking. So I prefer a plastic straw.
젖다(soak: 적시다) / 망가지다

W: But plastic straws can <u>harm</u> the <u>environment</u>.
해를 끼치다 / 환경

M: Protecting the environment is all good, but my drink <u>tastes bad</u> with paper straws.
맛이 없다

W: If so, there are other types of straws to enjoy your drink that <u>cause less harm to</u> the environment.
~에 해를 덜 끼치다

M: I didn't know there were other kinds. Can you <u>name</u> some of them?
말하다

W: Have you heard of a silicone straw?

M: No, I haven't. It sounds interesting.

W: There are also straws <u>made of</u> glass or metal. They're <u>reusable</u> and don't <u>affect</u> the taste of your drink.
~으로 만든 / 재사용할 수 있는 / 영향을 주다

M: (Thanks for letting me know. I should try using them.)

해석

여: Fred, 내가 우리가 주문한 블루베리 주스를 받았어.

남: 고마워, Kathy. 오, 종이 빨대가 있구나. 플라스틱 빨대는 없어?

여: 종이 빨대에 무슨 문제라도 있니?

남: 그것은 음료를 마시는 동안 젖어서 망가질 수 있잖아. 그래서 나는 플라스틱 빨대를 선호해.

여: 하지만 플라스틱 빨대는 환경에 해를 끼칠 수 있어.

남: 환경을 보호하는 것은 다 좋지만, 내 음료는 종이 빨대를 쓰면 맛이 없어.

여: 그렇다면, 환경에 해를 덜 끼치고 음료를 즐길 수 있는 다른 종류의 빨대들이 있어.

남: 나는 다른 종류가 있는지 몰랐어. 그것들 중 몇 가지를 말해주겠니?

여: 실리콘 빨대에 대해 들어봤니?

남: 아니, 없어. 흥미롭게 들리는데.

여: 유리나 금속으로 만든 빨대들도 있어. 그것들은 재사용할 수 있고 음료의 맛에 영향을 주지 않아.

남: (알려줘서 고마워. 나는 그것들을 사용해 봐야겠어.)

✓ 알려줘서 고마워. 나는 그것들을 사용해 봐야겠어.

② 맛이 좋구나. 나는 이 주스의 조리법이 궁금해.

③ 걱정하지 마. 나는 내가 사용하는 빨대의 종류에 신경 쓰지 않아.

④ 네 말이 맞아. 나는 앞으로 실리콘 빨대를 쓰지 않는 것이 좋겠어.

⑤ 나는 이미 그것들을 다 써 봤지만, 여전히 종이 빨대를 선호해.

문제 풀이

환경에 덜 해로운 다른 종류의 빨대들에 대해 묻는 남자의 질문에 답하면서 여자는 그 빨대들은 재사용이 가능하고 음료의 맛에 영향을 미치지 않는다고 설명한다. 이에 대한 남자의 응답으로 가장 적절한 것은 ① 'Thanks for letting me know. I should try using them.(알려줘서 고마워. 나는 그것들을 사용해 봐야겠어.)'이다.

15 다음 상황에서 Nick이 Annie에게 할 말

정답률 70% ▶ 정답 ②

M: Nick and Annie are partners for an <u>art project</u>. They are
미술 과제
supposed to <u>make a presentation</u> on the life of Vincent van Gogh.
발표를 하다
However, while <u>researching</u> and working on their project, they
조사하는(research)
<u>realized</u> that some of the <u>content</u> they found was <u>conflicting</u>.
깨달았다 / 내용 / 상충되는
For example, there was a <u>disagreement</u> about when exactly Van
의견 차이
Gogh started painting. Nick <u>gathered</u> his information from the
모았다
books in the library, while Annie <u>collected</u> hers from the Internet.
수집했다
Nick and Annie are not sure which one to trust. Nick wants their
믿다

presentation to <u>be as precise as possible</u>, so he thinks that they
가능한 한 정확하다
(as A as possible: 가능한 한 A한, precise: 정확한)
should ask their <u>professor</u> for help with deciding which <u>source</u> is
교수   출처
<u>more reliable</u>. In this situation, what would Nick most likely say to
더 신뢰할 수 있는
Annie?

Nick: (We'd better ask our professor about which source to trust.)

해석

남: Nick과 Annie는 미술 과제의 파트너이다. 그들은 Vincent van Gogh(빈센트 반 고흐)의 삶에 대해 발표를 하기로 되어 있다. 하지만, 과제에 대해 조사하고 작업하면서, 그들은 자신들이 찾은 내용 중 일부가 상충된다는 것을 깨달았다. 예를 들어, 정확히 언제 Van Gogh가 그림을 그리기 시작했는지에 대해 의견 차이가 있었다. Nick은 도서관에 있는 책들로부터 정보를 모은 데 반해 Annie는 인터넷에서 정보를 수집했다. Nick과 Annie는 어떤 것을 믿어야 할지 확신하지 못한다. Nick은 자신들의 발표가 가능한 한 정확하기를 원하므로, 어떤 출처가 더 신뢰할 수 있는지를 결정하는 데 있어 교수님에게 도움을 요청해야 한다고 생각한다. 이러한 상황에서, Nick은 Annie에게 뭐라고 말하겠는가?

Nick: (우리는 교수님에게 어떤 출처를 믿어야 할지에 대해 여쭤보는 게 좋겠어.)

① 나는 당장 내 내용을 네 것으로 바꾸고 싶어.
✓ 우리는 교수님에게 어떤 출처를 믿어야 할지에 대해 여쭤보는 게 좋겠어.
③ 네 정보는 인터넷에 있는 것과 달라.
④ 너는 발표를 위해 더 많은 조사를 했어야 했어.
⑤ 나는 Van Gogh가 10대 초반에 그림을 그리기 시작했다고 생각해.

16~17 1지문 2문항

W: Welcome back to <u>Tips for Entrepreneurs</u>. Last time, we talked
기업인을 위한 조언들
about this year's trendy colors. Now let's talk about <u>how to use</u>
최신 유행의   사용하는 방법
(how to V: ~하는 방법, use: 사용하다)
them in design for your brand. Understanding the <u>art</u> of using
기술
colors can help <u>create</u> more <u>effective</u> and <u>memorable</u> designs.
만들다   효과적인   기억에 남는
For example, using red for important <u>elements</u> will make it hard
요소들
to <u>ignore</u> them. <u>It's no coincidence that</u> so many fast food logos
무시하다   ~은 우연이 아니다
are red. Orange <u>communicates</u> <u>creativity</u> and <u>youth</u>, which is
전달하다   창의성   젊음
perfect for a <u>bold</u> brand. If you're trying to get your <u>customers</u>
과감한   고객들
excited about something, go for orange. Green, <u>on the other</u>
                                                반면에
<u>hand</u>, can communicate lots of different ideas, like luck, <u>wealth</u>,
~을 선택하다   부
and <u>freshness</u>. Green is also a <u>common</u> choice to communicate
신선함   일반적인
<u>environmentalism</u> and <u>sustainability</u>, as well as <u>comfort</u> and
환경 보호주의   지속 가능성   편안함
<u>prosperity</u>. Lastly, for a cool and <u>calm</u> feel, choose blue. Brands
번영   차분한
that <u>supply</u> ice or <u>cooling solutions</u> can communicate this literal
공급하다   냉각 솔루션들   문자 그대로의
coolness through blue logos. So, to design your brand <u>effectively</u>,
효과적으로
use colors <u>wisely</u>!
현명하게

해석

여: Tips for Entrepreneurs(기업인을 위한 조언)에 다시 오신 것을 환영합니다. 지난 시간에, 우리는 올해의 최신 유행 색깔들에 대해 이야기했습니다. 이제 여러분의 브랜드를 위한 디자인에 그것들을 사용하는 방법에 대해 이야기해 보겠습니다. 색깔을 사용하는 기술을 이해하는 것은 더 효과적이고 기억에 남는 디자인을 만드는 데 도움을 줄 수 있습니다. 예를 들어, 중요한 요소들에 빨간색을 사용하는 것은 그것들을 무시하기 어렵게 만들 것입니다. 매우 많은 패스트푸드 로고가 빨간색인 것은 우연이 아닙니다. 주황색은 창의성과 젊음을 전달하는데, 그것은 과감한 브랜드에 안성맞춤입니다. 여러분의 고객들이 무언가에 흥분하도록 만들고자 애쓰고 있다면, 주황색을 선택하십시오. 반면에, 초록색은 행운, 부, 그리고 신선함과 같은 많은 다양한 생각들을 전달할 수 있습니다. 초록색은 또한 편안함과 번영뿐만 아니라, 환경 보호주의와 지속 가능성을 전달하기 위한 일반적인 선택입니다. 마지막으로, 시원하고 차분한 느낌을 위해서, 파란색을 선택하세요. 얼음이나 냉각 솔루션을 공급하는 브랜드는 파란색 로고를 통해 이러한 문자 그대로의 시원함을 전달할 수 있습니다. 그러므로, 여러분의 브랜드를 효과적으로 디자인하기 위해서, 색깔들을 현명하게 사용하세요!

16 여자가 하는 말의 주제
정답률 85% ▶ 정답 ⑤

① 집을 설계하기 위해 사용되는 자원들
② 디자인 회사를 설립하는 방법
③ 색깔의 종류와 분류
④ 다양한 색깔 사용의 예술적 가치
✓ 브랜드 디자인을 위한 효과적인 색깔 사용

17 언급된 색깔이 아닌 것
정답률 90% ▶ 정답 ②

① 빨간색 ✓ 노란색 ③ 주황색
④ 초록색 ⑤ 파란색

20 2023년 9월 학력평가

01	⑤	02	③	03	②	04	④	05	①
06	①	07	⑤	08	④	09	③	10	②
11	②	12	①	13	①	14	②	15	⑤
16	②	17	④						

01 남자가 하는 말의 목적
정답률 85% ▶ 정답 ⑤

M: Good afternoon. I'm Tom Anderson, the <u>student council president</u>.
학생회장
I'm glad to <u>announce</u> that the student council is <u>recruiting</u>
알리다   모집하고 있다(recruit)
<u>volunteers</u> for our campus tour event. Next Saturday, our school
자원봉사자들
will be welcoming <u>middle schoolers</u> who are <u>interested in</u>
중학생들   ~에 관심이 있는
attending our school. Student volunteers will show the middle
schoolers around our campus, and <u>provide them with useful</u>
그들에게 유용한 정보를 제공하다
(provide A with B: A에게 B를 제공하다,
useful: 유용한, information: 정보)
<u>information</u> about our school's <u>extracurricular activities and</u>
과외 활동과
<u>traditions</u>. To <u>sign up</u> to volunteer, please visit our school website.
전통들   신청하다
Your <u>participation</u> will be a great help to those who wish to attend
참여
our school.

해석

남: 좋은 오후입니다. 저는 학생회장인 Tom Anderson입니다. 학생회가 캠퍼스 투어 행사를 위한 자원봉사자들을 모집하고 있다는 것을 알려드리게 되어 기쁩니다. 다음 주 토요일에, 우리 학교는 우리 학교에 다니는 데 관심이 있는 중학생들을 맞이할 것입니다. 학생 자원봉사자들은 중학생들에게 우리 캠퍼스를 둘러보도록 안내하고, 그들에게 우리 학교의 과외 활동과 전통에 대한 유용한 정보를 제공할 것입니다. 자원봉사를 하기 위해 신청하려면, 우리 학교 웹사이트를 방문해 주세요. 여러분의 참여는 우리 학교에 다니기를 원하는 사람들에게 큰 도움이 될 것입니다.

① 학생회 운영 방침을 설명하려고
② 학교 웹사이트 활용을 독려하려고
③ 진학 설명회 일정 변경을 공지하려고
④ 교내 봉사 활동 시 유의점을 안내하려고
✓ 캠퍼스 투어 행사 자원봉사자를 모집하려고

02 여자의 의견
정답률 90% ▶ 정답 ③

W: David, the <u>screen</u> on your cell phone looks <u>cracked</u>. What
화면   깨진
happened?

M: I accidentally dropped it on the bathroom floor last week.
　　　　　　　떨어뜨렸다(drop)　　　　　　　　　바닥
W: That's too bad, but why haven't you fixed it yet?
　　　　　　　　　　　　　　　　　　　수리했다(fix)
M: It's working perfectly fine, so I don't think I need to fix it.
　　작동하고 있다(work)
W: Well, I think it's better to get a phone fixed immediately when the
　　　　　　　　　　　　　휴대 전화를 수리하다　　　　즉시
　screen is cracked.
M: I don't think a small crack like this is a big deal.
　　　　　　　　　　　균열　　　　　　　큰 문제
W: It may look okay, but a single crack can break the whole screen
　　　　　　　　　　　　　　　　　　　　　　　깨뜨리다
　over time.
　시간이 지나서
M: Really? I didn't know that.
W: Also, tiny pieces of glass from the cracked screen could cut your
　　　작은 조각들　　　　　　　　　　　　　　　　　　　베다
　face or your fingers.
M: Hmm.... That could be dangerous.
　　　　　　　　　　　위험한
W: Exactly. That's why you should fix a cracked phone screen as soon
　as possible.　　　　　　　　　　　　　　　　　　가능한 한 빨리
M: You're right. I'll get it repaired today.
　　　　　　　　　그것을 수리하다

해석

여: David, 네 휴대 전화의 화면이 깨진 것 같아. 어떻게 된 거야?
남: 지난주에 실수로 욕실 바닥에 그것을 떨어뜨렸어.
여: 정말 안됐구나, 그런데 왜 아직도 수리하지 않았어?
남: 완벽하게 잘 작동하고 있어서, 수리할 필요가 없을 것 같아.
여: 음, 화면이 깨졌을 때 휴대 전화를 즉시 수리하는 게 더 좋을 것 같아.
남: 이런 작은 균열은 큰 문제가 아닌 것 같은데.
여: 괜찮아 보일 수도 있지만, 하나의 균열이 시간이 지나면서 전체 화면을 깨뜨릴 수 있어.
남: 정말? 나는 몰랐어.
여: 또한, 깨진 화면에서 나오는 작은 유리 조각들이 얼굴이나 손가락을 벨 수도 있어.
남: 흠.... 그것은 위험할 수 있겠네.
여: 맞아. 그러니까 가능한 빨리 깨진 휴대 전화 화면을 수리해야 해.
남: 네 말이 맞아. 오늘 그것을 수리하도록 할게.
① 휴대 전화는 정기적으로 소독해야 한다.
② 학생 대상 스마트 기기 활용 교육을 강화해야 한다.
✓③화면이 깨진 휴대 전화는 되도록 빨리 수리해야 한다.
④ 숙면을 위해 취침 전 전자 기기 사용을 자제해야 한다.
⑤ 휴대 전화 화면 밝기는 주변 밝기에 맞게 조절해야 한다.

03　두 사람의 관계

정답률 85%
▶ 정답 ②

[Phone rings.]
W: Hello.
M: Hello. Can I speak to Ms. Norton?
W: This is she.
M: Hi, this is Mark Kelly from Polaris Studio. I heard you were a
　scientific advisor on the movie *Space Dynasty*.
　과학 자문가
W: Yes, I helped the writers with the script.
　　　　　　　　　작가들　　　　　　대본
M: I thought the script was well written and had many entertaining
　scenes related to science.　　　　　　　　　　　　　　　재미있는
　장면들　~과 관련된
W: Thank you. It was a lot of fun.
M: I'm actually writing a script for a science fiction movie right now,
　　　사실　　　　　　　　　　　　공상과학 영화
　and I was wondering if you could help me with your expertise.
　　　　　　　　　　　　　　　　　　　　　　　전문 지식
W: Okay. What's the movie about?
M: It's about natural disasters caused by global warming. I need
　　　　　자연 재해들　　　　　　　　지구 온난화
　advice from science experts like you to make it more realistic.
　　　　　　　　전문가들　　　　　　　더 사실적인
W: I'd be interested. I've done a lot of scientific research on global
　　　　　　　　　　　　　　　　　　　　　　　　연구
　warming in my lab. My findings might be useful for you.
　　　　　연구실　　연구 결과들
M: Fantastic! I'll send you my script. Thank you so much.

해석

[전화벨이 울린다.]
여: 여보세요.
남: 여보세요. Norton 씨와 통화할 수 있을까요?
여: 전데요.

남: 안녕하세요, 저는 Polaris Studio의 Mark Kelly입니다. 당신이 영화 'Space Dynasty'의 과학 자문가였다고 들었어요.
여: 네, 제가 작가들의 대본에 도움을 줬어요.
남: 저는 그 대본이 잘 쓰였고 과학과 관련된 재미있는 장면들이 많다고 생각했어요.
여: 감사해요. 그것은 정말 즐거웠어요.
남: 사실 제가 지금 공상과학 영화 대본을 쓰고 있는데, 당신의 전문 지식으로 저를 도와주실 수 있는지 궁금해요.
여: 좋아요. 무슨 영화인가요?
남: 지구 온난화로 인한 자연 재해에 대한 영화예요. 그것을 더 사실적으로 만들기 위해서 당신과 같은 과학 전문가들의 조언이 필요해요.
여: 관심이 있어요. 저는 연구실에서 지구 온난화에 대한 많은 과학적 연구를 해 왔어요. 제 연구 결과가 당신에게 유용할 수 있겠네요.
남: 환상적이네요! 제 대본을 보내드릴게요. 정말 감사합니다.

① 방송 연출가 — 배우
✓②영화 각본가 — 과학자
③ 신문 기자 — 환경 운동가
④ 영화감독 — 영화 비평가
⑤ 잡지 구독자 — 잡지 편집장

04　그림에서 대화의 내용과 일치하지 않는 것

정답률 85%
▶ 정답 ④

M: Hello, Ms. Clark. How's it going with rearranging your classroom?
　　　　　　　　　　　　　　　　　　　　재배치하는 것(rearrange)
W: Good morning, Mr. Cooper. It's almost done. Do you want to see a
　　　　　　　　　　　　　　　　　거의
　picture of what it looks like?
M: Sure. [Pause] Oh, I see a round clock on the wall. It looks nice.
　　　　　　　　　　　　원형 시계
W: Yes. I replaced the old clock with a new one.
　　　　오래된 시계를 새 시계로 교체했다
　　　　(replace A with B: A를 B로 교체하다)
M: I also like the bookcase under the window.
　　　　　　　　책장
W: I put it there to make it easier for students to read books. How do
　you like the stripe-patterned rug?
　　　　　　　줄무늬의　　　깔개
M: I like it. It goes well with the classroom. By the way, what are the
　　　　　　　　~과 잘 어울리다
　two boxes on the table for?
　　두 개의 상자
W: I'll put some classroom supplies in them. I also put a flower pot in
　　　　　　　　　　　비품들　　　　　　　　　　　　　화분
　the corner.
M: Great idea! I think your students will really like the new classroom.
W: Thank you.

해석

남: 안녕하세요, Clark 선생님. 교실을 재배치하는 일은 어떻게 되어 가고 있어요?
여: 안녕하세요, Cooper 선생님. 거의 다 됐어요. 어떤 모습인지 사진으로 보여드릴까요?
남: 네. [잠시 후] 오, 벽에 원형 시계가 보이네요. 좋아 보여요.
여: 네. 오래된 시계를 새 시계로 교체했어요.
남: 창문 아래에 있는 책장도 마음에 드네요.
여: 학생들이 책을 읽는 것을 더 쉽게 하기 위해서 거기에 놓았어요. 줄무늬 깔개는 어때요?
남: 마음에 들어요. 교실과 잘 어울리네요. 그런데, 책상 위에 있는 두 개의 상자는 무슨 용도인가요?
여: 교실 비품들을 그 안에 넣을 거예요. 저는 구석에 화분도 놓았어요.
남: 좋은 생각이네요! 학생들이 새 교실을 정말 좋아할 것 같아요.
여: 감사해요.

정답률 85%

05 남자가 할 일

▶ 정답 ①

M: Mom, I'm home.
W: Hi, Brian. How was your violin lesson?
바이올린 레슨
M: It was fun. I think my violin skills have improved a lot.
실력
W: Good! By the way, did you see the pile of clothes in the living room?
옷 무더기
M: Yeah. I wore those clothes when I was a little kid. Are you going to
입었다(wear)
throw them away?
그것들을 버리다
(throw A away: A를 버리다)
W: No. I'm going to give them to charity today.
자선 단체
M: Oh, so you want to donate the clothes?
기부하다
W: Yes. They're all in good condition and they've been dry-cleaned.
상태가 좋은
M: That's great. Is there anything I can help you with?
W: Well, I need some boxes to put the clothes in.
M: No worries. I'll bring some from the garage.
차고
W: Thanks, but be careful. The lights in the garage aren't working.
조심하다 전등들
M: I got it, Mom. I'll be right back.

해석
남: 엄마, 저 왔어요.
여: 안녕, Brian. 바이올린 레슨은 어땠니?
남: 재미있었어요. 제 바이올린 실력이 많이 향상된 것 같아요.
여: 잘됐구나! 그런데, 거실에 있는 옷 무더기를 봤니?
남: 네. 제가 어렸을 때 그 옷들을 입었잖아요. 그것들을 버리실 거예요?
여: 아니. 오늘 자선 단체에 줄 거야.
남: 오, 그럼 옷들을 기부하고 싶으신 거예요?
여: 그래. 모두 상태가 좋고 드라이클리닝을 했어.
남: 잘됐네요. 제가 도와드릴 일이 있나요?
여: 음, 옷들을 넣을 상자 몇 개가 필요하구나.
남: 걱정하지 마세요. 제가 차고에서 가져올게요.
여: 고마워, 그런데 조심하렴. 차고의 전등이 작동하지 않는구나.
남: 알겠어요, 엄마. 금방 돌아올게요.

✔ 상자 가져오기
② 거실 청소하기
③ 전구 구입하기
④ 세탁물 맡기기
⑤ 바이올린 레슨 신청하기

정답률 85%

06 여자가 지불할 금액

▶ 정답 ①

M: Welcome to Platinum Hillside Resort. How can I help you?
W: Hi. I want to reserve an outdoor barbecue table for tonight.
예약하다 야외 바비큐 테이블
M: Okay, right now we have small tables for four people and large tables for eight people available.
이용 가능한
W: I'd like to reserve two small tables.
M: Sure, it's $25 per table. Do you also want to try our salad bar?
샐러드 바
W: How much is it?
M: It's $30 per table.
W: No, thanks. That won't be necessary. I'll just reserve the two tables.
필요한
M: Okay. Are you currently a guest at our resort? If you are, you can
현재 투숙객
get a 10% discount.
10% 할인을 받다
W: Yes, I'm staying in room 609. My name is May Jones.
M: *[Typing sound]* Okay, Ms. Jones. We've confirmed you're a guest.
확인했다(confirm)
How would you like to pay for your tables?
W: I'll pay by credit card.

해석
남: Platinum Hillside Resort에 오신 것을 환영합니다. 어떻게 도와드릴까요?
여: 안녕하세요. 오늘 저녁에 야외 바비큐 테이블을 예약하고 싶은데요.
남: 알겠습니다, 지금은 4인용 작은 테이블과 8인용 큰 테이블이 이용 가능합니다.
여: 작은 테이블 2개를 예약하고 싶어요.
남: 네, 한 테이블에 25달러입니다. 저희의 샐러드 바도 이용해 보시겠습니까?
여: 얼마인가요?
남: 한 테이블에 30달러입니다.
여: 아니요, 괜찮아요. 그것은 필요하지 않을 거예요. 테이블 2개만 예약할게요.
남: 알겠습니다. 현재 저희 리조트의 투숙객이신가요? 투숙객이시면, 10% 할인을 받으실 수 있습니다.
여: 네, 609호에 묵고 있어요. 제 이름은 May Jones예요.
남: *[타자 치는 소리]* 네, Jones 씨. 투숙객이신 것을 확인했습니다. 테이블에 대한 지불은 어떻게 하시겠습니까?
여: 신용카드로 지불할게요.

✔ $45	② $50	③ $55
④ $72	⑤ $80	

문제풀이
한 테이블에 25달러인 4인용 작은 테이블 2개만 예약하고, 한 테이블에 30달러인 샐러드 바는 이용하지 않기로 했으므로 총액은 50달러이다. 리조트의 투숙객은 10% 할인을 받을 수 있다고 했기 때문에 여자가 지불할 금액은 5달러가 할인된 45달러이다. 따라서 답은 ① '$45'이다.

정답률 75%

07 남자가 식당에서 식사를 하지 못한 이유

▶ 정답 ⑤

W: Hey, Mike. How was dinner at the French restaurant downtown last weekend? I heard it was recently renovated.
최근에 보수되었다
(recently: 최근에, renovate: 보수하다)
M: Well, I went there, but I didn't get to eat anything.
W: Why? Were there too many people waiting in line?
줄을 서서 기다리는(wait in line)
M: Not really. There were tables available.
W: Did you bring your dog and the restaurant said no?
M: No, I checked their website and it said I could sit with my dog at an outdoor table.
W: Okay, so then why couldn't you eat anything?
M: The restaurant said they ran out of ingredients, so I left.
~이 다 떨어졌다(run out of) 재료들 나왔다(leave)
W: Oh, you must have been disappointed. How about we go there for
실망했음에 틀림없다
(must have p.p.: ~했음에 틀림없다, disappointed: 실망한)
lunch this Saturday?
M: Sounds great! They don't take reservations on weekends, so we should get there early.
예약을 받다
W: Good idea. I look forward to it.
~을 기대하다

해석
여: 안녕, Mike. 지난 주말에 시내에 있는 프랑스 식당에서 저녁 식사는 어땠어? 나는 그곳이 최근에 보수되었다고 들었어.
남: 음, 거기에 갔었는데, 아무것도 못 먹었어.
여: 왜? 줄을 서서 기다리는 사람이 너무 많았니?
남: 그렇지 않아. 이용 가능한 테이블들이 있었어.
여: 네 반려견을 데려갔는데 식당에서 안 된다고 했니?
남: 아니, 웹사이트를 확인했더니 야외 테이블에 반려견과 함께 앉을 수 있다고 되어 있었어.
여: 알겠어, 그럼 왜 아무것도 못 먹었어?
남: 식당에서 재료가 다 떨어졌다고 해서, 나왔어.
여: 오, 너는 실망했음에 틀림없어. 이번 주 토요일에 점심 먹으러 거기에 가는 게 어떠니?
남: 좋아! 주말에는 예약을 받지 않으니까, 우리는 일찍 거기에 가야 해.
여: 좋은 생각이야. 나는 그것을 기대해.

① 반려견을 데려가서
② 예약을 하지 않아서
③ 보수 공사 중이어서
④ 대기자가 너무 많아서
✔ 음식 재료가 다 떨어져서

정답률 90%

08 Home Organization Class에 관해 언급되지 않은 것

▶ 정답 ④

M: Honey, check out this advertisement.
광고
W: Okay, let me see. *[Pause]* Oh, Home Organization Class? That sounds interesting.
집 정리 정돈 수업

20
23년 9월 학력평가

M: Yeah, it does. How about we take the class together? We can learn some tips for organizing and cleaning our house.
요령들
W: Great idea. Look, the class will be held at the community center.
열리다(hold: 열다, 개최하다)   지역 문화 회관
It's just a ten-minute walk from here.
M: Right. And it's on Saturday, September 30th, from 2 p.m. to 6 p.m. Is that okay with you?
W: Yes, my schedule is free on that day. How much is the class?
일정   없는
M: It's $20 per person.
W: That's reasonable. Is there anything we need to prepare for the
합리적인   준비하다
class?
M: Yes. We have to bring some pictures of our living room and other rooms in our house.
W: Okay. I'll do that.
M: Great. Let's sign up for the class.

해석

남: 여보, 이 광고 좀 봐요.
여: 알겠어요, 어디 보자. [잠시 후] 오, Home Organization Class(집 정리정돈 수업)? 재미 있겠네요.
남: 네, 그래요. 같이 그 수업을 듣는 게 어때요? 집을 정리 정돈하고 청소하는 요령을 배울 수 있잖아요.
여: 좋은 생각이에요. 보세요, 수업은 지역 문화 회관에서 열릴 거예요. 그것은 여기서 걸어서 10분 거리에 있어요.
남: 맞아요. 그리고 9월 30일 토요일 오후 2시부터 6시까지네요. 당신은 괜찮아요?
여: 네, 그날은 일정이 없어요. 수강료가 얼마죠?
남: 1인당 20달러예요.
여: 합리적이네요. 수업을 위해 우리가 준비해야 할 것이 있어요?
남: 네. 우리 집의 거실과 다른 방들의 사진을 가져가야 해요.
여: 알겠어요. 제가 할게요.
남: 좋아요. 수강 신청을 합시다.

① 장소   ② 일시   ③ 수강료
✔④ 수강 인원   ⑤ 준비물

---

09 2023 Board Game Design Contest에 관한 내용과 일치하지 않는 것 ▶ 정답 ③

정답률 85%

W: Hello, viewers. The 2023 Board Game Design Contest is an
보드 게임 디자인 대회
annual event for designing board games. It's open to board game
연례 행사
fans of all ages around the world. The contest is split into two
~으로 나누어지다
rounds. In round one, contestants must submit a 2-minute video
참가자들   제출하다
introducing their games. In round two, contestants must hand in
제출하다
a document that explains how to play their game. During round
문서   설명하다
two, contestants get the chance to work with experienced game
기회   경험이 있는
designers who will help each contestant with establishing the rules
정하는 것(establish) 규칙들
for their game. The final winner of the contest receives $1,000,
최종 우승자
plus a chance to release his or her game. Registration closes on
출시하다   등록
Friday, September 15th. Show us your skills as a game designer!

해석

여: 안녕하세요, 시청자 여러분. 2023 Board Game Design Contest(2023 보드 게임 디자인 대회)는 보드 게임을 디자인하는 연례 행사입니다. 그것은 전 세계의 모든 연령대의 보드 게임 팬들에게 열려 있습니다. 대회는 2개의 라운드로 나누어집니다. 1라운드에서, 참가자들은 자신의 게임을 소개하는 2분짜리 영상을 제출해야 합니다. 2라운드에서, 참가자들은 자신의 게임을 하는 방법을 설명하는 문서를 제출해야 합니다. 2라운드 동안, 참가자들은 각 참가자가 자신의 게임을 위한 규칙을 정하는 것을 도와줄 경험이 있는 게임 디자이너들과 함께 일할 기회를 얻습니다. 대회의 최종 우승자는 자신의 게임을 출시할 수 있는 기회와 더불어 1000달러를 받습니다. 등록은 9월 15일 금요일에 마감됩니다. 여러분의 게임 디자이너로서의 실력을 보여주세요!

① 참가 연령에 제한이 없다.
② 1라운드에서는 게임 소개 영상을 제출해야 한다.
✔③ 2라운드에서는 게임 디자이너의 도움을 받지 못한다.
④ 최종 우승자는 1,000달러를 받는다.
⑤ 9월 15일에 등록이 마감된다.

문제 풀이

게임 규칙을 정하는 작업을 해야 하는 2라운드에서 경험이 있는 게임 디자이너들이 참가자들을 도와줄 것이라고 했으므로 ③ '2라운드에서는 게임 디자이너의 도움을 받지 못한다.'는 내용과 일치하지 않는다.

---

10 표에서 두 사람이 주문할 제품

정답률 75% ▶ 정답 ②

W: Sean, look what I found for mom for her birthday.
M: Oh, an electric mug warmer set? What is it?
전기 머그잔 워머 세트
W: It's a set that includes a mug and a warmer, and the warmer keeps
포함하다
beverages warm.
음료들
M: Cool! How much can we spend on this?
W: Well, we didn't buy a cake yet, so we'd better not spend more than
쓰지 않는 게 좋다
$50.
(had better V: ~하는 게 좋다)
M: I see. The mugs come in three different materials. Which one
소재들
would she like?
W: She already has glass mugs, so let's choose from the other materials.
M: Good idea. How about the capacity of the mug?
용량
W: I think less than 500ml will be appropriate.
적당한
M: Yeah, that makes sense. Do you think it's better to buy a set with
일리가 있다
the LED display?
표시 장치
W: Yes. I think it's better because it allows you to check the
네가 확인할 수 있게 해주다
temperature.
온도   (allow A to V: A가 ~할 수 있게 해주다)
M: I like it, too. Let's order this one.

해석

여: Sean, 내가 엄마 생신을 위해 찾은 것을 봐.
남: 오, 전기 머그잔 워머 세트? 그게 뭐야?
여: 머그잔과 워머를 포함한 세트로, 워머는 음료를 따뜻하게 유지해 줘.
남: 멋지다! 우리는 이것에 얼마를 쓸 수 있어?
여: 글쎄, 아직 케이크를 사지 않았으니까, 50달러 이상은 쓰지 않는 게 좋아.
남: 알겠어. 머그잔은 세 가지의 다른 소재로 나와. 엄마께서는 어떤 것을 좋아하실까?
여: 유리 머그잔은 이미 가지고 계시니까, 다른 소재 중에서 고르자.
남: 좋은 생각이야. 머그잔의 용량은 어때?
여: 500ml 이하가 적당할 것 같아.
남: 그래, 일리가 있네. LED 표시 장치가 있는 세트를 사는 것이 더 좋을까?
여: 응. 그것은 네가 온도를 확인할 수 있게 해 주기 때문에 더 좋을 것 같아.
남: 나도 좋아. 이것을 주문하자.

전기 머그잔 워머 세트

	세트	가격	머그잔 소재	머그잔 용량	LED 표시 장치
①	A	26달러	유리	250ml	X
✔②	B	32달러	도자기	350ml	O
③	C	37달러	도자기	450ml	X
④	D	42달러	스테인리스 스틸	550ml	O
⑤	E	55달러	스테인리스 스틸	590ml	X

---

11 남자의 마지막 말에 대한 여자의 응답

정답률 85% ▶ 정답 ②

M: Clara, I finished designing the poster for our school's musical
포스터
auditions. Have a look.
뮤지컬 오디션들
W: Wow, it looks fantastic! And why don't we put a QR code on it for
QR 코드를 넣다
registration? It'll make it easier for students to sign up.
등록   지원하다
M: Great idea, but I don't know how to make QR codes. Could you help
만드는 방법(how to V: ~하는 방법)
me with that?
W: (Sure. I'll create one and send it to you.)

해석

남: Clara, 우리 학교의 뮤지컬 오디션을 위한 포스터 디자인을 끝냈어. 한번 봐.
여: 와, 환상적인 것 같아! 그리고 등록을 위한 QR 코드를 넣는 게 어때? 그것은 학생들이 지

원하는 것을 더 쉽게 만들어 줄 거야.

남: 좋은 생각이지만, 나는 QR 코드를 만드는 방법을 몰라. 네가 그것을 도와줄 수 있을까?

여: (물론이지. 내가 그것을 만들어서 네게 보내줄게.)

① 미안해. 너는 여기에 포스터를 게시할 수 없어.

✔ 물론이지. 내가 그것을 만들어서 네게 보내줄게.

③ 아니야. 이 QR 코드가 작동하지 않는 것 같아.

④ 맞아. QR 코드를 스캔하고 신청하면 돼.

⑤ 응. 너도 오디션에 참가할 수 있어.

---

12 여자의 마지막 말에 대한 남자의 응답

정답률 75% ▶ 정답 ①

W: Harry, have you decided what school club you will join?
　　　　　　　　　　　　　　　　　　학교 동아리　　　　　가입하다

M: Not yet. I'm thinking of joining either the poetry club or the history
　　　　　　　　　　　　　　　　시 낭독 동아리나 역사 동아리 둘 중 하나
club.
(either A or B: A나 B 둘 중 하나)

W: I've heard the history club is already full, so they're not accepting
　　　　　　　　　　　　　　　　　　　　만원의
any more new members.
　　　　　　신입 회원들

M: (Then, I'll apply for the poetry club.)
　　　　　　　　~에 지원하다

해석

여: Harry, 어떤 학교 동아리에 가입할지 결정했니?

남: 아직이야. 시 낭독 동아리나 역사 동아리 둘 중 하나에 가입할까 생각 중이야.

여: 역사 동아리는 이미 만원이라서, 더 이상 신입 회원을 받지 않는다고 들었어.

남: (그럼, 나는 시 낭독 동아리에 지원할게.)

✔ 그럼, 나는 시 낭독 동아리에 지원할게.

② 그래, 내가 너에게 좋은 동아리를 추천할 수 있어.

③ 말도 안 돼. 우리는 신입 회원을 받을 수 없어.

④ 좋아! 방과 후에 역사 동아리에서 봐.

⑤ 정말? 내가 이 동아리에 가입할 수 있게 해줘서 고마워.

---

13 남자의 마지막 말에 대한 여자의 응답

정답률 80% ▶ 정답 ①

W: Dad, did you throw away all the empty plastic bottles?
　　　　　　　　　버리다　　　　　빈

M: Yes. Why?

W: I need plastic bottle caps for our school's zero waste challenge.
　　　　　　　　　뚜껑들　　　　　　쓰레기 배출 줄이기 운동

M: Interesting. So what are you doing with the caps?

W: We'll send them to an upcycling company, and they make products
　　　　　　　　　　　업사이클링 업체　　　　　　　　　제품들
like chairs and hairpins from the caps.

M: That's cool.

W: Yeah, and the teacher said if we bring in more than 20 bottle caps,
　　　　　　　　　　　　　　　　가져오다
she'll give us a bamboo toothbrush as a prize.
　　　　　　　　　　　　　상품으로

M: Great. How many bottle caps have you collected so far?
　　　　　　　　　　　　　　　　　　　　지금까지

W: I've collected only eight bottle caps. I need some more.

M: Hmm, I threw the plastic bottles away just an hour ago, so they
should be in the recycling area.
　　　　　　재활용 구역

W: (Okay. I'll go there to check if I can find more caps.)

해석

여: 아빠, 빈 플라스틱 병을 다 버리셨어요?

남: 응. 왜?

여: 저희 학교의 쓰레기 배출 줄이기 운동을 위해 플라스틱 병뚜껑이 필요해요.

남: 흥미롭구나. 그럼 병뚜껑으로 무엇을 하는 거니?

여: 그것들을 업사이클링 업체에 보내면, 병뚜껑으로 의자와 머리핀 같은 제품들 만들어요.

남: 멋지구나.

여: 네, 그리고 선생님께서 20개 이상의 병뚜껑을 가져오면, 상품으로 대나무 칫솔을 주신다 고 하셨어요.

남: 좋아. 지금까지 몇 개의 병뚜껑을 모았니?

여: 겨우 8개의 병뚜껑을 모았어요. 좀 더 필요해요.

남: 흠, 한 시간 전에 플라스틱 병을 버려서, 그것들은 재활용 구역에 있을 거야.

여: (알겠어요. 제가 거기에 가서 병뚜껑을 더 찾을 수 있는지 확인해 볼게요.)

✔ 알겠어요. 제가 거기에 가서 병뚜껑을 더 찾을 수 있는지 확인해 볼게요.

② 잠시만요. 병뚜껑과 병을 분리하는 것을 잊어버렸어요.

③ 좋아요. 우리는 예술 작품에 병뚜껑을 사용할 수 있어요.

---

④ 걱정하지 마세요. 제가 이미 쓰레기를 버렸어요.

⑤ 아니요, 괜찮아요. 우리는 충분한 칫솔을 가지고 있어요.

---

14 여자의 마지막 말에 대한 남자의 응답

정답률 85% ▶ 정답 ②

[Cell phone rings.]

W: Hi, honey. What's up?

M: Hey, sweetheart! I have good news.

W: What is it?

M: I'm at the mall, and I just saw the hiking shoes you wanted are on
　　　　　　　　　　　　　　　　　　등산화　　　　　　　　　　할인 판매 중인
sale.

W: Really? We didn't buy them the other day because they were too
　　　　　　　　　　　　　　일전에
expensive.

M: Yeah, but they're 50% off now. Do you want me to buy you a pair?
　　　　　　　　　　　　　　　　　　　　　　　　　　한 켤레

M: You wear a size six for your shoes, right?

W: Yeah, but for hiking shoes, I usually wear a size seven.
　　　　　　　　　　　　　　　　보통

M: Hmm…. Wouldn't they be too big for your feet?

W: No, they're fine. My feet get easily swollen while hiking, so I prefer
　　　　　　　　　　　　　　쉽게 붓다
wearing hiking shoes that aren't too tight.
　　　　　　　　　　　　　　꽉 조이는

M: Oh, I see.

W: Plus, I usually wear thick socks when hiking, so buying a size six
　　게다가　　　　　　　두꺼운
wouldn't work for me.

M: (I got it. I'll buy a size seven for your hiking shoes.)

해석

[휴대전화가 울린다.]

여: 안녕, 여보. 무슨 일이에요?

남: 안녕, 여보! 좋은 소식이 있어요.

여: 뭔데요?

남: 지금 쇼핑몰에 있는데, 당신이 사고 싶어 했던 등산화가 할인 판매 중인 것을 봤어요.

여: 정말이에요? 일전에 그것들이 너무 비싸서 사지 않았잖아요.

남: 네, 그런데 지금은 50% 할인을 하고 있어요. 내가 한 켤레를 사줄까요?

여: 네, 그러면 정말 좋겠어요.

남: 당신은 6사이즈의 신발을 신잖아요, 그렇죠?

여: 네, 하지만 등산화는 보통 7사이즈를 신어요.

남: 흠…. 당신의 발에 너무 크지 않겠어요?

여: 아니요, 괜찮아요. 등산할 때 발이 쉽게 부어서, 너무 꽉 조이지 않는 등산화를 신는 게 더 좋아요.

남: 오, 그렇군요.

여: 게다가, 등산할 때는 보통 두꺼운 양말을 신어서, 6사이즈를 사는 것은 저에게 맞지 않을 것 같아요.

남: (알겠어요. 당신의 등산화를 7사이즈로 살게요.)

① 걱정하지 마요. 그 신발을 더 작은 사이즈로 교환할게요.

✔ 알겠어요. 당신의 등산화를 7사이즈로 살게요.

③ 미안해요. 당신이 원하는 신발 모델은 할인 판매하지 않고 있어요.

④ 물론이죠. 등산을 가기 전에 신발을 확인해요.

⑤ 당신 말이 맞아요. 그 신발을 사기 위해 할인 판매를 기다릴게요.

문제 풀이

평소에 6사이즈의 신발을 신는 여자에게 7사이즈의 등산화는 크지 않겠냐고 묻는 남자의 말 에 여자는 발이 붓고 두꺼운 양말을 신기 때문에 6사이즈의 등산화를 사는 것은 적절하지 않 다고 대답한다. 이에 대한 남자의 응답으로 적절한 것은 ② 'I got it. I'll buy a size seven for your hiking shoes.(알겠어요. 당신의 등산화를 7사이즈로 살게요.)'이다.

---

15 다음 상황에서 Kate가 Claire에게 할 말

정답률 85% ▶ 정답 ⑤

M: Kate and Claire are new members of the school orchestra. They'll
perform with the orchestra for the first time next month. Today,
　공연하다　　　　　　　　　　　　　　처음으로
they go to a dress shop together and look for a formal dress to
　　　　　　　　　　　　　　　　　　　　　　　　　정장
wear for their concert. They look around the shop and try on the
　　　　　　　연주회　　　　　둘러보다　　　　　　입어 보다
dresses they like. However, after asking the clerk about the prices,
　　　　　　　　　　　　　　　　　　　　　　점원
they find the dresses are too expensive for their budget. At this
　　　　　　　　　　　　　　　　　　　　　　　예산

moment, Kate <u>realizes</u> that it'd be better to <u>rent</u> the dresses for
깨닫다   빌리다
their concert at a <u>rental shop</u>. So, Kate wants to suggest to Claire
대여점
that they <u>borrow</u> dresses rather than spend a lot of money on
빌리다
buying new dresses. In this situation, what would Kate most likely
say to Claire?
Kate: (How about renting dresses <u>instead of buying</u> new ones?)
                                 사는 대신에(instead of V-ing: ~하는 대신에)

해석

남: Kate와 Claire는 학교 오케스트라의 신입 단원이다. 그들은 다음 달에 처음으로 오케스트라와 함께 공연할 것이다. 오늘, 그들은 함께 의류 매장에 가서 연주회에서 입을 정장을 찾는다. 그들은 매장을 둘러보고 마음에 드는 옷들을 입어 본다. 그러나, 점원에게 가격에 대해 물어본 후에, 그들은 옷들이 자신들의 예산에 비해 너무 비싸다는 것을 알게 된다. 이 순간에, Kate는 대여점에서 연주회에 입을 옷을 빌리는 것이 더 낫다는 것을 깨닫는다. 그래서, Kate는 Claire에게 새 옷을 사는 데 많은 돈을 쓰는 것보다 옷을 빌릴 것을 제안하고 싶다. 이러한 상황에서, Kate는 Claire에게 뭐라고 말하겠는가?

Kate: (새 옷을 사는 대신에 옷을 빌리는 게 어떠니?)

① 우리는 복장 규정을 따라야 할 것 같아.
② 점원에게 옷에 대한 환불을 요청하자.
③ 오케스트라 연주회의 티켓을 사는 게 어떠니?
④ 다가오는 연주회를 위해 더 열심히 연습하는 게 좋겠어.
✔️ 새 옷을 사는 대신에 옷을 빌리는 게 어떠니?

16~17 1지문 2문항

W: Hello, students. <u>Weddings</u> are held all over the world, but the
                    결혼식들
way they're celebrated <u>varies</u> <u>greatly</u>. Today, we'll learn about
                        거행되다 다르다 매우
                    (celebrate: 거행하다, 축하하다)
unique wedding <u>customs</u> in different countries. In <u>Germany</u>, for
                풍습   독일
example, <u>newlyweds</u> cut a <u>log</u> in half using a large <u>saw</u>. By cutting
         신혼부부   통나무   톱
the log together, the couple shows their <u>willingness</u> to <u>cope with</u>
                                          의지   ~을 극복하다
difficulties in their <u>marriage</u>. Next, in Cuba, wedding <u>guests</u> have
                      결혼 생활   하객들
to pay to dance with the <u>bride</u>. The money is then used to pay for
                          신부
wedding <u>expenses</u>. Thirdly, it's <u>traditional</u> to <u>have a tea ceremony</u>
        비용   전통의   차 의식을 행하다
at weddings in China. The couple <u>serves</u> tea to both sides of their
                                  대접하다
families to show their <u>respect</u> and <u>gratitude</u>. Lastly, in Australia,
                       존경   감사
guests hold stones during the wedding ceremony. When it's over,
they <u>place</u> the stones in a <u>decorated bowl</u>, and it's given to the
     놓다   장식된 그릇
couple as a <u>reminder</u> of the <u>support</u> from their family and friends.
            기념품   지지
Now, let's watch a video of these wedding customs.

해석

여: 안녕하세요, 학생 여러분. 결혼식은 전 세계에서 열리지만, 결혼식이 거행되는 방식은 매우 다릅니다. 오늘, 우리는 여러 나라의 독특한 결혼식 풍습에 대해 배울 것입니다. 예를 들어, 독일에서는 신혼부부가 큰 톱을 사용하여 통나무를 반으로 자릅니다. 통나무를 함께 자름으로써, 커플은 결혼 생활의 어려움을 극복하려는 의지를 보여줍니다. 다음으로, 쿠바에서는 결혼식 하객들이 신부와 춤을 추기 위해 돈을 지불해야 합니다. 그 후에 그 돈은 결혼식 비용을 지불하는 데 사용됩니다. 세 번째로, 중국에서는 결혼식에서 차 의식을 행하는 것이 전통입니다. 커플은 존경과 감사를 표하기 위해 양가의 가족 모두에게 차를 대접합니다. 마지막으로, 호주에서는 하객들이 결혼식 동안에 돌을 들고 있습니다. 결혼식이 끝나면, 그들은 돌을 장식된 그릇에 놓고 그것은 가족과 친구들의 지지에 대한 기념품으로서 커플에게 주어집니다. 이제, 이러한 결혼식 풍습에 대한 동영상을 시청하겠습니다.

16 여자가 하는 말의 주제
▶ 정답 ②   정답률 85%

① 결혼식 비용을 줄이는 다양한 방법들
✔️ 여러 나라에 걸친 다양한 결혼식 전통들
③ 결혼 피로연 음식의 문화적 의미
④ 전 세계의 변화하는 결혼 경향들
⑤ 여러 나라의 웨딩드레스 역사

17 언급된 나라가 아닌 것
▶ 정답 ④   정답률 90%

① 독일   ② 쿠바   ③ 중국
✔️ 나이지리아   ⑤ 호주

---

21 2023년 11월 학력평가

01	①	02	②	03	③	04	⑤	05	⑤
06	③	07	③	08	⑤	09	④	10	②
11	②	12	②	13	①	14	②	15	②
16	④	17	④						

01 남자가 하는 말의 목적
▶ 정답 ①   정답률 90%

M: Hello, *City Talk Radio* listeners! This is Tony Moore. As some of
you know, the <u>International Motor Show</u> is coming to our city
              국제 모터쇼
this weekend. I'm here to <u>inform</u> you that the city will <u>operate a</u>
                          알리다   운영하다
<u>temporary parking lot</u> for visitors' <u>convenience</u>. It's because a
임시 주차장   편의
<u>huge crowd</u> is expected to visit the motor show. The temporary
엄청난 수의 관중
parking lot is <u>a five-minute walk from</u> the <u>main entrance</u>. Also,
               ~에서 걸어서 5분 거리   정문
parking is <u>free</u> for all visitors. Once again, I <u>announce</u> that a
           무료의   알리다
temporary parking lot will <u>be set up</u> and run for visitors. You can
                           설치되다(set up: 설치하다)
enjoy the motor show without parking problems. I'll <u>be back</u> after a
                                                    돌아오다
short <u>commercial break</u>. Stay tuned!
      광고 시간

해석

남: 안녕하세요, 〈City Talk Radio〉 청취자 여러분! 저는 Tony Moore입니다. 여러분 중 일부가 아시다시피, 이번 주말에 International Motor Show(국제 모터쇼)가 우리 시에 올 것입니다. 방문객들의 편의를 위해 시가 임시 주차장을 운영할 것임을 여러분께 알려드리고자 합니다. 왜냐하면 엄청난 수의 관중이 모터쇼를 방문할 것으로 예상되기 때문입니다. 임시 주차장은 정문에서 걸어서 5분 거리에 있습니다. 또한, 모든 방문객들에게 주차는 무료입니다. 다시 한 번, 방문객들을 위해 임시 주차장이 설치되어 운영될 것임을 알려드립니다. 여러분께서는 주차 문제없이 모터쇼를 즐기실 수 있습니다. 짧은 광고 시간 후에 돌아오겠습니다. 채널 고정해 주세요!

✔️ 모터쇼 임시 주차장 운영을 안내하려고
② 방송국 방문 등록 방법을 설명하려고
③ 모터쇼 입장 시간 변경을 알려주려고
④ 공영 주차장 요금 인상을 공지하려고
⑤ 라디오 행사 지원 팀을 모집하려고

02 여자의 의견
▶ 정답 ②   정답률 90%

W: Honey, since you're a fruit lover, I bought some fruits.
M: Wow, they look so <u>fresh</u> and <u>delicious</u>.
                      신선한   맛있는
W: Yes. Let's have some now.
M: Oh, is it okay to have fruits before lunch?
W: Of course. Actually, <u>consuming</u> fruits before a <u>meal</u> can have
                        섭취하는 것(consume)   식사
<u>beneficial effects on</u> your health.
~에 유익한 영향을 주다
(have an effect on: ~에 영향을 주다, beneficial: 유익한)
M: What kinds of <u>benefits</u> are you talking about?
                 이점들
W: For example, eating fruits before a meal can <u>aid in</u> <u>weight</u>
                                                도움이 되다 체중 관리

management because it helps you feel full.
포만감을 느끼다
M: Hmm... That makes sense.
W: Also, nutrients are better absorbed when fruits are eaten before a
영양소들   더 잘 흡수되다(absorb: 흡수하다)
meal.
M: I see. I didn't know that when we eat fruit has so much to do with
~과 그렇게 많은 관계가 있다
our health.   (have to do with: ~과 관계가 있다)
W: Exactly. Having fruits before a meal can improve your health.
증진시키다
M: Okay. Then I'll wash them for us.

해석

여: 여보, 당신이 과일을 좋아하는 사람이어서, 제가 과일을 좀 샀어요.
남: 와, 정말 신선하고 맛있어 보이네요.
여: 네. 지금 좀 먹어요.
남: 오, 점심 식사 전에 과일을 먹어도 괜찮아요?
여: 물론이죠. 사실, 식사 전에 과일을 섭취하는 것은 건강에 유익한 영향을 줄 수 있어요.
남: 어떤 종류의 이점을 말하는 거예요?
여: 예를 들어, 식사 전에 과일을 먹는 것은 포만감을 느끼도록 돕기 때문에 체중 관리에 도움
   이 될 수 있어요.
남: 흠... 일리가 있네요.
여: 또한, 식사 전에 과일을 먹으면 영양소가 더 잘 흡수돼요.
남: 그렇군요. 과일을 언제 먹는지가 건강과 그렇게 많은 관계가 있는지 몰랐어요.
여: 맞아요. 식사 전에 과일을 먹는 것은 건강을 증진시킬 수 있어요.
남: 알겠어요. 그럼 우리를 위해 그것들을 씻을게요.

① 충분한 영양 섭취를 위해 다양한 과일을 먹어야 한다.
✓식사 전에 과일을 먹는 것이 건강에 도움이 된다.
③ 과일을 먹기 전에 껍질을 깨끗이 씻어야 한다.
④ 규칙적인 생활 습관이 체중 관리에 중요하다.
⑤ 늦은 밤중에 먹는 음식은 숙면을 방해한다.

03 남자가 하는 말의 요지
정답률 90%
▶ 정답 ③

M: Hello, everyone. Welcome to our environmental lecture, *Love Our*
환경 강연
Planet. You've all heard that "Plastic is bad for the environment!,"
플라스틱
but do you actually know how bad it is? Plastic items take 1,000
실제로   제품들   (시간이) 걸리다
years to degrade in landfills. Plus, only a small percentage
분해되다   매립지들
of plastic items are actually recycled. To overcome the plastic
극복하다
pollution crisis, you can start by taking personal action. As a
오염 위기   개인 행동을 취함으로써
                          (by V-ing: ~함으로써, take action: 행동을 취하다, personal: 개인의)
first step, you ought to carry your own tumbler. It helps you work
가지고 다니다   텀블러
towards reducing plastic waste and make your carbon footprint
줄이는 것(reduce)   쓰레기   탄소 발자국
smaller. Why don't you carry a tumbler to cut down on plastic
waste? Let's act now for our planet.   ~을 줄이다

해석

남: 안녕하세요, 여러분. 저희의 환경 강연 〈Love Our Planet〉에 오신 것을 환영합니다. 여러
   분 모두 "플라스틱은 환경에 해롭습니다!"라고 들어본 적은 있지만, 실제로 얼마나 해로운
   지 알고 있습니까? 플라스틱 제품은 매립지에서 분해되는 데 1,000년이 걸립니다. 게다
   가, 플라스틱 제품의 극히 일부만이 실제로 재활용됩니다. 플라스틱 오염 위기를 극복하
   기 위해, 여러분은 개인 행동을 취함으로써 시작할 수 있습니다. 첫걸음으로, 여러분 자신
   의 텀블러를 가지고 다녀야 합니다. 그것은 플라스틱 쓰레기를 줄이기 위해 노력하고 탄
   소 발자국을 더 작게 만드는 데 도움을 줍니다. 플라스틱 쓰레기를 줄이기 위해 텀블러를
   가지고 다니는 게 어떠세요? 우리의 지구를 위해 지금 행동합시다.

① 환경 교육 프로그램에 적극적으로 참여해야 한다.
② 쉽게 분해될 수 있는 플라스틱 제품 개발이 필요하다.
✓플라스틱 쓰레기를 줄이기 위해 텀블러를 가지고 다녀야 한다.
④ 플라스틱병 재활용률을 높이려는 새로운 정책이 요구된다.
⑤ 텀블러 구매 시 유해 성분 포함 여부를 확인해야 한다.

04 그림에서 대화의 내용과 일치하지 않는 것
정답률 90%
▶ 정답 ⑤

W: Hi, Daniel. What are you looking at on your phone?
M: Hello, Jenny. It's a picture I took last Christmas Eve.

W: That's almost a year ago. Oh, I like the chimney on the roof of your
거의   굴뚝   지붕
house. You know, Santa Claus comes in through that.
M: Right. Look at the star-shaped light at the top of the tree. I hung it
별 모양의   조명   ~의 꼭대기에   걸었다(hang)
myself.
W: Great. There's a snowman wearing a stripe-patterned scarf.
눈사람   줄무늬의   목도리
M: I made him with my younger sisters. What do you think about the
ribbon on the door?
리본
W: I think it looks lovely and welcoming.
사랑스러운   반갑게 맞이하는
M: Yes. It really suits the Christmas mood.
어울리다   분위기
W: What are the three boxes under the table?
상자들
M: They're Christmas presents for my parents. My sisters and I
선물들
prepared them together.
준비했다
W: Your parents must have been touched. Looks like you had a great
틀림없이 감동했을 것이다
time.
(must have p.p.: 틀림없이 ~했을 것이다, touched: 감동한)

해석

여: 안녕, Daniel. 휴대폰으로 무엇을 보고 있니?
남: 안녕, Jenny. 작년 크리스마스 이브에 내가 찍은 사진이야.
여: 거의 1년 전이잖아. 오, 나는 네 집의 지붕에 있는 굴뚝이 마음에 들어. 알다시피, 산타클로
   스는 그것을 통해 들어오잖아.
남: 맞아. 나무 꼭대기에 있는 별 모양의 조명을 봐. 내가 직접 걸었어.
여: 멋지다. 줄무늬 목도리를 두른 눈사람이 있네.
남: 그것을 여동생들과 함께 만들었어. 문에 있는 리본에 대해 어떻게 생각해?
여: 사랑스럽고 반갑게 맞이하는 것 같아.
남: 그래. 크리스마스 분위기에 정말 잘 어울리지.
여: 테이블 밑에 있는 세 개의 상자는 뭐니?
남: 부모님을 위한 크리스마스 선물이야. 여동생들과 내가 함께 준비했어.
여: 네 부모님께서 틀림없이 감동하셨을 거야. 너는 즐거운 시간을 보낸 것 같구나.

05 여자가 할 일
정답률 90%
▶ 정답 ⑤

W: Hi, Mr. Williams. How are you doing with making our school
promotion video?
홍보 영상
M: Hello, Ms. Watson. I've been working on it for two weeks, and I've
almost finished.
W: The video will provide useful information for newcomers who are
유용한   신입생들
interested in our school.
~에 관심이 있는
M: I hope so. Do you want to watch it?
W: Of course. *[Pause]* Oh, you included interviews with teachers in the
담았다
video.
M: Yes. Many teachers participated.
참여했다
W: That's so kind of them. You know every teacher is busy.
바쁜
M: Right. I also filmed the science lab.
촬영했다 과학실
W: Great! Did you insert the subtitles into the video yourself? They're
넣다   자막들
eye-catching.
눈길을 끄는
M: Thank you for mentioning that. I've also been thinking about
background music. Can you choose some?
배경 음악   고르다

W: Sure. I'll do that for you. As you know, I have a big music collection.
음악 모음집
M: Thank you. That'd be really helpful.

해석

여: 안녕하세요, Williams 선생님. 학교 홍보 영상 제작은 어떻게 하고 계시나요?
남: 안녕하세요, Watson 선생님. 2주 동안 작업을 해 왔는데, 거의 다 마쳤어요.
여: 그 영상은 우리 학교에 관심이 있는 신입생들에게 유용한 정보를 제공할 거예요.
남: 그랬으면 좋겠네요. 그것을 보시겠어요?
여: 물론이죠. [잠시 후] 오, 영상에 선생님들과의 인터뷰를 담으셨네요.
남: 네. 많은 선생님께서 참여하셨어요.
여: 정말 친절하시네요. 모든 선생님들께서 바쁘신 거 아시잖아요.
남: 네. 저는 과학실도 촬영했어요.
여: 멋지네요! 영상에 자막을 직접 넣으신 거예요? 눈길을 끄는데요.
남: 그렇게 말씀해 주셔서 감사해요. 저는 배경 음악에 대해서도 생각하고 있어요. 좀 골라주실 수 있나요?
여: 그럼요. 제가 선생님을 위해 그 일을 할게요. 아시다시피, 제가 음악 모음집을 많이 가지고 있잖아요.
남: 감사해요. 정말 도움이 될 것 같네요.

① 과학실 촬영하기
② 영상에 자막 넣기
③ 홍보 문구 만들기
④ 선생님 인터뷰하기
✔ 배경 음악 선택하기

문제 풀이

학교 홍보 영상을 만들고 있는 남자가 여자에게 영상에 사용할 배경 음악을 골라줄 것을 부탁하고, 여자는 자신이 그 일을 해 주겠다고 대답한다. 따라서 답은 ⑤ '배경 음악 선택하기'이다.

06 남자가 지불할 금액
정답률 75%
▶ 정답 ③

W: Welcome to the National Costume Museum. How may I help you?
국립 의상 박물관
M: Hi. I'd like to buy admission tickets.
입장권
W: They're $20 for adults and $10 for children under the age of 12.
M: My daughter is 8 years old now, so I'll take two adult tickets and one child ticket, please.
W: Okay. Do you want to see the special exhibition?
특별전
M: Oh, special exhibition? What's that about?
W: It's about the jewel collection from the British royal family. It's open this month only.
보석 수집품   영국 왕실
M: That sounds interesting. How much is it?
W: It's originally $10 per person. But if you buy an admission ticket,
원래   1인당
you'll get a 50% discount on the ticket for the special exhibition.
50% 할인을 받다
M: Great. Then, I'll get three.
W: So, let me confirm. Two adults and one child admission tickets.
확인하다
Plus, three special exhibition tickets, right?
M: Yes. Here's my credit card.

해석

여: 국립 의상 박물관에 오신 것을 환영합니다. 어떻게 도와드릴까요?
남: 안녕하세요. 입장권을 사고 싶은데요.
여: 성인은 20달러이고 12세 미만 어린이는 10달러예요.
남: 제 딸은 지금 8살이니까, 성인 입장권 2장과 어린이 입장권 1장을 살게요.
여: 알겠습니다. 특별전을 보시겠어요?
남: 오, 특별전이요? 어떤 건가요?
여: 영국 왕실의 보석 수집품에 관한 거예요. 이번 달에만 열려요.
남: 흥미롭게 들리네요. 얼마인가요?
여: 원래 1인당 10달러예요. 하지만 입장권을 구매하시면, 특별전 티켓에 50% 할인을 받으실 거예요.
남: 좋네요. 그럼, 3장 살게요.
여: 그럼, 확인해 볼게요. 성인 2명과 어린이 1명의 입장권이죠. 거기에 더해, 특별전 티켓 3장이네요, 맞나요?
남: 네. 여기 제 신용카드가 있어요.

① $45   ② $60   ✔ $65
④ $75   ⑤ $90

문제 풀이

남자는 20달러인 성인 입장권 2장과 10달러인 어린이 입장권 1장을 구매하려고 하고 있으므로 입장권의 총액은 50달러이다. 1인당 10달러인 특별전 티켓 3장의 경우, 입장권 구매를 통해 50% 할인을 받게 되어 총 15달러에 살 수 있다. 따라서 남자가 지불할 금액은 65달러이므로 답은 ③ '$65'이다.

07 여자가 기타 동호회에 참석하지 못한 이유
정답률 90%
▶ 정답 ③

[Cell phone rings.]
W: Hello, Scott.
M: Hi, Reese. I didn't see you at the guitar club meeting yesterday.
기타 동호회 모임
W: I really wanted to go, but I couldn't.
M: Was there a problem with your guitar again?
W: Not at all. My guitar works fine now.
잘 기능하다
M: Oh, were you working late last night?
W: No. My team completed the project, so I left the office on time.
완료했다   퇴근했다(leave the office) 정시에
M: Is that so? Then why couldn't you come to the club meeting?
W: I've been feeling pain in my fingers when I play the guitar.
고통   연주하다
M: Oh, no. Maybe you should stop practicing for a while.
연습하는 것을 멈추다
(stop V-ing: ~하는 것을 멈추다, practice: 연습하다)
W: Yeah, but I'm concerned because I can't learn any new techniques.
걱정하는   연주법
M: Don't worry. I can teach you later if you want.
나중에
W: Thanks a lot.

해석

[휴대전화가 울린다.]
여: 안녕, Scott.
남: 안녕, Reese. 어제 기타 동호회 모임에서 너를 못 봤어.
여: 정말 가고 싶었는데, 갈 수 없었어.
남: 네 기타에 또 문제가 있었니?
여: 전혀 아니야. 내 기타는 지금 잘 기능해.
남: 오, 어젯밤에 늦게까지 일하고 있었니?
여: 아니. 우리 팀이 프로젝트를 완료해서, 정시에 퇴근했어.
남: 그래? 그럼 왜 동호회 모임에 오지 못했니?
여: 나는 기타를 연주할 때 손가락에 통증을 느껴왔어.
남: 오, 이런. 아마도 당분간 연습하는 것을 멈춰야겠구나.
여: 응, 그런데 새 연주법을 배울 수 없어서 걱정이야.
남: 걱정하지 마. 네가 원하면 내가 나중에 가르쳐 줄게.
여: 정말 고마워.

① 기타에 문제가 생겨서
② 늦게까지 일해야 해서
✔ 손가락에 통증이 있어서
④ 프로젝트에 참여해야 해서
⑤ 새 연주법을 익히지 못해서

08 2023 Laser Light Show에 관해 언급되지 않은 것
정답률 90%
▶ 정답 ⑤

M: Sandra, what are you looking at?
W: Dad, I'm looking at the 2023 Laser Light Show website.
M: Oh, it's been a yearly event for the past seven years. What's the theme of this year?
연례 행사   주제
W: It's 'Fly to the Sky.' Special effects will make the heavens glow.
특수 효과   빛나다
M: It sounds spectacular. When is the show?
장관인
W: It goes from December 22nd to 26th. And my final exams will be over by then.
기말고사
M: Perfect! Will it be held at Central Park again?
열리다(hold: 열다, 개최하다)
W: Yes. The park isn't far from home. We can walk to the park.
~에서 먼
M: Right. Hmm, do you see how we can book tickets?
예매하다
W: [Pause] The website says reservations should be made online only.
M: Okay. Let's book tickets now.
예약

해석

남: Sandra, 무엇을 보고 있니?

여: 아빠, 저는 2023 Laser Light Show 웹사이트를 보고 있어요.
남: 오, 그것은 지난 7년 동안 해 온 연례 행사구나. 올해 주제는 뭐니?
여: 'Fly to the Sky'인데요. 특수 효과가 하늘을 빛나게 할 거예요.
남: 장관일 것 같구나. 쇼는 언제 하니?
여: 12월 22일부터 26일까지 해요. 그리고 그때쯤이면 제 기말고사가 끝날 거예요.
남: 완벽하구나! 또 Central Park에서 열리니?
여: 네. 그 공원은 집에서 멀지 않아요. 공원까지 걸어갈 수 있어요.
남: 맞아. 흠, 어떻게 티켓을 예매할 수 있는지 알겠니?
여: [잠시 후] 웹사이트에는 온라인으로만 예약해야 한다고 되어 있어요.
남: 알겠어. 이제 티켓을 예매하자.

① 주제 　　　　② 기간 　　　　③ 장소
④ 예매 방법 　　☑입장료

09　Highville Fashion Pop-up Stores에 관한 내용과 일치하지 않는 것 　▶ 정답 ④

정답률 75%

W: Welcome, shoppers. We're pleased to be hosting the Highville Fashion Pop-up Stores next week. They'll run for three days starting on December 29th. These limited-time pop-up stores will be open on the fifth floor and operated by 10 different brands. You can purchase fashion items including gloves and knit hats to keep you warm during the winter. The pop-up stores will offer a 60 percent discount on certain fashion items. Also, they'll give away free coffee coupons to all shoppers who make a purchase. The coupon can be used at the cafe on the second floor in the mall. Don't miss this great chance to level up your style!

해석
여: 어서 오세요, 쇼핑객 여러분. 저희는 다음 주에 Highville Fashion Pop-up Stores (Highville 패션 팝업 스토어들)를 열게 되어 기쁩니다. 그것들은 12월 29일부터 3일 동안 진행될 것입니다. 이 기간 한정 팝업 스토어들은 5층에서 열릴 것이며 10개의 다른 브랜드들에 의해 운영될 것입니다. 여러분은 겨울 동안 여러분을 따뜻하게 해 줄 장갑과 니트 모자를 포함한 패션 상품들을 구매할 수 있습니다. 팝업 스토어들은 특정한 패션 상품들에 대해 60퍼센트 할인을 제공할 것입니다. 또한, 구매한 모든 쇼핑객들에게 무료 커피 쿠폰을 줄 것입니다. 쿠폰은 쇼핑몰 2층에 있는 카페에서 사용될 수 있습니다. 여러분의 스타일을 끌어올릴 수 있는 이 좋은 기회를 놓치지 마세요!

① 12월 29일부터 3일 동안 진행될 것이다.
② 5층에서 열릴 것이다.
③ 장갑과 니트 모자를 포함한 패션 상품을 구매할 수 있다.
☑ 전 상품에 대해 60퍼센트 할인을 제공할 것이다.
⑤ 모든 구매 고객에게 무료 커피 쿠폰을 줄 것이다.

10　표에서 남자가 구매할 하이킹 스틱 　▶ 정답 ②

정답률 90%

W: Welcome to Andy's Hiking Equipment Store. What can I do for you?
M: Hi. I'm looking for hiking sticks.
W: These are the five models we have in stock. What's your budget?
M: I'd like to keep it under $50.
W: Okay. We have three different materials. Do you have any preference?
M: Well, I don't like bamboo. It doesn't look strong.
W: I see.
M: And I prefer foldable sticks because they're easier to carry around.
W: Sure. Besides they'll take up less space in your backpack. Then there are two options left. Which do you like?
M: I like those blue ones. They look cool.
W: I agree. This model is the best for you.
M: Right. I'll buy them now.

해석
여: Andy's Hiking Equipment Store(Andy's 하이킹 용품점)에 오신 것을 환영합니다. 무엇을 도와드릴까요?

남: 안녕하세요. 저는 하이킹 스틱을 찾고 있어요.
여: 이것들이 저희가 재고로 가지고 있는 다섯 가지 모델이에요. 예산이 어떻게 되시나요?
남: 50달러 이하로 하고 싶어요.
여: 알겠습니다. 세 가지 다른 소재가 있어요. 선호하시는 것이 있으신가요?
남: 음, 대나무는 마음에 들지 않네요. 튼튼해 보이지 않아요.
여: 그렇군요.
남: 그리고 접이식 스틱이 휴대하기가 더 쉬워서 더 좋네요.
여: 물론이죠. 게다가 배낭에서 더 적은 공간을 차지할 거예요. 그럼 두 가지 선택지가 남았네요. 어떤 것이 좋으세요?
남: 파란색이 마음에 들어요. 멋져 보이네요.
여: 동의해요. 이 모델이 손님께 가장 적합해요.
남: 네. 지금 구매할게요.

하이킹 스틱

	모델	가격	소재	접이식	색상
①	A	37달러	대나무	X	갈색
☑②	B	39달러	알루미늄	O	파란색
③	C	43달러	탄소 섬유	X	검은색
④	D	47달러	알루미늄	O	갈색
⑤	E	52달러	탄소 섬유	O	파란색

11　여자의 마지막 말에 대한 남자의 응답 　▶ 정답 ②

정답률 80%

W: Hi, Mr. Smith, how many students signed up for the Green Recipe Contest?
M: Oh, Ms. White, almost 80 students signed up. So I have to change the location for the contest.
W: I think the auditorium has more space. Why don't you use that?
M: (Good idea. I'll go check if it's available.)

해석
여: 안녕하세요, Smith 선생님, 얼마나 많은 학생들이 Green Recipe Contest(그린 레시피 경연 대회)에 참가 신청을 했나요?
남: 오, White 선생님, 거의 80명의 학생들이 참가 신청을 했어요. 그래서 대회 장소를 변경해야 해요.
여: 강당의 공간이 더 넓은 것 같아요. 그곳을 사용하는 게 어때요?
남: (좋은 생각이네요. 가서 이용 가능한지 확인해 볼게요.)

① 걱정하지 마세요. 강당을 찾으실 수 있을 거예요.
☑ 좋은 생각이네요. 가서 이용 가능한지 확인해 볼게요.
③ 맞아요. 저는 당신의 수업을 신청하고 싶어요.
④ 문제없어요. 저는 제 레시피를 바꿀 수 있어요.
⑤ 네. 다음에는 당신이 대회에서 우승할 거예요.

12　남자의 마지막 말에 대한 여자의 응답 　▶ 정답 ③

정답률 90%

M: Hi, Amy. Have you heard that the central library started their e-book rental service?
W: Really? I need to borrow some books for my report. Can I try it now?
M: Sure. You can borrow e-books through the library app.
W: (Great! I'm going to download and try it out.)

해석
남: 안녕, Amy. 중앙 도서관에서 전자책 대여 서비스를 시작했다는 소식을 들었니?
여: 정말? 나는 보고서를 위한 책을 좀 빌려야 해. 지금 그것을 이용할 수 있어?
남: 물론이야. 도서관 앱을 통해서 전자책을 빌릴 수 있어.
여: (잘됐다! 그것을 다운로드해서 이용해 볼게.)

① 꼭 그렇진 않아. 나는 아직도 보고서를 작성하고 있어.
② 죄송합니다. 지금은 도서관 카드를 발급해 드릴 수 없습니다.
☑ 잘됐다! 그것을 다운로드해서 이용해 볼게.
④ 물론이지! 내가 내일 네 책을 반납할게.
⑤ 동의해. 나는 다양한 종류의 책을 읽어야 해.

13 여자의 마지막 말에 대한 남자의 응답

정답률 85%

▶ 정답 ①

M: Honey, what are you doing?
W: I'm organizing our daughter's closet. Look at these clothes.
　　　정리하고 있다(organize)　　　　　옷장
M: Many of them seem too small for her. Are you going to throw them away?
　　　　　　　　　　　　　　　　　　　　그것들을 버리다
W: No. I don't want to because some of them still look brand new.
　　　　　　　　　　　　　　　　　　　완전히 새것인
M: You're right. My co-worker says that lately many people buy and
　　　　　　　　　　직장 동료　　　　요즘, 최근에
sell second-hand items by using an online platform.
　　중고품들　　　　　　　　　　온라인 플랫폼
W: Really? We should try that.
M: I think so, too. Some people might want to buy these clothes.
W: I agree. Where do we start?
M: We need to take pictures of the clothes we want to sell and then
　　　　　～의 사진을 찍다
post them on the platform.
게시하다
W: Then I'm going to take pictures. But I don't know how to put them
on the website. Could you do that?　　올리는 방법(how to V: ~하는 방법)
M: (Of course. I'll post them after you're done.)

해석
남: 여보, 무엇을 하고 있어요?
여: 우리 딸의 옷장을 정리하고 있어요. 이 옷 좀 봐요.
남: 많은 것들이 그 애한테 너무 작아 보이네요. 그것들을 버릴 거예요?
여: 아니요. 일부는 아직도 완전히 새것처럼 보이기 때문에 그러고 싶지 않아요.
남: 당신 말이 맞아요. 제 직장 동료가 말하기를 요즘 많은 사람들이 온라인 플랫폼을 이용해서 중고품을 사고판다고 해요.
여: 그래요? 우리도 그것을 시도해 봐야겠네요.
남: 저도 그렇게 생각해요. 어떤 사람들은 이 옷들을 사고 싶어할 수도 있어요.
여: 동의해요. 어디부터 시작할까요?
남: 팔고자 하는 옷의 사진을 찍은 다음에 플랫폼에 게시해야 해요.
여: 그럼 제가 사진을 찍을게요. 그런데 사진을 웹사이트에 올리는 방법을 모르겠어요. 당신이 할 수 있겠어요?
남: (물론이죠. 당신이 끝낸 후에 제가 게시할게요.)
☑물론이죠. 당신이 끝낸 후에 제가 게시할게요.
② 왜 안 되겠어요? 온라인 후기를 검색해 봐야겠네요.
③ 알겠어요. 저는 경매로 사진을 좀 구매하고 싶어요.
④ 그렇군요. 저는 당신의 방을 위한 더 큰 옷장을 살 수 있어요.
⑤ 아니요. 그것들을 사고 싶어 하는 사람을 찾을 수 없었어요.

14 남자의 마지막 말에 대한 여자의 응답

정답률 85%

▶ 정답 ②

W: Hi, Kevin. How's the preparation going for your concert next week?
　　　　　　　　　　　　준비
M: Oh, Lisa. You haven't heard the news yet. My band decided to
delay the concert until next month.　　　연기하기로 결정했다
　　　　　　　　　　　(decide to V: ~하기로 결정하다, delay: 연기하다)
W: What happened? Is it because of the concert hall? You said the
facilities of the hall aren't so good.　　공연장
시설들
M: That's not it. We found a better one.
W: That's good to hear. Do you need more time to practice with your
band?　　　　　　　　　　　　　　　　　　　　　　연습하다
M: Not really. We've practiced a lot.
W: Then why did you put off the concert? You know a lot of fans are
looking forward to it.　　미루다
~을 기대하고 있다(look forward to)
M: Of course I do. The problem is the lead vocalist got a bad cold.
　　　　　　　　　　　　　　　　리드 보컬　　독감에 걸렸다
W: How awful! Did she lose her voice?　　　　　(get a bad cold)
　　끔찍한　　　　목소리가 나오지 않다
　　　　　　　(lose one's voice)
M: Yes. The doctor said she has to stop singing for two weeks until she
gets better.
호전되다
W: (Sorry to hear that. I hope she gets well soon.)

해석
여: 안녕하세요, Kevin. 다음 주에 있을 공연 준비는 어떻게 되어 가고 있나요?
남: 오, Lisa. 아직 소식을 못 들으셨군요. 저희 밴드는 공연을 다음 달까지 연기하기로 결정

했어요.
여: 무슨 일이 있나요? 공연장 때문인가요? 공연장의 시설이 별로 좋지 않다고 하셨잖아요.
남: 그게 아니에요. 더 좋은 곳을 찾았어요.
여: 다행이네요. 밴드와 연습할 시간이 더 필요하신가요?
남: 그렇지 않아요. 저희는 연습을 많이 했거든요.
여: 그럼 왜 공연을 미루셨나요? 많은 팬들이 그것을 기대하고 있다는 것을 아시잖아요.
남: 물론 알고 있죠. 문제는 리드 보컬이 독감에 걸렸다는 거예요.
여: 정말 끔찍하네요! 그녀는 목소리가 나오지 않았나요?
남: 네. 의사 선생님이 그녀가 호전될 때까지 2주 동안 노래를 하지 말아야 한다고 했어요.
여: (안타깝네요. 그녀가 빨리 회복하기를 바랄게요.)
① 당연하죠. 그녀는 연습을 더 해야 해요.
☑안타깝네요. 그녀가 빨리 회복하기를 바랄게요.
③ 별일 아니에요. 제가 그녀에게 시설에 대해 조언할게요.
④ 아쉽네요! 제가 당신과 함께 공연에 갔어야 했어요.
⑤ 맞아요. 당신은 병원에 며칠 더 입원하는 게 좋겠어요.

문제 풀이
독감에 걸린 리드 보컬의 목 상태에 대해 묻는 여자에게 남자는 리드 보컬의 건강이 호전될 때까지 노래를 할 수 없게 되었다고 말한다. 이에 대한 여자의 응답으로는 ② 'Sorry to hear that. I hope she gets well soon.(안타깝네요. 그녀가 빨리 회복하기를 바랄게요.)'이 가장 적절하다.

15 다음 상황에서 Ms. Parker가 Eric에게 할 말

정답률 85%

▶ 정답 ②

M: Eric is a high school student. He's been studying hard for the
exams next week. Every day he drinks caffeinated beverages
시험들　　　　　　　　　　　　　　카페인이 함유된　　음료들
instead of water because he thinks they can help increase his
concentration. However, caffeinated drinks interfere with his sleep
집중력　　　　　　　　　　　　　　　　　　～을 방해하다
at night. One day, he finds that he can't stay awake during class.
　　　　　　　　　　　　　　　　　　　　　　깨어 있는
Eric is worried about it and he decides to ask his teacher, Ms.
Parker, for advice. Ms. Parker thinks caffeinated beverages have
more disadvantages than advantages. She recalls an article about
단점들　　　　　　장점들　　　떠올리다　　기사
how drinking water can boost concentration. It says water carries
　　　　　　　　　증진시키다　　　　　　　　운반하다
nutrients to the brain to keep it healthy. So Ms. Parker wants to
영양소들
advise Eric to consume more water to enhance his ability to focus.
　　　　　섭취하다　　　　　　　　향상시키다　　집중력
In this situation, what would Ms. Parker most likely say to Eric?
Ms. Parker: (You'd better drink more water to improve concentration.)

해석
남: Eric은 고등학생이다. 그는 다음 주 시험을 위해 열심히 공부하고 있다. 매일 그는 물 대신 카페인이 함유된 음료를 마시는데 그것들이 그의 집중력을 높이는 데 도움을 줄 수 있다고 생각하기 때문이다. 하지만, 카페인이 함유된 음료는 밤에 그의 잠을 방해한다. 어느 날, 그는 자신이 수업 중에 깨어 있을 수 없다는 것을 알게 된다. Eric은 그것에 대해 걱정하며 Parker 선생님에게 조언을 구하기로 결심한다. Parker 선생님은 카페인이 함유된 음료는 장점보다 단점이 더 많다고 생각한다. 그녀는 물을 마시는 것이 어떻게 집중력을 증진시킬 수 있는지에 대한 기사를 떠올린다. 그것에 의하면 물은 영양소를 뇌로 운반해서 그것(뇌)을 건강하게 유지시킨다. 그래서 Parker 선생님은 Eric에게 집중력을 향상시키기 위해 더 많은 물을 섭취하라고 조언하고 싶다. 이러한 상황에서, Parker 선생님은 Eric에게 뭐라고 말하겠는가?
Parker 선생님: (집중력을 향상시키기 위해 더 많은 물을 마시는 게 좋겠구나.)
① 섭취하기 전에 식품 영양 성분표를 확인해야 해.
☑집중력을 향상시키기 위해 더 많은 물을 마시는 게 좋겠구나.
③ 학생들의 걱정을 덜어 주기 위해서 명상을 활용해야 해.
④ 재활용을 위해 물병을 분리하는 게 어떠니?
⑤ 공부할 때 일정을 계획하는 게 어떠니?

16~17 1지문 2문항

W: Good afternoon, students. Previously, we learned about interesting
　　　　　　　　　　　　　　　　이전에
facilities in airports. Today, we'll talk about city airports named
시설들　　공항들　　　　　　　　　　　　　　　　　～의 이름을 따서 명명된
after world-famous figures. First, in February of 1942 during the
인물들

Second World War, Edward O'Hare was flying a fighter plane. He
전투기를 조종하고 있었다
(fly: 조종하다, fighter plane: 전투기)
fought bravely in the war, and to honor him Chicago renamed an
용감하게   경의를 표하다   개명했다(rename)
airport after him. Then there's an airport called Jomo Kenyatta
Airport in Nairobi. As one of the most important individuals in
인물들
African history, Jomo Kenyatta played a central role in fighting
중심적인 역할을 했다
(play a role: 역할을 하다, central: 중심적인)
colonization. Next, Charles de Gaulle Airport is the main airport of
식민지화
Paris, one of the busiest hubs in Europe. It's named after Charles
중심지들
de Gaulle, who was best known as a French army officer and
육군 장교
later became the president. Finally, Jorge Newbery Airport serves
대통령   ~의 역할을 하다
as the main domestic gateway in Buenos Aires. Jorge Newbery
국내 관문
was a great pioneer who made the first flight across the Andes
개척자
Mountains. Which airport's name interests you the most? Now, I'd
like you to think of other examples.

해석

여: 안녕하세요, 학생 여러분. 이전에, 우리는 공항의 흥미로운 시설들에 대해 배웠습니다. 오늘, 우리는 세계적으로 유명한 인물들의 이름을 따서 명명된 도심 공항에 대해 이야기할 것입니다. 먼저, 제2차 세계대전 중인 1942년 2월에, Edward O'Hare(에드워드 오헤어)는 전투기를 조종하고 있었습니다. 그는 전쟁에서 용감하게 싸웠고, 그에게 경의를 표하기 위해 시카고는 그의 이름을 따서 공항을 개명했습니다. 그 다음에 나이로비에 Jomo Kenyatta(조모 케냐타) 공항이라고 불리는 공항이 있습니다. 아프리카 역사에서 가장 중요한 인물 중 한 명으로서, Jomo Kenyatta는 식민지화에 맞서 싸우는 데 중심적인 역할을 했습니다. 다음으로, Charles de Gaulle(샤를르 드 골) 공항은 유럽에서 가장 분주한 중심지 중 하나인 파리의 주요 공항입니다. 그것은 Charles de Gaulle의 이름을 따서 명명되었는데, 그는 프랑스 육군 장교로 가장 잘 알려져 있고 나중에 대통령이 되었습니다. 마지막으로, Jorge Newbery(호르헤 뉴베리) 공항은 부에노스아이레스에서 주요 국내 관문의 역할을 합니다. Jorge Newbery는 안데스 산맥을 가로질러 최초의 비행을 한 위대한 개척자였습니다. 어떤 공항 이름이 가장 흥미롭습니까? 이제, 다른 예들에 대해 생각해 보기를 바랍니다.

16 여자가 하는 말의 주제   정답률 90%   ▶ 정답 ④

① 공항 시설을 편리하게 이용하는 방법
② 공항 검색대를 더 빨리 통과하는 방법들
③ 유명한 건축가들이 설계한 미래형 공항들
④ 유명한 사람들의 이름을 따서 명명된 세계의 공항들
⑤ 국내선에서 국제선으로의 공항 환승을 위한 안내

17 언급된 도시가 아닌 것   정답률 85%   ▶ 정답 ④

① 시카고   ② 나이로비   ③ 파리
④ 자카르타   ⑤ 부에노스아이레스

---

22 **2024년 3월 학력평가**

01	③	02	①	03	①	04	④	05	⑤
06	③	07	②	08	⑤	09	⑤	10	①
11	①	12	①	13	②	14	②	15	②
16	⑤	17	③						

01 남자가 하는 말의 목적   정답률 85%   ▶ 정답 ③

M: Good morning, students. This is your vice principal, Mr. Gunning.
교감
I have an announcement regarding our 'Spring Flower Photo Day'
공지 사항   ~과 관련하여   봄꽃 사진의 날
event this afternoon. As you know, we planned to take pictures
of beautiful spring flowers as we walk around our neighborhood.
돌아다니다   동네
I regret to inform you that the event is canceled due to heavy rain.
알리게 되어 유감이다   취소되다(cancel: 취소하다)
(regret to V: ~하게 되어 유감이다, inform: 알리다)
I understand you've been looking forward to it, but unfortunately
~을 기대해 왔다(look forward to)   안타깝게도
it appears we won't be able to get the best photos today. We will
얻을 수 있다(be able to V: ~할 수 있다)
reschedule the event for a sunny day in the near future. Please
일정을 다시 잡다
understand that this decision was made to ensure that the event
결정   반드시 ~하게 하다, ~을 확실하게 하다
will be a success.
성공

해석

남: 좋은 아침입니다, 학생 여러분. 저는 교감인 Gunning 선생님입니다. 오늘 오후의 'Spring Flower Photo Day(봄꽃 사진의 날)' 행사와 관련하여 공지 사항이 있습니다. 아시다시피, 우리는 동네를 돌아다니면서 아름다운 봄꽃의 사진을 찍을 계획이었습니다. 폭우 때문에 행사가 취소된 것을 알리게 되어 유감입니다. 여러분이 그것을 기대해 온 것은 이해하지만, 안타깝게도 오늘은 최고의 사진을 얻을 수 없을 것 같습니다. 가까운 미래에 화창한 날로 행사의 일정을 다시 잡을 것입니다. 이번 결정은 행사가 반드시 성공하도록 하기 위해 내려진 것임을 이해해 주기 바랍니다.

① 꽃 사진 촬영 동아리 회원을 모집하려고
② 꽃 사진 촬영 시 유의 사항을 당부하려고
③ 꽃 사진 촬영 행사가 취소됨을 공지하려고
④ 꽃 사진 촬영에 적합한 장비를 소개하려고
⑤ 꽃 사진을 촬영하기에 좋은 장소를 안내하려고

02 여자의 의견   정답률 90%   ▶ 정답 ①

W: Liam, what's that bunch of paper in your hand?
종이 묶음
M: It's a deck of flashcards for memorizing new words, but it doesn't
플래시 카드 한 벌   암기하는 것(memorize)
work well for me.
W: Really? Why not? I think flashcards are helpful for learning
도움이 되는
vocabulary.
어휘
M: I thought so, too. But looking at the word on one side of the card
and the meaning on the back is too boring.
의미   지루한
W: Hmm, how about using them in a more interesting way?
더 재미있는 방법으로
M: A more interesting way to use flashcards? What do you mean?
W: Ask a friend to read the meaning on the back, and you shout out
외치다
the word as the answer.
답으로
M: Oh, you mean like asking and answering questions in a quiz?
질문들   퀴즈
W: That's right. By using flashcards for quizzes, you can learn new
활용함으로써(by V-ing: ~함으로써)
words while having fun.
M: I like your idea a lot. I'll give it a try!
한번 시도해 보다

해석

여: Liam, 손에 들고 있는 그 종이 묶음은 뭐니?
남: 새로운 단어를 암기하기 위한 플래시 카드 한 벌인데, 내게는 별로 효과가 없어.
여: 정말? 왜? 나는 플래시 카드가 어휘 학습에 도움이 된다고 생각해.

남: 나도 그렇게 생각했어. 그런데 카드 한 쪽에 있는 단어와 뒷면에 있는 의미를 보는 것이 너무 지루해.

여: 흠, 그것들을 더 재미있는 방법으로 활용하는 게 어떠니?

남: 플래시 카드를 활용할 수 있는 더 재미있는 방법이라니? 무슨 말이야?

여: 친구에게 뒷면에 있는 의미를 읽어달라고 부탁해. 그리고 네가 답으로 그 단어를 외치는 거야.

남: 오, 퀴즈에서 질문하고 답하는 것처럼 말이니?

여: 맞아. 플래시 카드를 퀴즈에 활용함으로써, 즐거운 시간을 보내면서 새로운 단어를 익힐 수 있어.

남: 네 생각이 정말 마음에 들어. 한번 시도해 볼게!

☑️ 플래시 카드를 퀴즈에 활용하면 단어를 즐겁게 익힐 수 있다.
② 퀴즈를 내는 활동을 통해 학습자의 약점을 파악할 수 있다.
③ 단어 학습에 가장 효과적인 방법은 개인마다 차이가 있다.
④ 그림과 글이 함께 포함된 플래시 카드는 학습에 효과적이다.
⑤ 플래시 카드를 활용한 단어 학습 프로그램 개발이 필요하다.

03 남자가 하는 말의 요지

정답률 85% ▶ 정답 ①

M: Hello, everyone. I'm Charlie Goodman, your speaker today. I'll be discussing the most effective way to maintain an organized room. Let's start by reflecting on the items in your room. Do you really use everything every day? Probably not. The most important thing to do to keep a clean room is to get rid of things you no longer need. Don't keep your room filled with items untouched for more than six months. If you haven't used an item in six months, it likely means you won't use it again! If you remove unnecessary items, you can keep your room nice and neat.

해석

남: 안녕하세요, 여러분. 오늘 강연자인 Charlie Goodman입니다. 저는 정리된 방을 유지하는 가장 효과적인 방법에 대해 논의할 것입니다. 여러분의 방에 있는 물건들을 되돌아보는 것으로 시작하겠습니다. 여러분은 정말 매일 모든 것을 사용하나요? 아마도 그렇지 않을 것입니다. 깨끗한 방을 유지하기 위해 해야 할 가장 중요한 일은 더 이상 필요로 하지 않는 물건들을 없애는 것입니다. 여러분의 방을 6개월 이상 손을 대지 않은 물건들로 가득 차게 두지 마세요. 어떤 물건을 6개월 안에 사용하지 않았다면, 그것은 아마도 그 물건을 다시 사용하지 않을 것이라는 의미입니다! 불필요한 물건들을 치우면, 여러분의 방을 멋지고 깔끔하게 유지할 수 있습니다.

☑️ 깔끔한 방을 유지하기 위해 필요 없는 물건을 없애야 한다.
② 쓰레기를 버릴 때는 환경에 미칠 악영향을 고려해야 한다.
③ 공간의 기능과 종류에 따라 효과적인 정리 방법이 다르다.
④ 사용하지 않는 물건은 보관하기보다 기부하는 것이 낫다.
⑤ 상자를 이용하면 물건을 효과적으로 보관할 수 있다.

04 그림에서 대화의 내용과 일치하지 않는 것

정답률 90% ▶ 정답 ④

W: I've just finished setting up my booth to sell used items. How does it look?

M: Wow! Everything looks nice, especially the banner hanging under the roof. People can see it well.

W: I think so, too. I also hope people like this striped dress in the corner.

M: I bet they will. What about the wooden box here? Is it a used one, too?

W: Yes. To make it look better, I put some flowers in it.

M: They really catch the eye. Also, the shoes on the table look almost new.

W: I haven't worn them much because they are a bit small for me. So I've decided to sell them. The guitar beside the table is almost new, too.

M: Oh, I like it the most. I hope you can sell everything you prepared!

해석

여: 나는 방금 중고품을 판매하기 위한 부스를 설치하는 것을 끝냈어. 어때 보여?

남: 와! 모든 게 멋져 보이는데, 특히 지붕 아래에 걸려 있는 현수막이 그래. 사람들이 그것을 잘 볼 수 있어.

여: 나도 그렇게 생각해. 사람들이 구석에 있는 이 줄무늬 원피스도 마음에 들어 했으면 좋겠어.

남: 분명 그럴 거야. 여기 있는 나무 상자는 어때? 그것도 중고품이니?

여: 그래. 더 좋아 보이게 하기 위해서, 그 안에 꽃을 좀 넣었어.

남: 그것들은 정말 눈길을 끄는구나. 또한, 테이블 위에 있는 신발은 거의 새것처럼 보여.

여: 내게는 좀 작기 때문에 잘 신지 않았어. 그래서 팔기로 결정했어. 테이블 옆에 있는 기타도 거의 새것이야.

남: 오, 나는 그것이 가장 마음에 들어. 네가 준비한 것을 다 팔 수 있었으면 좋겠다!

05 여자가 남자에게 부탁한 일

정답률 80% ▶ 정답 ⑤

W: We're almost done with our report on climate change. Why don't we check it together to see if everything is okay?

M: That's a good idea. Are you sure we included every graph we made?

W: Yes, they are all there in the report. They clearly show the causes of climate change that we've researched.

M: Good to hear that. How about the pictures? We've chosen the five best pictures.

W: They look very convincing. What do you think about the part discussing the students' awareness? Many of our friends participated in our survey.

M: The survey results show that many students know how serious it is. How about the action plans?

W: We have two action plans here, but I think we need more. Could you send me the data from our research?

M: Sure. I'll send the data this afternoon.

해석

여: 우리는 기후 변화에 대한 보고서를 거의 끝냈어. 모든 것이 괜찮은지 같이 확인해 보는 게 어때?

남: 좋은 생각이야. 우리가 만든 모든 그래프를 포함시킨 게 확실하니?

여: 그래, 보고서에 모두 있어. 그것들은 우리가 조사한 기후 변화의 원인들을 명확하게 보여줘.

남: 다행이네. 사진들은 어때? 가장 좋은 사진 5장을 골랐잖아.

여: 매우 설득력이 있어 보여. 학생들의 인식에 대해 논의하는 부분은 어떻게 생각해? 많은 친구들이 설문 조사에 참여했어.

남: 설문 조사 결과는 많은 학생들이 그것이 얼마나 심각한지 알고 있다는 것을 보여줘. 실행 방안은 어때?

여: 여기에 두 가지 실행 방안이 있는데, 더 필요할 것 같아. 내게 우리의 조사에서 나온 데이터를 보내줄 수 있겠니?

남: 물론이지. 오늘 오후에 데이터를 보내줄게.

① 설문 결과 정리하기
② 원인 조사하기
③ 그래프 제작하기
④ 사진 고르기
☑️ 데이터 전송하기

06 남자가 지불할 금액

▶ 정답 ③

W: Honey, how about getting a pizza from Toby's Place for dinner?
M: Sounds great! Let's try the new delivery app that I downloaded
  배달 앱
  recently. [Pause] Hmm... How about a potato pizza?
  최근에
W: I like that idea. How much is one large potato pizza?
M: It's $25. Oh, we have to order a minimum of $30 for delivery.
  주문하다 최소, 최소한
W: Then we can add some drinks. How much is a cola?
  추가하다   음료들
M: One small can is $2, and a large one is $3.
W: Then let's order two large cans.
M: Great, one large potato pizza and two large cans of cola. Now we
  can place the order.
  주문하다
W: Is there a delivery fee?
  배달료
M: Normally we have to pay $5, but it's free now because of the app
  보통   무료의
  promotion. So I'll pay using the app.
  판촉 행사
W: Thank you. I'm starving. I hope it gets here quickly.
  몹시 배고픈   빨리

해석
여: 여보, 저녁 식사로 Toby's Place에서 피자를 사 먹는 게 어때요?
남: 좋아요! 제가 최근에 다운로드한 새로운 배달 앱을 사용해 봐요. [잠시 후] 흠... 감자 피자
  는 어때요?
여: 좋은 생각이에요. 감자 피자 라지 사이즈 한 판에 얼마죠?
남: 25달러예요. 오, 배달을 위해 최소 30달러를 주문해야 해요.
여: 그럼 음료를 좀 추가하면 돼요. 콜라는 얼마죠?
남: 작은 캔 한 개는 2달러이고, 큰 캔 한 개는 3달러예요.
여: 그럼 큰 캔 두 개를 주문해요.
남: 좋아요, 감자 피자 라지 사이즈 한 판과 콜라 큰 캔 두 개네요. 이제 주문할 수 있어요.
여: 배달료가 있나요?
남: 보통 5달러를 지불해야 하는데, 앱 판촉 행사 때문에 지금은 무료네요. 그럼 앱을 사용해
  서 결제할게요.
여: 고마워요. 배가 무척 고프네요. 빨리 왔으면 좋겠어요.

① $25   ② $29   ✓ $31
④ $34   ⑤ $36

문제 풀이
25달러인 라지 사이즈 감자 피자 한 판과 한 캔에 3달러인 콜라 큰 캔 두 개를 주문하면 총액
은 31달러이다. 원래 5달러인 배달료는 앱 판촉 행사로 인해 지불하지 않아도 된다. 따라서
답은 ③ '$31'이다.

07 여자가 공연 동영상 파일을 보내줄 수 없는 이유

▶ 정답 ②

M: Hi, Kathy. How was your drama club's performance last week?
                                       공연
W: It was a huge success. Everyone liked it.
       대성공
M: Good to hear that. Then, can I include your performance video in
                                포함시키다   동영상
  our school promotion video? Did anyone record it?
         홍보   촬영하다
W: Yes, Mark recorded it.
M: Great! Could you send me the video file then?
                              파일
W: Sorry, I can't send it to you now.
M: Why not? Is it because you don't have the video file?
W: No, that's not it. Mark sent me the file yesterday.
M: Then, you don't want to be on the promotion video?
W: I'm okay with it. The problem is, without the club members'
                        문제
  approval, I cannot send the file to anyone outside the club.
  동의   ~의 밖에
M: Oh, I see. Can you ask your club members about it?
W: Sure. Once they say it's fine, I'll let you know.
      일단 ~하면

해석
남: 안녕, Kathy. 지난주에 있었던 연극 동아리의 공연은 어땠니?
여: 대성공이었어. 모든 사람들이 좋아했어.
남: 다행이네. 그럼, 우리 학교 홍보 동영상에 너희 공연 동영상을 포함시켜도 될까? 누군가
  그것을 촬영했니?
여: 응, Mark가 그것을 촬영했어.

남: 잘됐다! 그럼 동영상 파일을 내게 보내줄 수 있어?
여: 미안해, 지금은 보내줄 수 없어.
남: 왜 안 돼? 동영상 파일을 갖고 있지 않아서 그래?
여: 아니, 그런 거 아니야. Mark가 어제 나에게 파일을 보내줬어.
남: 그럼, 홍보 동영상에 나오고 싶지 않은 거야?
여: 그것은 괜찮아. 문제는, 동아리 부원들의 동의가 없으면, 동아리 밖에 있는 사람에게 파일
  을 보낼 수 없다는 거야.
남: 오, 그렇구나. 그것에 대해 동아리 부원들에게 물어봐 줄 수 있어?
여: 물론이지. 일단 그들이 괜찮다고 하면, 네게 알려 줄게.

① 동영상을 촬영하지 않아서
✓ 부원들의 동의를 구해야 해서
③ 동영상 파일을 갖고 있지 않아서
④ 공연을 성공적으로 마치지 못해서
⑤ 학교 홍보 영상에 나오고 싶지 않아서

문제 풀이
연극 공연 동영상 파일을 보내달라는 남자의 부탁에 여자는 동아리의 부원들이 동의하지 않
으면 공연 동영상을 외부 사람에게 보내줄 수 없다고 말한다. 따라서 답은 ② '부원들의 동의
를 구해야 해서'이다.

08 학급 캠핑에 관해 언급되지 않은 것

▶ 정답 ⑤

[Telephone rings.]
W: Green Forest camping site. How can I help you?
                   캠핑장
M: Hi, this is Daniel Baker, a teacher from Simon High School.
  I'm organizing a class camping trip for 25 students. Do you have a
  준비하고 있다(organize)
  camping site available?
            이용 가능한
W: Certainly, when do you plan on camping?
                      캠핑을 할 계획이다(plan on: ~할 계획이다)
M: From April 13th to 14th.
W: Let me see. [Typing] We have spots available for your students on
                            자리들
  that day. Do you want to reserve them now?
                     예약하다
M: Yes, please. Do you provide a tent rental service as well?
                              텐트 대여 서비스
W: Absolutely. We offer tents that are big enough for six people. We
                  제공하다   충분히
  also have sleeping bags for rent.
          침낭들
M: Sounds good. I'll rent five tents and 25 sleeping bags.
W: Alright, the total cost would be $90. You can pay it in advance or
             총 비용   미리
  onsite.
  현장에서
M: I'll pay onsite. Thanks, and see you then.

해석
[전화벨이 울린다.]
여: Green Forest 캠핑장입니다. 어떻게 도와드릴까요?
남: 안녕하세요, 저는 Simon 고등학교 교사인 Daniel Baker입니다. 제가 25명의 학생들을 위
  한 학급 캠핑 여행을 준비하고 있어요. 이용 가능한 캠핑장이 있나요?
여: 물론이죠, 언제 캠핑을 하실 계획인가요?
남: 4월 13일부터 14일까지입니다.
여: 제가 한번 볼게요. [타자 치는 소리] 그날 학생들이 이용 가능한 자리가 있네요. 지금 예약
  하시겠어요?
남: 네, 부탁드려요. 텐트 대여 서비스도 제공하시나요?
여: 물론이죠. 6명이 사용하기에 충분히 큰 텐트를 제공해요. 또한 대여용 침낭도 있습니다.
남: 좋네요. 텐트 5개와 침낭 25개를 빌릴게요.
여: 네, 총 비용은 90달러예요. 미리 결제하시거나 현장에서 결제하실 수 있어요.
남: 현장에서 결제할게요. 감사해요, 그때 뵐게요.

① 참여 학생 수   ② 날짜   ③ 대여 물품
④ 비용   ✓ 도착 시간

09 2024 AI Expo에 관한 내용과 일치하지 않는 것

▶ 정답 ⑤

W: Hello, listeners! Let's dive into the world of Artificial Intelligence at
                        ~로 뛰어들다   인공지능
  the 2024 AI Expo. It will be held on May 27th and 28th at the city
        박람회   열리다(hold: 열다, 개최하다)
  convention center. This year's theme is the use of AI in schools.
                            주제

From language learning to physical training, AI is widely used in
schools. For just $20, you can experience new AI technologies that
have been adopted in more than 50 countries. Come and see the
future of AI! And here's the best part. You can get a special portrait
drawn by AI used in art classes. If you purchase the admission
ticket on our website, you will get a 10% discount. Don't miss this
chance to have an unforgettable AI experience!

해석

여: 안녕하세요, 청취자 여러분! 2024 AI Expo(2024 AI 박람회)에서 인공지능의 세계로 뛰
어들어 봅시다. 그것은 5월 27일과 28일에 시 컨벤션 센터에서 열릴 것입니다. 올해의 주
제는 학교에서의 AI 활용입니다. 언어 학습에서 체력 단련까지, AI는 학교에서 널리 이용
됩니다. 단돈 20달러로, 여러분은 50개가 넘는 국가에서 채택된 새로운 AI 기술을 경험할
수 있습니다. 오셔서 AI의 미래를 보세요! 그리고 여기 최고의 부분이 있습니다. 여러분은
미술 수업에서 사용되는 AI에 의해 그려진 특별한 초상화를 받을 수 있습니다. 저희 웹사
이트에서 입장권을 구입하면, 10% 할인을 받을 것입니다. 잊을 수 없는 AI 경험을 할 이
기회를 놓치지 마세요!

① 5월 27일과 28일에 진행된다.
② 올해의 주제는 학교에서의 AI 활용이다.
③ 50개가 넘는 국가에서 채택된 AI 기술을 경험할 수 있다.
④ AI가 그려 주는 초상화를 받을 수 있다.
☑ 웹사이트에서 20% 할인된 가격에 입장권을 구입할 수 있다.

10 표에서 두 사람이 구매할 사진첩

정답률 85% ▶ 정답 ①

W: Dad, I found a website that provides a service to make photo
albums. How about creating one with the photos from our winter
holiday?
M: Great! Let me see. *[Pause]* Oh, it says all we need to do is choose a
few options and upload our photos.
W: Right. First, let's choose the cover material.
M: Umm... Leather might be too heavy.
W: You're right. Let's choose either paper or fabric.
M: Okay. For the number of pages, is 40 too many?
W: Yes. Let's just go for 20 or 30 pages. What color would be good for
the cover?
M: I want it to reflect our winter holiday. How about white?
W: Perfect. That leaves us with two options.
M: Then, let's choose the cheaper one.
W: Sounds great. I'll choose the best pictures and upload them.

해석

여: 아빠, 제가 사진첩 만드는 서비스를 제공하는 웹사이트를 찾았어요. 겨울 휴가 때 찍은 사
진들로 사진첩을 만드는 게 어떠세요?
남: 좋아! 어디 보자. *[잠시 후]* 오, 우리가 해야 할 일은 몇 가지 옵션을 선택해서 사진을 업로
드하는 것이 전부라고 되어 있구나.
여: 네, 우선, 표지 소재를 선택해요.
남: 음... 가죽은 너무 무거울 수도 있어.
여: 맞아요. 종이나 직물 둘 중 하나를 선택해요.
남: 알겠어. 페이지 수에 관해서는, 40 페이지는 너무 많니?
여: 네. 그냥 20 페이지나 30 페이지로 해요. 표지에 어떤 색상이 좋을까요?
남: 나는 그것이 우리의 겨울 휴가를 반영하기를 원해. 흰색은 어떠니?
여: 완벽해요. 그것은 우리에게 두 가지 선택지를 남겨요.
남: 그럼, 더 저렴한 것을 선택하자.
여: 좋은 것 같아요. 제가 가장 좋은 사진들을 골라서 업로드할게요.

사진첩

	모델	표지 소재	페이지	표지 색상	가격
☑	A	종이	20	흰색	16달러
②	B	종이	30	파란색	19달러
③	C	직물	30	흰색	22달러
④	D	직물	40	파란색	25달러
⑤	E	가죽	40	갈색	30달러

11 여자의 마지막 말에 대한 남자의 응답

정답률 85% ▶ 정답 ①

W: How was your weekend? Did you do anything special?
M: Yes, my older brother and I visited my grandparents who live on a
small island. We had a great time doing lots of outdoor activities
together.
W: That sounds lovely! What activity did you like the most there?
M: (Fishing on the boat was the best for me.)

해석

여: 주말은 어땠어? 어떤 특별한 것을 했니?
남: 그래, 형과 나는 작은 섬에 사시는 조부모님을 방문했어. 우리는 많은 야외 활동을 함께 하
면서 즐거운 시간을 보냈어.
여: 멋지구나! 그곳에서 어떤 활동이 가장 좋았니?
남: (나는 배에서 낚시하는 것이 가장 좋았어.)

☑ 나는 배에서 낚시하는 것이 가장 좋았어.
② 지난 주말에 조부모님께서 우리를 방문하셨어.
③ 네가 즐거운 시간을 보냈다니 정말 기뻐.
④ 섬까지 가는 데 너무 오래 걸렸어.
⑤ 일부 활동들은 취소되었어.

12 남자의 마지막 말에 대한 여자의 응답

정답률 85% ▶ 정답 ①

M: Hey, Jessica. Have you bought a birthday present for Olivia yet? Her
birthday is coming up soon.
W: Oh, not yet. I'm struggling to think of something good for her. What
do you think she'll like?
M: I heard her favorite writer published a new book recently. How
about buying the book as her birthday present?
W: (Good idea. I'll go to the bookstore tomorrow.)

해석

남: 안녕, Jessica. Olivia에게 줄 생일 선물을 이미 샀니? 그녀의 생일이 곧 다가오잖아.
여: 오, 아직이야. 그녀에게 좋은 것을 생각해 내려고 애쓰고 있어. 그녀가 무엇을 좋아할 것
같아?
남: 그녀가 가장 좋아하는 작가가 최근에 신간을 출간했다고 들었어. 그녀의 생일 선물로 그
책을 사는 게 어떠니?
여: (좋은 생각이야. 나는 내일 서점에 가야겠어.)

☑ 좋은 생각이야. 나는 내일 서점에 가야겠어.
② 미안하지만, 나는 그 책을 다 읽지 못했어.
③ 괜찮아. 나는 이미 도서관에 그 책을 반납했어.
④ 전혀 아니야. 나는 그녀의 생일 파티에 갈 수 있을 거야.
⑤ 고마워. 나는 항상 직접 책을 쓰고 싶었어.

13 여자의 마지막 말에 대한 남자의 응답

정답률 85% ▶ 정답 ②

M: Hello, welcome to Glow Cosmetics Shop. How can I help you?
W: Hi, I'm looking for sunscreen.
M: Certainly. Is it for you, or someone else?
W: It's for my husband. He asked me to buy one for him.
M: Okay, does your husband spend much time outdoors, playing
sports, or working outside?
W: No, not really. He works in an office and usually stays at home
after work.
M: In that case, he might not need one with strong sun protection. A

mild one is probably best for him.
    순한
W: Okay. I'll go with that.
      ~을 선택하다
M: We have two types of sunscreen, spray and cream type. Which one
   would he prefer?
W: I'm not sure but I guess he is used to cream type.
                        ~에 익숙하다(be used to)
M: (I see. Then this one is a perfect choice for him.)

해석

남: 안녕하세요, Glow Cosmetics Shop(Glow 화장품 가게)에 오신 것을 환영합니다. 어떻
   게 도와드릴까요?
여: 안녕하세요, 저는 자외선 차단제를 찾고 있어요.
남: 네, 고객님을 위한 건가요, 아니면 다른 분을 위한 건가요?
여: 남편을 위한 거예요. 제게 하나 사달라고 부탁했거든요.
남: 남편분께서는 운동을 하거나 밖에서 일을 하면서 야외에서 많은 시간을 보내시나요?
여: 아니요, 별로 그렇지 않아요. 그는 사무실에서 일을 하고 보통 퇴근 후에 집에 머물러요.
남: 그런 경우에는, 강한 자외선 차단 기능이 있는 제품은 필요하지 않을 수 있어요. 아마 순한
   제품이 가장 좋을 거예요.
여: 알겠어요. 그것을 선택할게요.
남: 스프레이 타입과 크림 타입의 두 가지 자외선 차단제가 있어요. 남편분께서 어떤 것을 선
   호하실까요?
여: 잘 모르겠지만 크림 타입에 익숙한 것 같아요.
남: (그렇군요. 그럼 이 제품이 남편분께 완벽한 선택이네요.)

① 걱정하지 마세요. 신용카드로 결제하실 수 있어요.
✓ 그렇군요. 그럼 이 제품이 남편분께 완벽한 선택이네요.
③ 괜찮을 거예요. 남편분께서 잠깐 들러서 그것을 가져가실 수 있어요.
④ 정말이에요? 외출하시기 전에 자외선 차단제를 바르시는 게 좋아요.
⑤ 맞아요. 강한 자외선 차단 기능이 있는 제품이 더 좋아요.

문제 풀이

제품을 추천하기 위해 남자가 선호하는 자외선 차단제의 타입을 묻는 남자에게 여자는 남편
이 크림 타입에 익숙할 것이라고 말한다. 이에 대한 남자의 응답으로는 ② 'I see. Then this
one is a perfect choice for him.(그렇군요. 그럼 이 제품이 남편분께 완벽한 선택이네요.)'
이 가장 적절하다.

---

14 남자의 마지막 말에 대한 여자의 응답

정답률 70%
▶ 정답 ②

M: Ms. Williams! Do you have a minute?
W: Sure. What is it?
M: I have to write an essay to get a scholarship, but I don't know what
           에세이를 쓰다   장학금을 받다
   to write about.
W: Maybe you can start by expressing your passion for learning and
                                            열정
   school life.
M: I already wrote about that, but it doesn't seem good enough.
W: Umm... How about mentioning a weakness you've worked on?
                                   약점
M: Weakness? Wouldn't that be a bad idea for an essay?
W: Not necessarily. If you describe how you've been trying to deal with
                        설명하다   ~에 대처하다
   it, your story will show your potential.
                                 잠재력
M: Well, I used to put my work off until the last minute. But by using a
          내 일을 미루곤 했다
        (used to V: ~하곤 했다, put A off: A를 미루다)
   planner, I make my schedule on an hourly basis. Now I no longer
     계획표   한 시간 단위로
   have any trouble finishing my work on time.
      끝내는 데 어떤 어려움을 겪다
      (have trouble V-ing: ~하는 데 어려움을 겪다)
W: That's perfect! That will be a great story to include in your essay for
   the scholarship.
M: Thank you for your help! That actually makes me feel a lot more
   confident.   훨씬 더 자신감을 갖는
W: (Good luck. Show them who you are, and you'll make it.)

해석

남: Williams 선생님! 잠시 시간 있으세요?
여: 물론이지. 무슨 일이니?
남: 장학금을 받으려면 에세이를 써야 하는데, 무엇에 대해 써야 할지 모르겠어요.
여: 아마 배움과 학교 생활에 대한 너의 열정을 표현하는 것으로 시작할 수 있을 거야.
남: 그것에 대해서 이미 썼는데, 만족스러운 것 같지 않아요.

여: 음... 네가 (개선하기 위해) 노력해 온 약점을 언급하는 것은 어떠니?
남: 약점이요? 에세이에 쓰기에 좋지 않은 생각이 아닐까요?
여: 꼭 그렇지는 않아. 네가 어떻게 그것에 대처하려고 노력해 왔는지를 설명한다면, 너의 이
   야기는 너의 잠재력을 보여줄 거야.
남: 음, 저는 마지막 순간까지 제 일을 미루곤 했어요. 하지만 계획표를 사용해서, 한 시간 단
   위로 일정을 잡아요. 이제는 더 이상 제시간에 일을 끝내는 데 어떤 어려움도 겪지 않아요.
여: 완벽하구나! 그것은 장학금을 위한 에세이에 포함시키기에 좋은 이야기가 될 거야.
남: 도와주셔서 감사해요! 실제로 저는 훨씬 더 자신감을 갖게 되었어요.
여: (행운을 빌어. 네가 누구인지 보여주면, 너는 성공할 거야.)

① 맞아. 가능하다면 약점은 감추는 것이 더 좋아.
✓ 행운을 빌어. 네가 누구인지 보여주면, 너는 성공할 거야.
③ 물론이지. 너는 숙제를 효과적으로 처리할 수 있어.
④ 동의해. 너는 계획표를 사용해서 일정을 잡을 수 있어.
⑤ 조심해! 약점은 네가 성장하지 못하게 해.

---

15 다음 상황에서 Lucy가 James에게 할 말

정답률 85%
▶ 정답 ②

W: Lucy is the head of her school's student council. She is concerned
               회장   학생회
   about the lack of proper recycling practices among students.
          부족   재활용 실천
   She notices that many students are not aware of the problem. To
        알아차리다   ~을 인식하는
   address this issue, she decides to create posters to emphasize
     처리하다   강조하다
   the importance of recycling. However, she lacks confidence in her
                                               자신감
   drawing skills. Lucy wants to seek help from her friend James, as
   그림 실력   ~에게 도움을 청하다
   he is talented in art and passionate about the environment. Lucy
           재능이 있는   열정적인   환경
   thinks collaborating with him will result in effective poster designs.
         협력하는 것(collaborate)   효과적인
   So, she wants to suggest to James that they work together on the
   recycling posters. In this situation, what would Lucy most likely say
   to James?
Lucy: (How about making posters with me about recycling?)

해석

여: Lucy는 학교 학생회의 회장이다. 그녀는 학생들 사이에 적절한 재활용 실천의 부족에 대
   해 걱정한다. 그녀는 많은 학생들이 그 문제를 인식하지 못한다는 것을 알아차린다. 이 문
   제를 처리하기 위해, 그녀는 재활용의 중요성을 강조하는 포스터를 만들기로 결정한다.
   하지만, 그녀는 자신의 그림 실력에 자신감이 부족하다. Lucy는 그녀의 친구인 James에
   게 도움을 청하고 싶어 하는데, 그가 미술에 재능이 있고 환경에 관해 열정적이기 때문이
   다. Lucy는 그와 협력하는 것은 효과적인 포스터 디자인이라는 결과로 이어질 것이라고
   생각한다. 그래서, 그녀는 James에게 재활용 포스터를 함께 작업하자고 제안하고 싶다.
   이러한 상황에서, Lucy는 James에게 뭐라고 말하겠는가?
Lucy: (재활용에 관한 포스터를 나와 함께 만드는 게 어떠니?)

① 우리 플라스틱 사용을 금지하는 캠페인을 시작하는 게 어때?
✓ 재활용에 관한 포스터를 나와 함께 만드는 게 어떠니?
③ 학생회 회의를 준비해 주겠니?
④ 나는 학교 예술제에 대한 네 의견을 듣고 싶어.
⑤ 적절하게 재활용하는 방법을 알려줄게.

16~17 1지문 2문항

M: Hello, students. Today, I'd like to talk about four great inventions
                                                      발명품들
   in history. Throughout history, humans have invented things
   that have transformed how we live. One of the most important
         변화시켰다(transform)
   inventions is the wheel. This simple yet powerful invention
                      바퀴
   revolutionized transportation. The wheel made it possible to
   대변혁을 일으켰다   운송
   travel far and wide, trade goods, and explore new lands. Another
   이동하다 널리   거래하다   탐험하다
   important invention is the printing press, which enabled books
                            인쇄기
   to be printed much faster. This change affected how knowledge
   책들이 인쇄될 수 있게 했다   영향을 미쳤다
   (enable A to V: A가 ~할 수 있게 하다, print: 인쇄하다)
   and education spread. Next is the light bulb. It lengthened our
                  전파되었다(spread)   전구   늘렸다

days, allowing for nighttime activities and opened the door to
many other modern technologies. The last invention I'd like to
mention is the telephone. With the telephone, people could
speak to each other instantly regardless of distance. As a result
of this transformation, people are connected as never before,
in business and social life. These are just a few examples of the
many inventions that have changed the course of human history.

해석

남: 안녕하세요, 학생 여러분. 오늘, 저는 역사상 위대한 네 가지 발명품에 대해 이야기하고자 합니다. 역사를 통틀어, 인류는 우리가 사는 방식을 변화시킨 것들을 발명해 왔습니다. 가장 중요한 발명품 중 하나가 바퀴입니다. 이 단순하지만 강력한 발명품은 운송에 대변혁을 일으켰습니다. 바퀴는 널리 이동하고, 상품을 거래하고, 새로운 땅을 탐험하는 것을 가능하게 만들었습니다. 또 다른 중요한 발명품은 인쇄기인데, 이것은 책들이 훨씬 더 빨리 인쇄될 수 있게 했습니다. 이러한 변화는 지식과 교육이 전파되는 방식에 영향을 미쳤습니다. 다음은 전구입니다. 그것은 우리의 낮 시간을 늘려서, 야간 활동을 할 수 있게 하고 다른 많은 현대 기술로 나아가는 문을 열어주었습니다. 마지막으로 언급하고 싶은 발명품은 전화기입니다. 전화기를 통해, 사람들은 거리에 상관없이 즉시 서로 이야기할 수 있었습니다. 이러한 변화의 결과로서, 사람들은 사업 및 사회 생활에서 전에 없이 연결되어 있습니다. 이것들은 인류 역사의 방향을 바꾼 많은 발명품의 단지 몇 가지 예일 뿐입니다.

16 남자가 하는 말의 주제 · 정답률 85% · ▶ 정답 ⑤

① 발명품에 영감을 준 역사적 사건들
② 어떻게 발명품이 예기치 않게 만들어지는가
③ 과학적 발명품 뒤에 숨겨진 이야기들
④ 문화적 정체성에 기반을 둔 독특한 발명품들
☑ 인류의 삶과 역사에 영향을 준 발명품들

17 언급된 발명품이 아닌 것 · 정답률 90% · ▶ 정답 ③

① 바퀴   ② 인쇄기   ☑ 증기 기관
④ 전구   ⑤ 전화기

---

23 2024년 6월 학력평가

01	④	02	①	03	①	04	⑤	05	④
06	①	07	③	08	③	09	⑤	10	①
11	④	12	⑤	13	②	14	④	15	⑤
16	②	17	③						

01 여자가 하는 말의 목적 · 정답률 85% · ▶ 정답 ④

W: Good morning, employees of ABC Company. I'm Tina White, a
senior manager. I've noticed that many of you have been
experiencing difficulties at work and are under a lot of stress these
days. Your well-being is important to us. Therefore, the company is
offering a counseling program during lunchtime every day starting
next week. Special counselors have been invited to help you deal
with your stress. I'm confident that our counseling program will
help you feel happier at work. If you are interested in this program,
please register for a session. I'm sure it'll be worth your time.

해석

여: 좋은 아침입니다, ABC Company의 직원 여러분. 저는 선임 관리자인 Tina White입니다. 저는 여러분 중 많은 분들이 요즘 직장에서 어려움을 겪고 있고 많은 스트레스를 받고 있다는 것을 알게 되었습니다. 여러분의 안녕은 저희에게 중요합니다. 그래서, 회사는 다음 주부터 매일 점심 시간에 상담 프로그램을 제공할 예정입니다. 여러분이 스트레스를 다루는 데 도움을 주기 위해 특별 상담 전문가들이 초청되었습니다. 저는 상담 프로그램이 여러분이 직장에서 더 행복하게 느끼도록 도와줄 것이라고 확신합니다. 이 프로그램에 관심이 있다면, (상담) 시간에 등록하십시오. 저는 그것이 여러분의 시간을 할애할 가치가 있을 것이라고 확신합니다.

① 휴식의 중요성을 강조하려고
② 직업 상담 전문가를 모집하려고
③ 스트레스 받는 이유를 설명하려고
☑ 회사의 상담 프로그램을 홍보하려고
⑤ 상담 프로그램의 일정 변경을 공지하려고

02 남자의 의견 · 정답률 85% · ▶ 정답 ①

M: Jane, are you feeling okay?
W: Well, I exercised at the gym and my muscles are hurting a bit now,
Dad.
M: Did you stretch after exercising?
W: No. I only stretched before.
M: Oh. You should definitely stretch after you finish exercising.
W: Really? I thought stretching after working out would put more
pressure on my muscles.
M: That's not true. Stretching afterward helps to loosen your tight
muscles and reduce injuries.
W: That makes sense. Are there any other benefits?
M: Absolutely. It allows both your body and mind to slow down and
helps you feel relaxed.
W: All right. I'll give it a try. Thanks for your tip, Dad.

해석

남: Jane, 몸은 괜찮니?
여: 음, 체육관에서 운동을 했는데 지금 근육이 조금 아파요, 아빠.
남: 운동을 한 후에 스트레칭을 했니?
여: 아니요. 운동을 하기 전에만 스트레칭을 했어요.
남: 오. 운동을 마친 후에 반드시 스트레칭을 해야 해.
여: 정말이요? 저는 운동을 한 후에 스트레칭을 하는 것이 근육에 더 많은 압박을 가할 것이라고 생각했어요.
남: 그렇지 않아. (운동을 한) 이후 스트레칭을 하는 것은 경직된 근육을 풀어 주고 부상을 줄이는 데 도움이 된단다.
여: 일리가 있네요. 다른 이점들도 있나요?
남: 물론이지. 그것은 너의 몸과 마음이 모두 느긋해지게 해 주고 편안한 기분이 들도록 도와줘.
여: 알겠어요. 한번 해 볼게요. 조언 감사해요, 아빠.

☑ 운동을 마친 후 스트레칭을 하는 것이 필요하다.
② 천천히 걷는 것은 근육통 완화에 도움이 된다.
③ 과도한 스트레칭은 부상을 유발할 수 있다.
④ 자신의 몸에 맞는 식단을 구성하는 것이 중요하다.
⑤ 몸과 마음의 건강을 위해 규칙적인 운동을 해야 한다.

03 여자가 하는 말의 요지 · 정답률 90% · ▶ 정답 ①

W: Good afternoon, listeners! Do you have a hard time figuring out
your emotions? Have you suddenly gotten really angry but
didn't know exactly what made you feel that way? If so, keeping
an emotion diary can be a powerful tool for understanding your
feelings. In an emotion diary, you write down in detail how you feel

in each situation. This will give you an <u>opportunity</u> to understand
　　　　　　　　　　　　　　　　　　　　기회
why you're feeling a <u>certain</u> way. Writing an emotion diary won't be
　　　　　　　　特정한
easy <u>at first</u>, but you'll soon <u>get used to</u> it. After the break, I'll tell
　　　　처음에는　　　　　　～에 익숙해지다
you how to keep an emotion diary <u>effectively</u>. Stay tuned!
　　　　　　　　　　　　　　　효과적으로

해석

여: 좋은 오후입니다, 청취자 여러분! 여러분은 자신의 감정을 이해하는 데 어려움을 겪습니
까? 갑자기 정말 화가 났지만 무엇이 여러분을 그렇게 느끼게 했는지 정확히 알지 못한 적
이 있습니까? 그렇다면, 감정 일기를 쓰는 것이 여러분의 감정을 이해하기 위한 강력한
도구가 될 수 있습니다. 감정 일기에는, 각각의 상황에서 여러분이 어떻게 느끼는지 자세
하게 씁니다. 이것은 여러분이 왜 특정한 방식으로 느끼는지를 이해하는 기회를 줄 것입
니다. 감정 일기를 쓰는 것이 처음에는 쉽지 않겠지만, 곧 그것에 익숙해질 것입니다. 광
고 후에, 감정 일기를 효과적으로 쓰는 방법을 알려드리겠습니다. 채널을 고정해 주세요!

✔️ 감정 일기 쓰기는 자신의 감정을 이해하는 데 도움이 된다.
② 자신의 감정을 절제하며 의견을 전달하는 것이 필요하다.
③ 타인과의 유대감은 감정 일기의 공유를 통해 증진된다.
④ 일기 쓰기는 규칙적인 생활 습관 형성에 효과적이다.
⑤ 가족과의 대화로 부정적인 감정을 해소할 수 있다.

문제 풀이

여자는 자신이 느끼는 감정에 대해 정확히 알지 못해서 힘든 시간을 보내는 사람들에게 감
정 일기를 쓰는 것이 감정 이해를 위한 강력한 도구가 될 수 있다고 말한다. 따라서 여자가 하
는 말의 요지로 가장 적절한 것은 ① '감정 일기 쓰기는 자신의 감정을 이해하는 데 도움이 된
다.'이다.

04　그림에서 대화의 내용과 일치하지 않는 것

정답률 80%　▶ 정답 ⑤

M: Hi, Julia. You were <u>amazing</u> in the <u>play</u> yesterday.
　　　　　　　　　　　놀라운　　　　연극
W: Thanks, Mason! Here's a picture from the <u>dressing room</u> after the
　　　　　　　　　　　　　　　　　　　　　　　분장실
play. Do you want to take a look?
M: Sure. [Pause] I see you're <u>holding</u> the flowers I gave you.
　　　　　　　　　　　　　들고 있다(hold)
W: They're so beautiful. Thanks again.
M: My pleasure. What are those two <u>boxes</u> on the <u>floor</u>?
　　　　　　　　　　　　　　　　상자들　　　　바닥
W: I <u>stored</u> some <u>items</u> for the play in them. I needed many items
　　보관했다　　　소품들
because I played <u>both a prisoner and the queen</u>.
　　　　　　　　　　죄수와 여왕 둘 다
　　　　　　(both A and B: A와 B 둘 다, prisoner: 죄수, queen: 여왕)
M: You wore that <u>striped T-shirt</u> on the <u>hanger</u> as a prisoner, right?
　　　　　　　　줄무늬 티셔츠　　　　옷걸이
W: Yes. Do you remember that <u>crown</u> on the table?
　　　　　　　　　　　　　　　왕관
M: I remember! You wore that as the queen. Wasn't it <u>difficult</u> to
　　　　　　　　　　　　　　　　　　　　　　　　　　　　어려운
change your <u>costume</u> during the play?
　　　　　　의상
W: Not really. But it was <u>hard</u> to see my <u>entire</u> <u>outfit</u> in that
　　　　　　　　　　　　힘든　　　　　　전체의　　옷
<u>star-shaped</u> <u>mirror</u> on the wall.
별 모양의　거울
M: I understand. Anyway, you did a great job.

해석

남: 안녕, Julia. 너는 어제 연극에서 놀라웠어.
여: 고마워, Mason! 여기 연극이 끝난 후에 분장실에서 찍은 사진이 있어. 한 번 볼래?
남: 물론이지. [잠시 후] 네가 내가 준 꽃을 들고 있는 게 보이네.
여: 그건 정말 아름다워. 다시 한 번 고마워.
남: 천만에. 바닥에 있는 저 두 개의 상자는 뭐야?
여: 연극을 위한 몇 가지 소품들을 그 안에 보관했어. 나는 죄수와 여왕 둘 다를 연기했기 때문
　에 많은 소품들이 필요했거든.
남: 죄수일 때 옷걸이에 걸린 저 줄무늬 티셔츠를 입었었지, 그렇지?
여: 응. 테이블 위에 있는 저 왕관 기억나니?
남: 기억나! 여왕일 때 그것을 썼잖아. 연극 중에 의상을 갈아입는 게 어렵지 않았니?
여: 별로 그렇지 않았어. 하지만 벽에 있는 저 별 모양의 거울로 옷 전체를 보기가 힘들었어.
남: 이해해. 어쨌든, 정말 잘했어.

05　남자가 할 일

정답률 90%　▶ 정답 ④

W: Honey, Mr. and Mrs. Brown are visiting today! What time <u>are they</u>
<u>supposed to come</u>?
그들이 오기로 되어 있다
(be supposed to V: ~하기로 되어 있다)
M: At seven o'clock. We haven't seen them <u>for a long time</u>. I'm so
　　　　　　　　　　　　　　　　　　　오랫동안
excited.
W: Me, too. Let's <u>check</u> if everything is <u>ready</u>.
　　　　　　확인하다　　　　　　　준비가 된
M: I'm <u>done cooking</u> tonight's dinner.
　　요리하는 것을 끝내다
　(be done V-ing: ~하는 것을 끝내다, cook: 요리하다)
W: Thanks for doing that. By the way, do we have <u>extra plates</u>?
　　　　　　　　　　　　　　　　　　　　　　　여분의 접시들
M: Yes, I already checked. There are <u>plenty</u>. Should we <u>prepare</u> some
　　　　　　　　　　　　　　　　　충분한 양　　　　　준비하다
<u>wine</u>?
와인
W: No, they told me they're bringing some. Did we get something for
<u>dessert</u>?
후식
M: Oh, I forgot. <u>I'll go buy a cake</u>.
　　　　　　　케이크를 사러 가다
W: Then I'll go to the <u>airport</u> to <u>pick them up</u>.
　　　　　　　　　공항　　　　　그들을 데리러 가다
M: Perfect. Thank you.

해석

여: 여보, Brown 씨 부부가 오늘 방문하잖아요! 그들은 몇 시에 오기로 되어 있어요?
남: 7시에 올 거예요. 우리는 그들을 오랫동안 보지 못했어요. 너무 기대되네요.
여: 저도 그래요. 우리 모든 것이 준비가 되었는지 확인해 봐요.
남: 저는 오늘 저녁 식사를 요리하는 것을 끝냈어요.
여: 그 일을 해 줘서 고마워요. 그런데, 우리에게 여분의 접시가 있나요?
남: 네, 이미 확인했어요. 충분한 양이 있어요. 우리가 와인을 좀 준비해야 할까요?
여: 아니요, 그들이 가져온다고 했어요. 후식으로 뭐 좀 샀어요?
남: 오, 잊어버렸네요. 제가 케이크를 사러 갈게요.
여: 그럼 제가 공항에 그들을 데리러 갈게요.
남: 완벽하네요. 고마워요.

① 저녁 식사 요리하기
② 여분 접시 확인하기
③ 와인 준비하기
✔️ 케이크 사러 가기
⑤ 공항에 마중 나가기

06　여자가 지불할 금액

정답률 65%　▶ 정답 ①

M: Welcome to the <u>World History Museum</u>. How may I help you?
　　　　　　　　　세계 역사 박물관
W: Hi, I'd like to <u>purchase</u> three <u>admission tickets</u>. What's the <u>fee</u> for
　　　　　　　　구매하다　　　　　　입장권들　　　　　　　　요금
an <u>adult</u>?
성인
M: An adult ticket is $10.
W: What about for <u>seniors</u>?
　　　　　　　어르신들, 노인들
M: If you look at the <u>price board</u>, people over 65 years of age <u>are</u>
　　　　　　　　　　　가격 게시판
<u>charged</u> $8.
부과되다(charge: 부과하다)
W: Okay, then I'll buy one senior ticket, and two adult tickets.
M: May I see an <u>identification card</u> for the senior?
　　　　　　　신분증
W: Yeah, just a moment. Here it is.

M: Thank you. And today is National Museum Day, so you can get 50% off the total price.
국립 박물관의 날
총액에서 50% 할인을 받다
W: Wow, that's amazing!
M: If you need audio guides, they're $5 each.
오디오 가이드들
W: No, thanks. Only the tickets, please. Here's my credit card.

해석
남: World History Museum(세계 역사 박물관)에 오신 것을 환영합니다. 어떻게 도와드릴까요?
여: 안녕하세요, 입장권 3장을 구매하고 싶어요. 성인 요금은 얼마인가요?
남: 성인 입장권은 10달러입니다.
여: 어르신들은 어떤가요?
남: 가격 게시판을 보시면, 65세 이상인 분들에게는 8달러가 부과됩니다.
여: 알겠어요, 그럼 노인 입장권 1장과 성인 입장권 2장을 살게요.
남: 어르신의 신분증을 보여주시겠습니까?
여: 네, 잠시만요. 여기 있어요.
남: 감사합니다. 그리고 오늘은 National Museum Day(국립 박물관의 날)라서, 총액에서 50% 할인을 받으실 수 있습니다.
여: 와, 정말 잘됐네요!
남: 오디오 가이드가 필요하시면, 개당 5달러입니다.
여: 아니요, 괜찮아요. 입장권만 주세요. 여기 제 신용카드가 있어요.

✓$14　　②$19　　③$24
④$28　　⑤$33

문제 풀이
8달러인 노인 입장권 1장과 10달러인 성인 입장권 2장을 사면 총액은 28달러이다. 여기서 50% 할인을 받게 되고, 오디오 가이드는 필요하지 않다고 했으므로 여자가 지불할 금액은 14달러이다. 따라서 답은 ① '$14'이다.

07 남자가 송별회에 참석할 수 없는 이유　정답률 90%　▶ 정답 ③

W: Hey, Tim. I didn't see you in Professor Jackson's class yesterday.
교수　수업
M: Hi, Kayla. I had a little stomachache. Did I miss anything important?
배탈　놓치다
W: As you know, Professor Jackson is retiring next week, so the students have decided to throw him a farewell party.
퇴직할 예정이다(retire)　그에게 송별회를 열어주다(farewell party: 송별회)
M: Sounds great. When is it?
W: It's this Saturday at 12 p.m. in Diamond Hall.
M: Umm... This Saturday? I can't go then.
W: Why not? Ah, you must have your club activity.
클럽 활동
M: It's not that. I don't have my club activity that day.
W: Then what is it? Do you need to take care of your brother again?
~을 돌보다
M: No. Actually, I have to participate in the marathon that day.
~에 참가하다　마라톤
W: Marathon? Oh, right. I know how hard you've been training for it. Good luck!
열심히　훈련해 왔다(train)
M: Thanks. Please congratulate the professor for me.
축하하다

해석
여: 안녕, Tim. 어제 Jackson 교수님 수업에서 너를 보지 못했어.
남: 안녕, Kayla. 배탈이 좀 났어. 내가 중요한 것을 놓쳤니?
여: 알다시피, Jackson 교수님이 다음 주에 퇴직할 예정이셔서, 학생들이 그에게 송별회를 열어주기로 결정했어.
남: 좋은 생각이네. 송별회는 언제야?
여: 이번 주 토요일 오후 12시에 Diamond Hall에서 해.
남: 음... 이번 주 토요일? 나는 그때 갈 수 없어.
여: 왜 안 돼? 아, 클럽 활동이 있는 거구나.
남: 그렇지 않아. 그날은 클럽 활동이 없거든.
여: 그럼 뭐야? 또 남동생을 돌봐야 하니?
남: 아니야. 사실, 그날 마라톤에 참가해야 해.
여: 마라톤? 오, 맞다. 나는 네가 그것을 위해 얼마나 열심히 훈련해 왔는지 알고 있어. 행운을 빌어!
남: 고마워. 나 대신 교수님을 축하해줘.

①동생을 돌봐야 해서
②클럽 활동에 가야 해서
✓마라톤에 참가해야 해서
④병원 진료를 받아야 해서
⑤교수님과 면담을 해야 해서

08 Noodle Cooking Contest에 관해 언급되지 않은 것　정답률 70%　▶ 정답 ③

W: Honey, I picked up a flyer about the Noodle Cooking Contest.
전단　면 요리 대회
M: What is it about?
W: It's a competition to cook the most creative dish using noodles.
대회　가장 창의적인　요리
M: Sounds interesting. Who can participate?
참가하다
W: Any city resident can participate. Why don't you give it a try?
시 거주민　시도하다
M: Let me take a look at the flyer. I should check the date first.
날짜
W: Here. It's on the 20th of June. Are you free then?
한가한
M: Luckily, I don't have any plans that day. Maybe I can apply for the contest.
다행히　계획들　~에 지원하다
W: You should! The winner will receive $500.
우승자　받다
M: Great! It says I have to send a recipe by e-mail to apply for the contest. Any suggestions?
조리법
W: Well, do you remember the cold noodle salad you made for my birthday? It was so good. You should use that recipe.
M: That's a great idea. I'll do it.

해석
여: 여보, 제가 Noodle Cooking Contest(면 요리 대회)에 관한 전단을 주웠어요.
남: 무엇에 관한 거예요?
여: 면을 이용해서 가장 창의적인 요리를 만드는 대회네요.
남: 흥미롭게 들려요. 누가 참가할 수 있나요?
여: 시 거주민이라면 누구나 참가할 수 있어요. 시도해 보는 게 어때요?
남: 전단을 좀 볼게요. 일단 날짜를 확인해야겠어요.
여: 여기 있어요. 6월 20일이네요. 그때 한가해요?
남: 다행히, 그날은 아무런 계획이 없어요. 대회에 지원할 수 있을 것 같아요.
여: 그래야죠! 우승자는 500달러를 받을 거예요.
남: 좋네요! 대회에 지원하려면 조리법을 이메일로 보내야 한다고 되어 있어요. 좋은 의견 있어요?
여: 음, 당신이 제 생일에 만들어준 냉면 샐러드 기억나요? 정말 맛있었어요. 그 조리법을 사용해 봐요.
남: 좋은 생각이에요. 그렇게 할게요.

①참가 대상　②대회 날짜　✓대회 장소
④우승 상금　⑤지원 방법

09 Library Plus에 관한 내용과 일치하지 않는 것　정답률 75%　▶ 정답 ⑤

M: Hello, I'm Tony Jones, a librarian at Greenfield Library. We're
사서
thrilled to tell you about a brand-new service called Library Plus.
매우 기쁜　새로운
Our library volunteers will deliver books straight to your home.
자원봉사자들　배송하다　바로
Our book delivery service is here to provide more people with
더 많은 사람들에게 기회를 제공하다
(provide A with B: A에게 B를 제공하다, opportunity: 기회)
the opportunity to read. All library members can use this service
회원들
free of charge. In order to get started, use the library's mobile
무료로　시작하기 위해서　모바일 앱
(in order to V: ~하기 위해서, get started: 시작하다)
application on your phone. You can borrow a maximum of five
빌리다
books at a time. Books may be borrowed for two weeks, but you
한 번에
can extend the borrowing period simply by giving us a call. You
연장하다　대출 기간
don't even need to come to the library to return your books. We'll
pick up the books at your place. For more information, visit our
수거하다
website. Thank you.

해석
남: 안녕하세요, 저는 Greenfield 도서관의 사서인, Tony Jones입니다. 저희는 Library Plus라는 새로운 서비스에 대해 알려드리게 되어 매우 기쁩니다. 도서관 자원봉사자들이 책을

여러분의 집으로 바로 배송할 것입니다. 저희의 책 배송 서비스는 더 많은 사람들에게 (책을) 읽을 수 있는 기회를 제공하기 위한 것입니다. 모든 도서관 회원은 무료로 이 서비스를 이용할 수 있습니다. 시작하기 위해서, 휴대폰의 도서관 모바일 앱을 이용하십시오. 한 번에 최대 5권의 책을 빌릴 수 있습니다. 책은 2주 동안 빌릴 수 있지만, 저희에게 전화만 하면 대출 기간을 연장할 수 있습니다. 책을 반납하기 위해 도서관에 올 필요도 없습니다. 저희가 여러분의 집에서 책을 수거할 것입니다. 더 많은 정보를 원하시면, 저희 웹사이트를 방문해 주십시오. 감사합니다.

① 도서관 자원봉사자들이 책을 집으로 배송한다.
② 도서관 회원은 무료로 이용할 수 있다.
③ 한 번에 최대 5권의 책을 빌릴 수 있다.
④ 전화로 대출 기간을 연장할 수 있다.
✓ 직접 도서관에 방문하여 책을 반납해야 한다.

10 표에서 두 사람이 구매할 반지
정답률 75%
▶ 정답 ①

W: Hey Adam, Mom's birthday is coming up. Why don't we buy a gold ring for her present?
금반지 / 선물

M: Good idea. I heard that jewelry online is cheaper than in stores. So let's buy one online.
보석류 / 더 저렴한(cheap)

W: Okay. Let me see... Rings are pretty expensive. What's our budget?
비싼 / 예산

M: We spent a lot for Mother's Day last month, so I don't think we can spend more than $400 on her present this time.
썼다(spend)

W: You're right. Let's decide on a color now. We have three options: white, yellow, and rose.
~을 정하다

M: Mom already has several yellow gold rings. We shouldn't choose yellow.
몇 개의

W: Good point. Both the white and rose ones look better anyway.

M: That's true. What about a stone for the ring?
보석

W: How about a ruby? It would go well with Mom's red earrings.
루비 / ~와 잘 어울리다 / 귀걸이

M: I agree. Oh, this one provides a gift-wrapping service.
선물 포장 서비스

W: We don't need that. I'd rather wrap it myself.

M: Okay, then let's order this one.
주문하다

해석

여: 얘 Adam, 엄마의 생신이 다가오고 있어. 선물로 금반지를 사드리는 게 어떠니?

남: 좋은 생각이야. 온라인에서 (파는) 보석류가 매장에서보다 더 저렴하다고 들었어. 그러니 온라인에서 구매하자.

여: 알겠어. 어디 보자... 반지가 꽤 비싸네. 우리의 예산은 얼마야?

남: 지난달에 어머니 날을 위해 돈을 많이 써서, 이번에는 선물에 400달러 이상을 쓸 수 없을 것 같아.

여: 맞아. 이제 색상을 정하자. 흰색, 노란색, 연홍색의 세 가지 선택권이 있어.

남: 엄마는 이미 노란색 금반지를 몇 개 가지고 계셔. 노란색은 선택하면 안 돼.

여: 좋은 지적이야. 어차피 흰색 금반지와 연홍색 금반지가 모두 더 좋아 보여.

남: 맞아. 반지에 넣을 보석은 어떻게 할까?

여: 루비는 어때? 엄마의 빨간색 귀걸이와 잘 어울릴 것 같아.

남: 동의해. 오, 이 제품은 선물 포장 서비스를 제공해.

여: 그것은 필요 없어. 차라리 내가 직접 포장하는 게 좋겠어.

남: 알겠어, 그럼 이 제품을 주문하자.

금반지

모델	가격	색상	보석	선물 포장 서비스
✓ A	300달러	흰색	루비	X
② B	330달러	노란색	루비	X
③ C	350달러	흰색	에메랄드	O
④ D	380달러	연홍색	루비	O
⑤ E	430달러	연홍색	에메랄드	X

11 남자의 마지막 말에 대한 여자의 응답
정답률 70%
▶ 정답 ④

M: Katie, we have to go to the Modern Art Center sometime this month for our art class project. How about this Sunday?
현대 미술관 / 미술 수업 과제

W: I have plans with my mom that day. Let's go another day.
~와 약속이 있다

M: But they have a special artist lecture only this Sunday. Would you consider changing your plans?
예술가 특별 강연 / 바꾸는 것을 고려하다
(consider V-ing: ~하는 것을 고려하다, change: 바꾸다)

W: (Yeah, just let me make sure it's okay with my mom first.)

해석

남: Katie, 우리 미술 수업 과제를 위해 이번 달 중에 Modern Art Center(현대 미술관)에 가야 해. 이번 주 일요일은 어떠니?

여: 그날은 엄마와 약속이 있어. 다른 날에 가자.

남: 하지만 이번 주 일요일에만 예술가 특별 강연이 있어. 약속을 바꾸는 것을 고려해 보겠니?

여: (그래, 우선 엄마가 괜찮은지 확인해 볼게.)

① 미안해. 우리는 오늘 미술 수업 과제를 끝낼 수 없어.
② 오, 네가 기회를 놓쳤다니 정말 안타까워.
③ 나는 그렇게 생각하지 않아. 표는 그렇게 비싸지 않아.
✓ 그래, 우선 엄마가 괜찮은지 확인해 볼게.
⑤ 왜 안 되겠어? 엄마와 나는 일요일에 아무런 약속도 없어.

12 여자의 마지막 말에 대한 남자의 응답
정답률 80%
▶ 정답 ⑤

W: Jake, are we going to drive to the restaurant for the dinner meeting with our client?
~에 운전해서 가다 / 저녁 식사 모임 / 고객

M: Yes. It would be best to go by car. The problem is the place doesn't have a parking lot.
차로 가다 / 문제 / 주차장

W: I'm sure we can find a place for the car around the restaurant.
~ 주변에

M: (Right. I'll check if there's any public parking nearby.)
공영 주차장

해석

여: Jake, 우리 고객과의 저녁 식사 모임을 위해 식당에 운전해서 갈 건가요?

남: 네. 차로 가는 것이 가장 좋을 것 같아요. 문제는 그곳에 주차장이 없다는 거예요.

여: 식당 주변에 차를 위한 장소를 찾을 수 있을 거라 확신해요.

남: (네. 근처에 공영 주차장이 있는지 확인해 볼게요.)

① 좋은 생각이네요. 당신이 저 대신 요리를 하면 돼요.
② 제 잘못이에요! 제가 저녁을 샀어야 했어요.
③ 유감스럽게도, 그 식당은 오늘 밤에 문을 닫아요.
④ 알겠어요, 그럼 우리의 약속을 취소해야겠네요.
✓ 네. 근처에 공영 주차장이 있는지 확인해 볼게요.

13 남자의 마지막 말에 대한 여자의 응답
정답률 75%
▶ 정답 ②

M: Hey Linda, what are you reading?

W: I'm reading Troy Morgan's new book. It's really interesting.
신간 / 흥미로운

M: You seem to really love his books.
~하는 것 같다

W: I do! Can you take me to his book signing event next week, Dad?
책 사인회

M: Sure, but didn't he already sign a book for you?
이미

W: Yes, but getting a book signed isn't my main purpose for going to the event.
주된 / 목적

M: Then why do you want to go?

W: It's because of his recent interview. He said he lost confidence in his writing.
최근의 / 잃었다(lose) / 자신감

M: Why? What happened?

W: He read some negative reviews about his last work.
부정적인 / 논평들 / 작품

M: Oh, really? It sounds like he needs to meet some fans like you to boost his confidence.
높이다

W: (I agree. That's why I want to go to the event to see him.)

해석

남: 얘 Linda, 무엇을 읽고 있니?

여: Troy Morgan의 신간을 읽고 있어요. 그것은 정말 흥미로워요.

남: 너는 그의 책을 정말 좋아하는 것 같구나.

여: 맞아요! 다음 주에 있을 그의 책 사인회에 저를 데려가 주실 수 있어요, 아빠?

남: 물론이지, 그런데 그가 이미 너를 위해 책에 사인해 주지 않았니?

여: 그렇죠, 하지만 책에 사인을 받는 것이 사인회에 가는 주된 목적은 아니에요.
남: 그럼 왜 가고 싶어 하는 거니?
여: 그의 최근 인터뷰 때문이에요. 그는 자신의 글에 대한 자신감을 잃었다고 했어요.
남: 왜? 무슨 일이 있었니?
여: 그의 최신 작품에 대한 부정적인 논평들을 읽었대요.
남: 오, 그래? 그는 자신감을 높이기 위해 너와 같은 팬들을 만나야 할 것 같구나.
여: (동의해요. 그래서 저는 사인회에 가서 그를 보고 싶어요.)

① 맞아요. 그에게 인터뷰를 도와줄 수 있는지 물어봐요.
✓동의해요. 그래서 저는 사인회에 가서 그를 보고 싶어요.
③ 와, 당신이 그의 책을 정말 많이 읽었다는 것을 알겠네요.
④ 네, 당신의 신간이 출판되어서 기쁘네요.
⑤ 아니요. 부정적인 논평이 제 경력에 도움이 될 수 있어요.

14 여자의 마지막 말에 대한 남자의 응답
정답률 80% ▶ 정답 ④

M: Hi, Sandra. You look excited.
W: Yeah, I just got my driver's license.
  운전 면허를 땄다(get one's driver's license)
M: Congratulations! Are you planning to buy a car?
W: Actually, I've been browsing cars online. But they're more expensive
  둘러보고 있다(browse)   더 비싼
  than I expected.
M: Then, what about a used car? My brother happens to be selling his
                        중고차   마침 팔고 있다
  car.   (happen to V: 마침 ~하다, sell: 팔다)
W: I was considering buying a used car, too. Can I see some pictures
  of his car?
M: Let me check... Here you go. He's had it for about three years.
W: Wow, it looks as shiny as new. Also, it's in my favorite color and
                    빛나는
  design.
M: I'm glad you like it. You'll be even more satisfied when you see it in
                              훨씬   더 만족하는
  person.
  직접
W: I hope so! Do you know how much he's selling it for?
M: He wants $10,000 for it.
W: That's within my budget. But I'd need to test-drive it first.
              예산   시운전하다
M: (No problem. We can schedule a time with my brother.)
            시간을 잡다

해석
남: 안녕, Sandra. 너 신나 보인다.
여: 그래, 방금 운전 면허를 땄거든.
남: 축하해! 차를 살 계획이니?
여: 사실, 온라인으로 차를 둘러보고 있어. 그런데 예상했던 것보다 더 비싸네.
남: 그럼, 중고차는 어때? 내 남동생이 마침 자신의 차를 팔고 있거든.
여: 나도 중고차를 사는 것을 고려 중이었어. 그의 차 사진을 좀 볼 수 있을까?
남: 어디 보자... 여기 있어. 그는 그것을 3년 정도 가지고 있었어.
여: 와, 새것처럼 빛나 보여. 게다가, 내가 가장 좋아하는 색상과 디자인이야.
남: 마음에 든다니 다행이야. 그것을 직접 보면 훨씬 더 만족할 거야.
여: 그랬으면 좋겠다! 그가 얼마에 그것을 팔고 있는지 아니?
남: 그는 그것의 가격으로 10,000달러를 원해.
여: 그것은 내 예산 범위 내에 있어. 그런데 먼저 그것을 시운전해 봐야 할 것 같아.
남: (문제없어. 우리는 내 남동생과 시간을 잡을 수 있어.)

① 걱정하지 마. 그는 곧 운전 면허를 딸 거야.
② 정말? 네가 내 차에 관심이 있는지 몰랐어.
③ 오, 아니야. 그럼 내 차를 정비소에 맡겨야겠어.
✓문제없어. 우리는 내 남동생과 시간을 잡을 수 있어.
⑤ 괜찮아. 나는 내일 다른 것을 살 거야.

문제 풀이
남자의 남동생이 팔려는 중고차가 마음에 든 여자는 구매 전에 차를 시운전해 보고 싶다고 말한다. 이에 대한 남자의 응답으로 가장 적절한 것은 ④ 'No problem. We can schedule a time with my brother.(문제없어. 우리는 내 남동생과 시간을 잡을 수 있어.)'이다.

15 다음 상황에서 Bill이 Susan에게 할 말
정답률 80% ▶ 정답 ⑤

W: Bill and Susan are second-grade high school students and friends.
  They are preparing for their final exams at the library after school.
                          기말고사   도서관

It used to be easy for Susan to focus on studying. However,
  예전에는 쉬웠다   ~에 집중하다
  (used to V: 예전에는 ~했다, easy: 쉬운)
these days she's noticing that she gets distracted easily at the
  요즘   산만해지다
library and doesn't know why she cannot maintain her attention.
                                        유지하다   집중력
So, she decides to get some advice from Bill, who gets high
    구하기로 결심하다   조언   높은 점수를 받다
  (decide to V: ~하기로 결심하다)
scores in school. When Bill hears her problem, he's suddenly
reminded of his own experience of losing focus. He recalls that
  ~이 갑자기 생각나다   기억해 내다
  (remind A of B: A에게 B를 생각나게 하다, suddenly: 갑자기)
he changed his study location and that really helped him get back
                        장소
his concentration. Therefore, he wants to suggest that Susan
      집중력
try studying in a different place to find her focus again. In this
situation, what would Bill most likely say to Susan?
Bill: (How about changing where you study to regain your focus?)
                                              되찾다

해석
여: Bill과 Susan은 고등학교 2학년 학생이고 친구이다. 그들은 방과 후에 도서관에서 기말고사를 준비하고 있다. Susan은 예전에는 공부에 집중하는 것이 쉬웠다. 하지만 요즘 그녀는 도서관에서 쉽게 산만해지는 것을 의식하고 있고 왜 자신이 집중력을 유지할 수 없는지 알지 못한다. 그래서, 그녀는 학교에서 높은 점수를 받는 Bill에게 조언을 구하기로 결심한다. Bill은 그녀의 문제에 대해 듣자, 집중력을 잃었던 자신의 경험이 갑자기 생각난다. 그는 공부 장소를 바꿨고, 그것이 집중력을 되찾는 데 정말 도움이 되었다는 것을 기억해 낸다. 따라서, 그는 Susan에게 집중력을 다시 찾기 위해 다른 장소에서 공부해 보라고 제안하고 싶다. 이러한 상황에서, Bill은 Susan에게 뭐라고 말하겠는가?
Bill: (집중력을 되찾기 위해 공부하는 곳을 바꾸는 게 어떠니?)

① 너는 휴식을 취할 적절한 시간을 찾아야 할 것 같아.
② 좋은 성적을 받는 것이 가장 중요한 것은 아니야.
③ 도서관에서 공부하는 것에는 분명히 많은 이점이 있을 거야.
④ 시험 준비를 위해 학습 계획을 세우는 게 어떠니?
✓집중력을 되찾기 위해 공부하는 곳을 바꾸는 게 어떠니?

16~17 1지문 2문항

M: Good evening, viewers. Last time, I introduced some paintings by
                                          소개했다
  well-known Western artists. Today, I'd like to talk about objects
  유명한   사물들
that have symbolic meanings in Western art. Let's begin with
          상징적인   의미들
mirrors. The reflection seen in mirrors can reveal a hidden truth
  거울들   모습   드러내다   숨겨진
or expose a lie. As you might imagine, a broken mirror generally
  폭로하다   깨진
represents bad luck. Second, candles. They can symbolize the
  나타내다   양초들
passing of time or show a timeline. This is seen in how much of the
  시간의 흐름   소요 시간
candles have burned. Third, let's talk about books. Books often
represent a higher educational status. They're also a symbol of
                    교육적인   지위
learning or of giving knowledge. Lastly, flowers can be a symbol
                        지식
of life. Blooming flowers are used to show power and growth. In a
  생명   피어나는   힘   성장
moment, I'll present some paintings with these symbols.
                  보여주다

해석
남: 안녕하세요, 시청자 여러분. 지난 시간에, 저는 유명한 서양 화가들의 그림을 소개했습니다. 오늘, 저는 서양 미술에서 상징적인 의미를 가지고 있는 사물들에 대해 이야기하고자 합니다. 거울부터 시작해 보겠습니다. 거울에 보이는 모습은 숨겨진 진실을 드러내거나 거짓말을 폭로할 수 있습니다. 여러분이 상상할 수 있듯이, 깨진 거울은 일반적으로 불운을 나타냅니다. 두 번째, 양초입니다. 그것들은 시간의 흐름을 상징하거나 소요 시간을 보여줄 수 있습니다. 이것은 양초가 얼마나 많이 탔는지에서 보입니다. 세 번째, 책에 대해 이야기해 보겠습니다. 책은 종종 보다 높은 교육적인 지위를 나타냅니다. 그것들은 또한 배움이나 지식을 주는 것의 상징입니다. 마지막으로, 꽃은 생명의 상징일 수 있습니다. 피어나는 꽃은 힘과 성장을 보여주기 위해 사용됩니다. 잠시 후에, 이러한 상징들이 있는 그림들을 보여드리겠습니다.

16 남자가 하는 말의 주제

정답률 85%
▶ 정답 ②

① 화가들이 사용하는 다양한 그림체
✓ 서양 미술에서 상징으로 쓰이는 사물들
③ 종교적 사물이 서양 문화에 미치는 영향
④ 역사를 거친 회화 도구의 변화
⑤ 사실적인 방법으로 사물을 그리는 방법

17 언급된 사물이 아닌 것

정답률 90%
▶ 정답 ③

① 거울   ② 양초   ✓ 조개껍질
④ 책   ⑤ 꽃

---

24 | 2024년 9월 학력평가

01	⑤	02	③	03	③	04	④	05	⑤
06	②	07	⑤	08	④	09	⑤	10	③
11	②	12	①	13	②	14	③	15	①
16	②	17	④						

01 여자가 하는 말의 목적

정답률 85%
▶ 정답 ⑤

W: Hello, community members. I'm Lena Smith, the leader of the Public Relations Team at the San Diego Art Museum. I'm excited to announce that our art museum will offer a free admissions event during next week. Our museum has been loved by the community for 50 years, so we're excited to give back to our loyal supporters and welcome new visitors. This event is a great chance for you to explore our extensive collections of famous artworks free of charge. Don't miss out on this incredible opportunity and spread the word to your family and friends.

해석
여: 안녕하세요, 지역 주민 여러분. 저는 샌디에이고 미술관의 홍보팀장인 Lena Smith입니다. 다음 주에 저희 미술관이 무료 입장 행사를 제공할 것을 알려드리게 되어 기쁩니다. 저희 미술관은 50년 동안 지역 사회의 사랑을 받아 왔기에, 충실한 지지자들에게 보답하고 새로운 방문객들을 맞이하게 되어 기쁩니다. 이 행사는 저희의 광범위한 유명 미술품 모음을 무료로 탐색할 수 있는 좋은 기회입니다. 이 놀라운 기회를 놓치지 마시고 가족과 친구들에게 소식을 전해주세요.

① 미술 대회 작품을 공모하려고
② 직원 채용 일정을 안내하려고
③ 전시회 취소에 대해 항의하려고
④ 어린이 미술관 건립을 제안하려고
✓ 미술관 무료 입장 행사를 홍보하려고

02 남자의 의견

정답률 90%
▶ 정답 ③

W: Hey, who are you talking to?
M: Hi, Jenny. I'm just talking to my plant.
W: Seriously? I've never heard of doing that.
M: You know what's interesting? Speaking to your plants can actually help them grow better.
W: No way! How so?

M: When we talk, we breathe out carbon dioxide, and plants love it. It's essential for their growth.
W: That makes sense.
M: And guess what? The vibrations from our voices when we talk can promote plant growth, too.
W: That's pretty cool!
M: Yeah. We can help our plants grow better by talking to them.
W: I see. I might just say 'hi' to my plants and see how they like it.

해석
여: 얘, 너 누구에게 말하고 있는 거야?
남: 안녕, Jenny. 내 식물에게 말하고 있는 거야.
여: 정말? 나는 그렇게 한다는 얘기를 들어본 적이 없어.
남: 흥미로운 게 뭔지 아니? 식물에게 말하는 것은 실제로 식물이 더 잘 자라는 데 도움이 될 수 있어.
여: 말도 안 돼! 어떻게 그렇지?
남: 말을 할 때, 우리는 이산화탄소를 내뿜고 식물은 그것을 정말 좋아해. 그것은 식물의 성장에 필수적이거든.
여: 일리가 있네.
남: 그리고 그거 알아? 우리가 말을 할 때 목소리의 진동도 식물의 성장을 촉진할 수 있어.
여: 정말 멋지다!
남: 그래. 우리는 식물에게 말함으로써 식물이 더 잘 자라는 데 도움을 줄 수 있어.
여: 그렇구나. 내 식물들에게 '안녕'이라고 말하고 식물들이 그것에 어떻게 반응하는지 봐야겠어.

① 식물을 실내에 두면 호흡기 건강에 해로울 수 있다.
② 지나치게 높은 온도는 실내 식물에 악영향을 미친다.
✓ 식물에게 말하는 것은 식물이 자라는 데 도움이 된다.
④ 상대방의 목소리를 통해 건강 상태를 파악할 수 있다.
⑤ 적절한 인사말은 대화를 자연스럽게 시작하는 데 필요하다.

03 남자가 하는 말의 요지

정답률 90%
▶ 정답 ③

M: Welcome back to our channel, Wellness Wisdom! Are you in the habit of eating fruit after your meals? Then this video is a must-watch for you. Fruit is packed with essential nutrients such as vitamins and minerals, but eating them immediately after a meal might lead to digestive issues. Fruit usually digests faster than other types of foods. So, when you have fruit right after a meal, the fruit may not digest fast because other foods stay in the stomach. This increases the pressure on the digestive system and may result in a stomachache and discomfort. Remember, choosing fruit as dessert may get your digestive system in trouble. Stay healthy, stay informed.

해석
남: 저희 채널 'Wellness Wisdom(건강 지혜)'에 다시 오신 것을 환영합니다! 여러분은 식사 후에 과일을 먹는 습관이 있나요? 그렇다면 이 영상은 여러분이 꼭 시청해야 할 영상입니다. 과일은 비타민과 미네랄 같은 필수 영양소로 가득 차 있지만, 식사 직후에 과일을 먹는 것은 소화 문제로 이어질 수 있습니다. 과일은 일반적으로 다른 종류의 음식물보다 더 빠르게 소화됩니다. 그래서 식사 직후에 과일을 먹으면, 다른 음식물이 위에 계속 있기 때문에 과일이 빠르게 소화되지 않을 수 있습니다. 이것은 소화 기관에 부담을 증가시키고 복통과 불편함을 초래할 수 있습니다. 기억하세요, 후식으로 과일을 선택하는 것이 여러분의 소화 기관에 문제를 일으킬 수 있습니다. 건강을 유지하고, 정보를 계속 얻으세요.

① 과일과 채소는 색깔에 따라 효능이 다르다.
② 규칙적인 식사는 혈당 수치 조절에 도움이 된다.
✓ 식사 직후의 과일 섭취는 소화 문제를 유발할 수 있다.
④ 일상생활의 스트레스는 소화 불량을 악화시킬 수 있다.
⑤ 음식물 섭취만으로 하루 권장 비타민양을 채울 수 있다.

04 그림에서 대화의 내용과 일치하지 않는 것

정답률 90%

▶ 정답 ④

M: Hello, Cindy. What are you looking at on your phone?

W: Hi, Tom. This is my own space in the metaverse.
공간

M: Wow, it's amazing. Oh, there's a heart-shaped door in your house.
하트 모양의
That's unique.
독특한

W: Yes. I can enter my home through the door like a real house.
들어가다   실제의

M: Fantastic! Is it possible to ride the bicycle next to the tree?
가능한   자전거를 타다

W: Of course. We can do everything in virtual reality.
가상 현실

M: Awesome. I love the two dogs looking at each other.

W: Yeah, they make my place so lovely.

M: I agree. I also like that striped-patterned mat on the ground.
줄무늬의   돗자리

W: Thanks.

M: Oh, there's a girl sitting on the bench. She looks a lot like you.

W: Yes, she's my avatar in the metaverse.
아바타

M: That's so cool. I also want to design my own space like yours.
디자인하다

해석

남: 안녕, Cindy. 휴대폰으로 무엇을 보고 있니?

여: 안녕, Tom. 여기는 메타버스에 있는 나만의 공간이야.

남: 와, 놀라운데. 오, 집에 하트 모양의 문이 있구나. 독특하네.

여: 응. 나는 실제 집처럼 그 문을 통해 집에 들어갈 수 있어.

남: 환상적이야! 나무 옆에 있는 자전거를 타는 것이 가능하니?

여: 물론이지. 가상 현실에서는 모든 것을 할 수 있어.

남: 대단하다. 나는 서로를 바라보는 두 마리의 개가 정말 마음에 들어.

여: 그래, 그들이 내 공간을 정말 사랑스럽게 만들어 줘.

남: 동의해. 나는 땅바닥에 있는 줄무늬 돗자리도 마음에 들어.

여: 고마워.

남: 오, 벤치에 한 소녀가 앉아 있어. 그녀는 너와 많이 닮았어.

여: 응, 그녀는 메타버스에 있는 나의 아바타야.

남: 정말 멋지다. 나도 네 것처럼 나만의 공간을 디자인하고 싶어.

05 여자가 할 일

정답률 80%

▶ 정답 ⑤

M: Hey, Sarah, the school's sports day is just a week away. Let's go
학교 운동회   점검하다
over our plan for the event.

W: Definitely, Alex. We're doing relays, a tug-of-war, and soccer, right?
계주   줄다리기

M: Yes. I'll manage the equipment, including whistles and the ropes.
장비   호루라기   밧줄들

W: Thanks. Can you also check our stock for soccer balls?
재고

M: Sure. I'll look into it. And, Sarah, I think we need some volunteers
~을 조사하다   자원봉사자들
to assist with the event as staff.
돕다   진행 요원

W: I already recruited some from the school's sports clubs.
모집했다

M: Perfect. I think we should make sure they know the basic rules of
기본 규칙들
the games.

W: I agree. Let's have a meeting with the volunteers tomorrow. I'll give
~와 모임을 가지다
them a phone call about the meeting.
그들에게 전화하다

M: Good idea. Then, I'll make the handout for the games' rules.
유인물

W: Deal. Let's make this sports day a success!
성공

해석

남: 안녕하세요, Sarah, 학교 운동회가 일주일밖에 남지 않았어요. 우리의 행사 계획을 점검해 봅시다.

여: 물론이죠, Alex. 우리는 계주, 줄다리기, 그리고 축구를 할 거예요, 맞죠?

남: 네. 제가 호루라기와 밧줄을 포함한 장비를 관리할게요.

여: 고마워요. 축구공의 재고 확인도 해 주시겠어요?

남: 그럼요. 조사해 볼게요. 그리고, Sarah, 진행 요원으로 행사를 도와줄 자원봉사자들이 좀 필요할 것 같아요.

여: 제가 이미 학교 운동 동아리에서 몇 명을 모집했어요.

남: 완벽하네요. 우리가 그들이 경기의 기본 규칙을 알도록 확실히 해야 할 것 같아요.

여: 동의해요. 내일 자원봉사자들과 모임을 가지죠. 제가 모임에 대해 그들에게 전화할게요.

남: 좋은 생각이에요. 그럼, 제가 경기 규칙에 대한 유인물을 만들게요.

여: 그래요. 이번 운동회를 성공시켜 봅시다!

① 운동 장비 대여하기

② 축구공 개수 확인하기

③ 스포츠 클럽 방문하기

④ 경기 규칙 유인물 만들기

☑ 자원봉사자들에게 전화하기

06 남자가 지불할 금액

정답률 85%

▶ 정답 ②

W: Welcome to Mobile Phone Oasis. How may I help you?

M: Hi, I'd like to get a new phone case.
휴대폰 케이스

W: Okay. What's your phone model?

M: It's a Quantum Plus. Do you have any recommendations?
추천 제품들

W: For your model, we have this silicone case and this leather wallet
실리콘 케이스   가죽 지갑 케이스
case. The silicone one is 20 dollars and the leather one is 30
dollars.

M: Hmm, I'll go with the silicone case.

W: Great choice. Is there anything else you need?
선택

M: I'd like to change the protective film on my phone.
바꾸다   보호 필름

W: Certainly. I'd recommend this clear film. It's slim and durable.
투명 필름   얇은   내구성이 있는

M: Fantastic. How much is it?

W: It's originally 10 dollars, but it's 20 percent off now.
원래

M: That's cool. I'll take it as well. Here's my credit card.

해석

여: Mobile Phone Oasis에 오신 것을 환영합니다. 어떻게 도와드릴까요?

남: 안녕하세요, 새 휴대폰 케이스를 사고 싶어요.

여: 알겠습니다. 휴대폰 모델이 무엇인가요?

남: Quantum Plus예요. 추천 제품이 있으신가요?

여: 고객님 모델의 경우에는, 이 실리콘 케이스와 이 가죽 지갑 케이스가 있어요. 실리콘 케이스는 20달러이고 가죽 케이스는 30달러예요.

남: 흠, 실리콘 케이스로 할게요.

여: 훌륭한 선택이네요. 다른 필요한 것이 있으신가요?

남: 휴대폰의 보호 필름을 바꾸고 싶어요.

여: 알겠습니다. 이 투명 필름을 추천할게요. 그것은 얇고 내구성이 있어요.

남: 환상적이네요. 얼마죠?

여: 원래 10달러인데, 지금 20퍼센트 할인하고 있어요.

남: 멋지네요. 그것도 살게요. 여기 제 신용카드가 있어요.

① $24   ☑ $28   ③ $30

④ $38   ⑤ $40

문제 풀이

여자가 구매하고자 하는 실리콘 휴대폰 케이스의 가격은 20달러이고, 투명 보호 필름의 가격은 10달러에서 20퍼센트가 할인된 8달러이다. 따라서 여자가 지불할 총액은 28달러이므로, 답은 ② '$28'이다.

07 여자가 대회에 출품할 사진을 촬영하지 못한 이유

정답률 90%

▶ 정답 ⑤

M: Hi, Clara. Everybody says that the science camp was a success.
과학 캠프

W: Yes. I'm glad the science camp ended well.
　　　　　　　　　　　　　　　　　　　끝났다
M: Me, too. By the way, did you take a picture to submit for the
　　　　　　　　　　　　　　사진을 찍다　　　출품하다
landscape photography competition? It's due today.
풍경 사진 대회
W: Unfortunately, I couldn't take a picture.
유감스럽게도
M: Oh, no! I thought the weather was perfect to take a picture last
　　　　　　　　　　　날씨
week.
W: Yeah. The weather was really nice.
M: Then what was the problem? Was your camera broken again?
　　　　　　　　　　　　　　　　　　　　　　고장난
W: No, there was nothing wrong with my camera.
M: Did you not feel well enough to go out?
　　　　몸 상태가 좋다　　　밖으로 나가다
W: No, I was fine.
M: Then why couldn't you take a picture?
W: Actually, I searched for some places with beautiful scenery, but I
　　　　　　　~을 찾아보았다　　　장소들　　　　경치
couldn't find the right place to take a picture of.
　　　　　　　알맞은
M: Sorry to hear that. I hope you'll have a better chance next time.
　　　　　　　　　　　　　　　　　　　　　　　　기회

해석
남: 안녕, Clara. 모든 사람들이 과학 캠프가 성공이었다고 말해.
여: 그래. 과학 캠프가 잘 끝나서 기뻐.
남: 나도 그래. 그런데 풍경 사진 대회에 출품할 사진은 찍었니? 오늘이 마감일이야.
여: 유감스럽게도, 사진을 찍지 못했어.
남: 오, 저런! 나는 지난주 날씨가 사진을 찍기에 완벽했다고 생각했는데.
여: 그래. 날씨가 정말 좋았지.
남: 그럼 문제가 뭐였어? 네 카메라가 또 고장났니?
여: 아니, 내 카메라에는 아무 이상이 없었어.
남: 밖으로 나가기에는 몸 상태가 좋지 않니?
여: 아니, 난 괜찮았어.
남: 그럼 왜 사진을 찍지 못했어?
여: 사실, 경치가 아름다운 몇몇 장소들을 찾아보았지만, 사진을 찍기에 알맞은 장소를 찾지 못했어.
남: 그 말을 들으니 유감이다. 다음에 더 좋은 기회가 있기를 바랄게.

① 카메라가 고장나서
② 몸 상태가 좋지 않아서
③ 촬영하기에 날씨가 나빠서
④ 과학 캠프와 일정이 겹쳐서
✓⑤ 적합한 촬영 장소를 찾지 못해서

08 Poetry Magic에 관해 언급되지 않은 것
정답률 90% ▶ 정답 ④

M: Hi, Alysa. What are you looking at?
W: I'm looking at a website for a poetry reading event.
　　　　　　　　　　　　　　　시 낭독 행사
M: Sounds interesting. Tell me more about it.
W: It's called "Poetry Magic." Many poets will be on stage for a
　　　　　　　　　　　　　시인들　　　　무대에 서다
reading. The famous poet, Sarah Mitchell, will be there, too.
　　　　　유명한
M: That's awesome! When will it be?
W: It'll be held at 7 p.m. on September 14th.
　　　열리다(hold: 열다)
M: Oh, that's next Saturday. I'm available then. Where's it taking
　　　　　　　　　　　　　　시간이 있는
place?
W: At the Bohemian Arts Center downtown. It's the best place for
　　　　　　　　　　　　　　　시내에
raising the love of poetry.
M: So how can I sign up?
　　　　　등록하다
W: You can just click the link here and fill this form out.
　　　　　　　링크를 클릭하다　　　이 서식을 작성하다
　　　　　　　　　　　　　　　　　(fill out: 작성하다, form: 서식)
M: Good, that's easy. I'll be there to enjoy the beautiful poetry.
　　　　　쉬운

해석
남: 안녕, Alysa. 무엇을 보고 있니?
여: 시 낭독 행사에 대한 웹사이트를 보고 있어.
남: 흥미롭게 들리네. 그것에 대해 더 말해줘.
여: 그것은 "Poetry Magic(시의 마법)"이라고 불려. 많은 시인들이 낭독을 위해 무대에 설 거야. 유명한 시인 Sarah Mitchell도 그곳에 있을 거야.
남: 굉장하다! 그게 언제니?

여: 9월 14일 오후 7시에 열릴 거야.
남: 오, 다음 주 토요일이네. 나는 그때 시간이 있어. 어디에서 열리니?
여: 시내에 있는 Bohemian Arts Center에서. 그곳은 시에 대한 사랑을 불러일으키기에 가장 좋은 장소야.
남: 그럼 어떻게 등록할 수 있어?
여: 여기 링크를 클릭해서 이 서식을 작성하기만 하면 돼.
남: 좋아, 쉽네. 나는 그곳에 가서 아름다운 시를 즐길 거야.

① 출연자　　　② 일시　　　③ 장소
✓④ 기념품　　　⑤ 등록 방법

09 Short-form Video Course에 관한 내용과 일치하지 않는 것
정답률 85% ▶ 정답 ⑤

W: Hello, listeners. Have you ever thought about boosting your
business with short-form videos? Then how about joining our
　　　　　　　　짧은 형식의 동영상들
Short-form Video Course? It's a free online course that is open
　　　　　　　　　　　　　　　　무료 온라인 강좌
to everyone interested in using social media for their business.
　　　　　　~에 관심이 있는
The course is made up of three stages that will teach you the
　　　　　　~로 구성되어 있다(be made up of)　단계들
art of planning, shooting, and editing videos like a professional.
기술　　　　　　　　　　　　　　　　　　　　전문가
Please visit our website at www.shortformclass.com to sign up.
　　　　　　　　　　　　　　　　　　　　　　　등록하다
The best part of this course is that you can take it at any time, over
　　　　　부분　　　　　　　　　　　　　　　언제든지
and over again. And guess what? We'll randomly pick some of
반복해서　　　　　　　　　　　　　　무작위로
the participants and give feedback on their work. Don't miss this
　　　참가자들　　　피드백을 제공하다　　　　　놓치다
chance to level up your business!
기회

해석
여: 안녕하세요, 청취자 여러분. 짧은 형식의 동영상을 통해 여러분의 사업을 활성화하는 것에 대해 생각해 보신 적이 있나요? 그렇다면 저희의 Short-form Video Course(짧은 형식의 동영상 강좌)에 참가하시는 것은 어떤가요? 그것은 사업을 위한 소셜 미디어 사용에 관심이 있는 모두에게 열려 있는 무료 온라인 강좌입니다. 강좌는 전문가처럼 동영상을 기획, 촬영, 편집하는 기술을 가르칠 세 단계로 구성되어 있습니다. 저희 웹사이트 www.shortformclass.com에 방문하여 등록하세요. 이 강좌의 가장 좋은 부분은 언제든지 반복해서 수강할 수 있다는 것입니다. 그리고 그거 아시나요? 참가자들 중 일부를 무작위로 선정하여 그들의 작품에 대한 피드백을 제공할 것입니다. 여러분 사업의 수준을 높일 수 있는 이 기회를 놓치지 마세요!

① 무료 온라인 강좌이다.
② 세 단계로 이루어져 있다.
③ 웹사이트에서 등록할 수 있다.
④ 언제든지 반복해서 수강할 수 있다.
✓⑤ 모든 참가자의 작품에 대해 피드백을 제공한다.

문제 풀이
무료 온라인 강좌에 참가한 사람들 중 일부만을 대상으로 하여 그들이 제작한 동영상에 대해 피드백을 해준다고 했으므로, 담화의 내용과 일치하지 않는 것은 ⑤ '모든 참가자의 작품에 대해 피드백을 제공한다.'이다.

10 표에서 두 사람이 주문할 백색 소음 기계
정답률 90% ▶ 정답 ③

M: Honey, what are you doing now?
W: I'm looking for a white noise machine. The machine plays white
　　　　　　　　　　백색 소음 기계　　　　　　　재생하다
noise to help people relax and fall asleep quickly.
　　　　　　　　　　휴식을 취하다　　잠들다
M: That's what we need. Shall we choose one together?
W: Okay, how much of the budget can we use?
　　　　　　　　　　예산
M: 40 dollars or less would be appropriate. How many tracks should
　　　　　　　　　　　　　　　사용하다　적절한　　　　　트랙들
the white noise machine play?
W: I think we'd better choose a model with more than 10 white noise
tracks. How about color?
M: I want to put it next to our bed, so I think white would look better
　　　　　　　　　　　　놓다
than black.
W: I agree. Look at this model. It has an alarm function.
　　　　　　　　　　　　　　　　　알람 기능

M: Great. It'll be useful for us.
　　　　　　　　　유용한
W: Let's order this model.

해석

남: 여보, 지금 무엇을 하고 있어요?

여: 백색 소음 기계를 찾고 있어요. 그 기계는 사람들이 휴식을 취하고 빠르게 잠들 수 있도록 도와주는 백색 소음을 재생해요.

남: 우리에게 필요한 것이네요. 함께 하나 고를까요?

여: 좋아요, 우리는 예산을 얼마나 사용할 수 있어요?

남: 40달러 이하가 적절할 것 같아요. 백색 소음 기계가 몇 개의 트랙을 재생해야 할까요?

여: 10개 이상의 백색 소음 트랙이 있는 모델을 선택하는 게 더 나을 것 같아요. 색상은 어때요?

남: 침대 옆에 놓고 싶으니까, 검은색보다는 흰색이 더 보기 좋을 것 같네요.

여: 동의해요. 이 모델을 봐요. 알람 기능이 있어요.

남: 잘됐네요. 그것은 우리에게 유용할 거예요.

여: 이 모델을 주문해요.

백색 소음 기계

	모델	가격	백색 소음 트랙 개수	색상	알람 기능
①	A	42달러	20	은색	X
②	B	38달러	18	흰색	X
✔③	C	35달러	15	흰색	O
④	D	30달러	12	검은색	O
⑤	E	25달러	8	검은색	X

11 여자의 마지막 말에 대한 남자의 응답   정답률 90%   ▶ 정답 ②

W: Honey, you know we often buy from the Best&Cost Online Shopping Mall, so how about getting a membership to it?
　　　　　　　　　　　　　　　　　　　　　　　~에 회원 가입을 하는 것(get a membership to)

M: Sounds good, but there is a five-dollar membership fee every month. Is it worth it?
　　　　　　　　　　　　　　　　　　회원비
　　　　　가치가 있는

W: Absolutely. The membership comes with free delivery and
　　　　　　　　　　　　　　　　　　　　　　　　무료 배송

discounts. We could actually save more money than the
　　　　　　　　　　　　　　　　절약하다
membership fee we pay.
　　　　　　　　지불하다

M: (Alright. Let's sign up for the membership.)
　　　　　　　　　~을 신청하다

해석

여: 여보, 알다시피 우리가 Best&Cost 온라인 쇼핑몰에서 자주 구매하니까, 거기 회원 가입을 하는 게 어때요?

남: 좋을 것 같지만, 매달 5달러의 회원비가 있어요. 그만한 가치가 있나요?

여: 당연하죠. 회원권은 무료 배송과 할인을 포함하고 있어요. 우리가 지불하는 회원비보다 더 많은 돈을 실제로 절약할 수 있어요.

남: (알겠어요. 회원권을 신청합시다.)

① 네. 배송이 방금 도착했어요.

✔② 알겠어요. 회원권을 신청합시다.

③ 오, 이런. 회원권을 갱신하는 것을 잊어버렸어요.

④ 잘됐네요. 그 쇼핑몰은 우리 집에서 가까워요.

⑤ 좋아요. 온라인 쇼핑을 줄이는 것을 고려해 볼게요.

12 남자의 마지막 말에 대한 여자의 응답   정답률 85%   ▶ 정답 ①

M: Cathy, this cafe offers a discount when a customer brings their
　　　　　　　　　　　　할인을 제공하다　　　　　　　고객
own tumbler for drinks. So, I brought mine.
　　　텀블러

W: Oh, that's a great idea. It'll help reduce the use of paper and
　　　　　　　　　　　　　　　　　　줄이다　　사용
plastic cups.

M: Yeah, it's a small step but can make a big difference. Would you
　　　　　　　작은 걸음　　　　　　　큰 차이를 만들다
like to join in as well?

W: (Sure. I'll bring my tumbler next time.)

해석

남: Cathy, 이 카페는 고객이 음료를 위한 자신의 텀블러를 가져오면 할인을 제공해요. 그래서 제 텀블러를 가져왔어요.

여: 오, 정말 좋은 생각이네요. 그것은 종이컵과 플라스틱 컵의 사용을 줄이는 데 도움이 될

거예요.

남: 네, 그것은 작은 걸음이지만 큰 차이를 만들 수 있어요. 당신도 함께 하시겠어요?

여: (물론이죠. 다음에는 제 텀블러를 가져올게요.)

✔① 물론이죠. 다음에는 제 텀블러를 가져올게요.

② 죄송하지만 안 되겠어요. 종이컵이 다 떨어졌어요.

③ 걱정하지 마세요. 제가 이미 음료를 준비했어요.

④ 죄송합니다. 카페는 할인을 제공하지 않습니다.

⑤ 왜 안 되겠어요? 텀블러를 환불 받읍시다.

13 여자의 마지막 말에 대한 남자의 응답   정답률 85%   ▶ 정답 ②

W: Dad, can you go shopping with me now?
　　　　　　　　쇼핑하러 가다

M: Sure, I can. But why, Allie?

W: I need to buy a white shirt today.
　　　　　　　　　흰색 셔츠

M: What do you need it for?

W: It's for the dance performance at the school festival next Friday.
　　　　　　　춤 공연　　　　　　　　　학교 축제

M: I see. But, wouldn't it be more convenient to order it online?
　　　　　　　　　　　　더 편리한　　　주문하다

W: Actually, I ordered a white shirt online a few days ago, but it hasn't
been delivered yet.　　　　　　　　　배송되지 않았다(deliver: 배송하다)

M: Sometimes that happens. There's still over a week left until the
festival day, though.　　　　　　　　　　　　　　남은(leave)

W: Right, but all of us decided to wear white shirts, even for
rehearsals.　　　　　　　　입기로 결정했다
예행연습들　　　　　(decide to V: ~하기로 결정하다, wear: 입다)

M: When do you start your rehearsals?

W: The first rehearsal is tomorrow. I'd like to be perfectly prepared for
it.　　　　　　　　　　　　　　　　　　　　완벽하게

M: (Okay. We'd better go buy your shirt right away.)

해석

여: 아빠, 지금 저와 함께 쇼핑하러 가실 수 있어요?

남: 그럼, 갈 수 있지. 그런데 왜 그러니, Allie?

여: 오늘 흰색 셔츠를 사야 해요.

남: 무엇 때문에 그것이 필요하니?

여: 다음 주 금요일 학교 축제에서 열리는 춤 공연을 위한 거예요.

남: 그렇구나. 그런데 온라인으로 주문하는 것이 더 편리하지 않을까?

여: 사실, 며칠 전에 온라인으로 흰색 셔츠를 주문했는데, 아직 배송되지 않았어요.

남: 가끔 그런 일이 있지. 하지만 축제일까지는 아직 일주일 이상 남았잖아.

여: 맞아요, 그런데 저희 모두가 예행연습에서도 흰색 셔츠를 입기로 결정했어요.

남: 예행연습은 언제 시작하니?

여: 첫 번째 예행연습이 내일이에요. 저는 그것을 완벽하게 준비하고 싶어요.

남: (알겠어. 당장 네 셔츠를 사러 가는 게 좋겠구나.)

① 훌륭한 선택이야. 이 셔츠는 네게 잘 어울려!

✔② 알겠어. 당장 네 셔츠를 사러 가는 게 좋겠구나.

③ 정말? 나는 예행연습이 취소된 줄 몰랐어.

④ 음, 공연을 위해 흰색 셔츠를 입는 게 어떠니?

⑤ 오, 네 공연을 놓쳐서 미안하구나.

14 남자의 마지막 말에 대한 여자의 응답   정답률 85%   ▶ 정답 ③

M: Hey, Jessica. How's the preparation for your business trip to
Singapore going?　　　　　　　준비　　　　　　　출장

W: It's going well. All the important documents are ready, and I'm
packing things for the trip.　　　　　　서류들
챙기고 있다(pack)

M: Glad to hear that.

W: Yeah, but I have a problem.

M: Oh, what is it?

W: You remember Tory, my five-month-old puppy? I need to find
someone to look after him while I'm away.　　　강아지
　　　　　　~을 돌보다

M: Why don't you leave him at your parents' house?
　　　　　　　　두고 가다

W: My mother is allergic to pet fur, so I don't think they can take care
of him.　　　　~에 알레르기가 있는　　　　　　　　　　　　~을 돌보다

M: Ah, got it. Have you considered a pet hotel?
　　　　　　　　　　　　　반려동물 호텔

W: Yes, I have. But I'm not sure about leaving Tory in those places <u>at such a young age</u>.
그렇게 어린 나이에
M: Hmm, fair point. You know what? I could <u>give a hand</u> if you're okay
도와주다
with it. Coco, my dog, will <u>welcome</u> a new friend.
환영하다
W: (I'd really appreciate it if you could take care of him.)

해석
남: 안녕, Jessica. 싱가포르 출장을 위한 준비는 어떻게 되어 가고 있니?
여: 잘 되어 가고 있어. 중요한 서류는 모두 준비가 되어 있고, 나는 출장을 위한 물건들을 챙기고 있어.
남: 다행이구나.
여: 그래, 하지만 문제가 하나 있어.
남: 오, 뭔데?
여: 5개월 된 내 강아지 Tory를 기억하지? 내가 없는 동안 그를 돌봐줄 사람을 구해야 해.
남: 부모님 댁에 두고 가는 게 어떠니?
여: 어머니께서 반려동물 털에 알레르기가 있으셔서, 부모님께서 그를 돌봐주실 수 없을 것 같아.
남: 아, 그렇구나. 반려동물 호텔을 고려해 봤니?
여: 응, 그랬지. 하지만 그렇게 어린 나이에 Tory를 그런 곳에 두고 갈 수 있을지 모르겠어.
남: 흠, 맞는 말이야. 그거 알아? 네가 괜찮다면 내가 도와줄 수 있어. 내 반려견 Coco는 새로운 친구를 환영해 줄 거야.
여: (네가 그를 돌봐 줄 수 있다면 정말 고마울 거야.)
① 반려견을 자주 산책시켜야 한다는 것에 동의해.
② 내 반려견이 반려동물 호텔에 머무는 것을 좋아했다니 기뻐.
✓ 네가 그를 돌봐 줄 수 있다면 정말 고마울 거야.
④ 여행에 필요한 물건들만 챙기는 것이 더 나아.
⑤ 네 반려견을 동물병원에 데려가는 것을 추천해.

문제 풀이
출장으로 집을 떠나 있는 동안에 자신의 강아지를 맡길 수 있는 사람을 찾지 못해서 걱정하고 있는 여자에게 남자는 자신이 도움을 줄 수 있다고 제안한다. 이에 대한 여자의 응답으로 가장 적절한 것은 ③ 'I'd really appreciate it if you could take care of him.(네가 그를 돌봐 줄 수 있다면 정말 고마울 거야.)'이다.

---

15 다음 상황에서 David가 Emily에게 할 말

정답률 85%   ▶ 정답 ①

M: David and Emily are members of the <u>school musical club</u>. The
학교 뮤지컬 동아리
club <u>has been preparing</u> their <u>creative musical performance</u> for
준비해 오고 있다   창작 뮤지컬 공연
a month. This time, David <u>takes a role</u> as the <u>stage director</u>, and
역할을 맡다   무대 감독
Emily as the <u>sound director</u>. Today, David and Emily <u>are checking</u>
음향 감독   확인하고 있다(check)
the music that will be used for the performance. After listening
to the music, David thinks that the <u>background music</u> for the last
배경 음악
<u>scene</u> is not <u>suitable</u>. So, David wants to ask Emily to <u>find</u> other
장면   적절한   찾다
music that <u>goes better with</u> the scene. In this situation, what would
~와 더 잘 어울리다
(go better with)
David most likely say to Emily?
David: (Can you look for <u>different</u> music for the last scene?)
다른

해석
남: David와 Emily는 학교 뮤지컬 동아리의 회원이다. 동아리는 한 달 동안 창작 뮤지컬 공연을 준비해 오고 있다. 이번에 David는 무대 감독, 그리고 Emily는 음향 감독 역할을 맡는다. 오늘, David와 Emily는 공연에 사용될 음악을 확인하고 있다. 음악을 들은 후에, David는 마지막 장면의 배경 음악이 적절하지 않다고 생각한다. 그래서 David는 Emily에게 그 장면과 더 잘 어울리는 다른 음악을 찾아달라고 부탁하고 싶다. 이러한 상황에서, David는 Emily에게 뭐라고 말하겠는가?
David: (마지막 장면을 위한 다른 음악을 찾아줄 수 있겠니?)
✓ 마지막 장면을 위한 다른 음악을 찾아줄 수 있겠니?
② 우리는 뮤지컬을 위해 연습을 더 많이 해야 할 것 같아.
③ 마지막 무대를 위한 일정을 확인해 줘.
④ 내가 몇몇 장면들을 바꿔도 될까?
⑤ 나는 네가 주인공을 연기했으면 좋겠어.

16~17 1지문 2문항

W: Hello, students. Nowadays, some <u>desserts</u> are very popular and
디저트들
well-known worldwide. Today, we'll learn about where and when
those desserts <u>might have originated</u>. First, <u>scones</u> are said to
유래했을지도 모른다   스콘들
(might have p.p.: ~했을지도 모른다, originate: 유래하다)
have come from Scotland in the early 1500s. Some historians
<u>assume</u> that it <u>was named after</u> the Stone of Scone, on which
추정하다   ~의 이름을 따서 명명되었다
(name after: ~의 이름을 따서 명명하다)
the kings of Scotland sat <u>while being crowned</u>. Secondly, <u>gelato</u>
왕위에 오를 때(crown: 왕위에 올리다)   젤라토
is thought to <u>have been invented</u> in Italy in the 16th century.
발명되었다(invent: 발명하다)
Historians aren't sure who invented it, but it's <u>generally believed</u>
일반적으로
that an Italian <u>architect</u>, Bernardo Buontalenti, created a <u>form</u> of
건축가   형태
the <u>modern-day</u> gelato. Thirdly, the first <u>marshmallows</u> are said
현대의   마시멜로들
to <u>have been produced</u> in Egypt around 2000 BC. Marshmallows
생산되었다(produce: 생산하다)
were offered only to the <u>ancient</u> Egyptian gods and <u>pharaohs</u> as
고대의   파라오들
a candy or dessert. Lastly, <u>cinnamon rolls</u> might have originated
시나몬 롤들
in Sweden in the 17th century. It's believed that cinnamon spice
향신료
started arriving in Sweden through <u>trade routes</u> and was <u>later</u> used
무역로들   나중에
in rolls and desserts. Now, I'd like you to search for more details of
these desserts.

해석
여: 안녕하세요, 학생 여러분. 요즘, 몇몇 디저트들이 매우 인기 있고 전 세계적으로 잘 알려져 있습니다. 오늘, 우리는 그 디저트들이 유래했을지도 모르는 장소와 시기에 대해 배울 것입니다. 첫째, 스콘은 1500년대 초에 스코틀랜드에서 생겨났다고 합니다. 일부 역사가들은 스코틀랜드의 왕들이 왕위에 오를 때 앉았던 Stone of Scone(스콘의 돌)의 이름을 따서 명명된 것으로 추정합니다. 둘째, 젤라토는 16세기에 이탈리아에서 발명된 것으로 생각됩니다. 역사가들은 누가 그것을 발명했는지 확신하지 못하지만, 일반적으로 이탈리아 건축가 Bernardo Buontalenti가 현대 젤라토의 한 형태를 만들었다고 여겨집니다. 셋째, 최초의 마시멜로는 기원전 2000년경에 이집트에서 생산되었다고 합니다. 마시멜로는 고대 이집트의 신과 파라오(고대 이집트의 왕)에게만 사탕이나 디저트로 제공되었습니다. 마지막으로, 시나몬 롤은 17세기에 스웨덴에서 유래했을지도 모릅니다. 시나몬 향신료는 무역로를 통해 스웨덴에 도착하기 시작했으며 나중에 롤과 디저트에 사용되었다고 여겨집니다. 이제, 이 디저트들에 대한 더 많은 세부 사항을 찾아보시기 바랍니다.

---

16 여자가 하는 말의 주제

정답률 85%   ▶ 정답 ②

① 음식을 보존하는 전통적인 방법들
✓ 유명한 디저트의 가능성 있는 기원들
③ 즉석 식품에 대한 건강상의 우려들
④ 인기 있는 디저트의 가격에 대한 논란
⑤ 새롭게 발명된 특별한 재료로 만든 디저트들

---

17 언급된 나라가 아닌 것

정답률 90%   ▶ 정답 ④

① 스코틀랜드   ② 이탈리아   ③ 이집트
✓ 프랑스   ⑤ 스웨덴

01 | 2018년 11월 학력평가   p.74

01. ensure the safety / a few regulations / cause / startle / prohibited
02. allowance / role of the parents / financially / proper spending habits
03. writing an article / diseases / help me treat patients / doctors
04. back of the stage / star-shaped / curtain / wearing
05. getting used to / do exercises / join / Can you lend
06. I'd like to buy / 30 / Two / off the total fare
07. thinking of / mall / wish / on a trip / pack
08. 16 to 25 / valid for / submit / It'll take / might as well
09. November 24th / entry fee / after lunch / in person
10. newly-released / trailer / fond of / special features / earlier
11. do you want / Have you been
12. two tickets / go together
13. Whose / if we're willing / take good care of / we'll have
14. facilities / having trouble / reopen / adopted / putting those details
15. packed with / used to / chronic coughing / purify / put plant pots
16~17. feeling sad / things to eat / fish / associated with / mood disorders / prevent / relieve / winter blues

02 | 2019년 3월 학력평가   p.79

01. vision problems / do to keep / nutritious / protective glasses / examined
02. item / authorized / can't trust / only at reliable
03. commercial for my restaurant / aired / broadcast / fix
04. rectangular / next to / uniform / letter / trophy beside the ball
05. housewarming / oven / fridge / forgot to replace / toilet
06. we've run / 15 / two / for a pack / discount
07. out of order / repair electronics / if possible / an appointment with
08. first episode / main character / directed / based on
09. promote / take place / unlimited / admission / not necessary
10. higher / 1,500 / good for / that's under / cool shot

11. had an accident / see a doctor
12. place / restaurant downtown
13. looking for / put / storing / seasons / any other advantage
14. too far / waste / downloaded it / keep track of
15. room temperature / calls / pays / tools / know
16~17. With technologies / made smarter / washers / strength / refrigerators / voice commands / vacuum cleaners

03 | 2019년 6월 학력평가   p.84

01. appreciate / announcement / has increased / in the afternoons
02. essay / improve my writing skills / first thing / sense / words
03. literature section / assignment / returned in a week / review / where it is
04. striped pattern / teddy bear / beside / flower pot / round clock
05. backpacking / extra clothes / sweet / grocery / could buy them
06. specific / has just released / 20 / three / 10
07. serious / submitted applications / challenge / develop your abilities / decision
08. Where will it / 17th / cost / specialist
09. theme / decorated / for a month / purchased at the gate
10. Electric kettles / at least / 30 / looks good / this time
11. new shopping mall / good about
12. light / uncomfortable to use
13. run for president / candidates / shy / assist / drawing
14. strategy / based on / Memorizing / effort / not so little anymore
15. act / nervous / discuss / experience / family or friends watched
16~17. ghosts / play an important role / memorable film / lion / fiction / dangerous dinosaurs / character

04 | 2019년 9월 학력평가   p.89

01. launch / emergency information / continue / an additional method / feel free
02. visual aids / considered recording / weak / gestures / improve
03. big fan / latest book / write that chapter / novelists
04. striped / between the poles / one round table / two stools / photo frame
05. translating / original text / first draft /

mind checking / feedback
06. to grow / four / liquid / 30 / credit
07. adopted / totally / environment / being alone / no one at home
08. brochure / held at / starts / tasting events / parking available
09. situated / diverse wildlife / drop-off / based on
10. using less oil / 100 / automatic switch off / at least / longer warranty
11. watched / did you like
12. arrive / was delivered
13. whenever I'm stressed / relieve / walking or stretching / Physical activity
14. annoyed / used to happen / blocks / prevent / that are not
15. majoring in / uncertain / regularly meets / worried / go see
16~17. tackle / closed to vehicles / France / bans / sharing / private transportation / Germany / acceptable emission level

05 | 2019년 11월 학력평가   p.94

01. opening of a new / provide / is now complete / served basis
02. trip / unexpected emergency / got injured / covered / go on
03. submitted in / compliment / As your art teacher / think of a title
04. striped / above the electronic / considerate / round table / lamp next to
05. one last check / stapled / just in case / snacks / I'll buy them
06. people are you with / 20 / we'll rent four pairs / off the total price
07. tasting the flavors / being held / my family plan to / profits
08. A guide explains / connected to / starts / register / a limit on
09. announce / food trucks and booths / Live music performances / zone / be cancelled
10. spending more than / matches / fixed / height / head and neck
11. coming home / take a train
12. pies and jam / Let me see
13. got there / want me to bring / passport instead / drawer
14. counseling / under stress / less special / behaves / you know what
15. selected / has been annoying / complain / encourage / more of a commitment
16~17. taken inspiration / no legs / surface / copied / soft and flexible / similar to an ant / inspired by

06 | 2020년 3월 학력평가   p.99

01. attention / is being repaired / open during regular / in use

02. peer teaching / enough time / helpful for your study / deeply / experience

03. broadcasting station / leader / deliver / want to host

04. theater / two different / bookshelf / rectangular mirror / at each end

05. What's keeping you / matching the articles with / I took / photo files

06. buy / so unique / 10 / four / discount off

07. chemistry / badminton lesson / ankle / flu shot / get some rest

08. working on / researchers are involved / budget / develop a new drug / within this period

09. interested / until late at night / check out / Snacks and beverages

10. less than / after a full charge / grey ones / keep my hands free

11. food / what it's made with

12. donate / the colors of

13. suspend / annual / on hold / after a month

14. scenery / completed and hung / won't be able / has an extra painting

15. running for / related to improving / replace / check if

16~17. details / changed through the agreement / excluded in / revived / disappeared from / its debut / additions

07 | 2020년 6월 학력평가   p.104

01. drama / auditions for actors / with passion / bulletin board

02. review / reading / better while listening / keeps me awake / give it a try

03. to rent / recommend in that area / separate from / included

04. between those two trees / striped / watermelon / playing the flute

05. preparations / difficulties inserting / finished decorating / Can you order

06. buy admission / rentals cost / any discounts / two

07. favorite artist / I'd really love to / delayed / science assignment

08. annual / next Friday / playground / our old stuff

09. a chance / start / Due to / not allowed to bring

10. need a suitcase / at least / 200 / darker / several umbrellas

11. present / buying her

12. stay / enjoy the nice weather

---

13. record his performance / nervous / impossible to reschedule / will be over

14. team workshop / look up / taking a bus instead / cut down on

15. decide to research / proposes / distribute / collect / and count / using the Internet

16~17. special occasion / depend on / promising / Ten is considered / thirteen is believed / airlines / captivating and mystical

08 | 2020년 9월 학력평가   p.109

01. president / clubs / how to sign up / fill out

02. distracted / having trouble focusing / pay attention to / notice

03. subscribers on / style of drawing / readers of our magazine / chance

04. armchairs / two flower pots / round table / lamp shade

05. moving / internet connection / compensation for / appointment to get

06. newborn niece / 50 / off that price / applies to purchases

07. tough / board games to celebrate / going skiing / suit

08. being held at / Who will perform / favorite / book them online

09. aims to promote / get a discount / run from / for free

10. 200 / longer than / unwanted / go with ones with / get dirty

11. bought / what's wrong with

12. delicious / Where did you learn

13. back hurt / with bad posture / stretch / can that happen

14. choose a topic / logical arguments / persuasive / send you the website

15. go to the gym / convenience store / harmful to / her own reusable bottle

16~17. wear glasses / foods that can help / surface / prevents / night

09 | 2020년 11월 학력평가   p.114

01. rules to follow / proper athletic / without permission / safely

02. wearing shoes / for your foot health / germs and bacteria / advice

03. I've been singing / make an easy dance / memorable / practice

04. above the fireplace / main character / bell on the door / can't wait

05. get ready / Roast chicken / arrival time / fill up

06. 20 / decoration / coffee cups / on all items

---

07. for not answering / made some changes / injured / medical check-up

08. brochure / surrounded by / convenient facilities / make a reservation

09. director / lasts for / limit / free postcards

10. wireless microphone / not enough / hands freely / don't want silver

11. give you a ride / wait for a second

12. almost halfway / car accident

13. business department / got accepted to / based on / what you love

14. decide on / determine / time to discuss / to the vote

15. fully understands / latest / tried to steal / keep up with

16~17. secret meanings / deeply admire / tulips / generally represent / have inspired / more than you think

10 | 2021년 3월 학력평가   p.119

01. field trip / explore / permission form / send it back

02. check out / convenient to listen to / short story / do chores

03. temperature / waves / thick wetsuits / not really necessary

04. heart with flowers / tied a ribbon / stars on / balloon dog

05. knitted hats / Luckily / science lab / get the ingredients

06. a pack of / four packs / originally / 50

07. job interview / career center / computer skill test / lecture

08. It'll be held on / long / entry fee / renovate

09. opportunity to sleep / staff-only areas / aged 5 and up / provided

10. crack / under 600 / 70 / doesn't like yellow

11. going camping / where the tent

12. opinion on / Shall I come back

13. hasn't been eating / regularly / at least an hour / on weekdays

14. post / debater / basically the same except / on your smartphone

15. reporters / drawing / better to put / use his work

16~17. celebrate / represents / greet / get rid of / empty suitcases / Greece / symbol of rebirth / unique

11 | 2021년 6월 학력평가   p.124

01. installed / rules / an excuse for / kick or push

02. general / many good points / understand historical events /

interesting to read

03. We're honored / make Italian dishes / recipes / after the show

04. banner hanging / flower vase / soccer ball / bird sculpture

05. cheer for / delivered / I've already chosen / buy hairbands

06. a wide selection of / appeared in / remote control / 50

07. reward ourselves / presentation for biology / planned a camping trip / some other time

08. purpose is to raise / views / we can choose from / participation fee

09. hosting / original written works / lead the discussions / you'll have to pay

10. chance to replace / how many shelves / White / cheaper

11. groceries / change my clothes

12. getting married / an invitation

13. search / good impression / bought those things / any other way

14. bad result / recommend / on foot / don't know how

15. take a trip / whatever / based on her experience / make plans

16~17. benefit your health / reduce the growth / positive effects / discomfort / traditionally / cause tooth decay

12 | 2021년 9월 학력평가   p.129

01. have conducted / responded / extend the survey period / improve the quality

02. recommended reading novels / another person's feelings / emotions / ability to share

03. company holiday party / live band / meet my clients' needs / how you've coordinated

04. carpet / spider web decoration / faces we carved / empty basket

05. outdoor activities / baseball game / on the way / Will you buy

06. 30 / our guests to take / five / you'll receive

07. book club meeting / missed / speech contest / take breaks

08. latest models / Various programs were available / takes place at / price

09. tradition where freshmen compete / consist of / chances / day of the event

10. willing to spend / prefer metal / storage / at least

11. straight / should take

12. passed / enough time to prepare

13. explain / audience understand / proper graphs and tables / give me

14. mountain peak / icy trails / dangerous / planning to see

15. frequently use / while riding / notice emergency situations / stop wearing

16~17. mathematical ability is widespread / strength in numbers / count / quite smart / desert ants / counting steps

13 | 2021년 11월 학력평가   p.134

01. renovation / making wider reading spaces / will be delayed / patience

02. make plans / in a limited time / put them in order / importance of the things

03. pick up / you can rent / full coverage / additional fee

04. bookshelf full of / ladder leaning against / two flower pots / introduce

05. weather / still packing / recommend / lend my speaker

06. striped neckties / 30 each / original price / two pairs

07. preview / book report / I'd like to join / my cousin's housewarming party

08. held in / play popular carols / be donated to / ticket sales start

09. Regardless of age / three categories / given as a prize / miss this opportunity

10. to spend over / floral scent / usually carries / pouch

11. bake some apple pies / How many

12. dinner after the conference / it's closed

13. recyclable packaging / reusable materials / reduce waste / around us

14. at the gym / exercising regularly / commuting time / walk either

15. supposed to choose / attends / field of architecture / watch him do

16~17. got their names / moves rapidly / largest / Mars has a reddish / caused many battles / discovered

14 | 2022년 3월 학력평가   p.139

01. announcement / drinking fountains installed / out of service / inconvenience

02. suit me well / approachable / wearer appear more friendly / go for

03. earlier than scheduled / arranging / took some nice photos / at our gallery

04. won a prize / above the board / basket / holding flowers

05. presentation for history / printed out / handout / made copies

06. 30 / loses his stuff / on sale / shipping fee

07. talent show / you'll do great / volunteer / help make a video

08. It'll be held at / starts on / Admission /

Ten great architects

09. professional opera singers / auditorium / take photos with / register in advance

10. it seems too much / capacity / more than 6 / baking pan

11. good shape / What kind of exercises

12. enter / how they will choose

13. working properly / tools and materials / Expert / nearest place

14. track / the amount of / diagnosed with / recommend it to anyone

15. president / mental and physical / improve / ask him for permission

16~17. live without food / oldest reptiles / extreme / spiders / As for penguins / sharks / deadly their hunting skills

15 | 2022년 6월 학력평가   p.144

01. retired / joined our school as / organized / such an enthusiastic

02. stupid mistakes / relieve your anxiety / lower levels / a proper amount of

03. What brings you here / get my hair colored / get a haircut / take care of

04. convenient for hanging / skateboard / speaker in the corner / safely store

05. weather forecast / one at a reasonable price / provide discount coupons to / I'll do that

06. see below / pay an additional / local residents / 5

07. What a bargain / Saturdays / medical check-up / play the piano

08. meet our neighbors / Guess where / as a gift / call the community center

09. a 3-day / former astronaut / through our telescopes / open two weeks before

10. 800 / not a good choice / would have more space / warranty periods

11. dying / how often

12. reservation / closed for repairs

13. out of the parcel / misdelivered / explain / wake him up

14. go to the gym / fee / work out / sign up soon

15. next to each other / given some tasks / no matter how fast / bring her son back

16~17. wasting / recycled and turned into / remove / Metals / melted down / Glass / bottles and jars / sorting

16 | 2022년 9월 학력평가   p.149

01. redesigned / conducting a survey / encouraged / your input is valuable

02. being the leader / different opinions /

make better decisions / reach

03. reading your articles / organized / Our readers have expressed / contain paintings featuring

04. square table / guitar next to / two / run around and bark

05. reviewed the candidates / arrange / How many graduates / take care of that

06. four / depends on the distance / delivery charge / correct

07. favorite musicians / plans / money to buy them / can't join you / though

08. view thousands of stars / per person / lodging / meals / and activities / dates

09. promote the importance / eager to find ways / online only / in advance at

10. it weighs / prefer / two cup holders / need a carry bag

11. couldn't concentrate on

12. decide on the topic

13. dropped it or anything / must be frustrated / would recommend / from the same model

14. can't get a connection / reinserting / push it slightly / You made my day

15. assigned / leave anything unfinished / loses track / pick her up

16~17. poorly planned diets / nutrient deficiency / nuts / and seeds / iron / vitamin B12 / consuming

---

17 | 2022년 11월 학력평가   p.154

01. convenient and eco-friendly / park them properly / misplaced / designated areas

02. brightest / screen is too bright / similar symptoms / damage your eye health

03. musical instruments / previous owner / used books / in a good condition

04. drew / basket on the round / three boxes next to / we took with

05. do a final check / considerate / laboratory gloves / first aid kit

06. take an intro session / 14 / rental fee / off the total price

07. borrowing some costumes / family gathering / soccer practice / musical audition scheduled

08. December 28th / they'll offer / participants will work together / complete the form

09. festive vibes / held from / recycled materials / at a discounted price

10. famous painting / We did / challenging than 400 / choose the frame

11. practicing / Who did you learn

12. register for / fully booked

13. bookcase you ordered / quite

---

complicated / searched for / There will be

14. thrown away / delicious and nutritious / buy ugly produce / at a reasonable price

15. teach literature / assigns / highly motivated / choose books for themselves

16~17. represent in different cultures / predator / crane stands for intelligence / wisdom / implied / healer and deliverer

---

18 | 2023년 3월 학력평가   p.159

01. important announcement / in use / temporarily closed / reopening

02. consider / does suit you well / stands out from / blend in

03. able to fix / precious / replaced it with / send me the bill

04. rented / hanging from the ceiling / star-shaped lamp / space shuttle

05. copy of my essay / did everything it says / city library / take you there

06. four extra / promotion / can afford / total shipping fee

07. pick up meals / restrictions / vaccination record / afraid I can't

08. runs for / guided tour to / for transportation / quite reasonable

09. three days starting / participate in up to / take longer than / attend

10. four or more / keep the brushes dry / drying function / staying under

11. might have watered / fix

12. hands are so dry

13. Old towels / keep the animals warm / in need of / propose

14. huge success / way to accommodate / interact with / how to start

15. sprains her wrist / take her solo part / too nervous to / encourage

16~17. commonly used / makes up / revolution / struggle for independence / natural element / peace and honesty / grasslands and forests

---

19 | 2023년 6월 학력평가   p.164

01. when you write / full of long / difficult words / convey the intention

02. up crying / something she likes / feel more comfortable / psychological

03. your new song everywhere / commercial / come up with / you've composed

04. square sign / tied to / star-patterned mat / ball is on the table

05. cover design / I'll add it / changes you

---

want / send the image file

06. guarantees clear vision / 40 / uses high-quality materials / discount on

07. move out of / get along with / issue is that / help look after

08. hosts it / take part / application by / only accepting

09. topic / living deep / huge screen / without having to make

10. 500 / install it anywhere / outdoors as well / not as accurate as

11. understand what I'm trying

12. earphones / can't use them until

13. missing / describe / Lost and Found / lady found it

14. soaked and fall apart / tastes bad / cause / reusable and don't affect

15. conflicting / gathered / which one to trust / ask their professor

16~17. design for your brand / memorable / no coincidence / bold / wealth / comfort and prosperity / literal coolness

---

20 | 2023년 9월 학력평가   p.169

01. recruiting volunteers / interested in attending / provide them with / Your participation

02. cracked / fixed immediately / break the whole / get it repaired

03. scientific advisor / entertaining scenes related to / expertise / findings might be useful

04. rearranging / round clock / two boxes / flower pot

05. have improved / throw them away / in good condition / bring some

06. small tables for four / 25 / won't be necessary / We've confirmed

07. recently renovated / waiting in line / sit with / ran out of ingredients

08. will be held at / How much / need to prepare / sign up

09. of all ages / submit / work with experienced / Registration closes

10. keeps beverages warm / we'd better not / capacity / display

11. why don't we put / how to make

12. either / not accepting

13. zero waste challenge / products / have you collected / recycling area

14. wanted are on sale / a pair / get easily swollen / thick socks

15. They'll perform / after asking the clerk / rent / borrow dresses rather than

16~17. way they're celebrated varies / Germany / willingness to cope with / pay for wedding expenses / Australia / as a reminder

01. operate a temporary / expected to / set up and run / commercial break
02. consuming fruits before / aid in weight management / better absorbed / improve
03. degrade / pollution crisis / carry your own / cut down on
04. chimney on the roof / stripe-patterned scarf / three boxes / must have been touched
05. useful information for newcomers / interviews / insert the subtitles / background music
06. 20 for adults / jewel collection / discount on / let me confirm
07. Was there a problem / completed / pain in my fingers / teach you later
08. theme / goes from / Will it be held / reservations should be made
09. operated by / gloves and knit hats / on certain / level up
10. keep it under / don't like bamboo / take up less space / blue
11. change the location / use
12. rental / through the library app
13. organizing our daughter's closet / second-hand items / buy these clothes / put them on
14. decided to delay / more time to practice / lead vocalist / stop singing
15. instead of / interfere with / boost / consume more water
16~17. named after world-famous / fought bravely / individuals / busiest hubs / serves as / flight across

01. announcement regarding / canceled due to / reschedule / ensure
02. memorizing / learning vocabulary / shout out / while having fun
03. maintain an organized / use everything / filled with items untouched / remove
04. banner hanging / wooden box / shoes on the table / guitar
05. included every graph / convincing / results show / send me the data
06. delivery app / 25 / add some drinks / free now
07. huge success / recorded it / want to be on / approval
08. for 25 students / spots available / tent rental service / total cost
09. Artificial Intelligence / physical training / adopted / purchase the admission ticket
10. cover material / either paper or fabric /

go for 20 / cheaper
11. live on / like the most
12. struggling / published a new book
13. spend much time outdoors / might not need / two types / used to
14. expressing your passion / mentioning a weakness / deal with / actually makes me feel
15. the lack of / emphasize the importance / talented in art / work together on
16~17. have transformed / revolutionized transportation / printing press / light bulb / opened the door to / connected as never before

01. experiencing difficulties / company is offering / deal with / it'll be worth
02. muscles are hurting / should definitely / afterward / feel relaxed
03. figuring out / powerful tool for understanding / a certain way / effectively
04. dressing room / you're holding / on the hanger / star-shaped mirror
05. haven't seen them / extra plates / get something for dessert / pick them up
06. purchase three admission / are charged / identification card / 50
07. stomachache / decided to throw / participate in the marathon / congratulate
08. Any city resident / 20th of June / winner will receive / apply for
09. volunteers will deliver / mobile application / extend / don't even need
10. jewelry online is cheaper / 400 / shouldn't choose / I'd rather
11. have plans / consider changing
12. parking lot / around
13. seem to really love / main purpose / lost confidence / boost
14. planning to buy / He's had it / selling it for / test-drive
15. gets distracted easily / suddenly reminded of / location / different place
16~17. objects / reveal a hidden truth / symbolize / represent / Blooming

01. free admissions / loyal supporters / extensive collections / spread the word
02. Speaking to your plants / essential for / promote / grow better
03. eating fruit / immediately after / digest fast / result in a stomachache

04. heart-shaped door / ride the bicycle / striped-patterned mat / design my own space
05. doing relays / volunteers to assist / basic rules / phone call
06. new phone case / 20 / go with / protective film / originally
07. landscape photography / perfect to take / feel well enough / find the right place
08. poetry reading / on stage for / September 14th / sign up
09. thought about boosting / open to everyone / planning / shooting / and editing / We'll randomly pick
10. relax and fall asleep / or less / white would look better / useful
11. getting / actually save more money
12. customer brings their own / join in
13. convenient to order / hasn't been delivered / decided to wear / perfectly prepared
14. packing things / someone to look after / Have you considered / give a hand
15. stage director / checking the music / last scene / goes better with
16~17. where and when / historians assume / Italy / created a form of / Egypt / originated in / trade routes

▶ **Don't hesitate to V :** 주저하지 마라
Please **don't hesitate to apply** for this volunteer work at our charity soccer match.
자선 축구 경기의 자원봉사 활동에 **지원하는 데 주저하지 마십시오**.
출처: 2024학년도 대학수학능력시험 01번

▶ **get into an argument :** 말다툼을 하게 되다
Tiffany and I **got into an argument** at school.
Tiffany와 제가 학교에서 **말다툼을 했어요**.
출처: 2024학년도 대학수학능력시험 02번

▶ **cut A off :** (말 등을) 끊다
That's why when somebody's talking, you shouldn't **cut them off**.
그래서 누군가 말할 때는 **그들의 말을 끊**지 말아야 한단다.
출처: 2024학년도 대학수학능력시험 02번

▶ **experience trouble V-ing :** ~하는 데 어려움을 겪다
But recently, more and more people are **experiencing trouble falling** asleep.
하지만 최근에 점점 더 많은 사람들이 잠드**는 데 어려움을 겪고 있습니다**.
출처: 2024학년도 대학수학능력시험 03번

▶ **eye-catching :** 눈길을 끄는
And isn't that striped tablecloth really **eye-catching?**
그리고 저 줄무늬 식탁보는 정말로 **눈길을 끌**지 않나요?
출처: 2024학년도 대학수학능력시험 04번

▶ **bother :** 괴롭히다, 귀찮게 하다
Then, are your allergy symptoms **bother**ing you again?
그럼, 알레르기 증상이 또 너를 **괴롭히는 거야?**
출처: 2024학년도 대학수학능력시험 07번

▶ **make it :** 성공하다, 도착하다
I'm afraid I can't **make it** this time.
미안하지만 이번에는 **갈 수 없어**.
출처: 2024학년도 대학수학능력시험 12번

▶ **look forward to V-ing :** ~하기를 기대하다
That's too bad. I was **look**ing **forward to seeing** you there.
아쉽다. 나는 거기서 너를 **보기를 기대하고 있었어**.
출처: 2024학년도 대학수학능력시험 12번

▶ **put A off :** 미루다, 연기하다
You make me think of my old passion to be a painter, but I **put it off** for too long.
당신은 화가가 되고 싶다는 저의 오랜 열정에 대해 생각하게 만드시지만, 저는 너무 오랫동안 **그것을 미뤘어요**.
출처: 2024학년도 대학수학능력시험 13번

▶ **hold :** 가지고 있다, 중단하다
Oh, there's one copy left there, but unfortunately we can't **hold** it for you.
오, 거기에 한 권이 남아 있는데 유감스럽게도 저희가 고객님을 위해 그것을 **예약해 드릴** 수는 없네요.
출처: 2024학년도 대학수학능력시험 14번

▶ **make sure :** 반드시 ~하다
make sure you visit our school library to submit your application.
신청서를 제출하기 위해 **반드시** 학교 도서관을 방문해 주십시오.
출처: 2023학년도 대학수학능력시험 01번

▶ **rich in :** ~이 풍부한
It said apple peels are **rich in** vitamins and minerals, so they moisturize our skin and enhance skin glow.
사과 껍질은 비타민과 미네랄**이 풍부해서**, 피부에 수분을 공급하고 피부 광채를 향상시킨다고 했어요.
출처: 2023학년도 대학수학능력시험 02번

▶ **It seems ~ :** ~인[한] 것 같다
It seems to include useful information.
유용한 정보를 포함하고 있는 **것 같아**.
출처: 2023학년도 대학수학능력시험 04번

▶ **remind A of B :** A에게 B에 대해 다시 한 번 알려주다
We need to **remind** our loyal customers **of** the event.
우리는 단골 고객들에게 행사에 대해 **다시 한 번 알려 줘야** 해요.
출처: 2023학년도 대학수학능력시험 05번

▶ **What about ~? :** ~은 어때?
What about the live music**?**
라이브 음악**은 어때요?**
출처: 2023학년도 대학수학능력시험 05번

▶ **be scheduled to V :** ~할 예정이다
I'm **scheduled to** shoot your school's graduation photos on Wednesday, November 23rd.
11월 23일 수요일에 선생님 학교의 졸업 사진을 촬영**할 예정이에요**.
출처: 2023학년도 대학수학능력시험 08번

▶ **in stock :** 재고가 있는
These are the ones we have **in stock**.
이것들은 **재고가 있는** 것들이에요.
출처: 2023학년도 대학수학능력시험 10번

▶ **be willing to V :** ~할 의향이 있는
How much **are** you **willing to** spend?
얼마를 쓰실 **의향이 있으신가요**?
출처: 2023학년도 대학수학능력시험 10번

▶ **fair :** 박람회; 공정한
Our son said he's going to a career **fair** and asked if we can come along.
우리 아들이 직업 **박람회**에 갈 거라고 우리가 함께 갈 수 있는지 물어봤어요.
출처: 2023학년도 대학수학능력시험 12번

▶ **have trouble with :** ~으로 곤란을 겪다
Is there anything specific you're **having trouble with**?
특별히 **곤란한 일이 있는** 거니?
출처: 2023학년도 대학수학능력시험 13번

▶ **for no reason :** 이유 없이, 공연히
Does your dog chew up your shoes or bark **for no reason** at times?
당신의 개가 당신의 신발을 씹거나 때때로 **이유 없이** 짖나요?
출처: 2022학년도 대학수학능력시험 01번

▶ **what do you think about[of]? :** ~에 대해 어떻게 생각해?
What do you think about the balloons next to the welcome banner**?**
환영 현수막 옆에 있는 풍선들**에 대해 어떻게 생각해?**
출처: 2022학년도 대학수학능력시험 04번

▶ **I guess (that) ~ :** ~이라고 생각하다
Oh, then **I guess** you have to study for the science quiz, right?
오, 그럼 과학 퀴즈를 위한 공부를 해야 **하는구나**, 그렇지?
출처: 2022학년도 대학수학능력시험 07번

▶ **on one's way to :** ~으로 가는 길[도중]에
Actually, I'm **on my way to** volunteer at the school library.
사실, 학교 도서관에 자원봉사를 하**러 가는 중**이야.
출처: 2022학년도 대학수학능력시험 07번

▶ **for free :** 무료로, 공짜로
We'll also give out a children's science magazine **for free**.
저희는 또한 어린이 과학 잡지를 **무료로** 나눠드릴 것입니다.
출처: 2022학년도 대학수학능력시험 09번

▶ **in advance :** 미리
There's no admission fee, but to participate, you must register **in advance**.
입장료는 없지만, 참가하시려면, **미리** 등록하셔야 합니다.
출처: 2022학년도 대학수학능력시험 09번

▶ **available :** 이용 가능한
Oh, only these rooms are **available**.
오, 이 룸들만 **이용 가능하**구나.
출처: 2022학년도 대학수학능력시험 10번

▶ **enough to V :** ~하기에 충분히 …한
We need a room big **enough to** accommodate six of us.
우리 6명을 수용**할 만큼 충분히** 큰 룸이 필요해.
출처: 2022학년도 대학수학능력시험 10번

▶ **since :** ~ 때문에, ~한 이래로
Since we're meeting for two hours, I don't think we can spend more than $20 per hour.
우리는 두 시간 동안 만나기로 했**기 때문에**, 시간당 20달러 이상은 쓸 수 없을 것 같아.
출처: 2022학년도 대학수학능력시험 10번

▶ **beyond :** ~을 초과한, ~을 뛰어넘는
It's **beyond** our budget.
그것은 우리의 예산을 **초과해**.
출처: 2022학년도 대학수학능력시험 10번

▶ **look up at :** ~을 올려다보다
Oh, so you went outdoors to **look up at** stars.
오, 그럼 별을 **올려다보**기 위해서 야외로 나갔겠구나.
출처: 2021학년도 대학수학능력시험 02번

▶ **become familiar with :** ~에 친숙해지다
And I think it helped my son **become familiar with** mathematical concepts.
그리고 그것은 내 아들이 수학 개념**에 친숙해지**도록 도와준 것 같아.
출처: 2021학년도 대학수학능력시험 02번

▶ **get used to N/V-ing :** ~에 익숙해지다
I think looking at stars is a good way for kids to **get used to** mathematical concepts.
별을 보는 것은 아이들이 수학 개념**에 익숙해지**는 좋은 방법인 것 같아.
출처: 2021학년도 대학수학능력시험 02번

▶ **be honored to V :** ~하게 되어 영광으로 생각하다
I'm **honored to** interview the person who designed the school I'm attending.
제가 다니는 학교를 설계하신 분을 인터뷰**하게 되어 영광으로 생각해요**.
출처: 2021학년도 대학수학능력시험 03번

▶ **fill A up with B :** A를 B로 가득 채우다
We're going to **fill** those **up with** donations of toys and books.
저희는 그것들을 장난감과 책 기증품들**로 가득 채울** 거예요.
출처: 2021학년도 대학수학능력시험 04번

▶ **need to V :** ~해야 한다
It was founded to deliver the message that we **need to** admit our failures to truly succeed.
그곳은 우리가 진정으로 성공하기 위해서는 우리의 실패를 인정**해야 한다**는 메시지를 전달하기 위해 설립되었어.
출처: 2021학년도 대학수학능력시험 08번

▶ **advance to :** ~에 진출하다
We had the most applicants in the history of this competition, and only 10 participants will **advance to** the final round.
이 대회의 역사상 가장 많은 지원자들이 있었으며, 오직 10명의 참가자들만 결선**에 진출할** 것입니다.
출처: 2021학년도 대학수학능력시험 09번

▶ **be about to V :** ~할 예정이다
You cannot park here because we**'re about to** close off this section of the parking lot.
저희가 주차장의 이 구획을 폐쇄**할 예정이**기 때문에 여기에 주차하실 수 없습니다.
출처: 2021학년도 대학수학능력시험 12번

▶ **be out of :** ~이 없다
We**'re out of** this model right now.
지금 당장은 이 모델**이 없어요**.
출처: 2021학년도 대학수학능력시험 13번

▶ **break down :** 고장 나다
My washing machine **broke down** yesterday.
제 세탁기가 어제 **고장 났어요**.
출처: 2021학년도 대학수학능력시험 13번

▶ **inform A of B :** A에게 B에 대해 알리다
We'd like to **inform** you **of** the special events going on through this weekend.
여러분**께** 이번 주말 동안 진행되는 특별 행사들**에 대해 알려드리고자** 합니다.
출처: 2020학년도 대학수학능력시험 03번

▶ **have something to do with :** ~과 관련이 있다
I didn't know how we sleep **has something to do with** digestion.
나는 우리가 잠을 자는 방식이 소화**와 관련이 있는** 줄은 몰랐어.
출처: 2020학년도 대학수학능력시험 04번

▶ **must have p.p. :** ~했음이 틀림없다
It **must have been** very difficult to get a reservation because our party is on December 24th.
우리 파티가 12월 24일이기 때문에 예약하는 게 매우 어려**웠음이 틀림없어**.
출처: 2020학년도 대학수학능력시험 10번

▶ **take a look at :** ~을 보다
Okay, Mr. White. Let's **take a look at** the flight schedule. 좋아요, White 씨. 비행기 시간표**를 봐요.**
출처: 2020학년도 대학수학능력시험 12번

▶ **share A with B :** B와 A를 공유하다
Yeah. You can **share** ideas **with** others in the group about the book you're reading.
그래. 네가 읽고 있는 책에 대해서 모임 내의 다른 사람들**과** 생각**을 공유할** 수 있어.
출처: 2020학년도 대학수학능력시험 14번

▶ **take care of :** ~을 챙겨주다, 돌보다, 다루다, 처리하다
Until now his mother has always **taken care of** his travel bag, so he doesn't have any experience preparing it himself. 지금까지 그의 어머니가 그의 여행 가방**을** 항상 **챙겨주**어서, 그는 그것을 직접 준비한 경험이 없다.
출처: 2020학년도 대학수학능력시험 15번

▶ **have access to :** ~을 이용[접근, 출입]할 수 있다
How did people send mail before they **had access to** cars and trains?
사람들은 그들이 자동차와 기차를 **이용할 수 있기** 전에 어떻게 우편물을 보냈을까요?
출처: 2020학년도 대학수학능력시험 16~17번

▶ **due to N :** ~ 때문에
Once again, today's game has been canceled **due to** heavy rain.
다시 한 번 말씀드리지만, 오늘의 경기는 폭우 **때문에** 취소되었습니다.
출처: 2019학년도 대학수학능력시험 03번

▶ **be supposed to V :** ~하기로 되어 있다
Today's baseball game **was supposed to** begin in twenty minutes.
오늘의 야구 경기는 20분 후에 시작**하기로 되어 있었습니다.**
출처: 2019학년도 대학수학능력시험 03번
Tip 원래는 무엇을 하기로 되어 있었으나, 계획에 변경이 생겼음을 말할 때 많이 사용돼요!

▶ **According to + N :** ~에 따르면
According to the forecast, the weather will only get worse.
일기예보**에 따르면**, 날씨가 더 나빠질 뿐입니다.
출처: 2019학년도 대학수학능력시험 03번

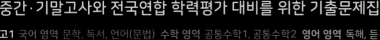

2025 마더텅 전국연합 학력평가 기출문제집 시리즈

학교 시험에 자주 출제되는 유형을 철저히 분석하여 적용한 유형별 기출문제집
중간·기말고사와 전국연합 학력평가 대비를 위한 기출문제집

NAME

book.toptutor.co.kr
구하기 어려운 교재는 마더텅
모바일(인터넷)을 이용하세요.
즉시 배송해 드립니다.

고1 국어 영역 문학, 독서, 언어(문법) 수학 영역 공통수학1, 공통수학2 **영어 영역** 독해, 듣기, 어법·어휘 **탐구 영역** 통합사회1, 통합사회2 통합과학1, 통합과학2
고2 국어 영역 문학, 독서, 언어(문법) 수학 영역 수학Ⅰ, 수학Ⅱ **영어 영역** 독해, 듣기, 어법·어휘 **과학탐구** 물리학Ⅰ, 화학Ⅰ, 생명과학Ⅰ, 지구과학Ⅰ

9차 개정판 2쇄 2025년 1월 15일 (초판 1쇄 발행일 2015년 12월 15일) **발행처** (주)마더텅 **발행인** 문숙영

책임 편집 정다혜, 성현영

해설 집필 변선영, 신재진

교정 신재진, 조해라, 류도이, 한수연, 윤병철, 마혜진, 김보란, 윤은채, 손유민 / 이성수, 신종윤, 강희원, 김다현, 김미희, 오정문, 장영민, 신철현, 이은혜, 김민정, 한선영, 전진성, 김도현, 박소유, 박지연, 이용민, 심가원, 윤수빈, 전진리, 전도윤

해설 감수 강산(EBS 영어), 김유경(올패스영어학원), 최주영(마더텅영어)

디자인 김연실, 양은선 **인디자인 편집** 허문희 / 박수경 **컷** 박수빈 / 곽원영

제작 이주영 **홍보** 정반석 **주소** 서울시 금천구 가마산로 96, 708호 **등록번호** 제1-2423호(1999년 1월 8일)

마더텅 교재를 풀면서 궁금한 점이 생기셨나요?

교재 관련 내용 문의나 오류신고 사항이 있으면 아래 문의처로 보내 주세요! 문의하신 내용에 대해 성심성의껏 답변해 드리겠습니다.
또한 **교재의 내용 오류** 또는 **오·탈자, 그 외 수정이 필요한 사항**에 대해 가장 먼저 신고해 주신 분께는 감사의 마음을 담아
네이버페이 포인트 1천 원 을 보내 드립니다!

* 기한: 2025년 12월 31일 * 오류신고 이벤트는 당사 사정에 따라 조기 종료될 수 있습니다. * 홈페이지에 게시된 정오표 기준으로 최초 신고된 오류에 한하여 상품권을 보내 드립니다.

🏠 홈페이지 www.toptutor.co.kr ▢ 교재Q&A게시판 ● 카카오톡 mothertongue ◉ 이메일 mothert1004@toptutor.co.kr
🎧 고객센터 전화 1661-1064(07:00~22:00) ✉ 문자 010-6640-1064(문자수신전용)

마더텅은 1999년 창업 이래 2024년까지 3,320만 부의 교재를 판매했습니다. 2024년 판매량은 309만 부로 자사 교재의 품질은 학원 강의와 온/오프라인 서점 판매량으로 검증받았습니다. [마더텅 수능기출문제집 시리즈]는 친절하고 자세한 해설로 수험생들의 전폭적인 지지를 받으며 누적 판매 855만 부, 2024년 한 해에만 85만 부가 판매된 베스트셀러입니다. 또한 [중학영문법 3800제]는 2007년부터 2024년까지 18년 동안 중학 영문법 부문 판매 1위를 지키며 명실공히 대한민국 최고의 영문법 교재로 자리매김했습니다. 그리고 2018년 출간된 [뿌리깊은 초등국어 독해력 시리즈]는 2024년까지 278만 부가 판매되면서 초등 국어 부문 판매 1위를 차지하였습니다.(교보문고/YES24 판매량 기준, EBS 제외) 이처럼 마더텅은 초·중·고 학습 참고서를 대표하는 대한민국 제일의 교육 브랜드로 자리잡게 되었습니다. 이와 같은 성원에 감사드리며, 앞으로도 효율적인 학습에 보탬이 되는 교재로 보답하겠습니다.

마더텅 학습 교재 이벤트에 참여해 주세요. 참여해 주신 **모든 분께 선물**을 드립니다.

이벤트 1 **1분 간단 교재 사용 후기 이벤트**

마더텅은 고객님의 소중한 의견을 반영하여 보다 좋은 책을 만들고자 합니다.
교재 구매 후, <교재 사용 후기 이벤트>에 참여해 주신 모든 분께는 감사의 마음을 담아 네이버페이 포인트 1천 원 을 보내 드립니다.
지금 바로 QR 코드를 스캔해 소중한 의견을 보내 주세요!

이벤트 2 마더텅 교재로 공부하는 인증샷 이벤트

인스타그램에 <마더텅 교재로 공부하는 인증샷>을 올려 주시면 참여해 주신 모든 분께 감사의 마음을 담아
네이버페이 포인트 2천 원 을 보내 드립니다.
지금 바로 QR 코드를 스캔해 작성한 게시물의 URL을 입력해 주세요!

필수 태그 #마더텅 #마더텅기출 #공스타그램

※ 자세한 사항은 해당 QR 코드를 스캔하거나 홈페이지 이벤트 공지 글을 참고해 주세요.

※ 당사 사정에 따라 이벤트의 내용이나 상품이 변경될 수 있으며 변경 시 홈페이지에 공지합니다.

※ 상품은 이벤트 참여일로부터 2~3일(영업일 기준) 내에 발송됩니다.   ※ 동일 교재로 두 가지 이벤트 모두 참여 가능합니다. (단, 같은 이벤트 중복 참여는 불가합니다.)

※ 이벤트 기간: 2025년 12월 31일까지 (*해당 이벤트는 당사 사정에 따라 조기 종료될 수 있습니다.)